PARENTING ACROSS THE LIFE SPAN

Biosocial Dimensions

PARENTING ACROSS THE LIFE SPAN

Biosocial Dimensions

Edited by

Jane B. Lancaster
Jeanne Altmann
Alice S. Rossi
Lonnie R. Sherrod

Sponsored by the
Social Science Research Council

ALDINE DE GRUYTER
New York

ABOUT THE EDITORS

Jane B. Lancaster is Professor of Anthropology, University of New Mexico. She chairs the Social Science Research Council's Committee on Biosocial Science Perspectives on Parental Behavior and Offspring Development as well as the General Anthropology Unit of the American Anthropological Association. She is the co-editor of "School-Age Pregnancy and Parenthood" and the co-author of "Eve and Adam: The Origins of Sex and the Family."

Jeanne Altmann is Associate Professor of Biology, University of Chicago. She was the American Editor of *Animal Behavior* and is consulting editor for the *American Journal of Primatology*. Dr. Altmann was chairperson and is a member of the scientific board of Karisoke Research Centre, Rwanda, and past President of the Animal Behavior Society.

Alice S. Rossi is Harriet Martineau Professor of Sociology, University of Massachusetts at Amherst. She has authored and edited numerous volumes including: "Gender and the Life Course," "Feminists in Politics," "The Feminist Papers," and "Academic Women on the Move." Dr. Rossi has served as President of the Eastern Sociological Society and the American Sociological Association.

Lonnie R. Sherrod, is Staff Associate, Social Science Research Council and Adjunct Assistant Professor, New York University. He is staff to numerous Council Committees and serves as Secretary-Treasurer of the Society for the Study of Social Biology. He has been a major contributor to various professional publications.

ALDINE DE GRUYTER (Formerly Aldine Publishing Company)
A Division of Walter de Gruyter, Inc.
200 Saw Mill River Road
Hawthorne, New York 10532

Library of Congress Cataloging-in-Publication Data

Parenting across the life span.

Bibliography: p.
Includes indexes.
1. Parenthood. 2. Life cycle, Human.
I. Lancaster, Jane Beckman, 1935–   . II. Social
Science Research Council (U.S.). Committee on
Biosocial Perspectives on Parental Behavior and
Offspring Development.
HQ755.8.P379 1987   306.8'74   86-21127
ISBN 0-202-30332-2 (lib. bdg.)

Printed in the United States of America
10 9 8 7 6 5 4 3 2 1

CONTENTS

Contents

ACKNOWLEDGMENTS

All aspects of the program of the Committee on Biosocial Perspectives on Parent Behavior and Offspring Development which resulted in the publication of this volume have been funded by the William T. Grant Foundation (New York). The committee and the Council are very appreciative of the support provided by the Foundation, and wish particularly to thank Dr. Robert Haggerty, President of the Foundation, for his deep interest and intellectual support. A previous grant to the Council from the National Institute of Child Health and Human Development provided funding for a series of planning workshops that led to the formation of the committee. The editors of the volume wish also to thank the Social Science Research Council for its support of the committee.

Among the early activities relating to the subject, Parenting Across the Life Span, was a conference held at the Belmont Conference Center, Elkridge, Maryland. The committee also wishes to express its appreciation to the staff of the Belmont Center.

During the planning and preparation of this volume, the editors were assisted by the members of the committee and the staff of the Social Science Research Council. A particular expression of appreciation is due Terry Ciatto at the SSRC who has handled all of the daily aspects of typing, mailing, distributing proofs, telephoning authors, and generally maintaining the progress of the volume. The management and staff at Aldine de Gruyter were of invaluable assistance throughout all phases of production of the volume.

LIST OF CONTRIBUTORS

Jeanne Altmann
Department of Biology
Allee Laboratory of Animal
  Behavior
Chicago, Illinois 60637

Vern L. Bengston
Andrus Gerontology Center
University of Southern California
Los Angeles, California
  90089-0191

Judith Blake
School of Public Health
University of California
Los Angeles, California 90024

Eric L. Charnov
Department of Psychology
University of Utah
Salt Lake City, Utah 84112

Patricia Draper
College of Human Development
Pennsylvania State University
University Park, Pennsylvania
  16802

Gunhild O. Hagestad
College of Human Development
Pennsylvania State University
University Park, Pennsylvania
  16802

Henry Harpending
Department of Anthropology
Pennsylvania State University
University Park, Pennsylvania
  16802

Dennis P. Hogan
Population Research Center
University of Chicago
Chicago, Illinois 60637

Michael E. Lamb
Department of Psychology
University of Utah
Salt Lake City, Utah 84112

Chet S. Lancaster
Technoserve Inc.
Norwalk, Connecticut
  06854

Jane B. Lancaster
Department of Anthropology
University of New Mexico
Albuquerque, New Mexico
  87131

Michael Leon
Department of Psychobiology
University of California
Irvine, California 92717

Jacqueline V. Lerner
College of Human Development
Pennsylvania State University
University Park, Pennsylvania
  16802

Richard M. Lerner
College of Human Development
Pennsylvania State University
University Park, Pennsylvania
  16802

James A. Levine
President, Media Center
Bank Street College of Education
New York, New York 10025

Robert A. LeVine
Graduate School of Education
Harvard University
Cambridge, Massachusetts 02138

James J. McKenna
Department of Sociology and
    Anthropology
Pomona College
Claremont, California 91711

Joseph H. Pleck
Department of Psychology
Wheaton College
Norton, Massachusetts
    02766

Alice S. Rossi
Social & Demographic Research
    Institute
University of Massachusetts
Amherst, Massachusetts 01003

Lonnie R. Sherrod
Social Science Research Council
New York, New York 10158

Maris A. Vinovskis
Department of History
University of Michigan
Ann Arbor, Michigan 48104

Thomas S. Weisner
Department of Psychiatry
University of California
Los Angeles, California 90024

Merry White
Graduate School of Education
Harvard University
Cambridge, Massachusetts 02138

FOUNDATIONS OF HUMAN BEHAVIOR

An Aldine de Gruyter Series of Texts and Monographs

Edited by
Sarah Blaffer Hrdy, *University of California, Davis*
Melvin Konner, *Emory University*
Richard W. Wrangham, *University of Michigan*

1 INTRODUCTION

Jane B. Lancaster
Jeanne Altmann
Alice S. Rossi
Lonnie R. Sherrod

THE BIOSOCIAL PERSPECTIVE

This volume is the second in a series sponsored by the Social Science Research Council's Committee on Biosocial Perspectives on Parent Behavior and Offspring Development. The committee, formed in 1980, is a multidisciplinary group (including biological, behavioral, and social scientists) that seeks to promote an exchange of concepts, methods, and data across disciplines on a variety of substantive issues on which the group shares intellectual and policy concerns. The goals of the committee's program are: to develop conceptualizations of social phenomena relying on biosocial science, to explore the interface between biological and social phenomena, and to advance our understanding of human social behavior. The first volume of this series, *School-Age Pregnancy and Parenthood: Biosocial Dimensions*, edited by J. Lancaster and B. Hamburg (Aldine, 1986), focuses on a particular segment of the life span and the challenges, problems, and opportunities inherent in parenthood during such an early phase of the reproductive years; there attention is focused on issues of timing during a specific transition period in the life span. The current volume achieves a broad sweep across the life span, examining parenthood as a commitment involving the entire life course. Of particular concern is the impact of modern changes in the timing, distribution, and intensity of commitment to parenthood on both parental and child behavior and experience throughout the life span.

Biosocial science is particularly relevant to research on human family systems and parenting behavior because the family is the universal social institution within which the bearing and care of children has been based and where cultural traditions, beliefs, and values have been transmitted to the young as individual actors fulfill their biological potential for reproduction, growth, and development. The biosocial perspective takes into account the biological substrate and the social environment as determinants of patterns of behavior, and pinpoints areas in which contemporary human parental behavior exhibits continuities with, and departures from, patterns evident throughout human history. Unless discontinuities in family behaviors and their overall costs and benefits are examined, we are not in a position to assess them objectively in terms of modern circumstances. The biosocial perspective, therefore, extends our understanding of parental behavior by sensitizing us to the variety of patterns among current practices as well as by highlighting the full range of parent-child patterns that have been represented in the evolutionary or historical past. Both the spectrum of options and the basis for making judgments about these options are expanded.

The term "biosocial" was selected to emphasize the functional unity of both biological and socioenvironmental factors. The mutual influences of these factors are more than additive; indeed, they are interrelated through reciprocal influences that can significantly alter the characteristics of each. The potential for change and variation in biological attributes is less well understood than is the potential for human learning and behavioral change. There has been a misleading tendency to perceive biological behaviors as being unlearned, independent of the environment and not readily susceptible to change. There also has been an expectation that there will be uniformity of response to a specific stimulus. For human beings, prior experience, motivation, and context will influence biological responses to all kinds of stimuli, whether they are pathogenic bacteria or social interactions. For example, the biosocial perspective is now being applied to physical health. Behavioral medicine is an emerging area of research and clinical practice (Hamburg, Elliott, and Parron, 1982). Recognition of the continuous, mutual, and inseparable interaction between biology and the social environment is one of the critical foundations of the biosocial perspective.

Armed with a commitment to a biosocial science perspective, 26 scientists from the disciplines of anthropology, sociology, psychiatry, human development, family studies, primatology, history, biology, psychology, psychobiology, and gerontology contributed chapters to this volume, discussing their own research and the knowledge of their respective disciplines about parenthood across the life span.

Approaches in the Biological and Social Sciences to Life-Span Research in Parent Behavior

By presenting and integrating recent research in the biological and social sciences regarding the life course of parenthood, this volume paves the way for a biosocial synthesis. The past decade has witnessed the independent maturation of two separate foci of science that deal with the life span. They represent a newly developed maturity in the data bases of both bodies of science regarding analytic approaches to issues of growth, maturation, development, and change through time. Until recent years these issues, particularly in regard to long-lived species, were most often approached through the synthesis of cross-sectional data into a projected trajectory of development (with the notable exception of growth studies in developmental psychology begun the 1920's). However, beginning in the 1950's and especially in the 1960's, modern biological and behavioral science began investing enormous amounts of time, energy, and resources into following individuals, birth cohorts, and local populations of both animals and humans through long periods, many of which represented the length of a generation or even a life span. For the first time information on the actual observed processes of change and maturation through time were gathered so that cross-sectional data drawn from different cultures, different cohorts, or different individuals no longer had to be the exclusive basis on which to construct composites of growth and development (see Migdol and Sherrod, 1981; Verdonik and Sherrod, 1984).

In the biological sciences, long-term, naturalistic field studies provided an impetus for fresh perspectives on parenthood and the life span. New theoretical models transformed evolutionary biology as behavioral ecology advanced the concept of life history strategies and tactics and sociobiology modeled parental investment theory. These theoretical frameworks emphasize the intimate interaction of biology and social behavior and the sensitivity of each to fluctuation in social and environmental resources. Definitions of evolutionary adaptation and fitness could assess long-range strategies and trade-offs of short-term loss for long-term gain in reproductive tactics (Hamilton, 1966; Stearns, 1976; Calow, 1979; Western, 1979). The fit between reproductive strategies and environmental resources and the shaping of the life course to optimize reproductive success in a given environment became a major focus of theoretical exploration (Cole, 1954; MacArthur, 1962; Schaffer, 1974; Pianka, 1976; Kirkwood and Holliday, 1979; Horn and Rubenstein, 1984). At the same time, the field of sociobiology formulated inclusive fitness and parental investment theory (Hamilton, 1964; Maynard Smith, 1964; Trivers, 1972; Dawkins and Carlisle, 1976; Maynard Smith, 1977; Clutton-Brock and Albon, 1982; Hausfater and Hrdy, 1984; Trivers, 1985). Using cost/benefit analyses drawn from economics, it emphasized the limited amount of parental resources (time, energy, attention) to be apportioned by a parent to its offspring over the course of the life spans of both (Wasser, 1983; Wasser and Waterhouse, 1983; Betzig, Mulder, and Turke, in press; Clutton-Brock, in press). Reproductive success could be measured over the entire life span both in respect to steady output as well as peak performance (Hausfater, 1975; Altmann, Altmann, and Hausfater, in press). A common characteristic of all these theoretical advances was the formulation of a series of alternative propositions that lent themselves to empirical testing through the use of observational data from long-term field studies.

At the same time that evolutionary biology felt the impact of long-term studies in its developing theories of inclusive fitness, life history, and parental investment strategies, the social sciences began formulating new perspectives on the processes of growth, development, and aging for the individual, and transformation and change for groups and societies. Although such work was initially based on adult developmental psychology and the sociological analysis of aging, the perspectives that emerged incorporated the biological as well as the social and behavioral sciences. New data bases drawn from long-term studies of individuals, birth cohorts, and groups demanded that processes of development and change no longer be expressed entirely in terms of stages artificially derived from cross-sectional research; rather, development was seen as pluralistic and multidirectional (Baltes, 1978; Baltes and Brim, 1980, 1982, 1983, 1984). New studies released developmental psychology from an exclusive focus on infancy and childhood to include the entire life span (Baltes, Reese, and Lipsitt, 1980; Lamb and Sutton-Smith, 1982), and the capacity for lifelong plasticity was recognized (Lerner, 1984). Aging was looked at differently as continuous growth, development, accommodation, and adaptation were observed; it was no longer defined in terms of declining function and capacity beginning at the onset of maturity (Datan and Ginsberg, 1975; Riley, Hess, and Bond, 1983; Rossi, 1980, 1985). Once research from long-term studies of individual development and from the collection of life histories was integrated, a new body of theory emerged incorporating life-span trajectories, birth-cohort effects, and the full course of human life.

In short, both the biological and social sciences now reap the benefits of mature science, with the development of rich data bases from long-term studies so that development, change, and growth no longer need to be synthesized from short-term cross sections. Despite this promising convergence of methods and orientation, there has been little actual interaction between biological and social research on the life course. And most contact between the fields has emphasized issues of health and the micro-level biological bases of behavior. Nonetheless, life course perspectives emerging from the social sciences explicitly incorporate a biosocial orientation, and biosocial perspectives in the life sciences necessarily approach phenomena from the orientation of the full life span. The purpose of this book is to encourage researchers of the life span working independently in the biological, biosocial, and social sciences to integrate their perspectives into a biosocial science of the life course. Parenthood proved to be a promising focus because of its lifelong nature and because it raises particularly important biosocial issues.

CURRENT BIOSOCIAL ISSUES IN LIFE-SPAN RESEARCH

The biosocial approach is characterized by its comparative dimensions: cross-species (evolutionary and biological), cross-cultural, and cross-time (historical and developmental). These dimensions enrich research by encouraging sensitivity to biological/physiological, ecological/contextual, and social/historical issues. Because the development of a biosocial perspective for life-span research, which weds the theoretical advances in the biological and social sciences, is still in its infancy, there are a number of major issues to confront. Four unifying themes appear in the following pioneering essays: parenthood as a life-span commitment; the value of the concepts of inclusive fitness and parental investment strategies in explaining species' patterns of parental behavior; the sensitivity of parental investment patterns to social and environmental context; and major evolutionary and historic change of the context in which human parental behavior is expressed. Together these themes underscore the need and utility of viewing current research on parenthood throughout the life span from a biosocial perspective.

Parenthood as a Life-Span Commitment

Past research on human parenthood tended to focus on the concerns of preadults and their relations to their parents, and, in fact, a major proportion of parenthood research is on mother–infant relations. However, as Altmann (this volume, Chapter 2) notes, the life history parameters of the higher primates (monkeys, apes, and humans), reveal a major commitment to rearing only a few costly, slowly developing young. Delayed timing in the onset of reproduction and the expansion of the infancy and juvenile periods of the life span place heavy burdens on the parent to foster its offspring from conception to reproductive maturity and even beyond.

In reality, parenthood is a lifetime commitment for many of the higher primates, and the fostering of an offspring may continue until the death of the parent. Conventional severance points of parent–offspring relations found in other animals, such as birth, weaning, or adolescence, represent shifts or transitions from one type of resource allocation or parental fostering in the higher primates to another. Birth as a marker of independence of the infant from the mother's body is just one step toward independent physiological functioning. So too, weaning and even the assumption of adult status do not mark the end of parental investment, just a shift in form in the physiological and social dependency typical of higher primates (see Altmann, Chapter 2; Leon, Chapter 4; Lancaster and Lancaster, Chapter 7; this volume).

For most of the higher primates the burden of rearing costly, slowly developing offspring falls on the mother. For this reason, most monkey and ape females support only a single nutritionally dependent youngster at a time. Humans, however, by capturing the energy of the father in contributing to the food supply of the family, permitted the nutritional dependency of two and even three young at a time and allowed humans to evolve an unusual stage of the life course: the juvenile period throughout which the weaned youngster was fed by its adult parents (Lancaster and Lancaster, Chapter 7, this volume). Humans then, early in the evolution of the species, vastly expanded the commitment to parenthood for both sexes and extended the period of development during which offspring were fed by adults through adolescence.

The course of human history shows a further intensification and extension of parenthood and parental investment even after adulthood is reached by the young, as the resources and skills necessary for reproduction became less and less free for the taking. The chapters herein by Lancaster and Lancaster (Chapter 7), Draper and Harpending (Chapter 8), Weisner (Chapter 9), LeVine and White (Chapter 10), and Vinovskis (Chapter 11) indicate that parents in recent human history have found that rearing healthy, fit offspring is not enough; they also seek to assure their children access to scarce resources to support their own reproduction. As Rossi (Chapter 3) as well as Draper and Harpending (Chapter 8) argue in this volume, world history in the past two hundred years reveals a number of societies in which the burden on parents to provide resources to their adult young through either inheritance or specialized training has become so heavy that parents limit the numbers of children produced in order to advantage existing offspring. This lengthening and expansion of parenthood in modern society has combined with a major demographic shift in life expectancy. Although the human span itself has probably not lengthened, the number of adults who live to the seventh, eighth, and ninth decades has increased so radically that many parents and offspring can expect to share 60 to 70 years of life on earth (see Bengtson, Chapter 16, and Hagestad, Chapter 15, this volume). For human beings parenthood is truly a lifetime commitment, with the lives of parents lengthening on average, at the same time that the resources needed to rear children have increased.

Parental Investment and Inclusive Fitness

Altmann (Chapter 2, this volume) introduces the concepts of inclusive fitness and parental investment strategies from evolutionary biology. These concepts are useful because they help us understand what at first appears to be a vast sea of variation in parental behavior among animal species and human groups. Inclusive fitness theory gives predictions about the evolutionary history and environmental constraints that lie behind the drawing in of male parental care or sibling care to supplement maternal investment. As Lamb, Pleck, Charnov, and Levine (Chapter 5, this volume) argue, human male parental investment, although a crucial element in human evolutionary history, cannot be analyzed as a closed biologically based system. Rather, it should be viewed as a pattern, the expression of which is clearly influenced by social and economic factors that define the context in which individuals make choices in the light of their predispositions and their presumed general goal—the maximization of inclusive fitness. Leon (this volume, Chapter 4) emphasizes the somatic costs of reproduction for female mammals and the inevitable trade of short-term loss for long-term gain inherent in mammalian reproductive effort and greatly elaborated in the rearing of slowly developing young.

McKenna (Chapter 6, this volume) presents a crucial concept in evolutionary biology and relates it to the presence or absence of maternal surrogates in the form of paternal and sibcare systems. There has been a tendency in evolutionary theory building to argue that whatever exists must be evolved and adaptive. McKenna shifts the focus to look at the role of environment in explaining the presence or absence of a particular pattern of surrogate parental care among the primates rather than at the degree of value or need for that behavior to the actors. For example, he argues that the presence of maternal surrogate care in colobine versus cercopithecine monkeys is based not on the infant's need for that care, but on the species' dominance system and hence the confidence of the mother that she can retrieve and monitor her infant. Similarly, the presence or absence of sibcare versus maternal care systems in human society discussed in chapters by Lancaster and Lancaster, Draper and Harpending, Weisner, LeVine and White, and Vinovskis rests on environmental constraints and facilitations such as the presence of multiple, dependent offspring of different ages, birth-spacing of two versus four years, and the introduction of universal education which removed older sibs from the pool of maternal aides.

Sensitivity of Parental Investment Patterns to the Social and Environmental Context

Just as inclusive fitness and parental investment theory predicts that the expression of various patterns of parental behavior will be affected by environmental constraints and facilitations, so too it predicts a fine-tuning of life history strategies and parental investment patterns to the availability of resources in the social and physical environment. As Lamb et al. (Chapter 5, this volume) emphasize, evidence for environmental influences does not constitute an alternative explanation for evolutionary adaptation; rather, such influences may be better viewed as characteristics of the relevant ecology within which parents make choices based on their behavioral predispositions, general goals, and ontogenetic experiences. The form of parental investment is sensitive to a series of trade-offs between costs and benefits in apportioning time and energy into a particular reproductive effort in the context of the life course, especially for the parents of expensive, slowly developing offspring.

LeVine and White (Chapter 10, this volume) propose a formulation to identify the optimal parental investment strategy for a given human society. This strategy is a function of (a) the expectable lifetime costs and contributions of each child to its parents and (b) the means available to enhance the lifetime cost-contribution ratio of a child from the average parent's point of view. However, among humans parental goals and means will always be culturally defined. For example, middle-class Japanese and American parents recognize education as crucial to rearing competitively fit offspring, but the implementation of this belief translates very differently in the two cultures, with the Japanese housewife staying home to tutor her children and the American mother going to work so that the family can afford to live in a particular school district or to pay for private education.

This sensitivity of parental investment and parental commitment to the environment through the life span is highlighted in cross-cultural and subgroup comparisons of human beings. Hogan (Chapter 12), Draper and Harpending (Chapter 8), and Weisner (Chapter 9) give examples of important ethnic and cultural variations in the way parental commitment and behavior is apportioned across the life span. Much of this variation is predictable on the basis of parental access to social and environmental resources. For example, Hogan describes differences among American blacks and whites in the timing of marriage and parenthood across the life course; nearly half of black infants are born to young women in mother-headed households. He notes that the opportunities for education, marriage, and employment are very different for the average black and white teenager, promoting an ever increasing divergence in their family formation and reproductive strategies.

The investment of parental attention in children also varies widely between cultures. Weisner (Chapter 9) notes that maternal behavior in middle-range societies practicing sibcare is largely supervisory rather than direct. This shifting of the burden of child care from parents to siblings permits an unexpected shift of direct child-care responsibilities to early in the life cycle, before puberty for the child—nurses, and reproduction to later in the life cycle, after marriage. Parental attention as a limited resource is underscored by Blake's study (Chapter 13), which indicates that in modern societies children from large sibships pay a cost in lesser parental attention irrespective of socioeconomic status or birth order, especially when measured by verbal skills.

Virtually every chapter in this volume emphasizes some aspect of the sensitivity of parental behavior, family formation patterns, and parental investment strategies to resources available in the social and physical environment. From the somatic costs of gestation and lactation to the complex predictions of modern parents about the availability of resources to their children and their grandchildren, an intricate interplay between biology and behavior is found. This highly evolved crucial aspect of species behavior, reproduction and parenthood, may be the most sensitive of all adaptive systems to environmental resources, constraints, and facilitations.

Evolutionary and Historic Change of the Context of Parenthood

Sensitivity to the social and physical environment is a fundamental feature of the evolutionary adaptation of parental investment patterns and life history strategies of both humans and animals. However, it is important to appreciate that humans, perhaps more than any other species, have witnessed a series of historic revolutions in the context within which parenthood is set. The transition to sedentism, confrontation with changes in resource availability, and a demographic restructuring of human populations have radically changed the factors to which human parents' behavior must respond. Many of the changes confronting human parents are really alterations in cost/benefit ratios in rearing children. Lancaster and Lancaster (Chapter 7, this volume) note the high cost of child rearing in terms of parental energy and attention in both forager and modern societies. The sibcare system and the value of child labor typical of middle-range societies probably marked a relatively brief period of human evolutionary history, when the cost of rearing children was at an all-time low and the direct benefits to parents in child labor and old-age support at an all-time high. Chapters by Draper and Harpending, Rossi, and Weisner (this volume) touch on various aspects of these major shifts to the parental calculus of investment in their young.

Human demographic changes have also had an overwhelming impact on the context of parenthood. Radical shifts in survivorship, the numbers of individuals who can expect to live out a human life span, typify much of the modern world (Rossi, Chapter 3; Bengtson, Chapter 16; Hagestad, Chapter 15, this volume). Many more parents and children can expect to share six or seven decades of life, and the three-generation family in which the middle generation is simultaneously burdened with both older and younger dependents could well become a major social issue in modern, developed societies. Relationships between generations in a three-generation family occur in a context of very rapid social change, so that each generation is confronted with a radically different world (Bengtson). Finally, as Lerner and Lerner (Chapter 14, this volume) emphasize, sensitivity to context and contextual variation is a complex, continuous two-way relationship in which children (and parents) contribute to the way that the social and environmental context impacts upon them. Individual, ethnic, and cultural differences in response to context must be continuously appreciated and evaluated.

Evolutionary and historic changes in the context of parenthood raise a whole series of theoretical issues relating evolutionary biology and social science. It is possible that historical change, going from hunter–gatherer to agricultural (middle-range societies) to modern industrial systems, in child-rearing practices, in family formation strategies, family size, and parental investment can be used as tests of predictions from parental investment and life history theory. Do parents alter the number of children produced in accordance with their assessment of the resources available in the social and physical environment, so as to rear children who will themselves be successful reproducers (Lancaster and Lancaster, Chapter 7; Draper and Harpending, Chapter 8, this volume)? What factors in the environment influence parental assessment of resource abundance (Hogan, Chapter 12; Draper and Harpending, Lancaster and Lancaster, this volume)? Do parents have a cost/benefit calculus that includes attention and emotion as well as physical resources (LeVine and White, Chapter 10; Weisner, Chapter 9; Vinovskis, Chapter 11; Blake, Chapter 13, this volume)? Does parental investment theory fit with demographic transition theory and data (Draper and Harpending, LeVine and White, this volume)? How much do social and historical differences in values and experience affect the ways in which parents assess resource availability and the appropriate ways to invest in children (Vinovskis, LeVine and White, Hogan, this volume)? The variability in parental behavior and parenthood through the life span so obvious in human history and in the cross-cultural record provides abundant and exciting opportunities to test the application of theory from evolutionary biology.

CONCLUSION

The biosocial perspective rests on a critical commitment to recognize the continuous, mutual, and inseparable interaction between biology and social behavior. To study aspects of a problem from conceptualizations that recognize the importance of only one of these factors or that set biology and behavior in causal competition is counterproductive. It is futile to study human behavioral systems involved with reproduction and parenthood without integration of all significant levels of causation. Recent developments in both theory and data bases for the biological and social sciences regarding the life span and research in parental behavior throughout the life course provide a rich possibility of unification and mutual stimulation between these two major fields of science.

As this brief overview suggests, we are a long way from any integrated biosocial science that simultaneously and conjointly deals with parenthood and life course. The state-of-the-art in theory building is still a very modest one. Hence, in many chapters in this volume the predominant focus is on biology, with minimal or only implicit attention to social influences; in other chapters the reverse holds, and the focus is predominantly on parental behavior and the life course. Some chapters focus on social behavior and only discuss biology in the sense that reproduction or aging are biological events. Others focus on evolutionary theory or reproductive biology and put less emphasis on individual and social variability in the way parental behavior is performed. There is excellent work in all these directions and sufficient diversity to provide the reader with a good sampling of what is occurring in parental behavior and life-span research in both the social and biological sciences.

REFERENCES

Altmann, S. A., Altmann, J., and Hausfater, G. Determinants of reproductive success in savannah baboons (*Papio cynocephalus*). In T. H. Clutton-Brock (Ed.), *Reproductive Success*. Chicago, IL: University of Chicago Press, in press.

Baltes, P. (ed.) *Life Span Development and Behavior*, Vol. 1. NY: Academic Press, 1978.

Baltes, P., and Brim, O. G., Jr. (Eds.). *Life Span Development and Behavior*. NY: Academic Press, 1980–1984 (Vols. II–VI).

Baltes, P., Reese, H., and Lipsitt, L. Life span development psychology. *Annual Review of Psychology*, 1980, *31*, 65–110.

Betzig, L. L., Mulder, M. G., and Turke, P. W. (Eds.). *Reproduction and Parental Investment in Humans*. NY: Cambridge University Press, in press.

Calow, P. The cost of reproduction—A physiological approach. *Biology Reviews*, 1979, *54*, 23–40.

Clutton-Brock, T. H. *Reproductive Success*. Chicago, IL: University of Chicago Press, in press.

Clutton-Brock, T. H., and Albon, S. D. Parental investment in male and female offspring in mammals. *Current Problems in Sociobiology*. Cambridge, NY: Cambridge University Press, 1982.

Cole, L. C. The population consequences of life history phenomena. *Quarterly Review of Biology*, 1954, *29*, 103–137.

Datan, N., and Ginsberg, L. H. (Eds.). *Life Span Development and Psychology: Normative Life Crises*. NY: Academic Press, 1975.

Dawkins, R., and Carlisle, T. R. Parental investment and mate desertion: A fallacy. *Nature (London)* 1976, *262*, 131–133.

Hamburg, D. A., Elliott, G. R., and Parron, D. L. *Health and Behavior: Frontiers of Research in Biobehavioral Sciences*. Washington, D.C.: National Academy of Sciences, 1982.

Hamilton, W. D. The genetical evolution of social behavior: Parts I and II. *Journal of Theoretical Biology*, 1964, *7*, 1–51.

Hamilton, W. D., The moulding of senescence by natural selection. *Journal of Theoretical Biology*, 1966, *12*, 12–45.

Hausfater, G. Dominance and reproduction in baboons (*Papio cynocephalas*): A quantitative analysis. *Contributions to Primatology*, Vol. 7. NY: S. Karger, 1975.

Hausfater, G., and Blaffer Hrdy, S. (Eds.). *Infanticide: Comparative and Evolutionary Perspectives*. NY: Aldine, 1984.

Horn, H. S., and Rubenstein, E. L. Behavioral adaptations and life history. In J. R. Krebs and N. B. Davies (Eds.), *Behavioral Ecology*. Sunderland, MA: Sinauer Press, 1984, pp. 279–298.

Kirkwood, T. B. L., and Holliday, R. The evolution of aging and longevity. *Proceedings of the Royal Society*, 1979, *205*, 531–546.

Lamb, M. E., and Sutton-Smith, B. (Eds.). *Sibling Relationships: Their Nature and Significance Across the Life Span*. Hillsdale, NJ: Erlbaum, 1982.

Lerner, R. *On the Nature of Human Plasticity*. NY: Cambridge University Press, 1984.

MacArthur, R. H. Some generalized theorems of natural selection. *Proceedings of the National Academy of Sciences*, 1962, *48*, 1893–1897.

Maynard Smith, J. Group selection and kin selection. *Nature (London)*, 1964, *201*, 1145–1147.

Maynard Smith, J. Parental investment: A prospective analysis. *Animal Behavior*, 1977, *25*, 1–9.

Migdol, S., and Sherrod, L. *An Inventory of Longitudinal Studies of Middle and Old Age*. NY: Social Science Research Council, 1981.

Pianka, E. R. Natural selection of optimal reproductive tactics. *American Zoologist*, 1976, *16*, 775–784.

Riley, M.; Hess, B.; and Bond, K. (Eds.). *Aging in Society: Selected Reviews of Recent Research*. Hillsdale, NJ: Erlbaum, 1983.

Rossi, A. S. Life span theories and women's lives. *Signs*, 1980, *6*, 4–32.

Rossi, A. S. (Ed.). *Gender and the Life Course*. NY: Aldine, 1985.

Schaffer, W. M. Selection for optimal life histories, the effects of age structure. *Ecology*, 1974, *55*, 291–303.

Stearns, S. C. Life history tactics: A review of the ideas. *Quarterly Review of Biology*, 1976, *51*, 3–47.

Trivers, R. L. Parental investment and sexual selection. In B. Campbell (Ed.), *Sexual Selection and the Descent of Man*. Chicago: Aldine, 1972, pp. 136–179.

Trivers, R. L. *Social Evolution*. Menlo Park, NJ: Cummings, 1985.

Verdonik, F., and Sherrod, L. *An Inventory of Longitudinal Research on Childhood and Adolescence*. NY: Social Science Research Council, 1984.

Wasser, S. K. (Ed.). *Social Behavior of Female Vertebrates*. NY: Academic Press, 1983.

Wasser, S. K., and Waterhouse, M. The establishment and maintenance of sex biases. In S. K. Wasser (Ed.), *Social Behavior of Female Vertebrates*. NY: Academic Press, 1983, pp. 19–35.

Western, D. Size, life history and ecology in mammals. *African Journal of Ecology*, 1979, *17*, 185–204.

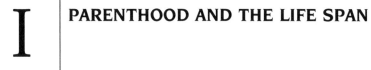

I

PARENTHOOD AND THE LIFE SPAN

2

LIFE SPAN ASPECTS OF REPRODUCTION AND PARENTAL CARE IN ANTHROPOID PRIMATES

Jeanne Altmann

INTRODUCTION

The close genetic relatedness and the asymmetry of survival abilities between parent and offspring result in this relationship being an obvious focus for consideration of the biological evolution of social behavior. The evolution of family relationships has been the subject of considerable theoretical investigation and speculation in the past ten years, occupying a major position particularly in the writings of behavioral and population biologists (e.g. Hamilton, 1964; Trivers, 1972, 1974; Alexander, 1974; West Eberhard, 1975; MacNair and Parker, 1978; Charlesworth, 1978; Wade, 1978; Stamps et al., 1978). These authors have considered factors that would promote or discourage the care of young by either or both parents and by nonparent caregivers (see review in McKenna, Chapter 6, this volume, for nonhuman primates), sibling competition or cooperation, and parent–offspring conflict.

The evolutionary models are economic in nature. Their key variables are the degree of genetic relatedness between the interacting individuals and the "costs" and "benefits" of performing behaviors, measured in terms of increments or decrements to the biological inclusive fitness of each party. Evolution through natural and sexual selection is viewed as having favored behavior that increases the actor's inclusive fitness; that is, behavior that enhances the sum of the actor's individual fitness plus an appropriate fraction of the individual fitness of the recipient kin (Hamilton, 1964). Thus, acts that are detrimental to the actor in the aid of another may be favored, particularly if the benefit to the recipient is high relative to the cost to the actor or if the genetic relatedness between the two is appreciable.

"Parental care" is a term that most people would probably understand to mean any behavior that is performed by a parent and that benefits its offspring. Some might restrict the term to include only behavior overtly directed toward the offspring, perhaps only behavior that serves little or no other purpose. "More care" would be understood to mean behavior that provided more benefit. In evolutionary models of behavior, however, it is not care or benefit per se but "parental investment," the ratio of or difference between benefit (to the offspring) and cost (to the parent) that is seen as the relevant variable affecting the evolution of these and other behaviors (see references above). This obviously important distinction has often been ignored in applications of these models to humans and to nonhuman species.

Several life-history characteristics of anthropoid primates, i.e., monkeys and apes, further suggest the evolution of complex, intense, and long-lasting parent–offspring interactions in these animals. Like humans, monkeys and apes are distinguished from most other mammals in ways that are particularly related to parental care and development. Relative to other mammals of comparable size, anthropoids give birth to their first offspring at a later age, have longer gestations, produce fewer (usually only one) young with each gestation, and have longer intervals between successive births (e.g., Sacher, 1978; Western, 1979). Both infancy and the juvenile stage last longer for these primate offspring than for other mammals. In the evolutionary "game" of survival and reproduction, we and our nearest relatives have adopted what is clearly a strategy of low reproduction, presumably compensated by concomitantly high gains in offspring survival (a so-called K-strategy in the jargon of population biology; see e.g., McNaughton and Wolf, 1973). It seems reasonable to expect that a long and effective period of primate parental care is a major contributor to any increases in the survival rate of the young.

Several other salient features set the stage for primate family interactions. Most monkeys and apes are, to varying degrees, sexually dimorphic, with males larger than females among adults. Social groups usually include fewer adult males than females—only one reproducing male in some species. Parental care in most of these species is primarily the province of the mother. Only the small-bodied apes, gibbons, and siamangs, among the Old World monkeys and apes, and some of the very small New World monkeys, primarily the marmosets and tamarins, are virtually monomorphic in size, monogamous in mating system, and demonstrate considerable paternal care. In monogamous species, offspring of both sexes disperse before reproduction, but in most other species of monkeys and apes, it is the males who disperse; females remain within their group of birth and reproduce (see Wrangham, 1980).

How does the behavior of parents and offspring mesh with primate life history characteristics to produce a successful, adaptive complex (Stearns, 1976)? To what extent does an evolutionary and ecological approach shed light on aspects of parental care, particularly the extent of care and its temporal distribution? What conditions favor greater paternal care? Why hasn't natural selection favored earlier or more frequent reproduction? This chapter provides an overview of reproduction and parental care across the life span in primates, considers the effects on reproduction and care of various seasonal or other differences in ecological conditions, and evaluates the compatibility and coordination of reproduction and care with nonreproductive activities both throughout an individual's life span and within the shorter rhythms of daily activities.

TEMPORAL ASPECTS OF REPRODUCTION
WITHIN THE LIFE SPAN

Onset of Reproduction

Reproductive maturation is gradual for nonhuman as well as human, primates, and the capability to produce young precedes completion of growth (Glassman et al., 1984; Watts, 1985). However, physical and social factors usually result in an appreciable gap between the time of initial reproductive potential and the time of actual reproduction. Among baboons, females who have recently attained menarche are often rejected as sexual partners by fully adult males. These adolescent females mate primarily with juveniles and adolescents, probably contributing to the females experiencing about a year of adolescent subfertility (Scott, 1984; Altmann et al., in press and unpublished data). Despite this subfertility period, sexually active females usually conceive for the first time before attaining their full adult size. One of the consequences for a primate female of this overlap in stages of growth and potential reproduction is the stress of simultaneously providing nutrition for her own growth as well as for that of her first offspring, more so if she conceives early in her potential reproductive span. This nutritional stress is probably one of the reasons that mortality rates for firstborn primate offspring are higher than for other offspring (see review in Lancaster, 1986; Altmann et al., in press, for wild baboons).

Especially in sexually dimorphic species, males also attain reproductive potential appreciably before their growth is complete (Watts, 1985). For example, baboon males experience testes enlargement and produce viable sperm when they are barely larger than adult females and only half the weight of full-grown males (Snow, 1967; Altmann et al., 1981; Altmann, unpublished data). As a result of both competition from older males and perhaps not being favored as mating partners by adult females, it is probably another two or three years before these young baboon males father infants in a social group (Altmann et al., in press). In addition, in various species males (or females) that normally disperse as adults often do not reproduce, for behavioral and/or physiological reasons, if they remain in their parental group, but will rapidly do so if they change groups or if their parents are removed from the group they are in (Abbott, 1984; Cheney and Seyfarth, 1983).

Recent evidence suggests that social exposure may sometimes accelerate reproductive maturation in nonhuman primates (reviewed in McClintock, 1983). For example, onset of the mating season in rhesus monkeys is stimulated, for both males and females, by the presence of mature females (Vandenbergh and Drickamer, 1974; Vandenbergh and Vessey, 1968), and in savannah baboons onset of menarche seems to be accelerated and coordinated by the presence of other females that have just reached menarche (Altmann et al., unpublished data).

Timing within the life span of menarche or the onset of the reproductive span is also ecologically labile in both human and nonhuman primates (for humans, see reviews in Eveleth and Tanner, 1976; Wyshak and Frisch, 1982; for nonhuman primates, see Altmann et al., 1977, 1981; Harcourt et al., 1980; Mori, 1979; Packer, 1979; Pusey, 1980; Strum and Western, 1982; Sugiyama and Ohsawa, 1982). Captivity, artificial feeding, or substantial natural increases in food availability lower the age of menarche and first birth in females and testes enlargement or descent and development of secondary sexual characteristics in males for almost all species that have been studied (but see Chism et al., 1984, for patas monkeys as an exception).

All other things being equal, we would expect earlier onset of reproduction to be favored by natural selection. As indicated above, this onset is quite susceptible to environmental and social factors. Earlier onset appears to have its costs, however. These may include increased nutritional competition between mother and offspring, interference with attainment of full adult size by the mother, increased infant mortality, and deficiencies in time spent by the mother learning foraging as well as social and other skills needed during adulthood (Johnston, 1982). The complexities and trade-offs of changes in aspects of social, reproductive, or other maturation remain relatively unexplored (Altmann, 1986, for nonhuman primates and other chapters in Lancaster and Hamburg, 1986, for humans).

Adulthood

After achieving her first conception, a primate female usually continues to produce young at regular intervals throughout adulthood. Like humans, most monkey and ape females experience an extended postpartum amenorrhea that probably is maintained to a considerable extent through frequent suckling (Konner and Worthman, 1980; Short, 1984). For example, unprovisioned wild baboons in nonexpanding populations do not resume menstrual cycles for about 10 to 12 months; then they experience three or four cycles, on average, before becoming pregnant, resulting in mean interbirth intervals of almost two years (Altmann et al., 1977; Nicolson, 1982). In contrast, if a baboon infant dies, its mother resumes menstrual cycles within a few weeks and has only one or two cycles before becoming pregnant (Altmann et al., 1978).

Unlike humans, baboons, and the great apes, most other anthropoids are seasonal breeders. Although some macaque females produce infants in successive years, those with surviving offspring are less likely to become pregnant in the first annual mating season after her infant's birth than are females who do not have a dependent offspring at the onset of the mating season (Tanaka et al., 1970). Only the marmosets and tamarins seem to lack a postpartum amenorrhea (French, 1983, and references therein); in captivity they usually conceive at a postpartum estrus, and unlike many rodents that have a postpartum estrus (Gilbert, 1984), they do not seem to have delayed implantation. Rather, a pregnancy and lactation commence simultaneously. It is not known the extent to which this reproductive overlap is facilitated by the fact that the mother provides little care other than suckling in these monogamous species, and to what extent simultaneous gestation and lactation is attributable to the rich nutritional conditions of captivity.

For the vast majority of species that do have a postpartum suppression of ovulation, those such as humans, gorillas, and baboons that exhibit little birth seasonality are probably better able than highly seasonal species to conceive promptly if an infant dies or if food becomes abundant. Many other primates must wait as long as six months, until the next breeding season, before they can start their next pregnancy, even if conditions otherwise seem optimal to do so. It is not well understood why even some closely related species exhibit major differences in the extent to which births are seasonally restricted (Hadidian and Bernstein, 1979).

For primate females the duration of interbirth intervals, like onset of reproduction, is affected by food abundance (see references above). Food availability interacts with infant survivorship and the extent to which a given species exhibits birth seasonality to determine the interbirth interval. Increased food availability usually leads to greater survivorship of the most susceptible age group, infants, thereby increasing interbirth intervals in species that exhibit lactational suppression of ovulation. However, among mothers with surviving infants, those with abundant food supplies conceive sooner than those with more restricted nutrition. As with humans, it is not known how much of this effect is due to better infant nutrition and how much to better maternal nutrition. A recent study of Japanese monkeys (Sugiyama and Ohsawa, 1982) suggests an additional consequence of abundant food supplies that are also spatially restricted. Under that condition, it is higher ranking females in the dominance hierarchy that benefit most; i.e., that have a greater reduction in interbirth intervals.

We know much less about the reproductive histories of primate males than primate females. This is partially because paternity is much harder to determine than maternity, especially in the semipromiscuous mating systems of most primates. Male reproductive histories are also harder to follow because most primate species are "matrilocal"—females spend their whole lives in the social group into which they were born, and males usually leave their natal group as young adults to join, if they survive to do so, another group in which they will father young. During adulthood a male may change social groups several times, and during his tenure in a group various factors such as dominance rank, alliances, and female choice will determine his access to females at the time of conception (Hausfater, 1975; Smuts, 1982; Strum, 1982).

The variance in reproductive success among males is commonly assumed to be greater than that among females, at least in animals that are polygynous. However, the extent of this difference may have been overestimated as a result of cross-sectional studies; male reproduction is probably much less evenly distributed throughout adulthood than is that of females. Males probably sire a disproportionate amount of their offspring when they are in prime physical condition, relatively young, and of high dominance rank. Longitudinal data from baboons, however, indicates that some reproduction continues well beyond loss of high rank (Strum, 1982; Altmann et al., in press). So little is known about most of the factors affecting the life course of male reproduction that it is hardly surprising that nothing is known of how the distribution of reproduction throughout adulthood is affected by environmental factors.

Reproductive Termination

Reproductive senescence has been demonstrated in only a few individual females of a few primate species (see chapters in Bowden, 1979); even in captivity, where primates live to much older ages than in the wild, reproductive senescence does not seem to proceed more rapidly or earlier than does senescence of other systems, and unlike humans, nonhuman primates experience no complete cessation of reproductive potential appreciably before the failure of other systems. However, some very aged monkey females in laboratories ceased reproduction at an age that would be comparable to about 70 years in humans. The most extensive data on aged primates are those for hamadryas baboons in a Russian laboratory where elderly females were found to have a large number of tumors and digestive disorders and to be of abnormally low weights (Lapin et al., 1979). It is not known to what extent nutritional deficiencies and weight loss contributed to reproductive failure in these old monkeys. Reproductive senescence does not occur in aged captive chimpanzees, the only great ape for which many data have been available (Graham et al., 1979). In sum, although little is known about reproductive senescence in nonhuman primate females, existing evidence suggests considerable quantitative, if not qualitative, differences from humans. These differences result in monkey and ape mothers caring for young offspring throughout adulthood until death.

Although elderly, weakened adult primate males are capable of fathering infants, like adolescent males they are probably excluded from reproduction in many normal social group settings. Thus, for social reasons it is possible that males more than females experience a postreproductive period in many nonhuman primates, but the question has not been addressed. In addition, data are needed on whether sperm counts or other physical aspects of reproductive capacity decline with age.

TEMPORAL ASPECTS OF PARENTAL CARE VIS-À-VIS OTHER ACTIVITIES

Maternal Care

Most primates are nonmonogamous, and for them parental care is overwhelmingly provided by an infant's mother, usually within a multifemale, single- or multimale social group. Quantitative developmental studies that formerly focused solely on social behavior, often in captive settings, have increasingly been supplemented by more ecological research in a range of situations (Berman, 1980; Rosenblum and Sunderland, 1982; Johnson and Southwick, 1984) that suggest the complexity of these females' lives. How does the care of young fit in with other aspects of an adult primate's life? Over three quarters of a baboon female's adulthood is spent caring for an infant or a growing fetus, and limited available information suggests that the same is true for the other anthropoids. On a daily basis this means that primate females spend the vast majority of days providing both for themselves, just as adult males and juveniles do, and for an offspring. During pregnancy the primary task is obtaining additional nutrition—no small feat when approximately 60% of the day is already spent in feeding and moving among food sites, as is the case for wild baboons. Females in late pregnancy are probably more susceptible to predation than cycling females; they hang behind the group and perhaps cannot flee predators as rapidly during attacks.

The stresses of providing parental care become much greater after the birth of an infant. The growing infant's nutritional needs keep increasing and must be satisfied through milk, probably a less efficient means of feeding than placental transfer (Reynolds, 1967). Unlike most other mammalian infants, anthropoid primate neonates can neither provide their own loco-motion (though most nonhuman primate infants can cling well to their mothers) nor be left in nests, burrows, or other hideaways. Rather, the infant clings and its mother carries it—all day in the case of far-ranging terrestrial species, somewhat less in the more arboreal species that often also travel shorter distances.

Primate mothers provide their infants with additional care through thermoregulatory assistance and through social grooming that provides ectoparasite removal. Finally, mothers protect against predators and against potentially dangerous conspecifics such as recent migrant males in some species or higher ranking adult females in species with strong dominance hierarchies. These tasks all require commitments of time, energy, and risk-taking that are interspersed with the normal and ongoing activities of "making a living." Among Amboseli baboons, not only is infant mortality high, but females with young infants have the highest mortality rates among adult females (Altmann et al., in press). As data become available for other nonexpanding populations of wild primates, it would not be surprising to find that this is often the case.

For baboons, the time course and extent of infant independence is affected by social and ecological factors on a monthly, daily, and even moment-by-moment basis. In Amboseli, mothers of low dominance rank are more restrictive of their young infants than are high-ranking ones and thereby seem to reduce the social stress and danger of kidnapping (see also Rowell, 1968, for captive anubis baboons). Apparently as a consequence, however, their infants are slower in becoming independent of their mothers, even long after the period of restrictive maternal care. Ecological influences are particularly apparent when infants are starting to do some locomotion slowly on their own. This exploration seems to be hindered if the season is one in which the animals are feeding much in the trees, or if the group must travel far and rapidly to reach key food resources. Under these conditions, infants stay in contact with their mothers more than on days of terrestrial feeding and short day-journeys. Thus, for nonhuman primates the season of birth, overall differences in habitats, or year-to-year habitat fluctuations may prove to have appreciable effects on parent–offspring relationships and development (see Lee, 1984, for vervet monkeys).

One of the most intriguing aspects of mothers' multiple tasks is the extent to which it is possible to perform simultaneously more than one of these tasks, and the developmental changes in this compatability. For example, when a baboon youngster is small and relatively inactive, it can ride and even suckle while its mother feeds uninterrupted. In fact, the mother's feeding would be interrupted if the infant were *not* in contact, because the infant is so young and needs constant attention and protection when not in contact. In contrast, an older, much larger and more active infant interferes with its mother's feeding when it is in contact with or next to her; it can detect many dangers on its own and rapidly run to its mother for protection when necessary. Thus, an older infant's mother can "afford" to have her infant in contact only when she is resting and needs to have it manage on its own while she feeds, whereas a neonate's mother can "afford" to attend to her exploring infant only when she is resting and needs to have it quietly riding on her while she is busy foraging. Similar results have recently been documented in rhesus monkeys in India and Nepal (Johnson and Southwick, 1984). Establishment of these fine contingencies between mother and infant behavior may provide the foundation for highly developed and crucial social sensitivities later in life.

Primate infants depend for a long time on their mothers for survival, and much of a mother's contribution to the next generation is tied up in her investment in each infant, increasingly so as an infant successfully survives the perilous early months. Consequently, evolutionary theorizing that attempts to isolate and predict behavior based on the self-interest of each family member must, to be regarded seriously, take into account the complexities of these dependencies. Attempts by an infant to garner additional care might, if successful, be self-destructive because (1) they will probably increase the mother's mortality risks and (2) retard independence in the infant which could lead to higher infant mortality if the infant is orphaned. Thus, it is in the interest of the infant as well as the mother to keep parental care below what might at first glance seem to be an optimal level.

Paternal Care

Paternal care has been best documented, and is most extensive, among the few monogamous primates (see Snowdon and Suomi, 1982, for a recent review). With the exception of the small-bodied apes, Asian gibbons, and siamangs, all of the monogamous anthropoids are very small monkeys, most of whom normally bear twins or even triplets, instead of the usual primate single births. In these twinning species the father and siblings provide virtually all nonnutritive care of the infants. The stresses of personal maintenance activities and those of reproduction and offspring care are thus divided among the family members, apparently facilitating greater reproductive output (see Lancaster, Chapter 7, this volume, for the importance of a division of labor in human parental care systems). Even in semipromiscuous, highly dimorphic and diethic primate societies, such as those of African baboons and Asian macaques, paternal care may be very important. In baboons, just the presence in close proximity of a mother's adult male associate (usually her infant's likely father based on behavioral and cycle state criteria), reduces harassment of the mother and results in her being less restrictive of her infant (Altmann, 1980). As the infant becomes partially independent, it spends time without its mother and with this adult male and benefits from this same passive, as well as occasionally active, protection. The infant also benefits from access to food sources that are available to the males and are not accessible to other group members. The older infant or young juvenile sometimes gets specific protection via retrieval and carrying by the male during a predator alarm. In the rare instances of yearling baboon orphans that survive, the survival is usually accompanied by virtual adoption by the same male associate. Good comparative data are needed that would examine, within and between species, rates of natality and infant mortality for anthropoid species under differing ecological constraints and differing systems of parental care. This is an area in which particular enrichment would come from interfacing experimental studies in captivity with experimental and nonexperimental field investigations.

DISCUSSION

Some aspects of parental care are more obvious, more easily identified, than are others. Direct provision of nutrition, carrying, hygienic care, overt teaching, are examples of the former. We have a much more difficult time identifying and evaluating long distance rather than contact behaviors, passive rather than active care, social learning without overt social teaching, assistance provided to many individuals as opposed to that directed toward a single one (Kleiman and Malcolm, 1981). In addition, individual, societal, academic, and other biases all too readily affect classification and measurement of behavior that is potentially harmful or helpful. Animal behavior research, including and perhaps particularly nonhuman primate research, has not escaped these pitfalls. Aggressive/harmful behaviors are more readily acknowledged, identified, and recorded in males than in females and the converse is true of nurturant ones, whether directed toward adults or infants. Operational, gender-free criteria, based in part on the kinds of cost and benefit analyses outlined in recent economic and evolutionary writings, are needed if we are to cross the temporal, cultural, and species boundaries in our efforts to understand parenting within the life span. Identification and measurement of paternal care in nonmonogamous primates suffers from both the aforementioned problems as well as from uncertainty of paternity.

Adulthood for nonhuman anthropoid females, like that for their human counterparts, is heavily committed to reproduction and care of dependent offspring on a minute-to-minute basis, from month-to-month and year-to-year. If anything, the reproductive years may normally encompass even more of their lifetime for nonhuman females than for women. In nonhuman primates care for first offspring often occurs before a female's own growth is complete, and successive infants continue to be born until a female's death; neither within nor among species is a postreproductive period a regular life stage.

Changes that occur in the lives of anthropoid females that receive extensive food enrichment, as in captivity, can be compared to those changes Rossi (Chapter 3, this volume) describes for western women in recent years. Food-provisioned anthropoid females start reproduction earlier, experience higher survivorship of their infants, have shorter interbirth intervals, and have longer periods of adulthood and reproduction (Altmann, 1986, Fig. 1). If mortality risks are reduced and nutrition is increased and easily obtained, these females may have a higher probability of experiencing a postreproductive period.

The lives of nutritionally enriched females are also probably more likely to overlap with the adulthood of more of their offspring and with the lives of their grandchildren. The opportunities for parental care continuing past infancy, for interactions with grandchildren, and for reciprocity with grown offspring are all increased in these situations. In our anthropoid relatives, unlike their modern human counterparts, there is no tendency to limit the number of offspring or to increase the length of the postreproductive period. We have much to learn about the consequences of these nutritionally induced life-history changes for individual behavior, family interactions, or social structure in our anthropoid relatives.

SUMMARY

Anthropoid primates share some important similarities in reproduction and parental care with their human relatives. Some striking contrasts are also evident. A long prereproductive period of gradual development and learning is followed by intensive and almost continuous care of each successive offspring. For most species, care is almost exclusively the province of the mother who, for months or years, suckles her infant, carries it, and protects it from danger, usually while simultaneously foraging to provide nutrition for them both. Fine coordination of activities between a mother and her developing, increasingly active and semi-independent infant appear to be critical to the mother's ability to meet these multiple demands. Such features of primate maternal care have implications for evolutionary models and the potential for parent–offspring conflict.

Patterns of reproduction and offspring survival and development are sensitive to social and ecological factors. Situations of extensive food enrichment, often accompanied by reduction in mortality risks, greatly change reproductive patterning. Females begin reproduction at a younger age, more of their offspring survive to adulthood, interbirth intervals are shortened, and the length of the reproductive span is increased. The result is often an increased overlap of generations and an increased opportunity for family interactions, within and between generations. Females are more likely to be alive when their own offspring are mature. There are greater chances for parental care to continue past infancy, for interactions between grandparents and grandchildren, and for reciprocity between parents and their adult offspring.

Extensive paternal care and major division of tasks within parental care is present only in the small, monogamous primates, almost all of which also produce twins. However, a greater degree of paternal care than previously was recognized is increasingly being demonstrated in a wide range of monkeys and apes. The paucity of data on male reproductive histories will continue to be hampered somewhat by the dispersal patterns in these primarily matrifocal animals and by the difficulty of ascertaining paternity without genetic analysis. However, the lack of information has also been a result of problems with academic biases, research design, and methodology, which may be changing.

ACKNOWLEDGMENTS

I am appreciative of the assistance of A. Samuels and C. Johnson with various aspects of manuscript preparation. S. Altmann, B. J. King, and J. Lancaster provided helpful comments on an earlier draft. Financial support of my research has been provided by the H. F. Guggenheim Foundation and by the American people through HD15007.

REFERENCES

Abbott, David H. Behavioral and physiological suppression of fertility in subordinate marmoset monkeys. *American Journal of Primatology*, 1984, *6*, 169–189.

Alexander, R. D. The evolution of social behavior. *Annual Review of Ecology and Systematics*, 1974, *5*, 325–383.

Altmann, J. *Baboon Mothers and Infants*. Cambridge, MA: Harvard University Press, 1980.

Altmann, J. Adolescent pregnancies in non-human primates: An ecological and developmental perspective. In J. Lancaster and B. Hamburg (Eds.), *School-Age Pregnancy and Parenthood: Biosocial Dimensions*. NY: Aldine, 1986, pp. 247–262.

Altmann, J., Altmann, S., and Hausfater, G. Primate infant's effects on mother's future reproduction. *Science*, 1978, *201*, 1028–1029.

Altmann, J., Altmann, S., and Hausfater, G. Physical maturation and age estimates of yellow baboons, *Papio cynocephalus*. *American Journal of Primatology*, 1981, *1*, 389–399.

Altmann, J., Altmann, S., Hausfater, G., and McCuskey, S. A. Life history of yellow baboons: physical development, reproductive parameters, and infant mortality. *Primates*, 1977, *18*, 315–330.

Altmann, J., Hausfater, G., and Altmann, S. Determinants of reproductive success in savannah baboons (*Papio cynocephalus*). In T. Clutton-Brock (Ed.), *Reproductive Success*. Chicago, IL: University of Chicago Press, in press.

Berman, C. M. Mother-infant relationships among free-ranging rhesus monkeys on Cayo Santiago: A comparison with captive pairs. *Animal Behaviour*, 1980, *28*, 860–873.

Bowden, D. M. *Aging in Non-Human Primates*. Reinhold Primate Behavior and Development Series. NY: Van Nostrand-Reinhold, 1979.

Charlesworth, B. Some models of the evolution of altruistic behaviour between siblings. *Journal of Theoretical Biology*, 1978, *72*, 297–319.

Cheney, D. L., and Seyfarth, R. M. Non-random dispersal in free-ranging vervet monkeys: Social and genetic consequences. *American Naturalist*, 1983, *22*, 392–412.

Chism, J., Rowell, T., and Olson, D. Life history patterns of female patas monkeys. In M. Small (Ed.), *Female Primates: Studies by Women Primatologists*. NY: Alan R. Liss, 1984, pp. 175–190.

Eveleth, P. B., and Tanner, J. M. *Worldwide Variation in Human Growth*. London: Cambridge University Press, 1976.

French, J. A. Lactation and fertility: An examination of nursing and interbirth intervals in cotton-top tamarins (*Saguinus. o. oedipus*). *Folia Primatologica*, 1983, *40*, 276–282.

Gilbert, A. N. Postpartum and lactational estrus: a comparative analysis in Rodentia. *Journal of Comparative Psychology*, 1984, *98(3)*, 232–245.

Glassman, D. M., Coelho, A. M., Carey, K. D., and Bramblett, C. A. Weight growth in savannah baboons: A longitudinal study from birth to adulthood. *Growth*, 1984, *48*, 425–433.

Graham, C. E., Kling, O. R., and Steiner, R. A. Reproductive senescence in female nonhuman primates. In D. M. Bowden (Ed.), *Aging in Non-Human Primates*. Reinhold Primate Behavior and Development Series. NY: Van Nostrand-Reinhold, 1979, pp. 183–202.

Hadidian, J., and Bernstein, I. S. Female reproductive cycles and birth data from an Old World monkey colony. *Primates*, 1979, *20(3)*, 429–442.

Hamilton, W. D. The genetical evolution of social behavior, I, II. *Journal of Theoretical Biology*, 1964, *7*, 1–52.

Harcourt, A. H., Fossey, D., Stewart, K. J., and Watts, D. P. Reproduction in wild gorillas and some comparisons with chimpanzees. *Journal of Reproduction and Fertility, Supplement*, 1980, *28*, 59–70.

Hausfater, G. Dominance and reproduction in baboons: A quantitative analysis. *Contributions to Primatology*, 1975, *7*, 1–150.

Johnson, R. L., and Southwick, C. H. Structural diversity and mother–infant relations among rhesus monkeys in India and Nepal. *Folia Primatologica*, 1984, *43*, 198–215.

Johnston, T. D. Selective costs and benefits in the evolution of learning. *Advances in the Study of Behaviour*, 1982, *12*, 65–106.

Kleiman, D. G., and Malcolm, J. R. Evolution of male parental investment in mammals. In D. J. Gubernick and P. H. Klopfer (Eds.), *Parental Care in Mammals*. NY: Plenum Press, 1981, pp. 347–387.

Konner, M., and Worthman, C. Nursing frequency, gonadal function, and birth spacing among !Kung hunter-gatherers. *Science*, 1980, *207*, 788–791.

Lancaster, J. Human adolescence and reproduction: An evolutionary perspective. In J. Lancaster and B. Hamburg (Eds.), *School-Age Pregnancy and Parenthood: Biosocial Dimensions*. NY: Aldine, 1986, pp. 17–37.

Lancaster, J., and Hamburg, B. *School-Age Pregnancy and Parenthood: Biosocial Dimensions*. NY: Aldine, 1986.

Lapin, B. A., Krilova, R. I., Cherkovich, G. M., and Asanov, N. S. Observations from Sukhumi. In D. M. Bowden (Ed.), *Aging in Non-Human Primates*. NY: Van Nostrand-Reinhold, 1979, pp. 14–37.

Lee, P. C. Ecological constraints on the social development of vervet monkeys. *Behaviour*, 1984, *91(4)*, 245–262.

McClintock, M.K. Pheromonal regulation of the ovarian cycle: Enhancement, suppression, and synchrony. In J. G. Vandenbergh (Ed.), *Pheromones and Reproduction in Mammals*. NY: Academic Press, 1983.

MacNair, M. R., and Parker, G. A. Models of parent-offspring conflict. II. Promiscuity. *Animal Behaviour*, 1978, *26*, 111–122.

McNaughton, S. J., and Wolf, L. L. *General Ecology*. NY: Holt, Rinehart and Winston, 1973.

Mori, A. Analysis of population changes by measurement of body weight in the Koshima troop of Japanese monkeys. *Primates*, 1979, *20*, 371–397.

Nicolson, N. *Weaning and the development of independence in olive baboons*. Ph.D. thesis. Cambridge, MA: Harvard University, 1982.

Packer, C. Inter-troop transfer and inbreeding avoidance in *Papio anubis*. *Animal Behaviour*, 1979, *27*, 1–37.

Pusey, A. E. Inbreeding avoidance in chimpanzees. *Animal Behaviour*, 1980, *28*, 543–552.

Reynolds, M. Mammary respiration in lactating goats. *American Journal of Physiology*, 1967, *212*, 707–710.

Rosenblum, L. A., and Sunderland, G. Feeding ecology and mother–infant relations. In L. W. Hoffman, R. Gandelman and H. R. Schiffman (Eds.), *Parenting, Its Causes and Consequences*. Hillsdale, NJ: Erlbaum, 1982, pp. 75–110.

Rowell, T. E. The effect of temporary separation from their group on the mother–infant relationship of baboons. *Folia Primatologica*, 1968, *9*, 114–122.

Sacher, G. A. Evolution of longevity and survival characteristics in mammals. In E. L. Schneider (Ed.), *The Genetics of Aging*. NY: Plenum Press, 1978.

Scott, L. M. Reproductive behavior of adolescent female baboons (*Papio anubis*) in Kenya. In M. Small (Ed.), *Female Primates: Studies by Women Primatologists*. NY: Alan R. Liss, 1984, pp. 77–100.

Short, R. V. Breast feeding. *Scientific American*, 1984, *250(4)*, 35–41.

Smuts, B. *Special relationships between adult male and female olive baboons* (Papio anubis). Ph.D. Thesis, Stanford, CA: Stanford University, 1982.

Snow, C. C. *The physical growth and development of the open-land baboon*, Papio doguera. Ph.D. Thesis, Tucson, AZ: University of Arizona, 1967.

Snowdon, C. T., and Suomi, S. J. Paternal behavior in primates. In H. E. Fitzgerald, J. A. Mullins, and P. Gage (Eds.), *Child Nurturance*. Vol. 3. *Primate Behavior and Child Nurturance*. NY: Plenum Press, 1982.

Stamps, J. A., Metcalf, R. A., and Krishnan, V. V. A genetic analysis of parent-offspring conflict. *Behavioral Ecology and Sociobiology*, 1978, *3*, 369–392.

Stearns, S. C. Life history tactics: A review of ideas. *Quarterly Review of Biology*, 1976, *51*, 3–47.

Strum, S. C. Agonistic dominance in male baboons: An alternative view. *International Journal of Primatology*, 1982, *3*, 175–202.

Strum, S. C., and Western, J. Variations in fecundity with age and environment in olive baboons (*Papio anubis*). *American Journal of Primatology*, 1982, *3*, 61–76.

Sugiyama, Y, and Ohsawa, H. Population dynamics of Japanese monkeys with special reference to the effect of artificial feeding. *Folia Primatologica*, 1982, *39*, 238–263.

Tanaka, T., Tokuda, K., and Kotera, S. Effects of infant loss on the interbirth interval of Japanese monkeys. *Primates*, 1970, *11*, 113–117.

Trivers, R. L. Parental investment and sexual selection. In B. Campbell (Ed.), *Sexual Selection and the Descent of Man*. Chicago, IL: University of Chicago Press, 1972, pp. 136–179.

Trivers, R. L. Parent-offspring conflict. *American Zoologist*, 1974, *14*, 249–264.

Vandenbergh, J. G., and Drickamer, L. C. Reproductive coordination among free-ranging rhesus monkeys. *Physiology and Behavior*, 1974, *13(3)*, 1–4.

Vandenbergh, J. G., and Vessey, S. Seasonal breeding of free-ranging rhesus monkeys and related ecological factors. *Journal of Reproduction and Fertility*, 1968, *15*, 71–79.

Wade, M. J. Kin selection: A classical approach and a general solution. Proceedings of the National Academy of Sciences U.S.A., 1978, *75*, 6154–6158.

Watts, E. Adolescent growth and development of monkeys, apes and humans. In E. S. Watts (Ed.), *Nonhuman Primate Models for Growth and Development*. NY: Alan R. Liss, 1985.

West Eberhard, M. J. The evolution of social behavior by kin selection. *Quarterly Review of Biology*, 1975, *50*, 1–33.

Western, D. Size, life history and ecology in mammals. *African Journal of Ecology*, 1979, *20*, 185–204.

Wrangham, R. W. An ecological model of female-bonded primate groups. *Behaviour*, 1980, *75*, 262–299.

Wyshak, G., and Frisch, R. E. Evidence for a secular trend in age of menarche. *New England Journal of Medicine*, 1982, *306*, 1033–1035.

3

PARENTHOOD IN TRANSITION: FROM LINEAGE TO CHILD TO SELF-ORIENTATION

Alice S. Rossi

INTRODUCTION

In the late 20th century parenthood is undergoing a profound and wrenching transformation in almost every part of the globe. It is an unprecedented transformation when viewed against the long stretch of human history. For most of that history there was a precarious balance between human fertility and mortality: life was short and societal survival depended on a fertility rate high enough to counter the heavy toll of infant and maternal mortality. Death was a familiar event in the lives of adults due to the loss of infants, children, and spouses, and few children grew to adulthood without intimate acquaintance with the death of a sibling and one or both parents.

Slow rates of population growth characterized most of the history of our species. That some societies lost the precarious battle for survival is suggested by the archeological record of extinct societies. In this century an unprecedented and critical issue facing the world is a reverse threat: a great excess of fertility over mortality in a fragile ecosystem whose population doubled in 50 years earlier in the century, and is now in the process of redoubling in only 25 years.

Because of the economic interdependence of the world system, global population pressure is a threat to all nations. The definition of what constitutes a population problem, however, varies from nation to nation. In Europe and North America, at a late stage of the demographic transition, nations face stable or declining population growth, while in Central and South America, Africa, and Asia, at an early phase, nations face rapidly expanding population growth that far outstrips their economic growth. With 42% of its population under 15 years of age, Mexico worries about the costs of educating children, while West Germany is concerned with the costs of supporting the elderly, and reports more deaths than births each year.[1] The

[1]Deaths exceed births in many European countries: by 1980, in addition to West Germany, these included Austria, Britain, East Germany, Luxembourg, Belgium, Denmark, Sweden, Czechoslovakia, and Hungary. By 1990 negative population

Chinese government pressures young people to marry late and restrict their fertility to one child, penalizing those who have more than two children, while the French government is offering 10,000 francs to couples having a third or later birth. The Scandinavian countries and most of those in the Soviet bloc have long relied upon child allowance and child-care systems to encourage fertility in their declining populations.

Population problems cut across the major political ideologies that divide the world community. Within the Communist bloc of nations, China copes with excess population while the Soviet Union and other East European countries cope with declining populations. The Chinese will be struggling to keep their population under one and a half billion in the next few decades; the Soviets have debated how to reverse their downward growth profile. Despite child allowances and child-care facilities, the Soviet population growth rate has continued to decline, from an annual rate of 1.3% for the census period 1959 to 1970 to only 0.9% for the period 1970 to 1979 (Weber and Goodman, 1981).[2] Hence, the Chinese have encouraged contraception, abortion, and sterilization, while the East European countries have resorted to restrictions on abortion and contraceptive access in a largely unsuccessful effort to increase the fertility rate (Finkle and McIntosh, 1980; Heeren, 1982; Westoff, 1978a).

Theorists of the demographic transition consider economic and technological change to be the chief stimulus to changes in population growth. Since death control is politically and psychologically more palatable than birth control, these theorists argue that the initial impact of industrialization is a drop in mortality, as public health measures, improved nutrition, and medical care prolong life and reduce infant mortality while the population continues to show its historic high fertility rates, the net effect being a rapid expansion of population size. The transition to a stable or declining population is completed only when the need and desire for high fertility declines under conditions of industrial work, urban residence, secular values, and contraceptive effectiveness.

The nature and timing of this demographic transition is quite different for

----

growth will also hold in Bulgaria, Greece, Italy, and Switzerland. France and the Netherlands will be added to the list by the year 2000 (Westoff, 1978a, 1978b, 1983). In the United States, because of the enormous short-run rise in the birth rate during the post-World War II era (1946 to 1960), deaths will not exceed births until 2035 (U.S. Bureau of the Census, 1983).

[2]The Soviets are also worried by the fact that infant mortality, instead of continuing to decline with expanded health care, has actually risen in recent years, from 22.9 per thousand in 1967 to an estimated 31.1 per thousand in 1976 (Davis and Feshbach, 1980). Western analysts of Soviet census data also report an unprecedented mortality increase among 20- to 44-year-old males (in their prime reproductive years), and suggest this is due to increased rates of serious alcoholism, occupational health risks, and psychological stress among young adult males in Soviet society (Davis and Feshbach, 1980; Weber and Goodman, 1981).

developing societies today than it was for western societies in the past, for several reasons. First, population expansion in western societies took place in an era when emigration was feasible, either because there were less populated places in the world that had not yet developed nationhood and lacked the means to curb in-migration, or places that, while populous, had neither the power nor the will to resist invaders. Hence, when European economies could not absorb their rising populations in the past, millions migrated to the New World. The same surplus population now faces developing societies: Kuhnen (1982) predicts that by the year 2000 the number of landless peasants in the world will approximate one billion. Migration is far less possible as a solution to this surplus, since the flow would have to be back to European and North American countries that now have immigration restrictions, mounting concern for technological unemployment among their own citizens, and racial prejudice or political ideologies that work against the relaxation of immigration policies to absorb black, Hispanic, and Oriental peoples.[3]

Second, the pace of modernization and industrialization was far more gradual in western history than it is in developing societies today. Many parts of the developing world had already been heavily drained of their natural resources by western nations before they achieved nationhood in the post World War II era, and were then subjected to a very rapid and wrenching injection of western industrial know-how and investment. The importation of modern industrial practices bypasses the stage when vast numbers of unskilled workers can be absorbed. Consequently, developing nations in recent years have only a small proportion of their population in urban industrial work, and the bulk of their production is destined for export, while the vast majority of their people continue to live in rural poverty or hover in the periphery of cities in urban poverty, as in many South American and African countries. Hence, population continues to grow at a pace that outstrips the economic growth necessary to feed, house, and clothe people at even minimal standards.

Third, western industrialization took hold through numerous individual entrepreneurs in small-scale firms widely spread in middle- and working-class sectors of society, and largely independent of those wielding political power. In developing societies today it is more typical for economic power to be fused with political power, so that industrialization redounds to the benefit of the elite stratum of society. Industrial wealth from manufacturing or extraction (as in the oil-producing Arab nations), like agricultural wealth in a landowner class in Latin countries, is fused with political power.

[3]A distinct exemption from this pattern are countries like Mexico, with a thousand-mile, readily passed border contiguous to a nation like the United States with sufficient need for unskilled workers (to perform the low-pay work of seasonal agricultural labor) to absorb illegal immigrants. The result has been an astonishing "latinization" of the United States, particularly in its southern states and coastal cities.

Powerful lineages thus continue to hold political power as they acquire economic power, with a growing gap in the standard of living between the upper and lower strata of the societies. Secular knowledge may dominate economic enterprises under such conditions, while traditional beliefs and customs continue to mark political and family life. In this context the economic elite who wield political power have very little motivation to restrict their own fertility, and no value base on which to encourage the restriction of fertility of other strata in their societies.

Four, significant changes had already taken place in family structure in western history before industrialization took hold. Recent family history and historical demography have now established that a small nuclear family system with minimal filial obligations on the part of adult children toward their elderly parents was fully in place before industrialization set in motion its own series of changes in the nature of work and the separation of the workplace from the domestic household. For centuries western European countries had evolved a pattern of retirement contracts, often with nonkin, to assure the elderly of maintenance and residence rights. People without money or property became the responsibility of parishes and municipalities. Emigration from Europe and westward migration in American history were youthful phenomena and therefore added a further impetus for minimal responsibility for elderly parents. Western welfare programs, including pension systems for the elderly, were therefore a logical outgrowth of this early pattern of minimal filial obligations (Cain, 1985).

Most developing societies today have had a very different history. They have been lineage-centered societies in which adult children were the only source of support for the elderly. With economic wealth highly concentrated in upper-class lineages, there is neither motivation nor appropriate values nor the economic means to provide pensions for the elderly. Consequently, adults continue to be highly motivated to produce a number of children, sons in particular, to assure their own support in old age.

From the perspective of concern for the plight of the world's parents and children, the scenario for the future bodes ill. Unless political unrest and revolution wrest power away from traditional lineage elites, the population in developing societies will continue to grow because most adults will need, want, and have large families, but at the price of continuing to live in poverty and suffering malnutrition and the diseases that follow in its wake. The only exceptions to this scenario will be secular states like China that have broken away from traditional religious and cultural beliefs and wield the authoritarian power to impose harsh penalties on those who violate a one- or two-child norm. This imposed policy may have unintended consequences, however, for rapid change of this sort in what has been historically a deeply rooted lineage system may entail not only individual psychological stress and anxiety, but serious distortion in the sex ratio, cohort size, and composition of the age stratification system.

The implication of this brief analysis is that the transition from high to low fertility will be a more difficult transformation in contemporary developing societies than it was in the history of western societies. This does not mean the West faces no problems of its own in population issues or the structure of the family and well-being of children. There are different kinds of problems ahead in the West, which shall be discussed later in this chapter. The nature of these problems is difficult to grasp from social science research on family life, since the research is conducted on microlevel samples of contemporary adults and children, which do not reveal the macrolevel trajectory of social change as it bears on parenting and child development. The trajectory can be glimpsed through demographic changes now taking place in western societies where there are hints of a second transformation taking place, from a child-centered set of values to an individual- or ego-centered set of values that imply a profound transformation in the social ambiance surrounding childbearing and rearing.

This chapter examines how parenthood is changing in western societies. It begins at the macrolevel of demographic trends on a selected number of dimensions: marriage, divorce, remarriage, fertility, longevity, and household composition. The second section examines recent developments in the medical treatment of birthing, and its potential impact on young adults as they undergo the transition to parenthood. The third section reviews gender differences in parenting as reflected in recent research on traditional and nontraditional family arrangements, with special attention on the effect of significant male investment in parenting on the child. With the evidence of this review, the adequacy of current explanations of gender differences in parenting will be assessed and the relevance of an expanded explanatory model that draws upon bioevolutionary theory and recent work in the neurosciences will be demonstrated. Thus the paper moves from a macrolevel historical analysis of social and economic change, through a hierarchy of sociological and developmental research on adult and child development and the short-term changes now taking place in this segment of social life, and on to the physiological and psychological characteristics adults bring to parenting roles as a consequence of gender differentiation rooted at least in part in our evolutionary heritage. Finally, the last section discusses the implications of the analysis for the larger global issues of population growth, family development, and individual choice.

DEMOGRAPHIC TRENDS AND THEIR IMPLICATIONS FOR CONTEMPORARY PARENTING

The postwar baby boom in western societies posed an unexpected challenge to western demographers, who had assumed that industrial societies had completed the demographic transition to low fertility. Debate raged throughout the decade of the 1950's on whether the sharp upturn in family size was a short-term deviation from the long-term trend toward a small family norm, or a significant turn of events that refuted the theory of the demographic transition. Though fertility rates in western societies began to decline in the early 1960's, it was another decade before demographers concluded that the baby boom was the aberration calling for special explanation and not a refutation of transition theory (Cherlin, 1981). But confidence that economic and technological change serve as the primary agents of historical change in fertility rates and population growth had been shaken. Coupled with the discovery by family historians and historical demographers that the nuclear family system *preceded* industrialization in western European societies, demographic researchers began to explore long-term changes in religious beliefs and trends toward secular thinking and philosophies to supplement strictly economic interpretations of changes in the family.

These efforts at exploring the impact of cultural belief systems on marriage and family characteristics have led to an exciting new vantage point from which to examine specific demographic trends in recent years. Any inspection of short-term, very recent indicators of social change may lead to the interpretation of a pattern as a significant reversal of direction rather than a short-run variation around a slow and steady single direction of change. Being more abstract and holistic, theories of ideational belief changes provide a comprehensive perspective from which to examine very discrete indicators of social behavior. Hence work by Philippe Ariés (1973) in France and Ron Lesthaeghe (1980, 1983) in Belgium is looked at first, before recent changes in highly discrete demographic indices on marriage, divorce, fertility, and so on are reviewed.

Philippe Ariés' book, *Centuries of Childhood*, first published in 1962, opened the way to a new understanding of changes in family structure and the value of children in western societies. Ariés pointed to a critical transformation in parental concern, from a priority on child *quantity* (the more hands on the land, the higher the productive output of a rural family) to that of child *quality* (the fewer the children, the better parents could equip them with the skills needed in adulthood). Both Ariés and Lesthaeghe trace this shift to the late 18th and early 19th century, first among the French and English bourgeoisie, then to other social classes during the second half of the 19th century. Lesthaeghe links this redefinition of parental responsibilities not to industrialization and urbanization, but to the philosophers of the Enlightenment near the end of the 18th century; in particular, to their redefinition of the position of the individual relative to his/her universe by legitimizing the principle of individual freedom of choice. Lesthaeghe suggests this principle of individual freedom dominated the social, economic and political transformations that were to occur in the following two centuries and probably constitutes one of the most important historical legacies in the West (Lesthaeghe, 1983, p. 413).

The new focus on individual choice did not replace but joined other beliefs. In other words, there was no license for an "absolute" individualism as Enlightenment ideas spread throughout western European societies, because the new principle joined others in a European "mentalité" rooted in such beliefs as altruism, humanistic responsibilities, the Judeo-Christian religion, and the concept of a social contract.

Concern for child quality, which Ariés sees as the start of the era of "l'enfant-roi", was thus part of a significant shift in larger ideational beliefs. Child quality in turn could only be achieved through the control of marital fertility, since it is only by restricting births to a few children that parents could assure their proper rearing and schooling. Lesthaeghe notes the remarkable coincidence of the fact that the two countries that had revolutions premised in the ideals of the Enlightenment—France and the United States—were the same two countries where control of marital fertility began as early as the end of the 18th and beginning of the 19th century, when both countries were predominantly rural and agricultural.[4]

By this argument, fertility control preceded industrialization and urbanization. The latter processes contributed to the momentum toward control of marital fertility and set in motion changes in other elements of western belief systems. The units of society involved in concepts of solidarity were undergoing transformation: The idea of a social contract shifted from family, church, and community to new axes of solidarity reflecting the restructuring of society along the lines of interest groups, social class, and class-based political parties. These latter three organizational entities share a primary focus on common economic goals. Social embeddedness in primary groups of family, lineage, friendship, and neighborhood was loosened and replaced by affiliation with secondary groups in the occupational and political systems. This left much more latitude for individual choice, while providing less secure anchorage in primary groups to reinforce traditional beliefs. Over time, the young broke away from family control, married at younger ages, and controlled fertility within marriage. Despite the fact that adultery remained the sole ground for divorce, people began in large numbers to seek divorce by the late 19th century. Emile Durkheim captured the social anomie of this period as well, as indexed by a sharp rise in the suicide rate; he reported this in his classic study of suicide (1951).

Hence, Ariés and Lesthaeghe claim it was the underlying pattern of change toward an increasing centrality of individual goal attainment and the

---

[4]In many European countries—Portugal, Spain, Holland, France, Italy—secularism and radical political beliefs were not confined to urban centers, but were entrenched in many rural areas as well.

right and freedom of the individual to define those goals that provided the context within which family structure and the motivation underlying parenting and the goals of child rearing changed. This first significant change may be summarized as going from a lineage- to a child-centered value orientation in western societies.

Lesthaeghe's work has particular relevance to the present concern for further changes in family life, because he argues that western societies are undergoing a second fundamental transformation of basic values, a shift from a child-centered to an individual or self-centered orientation. This second transformation is a further development in the ongoing erosion of traditional beliefs under the impact of increasing secularism, the loosened hold of religion over private behavior, and the further application of the concept of individual freedom of choice to the private world of family. Westerners are now shifting from concern for their children's futures to a self-orientation that gives priority to individual desires rather than to the needs of spouses or children.

Implicit in this theoretical perspective is the view that once cultural belief systems begin to change, they develop their own momentum, inexorably moving toward an expansion of the basic principles underlying the belief system. There will be pockets of resistance to such change, rooted in ethnicity, class, or religious commitments, but among the native-born, better-educated, and most secularized sectors of western societies, an analyst can identify the direction of future change in beliefs and behaviors.

Lesthaeghe does not reject the influence of economic factors in his analysis. In fact, he points to economic factors as critical to the *timing* of the inflection points on the long-term changes involved. He claims these inflection points tend to occur in the later half of periods of rapid increases in economic affluence, when real income is expanding rapidly. Thus, he points out that it was between 1860 and 1910, when real income doubled, that marital fertility began to fall, from 1880 onward in most countries in western Europe. By 1910 concern for child quality was the dominant motivation for restricting marital fertility. Lesthaeghe claims the second transition, from child orientation to self-orientation, took place from 1963 onward, for by 1963 real income had nearly tripled over the course of the preceding decade, and marital fertility again underwent a decided decline, a process still under way in western societies. Lesthaeghe's reason for associating economic growth with change in the demographic parameters of family formation is that

> rapid increases in real income fuel individual aspirations and . . . the opening up of new employment opportunities creates an impression of lowered economic vulnerability. This in turn allows individuals to be more self-reliant and more independent in the pursuit of their goals, which ultimately stimulates self-orientation and greater aversion to long-term commitments (Lesthaeghe, 1983, p. 430).

The empirical question raised by this claim that western peoples are now shifting from a child- to a self-centered orientation is: What evidence in demographic trends in recent years is consistent with an upturn in "aversion to long-term commitments"? One may posit several trends that would be consistent with this theory: a lowering of the marriage rate, a rise in the age at marriage, a rise in the divorce rate, a drop in the remarriage rate following divorce, and an increase in childlessness. Since it has become apparent over the past few decades that demographic, attitudinal, and institutional change in the Scandinavian countries often precedes comparable developments in the United States, an array of demographic indicators in both western European countries and the United States will be reviewed.

Marriage, Divorce, and Remarriage

There has been a steady rise in the age at marriage and a drop in the marriage rate over the past 20 years in the United States, as in many European countries. Using an index that equates the 1960 rate to 100, Lesthaeghe shows that the age-specific first marriage rate per thousand single women in eight European countries fell steadily between 1960 and 1970, and continued to decline further between 1970 and 1979. In Sweden, for example, the index was only 64 by 1970, and then dropped even further by 1979, to 53. In the course of the 1970's, the same dramatic drop was shown in Denmark (82–57) and West Germany (92–60). An older age at marriage is associated with rising levels of educational attainment, but even if attention is limited to adults in their late 20s, when most schooling has been completed, there has been a dramatic rise in the proportion of never-married adults. In the United States there was a tripling of the proportion of women not married by their late 20s in 1980 (30%) compared to as short a time ago as 1967 (9%). Masnick and Bane (1980) predict that by 1990, half the men and more than a third of the women in their late 20s will still be unmarried.

Fewer marriages are being formed, and those that are, come at later ages and are more fragile than in the past. This was not a trend that demographers expected, since for a long time it was argued that, with a rise in the age at marriage, divorce rates would drop because older couples enter marriage with greater maturity and a firmer commitment to making their relationship work than younger couples do. But in western Europe as in the United States, total divorce rates doubled by 1978, compared to 1970. Even in a country like Sweden, which had a very high divorce rate in the 1950's, there has been a dramatic recent rise in the marriage-duration-specific divorce rate, from 160 per thousand marriages in the period 1955–1964 to 427 in 1979 to 1980. A country like Belgium, which began with lower divorce rates than Sweden, has rapidly followed the trend, with comparable rate increases from 74 to 187. The index for England and Wales showed even sharper changes, from 75 to 367 in the most recently available year (Lesthaeghe, 1983).

When these marriage and divorce trends were first noted by family sociologists and demographers in the early 1970's, they argued that what was happening was not an indication of disenchantment with the institution of marriage, because divorce was typically followed by remarriage. It was a particular spouse that was found wanting, not marriage itself. This interpretation is challenged, however, by recent evidence of a drop in the remarriage rate among divorced adults. Using an age-specific remarriage rate per thousand divorced persons and an index equating the rate in 1960 at 100, several European countries have shown a decline by 1970, and an even more dramatic drop by the end of the decade (e.g., in Sweden the index dropped to 62 by 1979).

Following a review of trends such as these, and the observation that for many women, from half to two thirds of their adult lives will be without husbands, Davis and van den Oever (1982) suggest that marriage is "falling out of fashion." Lesthaeghe would add that the marriage, divorce, and remarriage trends are indicators of an aversion to "long-term commitments" in favor of individual freedom and self-indulgence.

Longevity

Marriage and divorce largely involve people in early through middle age, and reflect choices that are voluntary preferences (or the voluntary preference of at least one spouse where there is no mutuality in opting for divorce). The major trend affecting late-middle and old age is the greatly extended sheer length of life. Longevity increases are not so much freely chosen as an unintended gift that reflects the cumulative effects of improved health care and better nutrition in developed societies. The second development affecting people in the last third of life is a growing gender gap in expected longevity. Davis and van den Oever (1982) calculate the life expectancy for men in 20 developed nations at 68 years for men and 75 for women (as of the late 1970's). The estimates are lower, of course, for those in developing nations: 60 for men, 64 for women.

These figures underestimate the prevalence of widowhood among the elderly, since they concern the overall trend in the population and do not take into account an invariant pattern across most known societies for men to marry women younger than themselves. The age difference between spouses has narrowed in first marriages in western societies, but the sharp rise in the divorce rate is followed by an increasing age difference in remarriages, so there is still a strong pattern of age hypergyny in western societies, and therefore a much greater probability that women will live out their elderly years alone, while most men still have wives when they die. By 1982, 85% of the widowed population in the United States were women (U.S. Bureau of the Census, 1983).

The pattern of age hypergyny in marriage formation has the effect of producing markedly different sex ratios within specific age groups of married and unmarried adults. Thus, for example, among young American adults between 20 and 24, there are on average about 60 unmarried women for every 100 unmarried men; by ages 50 to 59, the ratio is more than 250 unmarried women for every 100 unmarried men. The profile is remarkably similar in developing societies, prompting the suggestion that this phenomenon is "so fundamental that it is independent of economic development" (Davis and van den Oever, 1982, p. 501). These authors interpret the pattern as a maximization of the possibility for mating and reproduction by women during their reproductive years. In addition, remaining unmarried to the age of 35 has none of the risk of remaining childless for a man that it does for a woman. Hence, the increased longevity that is now enjoyed by a modern woman does not increase her reproductive potential, while it considerably extends that potential for men.[5]

Fertility

Recent trends in marriage, divorce, and remarriage are consistent with the view that young adults in western societies are becoming less enthusiastic about long-term commitments to intimate relationships. Whether becoming a parent is also falling out of fashion is less certain. Marriages that turn sour can be terminated, so individuals can move in and out of the married status, while parenthood turned sour has more limited solutions. One can have an ex-spouse more readily than an ex-child. Furthermore, the dissolution of a marriage leaves two individuals free to marry again or not, but parenthood continues beyond a divorce for at least one of the parents, typically the mother.

Most demographers today would concur with Westoff's view that the "primary forces of social change conducive to later marriage and low fertility will persist" (Westoff, 1983, p. 99). Recent research shows that

[5]For a long time it was assumed that only maternal age was a relevant factor predictive of genetic defects in offspring like Down's syndrome. More recently, a paternal contribution to Down's syndrome has been recognized. Cytogeneticists have, in some proportion of cases, traced the parental origin of chromosomes by means of idiosyncratic markers; in a number of these, the anomalous chromosome is paternal and must have originated in the sperm (Hulten, 1974). Stene and Stene (1977) in a Danish study found a higher rate of Down's syndrome with very old fathers. One American study (Erickson, 1978) contradicts the Danish study, while Susser (1981) suggests the crucial link between idiosyncratic markers of trisomic chromosomes and paternal age has yet to be made.

lifetime birth expectations of young women in the United States are below replacement level for their generation, and employment status has only a modest effect on these expectations (National Center for Health Statistics, 1982).[6]

What the future holds in terms of the incidence level of voluntary childlessness is uncertain at this time. Clearly families are becoming smaller, and recent research shows a desire to postpone parenthood after marriage (Knaub, Eversoll, and Voss, 1983), but the estimates vary on what proportion of young adults will remain childless. Blake (1974, 1979, 1982) suggests that fewer than 10% of American women enter adulthood with no desire or expectation for children. However, the proportion childless in Scandinavian countries in recent cohorts has been over 20%. Bloom (1982), in an application of the Coale nuptuality model, estimates a childless rate between 20 and 30% for women born after 1950. Changing attitudes toward childlessness are suggested by Huber and Spitze (1983), who report a dramatic drop in the view that remaining childless is "selfish": only 21% of the women in their 1978 sample took this view, while more than 70% endorsed it in surveys five years earlier. Lesthaeghe reports an increase in acceptance of voluntary childlessness in public opinion polls in the Netherlands, from 21% in 1965 to 65% in 1974 (Lesthaeghe, 1983, Table 6, p. 419). If as many as 20% of young women expect to remain childless while public attitudes are still in a state of flux, it would seem highly likely that voluntary childlessness might rise even higher than one in four young adults once public attitudes toward childlessness undergo further softening.

Other data on fertility patterns suggest that parenthood is less securely linked to marriage than it has been in the past. In the 1980's the overall rate of out-of-wedlock childbearing for unmarried women 15–44 years of age (29.4 per 1000 women) is the highest ever recorded, and represents 18% of all American births. In the past sociologists tended to view such births as an unfortunate consequence of economic hardship, sexual exploitation of women, family disorganization, and lack of access to contraception and abortion. It has clearly not been seen by American social scientists as a pattern freely chosen by women. Yet such a trend has been in place for some time in Scandinavian countries (Westoff, 1978b), where out-of-wedlock births are not stigmatized and unmarried mothers are not subjected to the "putdown" of characterizing their children as fatherless rather than as having a status derived from their mothers. Blake (1982) suggests a comparable trend is occurring in the United States.

What proportion of these births is motivated by a desire for a child coupled with no wish for a spouse is unknown. It is an infrequent pattern today, but may become more prevalent in the future as economically

---

[6]As of June 1980, the lifetime birth expectations of women aged 18 to 24 was 2023 births per 1000 women (National Center for Health Statistics, 1982).

independent women rely on sperm banks and artificial insemination rather than marriage. Current users of such facilities are largely women who seek artificial insemination because of infertility on the part of their partners, but there are other women in their late 20s and early 30s who have no "Mr. Right" on the horizon and strong desires for a child before they run out of reproductive prime time. One health center in Oakland, California, reports that one third of their inseminations involve single women who wish children but not marriage (Bagne, 1983). As economic independence increases for women in western societies, this trend to purposive births without marriage may also increase.

In terms of fertility, we can see a slow rise in voluntary childlessness, a rapid increase in the proportion of women who rear children by themselves after a divorce, small family size, and closely spaced births. Instead of a parental death preceding the adulthood of a child, increased longevity now assures that most parents will have adult children for many more years than they devote to child rearing. A much larger proportion of men than women will be parents of children separated by a generation in age, with children in their 20s from a first marriage and child or two born after a second marriage to a much younger woman. The incidence of this latter pattern is not nearly so prevalent as the single-female parent carrying solo responsibility for child rearing. Hence, while there is evidence that parenting is being slowly separated from marriage, as sex was separated from marriage in an earlier period, there is a widening gap in the proportion of each sex carrying family responsibilities. The evidence then for an increasing "aversion to long-term commitments" that Lesthaeghe suggests is a characteristic of contemporary western societies may require the qualification that it applies more to men than it does to women.

Household Composition

One last indicator of change in the social ambiance surrounding parenthood and child rearing concerns household composition. The trends already reviewed combine to effect a dramatic change in household composition in western societies. Postponement of marriage, rising rates of separation and divorce, a decline in the marriage and remarriage rates, smaller families with closely spaced births, and the growing gender gap in longevity have combined to produce a shift in the modal household in the United States, from one headed by a marital pair rearing dependent-age children to a household headed by a single adult (Kobrin, 1976a, 1976b; Masnick and Bane, 1980). In 1960, the proportion of single-adult-headed households was 25%, but this increased to 35% by 1975 and will be a projected 45% of all households by 1990. The trend to independent residence is particularly striking among young adults. Masnick (1983) has recently shown that as late as 1950, only 17% of unmarried women in their late 20s headed their own households; by 1980 this had jumped to 60%.

For an increasing proportion of well-educated young adults, there is now almost a decade between departure from their parents' household and the formation of a marital household. This moratorium from family living in early adulthood may eventually have positive effects, in the sense of greater equity upon gender roles in employment and household division of labor, but less positive if not negative effects upon adjustment to parenthood. Increasing proportions of women are acquiring economic and social self-sufficiency through career commitment and employment continuity, which in turn reinforces independent political and social values and an expectation of equitable sharing of family and household responsibilities after marriage. By the same token, more young men are living on their own, acquiring competence in the domestic skills they bring to marriage.

What is not clear is the impact of early adult independence upon a couple's ability to shift concerns from their own personal gratifications to a shared and greater concern for the welfare and care of children. Solo living may increase skills in household maintenance, cooking, and personal care, but it contributes nothing to the skills needed in caring for a child, or placing the needs and desires of others above one's own. Premarital independent living and postponement of childbearing after marriage may pave the way, for some couples, to an eventual decision to remain childless. That there may be greater difficulty when parenting is opted for was suggested in a pilot study of mine, in which late timing of parenthood was associated with greater reported difficulty in child rearing than early "on-time" parenting (Rossi, 1980a, 1980b).

Looking back over these various demographic trends suggests two general points relevant to the place of parenthood in individual lives and the ambiance surrounding child rearing in the larger society. First, small families with closely spaced births coupled with greatly extended life spans means childbearing and child rearing have become truncated, sharply contracted as a phase of life that previously occupied a significant proportion of adulthood. Only one in four American households now includes even one dependent-age child. On a societal level, this implies an erosion of a major source of social integration. Slater (1964) pointed out 20 years ago that parenting serves social functions by linking dyads to the community. More recently, Fischer et al. (1977) and O'Donnell (1983) found that parents in the active stages of child rearing are more involved in neighborhood and community affairs than childless or postparental adults. For the future, children's needs may have a lower priority on public agendas, since only a minority of political constituents will be rearing children, thus undercutting the responsiveness of elected public officials to the needs of the very young.

Second, there is a growing difference in the proportion of each sex that is carrying family responsibilities. Despite a slight shift toward shared or primary father custody of children, women overwhelmingly carry the major child rearing responsibility following divorce, and an increasing proportion of women are having children outside marriage. Together these trends imply that a larger proportion of women than men are tied into communal activities and institutions.

This gender gap in embeddedness in the caring institutions of society also carries broader political and social deviance implications. One may not go as far as French social scientist Gaston Bouthol (1969), who argues that the best predictor of war is a surplus in the number of young unattached males, but it is this same subpopulation group that predominates in sexual violence and other crime, alcohol and drug abuse, terrorism, and military adventurism. Unattached males roam the interstices between socially cohesive groups, kill, and are themselves killed and maimed, but the machine cultures of the West have shown no inventiveness in developing new social institutions capable of providing individual loyalty and social integration to replace the bonds of family. Durkheim's prediction that occupations would provide such a base for social cohesion has not been borne out, and we have learned to our sorrow that expansive nationalism may be the consequence of intense identification with a centralized state. Yet should altruism be replaced by egotism in western societies while the world shrinks and becomes more interdependent, the prospects for global harmony are dim indeed.

Social anthropologists have at times suggested that there is a common core of identical human experience that cuts across the very great world diversity of culture, economy, religion, and ecological settings. The "family of man" was seen as a universal social unit in all societies, and the bond between man and woman and their offspring the most treasured relationship of people everywhere. One implication of the demographic trends in developed societies compared to the very different profile of developing societies is that this common, shared base is being eroded. Hence the same decline in the proportion of American adults who are embedded in marriage and child rearing that may trigger a lack of concern for child welfare in domestic politics could be even more dramatically extended to a lack of concern for child welfare in countries abroad. The unmarried, divorced, childless, and postparental adults in western societies may have little sympathy for and lend little political support to programs to help other countries facing famine and death as a consequence of uncontrolled population growth. Conflict and political cleavage in the world have been seen as divisions between East and West, communist and democratic states, but conflict and political unrest on the grounds of population issues are divisions between Northern and Southern Hemispheres, Europe and North American versus Africa, Latin America, and Asia. The substantive issues at stake vary across this major division, but in almost all nations of the world parenthood is undergoing a profound transformation.

TRANSITION TO PARENTHOOD: BIRTH MANAGEMENT

Major events along the life span that carry both emotional significance for individuals and social significance for the larger society are apt to be marked by special rules and rituals. The birth of a child is surely a major experience in the biography of most adults, as is true in the history of all societies. There is great cultural diversity in the rules imposed on pregnant women and the way that birth is managed, but within any given society birthing procedures tend to be uniform with respect to where a birth takes place, who may be present to assist or observe, and what must be done to celebrate the event in the larger family and community to which the parents and infant belong.

How birth is managed by the parturient woman herself and her attendants tells us much about a society. Pregnancy and birth may be feared, hidden, and fraught with pain, or welcomed, publicized, and managed with equanimity. Thus, Mead and Newton (1967) report that labor is remarkably short and childbirth relatively painless in a society with relaxed sexual attitudes—such as that of the South American Siriono, where birth is an easy, public event controlled by the mother herself—but that it is a prolonged, painful process among the Cuna in Panama who prevent young girls from learning about either coitus or childbirth until the final stages of the marriage ceremony. Historically, western societies have approximated the Cuna far more than the Siriono, reflecting their conflictual image of women and natural body processes symbolized by the split image of woman as temptress Eve and saintly, Virgin Mary. Until the emergence of modern medicine, birthing was secluded and managed by women.

In more recent times, birthing, like working, moved from the domestic household to specialized settings; in the case of birth, to maternity clinics and hospitals, where the overwhelming majority of babies in western societies are now born. We begin this review of changes in contemporary parenting with birth itself because it is undergoing significant and contradictory changes while remaining a critical phase in the role induction to parenthood. Birth management also represents an important but neglected dimension of family life, one on which there is little overlap between medical and obstetrical research on the one hand and psychological and sociological research on the other. If a biosocial perspective has relevance to an understanding of family structure and family process, then it is surely relevant to an examination of current practice and research on birth management.

Psychological research has focused on the prediction of pregnancy complications as a function of psychological variables such as attitudes to sex, life event stress, social support networks, motivation for having a child, emotional stability, and anxiety (Beck et al., 1980; Colman and Colman, 1973; Gorsuch and Key, 1974; Grimm, 1969; Helper et al., 1968; McDonald, 1968; Newton, 1973; Norbeck and Tilden, 1983; Shereshefsky and Yarrow, 1973; Standley *et al.*, 1979). Thus, for example, Grimm and Newton report that good sexual adjustment is related to a low incidence of nausea during pregnancy, easier and shorter labor, desire for and success at nursing, and preference for natural childbirth. Some developmental psychologists have been concerned with determining whether there is a sensitive phase for mother–infant attachment immediately following birth, and have sought to connect mother–neonate separation or varying amounts of contact with the neonate in the first few days after birth to the quality of the mother–infant relationship several months later (Barnett *et al.*, 1970; DeChateau, 1977; Dennenberg, 1964; Klaus and Kennell, 1976).

Sociological research has only recently focused on the transition to parenthood, as interest shifted from static portrayals of stages of the family life cycle to research on topics such as the impact on a couple of having the father present during birth, the determinants of parental involvement in child care, or the impact of a first birth upon marital division of labor (Fischer, 1979; LaRossa and LaRossa, 1981; Shapiro, 1979). Hence, psychologists have emphasized the impact of longstanding stress and anxiety on labor complications or early parental emotional adjustment, while sociologists have tended to focus on the impact of birth on marriages and gender roles. Until the recent work of Entwisle and Doering (1981), social scientists have not included measures of medical management of birth as they relate to parental preferences on the subject, or the consequences of medical management of birth on early adjustment to the parenting role.

The medical literature has similarly focused very narrowly on advances made in obstetric care, and rarely shows concern for the psychological and emotional impact of obstetric birth management upon the mother and the quality of her relationship with the infant following hospital discharge. As we shall see, obstetrics, like other medical specialties, has primary concern for technological advance and a narrow criterion of medical success: survival of the patient. In this context, the quality of the birth experience for the mother or the problems facing a family with a severely handicapped infant are not considered. Yet there are technological developments in modern obstetrics that carry profound significance for the condition of the infant new parents have in their charge.

Birth, in a modern western hospital, involves procedures that would impress mothers in many other parts of the world as nothing short of bizarre: shaving of the genital area, administration of an enema, confinement to bed, surgical incision of the perineum (episiotomy), use of drugs, withholding of food, forceps delivery, the whisking away of the infant to be bathed and kept from the mother while she recovers from anesthesia, all in an unfamiliar setting with largely unknown persons in attendance. Becoming a parent in western societies is a medical event, in the hands of professionals who are paid and praised for a "safe delivery."

When any of these obstetric procedures have been challenged (by young couples seeking a more natural, less medical approach to birth, or by midwives and obstetricians from the Netherlands where natural childbirth is the dominant mode), the response is apt to be a citation of improved infant mortality statistics over the decades that birth moved from home to the hospital. What is not clear is the extent to which the improved infant mortality figures is attributable to medical management of birth and how much to the generally improved physical condition of the population brought about by improved nutrition and personal hygiene.

The history of obstetric practice does not give confidence that the profession is able or willing to undertake the scientific studies necessary to test the efficacy of new obstetrical procedures, or to change those procedures once the scientific evidence is in. For example, a randomized prospective trial conducted as early as 1922 showed that genital shaving did not reduce the incidence of infection (Johnston and Sidall, 1922). A further prospective trial conducted in 1965 confirmed this finding (Kantor et al., 1965). The procedure is not followed in most maternity clinics in the Netherlands, which has one of the lowest infant and maternal mortality and morbidity rates in the world, yet it is still standard procedure in most American hospitals.

A similar story can be told concerning the almost routine reliance on a surgical incision of the perineum: American obstetricians claim that episiotomies facilitate perineal healing and assure a tighter vaginal opening, yet no evidence of delayed healing or sexual complaints has appeared in countries that do not routinely perform episiotomies.

What is striking to an observer of medical developments in western countries is the fact that there is such enormous diversity in obstetric procedures, while the treatment of diseases of the thyroid, or prostatic enlargement, or of common fractures, varies only marginally between different practitioners or different countries. Yet an English woman is nearly three times as likely to have her labor induced as a Norwegian woman (Diggory, 1981); and within England itself, induction rates vary among hospitals from 15 to 55% of all deliveries (Chalmers and Richards, 1977). The justification for reliance on induction is that it reduces fetal respiratory distress and perinatal mortality. However, inspection of evidence gathered by Chalmers and Richards (1977) clearly indicates that the perinatal mortality rate has shown the same decline between 1967 and 1974 in both England and Norway, while the induction rate rose sharply during the same years in England but only modestly in Norway, suggesting that induction of labor has very little effect on reducing infant mortality.

Over the past two decades there has been a sharp increase in the use of technological equipment in obstetric practice. New procedures employed during pregnancy include: *amniocentesis* (puncturing the uterus to collect a sample of amniotic fluid) to detect a range of potential abnormalities in fetal development, including hydrocephaly and mongolism; *fetoscopy* (transuterine telescopic visualization of the fetus), also to detect fetal abnormality; and *ultrasound* (the use of reflected sound waves to outline contents of the uterus) to assess the age of the fetus, the number of fetuses if multiple births are suspected, or the situation of the placenta (Beard, 1981).

Electronic Fetal Heart Monitoring

The major new procedures used during labor and delivery are fetal heart rate monitoring and fetal blood sampling. Electronic fetal heart rate monitoring provides more detailed information than the customary stethoscope to determine the average heart rate of the fetus. The monitoring equipment requires the pregnant woman to remain immobilized in a prone position throughout labor, with a wide belt around her abdomen through which wires record the fetal heart rate. The purpose of the device is to detect abnormal shifts in heart rate that may indicate serious lowering of oxygenation in the fetus. Alone, however, the monitoring charts cannot tell if the pattern is produced by oxygen loss, the drugs being administered to the mother, or the compression of the fetal head in the birth canal. Consequently the procedure is often combined with direct fetal blood sampling. When this blood sampling procedure was first used in the early 1960's, it was done by passing a metal tube up the vagina through the cervix so that the head of the baby could be pricked and a small mount of blood collected for testing. (The acidity of the blood was a measure of tissue asphyxia.) More recently, fetal blood sampling is being used in a more continuous way, by attaching a small electrode to the head of the fetus via the cervix and transmitting the signal from each heartbeat directly to a small computer (Beard, 1981). Thus both the laboring woman and her baby are attached to machines.

If such equipment were used only for high-risk pregnancies, one might consider the restriction of physical mobility of the mother to be a justified price to pay in exchange for greater assurance of a healthy baby at birth. But there is growing pressure in American and English obstetrics to extend the continuous recording of the fetal heart rate as part of medical surveillance of all babies during labor. Since high-risk pregnancies represent less than 5% of all deliveries, one might expect to find fairly persuasive evidence from clinical trials that this equipment contributed to the successful outcome of labor. There have been four reports of clinical trials involving a comparison of labor managed by the use of electronic fetal monitoring and labor managed by clinical assessment only. Diggory's judgment after reviewing these studies was that none showed any superiority of the new technology over clinical assessment methods (Diggory, 1981). What was found, however, was that in all four trials, the Caesarean section rate was *doubled* for those women who were monitored compared to those who were not, but with "no demonstrable improvement in fetal outcome" (Diggory, 1981, p. 30).

Here is a clue to another shocking statistic on obstetric practice: over the ten-year period 1969 to 1979 there has been a *tripling* in Caesarean sections as a proportion of all deliveries in the United States (Marieskind, 1979), from slightly less than 5% in 1969 to 16% in 1979. There is no reason to think that today's pregnant women are in poorer health than women of a decade ago, yet the Caesarean section rate has been rising so steeply as to prompt two major studies in the Department of Health, Education and Welfare (Marieskind, 1979) and the National Institutes of Health (Perry and Kalberer, 1980). Chalmers (1981) summarized the results of these investigations and noted a number of nonclinical factors affecting obstetric decisions to deliver by Caesarean section. Among them are the greater availability of personnel, beds, and equipment (reflecting the declining fertility rate after a period of rapid rise, which has left expensive hospital facilities underutilized); the growing fear of malpractice litigation, which prompts physicians to move to a surgical delivery more quickly than they did in the past if there is any hint of fetal distress; commercial pressure from drug and equipment manufacturers; and reliance on electronic fetal heart rate monitoring that produces massive amounts of data that physicians are poorly trained to interpret. When in doubt, operate, seems therefore to have become the guiding principle behind many obstetric decisions. Despite the lack of evidence that electronic monitoring works better than traditional clinical procedures and the clear implication that, to the contrary, use of such equipment has only led to greater reliance on surgical intervention, the British Select Committee on Perinatal and Neonatal Mortality recommended in 1980 that the continuous recording of the fetal heart rate should become part of the surveillance of all babies during labor (House of Commons, 1980).[7]

A review of the evidence on the new fetal heart monitoring procedure led one English professor of obstetrics, Peter Diggory, to change his mind about the new technology: he admits that prior to his review he expected to find that the use of fetal monitoring was an important advance in obstetrics, and that with more doctors and better equipment many avoidable deaths and cases of handicap would be eliminated; but having reviewed the medical

---

[7]Chalmers (1981) suggests there were commercial interests involved in the British House of Commons' strong support for customary reliance on the monitoring device. Thus, at the press conference at which their report was launched, the committee went out of its way several times to mention the name of the British manufacturer of fetal monitors. Banta and Thacker (1979) have also argued that perinatal intensive care is big business, which applies its own pressure to extend the use of such equipment. They conclude that the public should feel some skepticism when confronted with an epidemic of medical intervention in birth management and technology.

literature he admits: "I cannot honestly say any of these things" (Diggory, 1981, p. 35).

Intensive Care of Premature Babies

The widespread development of intensive care units for premature babies is a second example of a new technology taking on its own momentum. Obstetric technology is partially responsible for the emergence of a new specialty in pediatrics—neonatology. No one would question the desirability of exerting every effort to spare the life of a premature 7-month baby weighing four to five pounds; the amount of effort required is questionable, however, when one reads a report, from Australia, that showed 40% of babies weighing between one and one-and-a-half pounds survived to the point of hospital discharge (Yu and Hollingsworth, 1980). Clearly these are high-risk fetuses whose development is severely retarded even with the best of intensive care equipment compared to development *in utero*.

The medical literature contains very few studies of the long-term physical and mental effects of intensive care on premature babies who survive to the point of discharge from the ICUs, much less the impact of incorporating such infants into a family and the special problems they pose to the parents' marriage, finances, or relation to other, healthy children in the family. One English study surveyed 357 babies with very low birth weights over the years between 1961 and 1975, and found at follow-up that only 27% of the babies were normal, 11% had physical handicaps, and the remainder, 62%, had died. Despite increasing complexity of hospital care over the 14-year span of these births, there was no difference in survival or health of the babies in the last several years compared to the earlier period (McIlwaine et al., 1979).

Kitchen and his associates (1979) conducted the only randomized prospective trial on the effect of intensive care versus standard care of low birth weight infants in Melbourne, Australia, between 1966 and 1970. They found a significantly higher survival rate for newborns receiving intensive care, but achieved at the expense of producing severely handicapped children. S. Leiderman (personal communication, 1982) reports an American follow-up study of premature babies compared to full-term babies of normal weight. He reports that families with low-weight premature babies experienced higher overall family stress and a markedly higher separation and divorce rate within two years of the premature infants' birth compared to families with full-term babies.

No one would doubt that there is a good deal of anguish for a parent who loses a premature three-pound baby. On the other hand, that loss must be measured against a different but longer period of anguish in rearing a severely handicapped child who will never lead a normal life, particularly when the loss of an impaired infant at birth might be followed by the joy of a normal full-term baby later.

One additional factor should be considered as intensive care of premature infants becomes an increasingly prevalent pattern in western societies. This concerns the likely impact of saving such babies upon the sex ratio of the upcoming generation. Countries that led the world in reducing infant mortality now show a male surplus well into the fourth decade of life. In the United States between 1910 and 1980, the sex ratio rose among those under 50 years of age, while it declined among those over 50 years of age (Davis and van den Oever, 1982).[8]

Improved diet and prenatal care for pregnant women affect the sex ratio for a reason rooted in a genetic difference between male and female: there are more points at which aberrations may occur in the fetal development of the male than the female. Indeed, the estimated sex ratio at conception is about 125, which compensates for the higher rates of spontaneous abortion of male fetuses and the higher neonatal death rates of male babies that characterized most of human history.[9] It is very likely that intensive care of ever smaller infants involves a larger proportion of male than female babies, since the closer to conception, the higher the sex ratio. None of the medical research reviewed herein identified the sex distribution of the tiny premature babies under study; hence the imbalance in the sex ratio noted here may well have gone unnoticed by the medical profession.

Chalmers (1981) and Diggory (1981) both conclude that obstetric practice in western nations is foolishly focused on a narrow criterion of success: the avoidance of death at all costs, and hence the reduction of perinatal mortality regardless of the physical and emotional consequences for parents and other children in the family. Technology designed for a very small proportion of cases takes on a momentum of its own and is applied to low-risk cases that would progress as well or better in its absence. Thus, electronic fetal heart monitoring was devised as a means for dealing with the possible failure of oxygenation in the last phase of labor and during delivery. Yet only 13% of perinatal deaths occur during labor (McIlwaine et al., 1979); most involve pregnancies that were a special risk long before labor started, as a consequence of congenital abnormality or unsatisfactory intrauterine development. Only 5–6% of births each year involve any form

[8]This explains why the overall sex ratio in developed countries is not lower than it is: mortality reduction that produces a female surplus in old age is balanced by mortality reduction in infancy and childhood that produces a male surplus in the younger years. Thus, Davis and van den Oever (1982, p. 497) report the sex ratio of Americans under 50 rose from 101.9 in 1910 to 103.7 by 1980, while among adults over 50 years of age the sex ratio declined from 92.4 to 84.9 over the same span of years.

[9]The male surplus among the young is not unprecedented in human history. In fact, a male surplus characterized all known traditional societies in virtually all of Eurasia until the 19th century, as a consequence of female infanticide or neglect that led to higher mortality rates among female infants than male (Jane Lancaster, personal communication).

of physical handicap or mental retardation, and of these, less than 3% are due to perinatal events. Further, premature fetuses can sustain oxygen deprivation better than mature fetuses can, and short periods of oxygen lack during labor, even when severe, are less damaging than prolonged lack of oxygen *in utero*. With such a low incidence of even potentially relevant cases justifying the use of fetal monitoring, it is extraordinary that such equipment has been proposed as appropriate for all obstetric patients.

Additional research is clearly needed on this issue. There are critical bioethical issues involved, and research evidence is as yet quite scant. What seems called for is new research that would involve developmental psychologists and sociologists in collaboration with biomedical researchers and practitioners in obstetrics and neonatology. Such collaborative research might encourage the medical profession to pay more attention to the social and psychological sequelae of their "success" in keeping impaired neonates alive, including damage to the relationships within the family when such babies finally go home. It might also encourage developmental social scientists to deal with critical life-and-death issues that have significant impact on parents and children. Compared to the plight of parents with physically and mentally impaired newborns, developmental research that tests whether a half-hour more a day of contact with the baby in the hospital will contribute to mother–infant attachment seems trivial in the extreme.

Results from such studies might also contribute to the empowerment of parents facing labor and delivery. At the moment, such parents are highly vulnerable to medical persuasion, since the rationale for using medical intervention given to them by physicians is to assure the safe delivery of a healthy baby. Under such pressure, few couples protest any medical procedure unless they are far better informed than they usually are. This pattern is already well substantiated in Entwisle and Doering's study of first births (1981), and in Shapiro's study of first and second births (1979). Most of the subjects in these studies had taken childbirth preparation classes and anticipated a drug-free natural childbirth experience, but the majority of the women were given drugs against their wishes, and a high proportion had either a forceps delivery under spinal or full anesthesia, or a Caesarean section.

This is a propitious decade in which to attempt a change in procedures in western obstetrics, because a declining birth rate makes obstetrics a buyers' market. Parents are in a good bargaining position to seek changes in birth management, and indicators of some success in efforts to provide parents with a more natural experience of birth do exist. Some obstetricians, alerted to the harmful effects of drugs on the fetus, have become cooperative with couples who wish to have natural childbirth, to be together throughout labor and delivery, and to handle the infant as soon as it is born. Physicians and hospital administrators increasingly support preparation classes for prospective parents. A more homelike decor is occasionally provided in maternity wards and birth clinics. Women are gaining the courage to assert their desire to be in charge of their own deliveries and to oppose efforts to make them passive creatures controlled by the physician. But there is still a great deal of counterpressure stemming from the fear of malpractice and the medical profession's attraction to complex new technology.

GENDER DIFFERENCES IN PARENTING

There has been a significant shift in the language used in the social sciences to refer to human parenting. Twenty years ago parenting meant mothering, and either studies frankly labeled their subjects "mothers" or one quickly learned that all the subjects were women, though the title referred to parents. A decade ago one began to see the label "care giver," presumably to project the notion that parenting can be done not only by fathers as well as mothers but by nonparent surrogates too (Lewis and Rosenblum, 1974). By the 1980's, the research literature has become richer and we can begin to compare fathering and mothering.

Three types of research permit a close-up view of what it is that men do when they carry primary child-care responsibility and how they differ from the more traditional circumstance of women carrying this responsibility. The first type concerns solo fathers, men whose wives have died or who hold custody of their children following divorce; these studies permit us to compare solo fathering with the more prevalent pattern of solo mothering. The second type involves men in nontraditional family circumstances— communal groups or social contract couples. The third type centers on men in intact marriages who carry primary child-care responsibilities out of a commitment to marriage and parenthood as a full partnership.

Solo Fathers

The best research on solo fathering has been conducted in England, where Hipgrave (1981) estimated fathers constituted 12% of all solo parents.[10] Three factors are found in common between solo fathers and solo mothers: a more restricted social life; a somewhat more democratic style in family management; and, when a new partner enters the domestic setting, some difficulty in deciding what responsibilities to delegate to the partner. Although solo mothers are far more apt to slip below the poverty level than solo fathers, there is a considerable negative impact on income for solo

[10]Ferri (1973, 1976) estimated that solo fathers were twice as likely to be rearing sons as daughters, while solo mothers were only slightly more apt to be rearing girls than boys, and 90% of the fathers who took on primary care, did so when the children were over 5 years of age (Ferri, 1976).

fathers as well. Hipgrave found that *half* the men experienced a decline in income after taking on child rearing responsibilities, only 12% of which was attributable to the loss of a wife's earnings. In another study, some 35% of solo fathers left their jobs in order to meet their parental responsibilities for young children (George and Wilding, 1972). Most of the income drop was a direct result of increased parental responsibility: a shift to less demanding, lower-paying jobs; loss of overtime pay in order to mesh with children's schedules; absenteeism to care for ill children; and a drop in social ties with business or professional associates that had increased income in the past.

The problems of solo parenting differ for men and women. Solo fathers receive more volunteer help from friends and kin, probably because men are assumed to be less capable of child rearing than women, but when men need and do not receive unsolicited help, they are less apt to seek it than solo mothers. Solo fathers make fewer new social contacts than solo mothers because men make such contacts primarily through informal association with work colleagues, which they have little time for once they become solo parents.[11]

Solo fathers show anxiety about their role just as solo mothers do, but on different grounds: many men report that although their children seemed to be faring well at the moment, they expect trouble in the future, some anticipating a "volcanic eruption" when their children enter puberty. The men feel they fail to provide intimate emotional support to their children, particularly their daughters, a finding also reported in American studies (Santrock and Warshak, 1979; Santrock, Warshak and Elliott, 1982). Solo mothers' anxiety centers on the inability to maintain past living standards and a breakdown of disciplinary control, particularly where sons are concerned. Discipline problems do not emerge in the experience of solo fathers, who follow stricter rules and are more consistent in disciplining their children.

The reality of these parental concerns is suggested by the changes that attend remarriage by solo parents. Daughters in solo father households benefit with the entry of a stepmother—as sons do in solo mother households with the entry of a stepfather. Wallerstein and Kelly (1980) report

---

[11]Social expectations also play a role in the response of neighbors to solo fathers, particularly if the fathers had to leave their jobs, as 35% of solo fathers did in a study by George and Wilding (1972): many of these fathers report suspicion and malicious gossip from neighbors concerning their being at home full time. Similar themes emerge in intact egalitarian couples when the fathers are at home a good deal in the daytime: Russell's (1982) study of Australian couples also reports social disapproval of paternal child care from friends who thought him a "bit of a woman" and from neighbors who would not let their children play in the home of a male primary care giver, suggesting an element of sexual and aggression fear linked to intimacy between men and unrelated young children.

increased self-control and a growth of emotional maturity in boys who acquire stepfathers, and increased emotional maturity and subjective self-confidence for girls who acquire a stepmother. Hence, it seems to be the absence of a same-sex parent that has a negative impact on children, while the *kind* of impact varies by gender.

Alternate Family Forms

The best single study of the impact of alternate family forms upon child development is a longitudinal study in Los Angeles that has run for six years, beginning with a first interview with the mothers in their third trimester of pregnancy (Eiduson et al., 1982). Four family forms are being studied: communal living groups, unmarried social contract couples, unmarried solo mothers, and traditional married two-parent families.

Two findings hold for all four family types. One is a shift to greater social conventionality, predictable from the assumption that parenthood ties adults more closely to social institutions. In addition, the reversion to more traditional gender roles that has been noted in other studies of the transition to parenthood (Entwisle and Doering, 1981; Fischer, 1979; Shapiro, 1979) is found in the nontraditional family types in Eiduson's study. The second pattern shown in all four family types is for the mother to provide the primary care for the children up to the age of eighteen months. Men enter the child-care scene only when the child is walking and talking.

The unmarried mothers in this study are of special interest because they consist of two distinct types: predictably, most are young women who accepted unintended pregnancies and kept their babies; the second type are nest-building women who became pregnant intentionally, are well-educated, hold good jobs, and enjoy reasonable incomes—a first empirical example of the type discussed earlier. As a group, the solo mothers report a problem similar to that found in studies of divorced mothers, though their children are still too young to see its full ramifications: their sons verge on problem behavior more often than daughters or sons in the other three family types. In none of the family arrangement types have men played any significant role in child rearing. Hence, marital styles seem more amenable to change than parenting styles.

Egalitarian Fathers

The most interesting study, for our purposes, of intact couples in which the father carried primary child-care responsibility was conducted by Radin (1982) who studied middle-class Michigan couples with a child between 3 and 6 years of age. She compared families in which men took on primary child care while their wives worked or attended school with traditional couples in which women were the primary caregivers. Her interest in doing the study was to test whether it was sex or social role that explains the unique effects of fathers on children and their different treatment of sons and daughters.

One important finding is the absence of any differences between parents in egalitarian and traditional families on sex role orientation (Bem scale) or strictness. That may seem surprising until one notes that while the *children* in egalitarian families perceived their fathers to be more forceful, assertive, and strict than children from traditional families did, it was their daily exposure to the egalitarian fathers that mattered, since these men followed the rules they felt were important and enforced discipline on their children.[12] Traditional fathers were simply not there to exercise the values they espoused to the researcher.

A second finding relevant to Radin's major question concerning sex versus social role is a difference in the child-rearing problems men and women experienced. The majority of the egalitarian fathers reported impeded careers as their major problem, while their wives complained of loss of close involvement with their children. This finding prompts Radin to conclude that "even when parents choose to violate sex role expectations, there are still internal pressures to fulfill the tasks for which they were socialized" (Radin, 1982, p. 198). It is dubious whether these results merely reflect residual effects of prior socialization.

Finally, there are decided differences in the effect on the child between the egalitarian and traditional patterns of child rearing: egalitarian fathers engage in more cognitive stimulation of both sons and daughters than occurs in traditional families. They engage in more direct teaching efforts, and their children show the effect of such input by scoring higher on tests measuring internal locus of control and verbal intelligence than the children in traditional families. These children were too young to test for arithmetic ability, but the results are consistent with Biller's finding that children of solo mothers score lower on mathematical aptitude tests than children in intact families (Biller, 1974).

In none of the extant studies were primary care-giver fathers in charge of babies and toddlers. All the children were three years of age or older. Why 18 months of age is a significant watershed in paternal child care is not readily apparent, particularly since breastfeeding although on the increase at birth, is rarely practiced by contemporary American mothers beyond 2 or 3 months of age. Some clues are provided in qualitative material on a

[12]Russell's study of Australian couples (1982), comparable in many ways to Radin's American study, reports that both spouses in coparenting couples consider the father to have higher standards for child behavior and to be stricter in rule enforcement than men in traditional families.

couple in LaRossa and LaRossa's study (1981) of the transition to parent-hood, unusual in that the husband was caring for an infant son on a regular basis.

Stuart is a history professor who devoted four mornings a week to infant care while his wife taught and an older child attended nursery school. The father reported that things went well for the first three months because the baby slept most of the morning and he could spend three hours on lecture preparations. As the baby began to sleep less, trouble began, and Stuart reports he was unable to comfort the child. Asked about his feelings under such circumstances, he reports he felt "anger, frustration, sometimes I go pound my fist on the wall or something like that."

By contrast, he takes increasing pleasure in his 2-year-old daughter. Note what it is that delights Stuart in this passage from an interview:

> my older child now is verbal . . . she dresses herself, takes care of herself, goes to the bathroom by herself, everything, a more or less autonomous being . . . and I just enjoy that tremendously (LaRossa and LaRossa, 1981, p. 193–94).

The daughter's skills in taking care of herself reduce the need for physical care giving by the father; she is accessible to verbal communication and her autonomy permits Stuart to get on with his own work.

Fathering for Stuart involves being in charge and teaching the child. This makes for a good part of his frustration in dealing with his infant son. As much as he is able to, he seems to avoid direct interaction. Asked what he does when the baby is awake, Stuart says:

> I try to do something constructive still, maybe a little reading or some project around the house. . . . Sometimes I'll be in here in the same room with him, other times I'll just let him play by himself (LaRossa and LaRossa, 1981, p. 194).

When the interviewer suggests Stuart seems not to interact much with his son, he explains:

> Uh, not on a continuous basis. . . . I mean, I give him a bottle; he's just learning to hold it up for himself now. I continually will teach him things or try to: how to hold his bottle, how to get it if it's fallen over to one side. . . . Right now I am trying to teach him how to roll over. . . . He should know by now, but he's got this funny way. He tries to roll over with his arms stuck straight out. . . . Also, I will interact with him . . . by trying out new toys (LaRossa and LaRossa, 1981, p. 195).

Later in the interview Stuart confesses to finding a "certain degeneracy" in himself. He reports that when the baby is too fussy to permit him to concentrate on his work, he invents little things to do "to sort of occupy my time." Eating is one of these things, and he admits he has put on "fifteen or twenty pounds" since his son's birth.[13]

Most of the fathers in the LaRossa study did not even try to become significantly involved in the care of the newborn. The LaRossas use two concepts to capture the contrast between the mothers and fathers in their early induction to the parenting role: *role distance* and *role embracement*. They suggest men distance themselves from the parental role in early infant care; they act clumsy when handling the baby and show less skill than they actually possess when in the company of others. The fathers also tended to "reify" the baby—that is, act as if the infants were "things" rather than persons with whom they can interact.

Women, by contrast, tend to embrace the mother role, submerging themselves in it and trying to act with more skill than they in fact feel they have. Role embracing mothers deny that one cannot interact with a baby, pointing out that one must simply interact on a largely nonverbal level. Hence, the new mothers quickly gain the sense that the infant has "interpersonal competence," while fathers by and large see no such competence and prefer to relate to an older child.

Were it the case that this gender difference in early parenting merely reflected the lesser opportunity men have earlier in life from sibcare or baby-sitting to learn the skills involved in handling an infant, one would predict that second-time fathers feel more comfortable and become more involved in the care of the second infant than the first. Shapiro's study (1979) does not confirm this expectation, however. Second-time fathers showed no greater familiarity with babies: they were enamored with the growing abilities of their 2- and 3-year-olds and left the new infant to the mother while they took over more of the care of the older child. Their wives encouraged this because they themselves felt more experienced in infant care by this time and were pleased to have their husbands' help with the older child while they enjoyed the new infants.

Several general results emerge from this review of research. For one, solo fathers, like solo and traditional mothers, experience social isolation, income loss, and career restrictions as a consequence of primary responsibility for child care. Second, coparenting in intact families, like solo fathering, tends to involve children beyond the toddler stage, rarely infants under 18 months of age. Third, solo parenting involves anxiety for the parents primarily where the opposite sex child is concerned, with daughters of solo fathers experiencing emotional deprivation and sons of solo mothers

[13]At last follow-up, Stuart was back at the university full-time, his wife teaching part-time, and a baby-sitter was taking care of his son during the morning. A similar reversion to a more traditional pattern is found in Russell's (1982) Australian coparenting couples, only a fifth of whom continued the primary father care giver pattern in a two-year follow-up.

disciplinary problems. Fourth, exclusive or high levels of paternal investment in child rearing yields an internal locus of control and cognitive growth in the child, while exclusive rearing by women restricts young children's environmental exploration and encourages emotional dependence. We do not know if children of solo mothers show greater empathy and social skills than children of solo fathers, since this has not been investigated, though there was a hint of this being the case in Eiduson's Los Angeles study.

The consistency with which one finds low paternal involvement with very young infants who can neither walk nor talk is of particular interest. Experimental work on response to infants supports the view that the underlying psychophysiological responses to infants are similar in men and women, but their behavioral responses differ in a way consistent with role distancing in the male and role embracing in the female: women show approach behavior of a nurturant kind toward the infant, while men respond by ignoring or withdrawing from the infant (Frodi and Lamb, 1978). Lamb (1977) and Lamb and Goldberg (1982) have found that fathers differ in the *type* of interaction they engage in with children under a year old: fathers hold babies to play with them, mothers to take care of and soothe them. Altogether, it seems that men tend to avoid major involvement in infant care because infants do not respond to their repertoire of skills, and men have difficulty acquiring the skills needed to comfort the infant.

What shows in this new research on parenting are gender differences similar to those that emerge in psychological research: greater empathy, affiliation, sensitivity to nonverbal cues and social skills in women, greater emphasis on skill mastery, autonomy, and cognitive achievement in men. The other side of these generally desirable attributes is a tendency for men to feel discomfort with intimacy and women to be uncomfortable in impersonal situations. Gilligan (1982), using TAT storytelling protocols varying whether the central characters are in isolated competitive situations or intimate relational ones, found that women perceive danger and project violence into impersonal achievement situations, while men perceive danger and project violence into close personal situations.[14] Intimacy is threatening to the male, and impersonality to the female. These results are consistent with the role distancing by men and the role embracement by women in relating to the newborn child, since infant care involves a high degree of physical and emotional intimacy.

[14]These gender differences are found not only in samples of average college students, but among Harvard and Radcliffe men and women who went on to law and medical schools, where one might expect self-selection to produce a closer approximation to the male response among the women students (Gilligan, 1982).

Prior socialization no doubt presents difficulties to contemporary young adults who attempt coparenting and solo fathering. They are negotiating new turf with few cultural guidelines and little social support. On the other hand, the fact that the same gender differences between solo mothers and solo fathers are found between men and women in intact families and in general psychological research of the kind Gilligan and others have conducted suggests there is more involved than a need to unlearn old habits and learn new ones specific to parenting. That the issue is not simply past socialization running against current ideological commitment is also suggested by recent studies on the Israeli kibbutzim. Spiro's (1980) 25-year follow-up on the kibbutz he first studied in the 1950's shows that it is women in the *sabra* generation—those born and reared totally under the collective child rearing of the kibbutz—who have pressed the hardest for greater contact with children, overnight visiting privileges for children, and more room for home-based family activities.[15]

Spiro concluded, against his earlier presuppositions as a cultural anthropologist, that "precultural sex differences" must be at work, but he gives no detail on what he thinks those precultural factors might be. Neither does Gilligan propose any theory to explain *why* intimacy is threatening to men and impersonality to women, or *why* she finds women's mode of thinking to be contextual and narrative while men's is formal, linear, and abstract. She merely argues that theories of human development have used male lives as a norm and tried to fashion women out of a masculine cloth that does not fit.

Still another example of a lack of explanation of gender differences is found in studies demonstrating a sex-role inversion in the later years of the life span. It has been noted in a variety of studies that with age, men become less assertive and more tender and nurturant, while women become more self-assured and assertive (Gutmann, 1964, 1969, 1975; Neugarten and Gutmann, 1968). The same massive involution of gender role with age was found in four very different societies, but the researchers have not proposed any biosocial or biopsychological mechanism through which this transformation takes place in the postparental years of life. The lack of explanatory specificity in all three examples—Spiro, Gilligan and Gutmann—is based on the entrenched but erroneous view that biology is properly left outside the ken of the social sciences.

---

[15]There is great controversy in the interpretations given for the departure from sex equality on the kibbutzim (Palgi, 1983). Blumberg (1983) argues that women never had a real chance, since they were "integrated into 'male' economic and political roles, but there was no systematic attempt to integrate kibbutz men into 'female' roles" (p. 136). See also Blasi (1983) for another critical perspective on Spiro's argument that the shift back to traditionalism reflects the greater strength of "precultural sex differences."

EVOLUTIONARY PERSPECTIVE ON GENDER AND PARENTING

Parenting styles show the same gender differences found in other contexts than the family, which refutes the idea that there is something particular to pregnancy and birthing that "predisposes" or "triggers" maternal attachment to the newborn. It is not to a maternal instinct or hormonal priming at birth that one should look, but to gender differences that are in place long before a first pregnancy. This makes very dubious a view prevalent in the infant development literature in the last decade that close contact of the mother with her newborn during the first hours after birth, when hormonal levels are still very high, is important to subsequent mother–infant attachment. Lamb and Hwang's (1982) review of this literature concludes that the postbirth period is neither a critical nor a sensitive period[16] for maternal attachment.[17]

Indeed, a rethinking of this issue from an evolutionary perspective suggests it is highly unlikely that small variations in early contact could be critical to human attachment to infants. For a complex organism like a human being, fixing of an essential bond is not likely to be dependent on a brief period or a specific experience following childbirth. There will be considerable redundancy in the processes that assure activation of parental attachment to a child, and this will take place over a considerably longer period than a few hours or days after birth.

Animal research shows that it is possible to experimentally invoke nurturant behavior toward the young through the administration of female sex hormones to virgin, prepubescent males and females, so some hormonal factors implicit in sex dimorphism are implicated (Moltz et al., 1970; Rosenblatt, 1967, 1969; Terkel and Rosenblatt, 1968). It is also the case that normal males show nurturant behavior if exposed to pups for a period of

---

[16]A "critical" period refers to a discrete phase of development during which specific events *must* occur if development is to proceed normally, while a "sensitive" period refers to a phase during which an aspect of development may be *more readily* influenced than at other stages. Contact with the newborn in the hours after birth is neither a 'must' (in the critical-period sense) nor 'facilitative' (in the sensitive-period sense).

[17]The best known work in this area is that by Klaus and Kennell (1976), whose findings have not been replicated. Klaus and Kennell used poor young clinic patients who may have been affected by the projected model of good parenting behavior when they were designated for special treatment by being given more time with the newborn infants than other obstetric patients (Hawthorne effect). Studies with middle-class women at Stanford and in Sweden did not show any comparable effect of increased time with neonates for subsequent mother–infant attachment that Klaus and Kennell claim to have established. (See Lamb and Hwang (1982) for a detailed critical review.)

time. Adler (1973) suggests that hormones may *prime* nurturant behavior, but continuous proximity is necessary to *maintain* that behavior and may even stimulate it in the absence of hormonal priming.

For most primate species and most of human history, lactation assured the maintenance of proximity between mother and newborn. Then, too, the mother–infant dyad is not isolated but enmeshed in a group, whether a baboon troop, hunter–gatherer band, or contemporary family. Support by the group is enhanced by the general affiliative, socially responsive qualities of the female, since these qualities elicit aid from the group and assure persistence in providing nurturant care to the young by all the females in the group.[18]

Thus an evolutionary perspective suggests that no specific experience will be critical for parental attachment to and care of the young. It also argues against the possibility of leaving to a late stage of development, close to or following a pregnancy, the acquisition of qualities necessary for so important a function as child rearing. The attributes of mothering and fathering are inherent parts of sex differentiation that paves the way to reproduction.

If the parenting styles of men and women build upon underlying features rooted in basic sexual dimorphism, then increased male involvement in primary care of the very young child will not have the effect that some theorists expect. For example, Chodorow (1974, 1978) argues that gender differences are the consequence of the fact that it is women who do the parenting of both sons and daughters. By this thesis, if fathers had primary care responsibility for their same-sex child, boys, like girls today, would grow up with less individuation, greater relational affiliation, and less clearly demarcated ego boundaries.

But there is no evidence from the studies of solo or coparenting fathers to date to suggest this is a likely outcome. Men bring their maleness to parenting women bring their femaleness. Hence, the effect of increased male investment in primary care of sons is not to produce sons who would be more like daughters, but to either enhance gender differences or, if there is significant coparenting, to enlarge the range of characteristics shown by both sons and daughters.

---

[18]Gender-differentiated persistence in seeking contact with the newborn is found among siblings in both monkey and human groups. In monkey groups, mothers often try to keep both the male and female siblings away from the newborn, but pubescent females *persist* in seeking proximity while males do not (Suomi, 1982). Human toddlers show similar behavior, with girls seeking contact while boys go off more readily when the mother is with a newborn (Dunn and Kendrick, 1982; Nadelman and Begun, 1982). Ember (1973) found that helping to care for younger children increased nurturing and socially responsible behavior in boys.

BIOLOGICAL COMPONENTS OF GENDER

It is one thing to criticize psychosocial theories for their inadequacy in explaining empirical findings on gender differences in parenting. It is quite another to supplement them with biological factors. Sociologists share enough ground in theory and method with psychologists to readily work across both disciplines. This is not the case where biological contributions to gender differences are concerned. While treatment herein must be selective, it is nonetheless necessary to make a few general points.

One, it makes no sense to view biology and social experience as separate domains contesting for election as primary causes. Biological processes unfold in a cultural context and are themselves malleable, not stable and inevitable. So, too, cultural processes occur within and through the biological organism; they do not take place in a biological vacuum.

Second, there is a good deal of ferment in the biological sciences these days, in opposition to the Cartesian reductionism that has characterized western science for three centuries.[19] That model worked well in physics and chemistry and the technology they spawned. It has not worked well in embryology and the brain sciences. Reductionism in the biomedical fields works via the experimental mode in which one perturbs the normal working of the system under study, but as a consequence it runs the risk of confusing the nature of the perturbation with the cause of the system's normal functioning. An example from medical research illustrates this point: if you give patients the drug dopamine and it reduces Parkinsonian tremors, then Parkinson's disease is thought to be "caused" by a deficiency of dopamine (Lewontin, 1983). Sociobiologists rely on the same reductionist model: they consider properties of society to be determined by intrinsic properties of individual human beings; individuals in turn are expressions of their genes, and genes are self-replicating molecules. Following this logic leads to claims such as Dawkins' (1976) for a "selfish gene," others for an "altruistic gene." Under fire from social scientists, Edward Wilson has revised his earlier gene-determinist theory to include the evolution of culture itself, using the concept of "gene-culture coevolution" to explain the emergence of "mind" (Lumsden and Wilson, 1981, 1982). But the revision remains a reductionist theory.[20]

The challenge to the reductionist model has come from biological scientists here and in western Europe, particularly among Marxist biologists,

[19]Two books of essays from a 1980 conference in Bressanone, Italy, are a useful introduction to the dialectic perspective in biology (Rose, 1982a, 1982b). For a brief overview of the major ideas from this conference, see Lewontin's review of these books (Lewontin, 1983).
[20]See Gould (1983) for a review of Lumsden and Wilson's book, *Promethean Fire* (1982). A critical review of the companion volume, *Genes, Mind, Culture* (Lumsden and Wilson, 1981), can be found in Smith and Warre (1982).

who argue in favor of a dialectical model. This is based on an interesting set of assumptions: one, organisms grow and change throughout their life spans through an interplay of biological, psychological, and sociocultural processes (Parsons, 1982; Petersen, 1980; Riegel, 1976; Rose, 1982a, 1982b). Second, biological processes are assumed to have greater influence at some points in the life span than at others. For example, they are critical in fetal development, at puberty, during pregnancy, but less potent during latency or early middle age. Thus, for example, there are high correlations between testosterone level and aggression among young men, but no significant correlations among older men, since the latter's greater social maturation permits higher levels of impulse control (Persky, Smith, and Basu, 1971). So, too, Gutmann's theory of the parental imperative (1964) is based on an awareness of the ebb and flow of hormonal processes along the life span: childbearing and rearing take place during that phase of the life span with the greatest sex dimorphism in hormonal secretion and body morphology, and with very great pressure for adult males and females to perform in culturally specified ways. Along with the relaxation of social pressure from middle age on, there is also a change in body, a blurring of sexual and hormonal differences between men and women. It is the interaction of lowered inner hormonal pressures and lowered external social pressures with a psychological awareness of a limited life span that may produce the sex role involution noted in studies of personality in the later years.

In sum, organisms are not passive objects acted upon by internal genetic forces, as some sociobiologists claim, nor are they passive objects acted upon by external environmental forces, as some social scientists claim. Genes, organisms, and environment interpenetrate and mutually determine each other. To discuss biological predispositions is to attempt a specification of biological processes, in the same way sociologists try to specify social processes. Awareness of *both* social and biological processes adds a synergistic increment to knowledge that can then be used to provide the means for modification and change; it does not imply that we are locked into an unchangeable body or social system. Ignorance of biological processes may doom efforts at social change because we misidentify the targets for change, and hence our means to attain the change we desire.

But for social scientists to specify those biological processes relevant to the phenomenon they study can easily lead to flimsy argument by selective analogy of the aggressive-territorial-male-animal variety. One must adhere to some guidelines in exploring whether and in what specific way gender differences may be shaped by biological processes. The biological factors relevant to gender differences in social behavior will be located at some point on the chain of development that runs from genetic sex at conception (a female XX chromosome or a male XY chromosome), through gonadal differentiation during the first trimester of fetal development, to hormones produced by the gonads and related pituitary glands, to neural organization of the brain, and from there to social behavior.

The effect of variation at any one of these points on the chain can be studied for subsequent social behavior of the organism. For example, a normal conceptus has two sex chromosomes (XX or XY), but occasionally may have three, either an extra X (XXY) or an extra Y (XYY). The Y chromosome is critical in gonadal differentiation of the male and the level of androgenic hormones produced by the gonads. If androgens affect behavior, as they do, then we can see how social behavior and physical characteristics vary between a normal XY male and an XYY male or an XXY male. Compared to a normal male, the XYY male with his extra dose of maleness (so to speak) will be taller than average, more muscular, and have more body hair, higher activity levels, more impulsivity, and more acute visual-spatial abilities. A male with an extra dose of femaleness, the XXY male with Klinefelter's Syndrome, is shorter and less muscular, has less body hair, smaller testicles, lower sexual arousability, and is more timid and passive in behavior than the average male. Family and social circumstances will obviously affect the way and the extent to which the behavioral characteristics are shown, but we have identified a very specific and important biological component in the behavior of such males.

Sex hormones affect social behavior in one of two ways: they can have *direct* effects—what biologists call activational effects—or *indirect* effects— what biologists call inductive or organizational effects (Goy and McEwen, 1980; Hoyenga and Hoyenga, 1979). A direct effect means secretion level, hormone production rate or type of hormone is a *proximate* contributor to behavior. Think of the contrast in behavior of a 10- and an 18-year-old male; one contributor to the different social behavior they show is androgens: the older boy will have on average an eight times higher level of androgen secretion than a 10-year-old (Ellis, 1982), and a good deal of the behavior of the two males is affected by that difference.

The indirect or organizational effect of sex hormones refers to the influence of hormones during the critical phase of neural development in the third trimester of pregnancy, when the brain is undergoing rapid development and differentiation. Hormonal influence at this critical stage is important for gender differentiation, since brain cells acquire a "set" (like a thermostat setting) highly resistant to change after birth. It is this organizational effect of hormones on neural circuitry that led neuroscientists to speak of a "male" or a "female" brain at birth. Note, too, that a male fetus during the first trimester of pregnancy has the equivalent, by body weight, of four times the amount of androgen that he will have from birth to approximately 10 years of age (Ellis, 1982). Hormones, then, have powerful effects during fetal development, go into a relatively quiescent period for the first decade of life, and then rapidly increase again during the second decade of life. To the extent that hormones affect behavior, it is simply not true that an absence of a gender difference in behavior at age 4 and the emergence of such a difference at 14 means the difference is culturally produced, because the adolescent's behavior is strongly influenced by the activational effects of sex hormones.

With these comments as background, we can specify the criteria for determining whether biology is involved in a gender difference in social behavior. Parsons (1982) suggests four such criteria and proposes that if two or more of them are met, there is strong evidence implicating biology in the observed gender difference. Slightly modified from those Parsons proposed,[21] the criteria are: (1) consistent correlations between social behavior and a physiological sex attribute (body morphology, sex chromosome type, hormonal type and secretion level, neural organization in the brain); (2) the pattern is found in infants and young children prior to major socialization influences, or the pattern emerges with the onset of puberty when body morphology and hormonal secretion change rapidly; (3) the pattern is stable across cultures; and (4) similar behavior is noted across species, particularly the higher primates most genetically similar to the human species.

Using these four criteria, sex dimorphism with biological contributions can be claimed in four areas: (1) sensory sensitivity (sight, hearing, smell, touch) and body morphology; (2) aggression or, more aptly, general activity level; (3) cognitive skills in spatial visualization, mathematical reasoning, and to a lesser extent, verbal fluency; and (4) parenting behavior (Petersen, 1980).

Parenting as a sexually dimorphic pattern clearly meets two of the four criteria: in almost all cultures and most species it is primarily a female responsibility to care for the young. In most cultures siblings provide more care giving to the very young than fathers do (Weisner, 1982; Whiting and Whiting, 1975). Paternal care giving among nonhuman primates tends to be among New World monkeys who typically have multiple litters, unlike large apes and humans who typically have one infant at a time and a prolonged period of immature dependency (Redican, 1976).

Redican's assessment of the structural conditions that predict paternal involvement among nonhuman primates is remarkably similar to a comparable review by West and Konner (1976) of the conditions that predict human paternal involvement. For nonhuman primate males, paternal involvement is high when there is a monogamous social organization and paternity is readily identifiable; when males are not needed for the role of warrior–hunter; and when females are permissive and encourage paternal care giving. For human males, West and Konner observe that men take care of their children if they are sure they are the fathers, if they are not needed

---

[21] I have expanded Parsons' criterion "1" from just hormones to the factors cited in the text, and modified criterion "2" by including pubertal change.

as warriors and hunters, if mothers contribute to food resources, and if male parenting is encouraged by women.

The structural conditions specified by Redican and West and Konner apply for the most part to modern societies. There are limits of course on confidence in paternity, but sharing the economic provider role is increasingly the pattern and spills over to rising pressure from women for greater participation by their husbands in child care. We can assume, then, that structural conditions are ripe for higher levels of paternal involvement in the future. Two criteria remain at issue concerning biological implications: do the differences between male and female concerning hormones, sensory sensitivity, activity level, or social and cognitive skills lead one to predict different styles of parenting on the part of men compared to women as they move toward greater coparenting? It is this author's working hypothesis that all sexually dimorphic characteristics contribute to the species function of reproduction, and hence have persisted as biological predispositions across cultures and through historical time.

A profile of gender differences in sensory modalities reads like this:[22] females show greater sensitivity to touch, sound, and odor; and have greater fine motor coordination and finger dexterity. Sounds are judged to be twice as loud by women as men; women pick up nuances of voice and music more readily, and are six times more likely to sing in tune as men. The sense modality in which men show greater acuity than women is vision: men show greater sensitivity to light, responding more quickly to changes in its intensity than women do. At birth, females are four to six weeks more mature neurologically than males, which persists in their earlier acquisition of language, verbal fluency, and memory retention. Language disabilities like stuttering and dyslexia are several times more prevalent among males than females.

Gender differences in social and cognitive skills are also found: females are more sensitive to context, show greater skill in picking up peripheral information, and process information faster; they are more attracted to human faces and respond to nuances of facial expression as they do to nuances of sound. Males are better at object manipulation in space, can rotate objects in their mind, read maps and perform in mazes better, and show a better sense of direction. Males are more rule-bound, less sensitive to situational nuance. Most of these differences meet the criterion of precultural influence in that they show up at very early ages. Male infants are more attracted to the movement of objects, females to the play of expression on human faces. Girl babies startle to sound more quickly than

---

[22]Several sources contribute to this overview profile: Durden-Smith and DeSimone, 1983; Gove and Carpenter, 1982; Hoyenga and Hoyenga, 1979; Parsons, 1980, 1982.

boy babies and respond to the soothing effect of a human voice, while boys respond to physical contact and movement.

Viewed as a composite profile, there is some predisposition in the female to be responsive to people and sounds, an edge in receiving, interpreting, and giving back communication. Males have an edge on finer differentiation of the physical world through better spatial visualization and physical object manipulation. The female combination of sensitivity to sound and face and rapid processing of peripheral information implies a quicker judgment of emotional nuance, a profile that carries a put-down tone when labeled "female intuition." It also suggests an easier connection between feelings and their expression in words among women. Spatial perception, good gross motor control, visual acuity, and a more rigid division between emotional and cognitive responsivity combine in a counterpart profile of the male.

One ingenious study illustrates both the greater sound acuity of women and greater spatial perception of men. The test was simply to mentally search the alphabet for two types of capital letters: those with a curve in their shape like an "S", and those with a long "ee" sound like a "Z". As predicted, men were faster and made fewer errors than women on the shape task, while women were faster and more accurate on the sound task (Coltheart, Hull, and Slater, 1975).

When these gender differences are viewed in connection with caring for a nonverbal, fragile infant, women have a head start in reading an infant's facial expressions, smoothness of body motions, ease in handling a tiny creature with tactile gentleness, and soothing through a high, soft, rhythmic use of the voice. By contrast, men have greater tendencies to interact with an older child, with whom rough-and-tumble physical play, physical coordination, and teaching of object manipulation is easier. Note however, that these are general tendencies, many of them exaggerated through sex-differentiated socialization practices; they are neither biologically immutable nor invariant across individuals or cultures. Some cultures may reinforce these predispositions, as ours does, while others may socialize against or reverse them.

There is, however, a good deal of evidence in animal and human research to support the view that sex hormones and sex differentiation in neurological organization of the brain contribute to these differences. Androgens have been the most intensively studied for their effects on spatial visualization, maze running, aggression, and sexual behavior. Animals given androgen either neonatally or as adults show improvement in complex maze scores, while the administration of the female hormone, estrogen, depresses maze learning. Sons of diabetic mothers who were given estrogen during pregnancy show reduced spatial ability and more field dependence than control males. Turner's syndrome women, genetic females with only one sex chromosome (XO type), do not develop ovaries and hence are deprived of fetal androgens; they show poor spatial and numerical ability.

As noted earlier, hormones can operate in either an activational or organizational manner. There is evidence that certain of the gender differences cited above are not acquired after birth, when they could be the result of the interactive effect of both biological and social factors, but before birth, in the organization of the brain under the influence of gonadal hormones. Research in the neurosciences has established that the right hemisphere of the brain is dominant in emotions, facial recognition, music, visual tasks, and identification of spatial relationships, while language skills are dominant in the left hemisphere of the brain (Goy and McEwen, 1980; Kinsbourne, 1978). Human males show more rigid separation of function between the two brain hemispheres, while the female brain is less lateralized, less tightly organized than males. Thus, the brains of 4-year-old girls show more advanced cell growth in the left, language-dominant hemisphere, boys in the right, spatial perception-dominant hemisphere.[23]

Anatomical research has further established that a larger proportion of space in the right hemisphere is devoted to the visual-spatial function in males than females. McGuinness suggests that as a consequence males have more restricted verbal access to their emotions than females (Durden-Smith and DeSimone, 1983; McGuinness, 1976). Brain lateralization differences between men and women also suggest one reason that males show greater mathematical ability than females: females approach mathematical problems through left hemisphere *verbal* means, while males rely more directly on right hemisphere *symbols*, which is a more efficient route to problem solving.

Until 1982 why and how gender differentiation in hemisphere organization occurs was linked to the earlier maturation of girls generally. Lateralization, beginning earlier in girls, might give them an advantage in verbal skills, while delayed lateralization gives males an advantage in spatial skills (Harris, 1978). This interpretation has been challenged by new research, which finds that the divider between the brain hemispheres, called the *corpus callosum* (a bundle of fibers that carries information between the two halves of the brain), is larger and more bulbous in females than in males, suggesting greater ease and frequency of communication between the two hemispheres in females (DeLaCoste-Utamsing and Holloway, 1982; Durden-Smith and DeSimone, 1983).

If further research substantiates these findings, it does not mean we simply accept a gender difference in spatial visualization and mathematical ability as immutable. A postindustrial society in which an increasing proportion of

---

[23]Male victims whose left brain hemispheres were affected by stroke or epileptic seizure show more language impairment during recovery than female victims because of the much greater male reliance on the left hemisphere for language; female victims compensate by relying on their unimpaired right hemisphere.

occupations relies on mathematical and spatial skills, coupled with these findings, can as readily lead to a shift in mathematical training of girls, directing them away from dealing narrowly with their assumed "math anxiety" to biofeedback training to encourage greater direct reliance on symbols rather than words in problem solving.

Gender Characteristics in the Future

Assuming that the neurosciences continue to affirm what is a growing accumulation of evidence of biological processes that differentiate the sexes, and assuming further that the social trend toward greater coparenting continues in the future, what are the likely outcomes in gender characteristics of a future generation of children? The research findings appear to mean that at birth the child brings gender predispositions that interact with gender differences in the parents, whose own differences reflect biological predispositions either reinforced or discouraged by adult socialization and role pressure. Biological predispositions in the child do not preclude their supplementation by psychological qualities of the parents, or their encouragement by parents who do not themselves possess a given characteristic. Quite traditional parents encourage children to develop in ways they perceive to be useful when their children are adults, even when they themselves do not possess those qualities. Differences between parents and children do not mean that parental influence is nil, nor that children have rebelled under peer pressure. The qualities in question may have been actively encouraged by the parent.

Assuming further that there are many socially desirable attributes among traditional male and female traits, an equal exposure of children to parents who both invest a great deal in care giving could have the effect of encouraging more androgyny in the children. Several researchers have shown that cognitive ability and even scientific productivity is higher when subjects are neither strongly feminine nor strongly masculine, but possess in equal measure the socially desirable traits of both sexes. Spence and Helmreich (1978) show that when socially desirable attributes of men and women are measured, they vary independently of each other within each sex. In other words, masculine and feminine qualities do not preclude each other in the same person, although that combination is still not prevalent in American society. Furthermore, those with the highest levels of self-esteem and self-confidence were subjects *high* on *both sets* of attributes.

Spence and Helmreich used their masculinity–femininity scales in a study of established scientists that also included measures of work commitment, subject mastery, degree of overall competitiveness in work, and productivity. The measure of scientific productivity was an external criterion—the number of references to their subjects' publications in the Science Citation Index. They found that those scientists high on both the masculinity and the femininity scales were the most scientifically productive. Further analysis found the highest scientific attainment to be among those high in subject mastery and work commitment, and lowest in competitiveness, a profile that again combines traditionally feminine with masculine characteristics.

Productive labor in all sectors of the occupational system and creativity in critical professions may therefore benefit by a blending of the attributes traditionally associated with male and female. That blending may be encouraged by movement away from sex-segregated occupations with token minority representation of one sex toward compositional sex parity, on the assumption of an eventual reciprocal influence on each other of equal numbers of men and women incumbents.

But in the long run, on an individual as well as societal level, the socially desirable attributes of both sexes can be acquired by each sex only if we properly identify their sources in both biology and culture. Biological predispositions make certain things easier for one sex to learn than the other; knowing this in advance would permit development of ways to provide compensatory training for each sex, rear children within families, teach children in schools, or train adults on the job. No individual and no society can benefit when men fear intimacy and women fear impersonality.

As adults, there are limits on the extent to which we can change our deeply ingrained characteristics. But a first step is to understand and respect the qualities of each sex, and to actively encourage children to absorb the socially desirable attributes of both sexes. To the extent this is done, whether by solo fathers, solo mothers, or egalitarian coparents, a future generation of boys and men may temper competitive self-interest with affiliative concern for the welfare of others and skills in intimate relations, and girls and women may temper their affiliative concern for others with a sense of effective, actualized selves.

CONCLUSION

This chapter began with an overview of global population growth that is second only to the threat of a nuclear holocaust as the most pressing issue confronting the world community. Indeed, some would argue that differential population pressure is precisely the factor that produces internal political stress within nations as the gap widens between the haves and the have-nots. Such class conflict leads to civil unrest, political revolution, and international tensions and conflict between nations that might one day explode in nuclear confrontation. Hence, the two issues of population and war are intricately interrelated.

Over the shoulders of Ariés and Lesthaeghe, we have sketched the difference between developed western nations and the much larger proportion of the world's population in underdeveloped and developing nations. In the latter a difficult transition is taking place, from a lineage- to a child-centered orientation that is critical to a change in parental motivation from child quantity to child quality. In western industrial nations the transition we have traced is from a child- to a self-centered orientation. Both processes of change are painful for the individuals and the families involved, since many people are caught in the dilemma of having to reject a set of values they have internalized from childhood and replace them with a counterset of values in adulthood.

Everywhere in the world the place of parenthood in the lives of people in the late 20th century is undergoing a profound transformation. There is personal anguish in the decision to restrict one's family to a firstborn daughter and not to seek to bear three sons for a Chinese peasant woman, as there may be personal anguish in the decision to have no children at all in order to maintain the momentum of a scientific career for an American woman. A Soviet woman may experience anguish in facing a pregnancy she does not want when she is cut off from access to a medically safe abortion facility, while a Bolivian woman may experience anguish in facing a sixth pregnancy when the first five children cannot be fed. The childless American woman and the one-child Chinese woman may both have difficulty coping with the frustration of a hunger for children. Clearly the Chinese peasant has no assurance that she will be provided for in her old age should she become ill or otherwise unable to work to support herself. In other parts of the globe, unwanted children—poorly nourished, clothed, and schooled—will be robbed of hope, cheated of any prospect for even minimally adequate living conditions in what are apt to be equally impoverished adult lives.

Economic, military, and political power is in the hands of the developed industrial nations of the world. To the extent that such nations shift to greater competitive self-interest, the threat of global annihilation will become even graver than it is today. Hence, there is pressing need to raise probing questions about the etiology of egotism and altruism and explore the extent to which it is possible to rear children and change the definition of adult roles in work, politics, and family life toward a proper balance between concern for self and concern for others. The analysis of gender differentiation is a central issue in this regard. The demographic trends toward lower marriage rates, increased childlessness, and greater numbers of adults living alone, sketched earlier in this chapter, make it even more important that the affiliative, altruistic qualities associated with women become characteristic of boys and men, and the capacity for self-direction and creative use of abilities associated with men become characteristic of girls and women.

No society on this tiny planet provides a model for us to emulate. In recent years some have hoped that feminism would provide a guide to such a future, as it had been earlier that socialism did. But neither Marxism nor feminism, to say nothing of mainstream social science, has yet taken up the challenge of the biological component to human behavior, despite the fact that sexual dimorphism is important in both human production and reproduction. An ideology that does not confront this basic issue is an exercise in wishful thinking, and a social science that does not confront it is sterile. Whether one's motivation is rooted in a passionate commitment to solving major societal and global problems or in a passionate commitment to scientific advance, or both, it is my firm conviction and conclusion that goals sought are best approached through an integrated biosocial science.

SUMMARY

This chapter describes the transformation parenthood has undergone in western societies from three perspectives. First, the macrohistorical trans-formation in the social valuation of children, from concern for child *quantity* to child *quality* in the 19th century, followed by contemporary trends toward an increased centrality of *self-orientation* over family and child orientation. Demographic trends are shown to be consistent with this value transformation: with only one in four households containing even one dependent-age child, parenthood no longer provides a major axis for social integration, as it did in the past. Second, recent trends in birth management are reviewed for their implications concerning the transition to parenthood, with serious questions posed regarding the growing obstetrical trend toward handling birth as a medical event requiring complex technological and surgical intervention. Third, studies of solo parenting and parenting in alternative family forms are reviewed for clues to gender differences in parenting, an explanation of which is sought through an integration of biological, psychological, and social factors.

REFERENCES

Adler, N. The biopsychology of hormones and behavior. In D. A. Dewbery & D. A. Rethlingshafer (Eds.), *Comparative Psychology: A Modern Survey*. NY: McGraw-Hill, 1973, pp. 301–343.

Ariés, P. *Centuries of Childhood*. Harmondsworth, England: Penguin, 1973. [1962]

Bagne, P. High-tech breeding. *Mother Jones*, 1983, *8*, 23–29, 35.

Banta, H. D., and Thacker, S. B. Policies toward medical technology: The case of electronic fetal monitoring. *American Journal of Public Health*, 1979, *61*, 931–935.

Barnett, C. R., Leiderman, P. H., Grobstein, R., and Klaus, M. H. Neonatal sepa-ration, the maternal side of interaction deprivation. *Pediatrics*, 1970, *45*, 197–205.

Beard, R. W. Technology in the care of mother and baby: An essential safeguard. In R. Chester, P. Diggory, & M. B. Sutherland (Eds.), *Changing Patterns of Child-Bearing and Child Rearing*. London: Academic Press, 1981, pp. 1–11.

Beck, N. C., Siegle, L. J., Davison, N. P., Kormeier, S., Breitenstein, A., and Hall, D. G. The prediction of pregnancy outcome: Maternal preparation, anxiety and attitudinal sets. *Journal of Psychosomatic Research*, 1980, *24*, 343–351.

Biller, H. B. Parental and sex-role factors in cognitive and academic functioning. In J. K. Cole & R. Dienstbier (Eds.), *Nebraska Symposium on Motivation*. Lincoln, NE: University of Nebraska Press, 1974, pp. 83–123.

Blake, J. Can we believe recent data on birth expectations in the United States? *Demography*, 1974, *11*, 25–43.

Blake, J. Is zero preferred? American attitudes toward childlessness in the 1970s. *Journal of Marriage and the Family*, 1979, *41*, 245–257.

Blake, J. Demographic revolution and family evolution: Some implications for American women. In P. W. Berman & E. R. Ramey (Eds.), *Women: A Developmental Perspective*. U.S. Department of Health and Human Services, NIH Publication No. 82–2298, 1982, pp. 299–312.

Blasi, J. A critique of gender and culture: Kibbutz women revisited. In M. Palgi, J. R. Blasi, M. Rosner, & M. Safir (Eds.), *Sexual Equality: The Israeli Kibbutz Tests the Theories*. Norwood, PA: Norwood Editions, 1983, pp. 91–99.

Bloom, D. What's happening to the age at first birth in the United States? *Demography*, 1982, *19*, 351–370.

Blumberg, R. L. Kibbutz women: From the fields of revolution to the laundries of discontent. In M. Palgi, J. R. Blasi, M. Rosner & M. Safir (Eds.), *Sexual Equality: The Israeli Kibbutz Tests the Theories*. Norwood, PA: Norwood Editions, 1983, pp. 130–150.

Bouthol, G. *La Guerre*. Paris: Presses Universitaires de France, 1969.

Cain, M. Fertility as adjustment to risk. In A. S. Rossi (Ed.), *Gender and the Life Course*. Hawthorne, New York: Aldine, 1985, pp. 145–160.

Chalmers, I. Evaluation of perinatal practice: The limitations of audit by death. In R. Chester, P. Diggory & M. B. Sutherland (Eds.), *Changing Patterns of Child-Bearing and Child Rearing*. London: Academic Press, 1981, pp. 39–56.

Chalmers, I., and Richards, M. P. M. Intervention and causal inference in obstetric practice. In T. Chard (Ed.), *Benefits and Hazards of the New Obstetrics*. London: Spastics International Medical Publications, 1977, pp. 34–61.

Cherlin, A. J. Explaining the postwar baby boom. *Items*, *35*, 1981, 57–63. (NY: SSRC).

Chodorow, N. Family structure and feminine personality. In M. Z. Rosaldo & L. Lamphere (Eds.), *Women, Culture and Society*. Palo Alto, CA: Stanford University Press, 1974, pp. 43–66.

Chodorow, N. *The Reproduction of Mothering: Psychoanalysis and the Sociology of Gender*. Los Angeles, CA: University of California Press, 1978.

Colman, A., and Colman, L. Pregnancy as an altered state of consciousness. *Birth and the Family Journal*, 1973, *1*, 7–11.

Coltheart, M., Hull, E., and Slater, D. Sex differences in imagery and reading. *Nature* (London) 1975, *253*, 438–440.

Davis, C., and Feshbach, M. *Rising infant mortality in the USSR in the 1970s*. U.S. Bureau of the Census: International Population Report Series P-95, No. 74. Washington, D.C.: Department of Commerce, 1980.

Davis, K., and van den Oever, P. Demographic foundations of new sex roles. *Population and Development Review*, 1982, *8*, 495–511.

Dawkins, R. *The Selfish Gene*. London: Oxford University Press, 1976.

DeChateau, P. The importance of the neonatal period for the development of synchrony in the mother–infant dyad. *Birth and the Family Journal*, 1977, *4*, 10–23.

DeLaCoste-Utamsing, C., and Holloway, R. Sexual dimorphism in the human corpus callosum. *Science*, 1982, *216*, 1431–1432.

Dennenberg, V. H. Critical periods, stimulus input and emotional reactivity: A theory of infantile stimulation. *Psychological Review*, 1964, *71*, 335–351.

Diggory, P. The long-term effects upon the child of perinatal events. In R. Chester, P. Diggory, & M. B. Sutherland (Eds.), *Changing Patterns of Child-Bearing and Child Rearing*. London: Academic Press, 1981, 23–37.

Dunn, J., and Kendrick, C. Siblings and their mothers: Developing relationships within the family. In M. E. Lamb & B. Sutton-Smith (Eds.), *Sibling Relationships: Their Nature and Significance Across the Lifespan*. Hillsdale, NJ: Erlbaum, 1982, pp. 39–60.

Durden-Smith, J., and DeSimone, D. *Sex and the Brain*. NY: Arbor House, 1983.

Durkheim, E. *Suicide: A Study in Sociology*. Translated by J. A. Spaulding and G. Simpson. Glencoe, IL: Free Press, 1951. [1897].

Eiduson, B. T., Kornfein, M., Zimmerman, I. L., and Weisner, T. S. Comparative socialization practices in traditional and alternative families. In M. E. Lamb (Ed.), *Nontraditional Families: Parenting and Child Development*. Hillsdale, NJ: Erlbaum, 1982, pp. 315–346.

Ellis, L. Developmental androgen fluctuations and the five dimensions of mammalian sex (with emphasis upon the behavioral dimension and the human species). *Ethology and Sociobiology*, 1982, *3*, 171–197.

Ember, C. R. The effects of feminine task assignment on the social behavior of boys. *Ethos*, 1973, *1*, 424–439.

Entwisle, D. R., and Doering, S. G. *The First Birth: A Family Turning Point*. Baltimore, MD: Johns Hopkins University Press, 1981.

Erickson, J. D. Down's syndrome, paternal age, maternal age and birth order. *Annals of Human Genetics*, 1978, *41*, 289–298.

Ferri, E. Characteristics of motherless families. *British Journal of Social Work*, 1973, *3*, 91–100.

Ferri, E. *Growing Up in a One Parent Family*. Slough: National Foundation for Educational Research, 1976.

Finkle, J. L., and McIntosh, A. Policy responses in population stagnation in developed societies. In A. Campbell (Ed.), *Social, Economic and Health Aspects of Low Fertility*. Washington, D.C.: U.S. Government Printing Office, 1980, pp. 275–295.

Fischer, C., Jackson, R. M., Stueve, C. A., & Gerson, K. et al. *Networks and Places*. NY: Free Press, 1977.

Fischer, L. R. *When daughters become mothers*. Unpublished Ph.D. dissertation. Amherst: University of Massachusetts, 1979.

Frodi, A. M., and Lamb, M. E. Sex differences in responsiveness to infants: A developmental study of psychophysiological and behavioral responses. *Child Development*, 1978, *49*, 1182–1188.

George, V., and Wilding, P. *Motherless Families*. London: Routledge and Kegan Paul, 1972.

Gilligan, C. *In a Different Voice: Psychological Theory and Women's Development*. Cambridge, MA: Harvard University Press, 1982.

Gorsuch, R. L., and Key, M. K. Abnormalities of pregnancy as a function of anxiety and life stress. *Psychosomatic Medicine*, 1974, *36*, 352–362.

Gould, S. J. Genes on the brain. *New York Review of Books*, 1983, *30*, 5–6, 8, 10.

Gove, W. R., and Carpenter, G. R. *The Fundamental Connection between Nature and Nurture*. Lexington, Mass.: Lexington Books, 1982.

Goy, R. W., and McEwen, B. S. *Sexual Differentiation of the Brain*. Cambridge: MIT Press, 1980.

Grimm, E. E. Women's attitudes and reactions to childbearing. In G. Goldman & D. S. Milman (Eds.), *Modern Woman: Her Psychology and Sexuality*. Springfield, IL: Charles C. Thomas, 1969, pp. 129–151.

Gutmann, D. An exploration of ego configurations in middle and later life. In B. L. Neugarten (Ed.), *Personality in Middle and Later Life*. NY: Atherton, 1964, pp. 114–148.

Gutmann, D. *The country of old men: Cross-cultural studies in the psychology of later life*. Occasional papers in Gerontology, No. 5. Ann Arbor, MI: Institute on Gerontology, 1969.

Gutmann, D. Parenthood: A key to the comparative study of the life cycle. In N. Datan & L. H. Ginsberg (Eds.), *Life Span Development and Psychology: Normative Life Crises*. NY: Academic Press, 1975, pp. 167–184.

Harris, L. J. Sex differences in spatial ability: Possible environmental, genetic and neurological factors. In M. Kinsbourne (Ed.), *Asymmetrical Functions of the Brain*. Cambridge, MA: Cambridge University Press, 1978, pp. 405–522.

Heeren, H. J. Pronatalist population policies in some western European countries. *Population Research and Policy Review*, 1982, 137–152.

Helper, M. M., Cohen, R. L., Beitenman, E. T., and Eaton, L. F. Life-events and acceptance of pregnancy. *Journal of Psychosomatic Research*, 1968, *12*, 183–188.

Hipgrave, T. Child rearing by lone fathers. In R. Chester, P. Diggory, & M. B. Sutherland (Eds.), *Changing Patterns of Child-Bearing and Child Rearing*. London: Academic Press, 1981, pp. 149–166.

House of Commons. *Perinatal and neonatal mortality*. Second Report from the Social Services Committee, Session 1979–80. Vol. 1, *Report*. Cmnd. 661–1. London: HMSO, 1980.

Hoyenga, K. B., and Hoyenga, K. T. *The Question of Sex Differences: Psychological, Cultural and Biological Issues*. Boston, MA: Little-Brown, 1979.

Huber, J., and Spitze, G. *Stratification: Children, Housework, and Jobs*. NY: Academic Press, 1983.

Hulten, M. Chiasma distribution at diakineses in the normal human males. *Hereditas*, 1974, *76*, 55–78.

Johnston, R., and Sidall, R. S. Is the usual method of preparing patients for delivery beneficial or necessary? *American Journal of Obstetrics and Gynecology*, 1922, *4*, 645–650.

Kantor, H. I., Rember, R., Tabio, P., and Buchanon, R. Value of shaving the pudental-perineal area in delivery preparation. *Obstetrics and Gynecology*, 1965, *25*, 509–512.

Kinsbourne, M. (Ed.). *Asymmetrical Functions of the Brain*. Cambridge, MA: Cambridge University Press, 1978.

Kitchen, W. H., Richards, A., Ryan, M. M., McDougall, A. B., Billson, F. A., Hier, E. H., and Naylor, F. D. A longitudinal study of very low birthweight infants. II. Results of a controlled trial of intensive care and incidence of handicap. *Developmental Medicine and Child Neurology*, 1979, *21*, 582–589.

Klaus, M. H., and Kennell, J. H. *Maternal-Infant Bonding: The Impact of Early Separation or Loss on Family Development.* St. Louis, MO: C. V. Mosby, 1976.

Knaub, P. K., Eversoll, D. B., and Voss, J. H. Is parenthood a desirable adult role? An assessment of attitudes held by contemporary women. *Sex Roles: A Journal of Research*, 1983, 9, 355–362.

Kobrin, F. E. The fall in household size and the rise of the primary individual in the United States. *Demography*, 1976, *13*, 127–138. (a)

Kobrin, F. E. The primary individual and the family: Changes in living arrangements in the United States since 1940. *Journal of Marriage and the Family*, 1976, *38*, 233–239. (b)

Kuhnen, F. *Man and Land.* Fort Lauderdale, FL: Breitenbach Publishers, 1982.

Lamb, M. E. Father-infant and mother-infant interaction in the first year of life. *Child Development*, 1977, *48*, 167–181.

Lamb, M. E., and Goldberg, W. A. The father-child relationship: A synthesis of biological, evolutionary and social perspectives. In L. W. Hoffman, R. Gandelman & H. R. Schiffman (Eds.), *Parenting: Its Causes and Consequences.* Hillsdale, NJ: Erlbaum, 1982, pp. 55–73.

Lamb, M. E., and Hwang, C. P. Maternal attachment and mother-neonate bonding: A critical review. In M. E. Lamb & A. L. Brown (Eds.), *Advances in Developmental Psychology*, Vol. 2. Hillsdale, NJ: Erlbaum, 1982, pp. 1–38.

LaRossa, R., and LaRossa, M. M. *Transition to Parenthood.* Beverly Hills, CA: Sage, 1981.

Lesthaeghe, R. On the social control of human reproduction. *Population and Development Review*, 1980, *4*, 527–548.

Lesthaeghe, R. A century of demographic and cultural change in western Europe: An exploration of underlying dimensions. *Population and Development Review*, 1983, *9*, 411–435.

Lewis, M., and Rosenblum, L. A. *The Effect of the Infant on Its Caregiver.* NY: John Wiley, 1974.

Lewontin, R. The corpse in the elevator. *New York Review of Books*, 1983, *29*, 34–37.

Lumsden, C. J., and Wilson, E. O. *Genes, Mind, Culture.* Cambridge, MA: Harvard University Press, 1981.

Lumsden, C. J., and Wilson, E. O. *Promethean Fire: Reflections on the Origin of Mind.* Cambridge, MA: Harvard University Press, 1982.

McDonald, R. L. The role of emotional factors in obstetric complications: A review. *Psychosomatic Medicine*, 1968, *30*, 222–237.

McGuinness, D. Away from a unisex psychology: Individual differences in visual, sensory and perceptual processes. *Perception*, 1976, *5*, 279–294.

McIlwaine, G. M., Howat, R. C., Dunn, F., and Macnaughton, M. C. The Scottish perinatal mortality survey. *British Medical Journal*, 1979, *2*, 1103–1106.

Marieskind, H. *An Evaluation of Caesarean Section in the United States.* Washington, D.C.: U.S. Department of Health, Education and Welfare, 1979.

Masnick, G. Some continuities and discontinuities in historical trends in household structure in the United States. Unpublished discussion paper prepared for the Seminar on Family History and Historical Demography. Cambridge: Harvard Center for Population Studies, March 10, 1983.

Masnick, G., and Bane, M. J. *The Nation's Families: 1960 to 1990.* Cambridge, MA: Joint Center for Urban Studies, 1980.

Mead, M., and Newton, N. Cultural patterning of perinatal behavior. In S. A. Richardson & A. F. Guttmacher (Eds.), *Childbearing: Its Social and Psychological Aspects.* Baltimore, MD: Williams and Wilkins, 1967.

Moltz, H., Lubin, M., Leon, M., and Numan, M. Hormonal induction of maternal behavior in the ovariectomized nulliparous rat. *Physiology and Behavior,* 1970, *5,* 1373–1377.

Nadelman, L., and Begun, A. The effect of the newborn on the older sibling: Mothers' questionnaires. In M. E. Lamb & B. Sutton-Smith (Eds.). *Sibling Relationships: Their Nature and Significance Across the Lifespan.* Hillsdale, NJ: Erlbaum, 1982, pp. 13–38.

National Center for Health Statistics. Advance report of final natality statistics, 1980. *Monthly Vital Statistics Report,* 1982, *31* (8th Suppl.).

Neugarten, B. L., and Gutmann, D. Age-sex roles and personality in middle age: A thematic apperception study. In B. L. Neugarten (Ed.), *Middle Age and Aging.* Chicago, IL: University of Chicago Press, 1968, pp. 58–71.

Newton, N. Interrelationships between sexual responsiveness, birth and breast feeding. In J. Zubin & J. Money (Eds.), *Contemporary Sexual Behavior.* Baltimore, MD: Johns Hopkins University Press, 1973, pp. 77–98.

Norbeck, J. S., and Tilden, V. P. Life stress, social support, and emotional disequilibrium in complications of pregnancy: A prospective multivariate study. *Journal of Health and Social Behavior,* 1983, *24,* 3–46.

O'Donnell, L. The social world of parents. *Marriage and Family Review,* 1983, *5,* 9–36.

Palgi, M., Blasi, J. R., Rosner, M., & Safir, M. (Eds.). *Sexual Equality: The Israeli Kibbutz Tests the Theories.* Norwood, PA: Norwood Editions, 1983.

Parsons, J. E. (Ed.). *The Psychobiology of Sex Differences and Sex Roles.* Washington, D.C.: Hemisphere, 1980.

Parsons, J. E. Biology, experience and sex dimorphic behaviors. In W. R. Gove, & G. R. Carpenter (Eds.), *The Fundamental Connection between Nature and Nurture.* Lexington, MA: Lexington Books, 1982, pp. 137–170.

Perry, S., and Kalberer, J. T. The NIH consensus-development program and the assessment of health-care technologies. *New England Journal of Medicine,* 1980, *303,* 169–172.

Persky, H., Smith, K. D., and Basu, G. K. Relation of psychologic measures of aggression and hostility to testosterone production in man. *Psychosomatic Medicine,* 1971, *33,* 265–277.

Petersen, A. C. Biopsychosocial processes in the development of sex-related differences. In J. E. Parsons (Ed.), *The Psychology of Sex Differences and Sex Roles.* Washington, D.C.: Hemisphere, 1980, pp. 31–56.

Radin, N. Primary caregiving and role-sharing fathers. In M. E. Lamb (Ed.), *Nontraditional Families: Parenting and Child Development.* Hillsdale, NJ: Erlbaum, 1982, pp. 173–204.

Redican, W. K. Adult male-infant interactions in nonhuman primates. In M. E. Lamb (Ed.), *The Role of the Father in Child Development.* NY: Wiley, 1976, pp. 345–386.

Riegel, K. F. The dialectics of human development. *American Psychologist*, 1976, *31*, 689–700.

Rose, S. (Ed.). *Against Biological Determinism*. NY: Schocken, 1982. (a)

Rose, S. (Ed.). *Towards a Liberatory Biology*. NY: Schocken, 1982. (b)

Rosenblatt, J. S. Nonhormonal basis of maternal behavior in the rat. *Science*, 1967, *156*, 1512–1514.

Rosenblatt, J. S. The development of maternal responsiveness in the rat. *American Journal of Orthopsychiatry*, 1969, *39*, 36–56.

Rossi, A. S. Aging and parenthood in the middle years. In P. Baltes & O. G. Brim Jr. (Eds.), *Life Span Development and Behavior*, Vol. 3. NY: Academic Press, 1980, pp. 137–205. (a)

Rossi, A. S. Life span theories and women's lives. *Signs: Journal of Women in Culture and Society*, 1980, 6, 4–32. (b)

Russell, G. Shared-caregiving families: An Australian study. In M. E. Lamb (Ed.), *Nontraditional Families: Parenting and Child Development*. Hillsdale, NJ: Erlbaum, 1982, pp. 139–171.

Santrock, J. W., and Warshak, R. A. Father custody and social development in boys and girls. *Journal of Social Issues*, 1979, *35*, 112–125.

Santrock, J. W., Warshak, R. A., and Elliott, G. L. Social development and parent-child interaction in father-custody and stepmother families. In M. E. Lamb (Ed.), *Nontraditional Families: Parenting and Child Development*. Hillsdale, NJ: Erlbaum, 1982, pp. 289–314.

Shapiro, E. R. *Transition to parenthood in adult and family development*. Unpublished Ph.D. dissertation. Amherst: University of Massachusetts, 1979.

Shereshefsky, P. M., and Yarrow, L. J. (Eds.). *Psychological Aspects of a First Pregnancy and Early Postnatal Adaptation*. NY: Raven Press, 1973.

Slater, P. Social limitations on libidinal withdrawal. In R. L. Coser (Ed.), *The Family: Its Structure and Functions*. New York: St. Martins Press, 1974 (2nd ed.), pp. 111–133. [1964]

Smith, J. M., and Warre, N. Models of cultural and genetic change. *Evolution*, 1982, *36*, 620–621.

Spence, J. T., and Helmreich, R. L. *Masculinity and Femininity: Their Psychological Dimensions, Correlates and Antecedents*. Austin, TX: University of Texas Press, 1978.

Spiro, M. E. *Gender and Culture: Kibbutz Women Revisited*. NY: Schocken, 1980.

Standley, K., Soule, B., and Copans, S. Dimensions of prenatal anxiety and their influence on pregnancy outcome. *American Journal of Obstetrics and Gynecology*, 1979, *135*, 22–26.

Stene, J., and Stene, E. Statistical methods for detailing a moderate paternal age effect on incidence of disorder when a maternal one is present. *Annals of Human Genetics*, 1977, *40*, 343–353.

Suomi, S. J. Sibling relationships in nonhuman primates. In M. E. Lamb & B. Sutton-Smith (Eds.), *Sibling Relationships: Their Nature and Significance Across the Lifespan*. Hillsdale, NJ: Erlbaum, 1982, pp. 329–356.

Susser, M. Environment and biology in aging: Some epidemiological notions. In J. L. McGaugh & S. B. Kiesler (Eds.), *Aging and Behavior*. NY: Academic Press, 1981, pp. 77–96.

Terkel, J., and Rosenblatt, J. S. Maternal behavior induced by maternal blood plasma injected into virgin rats. *Journal of Comparative and Physiological Psychology*, 1968, *65*, 479–482.

U.S. Bureau of the Census. *Projections of the population of the United States: 1982 to 2050.* Advance Report, P-35, No. 922. Washington, D.C.: Department of Commerce, 1983.

Wallerstein, J. S., and Kelly, J. B. *Surviving the Breakup: How Children and Parents Cope with Divorce.* NY: Basic Books, 1980.

Weber, C., and Goodman, A. The demographic policy debate in the USSR. *Population and Development Review*, 1981, *7*, 279–295.

Weisner, T. S. Sibling interdependence and child caretaking. A cross-cultural view. In M. E. Lamb & B. Sutton-Smith (Eds.), *Sibling Relationships: Their Nature and Significance Across the Lifespan.* Hillsdale, NJ: Erlbaum, 1982, pp. 305–328.

West, M. M., and Konner, M. L. The role of the father: An anthropological perspective. In M. E. Lamb (Ed.), *The Role of the Father in Child Development.* NY: John Wiley, 1976, pp. 185–218.

Westoff, C. F. Marriage and fertility in the developed countries. *Scientific American*, 1978, *239*, 51–57. (a)

Westoff, C. F. The future of marriage and the family. *Family Perspectives*, 1978, *10*. (b)

Westoff, C. F. Fertility decline in the west: Causes and prospects. *Population and Development Review*, 1983, *9*, 99–105.

Whiting, B., and Whiting, J. W. *Children of Six Cultures: A Psycho-Cultural Analysis.* Cambridge, MA: Harvard University Press, 1975.

Yu, V. Y. H., and Hollingsworth, E. Improved prognosis for infants weighing 1000 g. or less at birth. *Archives of Diseases in Childhood*, 1980, *55*, 422–426.

II BIOSOCIAL PERSPECTIVES AND PARENTAL INVESTMENT

4 SOMATIC ASPECTS OF PARENT–OFFSPRING INTERACTIONS

Michael Leon

> And hark! how blithe the throstle sings!
> He, too, is no mean preacher:
> Come forth into the light of things,
> Let Nature be your teacher.
> Wordsworth

INTRODUCTION

Why should social scientists, who focus their research on human interactions, be interested in the study of analogous behaviors in other species? In the biomedical sciences one is forced to resort to animal models of human function to be able to investigate mammalian physiology using the powerful invasive techniques at the disposal of modern researchers. Parental behavior, however, along with its somatic consequences, can be observed and measured in humans. Clearly, one can be interested in the study of the parental behavior of other species for its own sake, much as one might appreciate works of art or any well-done scientific research program. Alternatively, observations of parental interactions with young animals may touch one's emotions, and one might want to know more about the biological basis of such behaviors. Aesthetics and emotions aside, however, why deal with nonhuman animal research rather than concentrating on human research?

It is possible that a real understanding of the basis of reproductive physiology and behavior in nonhuman animals will ultimately result in new insights into the study of human reproduction. First, the study of animals brings to light mechanisms and strategies for dealing with the world that may help to explain human physiology and behavior, or to suggest new hypotheses to be examined in humans. Even a brief look at the animal literature will reveal a wide range of mechanisms and strategies for dealing with the energetic stresses associated with reproduction. Some species delay reproduction under limiting environmental conditions. Others terminate their reproductive attempt, and still others compensate with altered behavior or physiology and are thereby able to continue their reproductive attempt.

This sort of variation may exist in a single species living under different circumstances, suggesting that there is not necessarily one "natural" way for a species to care for its young.

Variation in human reproductive patterns may be less surprising if one is familiar with the variation in these patterns among other animals. For example, human infanticide may be perceived differently if one is familiar with the mammals that routinely engage in such behavior. One can then analyze the behavior in humans rather than treating infanticide, however alien to western customs, as an aberration.

The second advantage derived from a knowledge of the animal world is that it brings the social scientist in touch with contemporary evolutionary biology. There has been an explosion of reasearch and theory in this field within the last few years that has revolutionized the way animal behaviorists formulate their hypotheses and interpret their data. While the example of infanticide may be less surprising in the light of the behavior of other animals, it remains a puzzle for evolutionary theory. At this point in its development, the resolution of evolutionary puzzles rather than the search for confirming data stimulates much of the recent work in the field.

Much of this work has dealt with situations in which individuals seem to engage in behaviors that increase the reproductive success of others, thereby decreasing their own relative contribution to the population gene pool, or in behaviors that appear to decrease their own reproductive success directly. Destruction of one's own offspring, of course, would fall into the latter category. Such behavior can be reconciled with natural selection only if the long-term consequences outweigh the short-term ones. For example, one could more readily understand the short-term reproductive loss if it resulted in a greater lifetime reproductive output for the individual. This long-term perspective is one of the contributions of modern evolutionary thought. Moreover, an evolutionary perspective demands that more be explored about the situation in which infanticide takes place to determine whether its predictions are justified.

While most biologists have seen the advantage of using the powerful conceptual tools forged by this new generation of evolutionary thought, most social scientists have not used these concepts to their advantage. Indeed, there has been a somewhat violent rejection of these ideas in the social sciences. Part of the problem has been the enthusiasm of some evolutionary biologists for generating facile, deterministic explanations of human behavior. Given the rational, humanistic traditions of the social sciences, those initial attempts by biologists to explain human behavior were perceived as naive at best, and intellectually and politically dangerous at worst. While not the only way in which the world can be analyzed, an evolutionary level of analysis is important and useful, along with other types, to understand the world in which we live.

Those social scientists that have access to these new concepts will have a distinct advantage over their colleagues who are not familiar with the material. They will formulate very different questions and draw different conclusions from their data when the evolutionary level of analysis is appropriately used. The problem for the ambitious social scientist is that most of the concepts have been tested and explained using nonhuman animals. A researcher can either read the animal literature now and use the new concepts in one's own work, or wait until sufficient work has been done with humans to make the new material palatable.

Ironically, evolutionary biology has borrowed the cost/benefit method of analysis from the social sciences. The costs and benefits of living in this world and engaging in different behaviors for varying amounts of time, or of choosing one reproductive strategy over another, have been useful in understanding the workings of the animal world. This chapter will deal principally with some of the costs to the parent of reproduction and the benefits to be gained in the currency of its offspring. In many cases it becomes easier to understand the variability in parental patterns if the individual's situation is subjected to a cost/benefit analysis. The somatic costs of reproduction are the most easily measured and, therefore, the most widely studied reproductive costs. Returning to infanticide, such behavior might be more understandable if it could be demonstrated that the energetic costs of nursing one more baby under difficult environmental conditions would make the mother physically unable to bear more children.

This chapter will review the kinds of energetic stresses that affect reproducing mammals, along with the solutions to these stresses that different animals have developed. Moreover, both the long- and short-term costs of these solutions will be presented.

Mammalian mothers attempt to reproduce repeatedly over the course of a lifetime, driven as they are to maximize their reproductive contribution. The production of mammalian young, however, is energetically costly, time-consuming, and potentially dangerous in a world with unpredictable re-source availability, limited time, and the threat of predation. Mothers must therefore engage in a series of trade-offs between the number of times that they can breed, either during each season or during their lifetime, and the apportionment of their time and energy into any one reproductive attempt. In an often quoted seminal insight into the problem, R.A. Fisher (1930) wrote:

> It would be instructive to know not only by what physiological mechanism a just apportionment is made between nutriment devoted to the gonads and that devoted to the rest of the parental organism, but also what circumstances in the life-history and environment would render profitable the diversion of a greater or lesser share of the available resources towards reproduction.

His question eventually led to a consideration of the lifetime reproductive strategies of various invertebrates and vertebrates (Calow, 1979; Cole, 1954;

Pianka, 1976). Relatively little work, however, has been devoted to an analysis of the apportionment of resources for reproduction in species that care for their offspring, no doubt due to the difficulties associated with quantifying the cost of parental care over the course of a lifetime under natural or even seminatural circumstances. While a complete picture of the lifetime costs and benefits of mammalian parental care is not available, some of the somatic consequences of pregnancy and lactation can be examined in this context.

REPRODUCTIVE LIFE SPAN

One of the most difficult questions in biology is why a reproductive life span exists at all, for it is not obvious why young mammals delay their reproduction or why old animals cease to reproduce. If animals are geared to maximize their reproductive contribution, one would expect there to be a strong selection for all animals to reproduce over the entire life course, unless some great cost of early or late reproduction would decrease the total lifetime reproductive contribution of the parent. One might expect that there would be a strong selection for females to start breeding, as a small reduction in the age of reproductive onset greatly increases the reproductive potential of a population (Cole, 1954). Early reproduction, however, might decrease the somatic and/or reproductive life span of the animal and thereby decrease the total reproductive capabilities of the organisms. Alternatively, early reproduction may simply decrease the number or viability of offspring, if the younger mother cannot provide them with sufficient energy to ensure their growth, or if providing for the young permanently drains the young parent to the extent that future reproduction suffers.

This chapter deals principally with mammals, referring to other species only when no mammalian example can be found. The first example presented is a rotifer. This invertebrate actually seems to have a clear trade-off between life span and reproduction. Those that reproduce early in their life have a higher fecundity than the rotifers that reproduce later in life, but the former have a reduced survival time (Snell and King, 1977). Lawlor (1976) also related age and reproduction in a terrestrial isopod. In these animals body size correlates with age and fecundity with body size, as in most animals, the exceptions being birds and mammals. Those young invertebrates that forego early reproduction eventually grow to be larger, and produce more offspring, than would have been the case had they begun to reproduce early in life. Here, then, are examples of a short-term loss coupled with a long-term (lifetime) gain.

The importance of short-term reproductive costs for long-term reproductive ability have not really been demonstrated for mammals. It remains possible that, under most circumstances, the ability of mammalian mothers to compensate for or to recover from the short-term costs of reproduction limit the cumulative importance of the short-term costs.

Mammals delay the onset of their reproduction until a considerable portion of their life has expired. Moreover, the reproductive systems of these animals may be functionally mature and capable of being activated well before puberty. In Norway rat females, for example, the brain is capable of secreting releasing hormones, the pituitary is capable of secreting an ovulatory surge of LH, and the ovaries are capable of both ovulating and producing steroid hormones at about 20 days of age, while puberty does not normally arrive in females until about 40 days (Ramaley, 1982). During that period the system is inhibited. It can, however, become activated in a number of ways including: the administration of estrogen (Ramirez and Sawyer, 1965; Docke and Dorner, 1965), introduction of brain lesions (Donovan and van der Werff ten Bosh, 1956), exposure to the odor of male rats (Vandenbergh, 1980), and constant light (Fiske, 1941).

One possibility for the delay is that the rats have a mechanism that suppresses the onset of reproduction until there is sufficient body weight or fat stores to support pregnancy and lactation. Kennedy (1967) suggested that there was some metabolic cue linked to fat stores that allowed young Norway rat females to mature sexually. Females reared on a high-fat diet had a higher ratio of body fat to total weight at puberty and reached puberty earlier than females on a low-fat diet (Frisch, Hegsted, and Yoshinaga, 1977; Wilen and Naftolin, 1978); malnutrition further delayed the onset of reproduction (Kennedy and Mitra, 1963). The mechanism of the delay may be in the inability of the ovary of malnourished females to secrete sufficient estrogen to trigger the onset of puberty (Ronnekleiv, Ojeda, and McCann, 1979).

Women also seem to require a minimum fat store before menarche will occur; this store has been calculated to meet the energetic requirements of pregnancy and up to three months of lactation (Frisch and McArthur, 1974). The declining age at which menarche has been occurring in industrial societies (Tanner, 1962) may reflect the improvement in the diet of grandmothers, mothers, and children that allows a critical amount of corporal fat to be stored earlier in life. It may also be the case that there is a strong selection for early reproduction that is manifested only when the individuals can support an early pregnancy and lactation (short-term) without having long-term decline in reproduction.

A rapid change in the time of menarche can be shown to accompany a change in the accessibility of food and water. When !Kung families move from a hunter–gatherer life style to an agricultural life, with easier, more reliable access to food and water, the average age of menarche drops (Howell, 1976).

There also appears to be a period of sterility before successful reproduction commences in humans. For example, young girls of the !Kung reach menarche at l6.5 years, but typically do not conceive until three years later

(Howell, 1976; 1979). This kind of delay may be accounted for by the availability of energy stores to adolescent girls (Frisch and McArthur, 1974).

Given these data, one would expect females in whom precocious puberty has been induced to have severe problems in maintaining pregancy or lactation. Eisen (1975) and Eisen and Leatherwood (1976) found that juvenile house mice in which puberty was advanced by contact with an adult male (see Vandenbergh, 1980) had a weight gain greater than that of the adult pregnant females. While there was no difference in the amount of food eaten by the females in the two groups, the efficiency with which food was utilized by the juvenile group was greater that that of the adult pregnant group. Juvenile pregnancy also accelerated weight gain relative to virgin controls, raising the possibility that these females were able to gain enough in energy stores once they were committed to reproduction to maintain their pups. Indeed, no difference in the number of pups born, the total litter weight, or the body composition of the litters was found, although there was a somewhat greater pup mortality rate at birth in the juvenile pregnant dams (Eisen, 1975; Vandenbergh, Drickamer, and Colby, 1972).

Wilson, Walker, and Gordon (1983) found that while most young rhesus monkey females begin to breed when they are 4 years old, about a quarter of them begin to breed a year earlier. Most of the 3-year-old breeders are the offspring of high-ranking mothers. While the early breeding start resulted in a short-term reproductive gain relative to the less precocious females, the former had a longer sterile period than the latter group of females before their second lactation. The authors speculate that the younger females took longer to recover from their nutritional drain than the older females. Over the course of their reproductive lives, however, the number of offspring produced by the two groups did not differ.

Senescence may be a more difficult phenomenon to handle from a theoretical standpoint. While most animals in the wild succumb to disease or predation before they reach the end of their reproductive cycle, it is perplexing to find that the animals that do survive stop reproducing, even under seemingly optimal conditions (Medawar, 1952). Perhaps the most compelling explanation for the appearance of senescence is the benefit of having genes that confer an early advantage on the individual (Williams, 1957). Kirkwood (1977) and Kirkwood and Holliday (1979) have expanded on this idea by proposing that senescence occurs because animals that reproduce repeatedly through their lifetimes allocate only enough resources to somatic repair to retain their ability to reproduce throughout their normal expectation of life in the wild. Those that outlive their expected lifetime begin to experience the degeneration of their soma.

While such a theory implies that the duration of life span is programmed, there are some data that suggest that life span, as well as the period of reproductive activity, is subject to environmental modification. Asdell and Crowell (1935) and McCay (1942) kept Norway rats on a greatly reduced diet. These rats did not reach sexual maturity but had an expanded life span. Berg (1960) restricted the diet of weanling rats, and when he reinstated their full diet far after the time of normal adult senescence, their estrous cycle began. Two thirds of the females conceived, although their litters were small and the mortality rate was high. House mice, subjected to food restriction and later returned to an ad lib diet long after control mice had reached senescence, reached puberty, conceived, and weaned their pups. Indeed, the offspring of these old dams fared as well as those in litters reared by much younger dams (Merry and Holehan, 1979). Thus, as in the case of somatic life span, reproductive life span also appears not to be entirely preprogrammed.

It may be that reproductive life span actually contributes to the determination of the duration of somatic life span. Finch (1978) has presented evidence consistent with the idea that senescence in mice is induced by repeated exposure to estrogen during the estrous cycle. Given the suppressive effects of diet restriction on hormone levels, diet-restricted females may have been relieved of cyclic estrogen exposure. Moveover, absence of the cyclic repair necessitated by reproductive functioning may have allowed the animals to husband their resources and extend their lives. In fact, Calow (1979) has been able to extend the lives of invertebrate species that reproduce only once in their lives simply by preventing reproduction. Similarly, both male and female fruit flies that are allowed to reproduce die sooner than those who do not (Maynard-Smith, 1958; Partridge and Farquhar, 1981).

SOMATIC BASIS FOR THE INITIATION OF REPRODUCTION

The environment in which individuals live imposes direct and indirect constraints on their ability to reproduce. Mammals tend to reproduce seasonally, and their yearly reproductive readiness often is induced by an endogenously provoked set of neuroendocrine events cued by predictable changes in the length of daylight (Zucker, Johnston, and Frost, 1980). The internal programming of reproductive readiness allows mammals, even those that hibernate, to synchronize their reproduction both with conspecifics and with favorable environmental circumstances. In addition to this endogenous reproductive control mechanism, there are other species that may rely, to different degrees, on changes in resource availability to trigger the initiation of reproduction. For example, house mice can breed continuously, both in some wild populations (Lidicker, 1966; Pearson, 1963; Smith, 1954) and in the laboratory (Lidicker, 1965). There is some evidence linking food availability to their ability to initiate reproduction.

Food deprivation reduces mating and increases abortion in mice (McClure, 1962; 1966). Diet restriction has also been shown to suppress the hormone secretion patterns in rodents that are essential for reproduction to occur (Campbell, Kurcz, Marshall, and Meites, 1977). Even the ad lib availability of diets of marginal quality depressed the ability of the mice to produce offspring (Pryor and Bronson, 1981). Conversely, the provision of food to wild mouse populations prevented the normal winter cessation in breeding (Delong, 1967).

Provisioning feral populations of old field mice and white-footed mice also increased their populations (Bendell, 1959; Smith, 1971). Pine voles living in an area with high-quality food available bred more often and continued to breed into the late fall and winter (Cengel, Estep, and Kirkpatric, 1978). Smyth (1966) found that winter breeding in woodland mice and bank voles was associated with abundant natural food supplies. Flowerdew (1973) and Watts (1970) found that provisioning these species in the absence of a natural abundance of food could lengthen the breeding season.

Women may impose a restricted diet on themselves, and such women may experience a suppression of menstrual cyclicity (Bates, Bates, and Whitworth, 1982; Frisch and McArthur, 1974; Knuth, Hull, and Jacobs, 1977), which can be restored by an elevation of body weight (Bates, Bates, and Whitworth, 1982). Indeed, gonadotrophin secretion levels that mediate normal menstrual cyclicity are related to the body weight of such women (Bates, Bates, and Whitworth, 1982; Knuth and Schneider, 1982). Other human populations may experience diet restriction because of a natural limitation on available food. In the !Kung, desert-dwelling hunter-gatherers, the peak birth period occurs nine months after the yearly maximum female body weight. The time of conception is associated with the time of maximum food supplies (Van der Walt, Wilmsen, and Jenkins, 1978).

Water availability also limits the ability of mammals to reproduce. Yahr and Kessler (1975) found that water restriction of Mongolian gerbil completely stopped their reproduction. Bodenheimer (1949) found that Levant voles living in irrigated fields continued to breed after other voles in arid fields ceased breeding.

Although the winter cessation of breeding demonstrated by many species may reflect the associated limits on food intake, there is some evidence indicating that ambient temperature itself may play a role in limiting the onset and termination of breeding. The rate of house mice reproduction was depressed at low ambient temperatures, regardless of the diet ingested, although the mice continued to breed (Barnett and Manly, 1959; Pryor and Bronson, 1981).

The elevated energetic and/or nutritional requirements of reproduction may limit directly the duration of the breeding season to those portions of the year when the food and/or water supply is abundant. In species that initiate breeding regardless of the immediate availability of critical resources, these factors may contribute to the success or failure of the reproductive episode.

SOMATIC RESPONSES TO PREGNANCY

Mothers may respond to excessive energy demands during pregnancy by terminating that pregnancy (MacFarlane, Pennycuik, and Thrift, 1957). Termination of the parental investment may occur at a point that allows the mother to survive and to reproduce again.

Mothers may also respond to a variety of predictable and unpredictable energy demands with a flexibility of behavior and physiology that allows them to compensate for these demands with few adverse consequences for their offspring. The support of the fetuses during gestation increases the energy needs of the mother, and many mammals deal with this need by increasing their food intake during pregnancy (Cole and Hart, 1983; Hytten and Thompson, 1968; Kaczmarski, 1966; Migula, 1969; Millar, 1975; Randolph, Randolph, Mattingly, and Foster, 1977).

Not all of the gestational food intake, however, need serve the immediate energy requirements of the mother. A significant portion of the gestational energy intake may be stored and then mobilized to help meet the energy requirements of the dams during lactation. This phenomenon has been documented in cotton rats (Randolph, Randolph, Mattingly, and Foster, 1977), white-footed mice (Millar, 1975), pigs (Elsley, 1971), cows (Reid, 1961), and humans (Hytten and Thompson, 1968). The short-term cost of acquiring the food over the amount that is needed for immediate use may well be compensated for by the benefits of an energy reserve during the stresses of lactation.

Gestation lasts for about 22 days in Norway rats, but while food intake rises soon after conception (Cole and Hart, 1938; Menaker and Navia, 1973), each fetus weighs only about 0.04 g by the end of the second week (Stotsenburg, 1915). Females require only a fraction of their increased food intake to support fetal growth to that point, resulting in a maternal weight gain in excess of fetal tissues (Rosso, 1977). Specifically, there is an increase in fat stores of 35 to 45% by that time (Naismith, 1966; Beaton, Beare, Ryu, McHenry, 1954) due to the elevated food intake (Menaker and Navia, 1973), the elevated insulin secretion (Knopp, Saudek, Arky, and O'Sullivan, 1973), and the elevated lipoprotein lipase activity (Hamosh, Clary, Chernick and Scow, 1970) associated with pregnancy.

An increase in protein incorporation occurs during the first and second trimesters of the rat pregnancy (Naismith, 1969; 1973), as the dams increase both their protein intake and the efficiency of its utilization (Tagle, Ballester, and Donoso, 1967). Food utilization efficiency also may be further elevated when the pregnant females are food restricted (Lederman and Rosso, 1980).

During the last week of pregnancy, however, there is an abrupt reversal of the anabolic situation, with the dams mobilizing both protein and fat stores to support fetal growth (Knopp, Saudek, Arky, and O'Sullivan, 1973; Naismith, 1966). Even following this gestational catabolic period, the dams maintain an elevated corporal store that may be mobilized during lactation (Leon and Woodside, 1983; Rosso, 1977). The ability to mobilize stored fat and protein also may allow food-restricted rats to go to term, although they may still bear underweight pups (Berg, 1965).

The effects of malnutrition in pregnancy may not be restricted to primary caloric or nutritional deficiencies, for there is a decrease both in total plasma volume and in uterine blood flow in diet-restricted pregnant rats (Rosso and Streeter, 1979; Rosso and Kava, 1980). The blood flow reduction therefore may have been the primary factor in both the reduced transfer of nutrients to the fetus and the depressed fetal growth (Lederman and Rosso, 1980).

Humans may undergo a comparable change from anabolism to catabolism over the course of their pregnancies (Naismith, 1981). On the other hand, some women may not increase their food intake while pregnant, and some may even decrease food intake in the third trimester (Darby, McGanity, Martin, Bridgforth, Densen, Kaser, Ogle, Newbill, Stockell, Ferguson, Touster, McLellan, Williams, and Cannon, 1953; Hytten and Leitch, 1971; Papoz, Eschwege, Pequignot, and Barrat, 1981). Indeed, metabolic economies in previously well-nourished women may allow pregnancy to proceed without the need for an elevation of maternal dietary requirements.

Previously chronically underfed women, however, have babies with depressed birth weights, and have both higher neonatal mortality and morbidity rates than their previously well-nourished counterparts (Iyenger, 1974; Sibert, Jadhav, and Inbaraj, 1978). Diet supplementation during the pregnancies of the former group can result in a somewhat elevated birth weight (Iyengar, 1974). Diet supplementation in the marginally malnourished poor of western industrialized countries, however, has not been found to facilitate fetal growth or health (Rush, Stein, and Susser, 1980). Birth weight, therefore, normally seems to be largely dependent on previous maternal nutritional status; elevated diet intake during pregnancy may compensate to some extent for previous deficiencies. Even in industrialized societies, thin women must elevate their gestational food intake and gain more weight than heavy mothers to avoid giving birth to low birth-weight babies (Papiernik, Frydman, Hajeri, Spira, and Bachelier, 1976; Naeye, Blanc, and Paul, 1973).

SOMATIC RESPONSES TO LACTATION

Reproductive Tactics during Lactation

The energy demands of lactation far exceed those of pregnancy (Brody, Riggs, Kaufman, and Herring, 1938). Lactating females must meet the elevated energy requirements of milk production while caring for their offspring. Since this is often incompatible with obtaining food, the time necessary to deliver milk may be diminished by the time needed to obtain the wherewithal to produce the milk. Various mammalian species have solved this problem in very different ways. Marsupials, such as the red kangaroo, initially maintain constant contact with their offspring in their pouch, an adaptation that allows the mothers to forage while keeping the young fed on demand under relatively constant conditions (Frith and Sharman, 1964; Sharman and Calaby, 1964). The mothers of other species, particularly ungulates, give birth to young that to varying degrees are able to follow them through the environment shortly after parturition (Altmann, 1958; David, 1975; Lent, 1966).

Primates are able to cling to the mother while she moves through her habitat, thereby maintaining contact while allowing the dam to obtain food (Mowbray and Cadell, 1962; Lindburg, 1973; Tinklepaugh and Hartman, 1932). Even among the primates there are marked differences in the strategies used to care for offspring while mothers meet the elevated energy demands of lactation. For example, green monkeys surprisingly decrease the time that they spend feeding while they are lactating, despite their increased energy needs (Harrison, 1983). What these monkeys apparently do is to decrease their energy expenditure by increasing the time that they spend resting, perhaps draining their reserves to make up the balance of the energy deficit. The green monkeys bear their young during the dry season, when there is little for the mothers to eat and when it may be very difficult to find sufficient food to make the energy expenditure of foraging result in a net energy gain. The relatively short lactational period of this species, the clear seasonality of the births, and, therefore, the reliable occurrence of the rainy season at the time of weaning may allow the mothers to absorb the energy needs of the young. Mothers greatly increase the time spent feeding during the wet season, and may thereby restore their own body stores (Harrison, 1983; Riopelle, Hill, Li, Wolf, Seibold, and Smith, 1974).

On the other hand, yellow baboons have a prolonged lactation (Altmann, 1980), and may not be able to absorb its costs as readily as green monkeys. Yellow baboons are not strongly seasonal in their births, but they are able to utilize different foods during the year to support lactation (Altmann and Altmann, 1970). These females increase their feeding time during lactation, further increasing it when the needs of the young increase (Altmann, 1980). Even under these conditons, the mothers eventually cannot keep up with the energy demands of the young and probably call on their corporal reserves to supply them with milk (Altmann, 1980).

Corporal Reserves

Some species handle the increased energy demands of lactation by simply not eating during the period in which they care for their offspring.

Northern elephant seal mothers remain near their young on the shore, fasting during the entire lactational period (LeBoeuf, Whiting, and Gantt, 1972). Both male and female emperor penguin parents lose a large proportion of their body weight during the fast that they maintain during the incubation of their young (LeMaho, 1977). While the penguins incubate their young 200 km from the sea, which is the source of their food, Burmese red jungle fowl drastically reduce their food intake even when it is readily accessible (Sherry, Mrosovsky, and Hogan, 1980). Similarly, several species of lactating whales do not eat while caring for their young, despite the presence of appropriate prey in their calving grounds (see Brodie, 1975). Black bears initially remain in their den while nursing their young, foregoing foraging excursions into the snow during that period (Hock, 1966). All of these species are able to support themselves and their young by mobilizing great quantities of corporal stores.

Mother–Young Contact

There are many species, however, in which the mother does not carry the young, nor do the young follow the mother, nor do the dams stop eating while they lactate. In such species the female leaves the offspring periodically to obtain food. The time spent away from the young by the mother may be minimized by having male and nonreproductive helpers bring food to the den. This phenomenon has been described most extensively in canids (Bekoff and Wells, 1982; Kleiman and Eisenberg, 1973; Moehlman, 1979).

Other mothers are alone in caring for their young, and when absent leave them in a sheltered, insulated nest. The patterns of mother–young contact, however, vary greatly among these animals. Tree shrew mothers visit their offspring every other day, and then only briefly (Martin, 1966). Similarly, rabbits visit their young for a few minutes once a day (Zarrow, Denenberg, and Anderson, 1965). Norway rats initially spend most of their time in contact with the pups, a behavior pattern that should limit the amount of time that could be spent foraging (Grota and Ader, 1969; Leon, Croskerry, and Smith, 1978). As the pups grow and increase their milk intake, the dam increases her food intake (Babicky, Ostadalova, Parizek, Kolar, and Bibr, 1970; Ota and Yokoyama, 1967) and spends progressively less time with the young (Grota and Ader, 1969; Leon, Croskerry, and Smith, 1978). This pattern of declining mother–young contact can also be seen in humans (Konner, 1979) and nonhuman primates (Altmann, 1980; Struhsaker, 1967).

The large amounts of food that are hoarded by the rat dam (Calhoun, 1962), along with the corporal stores set down during gestation, may allow them to nurture the young effectively early in lactation without spending much of the time foraging. As lactation proceeds and the internal and external stores are consumed, the dam has the time to spend away from her pups and to forage for her progressively increasing food needs.

The mechanism that drives the mother rats off her pups after shorter and shorter contact bouts involves an acute hyperthermia that mother rats experience after being in contact with their offspring (Leon, Croskerry, and Smith, 1978). As the pups develop, they induce the hyperthermia in their mother after increasingly shorter intervals, driving the mother away and affording her an opportunity to forage to obtain the increased amounts of food that are needed by the older pups (Woodside, Pelchat, and Leon, 1980).

An interesting correlation emerges in mother–young contact patterns of a broad range of mammals and relates them to the quality of the milk delivered to the young. Those animals with continuous contact with their young have low-quality milk with low protein and lipid content. As the duration of the interval between contact bouts increases, the quality of the milk increases (Ben Shaul, 1962). The young are thereby carried through long maternal absences with milk of high caloric and nutritional value.

Dietary Limitations

Many mammals deal with the demands of lactation by increasing their food intake, and lactating females may experience a variety of physiological and anatomical changes that help to accommodate the elevated ingestion levels. In Norway rats, for example, a marked enlargement of the liver (Kennedy, Pearce, and Parrott, 1958), the heart (Canas, Romero, and Baldwin, 1982), and the gut (Campbell and Fell, 1964; Cripps and Williams, 1975; Poo, Lew, and Addis, 1939) accompany a more than doubled food intake (Cole and Hart, 1938; Cotes and Cross, 1954; Fleming, 1976; Ota and Yokoyama, 1967; Slonaker, 1925).

The nutritional intake of these dams is proportional to the number of pups in the litter and increases over the course of lactation (Ota and Yokoyama, 1967), suggesting a compensatory response of the dams to the energy and nutritional demands of the specific reproductive situation. The ability of rat dams to thus compensate for large litters is not complete, however, for the pups in the larger litters grow somewhat more slowly than pups in smaller litters (Dobbing and Widdowson, 1965; Fleischer and Turkewitz, 1977; Kennedy, 1957; Knittle and Hirsch, 1968).

When the quantity of the maternal food supply is restricted, there is again only a partial lactational compensation, for despite the mobilization of both fat and protein stores (Goswami and Srivastava, 1978), the growth rate of the pups is depressed under these conditions (Blackwell, Blackwell, Yu, Weng, and Chow, 1969; Hseuh, Simonson, Chow, and Hanson, 1974). Human mothers can also compensate to a great extent for energy shortages, although their young may eventually receive less milk than is needed for a continued high rate of growth (Whitehead, Hutton, Mueller, Rowland, Prentice, and Paul, 1978).

Food-restricted mother rats also increase the time that they spend with their offspring (Massaro, Levitsky, and Barnes, 1974; Wiener, Fitzpatrick, Levin, Smotherman and Levine, 1977), and even well-nourished dams increase pup contact time when the pups are malnourished (Fleischer and Turkewitz, 1981; Lynch, 1976). The increase in contact time appears to be due to a chronic depression in maternal heat load as a consequence of decreased fuel availability (Leon, Chee, Fischette, and Woodside, 1983). The continued contact with the pups, however, may serve to keep mother and young warm, thereby conserving their limited resources.

There is some evidence indicating that the sexes do not fare equally well under conditions of limited nutrition. Severe diet restriction in wood rats depresses pup weight, with the males growing more slowly than the females, and in all but one of the litters, all of the males died before any females died. The reason for the accelerated weight loss and death in the males appeared to be due to an active rejection by the mothers (McClure, 1980). Female favoritism by parents under unfavorable circumstances was predicted by Trivers and Willard (1973), who argued that if adult reproductive success was related to the condition of the individuals early in life, the parents of polygamous species should favor males offspring only when sons can be of high quality. Daughters would be favored by mothers under suboptimal circumstances, for they would be expected to reproduce even under those conditions.

Mothers of other species cannibalize some of their offspring, reducing the litter to a size that they can rear (Day and Galef, 1977; Gandelman and Simon, 1978). Humans also engage in infanticide. !Kung mothers often kill a child born too soon after its older sibling, and frequently do away with one of a set of twins (Howell, 1976). This behavior may have an energy basis, for the cost of carrying another child in a hot, arid land may be more than !Kung mothers can handle. They may forsake the short-term benefit of an additional child for the long-term reproductive gain of conserving their resources, thus enabling them to reproduce several more times (Blurton-Jones and Sibley, 1978).

Norway rat dams can also compensate for a poor-quality diet. When their food was degraded with nonnutritive fiber, the dams were able to increase their food intake to the point where the total amount of nutritive substance equaled that of controls, and their pups grew as fast as controls (Leon and Woodside, 1983). These data suggest that dams are not normally limited in their food intake by the capacity of their gut. Rather, the limitation may exist in their ability to produce milk. Moreover, these data suggest that dams with intermediate-size litters could eat more than they actually do and probably support a higher growth rate for their pups. It may be the case, therefore, that dams do not support a maximal growth rate for their pups.

Many species, such as *Cercopithecus* monkeys, increase their intake of high-protein foods during pregnancy and lactation (Gauthier-Hion, 1980).

Protein deprivation has not been shown to have immediate effects during pregnancy, but does induce depressed growth rate for baboon offspring (Buss and Reed, 1970). The young were able to make up their body-weight deficit, however, once they started eating a diet adequate in protein.

Nutrient Demands

Richter (1956) found that lactating rats consumed more of a compounded diet, in terms of both calories and amount of food than they ate when the various components of the diet were presented separately. The elevated intake of the compounded diet may therefore have been induced less by a need for increased calories than a need for a particular nutrient in the diet. The intake of that nutrient may have been elevated when the diet was presented in its components, without increasing caloric intake.

One critical lactational nutrient may be calcium, for its intake is elevated throughout pregnancy and lactation (Richter, 1956). In addition, while calcium is normally stored during gestation (Ellinger, Duckworth, Dalgarno, and Quenoville, 1952; Goss and Schmidt, 1930; Spray, 1950), Norway rat dams typically surrender to the milk about 60% of the calcium in their bodies (Toverud and Boass, 1979). While much of that calcium is normally garnered from increased ingestion, a large portion is normally drawn from skeletal reserves. When calcium is deficient in the diet, there is an even more intense drain on those reserves (deWinter and Steendijk, 1975; Ellinger, Duckworth, Dalgarno, and Quenoville, 1952).

There may be, however, long-term consequences of such calcium withdrawals for rat mothers over the course of their reproductive lives (Simmonds, 1924). In mice on calcium-adequate diets, for example, the amount of stored calcium declines with repeated pregnancies (Johnson, 1973). Women on calcium-rich diets appear to have these levels restored after the third month postpartum, whether or not lactation persists (Lamke, Brundin, and Moberg, 1977).

Water Balance

Milk consists largely of water, and the loss of large amounts of water during lactation constitutes an osmoregulatory challenge for mothers (Fitzsimons, 1979), which can be met by increasing water intake and/or elevating fluid conservation. Some species, such as the Norway rat, greatly increase their water intake during lactation (Kaufman, 1981). When these females are deprived of water, they are able to maintain pup weight gain, at least over a short term, either by mobilizing water from their own body or by minimizing the water content of their milk. These females also seem to have a reduced response to dipsogenic stimuli, perhaps indicative of an ability to withstand at least temporary water imbalance to compensate for the needs of the young (Kaufman, 1981). In fact, their water intake during the daytime, when the dams are most often with their pups (Ader and Grota, 1970), is actually less than for nonlactating females (Kaufman, 1981).

Other rodents with a naturally limited access to free water during lactation have a small or no increase in their water intake (Baverstock and Watts, 1975). The dams continue to lactate under conditons of water restriction, but the result is a reduced rate of growth for the young. These females, as well as Norway rat dams, seem to cope with the demands of lactation by increasing fluid conservation through an elevated glomerular concentration rate, elevated water reabsorption, and elevated sodium reabsorption (Arthur and Green, 1981; Baverstock and Watts, 1975; Atherton and Pirie, 1978). Both desert rodents and Norway rats also recycle the water through their pups by drinking the pup urine, efficiently conserving a large portion of the water initially given to the young in the milk (Baverstock and Green, 1975; Friedman, Bruno, and Alberts, 1981).

Seals voluntarily abstain from both food and water intake during lactation. The females increase the fat content of their milk as lactation proceeds, thereby minimizing the fluid drain (Lavigne, Stewart, and Fletcher, 1982; Riedman and Ortiz, 1979; Stull, Brown, and Kooyman, 1967). As the pups grow, they become more and more able to metabolize lipids to derive water (Riedman and Ortiz, 1979).

Water is also needed by many species for temperature regulation; water loss through the milk is minimized under high ambient temperature conditions by decreasing milk production. The proportion of water in the milk that is produced by both rats (Yagil, Etzion, and Berlyne, 1976) and cattle (Bianca, 1965) decreases with increased ambient temperature. Camels appear to be the exception, maintaining their milk production and actually increasing the proportion of water in the milk under drought conditions (Yagil and Etzion, 1980a, b).

CONCLUSIONS

Mammals seem to have great flexibility in dealing with both the predictable and the unpredictable needs of reproduction. They can delay reproduction until the environmental conditions are appropriate, or they can have it coincide with the time of year that is most likely to allow them to reproduce effectively. Once reproduction has begun, environmental variables may terminate pregnancy, or dams may adjust to the needs of the pregnancy and even increase somatic stores during that period. Lactation poses the greatest energy test for reproducing females, and the mothers may deal with this challenge by elevating food and water intake and mobilizing corporal stores of lipids, protein, and calcium. Other species may simply drain their energy reserves to provide milk to their offspring. Even the duration of life seems to be flexible and may be linked to energy/ reproductive considerations. If there is a pattern that emerges from a comparative view of the somatic consequences of reproduction it is that there is a variety of ways in which mothers deal with the physical stresses imposed upon them as by parenthood.

While there has been significant progress in understanding the somatic costs of reproduction in mammalian mothers, we still know very little of even the short-term costs of reproduction for males, for allomothers, or for parental helpers. Indeed, we still know little of the long-term costs of reproduction in mammalian mothers. Perhaps as more and more researchers appreciate the importance of the issues involved, our understanding of these factors will continue to grow.

SUMMARY

The energy limitations imposed on reproducing mammals are considered in this chapter. Different strategies for dealing with the caloric, nutrient, and thermal challenges of gestation and lactation are discussed from both a physiological and an evolutionary perspective. Finally, the importance of energy considerations for the onset of puberty and senescence is described.

ACKNOWLEDGMENT

This work was supported by NSF grant BNS 8023107 and NIMH Grant MH39620 to the author, who holds a Research Scientist Development Award MH00371 from ADAMHA, NIMH.

REFERENCES

Ader, R., and Grota, L.J. Rhythmicity in the maternal behaviour of *Rattus norvegicus*. *Animal Behavior*, 1970, *18*, 144–150.

Arthur, S.K., and Green, R. Renal function during lactation in the rat. *Journal of Physiology*, 1981, *316*, 49–50P.

Asdell, S.A., and Crowell, M.F. The effect of retarded growth upon the sexual development of rats. *Journal of Nutrition*, 1935, *10*, 13–24.

Atherton, J.C., and Pirie, S.C. Glomerular filtration rate and sodium and water reabsorption in the early post-partum rat. *Journal of Physiology*, 1978, *285*, 43P.

Altmann, J. *Baboon Mothers and Infants*. Cambridge, MA: Harvard University Press, 1980.

Altmann, M. Social integration of the moose calf. *Animal Behavior*, 1958, *6*, 155–159.

Altmann, S.A., and Altmann, J. *Baboon Ecology: African Field Research.* Chicago, IL: University of Chicago Press, 1970.

Babicky, A., Ostadalova, I., Parizek, J., Kolar, J., and Bibr, B. Use of radioisotope techniques for determining the weaning period in experimental animals. *Physiologica Bohemoslovaca*, 1970, *19*, 457–467.

Barnett, S.A., and Manly, B.M. Effects of low environmental temperature on the breeding performance of mice. *Proceedings of Royal Society of Biology*, 1959, *151*, 87–105.

Bates, G.W., Bates, S.R., and Whitworth, W.S. Reproductive failure in women who practice weight control. *Fertility and Sterility*, 1982, *37*, 373–378.

Baverstock, P.R., and Green, B. Water recycling in lactation. *Science*, 1975, *187*, 657–658.

Baverstock, P.R., and Watts, C.H.S. Water balance of small lactating rodents. I. Ad libitum water intakes and effects of water restriction on growth of young. *Comparative and Biochemical Physiology*, 1975, *50A*, 819–825.

Beaton, G.H., Beare, J., Ryu, M.H., and McHenry, E.W. Protein metabolism of the pregnant rat. *Journal of Nutrition*, 1954, *54*, 291–304.

Bekoff, M., and Wells, M.C. Behavioral ecology of coyotes: social organization, rearing patterns, space use, and resource defense. *Zeitschrift fur Tierpsychologie*, 1982, *66*, 281–305.

Bendell, J.F. Food as a control of a population of white-footed mice, *Peromyscus leucopus novaboracensis* (Fischer). *Canadian Journal of Zoology*, 1959, *37*, 173–209.

Ben Shaul, D.M. The composition of the milk of wild animals. *International Zoo Yearbook*, 1962, *4*, 333–342.

Berg, B.N. Nutrition and longevity in the rat. I. Food intake in relation to size, health and fertility. *Journal of Nutrition*, 1960, *71*, 242–254.

Berg, B.N. Dietary restriction and reproduction in the rat. *Journal of Nutrition*, 1965, *87*, 344–348.

Bianca, W. Reviews of the progress of dairy science. Section A. Physiology: Cattle in a hot climate, *Journal of Dairy Research*, 1965, *32*, 291–345.

Blackwell, B.N., Blackwell, R.W., Yu, T.T.S., Weng, Y.S., and Chow, B.F. Further studies on growth and feed utilization in progeny of underfed mother rats. *Journal of Nutrition*, 1969, *97*, 79–84.

Blurton-Jones, N.G., Sibley, R.M. Testing adaptiveness of culturally determined behavior: Do Bushman women maximise their reproductive success by spacing births widely and foraging seldom? In N.G. Blurton-Jones and V. Reynolds (Eds.), *Human Behavior and Adaptation*, Symposium No. 18, Society for the Study of Human Biology. London: Taylor and Frances, 1978.

Bodenheimer, F.S. Problems of vole populations in the Middle East: Report on the population dynamics of the Levant vole (*Microtus guentaeri*). *Research Council of Israel*, 1949, *77*.

Brodie P.F. Cetacean energetics: An overview of intraspecific size variations. *Ecology*, 1975, *56*, 152–161.

Brody, S., Riggs, J., Kaufman, K., and Herring, V. Energy metabolism levels during gestation, lactation and postlactation rest. *Research Bulletin University of Missouri Agriculture Experiment Station*, 1938, *281*, 1–43.

Buss, D.H., and Reed, O.M. Lactation of baboons fed a low protein maintenance diet. *Laboratory Animal Care*, 1970, *20*, 709–712.

Calhoun, J.B. *The Ecology and Sociology of the Norway Rat.* Public Health Service Publication No. 1008. Washington, D.C., 1962.

Calow, P. The cost of reproduction—A physiological approach. *Biology Reviews*, 1979, *54*, 23–40.

Campbell, G.A., Kurez, M., Marshall, S., and Meites, J. Effects of starvation in rats on serum levels of follicle stimulating hormone, luteinizing hormone, thyrotropin, growth hormone and prolactin; response to LH-releasing hormone and thyrotropin-releasing hormone. *Endocrinology*, 1977, *100*, 580–587.

Campbell, R.M., and Fell, B.F. Gastro-intestinal hypertrophy in the lactating rat and its relation to food intake. *Journal of Physiology*, 1964, *71*, 90–97.

Canas, R., Romero, J.J., and Baldwin, R.L. Maintenance energy requirements during lactation in rats. *Journal of Nutrition*, 1982, *112*, 1876–1880.

Cengel, D.J., Estep, J.E., and Kirkpatric, R.L. Pine vole reproduction in relation to food habits and body fat. *Journal of Wildlife Management*, 1978, *42*, 822–833.

Cole, H., and Hart, G. Effect of pregnancy and lactation on growth in the rat. *American Journal of Physiology*, 1938, *123*, 589–597.

Cole, L.C. The population consequences of life history phenomena. *Quarterly Review of Biology*, 1954, *29*, 103–137.

Cotes, M., and Cross, B. The influence of suckling on food intake and growth of adult female rats. *Endocrinology*, 1954, *10*, 363–367.

Cripps, A.W., and Williams, V.J. The effect of pregnancy and lactation on food intake, gastrointestinal anatomy and the absorptive capacity of the small intestine in the albino rat. *British Journal of Nutrition*, 1975, *33*, 17–32.

Darby, W.J., McGanity, W.J., Martin, M.P., Bridgforth, E., Densen, P.M., Kaser, M.M., Ogle, P.J., Newbill, J.A., Stockell, A., Ferguson, M.B., Touster, O., McLellan, G.S., Williams, C., and Cannon, R.O. The Vanderbilt cooperative study of maternal and infant nutrition. IV. Dietary, laboratory and physical findings in 2129 delivered pregnancies. *Journal of Nutrition*, 1953, *51*, 565–597.

David, J.H.M. Observations on mating behaviour, parturition, suckling, and the mother-young bond in the bontebok (*Damaliscus dorcas dorcas*). *Journal of Zoology*, 1975, *177*, 203–223.

Day, C.S.D., and Galef, B.G. Pup cannibalism: One aspect of maternal behavior in golden hamsters. *Journal of Comparative and Physiological Psychology*, 1977, *91*, 1179–1189.

Delong, K.T. Population ecology of feral house mice. *Ecology*, 1967, *48*, 611–634.

deWinter, F.R., and Steendijk, R. The effect of a low-calcium diet in lactating rats, observations on the rapid development and repair of osteoporosis. *Calcified Tissue Research*, 1975, *17*, 303–316.

Dobbing, J., and Widdowson, E.M. The effect of under-nutrition and subsequent rehabilitation on myelination of rat brain as measured by its composition. *Brain*, 1965, *88*, 357–366.

Docke, F., and Dorner, G. The mechanism of the induction of ovulation by oestrogens. *Journal of Endocrinology*, 1965, *33*, 491–499.

Donovan, B.T., and van der Werff ten Bosh, J.J. Precocious puberty in rats with hypothalamic lesions. *Nature (London)*, 1956, *178*, 745.

Ebrahim, G.J. Cross-cultural aspects of breast-feeding. In *Breast-feeding and the Mother. Ciba Foundation Symposium 45*. North Holland: Elsevier, 1976, pp. 195–204.

Eisen, E.J. Influence of the male's presence on sexual maturation, growth and feed efficiency of female mice. *Journal of Animal Science*, 1975, *40*, 816–825.

Eisen, E.J., and Leatherwood, J.M. Effects of early pregnancy in growth, body composition and efficiency in mice. *Journal of Animal Science*, 1976, *42*, 52–62.

Ellinger, G.M., Duckworth, J., Dalgarno, A.C., and Quenoville, M.H. Skeletal changes during pregnancy and lactation in the rat: Effect of different levels of dietary calcium. *British Journal of Nutrition*, 1952, *6*, 235–253.

Elsely, F.W.H. Nutrition and lactation in the sow. In I.R. Falconer (Ed.), *Lactation*. London: Butterworths, 1971, pp. 341–347.

Finch, C.E. Reproductive senescence in rodents: Factors in the decline of fertility and the loss of regular estrous cycles. In E.L. Schneider (Ed.), *The Aging Reproductive System*. NY: Raven Press, 1978, pp. 193–212.

Fisher, R.A. *The Genetical Theory of Natural Selection*. Oxford: Clarendon Press, 1930.

Fiske, V.M. Effects of light on sexual maturation, estrous cycle and anterior pituitary in the rat. *Endocrinology*, 1941, *29*, 187–196.

Fitzsimons, J.T. *The Physiology of Thirst and Sodium Appetite*. Cambridge: Cambridge University Press, 1979.

Fleischer, S.F., and Turkewitz, G. Effect of neonatal stunting on development of rats: Large litter rearing. *Developmental Psychobiology*, 1977, *12*, 137–149.

Fleischer, S.F., and Turkewitz, G. Alterations of maternal behaviors of female rats caring for malnourished pups. *Developmental Psychobiology*, 1981, *14*, 383–388.

Fleming, A. Control of food intake in the lactating rat: Role of suckling and hormones. *Physiology and Behavior*, 1976, *17*, 969–978.

Flowerdew, J.R. The effect of natural and artificial changes in food supply on breeding woodland mice and voles. *Journal of Reproduction and Fertility, Supplement 19*, 1973, 259–269.

Friedman, M., Bruno, J.P., and Alberts, J.R. Physiological and behavioral consequences of water recycling during lactation. *Journal of Comparative and Physiological Psychology*, 1981, *95*, 26–35.

Frisch, R.E., and McArthur, J.W. Menstrual cycles: Fatness as a determinant of minimum weight for height necessary for their maintenance or onset. *Science*, 1974, *185*, 949–951.

Frisch, R.E., Hegsted, D.M., and Yoshinaga, K. Carcass components at first estrus of rats on high-fat and low-fat diets: Body water, protein and fat. *Proceedings of the National Academy of Science*, 1977, *74*, 379–383.

Frith, H.J., and Sharman, G.B. Breeding in wild populations of the red kangaroo (*Megaleia rufa*). *CSIRO Wildlife Research*, 1964, *9*, 86–114.

Gandelman, R., and Simon, N.G. Spontaneous pup-killing by mice in response to large litters. *Developmental Psychobiology*, 1978, *11*, 235–241.

Gautier-Hion, A. Seasonal variation of diet related to species and sex in a community of *Cercopithecus* monkeys. *Journal of Animal Ecology*, 1980, *49*, 237–269.

Goss, H., and Schmidt, L.L.A. Calcium and phosphorus metabolism in rats during pregnancy and lactation and the influence of the reaction of the diet thereon. *Journal of Biological Chemistry*, 1930, *86*, 417–432.

Goswami, T., and Srivastava, U. Maternal dietary deficiency and its effect on the metabolism of nucleic acids and proteins. Effect of exchanging the young, during the lactation period between the control and undernourished female. *Canadian Journal of Physiology and Pharmacology*, 1978, *56*, 274–286.

Grota, L., and Ader, R. Continuous recording of maternal behavior in *Rattus norvegicus*. *Animal Behavior*, 1969, *17*, 722–729.

Harrison, M.J.S. Age and sex differences in the diet and feeding strategies of the green monkey, *Cercopithecus sabaeus*. *Animal Behavior*, 1983, *31*, 969–977.

Hock, R.J. Growth rate of newborn black bear cubs. *Growth*, 1966, *30*, 339–347.

Howell, N. The population of the Dobe area !Kung. In R.B. Lee and I. DeVore (Eds.), *Kalabari Hunter-Gatherers*. Cambridge, MA: Harvard University Press, 1976.

Howell, N. *Demography of the Dobe !Kung*. NY: Academic Press, 1979.

Hseuh, A.M., Simonson, M., Chow, B.F., and Hanson, H.M. The importance of the period of dietary restriction of the dam on behavior and growth in the rat. *Journal of Nutrition*, 1974, *104*, 37–46.

Hytten, F.E., and Leitch, I. *The Physiology of Human Pregnancy*. Oxford: Blackwell, 1971.

Iyengar, L. Influence of diet on the outcome of pregnancy in Indian women. In *Proceedings of the IX International Congress of Nutrition*. Basel: Karger, 1974, pp. 53–58.

Johnson, C.L. Some aspects of changing body composition of mice during successive pregnancies and lactations. *Journal of Endocrinology*, 1973, *56*, 37–46.

Kaczmarski, F. Bioenergetics of pregnancy and lactation in the bank vole. *Acta Theriologica*, 1966, *11*, 409–417.

Kaufman, S. Control of fluid intake in pregnant and lactating rats. *Journal of Physiology*, 1981, *318*, 9–16.

Kennedy, G.C. The development with age of hypothalamic restraint upon the appetite of the rat. *Journal of Endocrinology*, 1957, *16*, 9–17.

Kennedy, G.C. Interactions between feeding behavior and hormones during growth. *Annals of New York Academy of Science*, 1967, *157*, 1049–1061.

Kennedy, G.C., and Mitra, J. Body weight and food intake as initiation factors for puberty in the rat. *Journal of Physiology*, 1963, *166*, 408–418.

Kennedy, G.C., Pearce, W.M., and Parrott, O.M.V. Liver growth in the lactating rat. *Journal of Endocrinology*, 1958, *17*, 158–160.

Kirkwood, T.B.L. Evolution of ageing. *Nature (London)*, 1977, *270*, 301–304.

Kirkwood, T.B.L., and Holliday, R. The evolution of ageing and longevity. *Proceedings of Royal Society*, 1979, *205*, 531–546.

Kleiman, D.G., and Eisenberg, J.F. Comparisons of canid and felid social systems from an evolutionary perspective. *Animal Behavior*, 1973, *21*, 637–659.

Knittle, J., and Hirsch, J. Effect of early nutrition on the development of rat epididymal fat pads: Cellularity and metabolism. *Journal of Clinical Investigation*, 1968, *47*, 2091–2098.

Knopp, R.H., Saudek, C.D., Avky, R.A., and O'Sullivan, J.B. Two phases of adipose tissue metabolism in pregnancy: Maternal adaptations for fetal growth. *Endocrinology*, 1973, *92*, 984–988.

Knuth, U.A., and Schneider, H.P.G. Influence of body weight on prolactin, estradiol and gonadrotropin levels in obese and underweight women. *Hormone Metabolism Research*, 1982, *14*, 142–146.

Knuth, U.A., Hull, M.G.R., and Jacobs, H.S. Amenorrhoea and loss of weight. *British Journal of Obstetrics and Gynaecology*, 1977, *84*, 801–807.

Konner, H.C. Maternal care, infant behavior, and development among the !Kung. In R.B. Lee and I. DeVore (Eds.), *Kalahari Hunter-Gatherers: Studies of the !Kung San and Their Neighbors*. Cambridge, MA: Harvard University Press, 1979.

Lamke, B., Brundin, J., and Moberg, P. Changes in bone mineral content during pregnancy and lactation. *Acta Obstetrica Gynecologica Scandinavia*, 1977, *56*, 217–219.

Lavigne, D.M., Stewart, R.E.A., and Fletcher, F. Changes in composition and energy content of harp seal milk during lactation. *Physiological Zoology*, 1982, *55*, 1–9.

Lawlor, L.R. Molting, growth and reproductive strategies in the terrestrial isopod *Armadillidium vulgare*. *Ecology*, 1976, *57*, 1179–1194.

LeBoeuf, B.J., Whiting, R.J., and Gantt, R.F. Perinatal behavior of northern elephant seal females and their young. *Behaviour*, 1972, *43*, 121–156.

LeMaho, Y. The emperor penguin: A strategy to live and breed in the cold. *American Science*, 177, *65*, 680–693.

Lederman, S.A., and Rosso, P. Effects of food restriction on maternal weight and body composition in pregnant and non-pregnant rats. *Growth*, 1980, *44*, 77–78.

Lent, P.C. Calving and related social behaviour in the barren-ground caribou. *Zeitschrift fur Tierpsychologie*, 1966, *23*, 701–756.

Leon, M., and Woodside, B. Energetic limits on reproduction: Maternal food intake. *Physiology and Behavior*, 1983, *30*, 945–957.

Leon, M, Croskerry, P.G., and Smith, G.K. Thermal control of mother–young contact in rats. *Physiology and Behavior*, 1978, *21*, 793–811.

Leon, M., Chee, P., Fischette, C., and Woodside, B. Energetic limits on reproduction: Interaction of thermal and dietary factors. *Physiology and Behavior*, 1983, *30*, 937–943.

Lidicker, W.Z. Comparative study of density regulation in confined populations of four species of rodents. *Research in Population Ecology*, 1965, *7*, 57–72.

Lidicker, W.Z. Ecological observations on the feral house mouse population declining to extinction. *Ecology Monographs*, 1966, *36*, 27–50.

Lindburg, D.G. The rhesus monkey in North India: An ecological and behavioral study. In L.A. Rosenblum (Ed.), *Primate Behavior*, Vol. 2. NY: Academic Press, 1973.

Lynch, A. Postnatal undernutrition: An alternative approach. *Developmental Psychobiology*, 1976, *9*, 39–48.

McCay, C.M. Chemical aspects and the effect of diet upon ageing. In E.V. Cowdry (Ed.), *Problems of Ageing*, 2nd edition. Baltimore, MD: William & Wilkins, 1942, pp. 680-727.

McClure, P.A. Sex-biased litter reduction in food-restricted wood rats (*Neotoma floridana*). *Science*, 1980, *211*, 1058–1060.

McClure, T.J. Infertility in female rodents caused by temporary inanition at or about the time of implantation. *Journal of Reproduction and Fertility*, 1962, *4*, 241.

McClure T.J. Infertility in mice caused by fasting at about the time of mating. *Journal of Reproduction and Fertility*, 1966, *12*, 243–248.

MacFarlane, W.V., Pennycuik, P.R., and Thrift, E. Resorption and loss of feotuses in rats living at 35°C. *Journal of Physiology*, 1957, *135*, 451–459.

Martin, R.D. Tree shrews: Unique reproductive mechanism of systematic importance. *Science*, 1966, *152*, 1402–1404.

Massaro, T.F., Levitsky, D.A., and Barnes, A.H. Protein malnutrition in the rat: Its effects on maternal behavior and pup development. *Developmental Psychobiology*, 1974, *7*, 551–561.

Maynard-Smith, J. The effects of temperature and of egg-laying on the longevity of *Drosophila pseudoobscura*. *Journal of Experimental Biology*, 1958, *35*, 832–842.

Medawar, P.B. H.K. Lewis, *An Unsolved Problem in Biology*. London: 1952.

Menaker, L., and Navia, J.M. Appetite regulation in the rat under various physiological conditions: The role of dietary protein and calories. *Journal of Nutrition*, 1973, *103*, 347–352.

Merry, B.J., and Holehan, A.M. Onset of puberty and duration of fertility in rats fed a restricted diet. *Journal of Reproduction and Fertility*, 1979, *57*, 253–259.

Migula, P. Bioenergetics of pregnancy and lactation in the European common vole. *Acta Theriologica*, 1969, *14*, 167–179.

Millar, J.S. Tactics of energy partitioning in breeding *Peromyscus*. *Canadian Journal of Zoology*, 1975, *53*, 967–979.

Moehlman, P.D. Jackal helpers and pup survival. *Nature (London)*, 1979, *277*, 382–383.

Mowbray, J.B., and Cadell, T.E. Early behavior patterns in rhesus monkeys. *Journal of Comparative Physiology and Psychology*, 1962, *55*, 350–357.

Naeye, R.L., Blanc, W., and Paul, C. Effects of maternal nutrition on the human fetus. *Pediatrics*, 1973, *52*, 494–503.

Naismith, D.J. The requirement for protein and the utilization of protein and calcium during pregnancy. *Metabolism*, 1966, *15*, 582–595.

Naismith, D.J. The foetus as a parasite. *Proceeds of the Nutrition Society*, 1969, *28*, 25–31.

Naismith, D.J. Adaptations in the metabolism of protein during pregnancy and their nutritional implications. *Nutrition Reports International*, 1973, *7*, 383–399.

Naismith, D.J. Diet during pregnancy—a rationale for prescription. In J. Dobbing (Ed.), *Maternal Nutrition During Pregnancy—Eating for Two?* NY: Academic Press, 1981, pp. 21–40.

Ota, K., and Yokoyama, A. Body weight and food consumption of lactating rats nursing various sizes of litters. *Journal of Endocrinology*, 1967, *38*, 263–268.

Papiernik, E., Frydman, R., Hajeri, H., Spira, A., and Bachelier, M. Intrauterine growth retardation and caloric deficiency during pregnancy. In *Fifth European Congress of Perinatal Medicine*. Stockholm, 1976, pp. 193–196.

Papoz, L., Eschwege, E., Pequignot, G., and Barrat, J. Dietary behaviour during pregnancy. In J. Dobbing (Ed.), *Maternal Nutrition in Pregnancy—Eating for Two?* NY: Academic Press, 1981, pp. 41–69.

Partridge, L., and Farquhar, M. Sexual activity reduces lifespan of male fruitflies. *Nature (London)*, 1981, *294*, 580–582.

Pearson, O. History of two local outbreaks of feral house mice. *Ecology*, 1963, *44*, 540–549.

Pianka, E.R. Natural selection of optimal reproductive tactics. *American Zoologist*, 1976, *16*, 775–784.

Poo, L.J., Lew, W., and Addis T. Protein anabolism of organs and tissue during pregnancy and lactation. *Journal of Biological Chemistry*, 1939, *128*, 69–77.

Priestnall, R. Effects of litter size on the behavior of lactating female mice (*Mus musculus*). *Animal Behavior*, 1972, *20*, 386–394.

Pryor, S., and Bronson, F.H. Relative and combined effect of low temperature, poor diet, and short daylength on the productivity of wild house mice. *Biology of Reproduction*, 1981, *25*, 734–743.

Ramaley, J.A. Current issues in the neuroendocrinology of puberty. In A. Vernadakis and P.S. Timiras (Eds.), *Hormones in Development and Ageing*. NY: Spectrum Publications, 1982, pp. 305–429.

Ramirez, V.D., and Sawyer, C.H. Advancement of puberty in the female rat by estrogen. *Endocrinology*, 1965, *76*, 1158–1168.

Randolph, P.A., Randolph, J.C., Mattingly, K., and Foster, M.M. Energy costs of reproduction in the cotton rat, *Sigmodon hispidus*. *Ecology*, 1977, *58*, 31–45.

Reid, J.T. Nutrition of lactating farm animals. In S.K. Kon and A.T. Cowie (Eds.) *Milk: The Mammary Gland and Its Secretion II*. NY: Academic Press, 1961, pp. 47–87.

Richter, C.P. Self-regulatory functions during gestation and lactation. In C.A. Villee (Ed.), *Gestation*. NY: Macy Foundation, 1956, pp.11–91.

Riedman, M., and Ortiz, C.L. Changes in milk composition during lactation in the northern elephant seal. *Physiology and Zoology*, 1979, *52*, 240–249.

Riopelle, A.J., Hill, C.W., Li, S.C., Wolf, R.H., Seibold, H.R., and Smith, J.L. Protein deprivation in primates. I. Non-pregnant adult rhesus monkeys. *American Journal of Clinical Nutrition*, 1974, *27*, 13–24.

Rolls, B.J., Rowe, E.H., and Fahrbach, S.E. Maternal weight loss is associated with obesity in the lactating rat. In L.A. Cioffi (Ed.), *The Body Weight Regulatory System: Normal and Disturbed Mechanisms*. NY: Raven Press, 1981, pp. 259–261.

Ronnekleiv, O.K., Ojeda, S.R., and McCann, S.M. Undernutrition, puberty and the development of estrogen positive feedback in the female rat. *Biology and Reproduction*, 1979, *19*, 414–424.

Rosso, P. Maternal nutrition, nutrient exchange, and fetal growth. *Current Concepts in Nutrition*, 1977, *5*, 3–25.

Rosso, P., and Kava, R. Effects of food restriction on cardiac output and blood flow to the uterus and placenta in the pregnant rat. *Journal of Nutrition*, 1980, *110*, 2350–2354.

Rosso, P., and Streeter, M.R. Effects of food or protein restriction on plasma volume expansion in pregnant rats. *Journal of Nutrition*, 1979, *109*, 1887–1892.

Rush, D., Stein, Z., and Susser, M. *Diet in Pregnancy: A Randomized Controlled Trial of Nutritional Supplements*. NY: Alan Liss, 1980.

Sharman, G.B., and Calaby, J.H. Reproductive behavior in the red kangaroo, *Megaleia rufa*, in captivity. *CSIRO Wildlife Research*, 1964, *9*, 58–85.

Sherry, P.F., Mrosovsky, N., and Hogan, J.A. Weight loss and anorexia during incubation in birds. *Journal of Comparative Physiology and Psychology*, 1980, *94*, 89–98.

Sibert, J.R., Jadhav, M., and Inbaraj, S.J. Maternal and foetal nutrition in South India. *British Medical Journal*, 1978, *1*, 1517–1518.

Simmonds, N. Observations on reproduction and rearing of young by the rat, as influenced by diet. *American Journal of Hygiene Supplement*, 1924, *4*, 1–108.

Slonaker, J. The effect of copulation, pregnancy, pseudopregnancy and lactation on the voluntary activity and food consumption of the albino rat. *American Journal of Physiology*, 1925, *71*, 362–394.

Smith, M.H. Food as a limiting factor in the population ecology of *Peromycus polionotus* (Wagner). *Annals of Zoology Fennici*, 1971, *8*, 109–112.

Smith, W.W. Reproduction in the house mouse *Mus musculus L.* in Mississippi. *Journal of Mammalogy*, 1954, *35*, 509–515.

Smyth, M. Winter breeding in woodland mice *Apodemus sylvaticus*, and voles, *Clethrionomys glareolus* and *Microtus agrestis*, near Oxford. *Journal of Animal Ecology*, 1966, *35*, 471–485.

Snell, T.W., and King, C.E. Lifespan and fecundity patterns in rotifers: The cost of reproduction. *Evolution*, 1977, *31*, 882–890.

Spray, C.M. A study of some aspects of reproduction by means of chemical analysis. *British Journal of Nutrition*, 1950, *4*, 354–360.

Stotsenburg, J.M. The growth of the fetus of the albino rat from the thirteenth to the twenty-second day of gestation. *Anatomical Record*, 1915, *9*, 667–682.

Struhsaker, T.T. Social behavior of mother and infant vervet monkeys (*Cercopithecus aethiops*). *Animal Behavior*, 1967, *19*, 233–250.

Stull, J.W., Brown, W.H., and Kooyman. Lipids of the Weddell seal *Leptonychotes weddelli*. *Journal of Mammalogy*, 1967, *48*, 642–645.

Tagle, M.A., Ballester, D., and Donoso, D. Net protein utilization of a casein diet by the pregnant rat. *Nutrition Diet*, 1967, *9*, 21–26.

Tanner, J.M. *Growth at Adolescence*, 2nd edition. Oxford: Blackwell Scientific Publications, 1962.

Tinklepaugh, O.L., and Hartman, C.G. Behavior and maternal care of the newborn monkey. *Journal of Genetic Psychology*, 1932, *40*, 257–286.

Toverud, S.U., and Boass, A. Hormonal control of calcium metabolism in lactation. *Vitamins and Hormones*, 1979, *37*, 303–347.

Trivers, R.L., and Willard, D.E. Natural selection of parental ability to vary the sex ratio of offspring. *Science*, 1973, *179*, 90–92.

Vandenbergh, J.G. Influence of pheromone on puberty in rodents. In D. Muller-Schwarze and R.M. Silverstein (Eds.), *Chemical Signals in Vertebrates and Aquatic Invertebrates*. NY: Plenum Press, 1980, pp. 229–241.

Vandenbergh, J.G., Drickamer, L.C., and Colby, D.R. Social and dietary factors in the sexual maturation of female mice. *Journal of Reproductive Fertility*, 1972, *28*, 397–405.

Van der Walt, L.A., Wilmsen, E.M., and Jenkins, T. Unusual sex hormone patterns among desert-dwelling hunter gatherers. *Journal of Clinical Endocrinology and Metabolism*, 1978, *46*, 658–663.

Watts, C.H.S. The effect of supplementary food on breeding in woodland rodents. *Journal of Mammalogy*, 1970, *51*, 169–171.

Whitehead, R.G., Hutton, M., Mueller, E., Rowland, M.G.M., Prentice A.M., and Paul, A. Factors influencing lactation performance in rural Gambian mothers. *Lancet*, 1978, *2*, 178–181.

Wiener, S.G., Fitzpatrick, K.M., Levin, R., Smotherman, W.P., and S. Levine. Alterations in the maternal behavior of rats rearing malnourished offspring. *Developmental Psychobiology*, 1977, *10*, 243–254.

Wilen, R., and Naftolin, F. Pubertal food intake and body length, weight, and composition in the feed-restricted female rat: Comparison with well fed animals. *Pediatric Research*, 1978, *12*, 263–267.

Wilson, M.E., Walker, M.L., and Gordon, T.P. Consequences of first pregnancy in rhesus monkeys. *American Journal of Physiological Anthropology*, 1983, *61*, 103–110.

Williams, G.C. Pleiotropy, natural selection and the evolution of senescence. *Evolution*, 1957, *11*, 398–411.

Woodside, B., Pelchat, R., and Leon, M. Acute elevation of the heat load of mother rats curtails maternal nest bouts. *Journal of Comparative Physiology and Psychology*, 1980, *94*, 61–68.

Yagil, R., and Etzion, Z. The effect of drought conditions on the quality of camel's milk. *Journal of Dairy Science*, 1980, *47*, 159–163. (a)

Yagil, R., and Etzion, Z. Milk yield of camels (*Camelus dromedarius*) in drought areas. *Comparative Biochemistry and Physiology*, 1980, *67A*, 107–209. (b)

Yagil, R., Etzion, Z., and Berlyne, G.M. Changes in rat milk quantity and quality due to variations in litter size and high ambient temperature. *Laboratory Animal Science*, 1976, *26*, 33–37.

Yahr, P., and Kessler, S. Suppression of reproduction in water-deprived Mongolian gerbils (*Meriones unguiculatus*). *Biology of Reproduction*, 1975, *12*, 249–254.

Zarrow, M.X., Denenberg, V.H., and Anderson, C.O. Rabbit: Frequency of suckling in the pup. *Science*, 1965, *150*, 1835–1836.

Zucker, I., Johnston, P.G., and Frost, D. Comparative, physiological and biochronometric analysis of rodent seasonal reproductive cycles. *Progress in Reproductive Biology*, 1980, *5*, 102–133.

5

A BIOSOCIAL PERSPECTIVE ON PATERNAL BEHAVIOR AND INVOLVEMENT

Michael E. Lamb
Joseph H. Pleck
Eric L. Charnov
James A. Levine

INTRODUCTION

Our goal in this chapter is to review selectively our current knowledge of fathering and father–child relationships in humans. Fathering (like mothering) includes a diverse array of activities involved in conceiving, feeding, provisioning, protecting, and rearing one's offspring. Psychologists have traditionally focused on the direct rearing activities and their correlates, so discussion of these issues constitutes the bulk of this chapter. Because the empirical literature is sparse and the constructs are ill-defined, we are able to say much less about the two other aspects of fathering. We discuss fathering as insemination and as protection and provisioning. For the most part, the literature we review pertains to the behavior of men in contemporary, Western, industrialized contexts. Similar questions might be asked about the behavior of men in other cultural contexts or about the behavior of fathers in other species. Our decision to focus on Western fathers rests on the need to limit the scope of the chapter in some way and to persuade social scientists that a biobehavioral approach is relevant, not only to the understanding of behavior in other species or more "primitive" societies, but to the behavior of humans in modern industrialized contexts as well.

Research on fathering and father–child relationships in Western societies has burgeoned recently, and it is thus necessary to limit our focus. We have chosen to concentrate on evidence concerning what fathers actually do *to* beget children, *for* their children (e.g., breadwinning), and *with* their children. In essence, it focuses on how much and what fathers do with and for their children, how well they perform as parents, what factors affect paternal involvement, and male procreative strategies.

Clearly, the recent increase in concern about father–child relationships is attributable in part to changing assumptions about the roles of men and women and to a resurgent belief that fathers can have a substantial influence on their children's development, both by way of their direct effect on children and by way of their influence on mothers, who in turn affect children (Belsky, 1981; Parke, Power, & Gottman, 1979). Lamb (1981b) reviews the literature suggesting that nurturant and at least somewhat involved fathers, as well as fathers who are emotionally and materially supportive of their wives, tend to facilitate the development of achievement motivation, cognitive and social competence, psychological adjustment, and sex-stereotyped role attitudes and attributions, particularly in sons. Continuing societal uncertainty and ambivalence about the roles of women seem to ensure that nurturant involvement can have a variety of effects on daughters, depending on the father's values and expectations. Unfortunately, the extensive literature on paternal effects cannot be explored here.

In our attempt to explain the data, we introduce a set of concepts drawn from behavioral ecology (e.g., Krebs & Davies, 1981). The exercise is largely heuristic, and illustrates our belief in the need for coherent theoretical approaches in this area. Whether or not it is subsequently shown to have explanatory power, behavioral ecology at least permits us to articulate testable hypotheses that invoke concepts applicable to the understanding of human behavior more generally, and that systematically address multiple levels of explanation and analysis. Unfortunately, it is clear that research in the behavioral sciences seldom addresses the issues of primary relevance to the questions raised by behavioral ecology; indeed, one has to wonder whether the constructs popular among sociologists and psychologists are the most useful when it comes to explaining even the immediate (i.e., proximate) determinants of human behavior. As will be apparent, there is a clear need for articulate theory construction in this area. We hope that behavioral ecology will help researchers define the questions, at multiple levels of analysis, that guide future research endeavors.

The issues and concepts basic to behavioral ecology are briefly discussed in the first section as a means of framing the analysis that follows. We then turn to male procreative strategies and provisioning/breadwinning, as they bear on the understanding of fathering in modern humans. In the third section evidence concerning the competence displayed by fathers is considered: compared with mothers, just how good are they as parents and as caretakers? The analysis of similarities and differences between mothers and fathers in parental competence leads to consideration in the fourth section of sex differences in the behavioral styles of mothers and fathers interacting with their children. In both sections, proximate (that is, immediate physiological and social/experiential determinants) and ultimate (that is, those related to biological function and evolutionary history) interpretations of the sex differences observed are discussed. In the fifth section studies designed to determine how much time fathers spend with their children, and how this compares with the extent of involvement by mothers, are considered. The focus then shifts to factors affecting degree of paternal involvement, beginning with factors accounting for sex differences between men and women and proceeding to factors accounting for individual differences among men.

FACTORS AFFECTING SEX DIFFERENCES IN PARENTAL BEHAVIOR

As in most of the great debates in psychology, popular and scientific discussions of sex differences in parental behavior frequently degenerate into debates between simplistic environmental determinism and simplistic biological determinism, neither of which proves very helpful in understanding the phenomenon. As indicated below, it seems that both biological and environmental factors are important, and that it is of little value to juxtapose these as competing rather than complementary positions.

Part of the problem lies in the multiple interpretations of the word "biology." This term is often used—incorrectly—to refer only to hard-wired deterministic influences on behavior, whereas it is more appropriately used to refer to *the tendencies on the part of organisms to make "decisions" based on behavioral predispositions and general goals* (i.e., maximizing inclusive fitness: Hamilton, 1964) *manifest or pursued in the context of, and dependent upon, the restrictions imposed or options made available by the social and physical ecology* (Krebs & Davies, 1981). In the discussion that follows, the term "physiology"[1] describes proposed hard-wired dispositions, whereas the term biology is used in its broader, more inclusive, sense. The environmental factors frequently viewed as alternative explanations of sex differences in parental behavior may better be viewed as characteristics of the relevant ecology within which mothers and fathers make choices based on their behavioral predispositions, general goals, and ontogenetic experiences. The environment, in other words, must be seen as one of the important factors involved in unraveling the biology of behavior.

As Tinbergen (1963) pointed out many years ago, any attempt to explain *why* individuals behave in a certain way involves addressing any or all of four equally legitimate types of "why" questions: ultimate *function* (survival and reproductive value), *causation* (internal and external proximate factors), ontogenetic *development*, and *evolutionary history*. Psychologists—even those who claim a concern with biological factors—have emphasized proximate causation and development; perhaps more attention to ultimate function and evolutionary history would expand and broaden our understanding. A preliminary attempt is made to explore these broader issues in this chapter.

[1]Clearly the term physiology is not used appropriately here, and hence inverted commas are used throughout the chapter. We are not aware of any term that appropriately represents the hard-wired view of "biology."

In efforts to explain the differential parental involvement of mothers and fathers, the more extreme biogenetically deterministic positions tend to focus on either ultimate (i.e., evolutionary) arguments or more proximate (i.e., hormonal) factors. In reality, of course, these two sets of factors are not incompatible, as they involve reference to different levels of explanation (different questions in Tinbergen's framework).

Let us first consider ultimate factors. Sociobiologists, stressing the principles of natural selection, point out that the goal of any individual organism is to maximize the representation of *its* genes in future generations (Krebs & Davies, 1981; Williams, 1966; Hamilton, 1964). This involves not only high levels of fertilization but also the rearing to reproductive maturity of one's offspring, taking into account the costs and benefits of the various activities that affect inclusive fitness. In many species, furthermore, there is a sex difference in the costs of child rearing and childbearing (Trivers, 1972). Among mammals, for example, females must invest considerable time and effort in the intrauterine maintenance, delivery, and postnatal care of youngsters who are, at least initially, wholly dependent on pregnant and later lactating mothers for survival. During this period, males are often free to mate with other females without affecting the likelihood of survival by their existing offspring, because previous female mates have so much invested in each litter (or child) that it would not be in the mothers' interests to abandon them and thus reduce their own inclusive fitness. The female role in reproduction thus makes it desirable for mammalian females to remain involved in the care of the young. Because males can count on females (who have more at stake) to care for their offspring, adult males can choose to maximize fitness through multiple matings rather than parental investment. On the basis of evolutionary principles and consideration of male and female roles in mammalian reproduction, therefore, one might expect sex differences in human parental involvement, with women being more involved in child care than men are.

The proximate (hormonal) argument, by contrast, proposes that women, who are hormonally prepared for pregnancy, parturition, and lactation, are primed similarly for the nurturant child-care tasks that are also essential for the survival of offspring. Men, who do not "need" to participate in child care, would not have these capacities. Thus, women would be biologically prepared for involvement in parenting while men would not be. This line of reasoning focuses on proximate rather than ultimate explanations, and could thus complement the sociobiological position just described, suggesting one of the possible physiological mechanisms whereby sex differences in parental involvement are achieved.

These arguments are plausible as far as they go. There probably are biogenetically determined sex differences in behavioral propensities. However, there is no reason to believe that these propensities are deterministic, mandating female involvement in parenting and precluding male involvement. It is probable that they make females more likely to seek out or encounter opportunities to learn child-care skills, and perhaps able to learn these skills more rapidly than boys (for analogous points, see Hamburg & Goodall, 1974; Rosenblatt, 1970). As demonstrated below, men can perform parenting tasks just as well as women can, and it is clear that they have become more involved in the last few decades (Pleck, 1983, 1984). This testifies to the plasticity of the "biological" (i.e., physiological) program and undercuts simplistic notions of biological determinism while being in no way incompatible with the principles of evolutionary biology as we now understand them.

A key tenet of sociobiology or behavioral ecology is that individuals are designed to maximize their fitness *in the context of the options available to them* given the physical, economic, and social ecology. The goal is individual inclusive fitness, not propagation of the family, group, or species. Behavior is only optimal (in terms of fitness) in the context of a specific environment (broadly defined), and thus it is necessary to consider the constraints or facilitators of behavior represented by the social and physical environment. Among the important, all interrelated, factors to be considered are: the number of young born simultaneously; their size and nutritional needs relative to those of adults; the interbirth interval; the species' mode of feeding (ranging from omnivorous to extreme selectivity); the nutritional richness of the ecology; and the species' typical social organization, particularly as it affects the options for reproduction and male certainty regarding paternity. In species like pygmy marmosets (*Callithrix jacchus*), for example, females, typically give birth to twins who are quite large relative to adults. It is physically impossible for females to feed these twins and themselves without assistance, so males assume the majority of child-care responsibilities, carrying the young at all times other than when they are nursing (e.g., Ingram, 1975). Freed of the burdens of carrying her offspring, the mother is able to nurse the twins, feed herself, and (as an added bonus to her and the loyal male) become pregnant again very rapidly. In this case, therefore, the reproductive fitness of females *and* males is enhanced by high paternal involvement. We also need to remember that within-species variability may often be desirable. For example, if most males adopt strategy A, it may be advantageous for some others to adopt strategy B. The system is in equilibrium when the fitness gains of pursuing strategy A are equal to those gained by pursuing strategy B.

The fact that these factors (among others) affect paternal involvement across species is important, because it undercuts simplistic, deterministic notions concerning the biogenetic constraints on parental (and especially paternal) behavior. Clearly, a biological perspective compels us to consider not only the physiological predispositions and potentiations, but also the ecological factors defining the environment in which the potential is displayed, whether that resembles the one for which it may have evolved or whether it is in many ways an evolutionarily novel context.

PROCREATION AND PROVISIONING

Procreation

Procreation must surely rank as one of the major activities involved in the attainment of inclusive fitness; it constitutes one of the most basic elements of fatherhood. American psychologists, however, have almost totally ignored this aspect of fatherhood, and the discussions by anthropologists and sociobiologists seldom go much beyond the issues raised in the previous section (cf., Symons, 1979; Van den Berghe, 1978, 1979). Some insight into the psychological significance of procreation in industralized countries can be obtained by examining research on the effects of infertility, however. Upon recognition of their infertility, many men experience prolonged impotence and depression (Berger, 1980), with a sequence of reactions that often resembles the reactions to diagnosis of cancer (Wilson, 1979). Interestingly, the reactions of men to voluntary sterilization by vasectomy do not appear to be so negative; indeed, some researchers report mainly positive reactions (Ager, Werley, Allen, Shea, and Lewis, 1974; Ferber, Tietze, & Lewit, 1967) while others report modest effects on psychological adjustment and self-concept (Horenstein & Houston, 1975; Bloom & Houston, 1976; Cord, 1972; Kendall, 1972). In the United States cultural attitudes toward vasectomy remain somewhat disapproving (Rodgers, Ziegler, & Levy, 1967).

According to sociobiologists (e.g., Trivers, 1972), reproduction almost certainly requires that males and females adopt different strategies in order to maximize their reproductive success. As mentioned earlier, females produce relatively few large gametes while males produce an essentially unlimited number of small gametes. Female mammals initially provide intraorganismic sustenance for their offspring, and during this time they are unable to conceive. Typically, there also follows a postnatal period of variable length during which maternal lactation is essential for survival. For all these reasons, the absolute number of offspring that any female can conceive is limited. During the lengthy pre- and postnatal period, by contrast, males are (in principle) free to mate without jeopardizing the survival of any existing conceptus. Because the female has so much invested in the young (by virtue of her pre- and postnatal involvement) and because the opportunity cost is so high, the male can count on her to look after their offspring.

This suggests that promiscuity should often be the reproductive strategy pursued by men. However, there are six major complicating factors. Most importantly, there is always some male uncertainty regarding paternity while there is certainty regarding maternity. By restricting access to females, particularly during fertile periods, males can increase the likelihood that the offspring conceived are their own progeny, but by so doing males reduce their potential for pursuing alternative females.

Second, in some mammalian species, probably including most early and contemporary hominids, pregnant and lactating mothers are partially dependent on others for provisioning and protection. The individuals most likely to provide these resources are those who have something at stake themselves, and the offsprings' fathers clearly have most at stake. To the extent that such provisioning and protection is desirable for females, it is advantageous for them to persuade males that they are the offsprings' fathers, and it is advantageous for males to have some reason for believing this. In this context, both sexes benefit if the males remain with the females.

Third, sexual encounters typically depend on both male and female participation. If females limit their sexual contacts, they may demand compensation from males—most likely in the form of protection and provisioning, particularly during the pre- and postnatal periods when they are most vulnerable and most in need of assistance. The males' contributions at this point can have a substantial influence on the females' inclusive fitness without real cost to the latter, since they cannot conceive again anyway. As Hrdy (1979) wrote, "The most plausible and widely cited hypothesis, advocated by Desmond Morris and others, is that continuous sexual attractiveness helped to elicit male support for the mothers of helpless human infants" (p. 313).

Fourth, at least up to a point, the more a male has invested in any particular offspring, the greater is the cost of later neglecting or abandoning it, although of course there will always be both costs and benefits (in a fitness sense) of either staying to parent or abandoning one's offspring.

Fifth, males may often need other males as allies (for example, in hunting), and to maintain such alliances, they may refrain from pursuing their allies' consorts.

Finally, because females are less fertile and often less sexually receptive while pregnant or lactating, it is to the advantage of males to dispose of offspring who are not their own, thus gaining access to receptive females. It is therefore important to putative fathers to protect their young (and female partners) against marauding males. This may be especially important in species, such as humans, in which offspring have a long period of relative dependency.

All these factors work together to ensure that males benefit by behaving in a less promiscuous fashion than a simple analysis of the situation would lead one to expect. Because all six conditions apply among humans, furthermore, we would expect these forces to be operative, with the pull of male promiscuity countered—but not counterbalanced—by the need to provision and protect females and young in order to maximize inclusive fitness. One also finds among humans social practices designed to maximize certainty about paternity. These practices include marriage (both monogamous and polygamous), harsh sanctions for adulterous women and tolerant attitudes toward vengeful cuckolds, the sexual double standard, and other social arrangements designed to keep women in relative seclusion from other males. Marital arrangements explicitly offer males a trade-off between greater certainty regarding paternity, on the one hand, and responsibility for the protection/provisioning of the family as well as reduced access to other females, on the other. Biosocial circumstances thus serve to ensure that the goal for modern males is not to maximize the number of sexual encounters and fertilizations, but to maximize the number of offspring—regarding whose paternity there is some confidence—who are conceived and raised in health to reproductive maturity and beyond. Although parents seldom verbalize desires to continue the family name or propagate one's genes as the reasons to have children, respondents, especially in rural third-world countries, do claim to consider the economic utility derived from children and the likelihood of their survival (Hoffman, Thornton, & Manis, 1978; Arnold, Bulatao, Buripakdi, Chung, Fawcett, Iritani, Lee, & Wu, 1975). Optimal reproductive strategies for both males and females may differ at different stages of the life span, however, so individuals may pursue mixed or variable strategies.

Provisioning or Breadwinning

In contemporary western societies the dominant family role played by men is that of economic breadwinner (e.g., Cazenave, 1979; Benson, 1968; Gronseth, 1972; Pleck, 1983). Fein (1976) and Yankelovich (1974) point out that most employees (at least in industrialized countries) view work not as a source of direct personal fulfillment but as a means of obtaining economic support, for themselves as well as for their families. Indeed, this is legally and socially defined as one of the primary duties or responsibilities of fathers (*American Jurisprudence*, 1968); surveys repeatedly suggest that men who are voluntarily derelict in this regard are frowned upon (Harris, 1971; Slocum & Nye, 1976). Recent public outrage about the failure of noncustodial fathers to pay child support illustrates these popular attitudes. It is also noteworthy that a man's success or potential success as a breadwinner serves as one important criterion for mate selection in both modern and "primitive" contexts, one consequence of which is the "marriage gradient," a term for the widespread tendency of women to marry men of higher status than themselves. Recent historical research, however, reveals that the male breadwinner role is a recent normative ideal (Pleck, 1976). Prior to this century women had a clearly defined and socially recognized economic role, albeit one that involved different provisioning activities than men undertook. (The same of course is true in almost all "primitive" societies.) Further, it is well known that increasing proportions of wives are employed and that there are growing numbers of employed single mothers (Glick & Norton, 1979). Nonetheless, family economic providing is typically defined today as a male's responsibility.

Even when women play a major role in family breadwinning (whether by gathering, agriculture, or paid work), both they and their offspring clearly benefit from the security provided by the presence and commitment of a male provider. Meanwhile, gender discrimination in market economies helps ensure that fathers/husbands remain the primary sources of family provisioning. Men's inability to provide materially for their families appears to be a major source of masculine self-humiliation and marital discomfort (Cavan, 1959; Campbell et al., 1976; Komarovsky, 1940; Voydanoff, 1983).

In sum, even though breadwinning has been deemphasized and devalued in recent examinations of "the changing nature of fatherhood," it may be that breadwinning/provisioning is as important—probably more important—to filial survival (and thus to paternal inclusive fitness) than direct father–child interaction. Indeed, it is probable that fathers have been able to incorporate direct father involvement into their roles only in recent, affluent times. In almost all cultures direct paternal involvement is a discretionary activity, whereas provisioning is mandatory. Finally, although it seems unlikely that women select mates on the basis of their child-rearing skills or propensities, women in both industrialized and nonindustrialized contexts certainly do consider wealth and breadwinning potential in selecting among suitors. Even after marital dissolution, societies emphasize the provisioning component of the father's role. Despite this, psychologists—especially recently—have been most concerned about fathers' direct interaction and involvement with children, and it is to such aspects of paternal behavior that we now turn.

PATERNAL COMPETENCE OR SENSITIVITY

In both the popular and professional literature it is commonly assumed that women are more competent as parents than men are. Two related questions are thus addressed in this section: do such differences exist, and if so, to what can they be attributed? The second of these questions, of course, can be posed at many levels: Why in an ultimate sense should women in general be more competent than men, and by what proximate mechanisms might these differences be brought about?

Sensitivity (or responsiveness) to infant signals is a topic that has been of interest to developmental psychologists for many decades because it has long been assumed that parental sensitivity determines the quality of parent–child relationships, which in turn is seen as the major determinant of the child's psychosocial development. Thus, sensitivity is a crucial aspect of parental competence. Unfortunately, the relevant research is of variable quality, and the concept itself has been operationalized in many different ways. Perhaps the most useful and popular formulation is that of the ethological attachment theorists (Ainsworth, 1973; Bowlby, 1969; Lamb, *theoretical base*

1978, 1981a; Lamb & Easterbrooks, 1981), who propose that human infants are biologically predisposed to emit signals (e.g., cries, smiles) to which parents are biologically predisposed to respond. When adults consistently respond promptly and appropriately to infant signals, infants come to perceive them as predictable and reliable. This perception may potentiate the formation of secure infant–parent attachments (Ainsworth, Bell, & Stayton, 1974; Lamb 1981a). By contrast, when adults do not respond sensitively, insecure attachments may result, and when they respond rarely, no attachments at all may develop. Although these hypotheses have not yet been substantiated empirically (Lamb, Thompson, Gardner, Charnov, & Estes, 1984), they remain plausible and make clear why it may be crucial to determine if fathers are appropriately responsive to their infants; when they are not, the likelihood of secure or high-quality father–infant relationships forming would be reduced.

There is another reason why research on paternal sensitivity is important. Several theorists (e.g., Klaus, Trause, & Kennell, 1975) have speculated that an innate predisposition to respond to infant signals is stronger in females than in males. If true, this would imply that biology limits the potential for males to have significant and direct influences on infant development. Unfortunately, the suggestion is based largely on evidence concerning hormonal influences on parental behavior in rodents and ungulates, and these animal models may be inappropriate (Lamb & Goldberg, 1982; Lamb & Hwang, 1982). In addition, recent studies have shown that fathers and mothers respond similarly to presentation of their newborn infants (Rodholm & Larsson, 1982), even though fathers do not experience hormonal priming, and that there is no "sensitive period" during which human mothers are primed to bond to their newborn offspring (Lamb, 1982a; Lamb & Hwang, 1982). Nevertheless, the implications of Klaus et al.'s suggestion are such that it merits serious consideration.

In an early interview study Greenberg and Morris (1974) reported that most fathers were elated by the birth of their infants and experienced strongly positive emotions that Greenberg and Morris termed "engrossment." No comparison with mothers' reactions were reported, however. Contrary to popular misconceptions, when mothers and fathers were observed in a maternity ward interacting with their newborn infants, the fathers were neither inept nor uninterested (Parke & O'Leary, 1976; Parke, O'Leary, & West, 1972; Parke & Tinsley, 1981). Indeed, all but a couple of measures showed that the fathers and mothers were equivalently involved in interaction. When later observed feeding their infants, both fathers and mothers responded to infant cues either with social bids or by adjusting the pace of the feeding (Parke & Sawin, 1977). Although the fathers were capable of behaving sensitively, they tended to yield responsibility for child-tending chores to their wives when not asked to demonstrate their competence for the investigators. However, fathers, like mothers, adjust their speech patterns when interacting with young children—they speak more slowly, use shorter phrases, and repeat themselves more often when talking to infants than when talking to adults (Phillips & Parke, 1979; Gleason, 1975; Golinkoff & Ames, 1979; Kauffman, 1977; Blount & Padgug, 1976).

Alternative ways of studying parental responsiveness to infant signals have been pursed by Feldman and Nash and by Frodi and Lamb. Both research teams have observed parents with unfamiliar infants rather than with their own. Although the reasons for responding to unfamiliar infants should—and probably do—differ from the reasons for responding to one's own offspring, these studies are still useful as tests of whether or not fathers are *capable* of "maternal responsiveness," regardless of whether they typically behave in this fashion (i.e., the competence/performance distinction).

Feldman and Nash (1977, 1978; Nash & Feldman, 1981; Feldman, Nash, & Cutrona, 1977) observed subjects individually while they sat in a waiting room containing an infant and its mother. They found that sex differences in "baby responsiveness" waxed and waned depending on the subject's age and social status. Females were more responsive than males in early adolescence and in early parenthood, whereas there were no sex differences among 8 year olds, childless couples, and unmarried college students. Feldman and Nash concluded that sex differences in responsiveness to infants are experientially rather than physiologically determined: They are evident when individuals are under increased social pressure to respond in a conventionally sex-typed fashion. The data indicated that in response to presumed social pressures, mothers were more responsive than fathers.

By contrast, the studies conducted by Frondi and Lamb revealed no sex differences in responsiveness to infants. In their first two studies (Frodi, Lamb, Leavitt, & Donovan, 1978; Frodi, Lamb, Leavitt, Donovan, Neff, & Sherry, 1978), the psychophysiological responses (heart rate, blood pressure, skin conductance) of mothers and fathers were monitored while the parents observed quiescent, smiling, or crying infants on a television monitor. Crying and smiling infants elicited characteristic and distinct psychophysiological response patterns in both mothers and fathers. In a later study, Frodi and Lamb (1978) found no sex differences in psychophysiological responses among either 8 to 14 year olds, whereas 14-year-old females were more behaviorally responsive than males in a waiting room situation similar to Feldman's. Like Feldman and Nash, Frodi and Lamb concluded that there were no physiologically based sex differences in responsiveness to infants and that behavioral dimorphisms emerged primarily in response to societal pressures and expectations. For a behavioral ecologist, of course, this conclusion begs the question: *Why* do almost all societies subject boys and girls/men and women to sex-differentiating pressures of these sorts?

The conclusion that socializing pressures constitute the best proximate explanation of sex differences in parental behavior appears to be consistent with all the relevant data currently available, including data from studies of nonparental adults and children (see Berman, 1980 for a review). Nevertheless, the fact that men *can* be as responsive as women does not mean that mothers and fathers typically *are* equivalently responsive. Fathers are not always highly responsive, and their responsiveness probably varies depending on the degree to which they participate in infant care, since caretaking experience appears to facilitate parental responsiveness (Zelazo, Kotelchuck, Barber, & David, 1977). It is also possible—if not probable— that females are more likely than males to seek out, be offered, and learn from opportunities to acquire child-care skills, so that physiological sex differences play a role in shaping—but do not determine or ensure—sex differences in parenting skills. As Lamb and Goldberg (1982) wrote:

> Parental behavior in humans must surely rank as one of the clearest examples of overdetermined behavior. In additon to hormonal influences, each young woman is subjected to many years of socializing pressures preparing her for the maternal role. . . . In the midst of such a complex and comprehensive set of influences, it seems unlikely that hormonal influences make unique and independent contributions to the emergence of parental behavior in humans. In other words, if hormonal influences do render women better prepared and suited for parental behavior than men, this advantage is secured largely by way of an extensive overlay of socialization (p.61).

Recent research, albeit with marmoset fathers, confirms that physiological and social factors work together in complex ways. Dixson and George (1982) showed that circulating levels of prolactin increased after male marmosets had carried their offspring. In this case it seemed that involvement produced the hormonal change, rather than the reverse. In terms of proximate causation, overall, it would seem that socialization and physiological factors work together; indeed, as far as individual behavior is concerned, they are probably deterministic. We should also ask, however, *why* it is that humans socialize females and males differently, and *why* there might be sex-differentiated predispositions. The answer, we propose, is that females "need" parenting skills in a way that males do not; child care is a much more important component of their total reproductive effort than it is for men, and their potential reproductive yield (in terms of live births) is so much smaller than men's that they cannot afford to risk the demise of their offspring.

PARENTAL STYLES OF MOTHERS AND FATHERS

Despite sex differences in parental responsiveness, fathers appear on average to be sufficiently responsive to their infants so that, with a sufficient amount of father–infant interaction, attachments should form. Observational studies indicate that most infants do form attachments to their fathers, and the attachments to mothers and fathers emerge at about the same time—in the middle of the first year of life (Belsky, 1979; Lamb, 1977; Kotelchuck, 1976).

This evidence, however, is not sufficient to demonstrate that fathers play a formatively significant role in child development. It could be argued, for example, that fathers are essentially redundant—that they are occasional mother substitutes who have little independent impact on child development. This possibility has stimulated research designed to determine whether mothers and fathers represent different types of experiences for their children and thus perhaps have distinct and independent effects. Related research has also been motivated by questions regarding the origins (i.e., societal or physiological) of gender-linked differences in the style of parental behavior.

Even in the first three months of life, fathers and mothers appear to engage in stylistically different types of interactions with their infants. When videotaped in face-to-face interaction, for example, fathers tended to provide staccato bursts of both physical and social stimulation, whereas mothers tended to be more rhythmic and containing (Yogman, Dixon, Tronick, Als, Adamson, Lester, & Brazelton, 1977). Mothers addressed their babies with soft, repetitive, imitative sounds, whereas fathers touched their infants with rhythmic pats (Yogman et al., 1977). During visits to hospitalized premature infants, mothers were responsive to social cues, fathers to gross motor cues (Marton & Minde, 1980).

Most of the data concerning the characteristics of interaction with older infants have been gathered in the course of naturalistic home observations. Lamb (1976, 1977) found that fathers tended to engage in more physically stimulating and unpredictable or "idiosyncratic" play than mothers did. Since these types of play elicited more positive responses from infants, the average response to play bids by fathers was more positive than the average response to maternal bids. Power and Parke (1979, 1982) and Clarke-Stewart (1978) later confirmed that American mothers and fathers engaged in different types of play, and Sagi, Lamb, Shoham, Dvir, and Lewkowicz (1985) reported similar differences in a study of Israeli kibbutznikim. Belsky (1979), by contrast, did not find any differences of this kind in a study of American parents and infants. However, both Lamb (1976, 1977) and Belsky (1979) found that mothers were more likely to hold infants in the course of caretaking, whereas fathers were more likely to do so in playing with the babies or in response to the infants' requests to be held. It is not surprising that infants responded more positively to being held by their fathers than by their mothers (Lamb, 1976, 1977). Clarke-Stewart (1978, 1980) found that fathers gave more verbal directions and positive reinforcements than mothers did, and were rated higher than mothers on the ability to engage children in play. For their part, babies showed more enjoyment and involvement when playing with fathers than with mothers, and came to prefer playing with them when they had a choice (see also Lamb, 1976; Lynn & Cross, 1974). When parents were asked to choose an activity in which to engage their infants, mothers—at least middle-class mothers—tended to choose intellectual activities, whereas fathers selected playful social-physical activities (Clarke-Stewart, 1978).

Data gathered by interview confirm that fathers are identified with playful interactions whereas mothers are associated with caretaking. According to Kotelchuck's (1975) informants, mothers spent a greater proportion of their total interaction time caretaking than fathers did (50 versus 25%), whereas fathers spent a greater proportion (75 versus 50%) of their interaction time in playful social interaction than mothers did. Similar differences were reported by Russell (1983) in a study of Australian families with somewhat older children: 82% of fathers' total interaction time involved play, while caretaking constituted 38% of mothers' total interaction time. Relative to the total amount of interaction, Clarke-Stewart's (1978) data also suggested that fathers were consistently notable for their involvement in play, although their relative involvement in caretaking increased over time. Rendina and Dickerscheid (1976) did not record maternal behavior (making a comparison of maternal and paternal behavior impossible), but it is clear that fathers spent most of their time in playful interaction; on average, only 3.8% of the time was spent in caretaking. A study of English families reported similar findings. From maternal interviews, Richards, Dunn, and Antonis (1975) found that at both 30 and 60 weeks, the most common father–infant activity in 90% of the families was play. Routine involvement in caretaking was rare: only 35% regularly fed their infants at 30 weeks and 46% at 60 weeks. Diaper-changing and bathing were the least common paternal activities.

Interestingly, the results of a recent study by Pedersen, Cain, and Zaslow (1982) suggest that the patterns of interaction may differ when both parents are employed full-time. When observed with their infants, employed mothers stimulated their infants more than nonemployed mothers did, and they were far more interactive than their husbands were. In accordance with the findings just reviewed, fathers with nonemployed wives played with their infants more than the mothers did, but this pattern was reversed in the families with employed mothers. Maternal responsibility for caretaking, however, did not differ depending on the mothers' working status.

There is little solid evidence available concerning the origins or effects of paternal and maternal play styles, although there has been much popular debate about whether they have physiological or social/experiential origins. In attempts to address this issue, two studies have focused on the behavioral differences between primary and secondary caretaking fathers (and, in one case, mothers). In the first, Field (1978) found that primary caretaking fathers behaved more like mothers than secondary caretaking fathers did, although there were still differences between primary caretaking mothers and fathers. Particularly noteworthy was the fact that playful and noncontaining inter- actions were more common among fathers regardless of their caretaking responsibilites. However, naturalistic observation of the interactions be- tween 3, 8, and 16 month olds and their Swedish parents in the second study showed that gender was a more powerful determinant of parental behavior than family type (Lamb, Frodi, Hwang, Frodi, & Steinberg, 1982c, d; Lamb, Frodi, Frodi, & Hwang, 1982a). In this study, there were few reliable differences associated with the caretaking role, or the interaction of caretak- ing role and gender, whereas there were several effects based on the gender of the parent, with mothers more likely to kiss, hug, talk to or smile at, tend to, or hold their infants than fathers were. Contrary to first impressions, these findings do not imply that there are physiologically based differences. It seems more likely that the differences are attributable—in a proximate sense—to the years of sex differentiated socialization and social interaction experienced by men and women. Whether these behavioral differences (a) directly serve any ultimate purpose, (b) are epiphenomena related to behavioral tendencies that have some ultimate purpose, or (c) have no direct or indirect ultimate purpose, remains unknown.

One unexplained and unexpected finding reported by Lamb et al. (1982a, d) in their longitudinal study of Swedish families was that the Swedish fathers were never distinguished for their playfulness like American, British, and Israeli fathers are. Lamb et al. (1983) also found that the Swedish infants, regardless of their fathers' degree of involvement in caretaking, consistently preferred their mothers over their fathers on attachment behavior measures. This suggests that, regardless of its origins, the typical playfulness of fathers may play a role in making interaction with them especially salient and affectively rewarding, so that attachments form despite the more limited amount of time infants spend with fathers than with mothers.

DEGREE OF PATERNAL INVOLVEMENT

In this section the amount of time that fathers spend with, and the degree of responsibility they assume for, their children is considered. For analytic purposes, it may be helpful to think of paternal involvement in terms of three components: interaction, availability, and responsibility (Lamb, Pleck, & Charnov, 1985). *Interaction* refers to the father's direct contact with his child through caretaking and shared activites. *Availability* is a related concept concerning the father's potential availability for interaction, by virtue of being present or accessible to the child whether or not direct interaction is occurring. *Responsibility* refers to the role the father takes in ascertaining that the child is taken care of and arranging for resources to be available for the child. For example, this might involve arranging for baby-sitters, making appointments with the pediatrician and seeing that the child is taken to him/her, determining when the child needs new clothes, and so on. Although this aspect of the parental role is extremely important, it has been researched much less thoroughly than have interaction and availability. In most cases, the degrees of interaction and availability are interrelated, and both appear to potentiate the development of a sense of responsibility on the father's part. Thus, there is a moderate (though imperfect) association among the three aspects of father involvement.

Fathers' Interaction with Their Children

In a reanalysis of data from a recent nationally representative time-diary study, the 1975–1976 Study of Time Use, Pleck (1982) examined fathers' time in caretaking and other interactive activities with their children. Employed fathers whose youngest child was aged 5 or under spent an average of 26 minutes per day in such interaction with their children. Fathers with a youngest child aged 6 to 17 reported spending an average of 16 minutes per day. In this study, fathers' interaction time with their children varied little in absolute terms, depending on whether the mothers were employed, although it did, of course, vary in relative terms. Depending on the age of the youngest child, fathers' interaction amounted to between a third and a half of the time reported by mothers who were employed outside the home, and between a fourth and a fifth of the time reported by mothers who were not employed. The 1965–1966 Study of Americans' Use of Time (Robinson, 1977) produced relatively similar figures (Pleck, 1982, 1983, 1984).

Several smaller-scale studies also provide data about fathers' time in interaction with their children. For example, Pedersen and Robson (1969), by interviewing mothers, found that fathers reportedly spent between 45 minutes and 26 hours per week (with a mean of 8 hours) interacting with their 8- to 9½-month-old infants. Much lower levels of interaction were reported by Lewis and Weinraub (1974): for their subjects, the average amount of father–infant interaction was between 15 and 20 minutes per day.

There have been relatively few small-scale studies focused on paternal interaction with children older than infants and toddlers, and all have involved intact, middle-class, and typically white, families. In one such time-diary study, parents reported that fathers spent about 4 hours per week in direct interaction with their third and fourth grade children (Zeigler, 1980). Mothers spent about 5 hours a week, and there were no differences related to the children's sex. Baruch and Barnett (1983), however, found that fathers spent a little over 2½ hours per day interacting with their kindergartners and older children up to fourth graders. In a study of Australian fathers from diverse socioeconomic backgrounds, Russell (1983) found that fathers spent an average of 11 hours per week interacting with their children, compared with 32 hours for mothers. In another study, Montemayor (1982) found that tenth graders in Salt Lake City reported spending about 1 hour per day in interaction with or engaged in the same activities as their fathers. The same amount of time was spent with mothers. In both cases, the amount is about equivalent to the time involved in eating meals and doing chores together.

Some of the studies discussed above noted great variation in the extent of fathers' interaction, and the growing number of studies focused on nontraditional families indicates there are at least some families in which fathers are as involved as, or more involved than, the mothers (DeFrain, 1979; Grønseth, 1975; Lamb, Frodi, Hwang, & Frodi, 1982b; Levine, 1976; Radin, 1982; Russell, 1982; Sagi, 1982). Since none of the studies involve random samples of the population, however, it is hard to estimate how common these sorts of families are. On the basis of his quasi-random sample of Australian families, Russell (1983) estimated that these families represent about 1 to 2% of the total.

Excluding these studies of nontraditional families, the estimates of fathers' interaction time range from about 15 minutes to about 2½ hours per day. This broad range is understandable in light of the many ways in which the studies themselves vary. First, they differ in how broadly or narrowly "interaction" is defined. Second, it is noteworthy that the highest figures come from studies of interaction with either infants or preschool-aged children. Third, the lowest figures tend to derive from studies using actual diaries of time use rather than estimates made by mothers or fathers themselves; the fact that time diaries yield such low figures is especially notable because they concern a father's time with *all* his children, not just a single child as in the other studies. An exception to both of the latter trends, however, is the fact that one of the lowest average figures comes from Lewis and Weinraub's (1974) study of father–infant interaction, which is based on estimates.

Fortunately, some of these studies also make possible estimates of the extent of fathers' interaction expressed as a proportion of mothers' interaction, and here the variability from study to study proves to be much less. Fathers' proportion of mothers' interaction appears to vary around a baseline figure of about a third. However, fathers' proportion of mothers' interaction appears to vary systematically in relation to other variables, from only a fifth of mothers' to nearly the same level. It is higher when the mother is employed and when the children are older. With school-age children, some studies (e.g., Montemayor, 1982; Zeigler, 1980) find that fathers' interaction level actually attains, or nearly attains, parity with mothers'.

Fathers' Availability to Their Children

As far as paternal availability is concerned, Robinson (1977) found that in the 1965–1966 Survey of Americans' Use of Time, men with at least one child under age four reported being available to their children between 2.0 and 2.7 hours per day, depending on the exact number of children in the home. Men whose children were all over four reported being available 2.5 to 3.9 hours per day. For employed wives, the comparable ranges were 2.9–5.8 hours per day and 2.4–4.0 hours per day, respectively; for nonemployed wives, the ranges were 6.5–7.8 hours and 3.8–6.0 hours, respectively (Robinson, 1977, Table 3.8). In these data, therefore, the availability of fathers with preschoolers varied between one third and two thirds of their wives', depending on their employment status. Fathers of school-age children reported between two thirds and nearly the same amount of availability as mothers.

Another national survey, the 1977 Quality of Employment Survey (Quinn & Staines, 1979), also provided data concerning parents' availability to their children (Pleck, 1981, 1983). Parents made separate estimates for working and nonworking days of "how much time they spent with their children," a concept that parents appeared to interpret quite broadly. Among fathers with a youngest child under age six, the average father reported spending 3.6 hours per day if the wife was employed, and 2.6 hours per day if his wife was not employed. Among fathers with youngest children ages 6 to 17, those with employed wives reportedly spent 2.1 hours per day, while those with nonemployed wives said they spent 2.0 hours per day (Pleck, 1982). These figures were between 50 and 65% of the amounts of time reported by the comparable group of employed mothers.

In Pedersen and Robson's (1969) study the mothers reported that the fathers were accessible an average of 26 hours per week, or almost 4 hours a day. From interviews with 180 middle-class mothers and fathers, Kotelchuck (1975) determined that fathers spent an average of 3.2 waking hours per day accessible to their infants, whereas mothers spent 9 hours. In a much smaller study ($N = 12$) Golinkoff and Ames (1979) reported that fathers were accessible for 3.2 hours per day on average, compared with 8.3 hours for mothers.

Russell's (1983) study of Australian fathers yielded considerably higher figures. On average, fathers were reportedly available to their young children roughly 33 hours per week, while the comparable figure for mothers was 76 hours. In a study of American fathers of kindergartners through fourth graders, Baruch and Barnett (1983) reported a similarly high estimate–5–6 hours a day. By contrast, Zeigler's (1980) study of third and fourth graders generated a smaller figure: 12.5 hours per week for fathers compared to 21 hours per week for mothers.

Studies of fathers' availability, like those of fathers' interaction, produce a range of results. Fathers are, on the average, available to their children between 1.75 and 4 hours a day. Considered as a proportion of mothers' availability, different studies find fathers are available from between a third as much as mothers to just as much as mothers. As was true for interaction, fathers' proportional availability appears higher when children are older and when mothers are employed, although in absolute terms availability declines as children grow older and increases only modestly in cases of maternal employment. Across the group of studies as a whole, the estimates appear to vary around a baseline proportion of about a half. Thus, while paternal interaction averages about a third of mothers', paternal availability is somewhat higher—around half of mothers'.

Fathers' Responsibility

Spending time with one's children or being available to them is not the same thing as being responsible for them. Kotelchuck (1975, 1976) and Russell (1983) both asked fathers and mothers about the fathers' degree of responsibility for their children. Only 7.5% of Kotelchuck's respondents claimed to share responsibility equally, and 75 percent did not take *any* responsibility for daily care. In Russell's study the average father was *solely* responsible for the children only 1 hour per week, compared with 40 hours for the average mother. Further, 80% of the fathers did not assume sole responsibility regularly, and 60% had never taken sole responsibility for their children (though their children were preschoolers). Likewise, in Baruch and Barnett's (1983) study 113 of 160 fathers reported being responsible for no child-care tasks, 35 were responsible for one, and 12 for two or three of the 11 specific tasks about which they were asked. In the 1977 Quality of Employment Survey (Quinn and Staines, 1979), fathers and mothers in two-earner families (but not married to each other) were asked, "If someone has to be home with your child (children) to do something for him (her, them) when you are both supposed to be working, which of you is more likely to stay home?" The father was more likely to stay home in only about 15% of the families; in only 5% did parents respond, "It depends." In comparison to studies of interaction and availability, research on the extent and nature of fathers' responsibility for their children is only beginning, but the data available so far show clearly that fathers are far less responsible for their children than mothers are.

Recent Changes in Paternal Involvement

Several studies indicate that the level of father involvement has increased over the last several decades. In a 50-year follow-up study, for example, Caplow and Chadwick (1979) reported that in 1924 about 10% of all fathers were reported by mothers to spend *no* time with their children, compared with 2% in 1976. Likewise, the proportion of fathers spending more than 1 hour a day with their children increased significantly (no data provided). In a follow-up of Walker and Woods' (1976) subjects, Sanik (1981) found that fathers with infants and toddlers were spending more time with their children in 1977 than in 1967, though there were no comparable changes among fathers of older children. Consistent with this, Daniels and Weingarten (1981) found (from interviews with 86 families in the Boston area) that twice as many children born in the 1970's received care form their fathers on a regular (daily) basis than was reportedly true of children born in the 1950's and 1960's. Finally, survey data gathered from a nationally representative sample in 1975 and a subsample in 1981 clearly show the increases in paternal involvement that have occurred in the last decade (Juster, in press). Juster reports that men in the prime child-rearing age range (18–44 years) spent 2.29 hours per week in child care in 1975 and 2.88 hours in 1981—an increase of 26%. For women, the amount rose from 7.96 to 8.54 hours—an increase of 7%.

Most time-diary studies report overall declines in the levels of women's total family work (Pleck, 1983). Thus, for example, Juster (in press) reported a decline of 23% from 1965 to 1975, and a further 3% between 1975 and 1981 among 25- to 44-year-old women. However, in the two most recent studies in which women's *child-care* involvement at two points in time was specifically compared, Juster found an increase of 7%, whereas Sanik (1981 who controlled for the ages of children) reported no historical change. Several hypotheses have been offered in an attempt to explain the overall declines in women's family work: increased maternal employment, smaller average family size, more efficient home care technology, and lower household standards of neatness and cleanliness (Robinson, 1982). Although there is some support for the first two hypotheses, support for the last two is, as yet, weak.

Previous investigations have, by contrast, offered no explanations for the increases in men's involvement in child care. The fact that this increase is occurring in the context of stable or only slightly rising maternal involvement in child care; declining overall family work participation by women, and declining family size suggests that increased motivation on the part of fathers to be involved is attributable to changing cultural values that encourage direct paternal involvement.

DETERMINANTS OF PATERNAL INVOLVEMENT

Many think that American fathers participate only minimally with their children, whereas others believe that contemporary fathers are highly involved. The truth lies somewhere between these extreme positions. There is no question that fathers, on the average, interact less with and are less available to their children than mothers. When mothers are employed, and/or when older children are involved, studies suggest that paternal availability—and in a few studies paternal interaction—approaches and even equals the levels of maternal availability and interaction. Rarely, however, do fathers assume responsibility for their children. In this section an explanation for these sex differences in parental involvement is explored.

As indicated earlier, male and female roles in reproduction are such that sex differences in parental involvement would be expected, all else being equal. However, the relevant ecology in the late 20th century North America may well differ substantially from our species' "environment of evolutionary adaptedness" (Bowlby, 1969): the inventions of the nursing bottle and of infant formula, to cite but two examples, changed the child-rearing environment in ways that potentially have a fundamental impact on parental behavior, in that they made it possible for persons other than lactating mothers to assume major infant-care responsibilities— namely, fathers. Some men have taken advantage of these opportunites, and the variability among fathers testifies to both the absence of deterministic and physiological barriers to paternal involvement and the influence of individual differences with respect to several personal and social-situational characteristics that appear likely to influence paternal involvement. As indicated earlier, these factors are not alternatives to a biological explana- tion; rather, they may represent crucial characteristics of the ecology within which mothers and fathers make choices regarding involvement. The net effect may be to override any predispositions that exist, although in most cases they tend to supplement or reinforce them. For analytic purposes, one can divide those factors explored by psychologists and sociologists into four categories: motivation, skills, supports, and institutional (workplace) barriers and opportunites. The fact that none of these factors accounts for more than a small proportion of the variance is revealing; it may mean that interactions are more important than simple main effects, or that social scientists have been exploring the wrong variables. In any event, it is important to recognize that these within-group explanations of variations in motivation for involve- ment are not necessarily the same factors important in explaining between- group (i.e., male versus female) differences. The latter could plausibly be attributed to years of sex-differentiated socialization based on assumptions regarding the differential propensities and likely future roles of men and women. Furthermore, in both cases, social scientists have not stepped back to ask why, in an ultimate sense, individual or gender differences might exist and what purpose might be served by the proximate mechanism on which social scientists focus.

Motivation

Clearly not all men want to be highly involved in the day-to-day care of their children, although large subgroups indicate that they are motivated to be more involved. In a 1977 national survey 51% of husbands said that if they worked fewer hours, they would spend the extra time with their families (Quinn & Staines, 1979). Another 40% said they would *like* to work fewer hours so they could spend more time with their wives and children, even if this meant earning less money. As with all interview studies in this area, unfortunately, social desirability effects may obscure the achieved number of fathers who *really* want to be highly involved in child care. Highly involved fathers and fathers who reportedly want to be highly involved are more likely to have androgynous sex roles, although whether this is a cause or consequence of high involvement is not yet clear (Frodi, Lamb, Frodi, Hwang, Försstrom, & Corry, 1982; Lamb, 1982b; Russell, 1978. See also Russell, 1981). In a recent study, Coysh (1983) found that fathers with higher self-esteem, better marital relationships, and higher levels of participation in household tasks prenatally were more likely to become involved in child care. In addition, some involved fathers report that their own fathers were highly involved (Manion, 1977; Sagi, 1982), whereas others report that they wish to avoid being like their own uninvolved fathers (e.g., Baruch & Barnett, 1983).

Skills

Even when men want to be involved in child care, their involvement may be limited by a perceived or real lack of skills. As indicated earlier, men appear as competent as women in basic baby care, but they have often been denied the exposure (through baby-sitting, home economics, or family life classes) to the skills necessary for success in and enjoyment of child care. As families become smaller and more isolated, this is less and less a problem for men only: increasing numbers of new parents, *both* male and female, have had little if any opportunity to learn child-care skills. Both have to learn it "on the job." Again, however, the apparent importance of this learning does not preclude a role for biology. For example, it may be that girls are more likely to seek opportunities to learn child-care skills, are offered these opportunities more often, and perhaps learn the skills more rapidly than boys (as is the case in rats: see Rosenblatt, 1970), although both males and females have the potential to perform equally well once learning has been achieved. Thus, physiological predispositions, if they exist, likely depend on differential opportunities and experiences for mediation of any observable effect on the behavior of men and women.

Supports

High paternal involvement is unlikely to occur and be maintained unless significant others—mothers, relatives, friends, workmates—approve of this behavior. Interestingly, national surveys indicate that many mothers do not want their husbands to be more involved than they currently are (Pleck, 1982). In one survey, for example, only 23% of employed and 31% of nonemployed wives said that they would like "more help with the children" from their husbands, whereas in another survey 42% of the wives (all of whom were employed) said that they wished their husbands would "spend more time taking care of or doing things with the children." Just over half of the husbands interviewed felt that their wives wished them to be more involved. Thus, while a substantial number of fathers may receive encouragement to be more involved, a large number of men is clearly not being encouraged by their partners, whether or not they either want or feel competent to be more involved. Furthermore, even when mothers are supportive, friends, relatives, neighbors, and workmates may not be. Indeed, studies of nontraditional families in the United States and elsewhere find that highly involved fathers encounter frequent hostility on the part of their acquaintances, relatives, and workmates (e.g., Russell, 1982, 1983; Hwang, Eldén, & Fransson, 1984).

Again, one can legitimately seek to explain societal disapproval in psychological and sociological terms that emphasize the socialization of adults (factors that surely are important and provide the best proximate explanations of societal reactions), or one can step back further and ask why—in an ultimate sense—these reactions and socialization processes might exist. Among factors affecting relative inclusive fitness in this situation might be the possibilites of cuckoldry, with the unemployed father having greater potential access to employed men's wives (Hipgrave, 1979, 1982), and concern that, by avoiding workplace hazards, the involved father may prolong his own survival and increase the workload and danger level for others.

Institutional Factors

Finally, men's employers may simply prevent fathers from being as involved in child care as they would like to be. There is considerable evidence that employers do disapprove of men whose first priority appears to be to their families, and that employees fear this disapproval could be translated into actions which adversely affect the fathers' careers (Hwang et al., 1984). However, it is also true that even when working hours or other circumstances permit increased family involvement without jeopardizing work roles or career advancement, the effect on family involvement is modest (Lamb, 1982c; Lamb & Levine, 1983; Pleck, 1982, 1983). Perhaps this should not be surprising. Changes in institutional practices should affect only those men who want to be more involved, feel they have the skills to do so, and are supported in their motivation. For those who lack motivation, skills, or supports, changing institutional practices should be of no significance; the lack of response to changing institutional practices on the part of these fathers would hide any major effect on the smaller subgroup of fathers within the total group who *were* affected. Furthermore, the psychological importance of work to the fathers' sense of identity may be crucial, not only the objective constraints placed by specific employers on their employees' family roles.

Summary

The current literature thus leads us to identify five types of factors that influence relative paternal involvement—one involving ultimate and four involving proximate reasons. Evolutionary pressures may account for sex differences in the propensity for involvement, but the phenotypic expression of those tendencies is clearly influenced by social and economic factors that define the context in which individuals make choices in light of their predispositions and their presumed general goal—the maximization of inclusive fitness. Four of the possible proximate explanations of individual differences in paternal involvement are briefly discussed here: motivation, skills, support, and institutional practices. The probable strength of these factors in explaining individual differences in involvement undercuts deterministic physiological explanations of parental involvement, but should be seen as part of a more general biological answer responsive to Tinbergen's four questions concerning parental involvement.

CONCLUSION

In the last decade the study of father–child relationships among humans has blossomed, and we have begun to gather descriptive information concerning the extent of paternal involvement and the characteristics of father–child interaction. However, much remains to be researched in this area, particularly regarding variations based on culture, age of child, and socioeconomics in paternal behavior and involvement and concerning components of the paternal role other than direct paternal involvement— that is, provisioning, protection, and procreation. In addition, relatively few systematic attempts have been made to explain variations in the quality or extent of paternal behavior and involvement. Particular attention might be paid in the future to the fact that reproductive, provisioning, and parenting strategies are likely to be conditional, and vary depending on social circumstances and resources. Thus, for example, very different strategies may prove optimal for poor people and wealthy people, just as strategies certainly vary interculturally. Space constraints have precluded our discussion of these issues in the present chapter. Where the correlates of paternal involvement have been studied (e.g., Pleck, 1983) in the past, recourse has been made to data initially gathered for other reasons. Furthermore, the focus has been on proximate explanations—usually in terms of psychological or sociological factors—without regard for ultimate factors which may, when viewed in the context of ecological characteristics and various proximate factors, provide a broader and more satisfying answer to questions about paternal behavior in humans. Whether or not such is the case, we suggest that there is some value in addressing all four of Tinbergen's (1963) questions, and that developmental psychologists need to view biology and experience as complementary rather than mutually exclusive constructs.

SUMMARY

Unlike the other chapters in this volume, the focus herein is on *paternal* (rather than *maternal*) behavior. Drawing upon the framework provided by evolutionary theory and behavioral ecology, an attempt is made to recast the available evidence concerning the behavior of human males. Fathers and mothers do not differ with respect to behavioral sensitivity or responsiveness early in their children's lives. Many studies have shown, however, that fathers spend much less time with their children than mothers do, although their involvement has been increasing. We suggest that the degree of paternal involvement is a function of the socioecological constraints upon parental behavior. The identification of mothers with child care and fathers with play may be influenced by biogenetic tendencies as well as the social roles prescribed for fathers and mothers in contemporary societies.

ACKNOWLEDGMENT

This chapter is based, in part, on work conducted by The Fatherhood Project, which was funded by the Ford, Levi Strauss, Ittelson, and Rockefeller Family foundations. We are grateful to these organizations for their support.

REFERENCES

Ager, J.W., Werley, H.H., Allen, D.V., Shea, F.P., and Lewis, H.Y. Vasectomy: Who gets one and why? *American Journal of Public Health*, 1974, *64*, 680–686.

Ainsworth, M.D.S. The development of infant-mother attachment. In B.M. Caldwell and H.N. Ricciuti (Eds.), *Review of Child Development Research*, Vol. 3. Chicago, IL: University of Chicago Press, 1973.

Ainsworth, M.D.S., Bell, S.M., and Stayton, D.J. Infant–mother attachment and social development: "Socialization" as a product of reciprocal responsiveness to signals. In M.P.M. Richards (Ed.), *The Integration of a Child into a Social World*. Cambridge: Cambridge University Press, 1974.

American Jurisprudence, Vol. 41. Rochester, NY: American Bar Association, 1968.

Arnold, F., Bulatao, R.A., Buripakdi, C., Chung, B.J., Fawcett, J.T., Iritani, T., Lee, S.J., and Wu, T.S. *The Value of Children: A Cross National Study*, Vol. 1. Honolulu, HI: East-West Center, 1975.

Baruch, G.K., & Barnett, R.G. *Correlates of fathers' participation in family work: A technical report*. Working Paper #106. Wellesley, MA: Wellesley College Center for Research on Women, 1983.

Belsky, J. Mother–father–infant interaction: A naturalistic observational study. *Developmental Psychology*, 1979, *15*, 601–607.

Belsky, J. Early human experience: A family perspective. *Developmental Psychology*, 1981, *17*, 3–23.

Benson, L. *Fatherhood: A Sociological Perspective*. NY: Random House, 1968.

Berger, D.M. Couples' reaction to male infertility and donor insemination. *American Journal of Psychiatry*, 1980, *137*, 1047–1049.

Berman, P.W. Are women more responsive than men to the young? A review of developmental and situational variables. *Psychological Bulletin*, 1980, *88*, 668–695.

Bloom, L.J., and Houston, B.K. The psychological effects of vasectomy for American men. *Journal of Genetic Psychology*, 1976, *128*, 173–182.

Blount, B.G., and Padgug, E.J. Mother and father speech: Distribution of parental speech features in English and Spanish. *Papers and Reports on Child Language Development*, 1976, *12*, 47–59.

Bowlby, J. *Attachment and Loss*, Vol. 1: *Attachment*. NY: Basic Books, 1969.

Campbell, A., Converse, P., and Rodgers, W. *The Quality of American Life*. NY: Russell Sage, 1976.

Caplow, T., and Chadwick, P. Inequality and lifestyles in Middletown, 1920–1978. *Social Science Quarterly*, 1979, *60*, 367–385.

Cavan, R. Unemployment-crisis of the common man. *Marriage and Family Living*, 1959, *21*, 139–146.

Cazenave, N.A. Middle-income black fathers: An analysis of the provider role. *Family Coordinator*, 1979, *27*, 583–593.

Clarke-Stewart, K.A. And daddy makes three: The father's impact on mother and young child. *Child Development*, 1978, *49*, 466–478.

Clarke-Stewart K.A. The father's contribution to children's cognitive and social development in early childhood. In F.A. Pedersen (Ed.), *The Father-Infant Relationship: Observational Studies in a Family Setting*. NY: Praeger Special Publications, 1980.

Cord, E.L. A study of certain personality factors incident to vasectomy as an adjustmental device. *Dissertation Abstracts International*, 1972, *33-B* (5), 2340–2341.

Coysh, W.S. *Predictive and concurrent factors related to fathers' involvement in childrearing*. Paper presented to the American Psychological Association, Anaheim, CA, August, 1983.

Daniels, P., and Weingarten, K. *Sooner or Later: The Timing of Parenthood in Adult Lives.* NY: Norton, 1981.

DeFrain, J. Androgynous parents tell who they are and what they need. *Family Coordinator*, 1979, *28*, 237–243.

Dixson, A.F., and George, L. Prolactic and parental behavior in a male New World primate. *Nature (London)*, 1982, *299*, 551–553.

Ehrhardt, A., and Baker, A. Fetal androgens, human central nervous system differentiation, and behavior sex differences. In R.C. Friedman, R.M. Richart, and R.L. Vande Wiele (Eds.) *Sex Differences in Behavior*. NY: Wiley, 1974.

Fein, R. Men's entrance into parenthood. *Family Coordinator*, 1976, *25*, 341–350.

Feldman, S.S., and Nash, S.C. The effect of family formation on sex stereotypic behavior: A study of responsiveness to babies. In W. Miller & L. Newman (Eds.), *The First Child and Family Formation*. Chapel Hill, NC: North Carolina Population Press, 1977.

Feldman, S.S., and Nash, S.C. Interest in babies during young adulthood. *Child Development*, 1978, *49*, 617–622.

Feldman, S.S., Nash, S.C., and Cutrona, C. The influence of age and sex on responsiveness to babies. *Developmental Psychology*, 1977, *13*, 675–676.

Ferber, A.S., Tietze, C., and Lewit, S. Men with vasectomies: A study of medical, sexual, and psychosocial changes. *Psychosomatic Medicine*, 1967, *29*, 354–366.

Field, T. Interaction behaviors of primary versus secondary caretaker fathers. *Developmental Psychology*, 1978, *14*, 183–184.

Frodi, A.M. and Lamb, M.E. Sex differences in responsiveness to infants: A developmental study of psychophysiological and behavioral responses. *Child Development*, 1978, *49*, 1182–1188.

Frodi, A.M., Lamb, M.E., Leavitt, L.A., and Donovan, W.L. Fathers' and mothers' responses to infant smiles and cries. *Infant Behavior and Development*, 1978, *1*, 187–198.

Frodi, A.M., Lamb, M.E., Leavitt, L.A., Donovan, W.L., Neff, C., and Sherry, D. Fathers' and mothers' responses to the faces and cries of normal and premature infants. *Developmental Psychology*, 1978, *14*, 490–498.

Frodi, A.M., Lamb, M.E., Frodi, M., Hwang, C.-P., Försstrom, B., and Corry, T. Stability and change in parental attitudes following an infant's birth into traditional and nontraditional Swedish families. *Scandinavian Journal of Psychology*, 1982, *23*, 53–62.

Gleason, J.B. Fathers and other strangers: Men's speech to young children. In D.P. Dato (Ed.), *Language and Linguistics*. Washington, D.C.: Georgetown University Press, 1975.

Glick, P.C., and Norton, A.J. Marrying, divorcing, and living together in the US today. *Population Bulletin*, *32* (whole number 5), 1979.

Golinkoff, R.M., and Ames, G.J. A comparison of fathers' and mothers' speech with their young children. *Child Development*, 1979, *50*, 28–32.

Greenberg, M., and Morris, N. Engrossment: The newborn's impact upon the father. *American Journal of Orthopsychiatry*, 1974, *44*, 520–531.

Gronseth, E. The breadwinner trap. In L. Howe (Ed.), *The Future of the Family*. NY: Simon & Schuster, 1972.

Grønseth, E. *Work-sharing families: Adaptations of pioneering families with husband*

and wife in part-time employment. Paper presented to the International Society for the Study of Behavioral Development, Surrey (England), July, 1975.

Hamburg, D.A., and Goodall, J.V.L. Factors facilitating development of aggressive behavior in chimpanzees and humans. In J. de Wit and W.W. Hartup (Eds.), Determinants and Origins of Aggressive Behavior. The Hague: Mouton,1974.

Hamilton, W.D. The genetical theory of social behavior. Journal of Theoretical Biology, 1964, 7, 1–52.

Harris, L. The Harris Survey Yearbook of Public Opinion 1970. NY: Louis Harris, 1971.

Hipgrave, T. Childrearing by lone fathers. In R. Chester, P. Diggory, and M. Sutherland (Eds.), Changing Patterns of Child Bearing and Child Rearing. London: Academic Press, 1982.

Hipgrave, T. When the mother is gone: The position of the lone father. Unpublished manuscript, University of Leicester, 1979.

Hoffman, L.W., Thornton, A., and Manis, J.D. The value of children to parents in the United States. Population: Behavioral, Social, and Environmental Issues, 1978.

Horenstein, D., and Houston, B.K. The effects of vasectomy on postoperative psychological adjustment and self-concept. Journal of Psychology, 1975, 89, 167–173.

Hrdy, S. The evolution of human sexuality: The latest word and the last. Quarterly Review of Biology, 1979, 54, 309–314.

Hwang, C.P., Eldén, G., and Fransson, C. Arbetsgivares och arbetskamraters attityder till pappaledighet. Rapport no. 1. Göteborg, Sweden: Psykologiska Institutionen, Göteborgs' Universitet, 1984.

Ingram, J.C. Parent–infant interactions in the common marmoset (Callithrix Jacchus) and the development of young. Unpublished Ph.D., University of Bristol, 1975.

Juster, F.T. A note on recent changes in time use. In F.T. Juster & F. Stafford (Eds.), Studies in the Measurement of Time Allocation. Ann Arbor, MI: Institute for Social Research, in press.

Kauffman, A.L. Mothers' and fathers' verbal interactions with children learning language. Paper presented to the Eastern Psychological Association, Boston, March, 1977.

Kendall, P.J. The relationship of vasectomy to self-concept. Dissertation Abstracts International, 1972, 33-B (3), 1307–1308.

Klaus, M.H., Trause, M.A., and Kennell, J.H. Human maternal behavior following delivery: Is it species specific? Unpublished manuscript. Cleveland, OH: Case Western Reserve University, 1975.

Komarovsky, M. The Unemployed Man and His Family. NY: Dryden, 1940.

Kotelchuck, M. Father caretaking characteristics and their influence on infant-father interaction. Paper presented to the American Psychological Association, Chicago, September, 1975.

Kotelchuck, M. The infant's relationship to the father: Experimental evidence. In M.E. Lamb (Ed.), The Role of the Father in Child Development. NY: Wiley, 1976.

Krebs, J.R., and Davis, N.B. An Introduction to Behavioural Ecology. Sunderland, MA: Sinauer, 1981.

Lamb, M.E. Interactions between eight-month-old children and their fathers and mothers. In M.E. Lamb (Ed.), The Role of the Father in Child Development. NY: Wiley, 1976.

Lamb, M.E. Father–infant and mother–infant interaction in the first year of life. *Child Development*, 1977, *48*, 167–181.

Lamb, M.E. Social interaction in infancy and the development of personality. In M.E. Lamb (Ed.), *Social and Personality Development*. NY: Holt, Rinehart & Winston, 1978.

Lamb, M.E. The development of social expectations in the first year of life. In M.E. Lamb & L.R. Sherrod (Eds.), *Infant Social Cognition: Empirical and Theoretical Considerations*. Hillsdale, NJ: Erlbaum, 1981. (a)

Lamb, M.E. *The Role of the Father in Child Development* (revised edition). NY: Wiley, 1981. (b)

Lamb, M.E. Early contact and mother–infant bonding: One decade later. *Pediatrics*, 1982, *70*, 763–768. (a)

Lamb, M.E. Generalization and inferences about causality in research on nontraditional families: Some cautions. *Merrill-Palmer Quarterly*, 1982, *28*, 157–161. (b)

Lamb, M.E. Why Swedish fathers aren't liberated. *Psychology Today*, 1982, *18*(10), 74–77. (c)

Lamb, M.E., and Easterbrooks, M.A. Individual differences in parental sensitivity: Origins, components, and consequences. In M.E. Lamb and L. R. Sherrod (Eds.), *Infant Social Cognition: Empirical and Theoretical Considerations*. Hillsdale, NJ: Erlbaum, 1981.

Lamb, M.E., and Goldberg, W.A. The father–child relationship: A synthesis of biological, evolutionary and social perspectives. In L.W. Hoffman, R. Gandelman, & H.R. Schiffman (Eds.), *Parenting: Its Causes and Consequences*. Hillsdale, NJ: Erlbaum, 1982.

Lamb, M.E., and Hwang, C.-P. Maternal attachment and mother–neonate bonding: A critical review. In M.E. Lamb & A.L. Brown (Eds.), *Advances in Developmental Psychology*, Vol. 2. Hillsdale, NJ: Erlbaum, 1982.

Lamb, M.E., and Levine, J.A. The Swedish parental insurance policy: An experiment in social engineering. In M.E. Lamb and A. Sagi (Eds.), *Fatherhood and Family Policy*. Hillsdale, NJ: Erlbaum, 1983.

Lamb, M.E., Frodi, A.M., Frodi, M., and Hwang, C.-P. Characteristics of maternal and paternal behavior in traditional and nontraditional Swedish families. *International Journal of Behavioral Development*, 1982, *5*, 131–141. (a)

Lamb, M.E., Frodi, A.J., Hwang, C.-P. and Frodi, M. Varying degrees of paternal involvement in infant care: Attitudinal and behavioral correlates. In M.E. Lamb (Ed.), *Nontraditional Families: Parenting and Child Development*. Hillsdale, NJ: Erlbaum, 1982. (b)

Lamb, M.E., Frodi, A.M., Hwang, C.-P., Frodi, M., and Steinberg, J. Effects of gender and caretaking role on parent–infant interaction. In R.N. Emde & R. Harmon (Eds.), *Development of Attachment and Affiliative Systems*. NY: Plenum, 1982. (c)

Lamb, M.E., Frodi, A.M., Hwang, C.-P., Frodi, M., and Steinberg, J. Mother- and father-infant interaction involving play and holding in traditional and nontraditional Swedish families. *Developmental Psychology*, 1982, *18*, 215–221. (d)

Lamb, M.E., Frodi, M., Hwang, C.-P., and Frodi, A.M. Effects of paternal involvement on infant preferences for mothers and fathers. *Child Development*, 1983, *54*, 450–458.

Lamb, M.E., Thompson, R.A., Gardner, W., Charnov, E.L., and Estes, D. Security of infantile attachment. Its study and biological interpretation. *Behavioral and Brain Sciences*, 1984, *7*, 127–147.

Lamb, M.E., Pleck, J., and Charnov, E.L. Paternal behavior in humans. *American Zoologist*, 1985, *25*, 883–894.

Levine, J. (1976) *And Who Will Raise the Children? New Options for Fathers and Mothers*. Philadelphia, PA: Lippincott, 1976.

Lewis, M., and Weinraub, M. Sex of parent versus sex of child: Socioemotional development. In R.C. Friedman, R.M. Richart, and R.L. Vande Wiele (Eds.), *Sex Differences in Behavior*. NY: Wiley, 1974.

Lynn, D.B., and Cross, A.R. Parent preferences of preschool children. *Journal of Marriage and the Family*, 1974, *36*, 555–559.

Manion, J. A study of fathers and infant caretaking. *Birth and the Family Journal*, 1977, *4*, 174–179.

Marton, P.L., & Minde, K. *Paternal and maternal behavior with premature infants.* Paper presented to the American Orthopsychiatric Association, Toronto, April, 1980.

Montemayor, R. The relationship between parent-adolescent conflict and the amount of time adolescents spend alone and with parents and peers. *Child Development*, 1982, *53*, 1512–1519.

Nash, S.C., and Feldman, S.S. Sex role and sex-related attributions: Constancy or change across the family life cycle? In M.E. Lamb and A.L. Brown (Eds.), *Advances in Developmental Psychology*, Vol. 1. Hillsdale, NJ: Erlbaum, 1981.

Parke, R.D., and O'Leary, S. Father–mother–infant interaction in the newborn period: Some findings, some observations, and some unresolved issues. In K.F. Riegel and J. Meacham (Eds.), *The Developing Individual in a Changing World, Vol. 2: Social and Environmental Issues*. The Hague: Mouton,1976.

Parke, R.D., and Sawin, D.B. *The family in early infancy: Social interactional and attitudinal analyses.* Paper presented to the Society for Research in Child Development, New Orleans, March, 1977.

Parke, R.D., and Tinsley, B.R. The father's role in infancy: Determinants of involvement in caregiving and play. In M.E. Lamb (Ed.), *The Role of the Father in Child Development* (Rev. ed.). NY: Wiley, 1981.

Parke, R.D., O'Leary, S.E., and West, S. Mother–father–newborn interaction: Effects of maternal medication, labor and sex of infant. *Proceedings of the American Psychological Association*, 1972, 85–86.

Parke, R.D., Power, T.G., and Gottman, J. Conceptualizing and quantifying influence patterns in the family triad. In M.E. Lamb, S.J. Suomi, and G.R. Stephenson (Eds.), *Social Interaction Analysis: Methodological Issues*. Madison, WI: University of Wisconsin Press, 1979.

Pedersen, F.A., and Robson, K.S. Father participation in infancy. *American Journal of Orthopsychiatry*, 1969, *39*, 466–472.

Pedersen, F.A., Cain, R., and Zaslow, M. Variation in infant experience associated with alternative family roles. In L. Laosa and I. Sigel (Eds.), *Families: Research and Practice*, Vol. 1. NY: Plenum, 1982.

Phillips, R., and Parke, R.D. *Father and mother speech to prelinguistic infants.* Unpublished manuscript, University of Illinois, 1979.

Pleck, E. Two worlds in one: Work and family. *Journal of Social History*, 1976, *10*, 178–195.

Pleck, J.H. *Changing patterns of work and family roles*. Paper presented to the American Psychological Association, Los Angeles, August, 1981.

Pleck, J.H. *Husbands' and wives' paid work, family work, and adjustment*. Wellesley, MA: Wellesley College Center for Research on Women (Working Papers), 1982.

Pleck, J.H. Husbands' paid work and family roles: Curent research issues. In H. Lopata and J.H. Pleck (Eds.), *Research in the Interweave of Social Roles, Vol. 3: Families and Jobs*. Greenwich, CT.: JAI Press, 1983.

Pleck, J.H. *Working Wives and Family Well-Being*. Beverly Hills, CA: Sage, 1984.

Power, T.G., and Parke, R.D. *Toward a taxonomy of father–infant and mother–infant play patterns*. Paper presented to the Society for Research in Child Development, San Francisco, March, 1979.

Power, T.G., and Parke, R.D. Play as a context for early learning: Lab and home analyses. In L.M. Laosa and I.E. Sigel (Eds.), *Families as a Learning Environment for Children*. NY: Plenum, 1982.

Quinn, R.P., & Staines, G.L. *The 1977 Quality of Employment Survey*. Arbor, MI: Survey Research Center, 1979.

Radin, N. Primary caregiving and role-sharing fathers. In M.E. Lamb (Ed.), *Nontraditional Families: Parenting and Child Development*. Hillsdale, NJ: Erlbaum, 1982.

Redican, W.K., and Taub, D.M. Male parental care in monkeys and apes. In M.E. Lamb (Ed.), *The Role of the Father in Child Development* (Rev. ed.). NY: Wiley, 1981.

Rendina, I., and Dickerscheid, J.D. Father involvement with first-born infants. *Family Coordinator*, 1976, *25*, 373–378.

Richards, M.P.M., Dunn, J.F., and Antonis, B. *Caretaking in the first year of life: The role of fathers' and mothers' social isolation*. Unpublished manuscript, Cambridge University, 1975.

Robinson, J. *How Americans Use Time: A Social-Psychological Analysis*. NY: Praeger, 1977.

Rodgers, D.A., Ziegler, F.J., and Levy, N. Prevailing cultural attitude about vasectomy: A possible explanation of postoperative psychological response. *Psychosomatic Medicine*, 1967, *29*, 367–375.

Rödholm, M., and Larsson, K. The behavior of human male adults at their first contact with a newborn. *Infant Behavior and Development*, 1982, *5*, 121–130.

Rosenblatt, J.S. The development of maternal responsiveness in the rat. *American Journal of Orthopsychiatry*, 1970, *39*, 36–56.

Russell, G. The father role and its relation to masculinity, femininity, and androgyny. *Child Development*, 1978, *49*, 755–765.

Russell, G. Shared-caregiving families: An Australian study. In M.E. Lamb (Ed.), *Nontraditional Families: Parenting and Child Development*. Hillsdale, NJ: Erlbaum, 1982.

Russell, G. *The Changing Role of Fathers?* St. Lucia, Queensland: University of Queensland Press, 1983.

Sagi, A. Antecedents and consequences of various degrees of paternal involvement in child rearing: The Israeli project. In M.E. Lamb (Ed.), *Nontraditional Families: Parenting and Child Development*. Hillsdale, NJ: Erlbaum, 1982.

Sagi, A., Lamb, M.E., Shoham, R., Dvir, R., and Lewkowicz, K.S. Parent-infant interaction in families on Israeli kibbutzim. *International Journal of Behavioral Development*, 1985, *8*, 273–284.

Sanik, M. Division of household work: A decade comparison—1967–1977. *Home Economics Research Journal*, 1981, *10*, 175–180.

Slocum, W., and Nye, F.I. Provider and housekeeper roles. In F.I. Nye (Ed.), *Role Structure and Analysis of the Family*. Beverly Hills, CA: Sage, 1976.

Symons, D. *The Evolution of Human Sexuality*. NY: Oxford University Press, 1979.

Tinbergen, N. On aims and methods of ethology. *Zeitschrift fur Tierpsychologie*, 1963, *20*, 410–433.

Trivers, R.L. Parental investment and sexual selection. In B.G. Campbell (Ed.), *Sexual Selection and the Descent of Men: 1871–1971*. Chicago, IL: Aldine, 1972.

Walker, K., and Woods, M. *Time Use: A Measure of Household Production of Family Goods and Services*. Washington, D.C.: American Home Economics Association, 1976.

Williams, G.C. *Adaptation and Natural Selection*. Princeton, NJ: Princeton University Press, 1966.

Wilson, E.A. Sequence of emotional responses induced by infertility. *Journal of the Kentucky Medical Association*, 1979, *77*, 229–233.

Van den Berghe, P. *Man in Society*. NY: Elsevier, 1978.

Van den Berghe, P. *Human Family Systems: An Evolutionary View*. NY: Elsevier, 1979.

Voydanoff, P. Unemployment as a family stressor. In H. Lopata and J.H. Pleck (Eds.), *Research in the Interweave of Social Roles*, Vol. 3: *Families and jobs*. Greenwich, CT: JAI Press, 1983.

Yankelovich, D. The meaning of work. In J. Rosow (Ed.), *The Worker and the Job*. Englewood Cliffs, NJ: Prentice-Hall, 1974.

Yogman, M.W., Dixon, S., Tronick, E., Als, H., Adamson, L., Lester, B.M., and Brazelton, T.B. *The goals and structure of face-to-face interaction between infants and their fathers*. Paper presented to the Society for Research in Child Development, New Orleans, March, 1977.

Zeigler, M. *The father's influence on his school-age child's academic performance and cognitive development*. Unpublished doctoral dissertation. Ann Arbor, MI: University of Michigan, 1980.

Zelazo, P.R., Kotelchuck, M., Barber, L., and David, J. *Fathers and sons: An experimental facilitation of attachment behaviors*. Paper presented to the Society for Research in Child Development, New Orleans, March, 1977.

6

PARENTAL SUPPLEMENTS AND SURROGATES AMONG PRIMATES: CROSS-SPECIES AND CROSS-CULTURAL COMPARISONS

James J. McKenna

INTRODUCTION

In a memorable scene from his recently released film, *The Lonely Guy*, comedian Steve Martin enters a very large, crowded, and obviously expensive restaurant. After a formal but nevertheless cordial greeting from the maître d', Martin is asked how many persons are in his party. When he responds, "Just one," a visibly shaken host gasps with disbelief and in a questioning tone of voice repeats, "Just one?" Instantly a deafening silence ensues while every person in the restaurant ceases to converse and turns to stare at a now terribly ashamed Martin as he is led, not inconspicuously, to his table. The silence and stares continue while Martin sits alone trying unsuccessfully not to feel self-conscious. Finally Martin calls back the maître d' and asks him to request the restaurant patrons to resume their prior activities; and with just a snap of his fingers a cacophony of voices rising from a hundred different conversations begins as the patrons shift their gaze away from "the lonely guy."

This scene is particularly amusing because most of us can identify with what Martin was feeling as well as with what those who were staring at him were feeling. It is an instructive scene because it reminds us of the kinds of social meanings we attach to companionship and the lack thereof, and how these social meanings affect the way we feel. In one sense, there is no question that the awkward and embarrassed Martin, the sympathetic maître d', and even the nosy patrons who, undoubtedly sad for Martin but glad it was not they who were alone, are simply reflecting some shared cultural values; but they are also displaying a sensitivity to companionship, and indeed sociality, that has an evolutionary as well as developmental basis. For example, like other primates who experience prolonged childhoods, the human infant begins to establish a series of "multiplex" relationships with individuals other than the parents shortly after birth. Some of these individuals offer direct assistance and care to the infant and, as a result, contribute substantially to the child's socioemotional development. Other

143

individuals, while not contributing directly to the care of the child, nevertheless associate with it and facilitate the emergence of the child's growing network of relationships that becomes important at different points in the life cycle.

The purpose of this chapter, then, is not to analyze any further the bases of the humor contained within the scene described above, but rather to use it as a point of departure to explore from both an evolutionary and developmental perspective the circumstances surrounding the supplemental care extended to infants—what motivates it, who is involved, how it occurs, and what effects it has on development. To what extent do early caretaking experiences contribute to social sensitivities and interdependence similar, but not identical, to the sensitivities displayed by Martin and the other actors in this scene? By utilizing a cross-species framework the purpose herein is to show that, however, circuitous the pathway that links up processes of natural selection with everyday cultural experiences such as Martin's extreme embarrassment at being discovered "alone" in a restaurant, it is only through a combined biological and social–psychological approach that a complete understanding of human behavioral characteristics eventually emerges.

QUERIES AND PROBLEMS

Perhaps because most of the nonhuman primates are intensely social, it should not be too surprising that among a great many species individuals other than the mother and father interact with infants in significant ways. In fact, because of the protracted period of infant development that occurs within what, for the most part, are tightly organized social groups, infant contacts with individuals other than the parents regularly take place; but whether or not others are extending care and, thus "helping" or increasing infant survival or future reproductive success remains a difficult question to answer. Even though on an intuitive level it appears that alloparenting has affected the social evolution of the primates (Wilson, 1975), it is amazing to think that there is very little data demonstrating it. Our awakening to the potential explanatory possibilities of kin selection theory and parental investment has enabled us to understand certain aspects of male–female or mother–father behavior, but we have had less good fortune in using the concepts to help us explain the adaptive significance of infant sharing or alloparenting (see reviews in Gubernick and Klopfer, 1981; Riemann, 1982; Rubenstein, 1982; Gadgil, 1982; MacDonald and Moehlman, 1982).

As mentioned above, one class of problems concerns the difficulties involved in distinguishing between direct care and indirect care, purposeful and incidental care, and in determining who actually benefits during alloparenting—the infant, the mother, the father, or the alloparent?

Another set of problems concerns our ability to recognize instances wherein natural selection has designed the forms and the function of alloparenting as opposed to instances in which substitute care emerges or develops in a group as a consequence of some other aspects of social structure, and, hence, some other biological and physiological adaptation that underlies it. In other words, the first question must be: To what degree has alloparenting actually evolved and to what extent was it designed by natural selection to take the form that it does?

The question of the benefits or effects of alloparenting must begin with a consideration of the role of each participant independently, and care must be taken to consider not simply how possible effects are distributed horizontally (across all participants at the time of the activity), but also vertically. For example, for each participant how, if at all, does the alloparenting experience affect future survival and reproductive success; in some way are alloparenting experiences projected to future contexts, contributing either positively or negatively to later stages in the life cycle? Moreover, for which participants, in how many of the interactions, do immediate benefits or deleterious consequences accrue and, if they do, what are they (see Hrdy, 1976; Kleiman and Malcolm, 1981; McKenna, 1981; Emlen, 1978; Riemann, 1982 for discussions)? It is important to consider that infant care giving by individuals other than the parents may not have any genetic basis per se, which is not to say that it does not have genetic consequences for the participants (McKenna, 1979; Bekoff, 1981). Indeed, when all the data have been collected and definitions of infant–nonmother, –nonfather contacts have been made more rigorous and standardized, we may find, for example, that while the time infants spend outside the custody of parents is not a particularly useful or safe time in itself, it may be critical for one of the parents or the siblings who may learn how to carry infants. The marmosets are a good example of this situation (Ingram, 1975). Alloparenting may prove to be as deleterious to some species as it proves to be neutral or helpful to others. At this point there appears to be much intragroup and interspecies variability (see McKenna, 1981).

From a methodological perspective it is most difficult to assess what internal and/or external immediate factors motivate individuals first to obtain access to infants and, then, to extend care to them. Are primates motivated in the same way as, for example, other mammals and birds—by signals emanating especially from the young communicating vulnerability and helplessness—that is, the "cute response"? To what extent are alloparents seeking proximity and responding in ways to protect, nurture, and/or touch, because infants are small, exhibit high-pitched cooing, have large eyes at the midline of the skull, have chubby cheeks necessary for good suckling, reflect different neonatal coat colors, and move in awkward ways? Or do alloparents respond as they do because infants are novelties or play objects in their environments, or because, first and foremost, it is simply possible for them to do so—that is, mothers or fathers will not act aggressively if alloparent–infant contact occurs. Does alloparenting occur only in instances wherein the coefficient of relatedness is high between the participants, or does it (can it) occur in instances wherein the coefficient of familiarity (irrespective of relatedness) is high (see Hood, 1978; Bekoff, 1981)? Among human beings, especially when infant care occurs outside the kin network within more urban societies, economic rewards serve as prime motivators. But the example of nonhuman primates, in particular, elicits a sense of wonder as to whether substitute care givers take infants only because they are there for the taking or whether alloparenting, for all species, represents a sound reproductive strategy.

One reason it is still extremely difficult to answer these questions is that we are just beginning to acquire the kind of longitudinal data that gives accurate geneologies permitting us to pinpoint, for example, who is related to whom, and how early experiences affect future reproductive success. In the vast majority of species that have been studied, kinship has mostly been inferred (if even addressed); in fact, some investigators have called attention to the excessive amount of theorizing that has occurred. For example, both Bekoff (1981) and Altman (1980) argue that all too frequently data have been made to account for kin selection theories rather than vice versa.

TENTATIVE HYPOTHESES

The amount of field and laboratory data on almost all aspects of primate sociobiology, including parenting systems, is accumulating at an astonishing rate. Eventually this will permit us to assess the utility of kin selection theories in explaining surrogate or supplemental care, as well as to propose alternative theories about the bases of such behavior among primates. But until that time a synthesis of the cross-species data, which includes socioecological and developmental concepts, permits the proposal of some tentative if not some provisional points for discussion and hypothesis testing. They include: (1) To explain alloparental care among primates, reference must first be made not to its possible benefits but rather to the ongoing social-structural features emerging out of unique biological, ecological, anatomical, and physiological adaptations—which alone create the conditions fostering access to infants and the kinds of alloparenting that can safely occur. (2) A set of necessary and sufficient conditions permitting alloparenting, which includes characteristics both internal and external to the participants, is recognizable, and these conditions seem to cut across diverse primate species. (3) It appears that alloparenting evolved independently to meet specific needs in different primate families, although early in the evolution of the primate order sufficient conditions for its emergence, such as an attraction to infants, may have existed. (4) While various benefits and/or negative genetic consequences can be attributed to specific instances of alloparental behavior, except in the most general sense, substitute infant care giving and the attachments that can accrue from such forms of care are not themselves coded on particular genotypes. (5) We can predict that where social rank (dominance) does not severely regulate relationships between members of the same sex, or regulate and differentiate males and females in ways that could inhibit infant monitoring and retrieval, it is possible for alloparenting to take place. (6) Especially with respect to males in polygynous societies, females, and not males themselves, act as a major constraint on adult male–infant attachment and potential male care giving roles. (7) Among humans monogamous-oriented primate species, supplemental or surrogate care giving will most likely be found within, rather than outside (including affinal), units.

ECOLOGICAL CONDITIONS AND THE EMERGENCE OF INFANT CARE BY INDIVIDUALS OTHER THAN THE MOTHER— A BRIEF SURVEY

Old World Monkey Primates: Cercopithecines and Colobines

A few years ago I became interested in the question of why only half the species constituting Old World monkeys regularly engaged in allomothering behavior while the other half did not. I wondered, in particular, why the colobus and langur monkeys of the Colobidae family (about 14 genera) regularly permitted 1-day-old infants to be passed around like toys to almost any female, when among the Cercopithecine subfamily (baboons, macaques, mangabeys, and guenons) such behavior does not occur nearly to the same degree or in the same form. Even though it now seems that the patas monkey (not a colobine but a cercopithecine) does exhibit regular allomothering to very young neonates (Chism and Olson: personal communication, 1982), it still seems apparent that half the Old World monkeys, the Colobidae family, exhibit a trend toward allomothering of 1-day-old infants while the other half of the Old World monkeys, the cercopithecines, mostly do not. By reviewing the available data on all primate species for which extensive alloparenting occurred, it appeared possible to elucidate a set of principles or conditions that seem to permit allomothering to take place. After securing these data my intention was to concentrate on the question of function, benefits, and adaptive significance. Too often our behavioral analyses propose explanations about certain behaviors based only upon their functional consequences (even when they are not yet proved). This approach makes it easy to confuse ideas about a behavior's function or benefits with an explanation for its origins. Although, of course, function and origin share an important relationship in behavior analysis, they are not necesarily the same (McKenna, 1979).

In order to understand the origins of parental systems within which care is extended in a regular way by caretakers other than the mother or father, one of the first issues to be addressed is under what kind of social structural and, thus, ecological conditions can a mother or father release her/his infant safely to another and, equally important, retrieve it. On an intuitive level it seems that through allomothering especially, younger females can practice or rehearse mothering behavior, thereby acquiring important care giving skills. Second, as Jones (1980) argues for howler monkeys, it may be that releasing the infant to a custodian permits the mother to forage more efficiently—it gives her more temporary mobility and reduces calorie demands. Third, bonds can be established and strengthened between members of groups which pass and share each other's infants. Fourth, the infants of mothers who have permitted others to handle them may have a greater chance of being adopted and, thus, increase the chances of survival, should the mother die (Boggess, 1976; Dolhinow, 1963; and McKenna, 1981). Finally, allomothering may hasten socialization (Hrdy, 1976) or even prepare the infant for a social life independent of the social assistance of its mother (McKenna, 1979).

Irrespective of whether or not these speculations are correct, and as will be pointed out later they all have some problems when tested against the data, they still tell us too little about the process by which alloparenting emerged to be useful. The question can still be asked: With all these possible benefits, why do not *all* monkeys (and apes) share their young? Female cercopithecines, like colobine females, are greatly motivated to seek out, touch, and obtain access to neonates just as colobine females are, but mothers are exceedingly reluctant to release their neonates to others and ordinarily do not; in fact, many baboon and macaque females attempt to avoid other group members by increasing interindividual proximity shortly after birth, so that their infants are less likely to be kidnapped (Altmann, 1980). These functional ideas, then, fail to reveal the evolutionary and/or the immediate proximate factors that coalesce to produce the proper social milieu within which allomothering is facilitated. Functional explanations are not the same as the origins or the processual factors that give rise to this parenting, or substitute-parenting, pattern.

In order to move beyond a functional explanation of alloparenting among monkeys and to answer the original question, it seems necessary to determine what morphologically and anatomically based adaptations of the colobines promoted the social structural circumstances (group structure, size, rank relations, composition, feeding and foraging patterns, defense, and so on) within which allomothering could be favorably selected, and why, then, this behavior could not evolve to the same degree among the cercopithecines.

A review of the literature on primate alloparenting seemed to produce five social-structural conditions within which allomothering could evolve. That is, the literature review indicated that there are necessary but not sufficient conditions for alloparenting among primates to occur (see Table 6.1). These conditions involve particular kinds of social structures which, in turn, are determined by ecological factors that also give rise to the animals' physiological and anatomical adaptations around which social structures emerge. For example, as is shown in Table 6.1, it appears that in order for alloparenting to emerge: (1) the size and basic composition of the social unit must make substitute female caretakers available; (2) neither allomothers nor other group members can afford to harm or injure neonates once they are away from their biological mothers; (3) at least with infants from within their own groups, allomothers must be strongly motivated and not lose interest in the infants, drop them, or leave the infants behind once in possession of them; (4) especially in the context of infant care, female–female competition and status differences must be reduced so that the dominance and/or status of the allomother cannot prevent a mother from retrieving her infant; and, finally (5) feeding and foraging patterns must be relatively cohesive and noncompetitive so that close spatial feeding and high rates of social interaction can facilitate infant transfer and enable a mother to monitor her infant visually for retrieval (McKenna, 1979, pp. 828–829).

Since conditions (1) through (3) seem, in most cases, to be applicable to the cercopithecine species, which do not transfer their young, conditions (4) and (5) are, perhaps, the most crucial ones. They indicate that dominance and rank systems [as originally suggested by Hrdy (1976) and Rowell (1972)] specifically in the context of feeding and foraging patterns provide the clues needed to understand the origins of allomothering—especially since the cercopithecine data clearly reveal that the presence of strict female dominance systems among and within matrilineages made it dangerous, and thus extremely unlikely, that a female of lesser rank (a subordinate) could release her infant to a female of higher rank. In fact, there are many examples in the literature illustrating how infants have been "kidnapped" by high-ranking females and have starved to death in their custody (see Hrdy, 1976; McKenna, 1979, 1981; Quiatt, 1979). Thus, the initial set of questions regarding allomothering must shift to ones that seek to determine the bases of social structural differences between alloparenting and nonalloparenting species. Consequently, the next question to answer is: If dominant systems or status differentials played out in the context of infant care prevented safe allomothering, as it apparently did for the cercopithecines (who seem to be highly motivated to obtain infants), what selective pressures promoted the evolution of status or rank systems among females; what occurred in colobine evolution to reduce the importance of dominance among females (see Dolhinow, McKenna, & von der Haar Laws, 1979)?

TABLE 6.1. Necessary and Sufficient Conditions for Occurrence or Facilitation of
             Alloparenting

1. Group composition makes substitute care givers available, i.e., permanent male
   and/or female(s), and/or siblings. (In order for sibling care to occur generations
   must overlap.)
2. Infants are born relatively in an altricial state and there is a protracted period of
   dependency on care givers so that: Infants are relieved from having to care for
   themselves (Bekoff, 1981).
3. Coefficient of familiarity, relatedness, or both is strong.
4. If separation from the mother or father occurs, care givers will be highly
   motivated and will not lose interest in, drop, or in any purposeful way injure the
   neonate.
5. Especially when nursing infants are cared for by others, alloparents must maintain
   proximity for parental monitoring and retrieval. This condition may not be
   applicable if, for species that forage independently, alloparenting is confined to
   periods in which they sleep or find and share shelter together. (a) Feeding and/or
   foraging is relatively noncompetitive; (b) status and/or rank systems do not
   regulate parent–alloparent interactions.

After much consideration of colobine life strategies and their supporting
physiological, anatomical, and structural bases (see McKenna, 1979), my
own hypothesis is that food competition necessitating rank differentiation is
much greater among and within groups of cercopithecines than it is among
colobine groups. This has been true since the two subfamilies diverged from
a stem cercopithecoid ancestor (see Table 6.2). It appears, then, that among
most cercopithecines, except possibly for the Patas monkey, matrilineages
infused with rather rigid dominance proscriptions may be one way in which
food competition is regulated and the process by which subgroups of related
females succeed to more and better food than others, especially during times
of resource stress or fluctuation (see Dittus, 1977; Hrdy, 1981; Wrangham,
1981, 1979).

Social structures within which status is a salient dimension of female life
preclude the emergence of supplemental care, unless, of course, status
barriers become irrelevant or less important in the context of infant care—
but among the vast majority of cercopithecine species such appears not to
be the case (McKenna, 1979).

This hypothesis is hinged upon whether or not, relative to the
cercopithecine groups, feeding competition and status differentials among
colobine females were diminished, and whether or not the ecological data
could account for this situation. Indeed, both the field and laboratory data
on the colobines revealed that females do not seem to compete directly with
each other at feeding sites; they tend to eat side by side, exhibiting affiliative
behavior without interanimal factionalism and squabbling. Of course, no
species can afford not to be concerned with food, and obtaining it is always
to a certain extent a competitive struggle; however, relative to the

TABLE 6.2. Socioecological Context of the Evolution of Alloparenting Among Old
World Monkeys

Cercopithecoid stem ancestor (high interest in neonates)	
FOREST ENVIRONMENTS Colobidae	FOREST-SAVANNAH MIXED ENVIRONMENTS Cercopithecidae
Physiological and morphological changes in the digestive system	Early adaptations to diverse environmental zones with less resource stability; need to regulate access to food
Leaf-eating adaptations (diverticulate stomachs; fermentation chamber)	
Langurs, Colobus, Proboscis	Baboons, Guenons, Macaques, Mangabeys
1. Breaks down cellulose to derive nutrients in dessicated leaves	1. Rise of kin-based (female-centered) societies—differential hierarchies (ranked lineages and individuals within lineages)
2. Breaks down some known secondary plant compounds	2. Emergence of cheek pouches (see Murray, 1975)
3. Can go without water for longer periods	3. Because males and females do not have the same reproductive interests, and status differences between them can be compromised, the possibility of systems of *Male Care* arises; males can contribute to survival of infants, *if females permit it*
4. Specialized molars which more effectively process food for absorption by digestive system	4. Competition between females precludes extensive allomothering in many species
Less emphasis upon matrilineages as means of regulating access to food during resource stress	
Reduced feeding competition—less interanimal aggression	
Increased female affiliation reduced emphasis upon status differentials among females, permits safe and relaxed transfer of infants (alloparenting)	

cercopithecines, the colobines seem to adjust to feeding stresses differently. Colobine monkeys cope with fluctuations and scarcities with biological and anatomical mechanisms more than with evolved social patterns. One study by Moreno-Black and Maples (1977), in which colobine and cercopithecine species lived in the same habitat, showed that while the cercopithecine species were greatly affected by resource fluctuations (their ranging, spacing, and intragroup behaviors), the group behavior of colobine species changed very little.

But what physiological or anatomical adaptations account for this? It is possible that the dietary regime of the colobines is extremely flexible and much more eclectic than earlier workers ever suspected. Primarily because of their unique masticatory and digestive systems, they are able to move swiftly to foodstuffs unavailable to most other primates. One might say that the digestive physiology of the colobines is best compared to that of a cow and not to other primates. It is the form and enzymatic activity of their digestive system that taxonomically differentiates them from their cercopithecine sisters: for example, the colobine stomach is four-chambered, sacculated or pouched, and diverticulate. By way of ruminant symbionts, the colobine stomach is able to neutralize and safely absorb some known secondary compounds (tannins, alkaloids) ordinarily retained in plants specifically to protect them from hungry herbivores. Moreover, the colobine stomach acts as a fermentation center capable of regularly breaking down cellulose from dry, dessicated leaves to obtain nutrients not available to other primates. And if these abilities are not advantageous enough, the colobines appear to be able to go without water for substantially longer periods of time than the cercopithecines (Jay, 1963). This means that if one were trying to guess whether colobine or cercopithecine would more dramatically change its behavior patterns in the face of changing availability of food resources, the colobines are *not* good candidates, since they have the option of shifting back and forth between high and low nutrition foods and more or less toxic ones.

Assuming the above hypothesis is correct, it means that throughout its evolution the colobine subfamily evolved physiological and anatomical systems that help head off (so to speak) the need to compete as fiercely and aggressively and in the same form as do other species for food when environmental change depletes preferred food resources. In contrast, the cercopithecines may have evolved in environments in which omnivory or physiological adaptations were not good enough; instead, natural selection favored the emergence of ways of reacting to food pressures, which included geneologically based social hierarchies of females supporting each other in *within-* and *between-*group feeding competition (McKenna, 1979 and Wrangham, 1979). This would have the effect of precluding safe, shared, infant care giving—a system of infant care compatible with and complementary to the more affiliative, less hierarchically oriented colobine species.

The most interesting aspect of such research has been the discovery that oftentimes factors which at first seem to be unrelated prove to be related after all. Irrespective of whether this hypothesis stands the test of time (already it has been made more precise by Kaplan and Zucker's 1980 data), it demonstrates the close relationship between aspects of social structure—in this case the influence (or lack thereof) of rank or status systems in a particular resource-specific context. It is fascinating to think that the kind of infant care the neonate langur or colobus monkey experiences (in this case it experiences many different caretakers) is possibly determined by the shape, morphology, and physiological abilities of its species' stomach!

New World Monkey Primates: Howlers, Marmosets, and Tamarins

Thus far, the two major families of Old World monkeys have been considered and have mostly focused upon one form of surrogate care giving,—namely, care extended by other females (allomothering). But there are several other kinds of supplemental surrogate care giving, each of which is, like the colobine adaptive complex, surrounded by a particular socioecological milieu. It is in reviewing these other forms of alloparenting and parenting itself that the diversity of mechanisms that both support and permit parenting systems and styles of care within those systems can be appreciated. Here the nature of parenting and alloparenting among a few New World monkeys, especially the howler monkeys, who exhibit some allomothering behavior, and the marmoset–tamarin species, wherein fathering and sibling alloparenting is extensive, is examined.

Jones' and Glander's analyses of howler monkey alloparenting as contrasted with the colobine-cercopithecine data is considered first. Glander (1975) argues that plant secondary compounds have reduced the amount of leaf nutrient resources to the point wherein, among arboreal foliovores of the New World forests, intraspecific competition for food has intensified. One means by which the calories of females can be conserved in environments of low nutrient and energy yields is through allomothering or "baby-sitting" behavior. While other individuals are holding or sitting with their infants, mothers are able to forage more efficiently and with less energy loss than they would expend if they were carrying their babies (Jones, 1980; Glander, 1975).

If Glander's hypothesis accords nicely with a model developed by Riemann (1982), which attempts to describe the varying conditions that give rise to alloparenting among mammals and birds, it is interesting that the very condition facilitating allomothering among this species (i.e., limited food supply) is the very condition that prevents it among the Old World monkey cercopithecines. However, it appears that among howlers competition and status itself become important to animals as they compete for very specific food reserves, and status is not defined by membership in particular lineages as it is among the cercopithecine species; in fact, matrilineages are not powerful organizational units that confer status and privilege across all aspects of social life. According to Jones (1980), rank is inversely related to age, and competitive advantages are more or less achieved by individuals acting alone in specific encounters over food. Moreover, infants are born during periods of high food availability, which diminishes feeding competition at this time.

The fact that limited amounts of allomothering occur among howlers even though status systems exist does not necessarily invalidate the notion that rank acts as a restraint on safe infant transfer. Recall that among howler monkeys rank is not always or necessarily generalizable to all aspects of social life—i.e., it does not permit animals to dominate over others in all goals. Most especially, status differences between females seem not at all to manifest themselves frequently and in the context of allomothering; this activity may well occur independent of dominance. In any event, the kinds of dominance and subordinance interactions common among howler monkeys occur with much less regularity and intensity than among the cercopithecines (see Glander, 1975; Jones, 1980), who do not ordinarily exhibit allomothering in relaxed and frequent ways.

There are, of course, bound to be many variations in the conditions within which allomothering is expressed, as well as in the factors that motivate it and its effects on the participants (see below). But it is important to note that, like the colobines, among the New World howler monkeys allomothering activities (assuming that Glander may be correct about secondary compounds limiting the howler diet) are influenced by the availability (or lack thereof) of foodstuffs. In this case it may be mostly the mother and not the infant, or the substitute care giver, who benefits, but more on this question later.

Perhaps one of the more interesting groups to consider when examining the conditions under which supplemental, substitute, and surrogate care giving emerged is the marmoset–tamarin group; taxonomically they are considered part of the superfamily Ceboidea and the family Callithricidae (see Table 6.3). This leads to a consideration of the possible evolutionary bases, the socioecological conditions, permitting male care of infants, or paternal behavior. It is well known that these callithricids are monogamous, not sexually dimorphic, and that both males and females as well as siblings are involved in infant care (see Epple, 1975, on tamarins, and Ingram, 1975, on marmosets). While it may be the case that allomothering emerged among colobines rather opportunistically, and without natural selection actually designing it (see McKenna, 1981), it can be hypothesized that among these small monogamous forms parental care may well be designed by selection. For example, Kleiman (1977) argues that the exceedingly high litter weight to maternal weight ratio characterizing callithricids necessitates the presence of at least one individual (logically an adult male) to help carry infants (since another female adult would compete for too many calories, particularly during her pregnancy). Most marmosets and tamarins give birth to twins, whose collective weight can approximate between 18 and 20% of the

TABLE 6.3. Possible Socioecological Context of Parenting and Alloparenting Among
          Marmoset-Tamarins

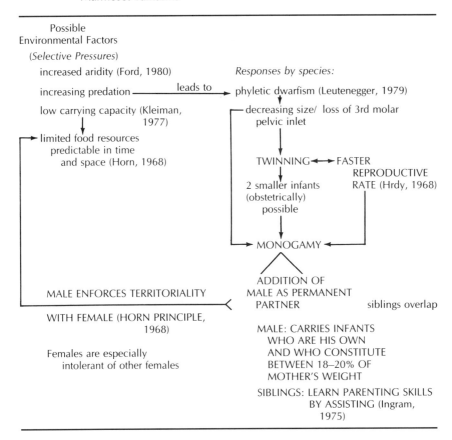

Possible
Environmental Factors
  (Selective Pressures)
    increased aridity (Ford, 1980)   Responses by species:
    increasing predation ——— leads to ——→ phyletic dwarfism (Leutenegger, 1979)
    low carrying capacity (Kleiman,   ┌— decreasing size/ loss of 3rd molar
                        1977)   pelvic inlet
  → limited food resources
      predictable in time
      and space (Horn, 1968)   TWINNING ←——→ FASTER
                                              ↓   REPRODUCTIVE
                                           2 smaller infants RATE (Hrdy, 1968)
                                           (obstetrically)
                                             possible

                                           → MONOGAMY ←

                                              ADDITION OF
    MALE ENFORCES TERRITORIALITY   MALE AS PERMANENT
                                              PARTNER   siblings overlap
    WITH FEMALE (HORN PRINCIPLE,
                  1968)   MALE: CARRIES INFANTS
                                              WHO ARE HIS OWN
    Females are especially   AND WHO CONSTITUTE
      intolerant of other females   BETWEEN 18–20% OF
                                              MOTHER'S WEIGHT

                                           SIBLINGS: LEARN PARENTING SKILLS
                                                     BY ASSISTING (Ingram,
                                                     1975)

mother's, thereby placing an excessive, if not impossible, physical burden on her.

Hrdy (1981) points out that compared with many other New World monkeys, especially the larger (cebids) variety, marmoset–tamarin females have extremely high reproductive rates; they become pregnant and some give birth to a new set of twins within a year following delivery, sometimes every 5 or 6 months. From this perspective Hrdy argues that (and this conforms to the data above) "mutual intolerance of mothers with big babies and their fast reproductive rate severely constrains the likely activity of males." In other words, male reproductive success is determined by the manner in which he accommodates female reproductive needs, and both of their reproductive success is determined by aspects of their changing environments requiring concealment from predation and adaptations to high, but limited, protein food reserves. In fact, Ingram (1975, p. 204, cited in Redican and Taub, 1981) argues that "the most plausible hypothesis for this involvement of the father in the care of the young is related to the freeing of maternal energy for milk production." She points out that the marmoset mother needs to forage for food continuously to support the cost of milk production. It is interesting to think that she can "conceive" again during her postpartum estrus, and that 2 weeks after having given birth to one set of twins she could be supporting another set *in utero*. This explains why mother marmosets do not share food with infants, whereas the fathers "may even chew solid food for infants during the first month" (Redican and Taub, 1981, p. 208).

The alloparenting of siblings who may, it has been reported, suppress their own reproductive capacity in the presence of adults, provides opportunities for males to learn how to manipulate and carry infants, which is critical to their own reproductive success (Epple, 1975, on tamarins; also see Riemann, 1982). A number of investigators, including Hearn and Lunn (1975) and Hoage (1977), have demonstrated that if they are deprived of caretaking experiences with younger siblings, marmosets will not successfully be able to care for their own offspring (Redican and Taub, 1981). There may be an interesting trade-off here: While sibling participation in care of the young increases the foraging efficiency of both parents, the parents might actually assist their older offspring in setting up their own territories in neighboring regions.

It is interesting to consider, then, that like the colobine-cercopithecine situation, several physiological and socioecological factors coalesce to create parenting patterns: Changing food availability and predation rates among the marmoset-tamarin groups have produced a trend toward smaller body size (phyletic dwarfism) that in turn promotes twinning and the social acquisition of a permanent adult male breeding partner whose assistance in child rearing is required by the female. This proves adaptive for the male, since he contributes to the survival of his own offspring, with whom half his genes are shared. Moreover, the inclusion of siblings in a social network of overlapping generations assures the perpetuation of parenting styles. Older siblings are able to practice care-giving behavior on their younger siblings, possibly increasing the fitness of all the participants (both immediately and in the long run). In all of this rank plays no role; males and females are equally dominant and rank between parents and siblings obviously does not play a significant role during alloparenting episodes.

Siamang and Chimpanzee

Ecological conditions, especially those related to food, once again become important when examining the experiences of the infant siamang, a lesser ape of Southeast Asia. Like the marmosets, siamangs live in isolated, extended family units, although females do not experience multiple (twin) births. Wrangham (1979) argues that monogamy and subsequent high male parental investment evolved as a direct consequence of the inability of females to maintain an exclusive territory, which they need and which can only be secured by the added contribution of a permanent, adult mate. Since females are a limiting resource in male reproductive success and are distributed at low densities due to concentrated and limited food resources, the male associates permanently with the female and participates in caring for his own offspring. In fact, Chivers (1971, 1972, cited in Redican and Taub, 1981) reports that after the first 12 to 16 months of life the infant siamang is carried, sleeps with, and is groomed by the father until they establish independence. Apparently while mother is the primary caretaker of the infant, father is the primary caretaker of the juvenile, and in this manner offspring develop important bonds with both parents at different stages in the life cycle.

It is now clear that male and female chimpanzees exhibit quite different foraging strategies and that males tend to be more gregarious (associate more frequently and for longer periods of time with others) than females (Wrangham, 1979b). The matricentric unit remains the most important network of social relations within the chimpanzee community and, depending upon the age of the infant and the unique characteristics of female and male siblings in the unit, alloparenting can occur (see Hamburg and McCown, 1979). Goodall (1971) describes the development of Flint, and the important role that Fifi, his sister, played in his care; she vividly documents how Fifi learned particular maternal skills from her mother, which she employed when she gave birth to her own infant. As Clark (1977) reports, there is tremendous variability in the amount of interest individuals other than the mother exhibit in infants, and mothers vary substantially from each other in terms of their willingness to submit their infants to the care of others—offspring included. Chimpanzee alloparenting, though certainly helpful to the participants in ways described below, does not appear to have been designed by natural selection, but may be a product of the prolonged and intense relationships shared by siblings and mothers.

Adult Male-Infant Interactions: More Than Meets the Eye

Thus far allomothers and the caretaking behavior of fathers have been discussed, but clearly there are many other instances in which related and nonrelated adult males care for infants (see Redican and Taub, 1981, for review). In fact, we are now beginning to realize that males affect the experiences of infants in important ways (see Hinde, 1983, for discussions). For example, studying the yellow baboon in Kenya, Altmann (1980) demonstrated that the presence of a male near a mother—infant pair increases the frequency with which the infant is out of physical contact with her, possibly hastening or contributing positively to its development of independence and status; clearly, Altmann demonstrated that the presence of a male who is primarily associating with the infant's mother improves the quality of the infant's experiences as judged by the fact that males act to inhibit kidnapping and pulling by other females. Taub (1979) has argued that Barbary macaque males develop important care giving relationships with infants that increase infant survival; moreover, female Barbary macaques may select mates using a criterion which includes how effectively the male administers infant care. Among anubis baboons, Packer (1980) has argued that by carrying infants, males decrease the probability of infants' being threatened by other males as well as protect themselves from possible attacks. Seyfarth's (1978) data on South African baboons also show that the presence of the adult male during the female's pregnancy and lactation probably assures that the quality of life of possibly his own offspring is improved.

In fact, the most recent data on many different species of baboons (anubis, yellow, olive) are beginning to reveal that male–female "friend-ships" and relationships exist beyond, around, and perhaps independent of events in the menstrual cycle (see Hinde, 1983, and especially Smuts, 1983). Infants accrue important benefits from mother's associates, not the least of which are relationships with particular adult males who, quite possibly, are their own fathers. It is important to point out that the precise interactions between the adult male and infant (whether it be care, protection, or grooming) may not have been directly designed by natural selection, though it may well have genetic consequences (see Redican and Taub, 1981; Katz and Konner, 1981 for reviews; Seyfarth, 1978; Packer, 1980; Busse and Hamilton, 1980; Altmann, 1980; Strum, 1983, for specific examples). It is also important to note that the genetic relationship that exists between the infant and the adult male associates of the infant's mother is not always known. If Taub (1979) is correct in thinking that Barbary macaque females choose particularly good caretaker males to be fathers of their offspring, then these macaques may well have a system of alloparenting that was designed by natural selection. Among the other species, however, it is not yet possible to say, although at present it appears that such adult male–infant interactions are fortuitous outcomes of male and female relationships (see Smuts, 1983, for discussion).

PROXIMATE MOTIVATION, ELICITORS, AND FACILITATION OF ALLOPARENTING BEHAVIOR

Biological and Social Factors

Even though any relationship between kin selection-parental investment theories and alloparenting is, at this point, uncertain, in many general ways the data support the theories. It is unfortunate that so little is known about the actual genetic relatedness of offspring and their caretakers, because a higher level of preciseness would be possible if this kind of data were available; but very few studies permit a comparison of behavior among individuals wherein the actual relationship is known (but see Altmann, 1980; Smith, 1981; Kurland, 1977; Silk, 1981, for exceptions), and this is likely to be the case for quite some time, although human data can clarify some of these issues (see Chagnon, Flinn, and Melancon, 1979).

However, several other important questions must be considered before the evolutionary process can be adequately addressed in detail, and these include: (1) what seems to motivate individuals other than the parent to care for the offspring, including immediate social and physiological phenomena; (2) what horizontal effects or benefits in an immediate sense does the alloparenting experience have on the participants; (3) what vertical effects, or less immediate but future effects or benefits, does alloparenting have on the participants; and (4) how uniform and consistent are the effects of alloparenting across primate species.

The question of what motivates an individual to increase proximity to infants and extend direct care to them, and/or to carry them, is a very difficult issue; it may be incorrect to separate factors that seem to be physiological motivators from social motivators. For example, contact with an infant by an alloparent can provide the caretaker with stimulation, including body warmth and body sensations, possibly of a positive nature (see Hofer, 1978), and, at the same time, infant care giving, or contact with an infant, has been known to raise the care giver's status (see Kurland, 1977) or assure immunity from attack/harassment by others (Deag and Crook, 1971). Perhaps the caretaker is, indeed, protecting the infant (Busse and Hamilton, 1980) from older male immigrants, or using the infant to maintain a peaceful relationship with another; perhaps the alloparent cares for an infant because the individual wants to construct a certain kind of relationship, to reduce social ambiguity with the infant's parent; perhaps the alloparent is motivated out of curiosity or is moved to interact with a novel, perhaps playful creature in its enviroment.

Infant Characteristics that Elicit Alloparenting and/or Parenting

Considering that the primate neonate is an evolved organism, preadapted to its developmental setting, it is expected that certain characteristics will evoke care and nurturance, or, at least, will tend not to elicit aggression (although the latter is not guaranteed) (Alley, 1980). Recall that the very characteristics which evoke nonaggressive responses (size, color, and so on) are those that at other times evoke killings. The fact that infanticide can and does occur suggests that while there is a social context within which individuals are biologically prepared to respond to infants positively, there is a different social context in which individuals are prepared to respond destructively (Hrdy, 1979).

Assuming that alloparents mostly find themselves in a context within which alloparenting can occur and that they have been socialized (have learned) to respond to infants, the following characteristics tend to elicit alloparental interest (see Figure 6.3). They include: (1) the infant's small size and neonatal (pelage) coat color (see Alley, 1980); (2) the infant's dimensions, including large head and ears with eyes falling at the midline of the skull, chubby cheeks (for nursing), rounded chin (evoke the "cute response"); (3) hairlessness or patch baldness; (4) high pitched, staccato vocalizations; (5) unfocused stares; (6) awkward body thrusts, limb movements; (7) the infant's smells; (8) the infant's soft, unpigmented skin. Obviously it is almost impossible to tell at this point what traits (morphological, kinetic, olfactory) or cues alloparents are responding to; and, of course, it is difficult to know the degree to which knowledge of immediate social benefits gained by caring for infants is affecting the strength of alloparents' responses to cues (see Alley, 1980, for review).

Moreover, it is likely that the strength and eagerness with which individuals respond to infant cues can partially be traced to their own experiences during development. Recall that the marmosets must be exposed to care giving during their premature years in order to deal with infants successfully as adults (see Ingram, 1975). In addition, Harlow describes "motherless" monkeys who were terrified when their own infants were born and consequently killed, mutilated, and/or rejected them (see Sackett et al., 1982, for review).

It is also important to consider the role that the infant plays in actively encouraging its own care, as Lewis and Rosenblum (1974) demonstrated a few years ago. While the precise age of the infant and its neurological maturity will affect the degree of infant manipulation, it now seems evident that the infant may control more of its own care than was previously believed. During a project in which 6-month-old Indian langurs were separated for 2 weeks from their mothers, Dolhinow (1980) was surprised to learn that despite the fact that Indian langur females are eager and frequent allomothers, the *infants* and not the adult females initiated and were largely responsible for their adoption by particular females. More surprising was the fact that most of the infants did not go back to their own mothers when they were reunited with them a mere 2 weeks later (see Dolhinow, 1980, and Dolhinow and De May 1983, for discussion of adoption).

During the next decade hypotheses testing different variables will, undoubtedly, be proposed, and the results will reveal the strength of infant signals on particular alloparents. At present an accurate picture of the effects of the immediate social circumstances on the ability of infants to elicit or

Table 6.4. Biological and Social Factors that Elicit Care

Infant Characteristics Promoting Care Giving, or the "Cute Response"

1. Large eyes, midline on skull
2. Chubby, nursing cheeks, rounded chin
3. Baldness, high-pitched cooing
4. Awkward locomotor movements
5. Neonatal coat color
6. Small size
7. Olfactory cues

	Act on	
Mother	Father	Alloparents (Allomothers and Allofathers)
1. Circulating estrogens, oxytocin, prolactin	1. Improves or continues access to female (mother) and, thus, the infant	1. Novelty item, play object
2. Nursing sensation	2. Association with female	2. Coefficient of familiarity, proximity
3. Learned social role	3. Body warmth	3. Relationship with infant's mother
4. Body warmth	4. Tactile stimulation	4. Increase in status when in association with infant
5. Tactile stimulation	5. Learned social role	5. Learned social role
6. Status increases		6. Reduce aggression inflicted by others
		7. Increases proximity to resources
		8. Improves status as a potential mate and eventual parent

161

induce care does not exist, and why some individuals are more motivated than others to exhibit alloparenting is also unknown.

Factors Blocking or Inhibiting Alloparental Care, Including "Significant Others"

Earlier in this chapter, it was argued that social circumstances, specifically rank or dominance systems among females, particularly when they affect feeding, foraging, and infant care, seriously act to inhibit allomothering. Here it should be stressed that mothers especially may act as a conservative line of defense against infant–nonmother contacts. Many researchers have found this to be the case, but the most interesting aspect that is not regularly considered is the extent to which mothers actively and with purpose prevent males from performing what might be regarded as serious caretaking roles. This is mentioned in passing because a general comparison of the frequency of male and female involvement in alloparental activities would lead one to believe that, perhaps due to hormonal regimes selected to optimize her "maternal" responses, females are more likely than males to respond to infant signals and cues; that is, on a biological level to protect the high metabolic investment that females experience by carrying and giving birth to infants (compared with the low biological investment of males), it should be expected that they will be more powerfully motivated to play care-giving roles. While this reasoning makes sense, in many respects the willingness of males to caretake and, subsequently, attach to infants is seriously constrained not by their own biology (or lack of certain kinds of biological attributes) but by the social aggression of females themselves.

Redican's (1975) fascinating data on Rhesus macaques, points out that if one bases a judgment only upon field data, it appears that Rhesus adult males are not interested in infants, or, at least, they are not *too* interested in them. But his data clearly reveal that given unrestricted access to infants (the adult males were housed alone with infants) and despite their aggressive reputations, the adult males will actively father and care for infants. As the investigator phrases it: "They will attach to them in ways that the field data would never have permitted us to predict." His study showed, and in retrospect not suprisingly, that mothers have a powerful effect in determining who interacts with infants and juveniles. This study appears to have some implications for human parenting roles, and reminds us that even among nonhuman primates the tasks animals are permitted to do and those they potentially could and would want to do may be quite different. In this case, the males may be in social circumstances that prevent them from using their biological capacity to respond to infants. In my own study of captive langurs, repeated instances were observed wherein one subadult male was immediately attacked by adult females when he gently carried and groomed a 4-month-old infant. His repeated attempts to do so in the face of imminent attack made it clear that this male was prepared to respond to infants, but that the nature of male langur social roles (or other unknown factors) would not permit it, at least not very easily.

WHICH EVOLUTIONARY PROCESSES ACCOUNT FOR WHICH KINDS OF ALLOPARENTAL AND PARENTAL CARE?

When one considers the degree of vulnerability experienced by the primate neonate it is not surprising that natural selection has produced a maturational setting within which a number of individuals are highly motivated to respond to infants. But the question of why animals respond in an immediate sense can prove to be different from why they "should" respond in an evolutionary sense, and in what way they should respond, and what processes are responsible.

In this section some of the problems that arise in using evolutionary processes to account for alloparenting are discussed (especially see Riemann, 1982; Dunbar, 1982; and MacDonald and Moehlman, 1982, for theoretical review). While kin selection theory and parental investment theory (per se) have provided an important framework for studying infant care, they may not fully or adequately account for the forms of alloparenting exhibited by caretakers, or perhaps, strictly speaking, the kinds of immediate social factors that make it useful for animals to act as caretakers. Moreover, degree of relatedness may not always be the determining factor in predicting who cares for offspring (Hood, 1978; Kurland, 1977; McKenna, 1979), and the fact that substitute care giving often detrimentally affects infants testifies to this point.

Consider Kleiman and Malcolm's (1981) review of the form, extensiveness, and evolutionary bases of mammalian male parental investment. Of course they concentrate on male parental investment, but their findings are instructive to the consideration of how to explain alloparenting in general. They note that between 9 and 10% of mammalian genera exhibit direct male parental investment, with direct investment by males being defined as "those acts which a male performs toward young that have an immediate physical influence on them which increases survivorship (feeding, carrying, sleeping with young, playing with young)" (Kleiman and Malcolm, 1981). This figure is surprisingly high, they point out, in light of the fact that male mammals cannot lactate, or, for the most part at least, provide as much physical care during the neonatal phase of development.

Kleiman and Malcolm's review indicates that the percentage of male mammals exhibiting direct parental investment is higher than the 7.7% of mammalian genera in which monogamy occurs (there are approximately 18% monogamous species among the primates). They observe that "the potential for direct male parental investment in mammals is considerable and is not necessarily tied to a monogamous mating system" (1981, p. 371) in which paternity certainty is high, as kin selection theories and, indeed, Trivers' parental investment theory might predict. "In summary, high levels of direct care appear to have evolved several times independently among the mammals. It is common in carnivores, perissodactyls, and primates, and may be found to be more common among rodents and insectivores" (Kleiman and Malcolm, 1981, p. 371). While they recognize the Trivers' notion of parental investment is a factor governing the operation of sexual selection, they consider that correlations between mating systems, variance in reproductive success, and differential investment are the result of "*coevolution* between factors rather than one directing the evolution of the other two" (Kleiman and Malcolm, 1981, p. 375).

Bekoff's perspective on why siblings are likely to participate in caring for each other provides clues about pertinent proximate variables that may explain the form and pattern of alloparenting for which kin selection cannot account. Bekoff (1981) maintains that animals are not selected to behave toward siblings in any particular way. He argues that there is nothing special about mammalian sibling identification, "although the consequences of sibling interactions are significant, since full siblings at least may serve as the major vehicle of shared gene propagation to future generations." In other words, a sibling is regarded as a sibling by virtue of early social experience, and "exposure is accomplished for the most part through developmental tracks." Thus, "if genetically unrelated, or distantly unrelated individuals grow up under the same environmental conditions that characterize a species typical sibling environment, it is predicted that they will behave as siblings because of a shared past history of repeated exposure and conse-quent familiarity with one another. The key proximate mechanism appears to be degree of familiarity that usually is strongly related to r, especially in species in which there are multi-individual litters and protracted periods of dependency on parents, and possible other caregivers, and by which fitness is enhanced" (1981, pp. 3l4–315). Bekoff calls this degree of familiarity a "coefficient of familiarity," and proposes a mathematical model as to how familiarity can be used as a guage to predict future sibling recognition and/or instances in which an animal may act in the interest of another—kin or nonkin.

Bekoff's point is well taken since there may well be "nothing special" about the adult male marmoset, or baboon, or even the mother's behavior, that cannot be explained by way of social experience and familiarity. Clearly, we are all familiar with the evidence which suggests that among primates, reproductive success depends largely upon early and continuous learning experiences, even for the mother. The question is, of course, how many or what kinds of genotypes have actually been selected for that underlie specific forms of care—or specific forms of learning?

Quiatt (1979) echoes some similar concerns about the manner in which kin selection theory especially has been utilized to explain alloparenting—in particular allomothering. For example, Quiatt points out that it is "subtly distorting to 'explain' aunting in terms of kin selection, which is not at all to say that it cannot be usefully explained within a framework of kin selection theory." To begin with, it is not always the close relatives, or relatives at all, who are doing the care giving. Quiatt argues that it is important to establish how natural selection operates to "produce specific kinds of outcomes," and to decide "which outcomes in a range of outcomes associated with a definite category of interactions are not likely to occur, and which of those that do occur appear to be selected for and are not fortuitous." It is his contention that, among species in which a good deal of infant transfer can be found, the potential for direct competition between mothers of varying skills (that is, skills in retrieving her infant, monitoring its care, and so on) is greater and, hence, "allomaternal behavior may be no more than a fortuitous outcome of selection for a behavioral orientation toward conspecifics that is essential to normal maternal performance . . . " (Quiatt, 1979, p. 316).

WHO BENEFITS, AT WHAT POINT IN THE LIFE CYCLE, AND AT WHAT COST?

Even though too much explanatory emphasis has been given to the possible beneficial effects of alloparenting, the "benefits" question is not unimportant. However, it may well be useful to consider the differences between beneficial effects and the function of a behavior, since the two are often used interchangeably. This is at worst incorrect, at very least imprecise. We will use the term "function" to imply an adaptation, i.e., for instances in which it is shown that alloparenting contributes to the individual's reproductive success and thus appears to have been designed by natural selection (after Symons, 1978).

Mother (or Father) as a Beneficiary

Depending upon the particular species, how "mother" benefits, or at least the degree by which she benefits, will vary. For example, howler and marmoset mothers may conserve calories while their infants are being held by others (see Tables 6.5 and 6.6). The howler mother's lactational and overall reproductive costs may not be as high as the fast-breeding, fast-metabolizing marmoset female who is nursing and gestating two sets of twins simultaneously; but, nevertheless, where environments provide low nutritious foods, most primate mothers conceivably could profit by having their infants temporarily cared for by alloparents. The degree of benefit depends on how often it occurs, how much mothers actually gain in nutrients once away from their infants, or the net gain of calories to the net loss incurred by, we can presume, traveling longer distances to obtain food. Of course, there are some possible risks involved that can counter the benefits—primarily the quality of care the infant receives in mother's absence, and whether or not continuous carrying by others, and the kind of monitoring and retrieving it required by mother actually burns up more calories than is gained by foraging independently. Altmann (1980) proposed the very interesting idea that completely dependent infants (ones continuously on mothers' ventrums) may be less calorically draining than semi-independent infants who require mothers' constant vigilance, monitoring, and collecting.

Alloparents as Beneficiaries

The possible benefits to alloparents include the learning of maternal skills and competence (the practice-makes-perfect idea, or learning-to-mother hypothesis). Exposure to infants, learning to transport and ventrally orient, clearly make sense, but so far there is little data except indirect evidence that allomothers, for example, become more competent. Maternal behavior skills do seem to be cumulative; among many species the infants of multiparous mothers experience much higher survival rates than primiparous mothers. Yet, in a captive colony of female langur monkeys wherein the most permissive kinds of allomothering occur, first-time mothers (even with all their practicing) had substantial numbers of infants die relative to the older, more experienced mothers (McKenna, 1975), although Indian langur infant mortality figures are, on the average, about 5 to 10% lower than those of nonsharing species. Therefore, there is some possibility that the alloparent can benefit from and contribute to the survival of its own offspring by practicing on some other individual's infants. Of course, with many incompetent caretakers practicing on the infants of competent caretakers, it need not be pointed out that whatever benefits the infant derives from its more skilled mother are negated by the less adequate care of the substitute mother. Still, as Quiatt (1979) notes, the competent mothers could be monitoring the care of the unskilled care giver to assure that the infants are not handled too roughly; however, based upon my own observations of langur caretaking, infants can experience extremely rough treatment (see McKenna, 1981).

Alloparents can also benefit by increasing their statuses as a result of handling infants and gaining access to social resources (grooming partners, proximity to dominant animals) and physical (preferred) resources while in possession of infants—the so-called "infant-as-a-social-passport" syndrome. The "agonistic-buffering" notion that Deag and Crook (1971) proposed

TABLE 6.5. The Question of Beneficial Effects Across the Life Cycle

Infants	Mothers	Fathers	Alloparents
1. Enriched socialization (Hrdy, 1976) and learning modes	1. Foraging independence expands and possibly calories are saved in nutrient-poor environments (Glander, 1975; Jones, 1980)	1. Releases male for patrolling activities, as well as for defense resource procurement	1. Practice-makes-perfect or the learning to mother and/or father hypothesis caretaking skills are transferred to increase survival chances of one's own infant
2. Hastens socialization	2. For species experiencing high reproductive rates, high milk production, i.e., marmosets/tamarins, mother is best able to support two sets of twins	2. Reduces calorie output	2. Care-giving skills are displayed to potential mates, i.e., the Barbary macaques (males) (Taub, 1979)
3. Increased chance of adoption should mother die, though infant age and infant's initiative may intervene here (Dolhinow, 1983)	3. Future reproductive success is increased relative to the number of resources (metabolic and others) not immediately siphoned off (Wiegle, 1982) by present litter or single offspring	3. Helps preserve resources for future reproduction (body resources)	3. Increases immediate status, and increases one's proximity to resources
4. As in the Colobines, infants are prepared to lead a life independent of mother's social network; at least mother's role in establishing the status or rank of the neonate is limited	4. With infrequent nursing ovulation is hastened, as lactational amenorrhea is shorter in duration	4. Bonds strengthened with alloparents (mostly siblings)?	4. Circumvents threats, aggression from others (the infant as a social passport syndrome)
5. Increased tactile and locomotor experiences hastening physical maturity	5. Bonds are strengthened, facilitated, or created with alloparents— group structure is strengthened?		5. Protects one's own infant, or the infant of a relative from aggression of immigrant males (Packer, 1980)

TABLE 6.6. The Question of Potential Costs and Risks of Alloparenting Across the Life Cycle to Major Participants

Infants	Mothers	Fathers	Alloparents
1. Nipple access is disrupted	1. Injuries to her infant diminish her "investment" in what amounts to an already "expensive" offspring	1. Injuries to infants affect father's "investment" as well; but his "losses" can be recovered more easily than can the mother's	1. Increased vulnerability to predators when carrying infants?
2. General disruption of sleep patterns varies with age	2. Stress increases during retrieval	2. Increased vulnerability to predators when carrying infants	2. Increased competition to obtain infants can lead to aggression
3. Serious injury in the custody of incompetent (especially) young care givers	3. Semi-independence of an infant may be calorically more expensive than complete dependence by the infant on the mother. How much energy is lost monitoring the location and handling of her infant? (Does it negate the gain? See Altmann, 1980)	3. Increased energy loss during infant care giving	3. Increased energy loss during care giving
4. In extreme cases, death, if mother is unable to retrieve the infant to feed it			4. Possible suppression of own reproduction?
5. Abuse suffered in the context of alloparenting may lead to abusive parenting detrimental to one's own offspring			

showed how males could use infants in triadic situations to lessen the potential of aggression being inflicted on them by other males; though for Barbary macaques Taub (1980) rejects this idea in favor of viewing such interactions in a much larger social context, which gives explanatory emphasis to the relationship existing between the particular male and the particular infant—and not to the allofather and his fellow adult male competitors.

The alloparent can also benefit from the bond-building that can occur by sharing and caring for another infant—the infant becomes a facilitator of social behavior of a wide variety, including the protective behaviors possibly of the parents when the alloparent gives birth to her own infant. With respect to male–infant interactions, females may "choose" males (so selection theory might predict) based upon nurturant skills, or in the case of Barbary macaques, overall paternal qualities (see Taub, 1979).

The "costs" to alloparents are, of course, the costs of parenting in general; that is, possible increased vulnerability to predation by being slower, more conspicuous, or less agile (all of these, or one or two). In addition, the metabolic costs of carrying or interacting with the infant must be considered as well, and these costs purely in energy loss (weight loss) are substantial. Altmann (1980) points out that mothers' chances of survival are diminished when carrying an infant during the first year of its life.

With respect to sibling alloparents, as in the case of marmosets, care extended to relations increases the reproductive efficiency and, indeed, survival of individuals (mothers, brothers, or sisters) with whom genes are shared. Successful reproduction by these individuals contributes to their own inclusive fitness (the sum total of one's own fitness plus that of one's relatives with whom genes by way of common descent are shared). Of course, the one important corollary to this is that there is some genetic component to sibling care; that is, some genotypes underlie the willingness to extend the care in the first place. If such is indeed the case for marmosets, and if this behavior by the father and the siblings actually contributes to increased reproductive success (as it appears to, since siblings need exposure to parenting to become successful parents and mothers require relief), then alloparenting has an adaptive function here—it was designed by natural selection to do what it does for those whom it was designed.

Infant as Beneficiary

The benefits of alloparenting for the infants lead to a somewhat contradictory situation. Several researchers have reported that among those species that exhibit extensive allomothering, the chances are increased that an infant will be adopted should its mother die; thus, the adoption means infant survival, and nobody will argue that this raises the infant's (and the mother's) fitness. Both Jay (1963) and Boggess (1976) studied langurs in very different environmental settings and observed instances where, indeed, infants who were extensively allomothered survived after their mothers' untimely demise. Kaufman's (1977) research on bonnet macaques in captivity also confirms the idea that allomothering can be linked to the increased survival chances of the infant upon loss of the mother.

However, allomothering does not assure adoptions, and Dolhinow's work suggests that the infant is largely responsible for it. Even among langurs (the permissive allomothers), where adoption is theoretically available, infants have died following mother loss (Dolhinow, 1980). The exact age and condition of the infant at the time of its mother's death probably has a lot to do with successful adoptions, since a very young infant adopted by a nonlactating female will die, regardless of the allomother's care. Moreover, there are other instances and circumstances in which primate young are adopted that could not have been predicted based on whether or not they were allomothered (Dolhinow, 1980). But since adoptions can occur, this must surely be included in the category of beneficial effect, though it is doubtful that selection designed this; it may be just a fortuitous outcome— a statistical summation (Symons, 1978, might say) of other behavioral adaptations and/or idiosyncracies of the participants.

Another possible beneficial effect involves the exposure to different personalities, to both competent and incompetent care-giving styles, to young and old animals, and to the social dynamics involved in infant transfers; these experiences may familiarize the infant with a whole range of emotions and species behavior patterns. Hrdy (1976) suggests that such experiences may hasten socialization for Indian langur neonates, although this might not be an advantage unless, of course, it leads to a longer reproductive career. Such a result still needs to be demonstrated.

Even permissive allomothers assert some control over who obtains their infants, though their actions in preventing or inhibiting access, or in retrieving the infant from an undesirable care giver (except if it is a male), are usually gentle and nonaggressive (McKenna, 1981). It is also important to point out that infants born successively to the same mother are treated differently by her; that is, Dolhinow (1977), found that for one infant a mother may be more restrictive throughout the infant's development and monitor it more diligently, but for some other infant, born at a future time, she may be continuously permissive and less careful about who handles it. This means that the quality of care infants experience, and thus the benefits they experience, vary from one infant to the next, even when they have the same mother. Many factors can account for these differences (Dolhinow, 1980; McKenna, 1979).

Among Barbary macaques, Burton (1972) showed that alloparenting encouraged the development of locomotor skills by requiring infants to walk to and approach the caretakers, while the infants' mothers did not require this of them. In fact, Taub (1979) found it significant that one infant who died in his study group was the one without a special allofather; he proposes that adult or subadult allofathers may be critical to the survival of infant Barbary macaques.

There is no doubt that infants can be the key losers in alloparenting episodes, at least judging from Hrdy's (1976) review and many other papers written subsequently. Both in the field and in captivity many Indian langur infants futilely resist and frequently protest their transfers—and it is no wonder. As reported elsewhere (see McKenna, 1981), during this author's year's study of captive Indian langurs it was not unusual to witness very young neonates being carried upside down, screaming, or being tugged simultaneously in two directions. Cuts, bruises, and mutilated tails often were the result of what might be considered excessive allomothering. Hrdy's (1977) field study reports similar instances wherein infants are roughed up during allomothering episodes.

After observing the death of a Rhesus macaque infant, which was "aunted to death" by a high-status female after its own lower status biological mother was unable to retrieve it, Quiatt supports the notion that in this and probably in many other unreported instances neither the infant nor the mother benefited. Possibly only the kidnapper gained some benefit, which for lack of data remains unspecified. Quiatt stresses that the consequences of aunting to the target infant and its mother may be of little or no benefit, or detrimental, while those to the aunt are likely to improve genetic fitness either indirectly, by providing her with training in advance of actual motherhood, or directly (because fitness is relative), by reducing the fitness of the competition, or in both ways at once" (1979). This kind of reasoning makes Quiatt's approach very useful. He has allowed for the possibility of multiple outcomes of a selected behavior, which may or may not have arisen because it favored one outcome over another. He disagrees with conclusions that juxtapose the terms "selfishness" and "altruism," because among primates the complexity and context of behaviors render these statements meaningless. With these terms dispensed with as explanatory tools, he concludes that allomothering tests maternal skills and acts as a conservative line of defense against inefficient mothers (see also McKenna, 1979).

ALLOPARENTING AND LIFE CYCLE CONNECTEDNESS

Attention in this section will be confined to two families of primates—the colobines and callithricids, and some comparative references to the cercopithecines and the apes will be made. The question of the extent to which early alloparenting experiences, either as the active participant (alloparent) or as the object of alloparenting (the infant), are projected to other phases in the life cycle needs to be addressed.

The best work has been done on the marmosets (reviewed by Redican and Taub, 1981), which shows that the young do, indeed, require exposure to infants (either observing and/or actual participation) before they can execute parenting skills. This includes the carrying behavior of the males (see Epple, 1975; Hearn and Lunn, 1975). Redican and Taub indicate that even though the data on marmosets "prove nothing about human beings . . . they do propose a potentially valuable question . . . : Might not an opportunity for human children to care for younger siblings or playmates reduce the likelihood that they will be abusive or neglectful parents? A simple prediction generated by this question is that children reared without younger siblings would be less effective parents than those reared with appreciably younger siblings whom they cared for" (1981, p. 210).

Among the langurs, assuming that neonates are not severely detrimentally affected during their alloparenting experiences, some connection can be proposed between neonatal experiences and adulthood; or more accurately, it can be assumed that the nonexclusive mother–infant relationship which occurs due to extensive allomothering among colobines does provide some insight into the kind of social structure into which the infant will be integrated and will play particular roles. In a sense, then, we are returning to the question of beneficial effects, and, again, it is not known whether natural selection designed the effects described below.

As argued elsewhere (McKenna, 1979, pp. 832–833), the constant and sometimes vigorous activity of infant transfer exposes the colobine langur neonate to a wide variety of female social contacts that differ in age, parity, temperament, and care giving competence (Dolhinow, 1977). The breadth of this form of social exposure is quite different from the kind experienced by the vast majority of cercopithecine infants, who have a more peaceful and exclusive relationship with their mothers. Even at very young ages these socialization experiences can affect the infants of these two taxa in different ways. For example, it may be that the infant transfer pattern among the Indian langurs prepares the infant for a social life characteristically not based upon exclusive and long-lasting special ties with members of one's lineage, but, rather, for a life based upon adult social relationships that develop independently from those of the mother. Although the field and laboratory data indicate that the social bonds between colobine langur females are the most conservative and, perhaps, the most critical in understanding social structures, present data indicate that those bonds are not built around specific kinship units or relatives to the degree characteristic of the macaques and baboons (Rosenblum, 1971; Ranson and Rowell, 1972, p. 126). Individual preference appears to constitute the primary basis of adult female–female bond formation (Dolhinow, 1977). While mothers may serve as central social focuses of the immature, at least through 2 years of age (see Curtin, 1976), the subadult and adult male and female langur monkeys appear to develop social nexuses quite separate from their mothers'.

In contrast, the exclusive and intensive relationship that characterizes many of the cercopithecine macaque mother–infant pairs may operate to familiarize the infant and the other group members with each other's genealogical matrilineal associations. From this recognition both the infant and other group members have bases upon which to build relationships and predict appropriate interactional behavior (McKenna, 1979). The exclusivity of the Japanese or Rhesus macaque mother–infant relationship, for example, may enable the infant to learn that its primary status is obtained, at least initially, from its mother, its siblings, and the lineage's associated adult male consorts. While the colobine langur learns to predict behavioral interactions from its experiences during infant transfer, the macaque infant learns to predict the effect of its actions on the basis of its defined position within a particular kin unit. Since studies conducted on the Japanese macaque demonstrate the role of powerful lineages in controlling access to desired resources, it is tempting to link the emergence of these influential kin units among this species with the competitively based feeding patterns. That notion fits well with the inclusive-fitness model: That is, buttressed by cohorts of related and supportive females, young macaques compete successfully for food resources. Rosenblum (1971) essentially supports the first part of that idea when he argues that the exclusivity of the mother–infant relationship, especially among the pig-tailed macaques, affects the degree of continued consanguineal associations during later development and helps establish the kin basis of group structure (also see Kurland, 1977; Hausfater, 1975; Altmann, 1980).

ALLOPARENTING AMONG HUMANS: FORM, CONTEXT, AND CONNECTEDNESS TO THE CROSS-SPECIES AND EVOLUTIONARY DATA

A comparison between the human and nonhuman primate data on alloparenting reveals some fascinating analogies. For example, there are similarities with respect to kinds of definitional and conceptual problems investigators face in this research area, and regarding the data itself there are similarities in the nature of socioecological conditions facilitating the development of alloparental or supplemental infant care. Moreover, like nonhuman primate females, human mothers often constrain or limit the role of the father as an active care giver (see Rossi, 1983). Obviously, there are differences, too, which cannot be minimized; but the similarities are striking. For example, the cross-cultural data on multiple care giving within what has been called "polymatric" societies, as compared with societies in which there is a single care giving figure, so-called "monomatric" societies, indicate that there is a need to better evaluate what constitutes infant care among humans. More attention needs to be focused upon what differentiates the kind of care that is given and at what age and under what amounts of supervision young care givers (or any care givers) are assuming responsibility for their infant charges (see Weisner and Gallimore, 1977; Whiting and Whiting, 1975; Super, 1981).

Weisner and Gallimore (1977) have called attention to the fact that in most societies around the world siblings spend, if not more time caring for children than mothers do, at least significant amounts of time with them. Unfortunately, much research on early child development tends to ignore these important contributions. Super (1981) argues persuasively that a "firm" enough empirical basis of quantitative, well-focused data as devoid of narrow presuppositions as possible is desperately needed. His excellent review demonstrates that the nature of supplemental care, its form and function, is but one of many sets of problems in need of serious rethinking among infant researchers.

It may well be important to point out that humans exhibit alloparenting behavior in frequencies that definitely exceed the nonhuman primate data. In fact, it is not simply rates or frequencies of alloparenting that differ, but its form as well. Human parents regularly leave infants in the care of others and move to greater distances from them and for longer periods of time than do monkey and/or ape parents (see Liederman and Liederman, 1977). However, the most important general hypothesis stated in the beginning of this chapter is borne out; that is, there is an important relationship between the physical environment as it relates to subsistence patterns (feeding, foraging, or growing food by humans), and the form and, indeed, the likely presence of alloparenting. Similar to the model proposed by Whiting and Whiting (1975) to explain human supplemental care and infant experiences, it has been shown how feeding and foraging pressures arising out of characteristics of the animals' environment create social structural conditions (group size, composition, nature and meaning of rank systems, defense, and so forth) that shape the early experiences of infants. Recall that among colobine Indian langur monkeys the early experience of the infant, which involves contact with an array of substitute care givers, possibly diminishing the strength of the infant's relationship with its mother, prepares it for an adult social life independent of maternal support or status. The marmoset-tamarin, possibly affected by environmental predation rates and increasing aridity, evolved a small body size that substantially changed not only the nature of the relationship between males and females, but also the relationship they have with their twin offspring; in effect, the high reproductive rate of the female, who nurses one set of twins while carrying another *in utero*, demands paternal care giving on nutritional grounds and sibling support as well. The marmoset-tamarin offsprings' learning environment prepares them for the shared parental roles they, too, will play as adults, and the degree of competence and experience gained in childhood from caring for siblings will later be translated into reproductive success.

With the examples of the Indian langurs and the marmoset-tamarin groups in mind, it is clear that biological and social characteristics are intimately intertwined; this is the case for humans as they, too, respond to environmental constraints (Konner, 1981; Whiting and Whiting, 1975).

Of course, human beings can adjust and respond to environmental pressures by way of technology; sociocultural change takes place much faster than biological or genetic change. Nevertheless, just as is the case for nonhuman primates, some general correlations can be seen between environmental conditions and the nature of social structures that create infant maturational settings within households which make parental substitutes necessary—i.e., maturational settings that, in the model of Whiting and Whiting (1975), create learning environments for children which reinforce the original structure and create the vehicles by which psychosocial differentiation and development among children occur.

Consider the fact that as a mother's contribution to the economic maintenance of the group increases (either due to need, desire, or both) there is a corresponding increase in the number of substitute care givers (other adults or siblings). Furthermore, the behavior of one parent surely affects what the other parent can and must do (Bekoff, 1981), so that the father's proximity to (if not direct care of) the infant also increases as the mother's roles change. Katz and Konner (1981, p. 181) state: "Fathers are more likely to be in proximity to their infants in monogamous, nuclear families, and nonpatrilocal cultures and subsistence adaptations in which mothers make a large contribution to the success of the family." Super's (1981) review confirms this finding, and also reveals that in traditional societies (horticulturists, pastoralists, and/or foragers) alloparenting tends to include related adults or siblings united by shared and reciprocal economic obligations; rarely are paid strangers involved in substitute care as can and often does occur in agricultural-urban societies.

Aside from these characteristics, reviews by Lamb (1981), Konner (1981), and Super (1981) clearly show that while the father cannot technically be considered an alloparent or substitute care giver, he exhibits much less direct care giving (dressing, changing, bathing, holding, and feeding) of infants than do siblings, mothers, or other female adult care givers. But the father's role, like that of other care givers, is greatly affected by the organization of the household (its density, size, composition, sex ratio), whose members are themselves affected by subsistence patterns. Moreover, the father's bond with a child is limited not so much by biological constraints as by the perceptions of responsibility he has regarding the infant and the duration of his association with it, and by the kind of care giving he extends (Lamb, 1981; Biller, 1981). In addition, the attitudes of the mother have a great deal to do with how the father interacts with his infant. The degree to which the nature of the infant's bond to *all* care givers, including the parents, is affected by the subsistence patterns and the general ecological conditions within which the society exists, is quite impressive. Just as is true for the nonhuman primates, the socioecological correlates to human alloparenting must be considered in attempting to understand how and why it emerges.

One can only speculate about what elicits infant care and, particularly, substitute care among humans, but it is certain that hormonal factors neither determine the quality of care nor assure that proper care will be administered; it seems that experience, exposure to infants, and learning are important, which is not to say that as "good mammals" we are not prepared to act nurturantly and protectively toward infants with all their adaptive neonatal (cute) traits. However, just as infanticide by male monkeys and apes can occur in full view of "neonatal care-eliciting" traits, so, too, will child abuse, neglect, and infanticide occur among humans if proper conditioning and parenting are not experienced by future parents, or if the prospects of the infants survival due to limited resources (social or physical) are doubtful. Among nonhuman primates care givers are mostly prepared to act protectively toward the young, but it is important to realize that they can also be prepared to act destructively toward them if social circumstances either in the past (improper socialization) or in the present (high density and male rivalry for nonhuman primates, religion, ideology, and values among humans) encourage it. Human infanticide is not rare and usually takes place if infants of one sex are thought to be needed and the other is born, or if a child is born too soon after the previous one, thereby jeopardizing the survival of both. Moreover, human infanticide can occur when perceived population needs affecting sex ratios are not being sustained (Dickeman, 1979).

With respect to "who benefits," or the effects of alloparenting among humans, Liederman and Liederman (1977), Weisner and Gallimore (1977), Goldberg (1977), Whiting and Whiting (1975), and Minturn and Lambert (1964) have described ways in which infants benefit (cognitively, emotionally, and socially) from substitute care giving, while Munroe and Munroe (1971, 1984) argue that both positive and negative effects can be measured, and Sutton-Smith (1977) worries about the negative effects—at least if younger siblings are providing the care. Liederman and Liederman (1977) studied Kikuyu infants in Africa and found that "regardless of familial income level, the caretaker appears to spend more daytime activity in talking to and playing with the infant than the mother does" (1977, p. 432). While monomatric infants (infants not cared for by others) showed less apprehensive behavior following the approach of strangers and the departure of mothers, polymatric infants, especially those cared for by mature caretakers, "are associated with higher infant performance on standardized tests even when the important variable of family socioeconomic level is controlled for" (Liederman and Liederman, 1977, p. 432). They conclude that: "Our findings emphasize the centrality of the infant's older peer as a socializing agent even in the postnatal period. The secondary care giver serving in a socializing role has the characteristics of both a child and an adult, and, thus, may have an advantage over the parent in passing on aspects of the culture to the infant and young children" (Liederman and Liederman, 1977, p. 432). It is interesting that Konner's (1981) suggestion that multiaged and not peer subgroups were the most common structural subgroup found in foraging peoples now and throughout hominid evolution, is compatible with the Liedermans' notion of who, in addition to the parents, most effectively socializes the young.

Basing his conclusion on a short-term longitudinal study in urban Zambia, Goldberg (1977) found a negative correlation between amount of mother activity with 4-month-old infants and cognitive development during latter months of the first year (cited in Munroe and Munroe, 1984). Whiting and Whiting (1975) suggest that care giving by siblings promotes prosocial and nurturant behaviors, while, studying the effects of alloparenting exhibited by Hawaiian boys, Gallemore (1984) found that boys attended to their peer tutors more and were more nurturant on standardized tests.

Super (1981) cites the work of Minturn and Lambert (1964), who found that "both between and within cultures household density is positively related to measures of maternal warmth" (p. 239); while Whiting's (1961, 1971) findings, cited in Super, indicate that if we assume that the amount of physical attention in some way measures "infant indulgence," then in a large worldwide sample it appears that such benefits to the infant increase as the number of adults living in the household (available care givers) increases (p. 234).

This last information accords nicely with one of the most interesting and long-running studies on the effects of substitute adult and sibling care givers on infants' cognitive and affective states. Studying the Bantu-speaking Logoli people in western Kenya, Munroe and Munroe (1971) elucidated not only how the local ecology, in this case the density of the household, affects infant holding rates and forms, but the effects of differential care. They focused on 12 infants, seven male and five female, beginning when the children were less than 1 year old. They found that in large households infants were responded to more frequently when they cried and were also held more frequently; it seemed that the mother had "less" to do with the baby in high membership households, and that she spent greater periods of time in the field gardening; in fact, there was a statistical (nonsignificant) trend indicating that as mothers spent more time in the field infants were increasingly in the care of older siblings (Munroe and Munroe, 1971). Four years later Munroe and Munroe returned to retest these children to determine the possible effects on affective dispositions of the child's first-year experiences. They found that "positive affective outlook at age five was correlated with the proportion of time the children had been held by their mothers during infancy" (Munroe and Munroe, 1984). As infant holding by mothers during the first year increased, and, thus, holding by siblings decreased, the amount of "optimism and trust" exhibited by the 5-year-olds increased. But, surprisingly, sibling care was unrelated to measures of childhood affective disposition.

Munroe and Munroe (1984; see also Munroe and Munroe, 1980, 1971) argue that while mother's holding is significantly related to a child's positive outlook on life, their tests of cognitive performance showed some different results. Using five measures of intellectual performance, they found that the child's cognitive performance "was superior when his or her involvement with the mother in infancy had been low and that runs counter to the direction of the findings for affect" (Munroe and Munroe, 1984).

The Munroes' data is especially important since it is longitudinal; however, as they point out, a small sample was used (11 infants in the follow-up study), and the continuity of care and nature of experiences since the first-year study can have important effects. Nevertheless, the data strongly suggest that the effects of early caretaking experiences of infants do not necessarily have one kind of beneficial or negative consequence.

In summary, the human and nonhuman data reveal that: (1) There are no uniform benefits or effects in general that infants, parents, or substitute care givers experience during alloparenting episodes. (2) Among all primates the conditions within which alloparenting can occur are similar and are mostly influenced by environmental factors that affect social structures, which in turn promote the specific circumstances within which alloparenting is possible (importance of group size, availability of care givers, socioeconomic roles of participants). (3) The existence of alloparenting does not seem to emerge due to the needs of the infants (at least direct needs) but to the needs of parents who have invested in the infants and who are largely responsible for their survival. (4) Characteristics of the infants (neonatal traits) do not guarantee or assure that alloparental care will take place, but it is rather the social experiences of the care giver and the immediate social context that determine the degree of nurturant/helpful "care" which will be administered. (5) Rank among parents and potential alloparents plays an important regulatory role in determining which individuals, if any, other than the parents, care for the infant. (6) A discussion of benefits or effects of alloparenting or surrogate care giving is essentially inadequate for understanding its origins. (7) With respect to the form of alloparenting, what one parent does is affected by what the other is doing, and the behavior of both determines the likelihood of sibling or surrogate care giving occurring (i.e., as mother's economic role and her distance from the infant increase, the father's proximity to the infant increases, or, as both mother's and father's distance from the infant increases, the proximity and role of sibling or substitute care givers increases). (8) It appears that with respect to siblings, the "coefficient of familiarity" may be a more powerful predictor of infant care than degree of relatedness, though degree of familiarity and relatedness are (themselves) ordinarily positively related. (9) Terminological problems concerning what constitutes "care" remain a major methodological handicap in this research area. (10) Finally, except for, perhaps, one group of primates, the marmoset-tamarins, alloparental care (even with all its possible effects in mind) probably was not designed by natural selection as a means of improving individual reproductive success for most of the participants.

REFERENCES

Alexander, R. D., Hoogland, J. L., Howard, R. D., Noonan, K. M., and Sherman, P. W. Sexual dimorphisms and breeding systems in pinnipeds, ungulates, primates, and humans. In N. A. Chagnon and W. Irons (Eds.), *Evolutionary Biology and Human Social Behavior: An Anthropological Perspective*. N. Scituate, MA: Duxbury Press, 1979.

Alley, T. R. Infantile colouration as an elicitor of caretaking behaviour in Old World Primates. *Primates*, 1980, *28*, 416–429.

Altmann, J. *Baboon Mothers and Infants*. Cambridge, MA: Harvard University Press, 1980.

Bekoff, M. Mammalian sibling interactions: Genes, facilitative environments, and the coefficient of familiarity. In D. Gubernick and P. Klopfer (Eds.), *Parental Care in Mammals*. NY: Plenum Press, 1981, pp. 307–333.

Blake, J. Family size and quality of children. *Demography*, 1981, *18*.

Boggess, J. E. *Social behavior of the Himalayan langur (Presbytis entellus) in Eastern Nepal*. Unpublished doctoral dissertation, University of California, Berkeley, 1976.

Burton, F. D. The integration of biology and behavior in the socialization of Macaca sylvana of Gibraltar. In F. Poirier (Ed.), *Primate Socialization*. NY: Random House, 1972, pp. 29–62.

Busse, Curt, and Hamilton, W. Infant carrying by male Chacma baboons. *Science*, 1980, *212*, 1281–1282.

Chagnon, N., Flinn, M. V., and Melancon, T. F. Sex ratio variation among Yanomamo Indians. In N. A. Chagnon and W. Irons (Eds.), *Evolutionary Biology and Human Social Behavior: An Anthropological Perspective*. N. Scituate, MA: Duxbury Press, 1979.

Clark, C. B. A preliminary report on weaning among chimpanzees of the Gombe National Park, Tanzania. In S. Chevalier-Skolnikoff and F. E. Poirier (Eds.), *Primate Bio-Social Development: Biological, Social, and Ecological Determinants*. NY: Garland, 1977, pp. 235–260.

Curtin, S. H. *Niche differentiation and social organization in sympatric Malaysian colobines*. Unpublished doctoral dissertation, University of California, Berkeley, 1976.

Deag, J. M., and Crook, J. H. Social behavior and 'agnostic buffering' in the wild Barbary macaque, *Macaca sylvana*. *Folia Primatologica*, 1971, *15*, 183–200.

Dickeman, M. Female infanticide and the reproductive strategies of stratified human societies. In N. A. Chagnon and W. Irons (Eds.), *Evolutionary Biology and Human*

Social Behavior: An Evolutionary Perspective. N. Scituate, MA: Duxbury Press, 1979.

Dittus, W. The social regulation of population density and age-sex distribution in the Toque macaque. *Behaviour,* 1977, *63,* 281–321.

Dolhinow, P. *Caretaking patterns of the Indian langur monkey.* Paper presented at the meeting of the American Association of Physical Anthropologists, Seattle, 1977.

Dolhinow, P. An experimental study of mother loss in the Indian langur monkey (Presbytis entellus). *Folia Primatologica,* 1980, *33,* 77–128.

Dolhinow, P., and De May, M. G. Adoption: The importance of infant choice. *Journal of Human Evolution,* 1982, *11,* 391–420.

Dolhinow, P., McKenna, J., and von der Haar Laws, J. Rank and reproduction among female langur monkeys: Aging and improvement (they're not just getting older, they're getting better). *International Journal of Aggressive Behavior,* 1979, *5,* 19–30.

Dunbar, R. I. Intraspecies variations in mating strategy. In P. P. G. Bateson and P. Klopfer (Eds.), *Perspectives in Ethology.* NY: Plenum Press, 1982, pp. 385–420.

Emlen, S. T. The evolution of cooperative breeding in birds. In J. R. Krebs and B. Davies (Eds.), *Behavioral Ecology: An Evolutionary Approach.* Sunderland, MA: Sinauer Associates, 1978, pp. 245–251.

Epple, G. Parental behavior in *Saguinus fusciollis spp. (Callithricidae). Folia Primatologica,* 1975, *24,* 221–238.

Ford, S. M. Callitrichids as phyletic dwarfs, and the place of the callitrichidae in platyrrhini. *Primates,* 1980, *21,* 31–43.

Gadgil, M. Changes with age in the strategy of social behavior. In P. P. G. Bateson and P. Klopfer (Eds.), *Perspectives in Ethology.* NY: Plenum Press, 1982.

Gallimore, R. M. Affiliation motivation and Hawaiian American achievement. *Journal of Cross-Cultural Psychology,* 1974, *5,* 481–491.

Glander, K. E. *Habitat and resource utilization: An ecological view of social organization in mantled howling monkeys.* Unpublished doctoral dissertation, University of Chicago, 1975.

Goldberg, S. Infant development and mother–infant interaction in urban Zambia. In P. H. Leiderman, S. R. Tulken, and A. Rosenfeld (Eds.), *Culture and Infancy: Variations in the Human Experience.* NY: Academic Press, 1977.

Goodall, J. Some aspects of mother–infant relationships in a group of wild chimpanzees. In H. R. Schaffer (Ed.), *The Origins of Human Social Relations.* NY: Academic Press, 1971.

Goodall, J. Infant killing and cannibalism in free-living chimpanzees. *Folia Primatologica,* 1977, *28,* 259–282.

Gubernick, D. J., and Klopfer, P. (Eds.), *Parental Care in Mammals.* NY: Plenum Press, 1981.

Hamburg, D., and McCown, E. *The Great Apes. Perspectives in Human Evolution,* Vol. 4. Menlo Park, CA: Benjamin, 1979.

Hampton, J. K., Hampton, S. H., and Landwehr, B. J. Observations on a successful breeding colony of the marmoset *Oedipomidas oedipus. Folia Primatologica,* 1966, *4,* 265–287.

Hausfater, G. Dominance and reproduction in baboons (*Papio cynocephalus*): A quantitative analysis. *Contributions to Primatology,* Vol. 7, Basel: S. Karger, 1975.

Hearn, J. P., and Lunn, S. F. The reproductive biology of the marmoset monkey *Callithrix jacchus. Laboratory Animal Handbooks*, 1975, *6*, 191–204.

Hinde, R. (Ed.). *Primate Social Relationships*. Sunderland, MA: Sinauer, 1983.

Hoage, R. Parental care in *Leontopithecus r. rosalia*: Carrying behavior. In D. G. Kleiman (Ed.), *The Biology and Conservation of the Callithrichidae*. Washington, D. C.: Smithsonian Institution Press, 1977.

Hofer, M. A. Hidden regulatory processes in early social relationships. In P. P. G. Bateson and P. H. Klopfer (Eds.), *Perspectives in Ethology*, Vol. 3. London: Plenum, 1978.

Hofer, M. Parental contributions to the development of their offspring. In D. Gubernick and P. Klopfer (Eds.), *Parental Care in Mammals*. NY: Plenum, 1981.

Hood, J. P. Dwarf mongoose helpers at the den. *Zeitschrift fuer Tierpsychologie*, 1978, *48*, 277–287.

Hrdy, S. Care and exploitation of nonhuman primate infants by conspecifics other than the mother. *Advances in the Study of Behavior*, 1976, 6.

Hrdy, S. B. *The Langurs of Abu*. Cambridge, MA: Harvard University Press, 1977.

Hrdy, S. B. Infanticide among animals: A review, classification, and examination of the implications for the reproductive strategies of females. *Ethology and Sociobiology*, 1979, *1*, 13–40.

Hrdy, S. B. *The Woman that Never Evolved*. Cambridge, MA: Harvard University Press, 1981.

Ingram, J. *Parent-infant interactions in the common marmoset (Callithrix jacchus) and the development of young*. Unpublished doctoral dissertation, University of Bristol, 1975.

Jay, P. *The ecology and social behavior of the North Indian langur*. Unpublished doctoral dissertation, University of Chicago, 1963.

Jones, C. B. Grooming in the mantled howler monkey, *Alouatta palliata* Gray. *Primates*, 1979, *20*, 289–292.

Jones, C. B. The functions of status in the mantled howler monkey (*Alouatta palliata* Gray): Intraspecific competition for group membership in a folivorous neotropical primate. *Primates*, 1980, *21*, 389–405.

Kaplan, J. R. and Zucker, E. Social organization in a group of free-ranging patas monkeys. *Folia Primatologica*, 1980, *34*, 196–213.

Katz, M. M. and Konner, M. The role of the father: An anthropological perspective. In M. Lamb (Ed.), *The Role of the Father in Child Development*. NY: Wiley, 1981.

Kaufman, I. C. Developmental considerations of anxiety and depression: Psychobiological studies in monkeys. In T. Shapiro (Ed.), *Psychoanalysis and Contemporary Science*. NY: International University Press, 1977.

Kleiman, D. G. Monogamy in animals. *Quarterly Review of Biology*, 1977, *52*, 39–69.

Kleiman, D. G., and Malcolm, J. R. The evolution of male parental investment in mammals. In D. J. Gubernick and P. H. Klopfer (Eds.), *Parental Care in Mammals*. NY: Plenum, 1981.

Konner, M. J. Aspects of the developmental ethology of a foraging people. In N. Blurton-Jones (Ed.), *Ethological Studies of Child Behavior*. Cambridge: Cambridge University Press, 1974.

Konner, M. J. The evolution of human infant development. In R. Munroe, L. Munroe, and B. Whiting (Eds.), *Handbook of Cross-Cultural Human Development*. NY: Garland Press, 1981.

Kurland, J. A. Kin selection in the Japanese monkey. *Contributions to Primatology*, Vol. 12. Basel: S. Karger, 1977.

Lamb, M. Father–infant and mother–infant interaction in the first year of life. *Child Development*, 1977, *48*, 167–181.

Lamb, M. Fathers and child development: An integrative overview. In M. Lamb (Ed.), *The Role of the Father in Child Development*, 2nd ed. NY: Wiley, 1981.

Lancaster, J. Carrying and sharing in human evolution. *Human Nature*, 1978, *1*, 82–89.

Liederman, P. H. and Liederman, G. F. Affective and cognitive consequences of polymatric infant care in the East African highlands. In A. D. Pick (Ed.), *Minnesota Symposia on Child Psychology*, Vol. 8. Minneapolis, MN: University of Minnesota, 1974. (a)

Liederman, P. H. and Liederman, G. F. Familial influences of infant development in an East African agricultural community. In E. J. Anthony and C. Koupernik (Eds.), *The Child in his Family—Children at Psychiatric Risk*, Vol. 3. NY: Wiley, 1974. (b)

Liederman, H. and Liederman, G. Economic change and infant care in an East African agricultural community. In H. Liederman, R. Tolkien, and A. Rosenfeld (Eds.). *Culture and Infancy*. NY: Academic Press, 1977, pp. 405–438.

Lewis, M., and Rosenblum, L. (Eds.) *The Effect of the Infant on its Caregiver*. NY: Wiley, 1974.

Leutenegger, W. Evolution of litter size in primates. *American Nature*, 1979, *114*, 525–531.

Macdonald, D. W., and Moehlman, P. D. Cooperation, altruism, and restraint in the reproduction of carnivores. In P. P. G. Bateson and P. H. Klopfer (Eds.), *Perspectives in Ethology*, Vol. 5. NY: Plenum, 1982.

McKenna, J. J. *An analysis of the social roles and behavior of seventeen captive hanuman langurs (Presbytis entellus)*. Unpublished doctoral dissertation, University of Oregon, 1975.

McKenna, J. J. The evolution of allomothering behavior among colobine monkeys: Function and opportunism in evolution. *American Anthropologist*, 1979, *8*, 818–840.

McKenna, J. Primate infant-caregiving behavior: Origins, consequences and variability with emphasis upon the common Indian langur. In D. Gubernick and P. Klopfer (Eds.), *Parental Care in Mammals*. NY: Plenum, 1981.

McKenna, J. J. *Fathers, infants and mothers in evolutionary perspective: Toward integrating psychiatry and anthropology*. Paper delivered at Second World Congress of Infant Psychiatry, Cannes, France, 1983.

Minturn, L., and Lambert, W. W. *Mothers of Six Cultures*. NY: Wiley, 1964.

Moreno-Black, G., and Maples, W. R. Differential habitat utilization of four cercopithecidae in a Kenyan forest. *Folia Primatologica*, 1977, *27*, 85–107.

Munroe, R. and Munroe, R. Household density and infant care in an East African society. *The Journal of Social Psychology*, 1971, *83*, 3–13.

Munroe, R. and Munroe, R. Infant experience and childhood effect: A longitudinal study among the Logoli. *Ethos*, 1980, *8*, 295–315.

Packer, C. Male care and exploitation of infants in *Papio anubis*. *Animal Behavior*, 1980, *28*, 512–520.

Quiatt, D. Aunts and mothers: Adaptive implications of allomaternal behavior of nonhuman primates. *American Anthropologist*, 1979, *81*, 310–319.

Ransom, T. W. and Rowell, T. E. Early social development of feral baboons. In F. Poirier (Ed.), *Primate Socialization*. NY: Random House, 1972.

Redican, W. K. A. *A longitudinal study of behavioral interactions between adult male and infant rhesus monkeys (Macaca mulatta)*. Unpublished doctoral dissertation, University of California, Davis, 1975.

Redican, W. and Taub, D. Male parental care in monkeys and apes. In M. Lamb (Ed.), *The Role of the Father in Child Development*. NY: Wiley, 1981.

Riemann, M. The evolution of alloparental care and adoption in mammals and birds. *Quarterly Review of Biology*, 1982, *57*, 405–435.

Rosenblum, L. Kinship interaction patterns in pigtail and bonnet macaques. *Proceedings of the Third International Congress of Primatology*, Vol. 3. Basel: S. Karger, 1971.

Rossi, A. *Parenthood in transition: Demographic and social pressures for change in human parenting in post-industrial society*. Paper delivered at the Belmont Conference on Parenting and Offspring Development in a Life Span Framework, under the auspices of the Social Science Research Council. Belmont, Maryland, May 1983.

Rossi, A. A biosocial perspective on parenting. *Daedalus*, 1977, *106*:1–32.

Rowell, T. *Social Behaviour of Monkeys*. London: Penguin, 1972.

Rubenstein, D. Reproductive value and behavioral strategies: Coming of age in monkeys and horses. In P. P. G. Bateson and P. Klopfer (Eds.), *Perspectives in Ethology*, Vol. 5. NY: Plenum, 1982.

Sackett, G., Gunderson, V., and Baldwin, D. Studying the ontogeny of primate behavior. In J. Fobes and J. King (Eds.), *Primate Behavior*. NY: Academic Press, 1982.

Seyfarth, R. Social relationships among adult male and female baboons. II. Behaviour throughout the female reproductive cycle. *Behaviour*, 1978, *64*, 227–247.

Silk, J. *Social behavior of female Macaca radiata: The influence of kinship and rank on cooperation and competition*. Unpublished doctoral dissertation, University of California, Davis, 1981.

Smith, D. G. The association between rank and reproductive success of male rhesus monkeys. *American Journal of Primatology*, 1981, *1*, 83–90.

Smuts, B. Dynamics of special relationships between adult male and female olive baboons. In R. Hinde (Ed.), *Primate Social Relationships*. Sunderland, MA: Sinauer, 1983, Chap. 6.9.

Strum, S. Agonistic dominance in male baboons: An alternative view. *International Journal of Primatology*, 1983, *3*, 175–202.

Super, C. Behavioral development in infancy. In R. H. Munroe, R. L. Munroe, and B. B. Whiting (Eds.), *Handbook of Cross-Cultural Human Development*. NY: Garland STPM Press, 1981.

Sutton-Smith, B. Comment on "My Brother's keeper: Child and sibling caretaking," by T. S. Weisner, and R. Gallimore, *Current Anthropology*, 1977, *18*, 184–185.

Symons, D. The question of function: Dominance and play. In E. O. Smith (Ed.), *Social Play in Primates*. NY: Academic Press, 1978.

Taub, D. M. Female choice and mating strategies among wild Barbary macaques (Macaca sylvanus). In D. G. Linburg (Ed.), *The Macaques: Studies in Ecology Behavior, and Evolution*. New York: Van Nostrand Reinhold, 1979.

Taub, D. Testing the agonistic buffering hypothesis. *Behavioral Ecology and Sociobiology*, 1980, *6*, 187–197.

Washburn, S. L. Human behavior and the behavior of other animals. *American Psychologist*, 1978, *33*, 405–418.

Weisner, T., and Gallimore, R. My brother's keeper: Child and sibling caretaking. *Current Anthropology*, 1977, *18*, 169–190.

Whiting, J. Socialization process and personality. In F. L. K. Hsu (Ed.), *Psychological Anthropology*. Homewood, IL: Dorsey Press, 1961.

Whiting, J., and Whiting, B. *Children of Six Cultures*. NY: Cambridge University Press, 1975.

Wilson, E. O. *Sociobiology: The New Synthesis*. Cambridge, MA: Harvard University Press, 1975.

Wolfe, L.D. A case of male adoption in a troop of Japanese monkeys. In A. B. Chiavelli and R. S. Corruccini (Eds.), *Primate Behavior and Sociobiology*. NY: Springer-Verlag, 1981.

Wrangham, R. W. On the evolution of ape social systems. *Social Science Information*, 1979, *18*, 335–368. (a)

Wrangham, R. W. Sex differences in chimpanzee dispersion. In D. Hamburg and E. McCown (Eds.), *The Great Apes Perspectives in Human Evolution*. Menlo Park, CA: Benjamin-Cummings Publishing, 1979. (b)

Wrangham, R. W. Drinking competition in vervet monkeys. *Animal Behavior*, 1981, *29*, 904–910.

III HUMAN VARIATION THROUGH TIME AND SPACE: HISTORIC CHANGE IN HUMAN PARENTHOOD

7

THE WATERSHED: CHANGE IN PARENTAL-INVESTMENT AND FAMILY-FORMATION STRATEGIES IN THE COURSE OF HUMAN EVOLUTION

Jane B. Lancaster
Chet S. Lancaster

PARENTAL INVESTMENT AND THE HUMAN FAMILY

In the course of human evolution there was a critical watershed that differentiated the parental-investment and family-formation strategies of human beings living in low-density, hunter–gatherer or long-follow horticultural societies from those living in high-density and stratified agricultural and urban societies. The crucial feature of this watershed was a changed perception by the human actors of the ratio between the numbers of human beings in a society and the resources essential to sustain life and successful reproduction. For most of human history, for most of the time, and probably for most people who have ever lived, human experience has been that there is a shortage of group members and that more children and more recruits are desirable for social, economic, and political reasons. Land and critical resources were free and openly accessible. Temporary shortages in local areas were buffered by systems of reciprocal access, visiting between neighbors, and migration.

Nearly everywhere in the world human populations eventually grew to the point where basic resources were no longer free for the taking. Although this change from resources-as-free-goods to resources-as-limited-goods has been a nearly universal feature of human experience, for many societies it came relatively late in history, perhaps only 2000–3000 years ago; for a few it has happened only recently. This shift in human experience had a profound impact on nearly every feature of human family life, because it altered the rules under which parents rear children. For most of human history it was sufficient for parents to raise to adulthood children who were healthy and possessed the social and survival skills appropriate for their society. Such young adults would have a reasonable assurance of living out their life spans, finding mates, and producing successful children of their own. However, once the resources necessary to rear children no longer appeared abundant and readily accessible to all fit adults, parents had an entirely new task set upon them: how to guarantee that their offspring would have access to the limited critical resources necessary for successful reproduction. In order to ensure such guarantees for their children, humans found that they must alter major features of human family life and relations between kin, including ways in which mates are chosen, ways in which marriages are formed and structured, how social position and property are passed from one relative to the next, the way that wealth is measured and displayed, how individuals are incorporated into or alienated from families, the way sexual behavior is patterned for each sex, and how parents invest time, energy, attention, and environmental resources in their offspring. The purpose of this chapter is to suggest the many ways in which the reproductive behavior of human beings is profoundly shaped is by their perception of the relative abundance of resources in the world around them, especially those most pivotal resources necessary to produce the next generation. This overview is a deliberate simplification of the various and complex paths followed by human history, but the goal is to establish a paradigm through which the various forms of the human family may be perceived.

The Evolution of the Human Family

In comparison to other large-bodied mammals, the higher primates, in general, and human beings, in particular, give birth to offspring at a later age, have longer gestation periods, produce fewer young with each gestation, have longer periods of lactation, experience longer intervals between successive births, and produce fewer young during the life span of the adult female (Altmann, this volume, Chapter 2). The higher primates and especially the great apes and humans produce high quality, highly invested young, reflecting both great cost and great value to the investing parent. The major burden of producing such valuable, costly offspring falls most heavily on the shoulders of adult females among the monkeys and apes. For them, the wide spacing between births allows the adult female to support a single *nutritionally dependent* youngster (infant) at the same time that she can foster and protect a second, *nutritionally independent* juvenile (Lancaster, 1984).

In contrast, the human family represents a specialized and very basic adaptation that greatly extended the investment parents could make in their offspring, especially furthering the survivorship of juveniles (Fig. 7.1) (Lancaster and Lancaster, 1983; and Lancaster and Lancaster, in press). This is especially important because, unlike monkeys and apes, human juveniles are not nutritionally independent. One of the most unusual behavioral patterns in the human repertoire is the collaboration of male and female parents in the feeding of weaned but nutritionally dependent juvenile offspring right up to their adulthood. The evolution of the division of labor

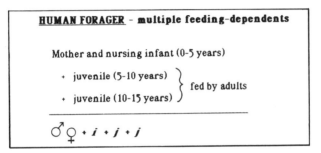

Figure 7.1.   Dependency in great ape and human forager societies.

between largely male hunting and largely female gathering not only allowed each sex to specialize in securing resources from different levels of the food pyramid but also permitted a system of reciprocal food sharing. This reciprocity benefited both sexes at the same time that it provided a protective umbrella over the most vulnerable part of the life cycle in mammals—the juvenile period during which the relatively inexperienced, small, and socially subordinant youngster must locate, garner, and compete for food. The evolution of the human husband-father role can be summarized as the channeling of male parental energy into the rearing of young (Lancaster and Lancaster, 1983; Katz and Konner, 1981). With the collaborate efforts of the male, human females are able to rear not only a nursing infant but one or more nutritionally dependent juveniles at the same time. Because of male parental investment, human beings, even without the benefit of modernized culture, are able to raise to adulthood, on the average, one out of every two children born in comparison to other primates and group-hunting carnivores where only 10–30% ever reach reproductive maturity (Lancaster and Lancaster, 1983).

    Studies of the relationship between mothers and their infants in modern hunter–gatherers indicate that, for most of human history, humans probably exhibited a very restrained pattern of reproduction featuring high levels of parental investment based on biological adaptations. Short (1978) suggests that the life cycle of the hunter–gatherer woman was characterized by a variety of biological adaptations supporting low fertility, such as late age of menarche followed by slowly developing fertility, first birth at the age of 18–19, a single infant nursed for three to four years, birth spacing between successive births of four years, early age of menopause with last birth before age 35, and a total lifetime production of only five surviving children.

Calculations by Blurton-Jones and Sibley (1978) indicate that such restrained reproductive output for hunter–gatherer women conforms well with parental investment theory and represents a maximization of the average number of children to reach maturity given the constraints of a mobile, foraging life style which places very high demands on maternal energy and in which children contribute little to the domestic economy. Such a limited production of offspring permits the kind of intensive, intimate mother–infant relationship reported for hunter–gatherers, in which the mother nurses her infant on demand, sleeps with it at night, and carries it on her hip during the day (Konner, 1976). Maternal responsibility and supervision of infants is very high for the entire period of lactation and it is only around the age of 4 to 5 that a youngster begins to spend long periods away from maternal supervision in a multiage play group (Draper, 1976; Konner, 1975).

The Impact of Sedentism

It was not until relatively late in human history, probably around the time of the abandonment of a mobile foraging life style and the beginnings of a sedentary life based on horticulture and hunting, that human women began to regularly bear children every other year, the rate most frequently reported for noncontracepting, breastfeeding women in recent times (Cohen, Malpass, and Klein, 1980; Hassan, 1981; Page and Lesthaeghe, 1981). The birth of a child every other year might have produced intolerable demands on energy, time, and attention budgets of individual mothers if it were not for two countervailing forces: sibcare systems widely practiced in village-based "middle-range" societies and the value of the labor of quite small children in horticultural routines, such as weeding, defending field crops, and the preparation of foods for cooking (Draper and Harpending, this volume, Chapter 8; Weisner, this volume, Chapter 9). These innovations permitted parents to produce children more often and to have larger families without major changes in the mental calculus for parental investment. The parental cost of rearing children was still kept at tolerable levels by the addition of the sibcare system, essentially the addition of parental surrogates drawn from the juvenile population to assist in rearing weaned 2- to 5-year-olds. Limitations on the number of children who could be successfully produced and reared came from the 2-year lactation period (perhaps long enough to establish sufficient immune-system competence) and not

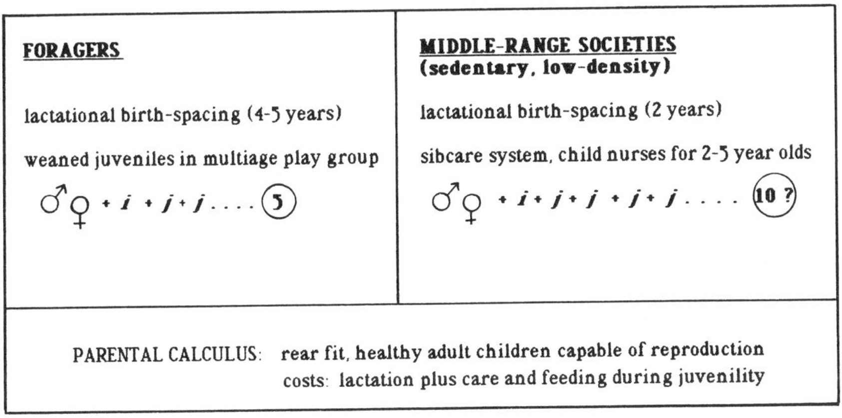

FORAGERS	MIDDLE-RANGE SOCIETIES (sedentary, low-density)
lactational birth-spacing (4-5 years)	lactational birth-spacing (2 years)
weaned juveniles in multiage play group	sibcare system, child nurses for 2-5 year olds
♂♀ + *i* + *j* + *j* . . . . ⑤	♂♀ + *i* + *j* + *j* + *j* + *j* . . . . ⑩ ?

PARENTAL CALCULUS: rear fit, healthy adult children capable of reproduction
costs: lactation plus care and feeding during juvenility

Figure 7.2. Dependency in human low-density societies.

from any parental sense that there might not be resources for these children to establish their own families once they reached reproductive age (Fig. 7.2).

The evolution of sedentary life styles due to the domestication of plants and animals did not radically transform human parental-investment and family-formation strategies as long as those life styles were based in relatively low-density, village-organized societies in which the resources necessary for reproduction were still equally accessible to all able-bodied adults. Sedentism is associated with shorter lactation, birth spacing of only two years, larger sibships, and a sibcare system of child rearing (Draper, 1975, Hassen, 1981) compared to the reproductive patterns of hunter–gatherers; historically its impact was to increase human reproductive efficiency by recruiting maternal aides and so lowering the cost of rearing individual children.

THE WATERSHED BETWEEN LOW- AND HIGH-DENSITY REPRODUCTIVE SYSTEMS

Trivers' (1972) original theoretical formulation of the evolutionary concepts of parental investment theory emphasized the differences in strategies between the sexes because of the much greater burden placed on the female who produces relatively few, but energetically costly, eggs. According to Trivers in species where one sex invests much more heavily than the other in the rearing of the young, the heavily investing sex becomes a limiting resource for which the opposite sex competes. This unbalanced cost function between sexes may lead to selection for successful competitors in promiscuous mating in the one sex while the other sex remains selective in mating and puts its energy reserves into parental investment rather than mating competition. As might be expected, among mammals where females are already committed to heavy investments in each offspring in terms of ovulation, gestation, lactation, and maternal care, sexual access to females often becomes the prize for a limited number of successful male competitors in each generation (Williams, 1966). An important point, which is often overlooked, is that there is one very significant deterrent to males that may bar many from an all-out pursuit of mating success: the degree to which it is necessary for the males of particular species to give aid to females in order for young to be successfully reared. Males, then, in the long run are not free to pursue their own strategies, but must mold them to fit the reproductive needs of females (Wrangham, 1975; Irons, 1983).

It has already been argued that, in the course of human evolution, the keystone in the foundation of the human family was the capturing of male energy into the nurturance of young, most specifically for the collaborative feeding of weaned juveniles. The human family is a complex organizational structure for the garnering of energy to be transformed into the production of the next generation, and its most essential feature is the collaboration of the male and female parent in a division of labor. For much of human history, the regulation and channeling of energy, once garnered, into the production of children was regulated by behavioral adaptations such as food sharing and the division of labor, as well as by biological adaptations such as exaggerated sexual dimorphism in the storage of energy as fat to support long lactation (Lancaster, 1984). The more slowly developing, costly, and valuable the offspring, the more it behooves the parent to ensure a steady, long-term access to food to support each egg from the point of fertilization to reproductive maturity. The older an offspring becomes, the more valuable it is since the cost of replacement increases with each year of life. The reproductive issue for K-selected animals is long-term access to energy for the rearing of costly young (see Altmann, this volume, Chapter 2 for an expanded discussion). For humans the earliest evolutionary history of the family can be understood in these terms, and later in history much of the cross-cultural variation in family formation can be understood as adaptations for the channeling of access to energy and resources within the family itself as behavioral adaptations are made to cope with increasing limitations within the social group on free access to resources.

The contrast between low- and high-density family formation strategies has been described by Lancaster and Lancaster (in press) (see also Goody, 1969, 1972, 1973, 1976, 1983; and C. Lancaster, 1976). The distinction between high and low density refers to a perceived difference in the ratio of group members to the resources available for each to successfully rear young. The distinction cannot be drawn on a simple basis of people per square mile but rather on a complex of evaluations by the actors themselves about the resources available in the environment, the energy and organization needed to extract them, and a cultural calculus regarding resources and experience necessary for adult status. However complex these assessments may seem to be, they are made and, at some point in history, a majority of humans in a given culture perceive that there are limited resources and that there are going to be major differentials in the success rate of individuals in converting energy and resources into a next generation. It is no longer sufficient to only rear fit, healthy adults, and parents must begin to calculate how to guarantee that children will have access to reproductive resources in a new reality of limited goods.

Low-Density Family-Formation Strategies

The most essential features of human family-formation strategies found in low-density contexts is the belief shared by family and group members that material resources necessary for life and reproduction (the pursuit of happiness) are sufficient so that all fit adults can expect to have access to them (Lancaster and Lancaster, in press). If such resources should occasionally be scarce, that scarcity is unpredictable and attempts to control access to them are impractical and costly. Given this perception, the true measure of wealth and power is, for human beings, expressed in terms of sociopolitical followings and factions. A thriving and "wealthy" family is large. Material productivity of the family is increased through increasing numbers of family members. Death of an adult provokes issues of succession to status and role within the sociopolitical system, not inheritance of property, the material needed for subsistence, which is held in common (Goody, 1966; Lancaster, 1981). Individuals are rarely alienated from their birthright, i.e., recognition of descent. Parents do not disinherit offspring from the material estate (held in common) since there is no need and no easy way to do so, children are not given up for adoption (but may be fostered by others), and children born out of marriage are not bastardized since no inheritance is at stake. Marriage is universal for men and women, and for women occurs at puberty with no delay in the life cycle. Marriages are formed through the transfer of services or goods from the groom and his family to the family of the bride, a transaction that serves to gain social recognition for his paternity of her children. Social attention is focused laterally toward peers instead of vertically because access to social power and critical aid comes from sibs and other close relatives in the same generation rather than through inheritance of access to resources between successive generations. There is relatively little attention to differentiation of role and status between same sex members of a sibship because of the assumptions that all have equal access to resources and death may lead one sib to step into the other's shoes and take up the latter's unfinished duties and responsibilities.

Low-density family-formation strategies do not focus on issues of regulating access to resources within the family because each family member has the same access to group resources as any other member of society. Instead, such strategies emphasize the equivalence of the same sex family members and a readiness to fulfill each other's role if necessary.

High-Density Family Formation Strategies

In contrast to low-density systems, high-density family-formation strategies emphasize the formation of reproductive units on a secured resource base (the treasured family estate) and the regulation of access to those resources between children born to the unit (Lancaster and Lancaster, in press). In a world perceived to have insufficient resources for all group members to successfully reproduce, wealth and power are measured in terms of access and control of the resources of the family estate, not in numbers of family members, which become a liability rather than an asset. Relationships within the family are regulated and negotiated on the basis of differential access to the resources controlled by the family with great attention to control of sexuality and reproduction, birth order, designated heirs, and possible alienation through bastardization, disinheritance, or disownment. Social attention focuses more on vertical intergenerational relations, because sib groups of potentially competing heirs have been reduced and estate-controlling parents are more important than peers and sibs for access to family wealth. Marriage is no longer a universal stage in the life cycle and is often delayed for years past puberty for both men and women, if not ruled out altogether. Marriages are negotiated on the basis of the presence of a sufficient resource base for reproduction and families of brides may even compete for quality grooms through dowry, just as families of grooms compete in a marriage settlement. Because social stratification is inevitable in high-density situations, some group members may be barred from marriage altogether. Those with unpredictable resource bases have to settle for lesser forms of reproductive alliance, such as concubinage, and each socioeconomic class may have to develop different sex-linked family-formation and parental-investment strategies.

Although, like low-density systems, high-density systems show great historical and cross-cultural variation in form, they all struggle with the same basic underlying issue of gaining control of and regulating access to scarce resources critical to reproductive success and maintaining the integrity of the family estate. Competition for access is not only between family groups but also between sibs and cousins within a family. Parents can no longer deem it sufficient to rear as many offspring as possible who are alive, healthy, and in command of the basic skills expected of adults.

TRANSFORMATIONS IN PARENTAL INVESTMENT STRATEGIES

A strong argument can be made that, among the higher primates, access to energy to support a long lactation is the principal concern of the adult female. This focus of interest lies behind species' differences in such aspects of female behavior as dispersion in geographic space, alliance formation and group structure, sexual assertiveness, pubescent wanderlust or attachment to natal group, and assertion of status (Wrangham 1975, 1980; Lancaster, 1984). Depending on feeding behavior and ecological context, some female primates are exceedingly aggressive in defending their territories or the social rank that allows them access to choice or concentrated food items. In contrast, among Old World monkeys of the colobine group, females can be only roughly labeled as high or low status and no hierarchies occur (McKenna, 1979). This is attributed to specializations of the digestive system of this large grouping of monkey species from Asia and Africa. Colobines can digest mature leaves, obtaining both nutrition and water from this abundant and dispersed resource for which differential access cannot be assured through competitive dominance.

Access to energy is a potent force in the parental-investment strategies of human women as well. Irons (1983) makes a strong case for the analysis of cross-cultural differences in family-formation patterns from the perspective of women. He suggests that women in a given culture focus on the value of certain alliances for the rearing of young. From the universe of networks created through kinship and marriage, women tend to emphasize those which offer them the most significant and assured access to energy sources during their child-rearing years. This may be a work group of women formed of female relatives, a husband, or an extended family of affines. The important point is that underlying a wide array of cross-cultural variation in family-structure and marriage patterns, we may still find an underlying theme conforming to predictions from parental-investment theory. Among women the networks most meaningful during their adult lives, given the cultural and ecological context in which they live, are those hat optimize their ability to foster and channel resources toward their children.

Parental-Investment Strategies in Low- and High-Density Systems

The principal task of low-density parental-investment strategies, is to produce the optimal number of children whose cost is measured in terms of energy and attention needed to produce healthy and fit individuals. Among hunter–gatherers, the limitation on the number of children produced appears to be found in the balance struck between the two roles of the mother as producer and reproducer (Blurton-Jones and Sibley, 1978; Lee, 1979). Given the crucial economic role of women in foraging societies in gathering and processing food and the high energetic demands of a long lactation and infant transport, such women can probably only regularly bear children every four years and remain healthy. Sedentism introduced savings in maternal energy output per child through the sibcare system and the

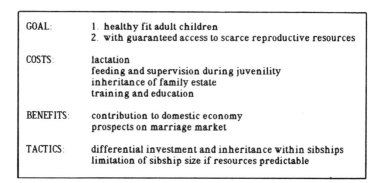

GOAL:	1. healthy fit adult children 2. with guaranteed access to scarce reproductive resources
COSTS:	lactation feeding and supervision during juvenility inheritance of family estate training and education
BENEFITS:	contribution to domestic economy prospects on marriage market
TACTICS:	differential investment and inheritance within sibships limitation of sibship size if resources predictable

Figure 7.3.   Parental calculus in high-density societies.

increase in the value of child labor, permitting the successful production of
children every two years. These "kin-centered" (Rossi, this volume, Chapter
3) systems of reproduction produce as many children as possible using a
parental investment calculus that only measures the cost of rearing fit adults
and not a need to assure specified access to reproductive "family estate"
resources during the later, adult portion of the offspring's life span (Fig. 7.2).

Historic change in parental investment was associated with the transition
from low- to high-density social systems (Fig. 7.3). One of the most salient
features of the later part of this transition is a lowered fertility referred to as
the "demographic transition," noted historically for European societies
somewhat before the impact of industrialization and currently as a demographic feature of modernization in some third-world countries (Shorter,
1975; Stone, 1977; Goody, 1983). Rossi (this volume, Chapter 3) describes
these as "child-centered" rather than "kin-centered" systems of parental
care; LeVine and White (this volume, Chapter 10) and Vinoskis (this volume,
Chapter 11) note the rising cost of child rearing as education and training
beyond the experience of individual parents became essential to producing
competitive offspring. Draper and Harpending (this volume, Chapter 8) note
the disappearance of the sibcare system for maternal helpers and data
presented by Blake (this volume, Chapter 13) suggest that large sibships may
dilute the resource of parental attention to the point where children's
success in the educational system is affected. Each of these authors touches
on facets of the same social transformation in which the parental calculus of
the costs and benefits of rearing children is revised to take into account that
the world in which each child is produced, and will in turn have to
reproduce, is one of limited resources and that parents need to adjust the
number of children in order to develop guarantees of access. Historically
parents first attempted to guarantee children access to the resources of land
and wealth, the family estate, and the flow of wealth passed from one
generation to the next (Caldwell, 1976; Lancaster and Lancaster, in press).
Later in history we find a growing emphasis of parental investment into

education and training of children to guarantee them adult lives with access to reproductive resources (LeVine and White; this volume, Chapter 10; Vinovskis, this volume Chapter 11). Paralleling this rise in the cost of producing competitive offspring, the value of child labor returned to low levels associated with hunter-gatherer societies because of the loss of the sibcare system and the need for the development of even greater skills before entering a labor market. Parental-investment strategies were altered to take into account the fact that the production of maximum numbers of healthy children was no longer sufficient, and that guarantees of access to resources in the form of education or inheritance were necessary in a world of limited goods. It would seem that this change in the human parental investment calculus is a potentially universal phenomenon inevitably unfolding from the changing ratio of human beings to the resources necessary for reproduction.

Control of Female Sexuality

The issue of male confidence in paternity is not one unique to humans. There is growing evidence that male mammals have evolved a variety of means to assess whether there is any probability that the particular offspring of a female could be their own progeny (Hausfater and Hrdy, 1984). Such mechanisms include familiarity with the mother, having mated with her during her last estrous period, or even recognition of family traits in phenotypic characters. Males may attempt to raise the likelihood of their sperm impregnating a female by guarding her, defeating other males in combat, depositing a copulatory plug to keep other sperm from entering her uterus, or by performing multiple copulations (a system of sperm competition). Parental investment theory predicts that, when a male goes beyond mating competition and also invests considerable time and/or resources into the rearing of young, the more sexual jealousy will typify males and females of the species since both sexes have much to lose to sexual competitors (Trivers, 1972; Hrdy and Williams, 1984).

Female sexual behavior in hunter-gatherer and horticultural societies is often described as unusually free from the perspective of modern ethnographers (Lancaster and Lancaster, in press; Lancaster, 1986). Typically, sexual behavior begins during childhood often preceding puberty, and virginity is not highly valued in a bride. Often young women have several years between menarche and their birth of their first child in which they are free to establish a number of sexual liaisons. However, sexual jealousy and socially disruptive sexual triangles are still a major factor in human social life. Lee (1979) in reviewing the literature on the causes of domestic violence in small-scale societies and data from the !Kung found sexual jealousy as the leading cause of fatal violence. Similarly, Daly, Wilson, and

Weghorst (1982), in reviewing violence in a modern city, found that in the case of murder by acquaintances, the vast majority of victims and perpetrators, both male and female, were members of sexual triangles or victims of sexual jealousy. Violence to intimidate a mate or eliminate a rival appear in similarly high frequencies in both small- and large-scale societies.

However, the transition to the family-formation and parental-investment strategies typical of high-density societies is associated with a major change in social perspective on female sexuality; it may become a threat to the social order itself. Instead of being the simple concern of the male and female actors immediately involved in drama, female sexuality becomes a central issue in the definition of sex roles, the separation of the sexes in space and activity, and a crucial element in bargaining over marriage agreements. Bridal virginity and wifely fidelity become central social values closely linked to the honor of the household. The guarding of female virtue becomes a primary concern for the families of the bride and groom, both before and after marriage. Dickemann (1981) points to the historic developments in Europe, East Asia, India, and the Middle East of the claustration of women in a variety of cultural forms emphasizing fidelity, tests of virginity, purdah, veiling, and other forms of seclusion, and a double standard allowing freer male sexuality—all in association with restricted reproductions coupled with a growing need for guaranteed resources in the form of land, animals, or wealth for the rearing of children.

In effect, the families of women, and the women themselves, collaborate in guaranteeing to grooms and husbands that the children receiving paternal investment will be their own offspring. The family of the groom has a strong interest because the wealth to be transferred or divided is family controlled and, just like male parental energy, should not be squandered on rearing the offspring of unrelated men. Sometimes the families of brides go even further and, besides guaranteeing paternity to the husband, also offer substantial payments in the form of a dowry in order to get a quality groom (Dickemann, 1979a). In the upper classes, male payments of bride service and bride wealth to guarantee social recognition of paternity may give way, or be complemented by, dowry competition between families of brides for high-status sons-in-law. It is particularly noteworthy that in such stratified societies, where those at the bottom of the social scale have little likelihood of attaining the resources needed for reproduction, the attractiveness of female "virtue" and the size of dowries progressively increase going up the social scale.

Manipulation of Parental Investment within Sibships

Another hallmark of the transition from low- to high-density reproductive systems among humans is the development of a wide variety of forms of manipulation of parental investment within sibships. In low-density systems, parents may manipulate their investment by practicing infanticide to increase birth spacing, thereby favoring an older child too young to be weaned, or occasionally by practicing female infanticide, particularly in small-scale societies where adult male lives are unusually dangerous because of hunting or warfare (McKee, 1984; Scrimshaw, 1984). This kind of female infanticide can be interpreted as manipulation of the sex ratio at birth—with an eye to potential skews in the sex ratio during adulthood and difficulties for those individuals seeking partners in a universal marriage market. In contrast to high-density systems, parental investment in foraging and horticultural societies does not seem to emphasize various forms of sexual or birth order favoritism but rather appears to attempt to optimize and equalize the opportunities of each child to develop into a healthy, fit adult.

High-density societies express a wide variety of patterns that indicate differential investment within the sibship, sometimes discriminating on the basis of sex and sometimes in terms of birth order. One of the most common forms of discrimination is differential inheritance and designated heirs (Goody, 1976). In order to keep the family estate intact and not dissipated by division through equal inheritance in successive generations, often a designated heir such as first- or lastborn son will inherit the bulk of the estate and other children will only receive portions large enough to help them get started independently. Frequently, the inheritance going to a daughter is received in the form of a dowry at marriage, in which her portion of the family estate is used to gain access to a quality groom. As Dickemann (1979a) has argued, dowry represents an uniquely human pattern of reproductive behavior in which the maternal grandparents invest resources to place a daughter in an advantageous position on the marriage market in order to enhance the reproductive success of their grandchildren. In other words, a dowry represents a long-range parental investment that gambles on a payoff in a yet-unborn, third generation.

The need to dower daughters, however, puts special pressures on high-status families that leads them to manipulate sex ratios within sibships, because rearing a larger proportion of daughters than sons could lead to a rapid dispersal of the family estate (Dickemann, 1979b). The higher the status of a family, the more likely it is to practice female infanticide to reduce the number of daughters to be dowered, or to use the institutions of spinsterhood or religious celibacy, to limit the number of daughters who marry. Such practices were widely spread throughout feudal Japan, China, Southeast Asia, India, the Middle East, and Europe, and the greatest intensity always came at the top of the social pyramid (Dickemann, 1979b).

Parents in high-density societies regularly respond to a calculus which evaluates the cost of rearing each child, its contribution to the domestic economy during both childhood and adulthood, and its chances on the marriage market given the resources of the family (Dickemann, 1979b); Guttentag and Secord, 1983; Hrdy, in press). One of the most difficult but not uncommon methods by which parents manipulate the cost of rearing particular children is by differentially investing in them during childhood. At first examination differential neglect or abuse of children within a sibship appears to run counter to parental-investment theory—if a child is allowed to survive infancy, why abuse it? However, such behavior conforms to theoretical predictions if the context is born in mind. Infanticide is based on an assessment by parents that conditions will not be favorable to raise that particular child during the next 15–20 years or that its reproductive prospects will not be good. However, given the long development of humans, such predictions are not easily made. Given the fluctuating conditions that occur among rural and urban poor, investment capacities which varies from year to year are expectable (Lightcap et al., 1982; Daly and Wilson, 1984; Scrimshaw, 1984). For example, Johannson (1984), in an elegant paper examining the death of young adults due to tuberculosis in 18th and 19th century Europe, found major fluctuations in the sex ratio of those dying that varied in accordance with the economic value of each sex in the domestic economy. When the value of female labor declined due to the mechanization of agriculture in the late 18th century, the tuberculosis death rate of young adult women rose above that of young men and remained high until the introduction of mills increased wage labor opportunities for young women. Johannson argues that tuberculosis is a sensitive instrument by which to measure parental investment, because diversion of family resources in the form of extra food, warmth, and rest to the afflicted was the only treatment available in the 18th and 19th centuries. As Johannson (1984) and Scrimshaw (1984) suggest, differential neglect, the most common form of female child abuse, may be a kind of "deferred infanticide"—a form likely when future resources fluctuate and are unpredictable.

Parental investment in high-density reproductive strategies is character-ized by two behavior patterns not found in low-density societies. The first is adjustments to do more than simply raise as many healthy, fit children as possible, but also to try to guarantee them access to reproductive resources when they reach adulthood through inheritance of wealth or special training and education. The second, is differential investment within a sibship through behavioral patterns such as designated heirs, unequal inheritance, female infanticide, or deferred infanticide through neglect. All of these disparate patterns represent a single underlying motive—the desire of parents to improve the future reproductive success of their children by enhancing their opportunities to gain access to the resources needed for successful reproduction.

CONCLUSION

The watershed between parental-investment and family-formation strategies in low- and high-density reproductive contexts marks a major shift in human behavior with respect to how human families produce children. Under low-density conditions in which actors perceive the resources necessary to sustain life and successful reproduction as abundant, parents will produce as many offspring as possible given the conditions of their social and ecological environment. Parental goals are simply to rear the maximum number of healthy, fit offspring. Under high-density conditions in which parents perceive that there are not enough free resources, for all children to have equal opportunities for reproduction, parents will revise their investment strategies in order to enhance their children's access to reproductive resources over that of other parents' children. Such revisions of family-formation and parental-investment strategies accompanied deep-seated adaptive changes in economic attitudes (see Lancaster, 1979) and virtually transformed human parental behavior, values, and goals. These revisions introduced a host of cultural practices ranging from regulation of the numbers of children reared, hypergyny, dowry competition, female infanticide and neglect during childhood, parental manipulation of investment within sibships, designated heirs, and control of female sexuality through claustration. All of these behavioral adaptations represent parental recognition of a transformation in the world around them in which the resources necessary for life and reproduction are no longer free and openly accessible to all fit adults.

SUMMARY

In the course of human history there was a critical watershed which differentiated the parental-investment and family-formation strategies of humans living in low-density, foraging or horticultural societies from those living in high-density and stratified agricultural and industrial societies. The crucial feature of this watershed was a changed perception of the ratio between the numbers of human beings in a society and the resources necessary to sustain life and successful reproduction. For most of human history, for most of the time, and perhaps for most people who have ever lived, human experience has been that there is a shortage of people and that more children and more recruits to the social group are desirable. Land and critical resources were freely accessible. Temporary shortages in local areas were buffered by systems of reciprocal access, visiting between neighbors, and migration.

In contrast, nearly everywhere in the world human, populations eventually grew to the point where basic resources were no longer free. Although this change from resources-as-free-goods to resources-as-limited-goods has been a nearly universal feature of human experience, for many societies it came relatively late in history, perhaps only 2000–3000 years ago; for some it is only happening today. This shift in human experience had a profound impact on nearly every feature of human family life and relations between kin, including ways in which mates are chosen, ways marriages are formed and structured, how social position and property are passed, the way that wealth is measured and displayed, the ways in which individuals are incorporated into or alienated from families, the way sexual behavior is patterned for each sex, and how parents invest time, energy, and resources in their offspring.

ACKNOWLEDGMENTS

The impetus to the first author for the writing of this paper came from a series of conferences and meetings organized by the Committee on Biosocial Perspectives on Parenthood and Offspring Development under the auspices of the Social Science Research Council. Support as a Senior Research Fellow in 1984 from the Wenner-Gren Foundation for Anthropological Research provided time free for the gathering and interpretation of material. Sara Hrdy, Patti Gowati, and Jim Chisholm gave helpful commentaries on an early version of the manuscript.

REFERENCES

Barkow, J. H., and Burley, N. Human fertility, evolutionary biology and the demographic transition. *Ethology and Sociobiology*, 1980, *1*, 163–180.

Blurton-Jones, N., and Sibley, R. M. Testing adaptiveness of culturally determined behavior: Do Bushmen women maximize reproductive success by spacing births widely and foraging seldom? In N. G. Blurton-Jones and V. Reynolds (Eds.), *Human Behaviour and Adaptation*. London: Taylor and Francis, 1978. pp. 135–157.

Caldwell, J. C. Toward a restatement of demographic transition theory. *Population and Development Review*, 1976, *2*, 321–366.

Cohen, M. N., Malpass, R. J., and Klein, J. G. (Eds.). *Biosocial Mechanisms of Population Regulation*. New Haven, CT: Yale University Press, 1980.

Daly, M., and Wilson, M. A sociobiological analysis of human infanticide. In G. Hausfater and S. Blaffer Hrdy (Eds.) *Infanticide: Comparative and evolutionary perspectives*. NY: Aldine, 1984, pp. 487–503.

Daly, M., Wilson, M., and Weghorst, S. J. Male sexual jealousy. *Ethology and Sociobiology*, 1982, *3*, 11–27.

Dickemann, M. The ecology of mating systems in hypergynous dowry societies. *Social Science Information*, 1979, *18*, 163–195.

Dickemann, M. Female infanticide, reproductive strategies and social stratification: A preliminary model. In N. Chagnon and W. G. Irons (Eds.), *Evolutionary Biology and Human Social Behavior*. N. Scituate, MA: Duxbury Press, 1979, pp. 321–367.

Dickemann, M. Paternal confidence and dowry competition: A biocultural analysis of purdah. In R. Alexander and D. Tinkle (Eds.), *Natural Selection and Social Behavior. NY: Chiron Press, 1981, pp. 417–438.*

Draper P., Social and economic constraints on child life among the !Kung. In I. DeVore and R. Lee (Eds.), *Kalahari Hunter-Gatherers*. Cambridge, MA: Harvard University Press, 1976, pp. 199–217.

Draper, P. Cultural contrasts in sex role egalitarianism in foraging and sedentary contexts. In R. Reiter (Ed.), *Toward an Anthropology of Women*. NY: Monthly Review Press, 1975, pp. 77–109.

Goody, Jack. *Succession to High Office*. Cambridge: Cambridge University Press, 1966.

Goody, Jack. Inheritance, property and marriage in Africa and Eurasia. *Sociology*, 1969, *3*, 55–76.

Goody, Jack. The evolution of the family. In P. Laslett and R. Wall (Eds.), *Household and Family in Time Past*. Cambridge: Cambridge University Press, 1972, pp. 103–124.

Goody, Jack. Bride wealth and dowry in Africa and Eurasia. In J. Goody and S. Tambiah (Eds.), *Bride Wealth and Dowry*. Cambridge: Cambridge University Press, 1973.

Goody, Jack. *Production and Reproduction: A Comparative Study of the Domestic Domain*. Cambridge: Cambridge University Press, 1976.

Goody, Jack. *The Development of the Family and Marriage in Europe*. Cambridge: Cambridge University Press, 1983.

Guttentag, M., and Secord, P. *Too Many Women? The Sex Ratio Question*. Beverly Hills, CA: Sage, 1983.

Hassan, F. *Demographic Archeology*. NY: Academic Press, 1981.

Hausfater, G., and Hrdy, S. Blaffer (Eds.). *Infanticide: Comparative and Evolutionary Perspectives*. NY: Aldine, 1984.

Hrdy, S. B. Sex biased parental investment among primates and other mammals: A critical evaluation of the Trivers-Willard hypothesis. In R. Gelles and J. Lancaster (Eds.), *Child Abuse and Neglect: Biosocial Dimensions*. NY: Aldine, in press.

Hrdy, S. Blaffer, and Williams, G. C. Behavioral biology and the double standard. In S. Wasser (Ed.), *Social Behavior of Female Vertebrates*. NY: Academic Press, 1983, pp. 3–17.

Irons, W. Human female reproductive strategies. In S. K. Wasser (Ed.), *Social Behavior of Female Vertebrates*. NY: Academic Press, 1983, pp. 169–213.

Johansson, S. R. Deferred infanticide: Excess female mortality during childhood. In G. Hausfater and S. Blaffer Hrdy (Eds.), *Infanticide: Comparative and Evolutionary Perspectives*. NY: Aldine, 1984, pp. 463–486.

Katz, M., and Konner, M. J. The role of the father: An anthropological perspective. In M. Lamb (Ed.), *The Role of the Father in Child Development*, rev. ed. NY: Wiley, 1981, pp. 189–222.

Konner, M. Relations among infants and juveniles in comparative perspective. In M. Lewis and L. Rosenblum (Eds.), Origins of Behavior. Vol. III: *Friendship and Peer Relations*. NY: Wiley, 1975.

Konner, M. Maternal care, infant behavior, and development among the !Kung. In

R. B. Lee and I. DeVore, *Kalahari Hunter-Gatherers*. Cambridge: Harvard University Press, 1976, pp. 218–245.

Lancaster, C. S. Women, horticulture, and society in sub-Saharan Africa. *American Anthropologist*, 1976, *78*, 539–64.

Lancaster, C. S. The influence of extensive agriculture on the study of socio-political organization and the interpretation of history. *American Ethnologist*, 1979, *6*, 329–348.

Lancaster, C. S. *The Goba of the Zambezi: Sex Roles, Economics and Change*. Norman, OK: University of Oklahoma Press, 1981.

Lancaster, C. S., and Lancaster, J. B. *Eve and Adam: Origins of Sex and the Family*. Norman, OK: University of Oklahoma Press, in press.

Lancaster, J. B. Evolutionary perspectives on sex differences in the higher primates. In A. Rossi (Ed.), *Gender and the Life Course*. NY: Aldine, 1984, pp. 3–27.

Lancaster, J. B. Human adolescence and reproduction: An evolutionary perspective. In J. Lancaster and B. Hamburg (Eds.), *School-Age Pregnancy and Parenthood: Biosocial Dimensions*. NY: Aldine, 1986, pp. 17–37.

Lancaster, J. B., and Lancaster, C. S. Parental investment: The hominid adaptation. In D. Ortner (Ed.), *How Humans Adapt: A Biocultural Odyssey*. Washington, D.C.: Smithsonian, 1983, pp. 33–65.

Lee, R. B. *The !Kung San: Men, Women and Work in a Foraging Society*. Cambridge: Cambridge University Press, 1979.

Lightcap, J. L., Kurland, J. A., and Burgess, R. L. Child abuse: A test of some predictions from evolutionary theory: *Ethology and Sociobiology*, 1982, *3*, 61–67.

McKee, Lauris (Ed). Child survival and sex differentials in the treatment of children. (Special Issue) *Medical Anthropology*, 1984, *8*, 1–108.

McKenna, J. J. The evolution of allomothering behavior among colobine monkeys: Function and opportunities in evolution. *American Anthropologist*, 1979, *8*, 818–840.

Page, J. J., and Lesthaeghe, R. (Eds.), *Child-Spacing in Tropical Africa: Traditions and Change*. NY: Academic Press, 1981.

Scrimshaw, S. C. M. Infanticide in human populations: Societal and individual concerns. In G. Hausfater and S. Blaffer Hrdy (Eds.), *Infanticide: Comparative and Evolutionary Perspectives*. NY: Aldine, 1984, pp. 439–462.

Short, R. V. The evolution of human reproduction. *Proceedings of the Royal Society*, 1976, *B195*, 3–24.

Shorter, E. *The Making of the Modern Family*. NY: Basic, 1975.

Stone, L. *The Family, Sex and Marriage in England, 1500–1800*. NY: Harper and Row, 1977.

Trivers, R. L. Parental investment and sexual selection. In B. Campbell (Ed.), *Sexual Selection and the Descent of Man*. Chicago: Aldine, 1972, pp. 136–179.

Weisner, Thomas S. Sibling interdependence and child caretaking: A cross-cultural view. In M. Lamb and B. Sutton-Smith (Eds.), *Sibling Relationships: Their Nature and Significance Across the Lifespan*. Hillsdale, NJ: Erlbaum, 1982, pp. 305–327.

Williams, G. C. *Adaptation and Natural Selection*. Princeton, NJ: Princeton University Press, 1966.

Wrangham, R. W. On the evolution of ape social systems. *Biology and Social Life*, 1975, *18*, 335–368.

Wrangham, R. W. An ecological model of female-bonded primate groups. *Behaviour*, 1980, *75*, 262–300.

8 PARENT INVESTMENT AND THE CHILD'S ENVIRONMENT

Patricia Draper
Henry Harpending

AN OVERVIEW

One of the puzzles in human sociobiology is that human beings limit their reproductive capabilities. That is, human groups voluntarily limit their population sizes even under circumstances of apparent resource abundance. The behavior of the middle and upper socioeconomic classes in industrialized nations is an example of this anomaly. If organisms have been designed by natural selection to make copies of themselves and to maximize fitness, then why do we not see high rates of reproduction among the human groups with the most favorable access to resources: why should not the more affluent sectors of the world population competitively outstrip the less favored populations?

Instead, what human population dynamics reveal over the past few thousands of years is a variable pattern of population increase and decrease in which the species has seen drastic alterations not only in crude numbers of individuals per unit of space but in the numbers of offspring born to individual women and in the ratio of surviving to deceased children. Associated with these kinds of population swings has been a regular set of adjustments in the kinds of institutions that humans establish under different conditions of population density, population increase, decrease, and overall mortality patterns. In other words, humans share with some other animals an ability to regulate their numbers not only on the basis of present essential resources, such as food and freedom from environmental stressors, but also on the basis of cognitions about the long-term quality of the environment through which they and their descendants will be moving. For humans and other social species, the institutions that regulate kinship, mating, and subsistence are important shapers of this perceptual estimation of environmental quality.

A general problem having been stated concerning the relationship between reproduction in humans and characteristics of an environment that will support it, attention is turned to the individual, and to the question: What is the nature of the stimuli with which individual humans deal and what role can they play in the assessment of environmental quality by that individual? It is known that, for humans, postnatal learning determines many of the options available. The nature of the conventional practices and understandings of the older members of the group further delimits the channels through which new members seek to play out their social and reproductive goals. It is believed that a fruitful place to look for environmental stimuli that can influence the individual's estimation of environmental quality is the experiences individuals have in the early years of life. This analysis pertains to a more restricted time period, namely, the toddler phase, but experiences before and after this developmental stage can also be contributory. A fuller justification of the significance of this period can be found later in this chapter.

The spirit behind the analysis developed here is a recognition of the fact that humans act largely but not exclusively on the basis of beliefs. The beliefs the individual holds arise both from the individual's direct experience and from what the individual learns to believe as a result of listening to what other people say. Natural selection is unlikely to have favored an organism that relies too heavily on received wisdom. Indeed, much of the current paradigm shift in the social sciences embodies an appreciation of the extent to which humans accommodate the appearances of behavior in a utilitarian way to the normative environment while simultaneously carrying out strategies that run counter to the standards approved by the group (Barth, 1969, 1973; Moore, 1975; Hewitt and Stokes, 1975; Wrong, 1961). In other words, people are not necessarily doing what they appear to be doing.

This way of looking at the relationship between culture and behavior makes culture change and intercultural variability much easier to understand. However, the study of humans from the point of view of their evolved status, their evolutionary past, causes one to keep track of what might be called "conservative forces" in human adaptation. Human beings have undergone a particular type of selection pressure, which means that some kinds of behaviors are more likely to be expressed by modern humans than others. Although there is plasticity in our behavioral responses, those with respect to certain "hard-core" behaviors can be expected to observe certain constraints. The hardest behaviors are those having to do with sexuality, reproduction, and parenting. Whereas there are many ways to capture energy, worship the divinity, and regulate social groups, there are relatively few ways in which humans can manage conceiving, nurturing, and rearing offspring such that the coresident group has continuity over time.

The validity of this assertion is not obvious even to well-informed people who are not accustomed to thinking about human origins. When most people think about human history, they think back to the Roman Empire, or the Renaissance, or perhaps to the Industrial Revolution that did away with the agrarian basis of Western civilization. They do not think about the fact that until perhaps 10,000 years ago the economic base to support larger numbers of people and more experimental forms of human association had not appeared.

The foundation for the reasoning in this chapter is as follows: The postnatal perceived environment of the individual will vary according to the nature of the parenting practices which support that individual in his/her dependency. In their turn, the perceptions of environmental resources will influence the person's reproductive behavior at sexual maturity.

INTRODUCTION

In this chapter is juxtaposed a theory of parenting in the spirit of contemporary evolutionary biology with some data from various societies around the world. There is a special concern with the interplay between biological factors, which will favor close and sometimes intense interaction between parent and offspring, and others, which favor dilution or dissolution of the parent–child bond. Humans are outstanding among animals for their high level of investment in offspring, yet there is much variation across cultures in the amount and the duration of parental care.

It is particularly interesting that in many societies where there is substantial surrogate caretaking of children there is also high fertility, while lower fertility is associated with direct parental care of offspring. This chapter discusses parenting and reproductive behavior and questions the immediate reciprocal influence of these two behaviors in social contexts. It is conventional in the social sciences to take reproduction and parenting (or child caretaking) as fixed quantities and to consider other factors such as residence pattern, economy, work load, education, and modernization (to name a few) as intervening variables that facilitate or inhibit parenting and/or reproduction. Here it is postulated that parent–offspring relations constitute a set with interesting internal dynamics which in and of themselves can be described and modeled independently of other aspects of social life.

There is a continuum of parenting among humans that ranges between two extremes: one in which biological parents are the primary socializers of children, and another in which children from about 18 months onward must turn to a multiaged group of peers for many essential services, including feeding, supervision, and protection. These will be regarded as two "types" of caretaking, but the types are simply ends of a continuum. It is easier, if inaccurate, to talk about types.

There are some general indicators of where to look in the ethnographic record for societies which exhibit the two types of caretaking. The parent caretaking system is most commonly found at the extreme ends of the continuum of sociocultural complexity: among nomadic hunter-gatherers and among the societies of the industrialized nations. The peer caretaking system occurs most frequently (although, of course, not in all cases) among what are known as tribal-level societies. Such societies contrast with the hunter–gatherers in that they have sedentary communities with substantially larger, nucleated communities. Subsistence entails food production (by plant and/or animal raising), food storage, and a labor organization sufficiently complex that men, women, and children are working harder and at a greater variety of tasks than is seen among foraging peoples. The subsistence work of women can be done at the homestead or close enough to the homestead that they can also supervise children by means of delegating much of the physical care and watching to older child caretakers. (See Weisner, 1982: and this volume, Chapter 9, for a discussion of the structural antecedents of sib caretaking systems.)

Surprisingly, the hunter–gatherers and the industrial societies share several institutional arrangements which combine to produce a system of parent caretaking, despite otherwise major differences in the two types of societies in terms of size and sociocultural complexity. The implications of an apparent "return" to parent caretaking in industrial society will be discussed later.

The reason for focusing on the two types of caretaking is as follows: a great deal of what a child learns is generally structured by the personnel of the settings in which he is reared. This notion was developed while an explanation was sought concerning how distinctive types of social interaction result from children spending time with certain classes of individuals who differentially reinforce children's social behavior (Whiting and Whiting, 1975; Whiting and Edwards, 1974). In particular, it is proposed here that an individual's perception of the availability of resources is shaped by the nature of the agents with whom he must bargain in early childhood. Children who are reared by their parents perceive resources as scarce and hard to come by; children who are reared in the context of a multiaged peer group perceive resources to be synonymous with the social milieu to which the child has access.

When dealing with a species as complex as humans and with an entity as potentially all-encompassing as resources, it is helpful to distinguish between perception of and cognition about a resource. A perception is a response (mediated by the organism's sensory organs) that is based on the stimulus properties of an object. A cognition is an acquired evaluation or understanding about a stimulus based on the organism's experience in a transactional sense with that stimulus. In this view, the translation between perception and cognition about of resources will be different for children reared under the types of caretaking. The differences in these translations will have a number of consequences, especially in terms of reproductive behavior. The dynamics by which perceptions and cognitions are joined are difficult to specify, particularly when a behavioral system such as reproduction is the issue. In long-lived, late maturing species such as humans, it is hard to know what mechanisms have been at work to shape responses that are not apparent until much later and that operate over a period in the developmental life span of the individual (Goude, 1981).

Thus far two types of social milieu which can predominate in the rearing of children are being contrasted. In the one case, the child and caretaker contacts are intergenerational, involving immature and adult interactants. In the other case, the contacts are intragenerational, between youngsters and other children. While there are differences among the children in the peer group (such as in the mastery of certain skills), the disparities will be less than the differences between adults (who are usually parents) and the dependent child.

Another aspect of contrast has to do with the degree of genetic relatedness between the child and the personnel who are most influential in the early years. Children who are reared in a multiaged peer group will be with several (or numerous) other children, only some of whom (full sibs) will be as closely related to the child as the child's parents. According to the current evolutionary theory, any individual should be willing to favor others of high genetic relatedness as long as the costs are not excessive. Therefore, other things being equal, a child who is the primary responsibility of one or both parents (usually the mother) will, on the average, be in a more favorable position to benefit nepotistically than a child reared in a peer group.

Humans, like other mammals, show advanced development of parental investment. The trend toward increased and prolonged parent investment finds it fullest expression in primates whose young are altricial (as are human neonates), as opposed to the precocial neonates of most ungulate species whose young can run beside the mother within hours after birth. Similarly, the parent, according to this formulation, is highly susceptible to signals from the offspring. It is predicted herein that decisions on the part of parents regarding how much of any resource to give to a particular offspring (in lieu of giving to future or living siblings of that offspring) and the amount of resources required by the offspring are heavily influenced by the nature of the access a child has to its parents. In other words, a child with unrestricted access to the parent can alter the congnitions that the parent forms of the offspring. This parent may subsequently be maneuvered into investing more heavily in that offspring than he/she might otherwise do.

This notion is essentially ethological and assumes that human parent-off-spring interactions are behaviors which have undergone intense selective pressures in our evolutionary past. A difficulty for social scientists who attend to human events within relatively recent historical times is that they ignore the fact that during much of the time span in which hominids evolved and *Homo sapiens* solidified its species characteristics, the social and economic life of humans was vastly different from what it is now. This applies to virtually all of the world's population, for nearly all humans today subsist by technologies that are only a few thousand years old and live in aggregations that are both more dense and more sedentary than would have been possible before the development of agriculture and animal domestication. A problem for scientists who view modern humans from the vantage point of the adaptive legacy they have brought with them from the past is that they do not know very much about the way people lived 30,000 or 40,000 years ago, when anatomically modern humans were spreading in such a rapid way over much of the globe.

Further pitfalls await those interested in speculative reconstructions. Postnatal learning has seemed so obviously a crucial component of our adaptation that it has been natural to look on all existing human cultural adaptations as equally plausible. They are there, after all, and in a manner of speaking, all working. This chapter argues that intense and prolonged parent–offspring relationships have been one of the more fixed aspects of human phenotypic (behavioral) adaptation, and that child caretaking systems which rely heavily on the use of surrogate caretakers are relatively recent.

Since modern biologists have paid attention to the fact that behavior as well as morphological attributes are subject to natural selection, such behaviors as parental investment and reproductive behavior (among others) have attracted closer examination. For mammalian species the matter of investment is especially critical, the more so among the more altricial species whose young are born in a neotonous state and where prolonged parental care is absolutely essential if any of the offspring are to survive. The higher primates (great apes and humans) extend a mammalian trend toward producing fewer and higher quality offspring whose prolonged period of juvenile dependency requires a degree of commitment of parental care which is extraordinary in comparison with other mammalian species.

An important point about the study of behavior from an evolutionary standpoint is that compared to form or physiology, the behavioral response of an organism seems less fixed by the genetic material. This becomes more pertinent as the more complex life forms are considered. For them the postnatal environment is a highly variable training ground for observing and practicing a variety of behaviors. In species such as apes and humans many behavioral predispositions are indeed wired in, but they require a certain type of social context and exposure to conspecifics before the individual can "learn" what he was born to be. The higher primates remain relatively generalized at a physical level, yet capable of huge gains of an intellectual sort through learning. This means that evolution works only partially on the physical form, since the individual can make postnatal adjustments to his environment through behavior. Natural selection, in this case, works not only on specific behavioral predispositions but also on the ability to learn and to modify behavior given relevant cues.

NOMADISM VERSUS SEDENTISM AND PARENTAL INVESTMENT

The human postnatal environment is mediated through social institutions and technology. It is believed that some institutions will foster a cognition of adequacy or abundance in resources; other institutions may foster a cognition of scarcity of relevant resources. As stated earlier, it is not clear how social science can get at the distinctions between perception of relevant stimuli (apparent resources) and the culturally patterned attitudes held by individuals which guide their evaluation response to these stimuli (Goude, 1981).

Under ancient hominid conditions, a prominent part of the environment for parents and dependent offspring must have been each other. They formed a durable set. Human young required, then as now, years of intense nurturance, and the mother was the one who delivered the bulk of the care, feeding, and carrying of young. This kind of pattern is described for most contemporary hunter–gatherer groups. Given the small size of social groups, the mobility and the absence of supplementary foods, the mother and her mate would have been the primary target of succorance requests by the child. The child played a major and active role in sustaining a high level of parental investment. While other group members could provide temporary assistance to the parents, it would be unlikely that a system of substantial surrogate caretaking would develop in this context. The parents, particularly the mother, must have been the significant caretaker of children under 4 years of age. She could not elude her offspring, although a mother or father could abandon or neglect a child, thereby terminating investment. However, the parent could not readily delegate major caretaking responsibility to others in the first several years of the child's life. The child living under these circumstances was in a position to actively regulate parental care.

A brief example from the hunter–gatherer society of the !Kung bushmen of the Kalahari Desert will illustrate some of these assertions. Their society lacks many of the features found in tribal-level societies which could support peer care. For example, group size is small: an average of around 35 people per group (Draper, 1973; 1976). The numbers of available children are correspondingly small. Given the tendency of !Kung to change bands, parents cannot routinely expect to find a sufficient number or an acceptable choice of older peers to mind their children.

The nature of the diet for these (and most other hunter–gatherers) is such that good quality supplementary infant food is not regularly available (Howell, 1976, 1979; Lee, 1972, 1979; Harpending, 1976). In agricultural societies where women are absent from the household while working in nearby fields, the surrogate caretakers can feed the infant a gruel made from the carbohydrate staple, and/or the surrogate can bring the infant to the mother for feeding. !Kung women are too far away on the days when they gather to be able to return home for feeding. Mothers instead opt to carry with them 2- and 3-year-old children on a day's gathering trip, whom they nurse during the day and feed from the foods they collect.

There comes a time when mothers discourage the dependence of their offspring, but they do this without finding another child or adult to take over major parts of the role they played as the child's caretaker. The most traumatic part of the weaning (from the child's point of view) comes when, as a result of its increased weight at 3 or more years of age, the mother insists that the child is too heavy to carry with her on gathering trips. This precipitates rather dramatic tantrums from the child who is being "weaned from the back." While the weaning separates the mother from her child during those days on which the mother gathers (in the !Kung society women gather about 3 or 4 days in a week), her reluctant "weanling" can be close to her on the days she remains in the camp. While she is gone other adults who are in camp maintain an informal watch over the children.

When the mother returns at the end of the day, she and her older child or children are reunited. Mother, father, and children continue to eat together at the same hearth and from the same pot, and all sleep together at night. It is not until adolescence that girls and boys move their sleeping place to join age mates or older kin of the same sex who do not have a mate. Neither a mother or father tries to peripheralize their children; in fact, parents often schedule their hunting and gathering on alternate days so that one of them can be with the children (Draper 1973; 1976).

One of the more critical elements in the technological transformation of the Neolithic has been the changes wrought on the parent–offspring dyad. Sedentism, increased food availability, changing forms of social organization, and later increased labor requirements have led to a number of new cultural practices. The relevant ones are those which have led to the casting of parent–offspring relationships in new forms wherein the intense and sustained, direct interaction between offspring and their biological parents is no longer essential for child survival. (Not all tribal-level societies will have developed a peer caretaking system. But as stated earlier, societies of this type are the place to look for this institution.) The uncoupling of parent–offspring mutuality has influenced fertility and the nature of parental care. When the set is broken, new sources of variation in reproduction and offspring care will appear.

In the next section the two types of parenting, parent care and peer care, will be expanded on. Examples of ethnographic cases will be cited and the notion of a linkage between types of parenting, fertility, and resource perception will be developed further.

THE MODEL: TWO KINDS OF CARETAKING

A child who is nurtured primarily by the parent(s) develops a distinctive set of cognitions about its environment. These cognitions contrast with those of a child who is reared by surrogate parents or, especially, by a multiaged and variable group of peers. Here attention is drawn to several attributes of the biological parent rearing condition that influence the kinds of things a child learns. In so doing a large and important literature will be bypassed on the ways in which sociocultural factors such as household structure, mother's work load, nature of economy, caretaker density, and others affect the care infants receive (Whiting and Whiting, 1975; Weisner, 1982; Goldberg, 1977; Ritchie and Ritchie, 1979; Leiderman et al., 1977; Greenfield, 1981; LeVine, 1974, 1980a, 1980b; Chisholm, 1981, 1983). Instead the focus is on the transactional nature of parent–child interaction from the standpoint of their genetic relatedness and the status differences between adult and child which promote a characteristic set or style of cognition on the part of the child.

For example, it will be argued that the high degree of genetic relatedness between parent and offspring constitutes a special context for the development of dyadic ties, one that is not duplicated in the case of other dyadic ties the child may have, even in the case of relationships with full siblings whose genetic relatedness is, on the average, the same.

BIOLOGICAL RELATEDNESS BETWEEN PARENT AND OFFSPRING

The genetic relatedness between parent and offspring should influence the nature of their interaction for two reasons; (1) the parent is selected to favor offspring and should not cease caring for a given offspring unless the parent judges its own ultimate fitness will be reduced by continued investment in a particular offspring; (2) because of the high degree of shared genetic material, the parent and child may be better able to read each other's signals and predict each other's behavior. It is likely that offspring will favor parents with something that might be described as heightened awareness. We know that infants develop strong bonds with their primary caretakers. The interpretation that this attachment drive is innate is strengthened by the many studies of human and nonhumans which show how normal development is deranged in the individual when the established attachment figure is removed or denied from birth (Harlow and Harlow, 1965, 1969; Harlow and Suomi, 1970; Bowlby, 1969).

As Trivers pointed out, there is potential theoretical complexity underlying the nature of communication between parent and offspring (Trivers, 1974). In sexually reproducing species they are incompletely related, their "interests" are not in general completely congruent, so transmission of both honest and dishonest messages should be expected.

Maynard Smith (1974), in a general discussion of interactions between animals, shows that there is little reason for animals to routinely convey accurate information about intentions or internal states to each other, while information about abilities or power may be advantageously transferred. His viewpoint is derived from a consideration of how confrontation strategies among animals should evolve, but his discussion assumes that the "players" of his game are unrelated. Genetic relationship should shift the balance of the game in the direction of increased accuracy, so a better assessment of states and needs between related individuals can be expected. These are very general grounds for anticipating more empathy and familiarity between natural parents and offspring than between adults and unrelated children (Maynard Smith, 1974).

If humans do in fact assess genetic relatedness (whether consciously or not), there are two obvious mechanisms that may be involved. First, the well-studied phenomenon of parent–offspring attachment may be the mechanism by which the dyad "learns" that its members are genetically related. This is clearly so in domestic animals such as goats, where an infant separated after birth from its mother is not recognized by the mother even a day later. The infant is a powerful stimulus at this time, but physical separation defeats the attachment mechanism. Of course, such dramatic effects are not known for humans, but the reports of failure of maternal bonding with premature babies who have been kept apart from the mother for a prolonged period lead to the suspicion that similar mechanisms are present in the human species.

Given a propensity to form attachments, an obvious strategy for a human mother who is resisting a child is to minimize face-to-face close interaction. Descriptions of peer group cultures often describe how the mother is less accessible to young children than any other adult of the village. The mother seems to make a conscious attempt to avoid the child's presence, probably because of the child's heightened salience. Women pursuing a prolonged high investment strategy, on the other hand, have much less to "fear" from their toddlers and do not avoid them.

A second mechanism for recognizing relatedness is to recognize phenotypic cues such as aspects of morphology, odor, and so on. These may be reliable indicators of relatedness, but little is known of the significance of phenotypic cues in human assessment. A possible indication is the prevalence of positive phenotypic assortative mating in groups where marriages are not arranged, such as in the United States. Humans seem to prefer to mate with those similar to themselves, but the effect is not large in most studies (Thiessen and Gregg, 1980).

Studies of childhood socialization have always been troubled by the fact that their subjects were being reared by their biological parents. Researchers overwhelmingly attribute outcome in the children to things parents do to the child. Studies of assortative mating show that additional mechanisms are at work that sort out certain sources of diversity between mates (Thiessen and Gregg, 1980). A research design which incorporated a longitudinal study of parent–offspring interaction in families where adoptive infants were followed by births of natural children would be useful for testing these ideas.

The question of whether children's interaction with peers varies according to degree of genetic relatedness will be an interesting one to pursue. We know of no published literature on the subject for humans. Studies of rhesus monkeys show some differences in peer interaction when siblings were concerned; particularly that bouts of aggression and sexual display were virtually nonexistent (see Golopol, 1979; cited in Suomi, 1982). Another study of rhesus monkeys for whom paternity data were known showed that mothers were much more tolerant of approaches and grabs of their infants when these approaches came from paternal half-sibs of the infant than when these attempts came from unrelated juveniles (Small and Smith, 1981). These data suggest that infant and juvenile monkeys are capable of differentiating kin on both the maternal and paternal sides from nonkin (Suomi, 1982; Wu et al., 1980). Presumably there is some perceptual basis for this social preference, which in the case of paternal half-sibs is "unlearned" or at least not mediated in an obvious way by the corearing maternal half-sibs receive.

Other indications that there is heightened salience with which parents and offspring recognize (at some level) each other's signals are weaker and more inferential. The growing literature on child abuse and neglect shows that child abusers are disproportionately found among stepparents (Lennington, 1981; Wilson et al., 1980; Daly et al., 1982; Daly and Wilson, 1980, 1981; Lightcap et al., 1982; Pelton, 1978; Polansky et al., 1981). Most interpretations of these findings, whether of sociobiological or environmentalist orientation, argue that the stepparent "knows" that the child of the current spouse is not his or her own, and therefore has a preexisting basis for depriving the stepchild in favor of natural children. Neither of these orientations recognizes the possibility that the stepchild is unattractive from the point of view of the stepparent because of a mutual failure to recognize each other's signals.

A test of this notion would require a study of stepparent–stepchild relations under a variety of conditions. It would be important to contrast stepparents who took charge of stepchildren when the stepchildren were quite young with those who acquired older stepchildren. A similar contrast should be arranged with respect to socioeconomic status within the study and control populations. Particularly appropriate for a study of this sort would be stepparent–stepchild relationships that began in the stepchild's infancy and among families of secure economic status.

STATUS CHARACTERISTICS OF PARENTS

In the parent socialization model it is not necessary that the parent be the only caregiver in the first 18 months, although the expectation is that the child will be primarily attached to its mother but willing to accept secondary care from other familiar individuals. There are now several excellent studies of surrogate caretaking of infants in traditional and underdeveloped societies. Examples include Goldberg, 1977; Leiderman and Leiderman, 1977; Martini and Kirkpatrick, 1981; Munroe and Munroe, 1971; Gallimore, Boggs, and Jordan, 1974. Herein the concern is with a later stage in the child's life, particularly the time a child learns to walk well on his own. This time is arbitrarily set at about 18 months.

The period of 18 months to about 2 years of age is promising for the model because of developmental changes occurring at this time, and because this is the age at which children in many societies are turned over to nonparental caretakers. While earlier in life the child required physical handling for transport, feeding, and toileting, the older child is now advanced in neuromotor terms. It can get about on its own and initiate separation from the parent, who increasingly must resort to language to control the child and increased vigilance to keep track of the child's whereabouts. Similarly, the more independent offspring must have ways of monitoring the parent, her whereabouts, her approval-disapproval, and so on. Therefore, toddlerhood should be a period during which infants are especially cognizant of parents and sensitive to their cues in new ways. Attachment theory, of course, incorporates the notion that the attachment behaviors have been selected because they promote the survival of an infant in a species such as ours, where the young mature slowly and remain dependent on intensive care from the mother for many years (Bowlby, 1969; Ainsworth, 1967; Rheingold and Eckerman, 1970).

During the toddler period the infant is maximally disposed to couple its own modus vivendi with that of the parent. However, this is precisely the point at which parents in certain kinds of societies deflect the child's attempts to gain their nearness and attention onto other care givers (Murphy and Murphy, 1974; Schuster, 1979; Weisner, 1982; LeVine and LeVine, 1981; Ritchie and Ritchie, 1979; Ritchie, 1957; Weisner, Chapter 9, this volume; DuBois, 1944; Kelekna, 1981; Korbin, 1981; Levy, 1968, 1969; Mead, 1928; Gallimore, Boggs, and Jordan, 1974).

Children clearly can succeed under a variety of caretaking regimes. There is no reason to assume that the western pattern is inherently superior. It is suggested, however, that being socialized in the post-18-month period by parents can have different outcomes for what is learned and how it is learned, in contrast with the alternate system in which children are socialized in early childhood by various others, especially including a multiaged peer group.

The parent is also at an important transition point from the point of view of this model (Trivers, 1974). She must decide whether to continue investing time and resources in this offspring or to terminate the conflict by weaning and training the child to redirect its requests for succorance to other members of the group. One can predict on the basis of evolutionary theory that the weanling will attend carefully to the mother at this time. This is when the parent can be expected to feel maximum ambivalence about the offspring, and, indeed, a child of this age in many societies experiences an abrupt discontinuity in its life. It is vulnerable to reduced parental care, and theory predicts it will accelerate its demands for attention, contact and other demonstrations of parental care. The mother is usually the preferred attachment figure; she is genetically closely related to the child, and as a model she is powerful, highly skilled, and already identified by the child as a supplier of resources.

Other properties of the parent seem relevant. From the child's point of view, the mother is a consistent and predictable source of interaction. As she is intellectually mature, she is likely to adjust her behavior toward the child in a way that takes account of its intellectual level. This is an example of a sensitivity on the part of the adult that should reduce confusion and anxiety in the child as it attempts to understand the parent's behavior. As a result, the intended and unintended consequences of the parent's behavior should be intensified.

Because of the status difference between parent and child, the child reared primarily by its parent spends relatively little time in dominance struggle and competitive manipulation of other people. This child knows where resources can be obtained, and they are handed over increasingly as the child masters adult competence. This attribute is important because the child is *not* learning that desirable things are held by a loose congregation of acquaintances whose goodwill must be maintained by constant social attention.

The toddler's dilemma is resolved by canalization in the sense that Waddington (1957) used the term in describing the constraints on biological or behavioral systems. Until the child is too heavy for carrying and too incompetent to walk on its own, it will require and receive care from the mother and whoever else will assist her. As the child matures, its demands become more insistent, onerous, and varied (because the child's communicative repertoire expands). It is being judged by others as less deserving (needful) of the quality of care it has previously enjoyed. To continue Waddington's metaphor of the "epigenetic landscape," once the child crosses certain thresholds of maturation it enters a different kind of topography of potential nurturance. If the child enters one behavioral system in which parents withdraw from their previous role, development will continue but along a different route and with different consequences. If the toddler's dilemma is resolved in favor of continued association with the parent, the probability of another set of outcomes is increased. The outcome will, in part, depend on the ways in which different sociocultural systems canalize the social choices available to the child.

A child whose parents retain the role of primary socializers enters a landscape in which the world is populated by powerful others whose dissimilarities with the child are marked. The parents and their adult surrogates are few in number and relatively stable in composition. As the rate of the child's mastery of adult skills is slow, he concludes that desirable goods are hard to obtain. A major probable consequence of this rearing environment is that it teaches the child an essentially conservative approach to the evaluation of apparent resources.

PEER GROUP CARETAKING

There are many societies and subgroups within societies where parental investment is terminated rather abruptly when a child reaches 18 months to 2 years of age. One of the most detailed descriptions of this pattern is found in Polynesia (Ritchie and Ritchie, 1979) although similar accounts turn up in ethnographies of other groups (LeVine and LeVine, 1966; Murphy and Murphy, 1974; Schuster, 1979; Korbin, 1981; DuBois, 1944; Kelekna, 1981).

According to the Polynesian practice, when the child has passed the stage of infancy and is judged to be capable of getting by on its own, it is not only turned loose for the daylight hours but also actively discouraged from returning to the parents for a continuation of the intensive nurturance it has received previously. (See also Levy, 1973; Ritchie and Ritchie, 1970; Howard, 1970, 1974; Gallimore, Boggs, and Jordan, 1974.) The child is denied the parent's attention and is discouraged from maintaining proximity by staying around the mother. The child joins a multiaged peer group and is often assigned to a particular older child who is expected to do most of the things that were previously done by the parent: feeding, dressing, disciplining, protecting. This peer group is a transient gang drawn from the neighborhood and houses of relatives. It varies in size and composition, depending on the time of day and the activity at hand. Descriptions of how parents achieve separation of children in toddler or transition stage are found in the account by Gallimore, Boggs, and Jordan of Hawaiian socialization practices.

> An infant that cries and fusses until picked up, fed, changed, and so on, is acceptable: a whining, clinging, demanding toddler is not. While babies live in the midst of an adult world, indeed, often at its very center, children are expected to function in a separate sphere that only overlaps with that of adults at the peripheries. To a large extent, they are not to intrude into adult activities except on invitation, or if they must have adult assistance, they should request it in a subtle and unobtrusive fashion, marking the presence of a need without making demands to which an adult must respond.
> . . . Other instances of reaction to intrusiveness include: scolding toddlers for approaching and responding to a field worker, pushing children away from groups of grown-ups, spanking a toddler for crying, and so on (pp. 119–120).

Experts disagree on whether or not this transition is traumatic for the child. For example, Ritchie and Ritchie maintain that parents are firm and insistent about the child separating itself, but not hostile. They say that the conflict for the child is ameliorated by prior experiences with multiple caretakers, which buffers the child's sense of loss upon being denied access to the parent (Ritchie and Ritchie, 1979; Gallimore, Boggs, and Jordan, 1974). Whether or not it is traumatic, it is very different from the way middle-class Americans think children should be raised.

Descriptions of rural, traditional child rearing in African societies mention many of the same features. The mother cares intensively for the infant in the first year of its life (though much of the "minding" may be delegated to an older child) and remains the person in authority (Weisner, 1982). Once the child is weaned it is turned over to older children, and from this point on the mother's investment in that particular child drops steeply. As the mother is already the main provider of food through her agricultural role, successive children are not looked upon as difficult to feed (LeVine, 1980b). Children are discouraged from seeking adult attention, asking too many questions, and in general from drawing unnecessary attention to themselves. Instead, they learn to direct most of their social interaction to their peers.

Children for whom major sources of socialization are other children, particularly older children, are "learning" different facts and different rules. What are the differences? A series of contrasts with the biological parent model presented earlier will be described below.

STATUS CHARACTERISTICS OF PEERS

The status difference between a child and its peer mentors will be less marked than for the child reared by the parent, and this will influence some types of learning. The disparity between the skills of a 3- to 5-year-old child and an 8- or 10-year-old child will be less. The older child, though acting with delegated authority, will be perceived by the child as less powerful than an adult and therefore less worthy of emulation (Whiting, 1960). As a result, the younger child may perceive its own shortcomings less acutely. This may well be advantageous in terms of emotional development, since a child will be associated at different times with children with whom he is closely matched as well as to whom he is inferior or superior, with respect to some skill.

Children's attention spans are short and their activities more rapidly changed; therefore, they are less likely to be as consistent as a parent would be in the examples they set for their charges or in their roles as rewarders and punishers. Hawaiian children show this pattern clearly:

> Some of the "older" siblings who may assume a caretaker role are relatively young themselves and new to the job, and consequently, they may be

unreliable. This condition is aggravated by compulsory school attendance of all over six years. A toddler is sometimes seen wandering from one sibling to another seeking some kind of assistance, sometimes approaching the parent. With experience, most learn to signal their needs unobtrusively, to which mothers may respond with the desired assistance, by ignoring, or by pointing out the problem to a sibling. At times, as in the case in any family there may be little satisfaction from any source (Gallimore, Boggs, and Jordan, 1974, pp. 124–125).

There are more personnel shifts under peer group socialization. This means the child is under less consistent scrutiny from his superiors: he can shift groups according to the task at hand and can get out from under negative evaluation by changing peer associations. This property of peer groups gives a child a degree of latitude that is probably lacking under the parent-rearing condition. Children have more opportunity to seek out satisfactions of whatever sort from various sources, and this in itself may promote learning and acquisition of skills for which the child is developmentally prepared.

The peer group can be an important source of vital resources for children who are trained not to direct dependent requests to the parents. A research project currently underway among the Mende of Sierra Leone details the extent to which peers are resources (Bledsoe and W. Murphy, personal communication, n.d.) Mende children are weaned and turned over to a variable group of peers, usually children of the polygynous and neighboring compounds (Bledsoe and Isingo-Abanihe, in press). Often a particular older child (ideally 7 or more years of age) is charged with the minding of a 2- or 3-year-old. The common practice with regard to meals is for one or more women in the compound to prepare one main meal each day. Children who are no longer deemed "infants" are fed together and separately from adults. They are served their food in a single common pot and are expected to share. However, adult supervision of their eating habits is not routine; older children manage to eat faster and to elbow younger children aside. Moreover, adults, particularly the men, receive larger portions of the higher quality food (meat, eggs, and fish), and the children's pot is likely to be skimpy on the sauce that contains animal protein.

While outright cases of child malnutrition are not rare, it seems that even children who appear to be adequately nourished are preoccupied wth food and describe themselves as frequently hungry. Children spend a substantial part of their days foraging, or, more properly, scrounging for food. They visit their peers from other households at mealtime when they have reason to believe extra food will be available. Several children cooperate in harvesting wild fruits when they are in season. Mende parents report that they do not look forward to the season of the year when wild fruits are available because the children are often gone (foraging) and parents cannot use threats of denying food as a way of disciplining children.

Peers exert strong pressure on each other to share purchased food; bottled drinks, breads, and candies bought from vendors are quickly divided, with each child receiving only a mouthful before the next child insists on his share. Peers provide each other a safe haven when they fall out of grace with their own parents. Since children's sleeping arrangements are informal, peers can move in with each other for one or more nights without causing consternation in either household.

Scientists who look into child nutrition in underdeveloped parts of the world sometimes encounter the apparent paradox of children who fail to show signs of undernutrition when other evidence would lead to the conclusion that they are sorely lacking in, for example, adequate protein or certain threshold levels of vitamins and minerals (Fleuret, 1979; Wilson, 1974). In the case of the East African Shambaa people described by Fleuret, many of the economic and social conditions considered to be associated with peer group rearing are indicated, albeit obliquely, by the author. The Shambaa are agricultural, and though using simple cultivating technology, have achieved densities in excess of 400 persons per square mile. Fleuret argues that in order to understand the nutritional intake of Shambaa children, it is necessary to actually follow or accompany them in their daily routines. In her discussion other relevant facts about their lives are revealed:

> Children over the age of two or three do not usually spend most of their time with the mother, as they have been weaned or even displaced by a subsequent birth. These children are too young to respond as informants [about their food intake] nor can their parents be asked to give a twenty-four-hour recall of their intake. . . . five children who were observed ranged in age from two and one-half to fourteen years; each already had specific household duties or were in the charge of an older sibling under conditions that took them away from the household during all or part of the day, and thus away from parental supervision. Snacking is common during these periods away from home, and fruit is commonly eaten. (p. 263)

From the point of view of the model, children who are reared in this context learn that there are multiple suppliers of resources. Friendship, approval, information, food, and protection can be had from different peers, depending on how many there are, how variable they are, and how good the child's access to individuals in his peer network is. This kind of child garners resources in proportion to his ability to manipulate social relations within his peer group; social skills are acquired early and are important adjuncts for survival. What is important is who the individual knows, who these people are, what they have, and how they are disposed toward the child.

Peer group rearing also seems to foster an individual who looks out on his social field and sees, regardless of objective perceptual reality, a host of potential resources based on culturally acquired evaluations and attitudes. He has grown up with the assumption that what he needs is "out there" and he must persuade someone else or some other group to help him obtain it.

In contrast, the child reared by a parent is freed from much of the burden of this kind of social work, since his social skills don't pay off in food and resources the way they do in a peer group context.

As stated earlier, the interest herein is the reciprocal influence of parent and offspring and the role each plays in promoting a given level of parental investment. The system of peer socialization described above in the form of an ideal type means that a parent is substantially shielded from attempts by the child to elicit resources, because the mother divests herself of a large measure of social and physical contact with the child (LeVine and LeVine, 1981). To the extent, then, that the child's presence and physical demands on the mother constitute a significant element in her congnitions about resource adequacy, the mother whose child is segregated in this way is less inhibited by the living child from conceiving another. Evidence for the operation of such factors is known from primate studies (Simpson et al., 1981; Suomi, 1982).

Discussion which parallels this account is found in the animal literature regarding mechanisms whereby parent–offspring relations can influence the nature of the dyadic ties and the fertility of the parent (Bateson and Klopfer, 1982). Suggestive findings for offspring effects on parents' reproductive behavior come from a wide range of animal studies (Clutton-Brock and Albon, 1982; Guinness et al., 1978; Harper, 1981; Simpson et al., 1981), which show that, depending on the species and factors of social structure and availability of resources, there can be a delay on the part of the mother in conceiving another, depending on the sex of the previous born offspring. For example, among rhesus macaques for whom the stable group structure centers around hierarchically organized female lineages, mothers who have daughters take a longer time to reconceive than mothers who have sons (Simpson et al, 1981). Clutton-Brock and Albon suggest that sex differences in the behavior of males and females may be indicated. For example, the lower activity levels of females and their preferences for remaining physically closer to the mother may mean that females may spend more time on the mother's nipples, which could lead to a longer period of postpartum amenorrhea after the female young are born (Clutton-Brock and Albon, 1982, p. 230; Konner and Worthman, 1980).

The parent versus peer model of caretaking being developed in this chapter makes no prediction for the effects of sex of child under the two regimens. It is possible that girls and boys are influenced differently by peer rearing, but such a discussion lies outside the purview of this chapter.

THE DEMOGRAPHIC TRANSITION, FERTILITY, AND PARENTING STYLE

In an earlier section of this chapter it was noted that among parents of western, industrialized nations there is an apparent return to a system of parent caretaking. Family life is much more like that of the nomadic !Kung, a hunting and gathering people whose parent–child relationships are similar to those of other nomadic peoples. Rates of child mortality are moderate among hunter–gatherers in comparison with those of primitive agriculturalists or contemporary underdeveloped countries. Low mortality among foragers has various causes, including low population density and especially long birth spacing. Children are nursed into their third year of life and sometimes later. The mother and father remain the primary caretakers of and are themselves responsible for feeding their children.

Among agricultural, tribal-level peoples it is more common for the birth spacing interval to be shortened to between 18 months and 2 years. This means that a toddler is weaned (to make room for its next sibling) at the same time that it is physically mobile and most capable of contracting disease from the environment. The mother's milk is replaced with a carbohydrate porridge substitute which, although perhaps high in calories, is low in animal protein. If food is limited or of low quality, older children will compete with younger children for the food. In all likelihood, the quality of the child's diet will worsen once it is weaned, especially if animal protein sources are limited or denied to children. The mother herself is less able to care directly for the toddler because she has a new infant and because her subsistence work load occupies many hours per day. If the child lives in a society in which peer caretaking is practiced, an additional set of risk factors can appear.

It is known from many studies of child mortality in the underdeveloped world that the postweaning period is a particularly vulnerable time for children and that a significant portion of child deaths take place at this point. Children are not deliberately underfed by their parents, but a number of factors simultaneously impinge in a way that can be detrimental to the child's welfare (Cassidy, 1980). Children of this age, because of the size, physical immaturity, and lack of social skills, are least able to cope with adversity, particularly in the form of unsympathetic care from child caretakers.

Children of foragers and children of the relatively affluent socioeconomic classes in modern society are similar in that they have direct access to adult sponsors, usually their parents. The mobility of adults in modern and hunter–gatherer societies is probably the single most important factor in bringing about the common element of parent caretaking. In modern society, married couples move, often several times, while their children are young. Not only are ties severed with relatives who might otherwise serve as surrogates, but frequent moves interfere with stable ties being formed with neighbors and their children. Parents and children must "go it alone." This makes for potentially very close emotional ties across the generations as well as a great deal of ambivalence in the relationships due to the inevitable conflicts that arise between parents and children. The potential for children to suffer acutely when the marriages of their parents fail is, of course, great under this arrangement, for there does not exist a network of other individuals from whom the child can draw support during a difficult time.

The parent caretaking system that is now normative in many parts of the industrialized world has developed from a far different set of domestic relationships than those characteristic of our recent historical past. In relatively recent times children in landed and aristocratic segments of European society grew up under conditions in which parent care was not prominent.

There is a substantial literature on the changes the family has undergone in western history in recent centuries. Historians and demographers have noted that prior to around the beginning of the 17th century the family, as defined today, was not evident. That is to say that the sort of family affect which embodies intense emotional ties of sentiment and loyalty between parents and offspring, which most westerners think of as natural, was not the prevailing norm in earlier historical periods in European history. Rather, the social interests of adults were directed toward other adult kin and neighbors whose activities were of primary importance to the adult, and indirectly to his or her offspring. The nuclear family did not form a conceptually separate unit with separate housing, substantial privacy, and mutual relationships protected from invasions by other competing relation-ships (Stone, 1977; Aries, 1962). On various grounds it can be inferred that the quality of parental investment in offspring was similarly different from that which is now common in the middle and upper classes in modern western society. Such practices as primogeniture, wet nursing, child foster-age, and the widespread use of lower status surrogate caretakers led to pronounced inequalities in the treatment of offspring and to greater risks in the lives of children.

Explanations for the shift in the nature of parent–offspring sentiment are controversial (Thadani, 1978). Some argue for the primacy of technological and economic factors, which broke up the ancient feudal basis of society. Technological changes that opened the way to commercial and manufac-turing developments favored the entry of nonaristocratic elements of the population into new positions of power. Such groups increasingly sought formal education for their offspring, particularly sons, since they knew that literacy and social skills would be needed to consolidate their new positions in society. Other interpreters of the transformation in family relations believe that ideological shifts were most important in explaining the change. They cite the breakup of the hold of the church and the new individualism that accompanied the Reformation. It is believed that this was not limited in its effects to a more individualistic conception of the relationship between man and God.

Scholars are interested not only in the pattern of functional relations between institutions but also in the mechanisms whereby changes in one sphere are translated into changes in another sphere. If there have been changes in the structure of the family and the extent to which children are nurtured by their biological parents, then what drives these changes? How are changes at the institutional level translated into changes in behavior and sentiment in interpersonal relations within the family?

Industrialization and labor migration do not necessarily bring about changes in family relationships, for there is much evidence that the transformation of family relationships preceded industrialization (Vinovskis, 1982; Stone, 1977; Shorter, 1975; Ryder, 1976). Similarly, it has been popular to argue that as child mortality fell due to better diet, improved hygiene, and knowledge of disease control, parents were willing to become more attached to their children at earlier ages. This argument also has been criticized, since there are many instances in which the family change precedes the fall in child mortality by several decades (Vinovskis, 1982). In sum, social historians appreciate the fact and significance of the change in family relationships in their social, economic, and sentimental form, but do not agree about the causal forces involved or about why parents would move toward greater occupation with the affairs of their children.

There is evidence from studies of developing nations that urbanization, wage work, education, individual and family mobility, the breakup of authoritarian control over young adults by elders, and other concomitants of economic development among the people of developing nations are associated in the long run with *reduced* fertility (Caldwell, 1976, 1978, 1979, 1980; Cochrane, 1979). It is not understood by what mechanisms these changes in people's lives lead to lowered fertility (LeVine, 1980a). In other words, if adults from backgrounds of high fertility and lowered child mortality enter into the more modern sectors of a developing economy, why don't they continue the parenting strategy of relatively low investment per child and high fertility, meanwhile benefiting from the increased child survivorship that comes with western medical care and improved public hygiene (Barkow and Burley, 1980)? Why should the parenting strategy change (Scrimshaw, 1978)?

According to the cost-of-children hypothesis, parents restrict fertility when they realize that each child requires a heavy outlay of parental resources. Entry into a cash economy seems to be a primary factor that triggers this perception by parents. In warm climates with a traditional subsistence economy, each additional child has little effect on domestic routines and work effort. However, parents cannot necessarily obtain the money required to provide for school fees, clothing, and western medicine for their offspring. (Parents, according to this line of reasoning, must have been persuaded that it is desirable for some or all of their children to receive these benefits.) Furthermore, children who are in school for most of their prepubertal years cannot contribute their labor in a regular way to the parents. Ironically, many parents find that once children are educated they are less willing to stay in the rural homelands and maintain relations with the very people who have helped finance their educations. In this way, the cost of rearing children goes up just as the benefit from their labor goes down.

The cost-of-children hypothesis is an example of reasoning about the ways in which changes in economic institutions are translated into changes in another system: namely, fertility. The mechanism that effects these changes is not specified. Presumably it is cognitive; that is, people are capable of rationally estimating the extent of change and its consequences for their and their children's welfare. They can "see" that a revision in fertility behavior will bring benefits.

While this type of inference is plausible and appealing because it conforms to the type of reasoning processes Westerners are thought to employ, it is faulty because it does not explain why some parents within a given society begin to reduce the numbers of their offspring and increase the amount of parental resources each receives and why other parents in the same community (and sometimes in the same kin network) do not.

One possibility is that parental care is an important source of behavioral variation among humans and that decisions about the numbers and quality of offspring are means whereby humans compete over resources. In thinking about the kinds of perceptual and cognitive processes adults undergo that can influence their fertility behavior, it is possible that an important attribute of "modernization" is changes introduced into the physical and social interaction between parents and children.

Many factors enter into a changed relationship. When young adults leave their natal and rural homes they lose the network of social support previously available. They enter new communities where the niche for children's peer groups is not developed. Other children may be available in the new communities, but if the parents lack confidence in the children or their parents because of language or ethnicity, they may discourage their children from mixing with other children. The population density of the community inhabited by the modernizing wage worker will probably be much higher than that in the rural area, with the result that land prices are higher, housing costs higher, and, especially, the amount of space available for the various activities of the members of a household will be greatly reduced. The reduced space means that parents and children will be forced into much more continuous association.

The parent who provides for a child under these circumstances is confronted with a different type of offspring; one who does not go away; one who directs its social and physical needs at the parent. This condition of high offspring salience may lead to a changed cognition on the part of the parent regarding the child's "needs." At some level, children all need about the same things: food, shelter, attention, social stimulation, predictable surroundings, and a secure attachment to one or more stable caretakers. Under conditions of peer care these child needs are met differently and by different personnel, but the ultimate outcome can be of good quality in terms of children who are able to assume the roles of adults. However, the singular feature of the parent caretaker system is that the child's needs are being met by the parents; they are the focus of the child's attention and are recipients of the child's requests. The stimulus value of offspring in this situation is different. Children loom larger, noisier, and needier in parental perceptions. As a result, the cognitions on the part of the parents are changed regarding how to deal with children and how to provide for them.

The above paragraphs have outlined how typical living conditions in the more urban areas (or in areas in which wage work can be found) lead to a necessary and unprecedented commingling of parent and child activity. There still remain several questions about why or to what extent parents undergoing modernization of the type described should change their fertility behavior and their style of parenting.

There is no reason to believe that all or most parents who are experiencing modernization in their own lifetime will respond appropriately or quickly with a new form of parental care. Different socioeconomic classes and ethnic sectors within the same population of a developing country are clearly at different stages in effecting the demographic transition in their own lives. Many underdeveloped countries are now at a point of continued high fertility and lowered mortality, leading to major population expansion and impressive levels of human misery in the form of ill health, child neglect, malnutrition, and underemployment.

Furthermore, many adults of reproductive age who are entering the modern sector are themselves products of peer group raising. This, as suggested earlier, is probably predictive of a reproductive strategy in favor of producing more offspring rather than fewer, and of investing relatively little in each child. These adults will be the ones who estimate resource availability in terms of their social network. Many modernizing young adults will probably commit much of their energies to establishing social access to other adults and to establishing sexual and marital relations as a means of accessing a source of supply. Their current and future children may not figure prominently in calculations for economic survival. Particularly where young adults maintain ties with relatives in the rural areas, children are often sent back to the villages for rearing. This strategy solves, temporarily, the problem of what to do with children when the familiar peer caretaking system is no longer available to absorb children. Parents who choose this option are continuing to behave as if resources are more or less abundant.

CONCLUSIONS

In the opening sections of this chapter it was suggested that children who are reared by their parents learn that resources are scarce. It is not clear what experiences lead such children to this cognition. It has been speculated that part of the explanation lay in the fact that the parent-reared child had to deal with only one or two central caretakers whose status was markedly superior to its own. For the parent-reared child the source of supply is finite (limited to resources only certain people can supply). The parents are the object of intense observation by the child, and it can see what work the parent must do in order to obtain goods; it can see what yield is realized by a given type of work. According to the model, the cognitions about resources are quite distinct from those which are fostered by peer raising.

Parent-reared children when grown are more likely to see that resources are not only scarce but linked to their own work. The prediction is that their decisions about reproduction will be similarly influenced. Interestingly, the perceptual field that is the basis for estimation of resources will in many cases be the same for parent-reared and peer-reared adults. Yet their cognitions about the availability of resources will be different due to the fact that their experiences have taught them different things.

A consequence of this new kind of family may be a generation adapted for resource competition and low fertility. The other type of family organization appears to foster skill in manipulating others (as a way to obtain resources) and high fertility. To the extent that parental care engenders a characteristic set of cognitions, economic development along a western model should be promoted.

REFERENCES

Ainsworth, Mary, D. S. *Infancy in Uganda: Infant Care and the Growth of Attachment.* Baltimore, MD: The Johns Hopkins Press, 1967.

Aries, Philippe. *Centuries of Childhood: A Social History of Family Life.* Translation by Robert Baldick. NY: Vintage Books, 1962.

Barkow, J. H., and Burley, N. Human fertility, evolutionary bigology, and the demographic transition. *Ethology and Sociobiology,* 1980, *1,* 163–180.

Barth, Frederick. On the study of social change. *American Anthropologist,* 1969, 71(6), 661–669.

Barth, Frederick. Descent and marriage reconsidered. In Jack Goody (Ed.), *The Character of Kinship.* NY: Cambridge University Press, 1973, pp. 3–19.

Bateson, P. P. G., and Klopfer, P. M. *Perspectives in Ethology,* Vol. 5. NY: Plenum, 1982.

Bledsoe, Caroline and Uche C. Isiugo-Abanihe n.d. Strategies of child fosterage among Mende grannies in Sierra Leone. Unpublished manuscript. Population Studies Center, University of Pennsylvania.

Bowlby, John. *Attachment and Loss,* Vol. 1. NY: Basic Books, 1969.

Caldwell, John C. Toward a reinstatement of demographic transition theory. *Population and Development Review,* 1976, *2,* 3–4, 321–366.

Caldwell, John C. A theory of fertility: From high plateau to destabilization. *Population and Development Review,* 1978, *4,* 553–578.

Caldwell, John C. Education as a factor in mortality decline: an examination of Nigerian data. *Population Studies, 1979, 33*(3), 395–413.

Caldwell, J. C. Mass education as a determinant of the timing of fertility decline. *Population and Development Review,* 1980, *6,* 225–255.

Cassidy, Claire Monod. Benign neglect and toddler malnutrition. In Lawrence S. Greene and Francis E. Johnston (Eds.) *Social and Biological Predictors of Nutritional Status, Physical Growth, and Neurological Development.* Academic Press, 1980, pp. 109–139.

Chisholm, James S. Residence patterns and the environment of mother–infant interaction among the Navajo. In Tiffany M. Field *et al.* (Eds.), *Culture and Early Interactions.* Hillsdale, NJ: Earlbaum, 1981, pp. 3–19.

Chisholm, James S. *Navajo Infancy: An Ethological Study of Child Development.* Aldine, 1983.

Clutton-Brock, T. H., and Albon, S. D. Parental investment in male and female offspring in mammals. In King College Sociobiology Group (Eds.), *Current Problems in Socio-Biology.* Cambridge: Cambridge University Press, 1982, pp. 222–247.

Cochrane, Susan H. *Fertility and Education: What Do We Really Know?* Baltimore, MD: Johns Hopkins University Press, 1979.

Daly, M., and Wilson, M. Discriminative parental solicitude: a biological perspective. *Journal of Marriage and the Family,* 1980, *42,* 277–288.

Daly, M., and Wilson, M. I. Abuse and neglect of children in evolutionary perspective. In R. D. Alexander and D. W. Tinkle (Eds.), *Natural Selection and Social Behavior.* NY: Chiron Press, 1981.

Daly, M., Wilson, M., and Weghorst, S. J. Male sexual jealousy. *Ethology and Sociobiology,* 1982, *3,* 11–27.

Draper, Patricia. Crowding among hunter–gatherers: The !Kung bushmen. *Science,* 1973, *182,* 301–303.

Draper, Patricia. Social and economic constraints on !Kung childhood. In Richard B. Lee and Irven DeVore (Eds.), *Kalahari Hunter–Gatherers.* Cambridge, MA: Harvard University Press, 1976, pp. 199–217.

DuBois, Cora. *The People of Alor: A Socio-Psychological Study of an East Indian Island.* Minneapolis, MN: University of Minnesota Press, 1944.

Fleuret, Anne. Methods for evaluation of the role of fruits and wild greens in Shambaa diet: A case study. *Medical Anthropology,* 1979, *3,* 249–69.

Gallimore, Ronald, Boggs, Joan W., and Jordan, Cathie. *Culture, Behavior, and Education: A Study of Hawaiian-Americans.* Beverly Hills, CA: Sage Publications, 1974.

Goldberg, Susan. Infant development and mother infant interaction in urban Zambia. In P. Herbert Leiderman, Steven R. Tulkin, and Anne Rosenfeld (Eds.), *Culture and Infancy: Variations in the Human Experience.* NY: Academic Press, 1977, pp. 211–243.

Golopol, L. A. Effects of the birth of a younger sibling on the behavior of male and female yearling rhesus monkeys. Unpublished M. A. thesis, Madison: University of Wisconsin, 1979.

Goude, Gunnar. On evolution and ontogenetic adaptation: Toward a psychobiological approach. In K. Immelmann, G. Barlow, L. Pefnovich, and M. Main (Eds.),

Behavioral Development: The Bielefeld Interdisciplinary Project. Cambridge: Cambridge University Press, 1981, pp. 131–145.

Greenfield, Patricia Marks. Child care in cross-cultural perspectives: Implications for the future organization of child care in the United States. *Psychology of Women Quarterly,* 1981, 6, 41–54.

Guinness, F. E., Albon, S. D., and Clutton-Brock, T. H. Factors affecting reproduction in red deer (*Cervus elaphus*) hinds on rhum. *Journal of Reproduction and Fertility,* 1978, 54, 325–34.

Harlow, H. F., and Harlow, M. K. The affectional systems. In A. M. Schrier, H. F. Harlow, and F. Stollnitz (Eds.), *Behavior of Nonhuman primates,* Vol. 2. NY: Academic Press, 1965.

Harlow, H. F., and Harlow, M. K. Effects of various mother-infant relationships on Rhesus monkey behaviors. In B. M. Foss (Ed.), *Determinants of Infant Behavior,* Vol. 4. London: Methuen, 1969.

Harlow, H. F., and Suomi, S. J. From thought to therapy: lessons from a primate laboratory. *American Scientist,* 1970, 59, 538–549.

Harpending, Henry. Genetic and demographic variation in !Kung populations. In Richard B. Lee and Irven DeVore (Eds.), *Kalahari Hunter–Gatherers.* Cambridge, MA: Harvard University Press, 1976, pp. 152–65.

Harper, Lawrence V. Offspring effects upon parents. In David J. Gubernick and Peter H. Klopfer (Eds.), *Parental Care in Mammals.* NY: Plenum Press, 1981, pp. 117–117.

Hewitt, John P. and Randall Stokes Disclaimers. *American Sociological Review,* 1975, 40, 1–11.

Howard, Alan. *Learning to Be a Rotuman.* NY: Columbia Teachers College Press, 1970.

Howard, Alan. *Ain't No Big Thing.* Honolulu, HI: University Press of Hawaii, 1974.

Howell, Nancy. The population of the Dobe area !Kung. In Richard B. Lee and Irven DeVore (Eds.), *Kalahari Hunter–Gatherers.* Cambridge, MA: Harvard University Press, 1976, pp. 137–151.

Howell, Nancy. *Demography of the Dobe !Kung.* NY: Academic Press, 1979.

Kelekna, Pita. Sex asymmetry in Jivaroan Achuara society: a cultural mechanism promoting belligerence. Unpublished Doctoral Dissertation, University of New Mexico, 1981.

Konner, M., and Worthman, C. Nursing frequency, gonadal function and birth spacing among !Kung hunter–gatherers. *Science,* 1980, 207, 788–791.

Korbin, Jill E. (Ed.). *Child Abuse and Neglect: Cross-Cultural Perspectives.* Berkeley, CA: University of California Press, 1981.

Lee, Richard B. The !Kung bushmen of Botswana. In M. Bicchieri (Ed.), *Hunters and Gatherers Today.* NY: Holt, Rinehart, and Winston, 1972, pp. 327–368.

Lee, Richard. *The !Kung San.* Cambridge: Cambridge University Press, 1979.

Leiderman, P. Herbert, and Leiderman, Gloria. Economic change and infant care in an East African agricultural community. In P. Herbert Leiderman et al (Eds.), *Culture and Infancy: Variations in the Human Experience.* NY: Academic Press, 1977, pp. 405–438.

Leiderman, P. Herbert et al. (Eds.). *Culture and Infancy: Variations in the Human Experience.* NY: Academic Press, 1977.

Lennington, Sarah. Child abuse: The limits of sociobiology. *Ethology and Sociobiology*, 1981, *2*, 17–29.

LeVine, R. A. Parental goals: A cross-cultural view. *Teachers College Record*, 1974, *78*, 226–239.

LeVine, R. A. Influences of women's schooling on maternal behavior in the Third World. *Comparative Education Review*, Special Supplement, 1980, 78–105. (a)

LeVine, R. A. A cross-cultural perspective on parenting. In M. Fantini and R. Cardenas (Eds.), *Parenting in a Multi-Cultural Society*. NY: Longman, 1980. (b)

LeVine, R. A., and LeVine, Barbara. *Nyansongo: A Gusii Community*. NY: Wiley, 1966.

LeVine, Sarah, and Levine, Robert A. Child abuse and neglect in sub-Saharan Africa. In Jill Korbin (Ed.), *Child Abuse and Neglect: Cross-Cultural Perspectives*. Berkeley, CA: University of California Press, 1981, pp. 35–55.

Levy, R. I. Child management structure and its implications in a Tahitian family. In E. Vogel and N. Bell (Eds.), *A Modern Introduction to the Family*. NY: Free Press, 1968.

Levy, R. I. On getting angry in the Society Islands. *Mental Health Research in Asia and the Pacific*, Vol. 1. Honolulu, HI: University of Hawaii Press, 1969.

Levy, R. I. *Tahitians*. Chicago, IL: University of Chicago Press, 1973.

Lightcap, Joy L., Kurland, Jeffrey A., and Burgess, Robert L. Child abuse: a test of some predictions from evolutionary theory. *Ethology and Sociobiology*, 1982, *3*, 61–67.

Martini, Mary, and Kirkpatrick, John. Early interactions in the Marquesas Islands. In Tiffany Field *et al.* (Eds.), *Culture and Early Interaction*. Hillsdale, NJ: Erlbaum, 1981, pp. 189–213.

Maynard Smith, J. The theory of games and the evolution of animal conflicts. *Journal of Theoretical Biology*, 1974, 47, 209–221.

Mead, M. *Coming of Age in Samoa*. NY: William Morrow, 1928.

Moore, Sally Falk. Epilogue: uncertainties in situations, indeterminacies in culture. In Sally Falk Moore and Barbara Meyerhoff (Eds.), *Symbol and Politics in Communal Ideology*. NY: Cornell University Press, 1975, pp. 210–239.

Munroe, Ruth H., and Munroe, Robert L. Household density and infant care in an East African society. *Journal of Social Psychology*, 1971, *83*, 3–13.

Murphy, Yolanda, and Murphy, Robert. *Women of the Forest*. NY: Columbia University Press, 1974.

Pelton, Leroy H. Child abuse and neglect: The myth of classlessness. *American Journal of Orthospsychiatry*, 1978, 48(4), 608–617.

Polansky, Norman A., Chalmers, M. A., Buttenwieser, E., and Williams, D. *Damaged Parents: An Anatomy of Child Neglect*. Chicago, IL: University of Chicago Press, 1981.

Rheingold, H. L., and Eckerman, C. O. The infant separates himself from his mother. *Science*, 1970, 168, 78–82.

Ritchie, Jane. *Childhood in Rakau*. Publications in Psychology, No. 10. Wellington, New Zealand: Victoria University, Department of Psychology, 1957.

Ritchie, Jane, and Ritchie, James. *Child Rearing Patterns in New Zealand*. Wellington: A. H. and A. W. Reed, 1970.

Ritchie, Jane, and Ritchie, James. *Growing Up in Polynesia*. Sydney: George Allen and Unwin, 1979.

Ryder, Norman B. *Some Sociological Suggestions Concerning the Reduction of Fertility in Developing Countries*. Honolulu, HI: East-West Population Institute, 1976.

Schuster, Ilsa M. G. *New Woman of Lusaka*. Palo Alto, CA: Mayfield, 1979.

Scrimshaw, Susan C. M. Infant mortality and behavior in the regulation of family size. *Population and Development Review*, 1978, *4*, 383–403.

Shorter, E. *The Making of the Modern Family*. NY: Basic Books Inc., 1975.

Simpson, M. J. A., Simpson, A. E., Hooley, J., and Zunz, M. Infant related influences on inter-birth intervals in rhesus monkeys. *Nature* (London), 1981.

Small, M. F., and Smith, D. G. Interactions with infants by full siblings, paternal half-siblings and non-relatives in a captive group of rhesus macaques *(Macaca mulata)*. *American Journal of Primatology*, 1981, *1*, 91–94.

Stone, Lawrence. *The Family, Sex and Marriage in England 1500–1800*. NY: Harper & Row, 1977.

Suomi, Stephen J. Sibling relationships in nonhuman primates. In Michael E. Lamb and Brian Sutton-Smith (Eds.), *Sibling Relationships: Their Nature and Significance Across the Lifespan*. Hillsdale, NJ: Erlbaum, 1982.

Thadani, Veena N. The logic of sentiment: The family and social change. *Population and Development Review*, 1978, *4*, 457–499.

Thiessen, Del, and Gregg, Barbara. Human assortative mating and genetic equilibrium: An evolutionary perspective. *Ethology and Sociobiology*. 1980, *1*, 111–140.

Trivers, R. L. Parent-offspring conflict. *American Zoologist*, 1974, *14*, 249–264.

Vinovskis, Maris A. Home, hearth, and history: American families in the past. Paper prepared for *Ordinary people and everyday life: Perspectives on the new social history*. Unpublished manuscript, February, 1982.

Waddington, Charles H. *The Strategy of the Genes*. Winchester, MA: Allen and Unwin, 1957.

Weisner, Thomas S. Sibling interdependence and child caretaking: A cross-cultural view. In Michael E. Lamb and Brian Sutton-Smith (Eds.), *Sibling Relationships: Their Nature and Significance Across the Lifespan*. Hillsdale, NJ: Erlbaum, 1982, pp. 305–327.

Whiting, J. W. M. Resource mediation and learning by identification. In I. Isco and M. Stevenson (Eds.), *Personality Development in Children*. Austin, TX: University of Texas Press, 1960.

Whiting, Beatrice B., and Edwards, Carolyn P. A cross-cultural analysis of sex differences in the behavior of children aged three through eleven. *Journal of Social Psychology*, 1974, *91*, 171–188.

Whiting, Beatrice B., and Whiting, John W. M. *Children of Six Cultures: A Psychocultural Analysis*. Cambridge, MA: Harvard University Press, 1975.

Wilson, Christine S. Child-following: A technique for learning food and nutrient intakes. *Journal of Tropical Pediatrics and Environmental Child Health*, 1974, *20*, 9–14.

Wilson, Margo I., Daly, Martin, and Weghorst, Suzanne J. Household composition and the risk of child abuse and neglect. *Journal of Biosocial Science*, 1980, *12*, 333–340.

Wrong, Dennis. The oversocialized conception of man in modern sociology. *American Sociological Review*, 1961, 26, 183–193.

Wu, H. M. H., Holmes, W. G., Medina, S. R., and Sackett, G. P. Kin preference in infant *Macaca nemestrina*. *Nature (London)*, 1980, *285*, 225–227.

9 SOCIALIZATION FOR PARENTHOOD IN SIBLING CARETAKING SOCIETIES

Thomas S. Weisner

INTRODUCTION

Parenting and day-to-day child care are viewed quite differently in other societies. In the American middle-class pattern (although not in some North American subcultures), acquiring a mate, marriage, establishment of a new household, and child care are seen as part of a common stage in the life course, part of a process of individuation and maturation. In many non-Western societies, however, these events are separated and occur in a different order. Child-care training comes first; marriage and new households come later; a permanent established role in one's new family of procreation comes later still (Brown, 1982). Adult parenting in many horticultural and pastoral societies involves important control and management activities—decisions about allocating resources and personnel, and the training of children in culturally appropriate conduct. These are the parenting skills adults in sibling caretaking settings are struggling to develop. Western parents may first experience many aspects of child care (such as discipline, feeding, carrying, or emotional or affective nurturance and support) only as adults, after marriage. New parents in many non-Western socities have already practiced such skills through participation in the sibling care, or shared management, family system. In this context, child care is, in parents' and children's own views, more a domestic task for children to learn than a specialized task of adulthood.

The training ground for parenting skills in many non-Western societies is the shared caretaking system, in which parents, other adults, and older children are jointly responsible for younger ones. A mixed age and sex group of children share the task of child management with one another and with parents and other adults. A cross-cultural view of training for child care and parenting, then, is that child-care training occurs within the sibling group during childhood; child-care skills are learned early, from ages 5 or 6; child-care skills are separated from the social roles of parenthood, which is a later stage in life that usually includes marriage, new household formation, and changes in relations with parents and siblings; and finally, the conditions that encourage sibling care seem to stem from ecocultural characteristics common to middle-range, labor-intensive economies and populations with high fertility rates. In most non-Western societies, training for competent, culturally appropriate child care is an active apprenticeship experience for children, usually completed by adolescence and learned along with the performance of domestic tasks essential for family, and often community, survival.

Training for parenting is a culturally expectable, "enterprise-engaged" activity (Tharp et al., 1981) that is part of normal child and early adolescent development in much of the world. It also appears to be a pattern which helps families adapt to their ecocultural circumstances; from this perspective, sibling care and shared caretaking more generally is a kind of parental investment strategy. Models of parental investment in children often separate five functions of parenting: safety and protection; provision of shelter and food; teaching and instruction in cultural meanings and scripts for appropriate conduct; direct child care (feeding, carrying, bathing, dressing, monitoring, and so on); and the provision of emotional and affective support and comfort.

There seems to be a pattern to the sequence of transfer of these care-giving functions from mothers and other adults to child caretakers in shared management societies. First, children learn direct child care, and to lend emotional comfort and support; these are gradually extended to the sibling group but remain shared with parents. Mothers gradually eliminate most direct care of older children and share affective and emotional support of older children with others. Direct commands and instruction continue from the mother, while enterprise-engaged learning increasingly occurs between sibs and peers. Fathers and mothers retain their roles in ensuring safety and security and in providing subsistence, and increasingly share these tasks with older children and adolescents. Furthermore, younger parents are not *themselves* usually fully in control of many parental investment decisions relating to subsistence, security, and domestic routines early in their own adult married life; they continue to share these responsibilities with their own brothers, sisters, cousins, and parents.

This sequence in the development of parenting skills seems almost reversed in Western societies. The Western young adult is expected first to leave the natal home and establish an independent household. Gradual independence from economic and emotional support from parents is expected to follow soon after. Thus, questions of personal and familial independence, safety, security, and responsibilities for provision of one's own food, shelter, and subsistence occupies the young Western adult first. Then it is expected that marriage occurs; children and parenthood come later still. Of course there are many obvious exceptions to this ideal pattern, and a variety of subcultural alternatives to it, but this kind of preparenthood path is a frequent, expectable, and culturally normative one for Western middle-class families.

The young adult in a shared function, sibling care family has had a very different experience and looks toward a different future. This youth already has had extensive experience in child care, providing instruction, emotional support, nurturance to others, and assistance in the management of the domestic and subsistence activities of his or her family. Marriage and parenthood occur relatively soon after menarche for girls, and may or may not involve the immediate formation of an independent household. In any event, a new parent typically continues to share decisions about community safety, subsistence, and domestic routines with parents and other siblings for some time to come. The new mother's sister or cousin may send a child to help out, or a younger sister will help out. Inheritance of land, livestock, a shop, or other trade and property by the wife or husband may remain some years in the future, and it only will be then that the parent will gain full control and responsibility for his or her own homestead.

There are ecocultural (Super and Harkness, 1980) constraints on such families that encourage the development of sibling care and shared management child-care systems. These conditions include maternal supports: the structure of the daily routine, workload, dangers and need for security, and others. Sibling care is associated with high fertility and mortality, heavy workloads for family members, and sustained functional interdependence of the sibling and cousin group across the life span, in domains such as inheritance, marriage payments, common defense and protection needs, and shared participation in essential rituals and ceremonies.

The middle-range societies that most typically practice shared management and early training in child-care skills arose recently on the scale of human sociocultural evolution and spread widely around the earth only within the past 5000 years or so. It appears unlikely that nomadic or seminomadic peoples, living through gathering and hunting, practiced the customs and trained for parenthood in the way described in this chapter (Draper, 1976; Draper, Chapter 8, this volume; Konner, 1976). Mothers probably retained responsibility for their infants for longer periods of time; large domestic compounds and multiage groups of neighboring children were not common; and formal child-nurse roles are not reported in contemporary foraging groups.

Training for parenting is shaped by a mix of (1) adaptations to ecocultural conditions of family survival and economic necessity; and (2) by parental goals and ideas concerning what Goody (1982) calls "social replacement." Social replacement includes providing children with civil and kinship status and personal identity; providing training and competence to meet adult roles; and sponsoring the child's transition into the adult world. Caretaking learned in the sibling group during childhood is influenced by ecocultural adaptations and cultural ideas about childhood and parenthood. The data that will be used to illustrate shared function parent training are drawn from mothers and children in two societies where sibling care is common: the Abaluyia of Western Kenya and Hawaiian-American families in Hawaii.

AN OVERVIEW OF SIBLING CARETAKING

The Experience of Sibling Care for Children

What is it like to be a sibling caretaker? Several persons in Kenya were asked to write down their childhood experiences as sibling caretakers. "Jane," a 24-year-old girl, third from last in a family of nine living children, is a student at the University of Nairobi, a Muluyia from the Abaluyia, a Bantu, horticultural and migratory wage labor-based society in western Kenya. She took care of her brothers and sisters while living in her own home, but since she was next to last-born in her sibling group and had done well in school, she was sent to stay in the city with her father's brother for a number of years. This pattern of sharing children among the parents' sibling groups is common among the Abaluyia and many other societies with shared child management and early child-care training for children. Jane was also cared for by her older sisters while still living at home with her parents on their rural homestead.

> . . . The first two children I took care of liked me so much. I would teach them Luluyia words and sing songs. We would play most of the time, walk around outside . . . . At meal times, they would want to sit by my side and would cry, even up to 5 years old, if their food was not by mine. They would rather have it by me than by their mother. They shared a bed with me and would cry if put to sleep somewhere else. I was called their "auntie." They imitated everything I would do.
> . . . It's not to say that it was all roses. The job was so tiresome sometimes . . . the children would cry and cry, and I would wish that I was not around . . . . Feeding and changing clothes and diapers were also things I never liked. I felt so frantic sometimes when they were sick, due to the attachments between us, but could do nothing to help them.
> But for me, it also brought me closer to their parents [her own brother and sister-in-law], and I learned a great deal about everything connected with child care . . . .
> Looking generally at child care, it is a definite duty for siblings. Some parents involve their children out of their own laziness, others sincerely out of a desire for proper role preparation. The level of family wealth and the amount of property the family has is a big influence. Very wealthy families can have children and can be parents without any labor on their parts, because they hire maids or get poorer relatives to help.
> I have found that younger children do not always manage their duties well. Do they really offer the motherly care desired? Do they come when the child

cries? Do they take the child's food, or bite, hit, or pinch it [the child]? Some child caretakers just see that their charge falls asleep, and then leave it . . . .

On the other hand, the company of other children is essential for language, work, singing, and dancing. The whole situation is that the child feels that he belongs [in the sibling group], that there is a group that appreciates a lot of things it does, that values its noise and appreciates a lot of things not even significant to parents and much older children. One cannot escape the strong impact of all this on younger children, making them at the same time submissive, reasonable, rude, polite, abusive, or cunning . . . .

Although as yet unmarried and, as an educated woman, in a new position in Kenya, Jane is comfortable and already familiar with children of a wide range of ages, with domestic management, with dealing with older women who have final authority over a home, and with the moods, conflicting emotions, and chicanery of children. She is likely in turn to rely heavily on such a shared caretaking system in her own family, although her university education might change that.

Characteristics of Sibling Caretaking

Children caring for other children is a common sight for even a casual traveler in non-Western cultures throughout most of the world. Descriptions can be found in life history and autobiographical materials by participants themselves (LeVine, 1979; Langness and Frank, 1981) and appear in novels, stories, and journalistic accounts.

Cross-cultural ratings and naturalistic observations within cultures confirm the importance of child caretakers and the frequency with which children are in situations where sibling care is expected. Barry and Paxson (1971) report that female children were the principal companions/caretakers of infants in 16.7% of their HRAF standard sample, and were principal caretakers of children during early childhood in 53.9% of the societies in their sample. Weisner (1979) found that children were involved in the role of caretaker or were cared for by another child in 41% of random naturalistic observations of Abaluyia girls aged 3–8, and 15.8% of the observations of boys 3–8. Although the Six Cultures Project (Whiting and Whiting, 1975; B. Whiting, 1963) did not directly record caretaking activities during field observations, three of those six societies had infant care by older children occurring some 25% of the time (Nyansongo, Juxtlahuaca, and Tarong), and occurring about 6% of the time in the other three cultures (Taira, Khalapur, and Orchard Town). Direct observations done after school among children aged 5–9 in Hawaiian-American families in urban Honolulu showed that sibling care occurred 29.5% of the time. These children were cared for by their mothers 40.0% of the time and were judged to be independent 30.5% of the time. If the situational circumstances for child–child care occurred during these visits (e.g., if two or more children were present together in the home or outdoors), caretaking responsibility by children was observed 48.9% of the time (Weisner, Gallimore, & Tharp, 1982). Children spend much of their time in multiage, multisex groups of children, sharing responsibilities for domestic chores including child care as a normal part of the daily routine.

Although children are pressed into service as child-minders and even do errands and domestic chores by age 4 or 5, the age during which children are most often involved ranges from 7 to 13 or 14. Child care more often involves girls than boys, especially where child care occurs along with other domestic chores required of girls. Beatrice Whiting (1983) has suggested that the 7–14 age period represents the time when girls have both the requisite cognitive skills and a strong identification with and desire to emulate the female/maternal role. Adolescence frequently brings a decline in participation in more routine child-minding and domestic drudgery. By this time, younger children are usually available, or marriage may have intervened, or the adolescent has moved out to live with other kin.

Nerlove, Roberts, Klein, Yarbrough, and Habicht (1974) identified two natural indicators of cognitive skill that develop during middle childhood and that seem important in the effective performance of child management activities: *self-managed sequencing* of activity and *voluntary social activities*. Self-managed sequencing refers to the child's ability to follow a precise sequence or series of acts autonomously. Washing clothes, for example, entails gathering up a basket, clothes, and soap, then putting the clothes in a basket, then going to water or the river, and so on. These tasks require, in a correct *order*, ". . . a scanning of the model and mapping of that model onto alternatives, remembering what one had already tried and how well it fit" (*Ibid.*, p. 287). Voluntary social activities involve self-directed, shared activity with others, which assumes shared goal and rule understandings. For language-related voluntary social activities, learning ". . . to name, recognize, and verbally relate functions or attributes of objects" to others (*Ibid.*, p. 287) is crucial. This set of cognitive skills includes having learned the major kinship rules and norms of appropriate cultural and family conduct. Effective performance of child care, as a part of competencies needed to perform domestic chores and even manage the domestic routine, probably requires a minimum level of both these kinds of skills in childhood.

In turn, domestic duties help to train children in the development of more general skills. Rogoff et al. (1975, 1980) identified the 5–7 age period as a widely recognized transitional point when such skills begin to be expected. Her review used cross-cultural data on cultural beliefs about maturation and reports of age of assignment of responsibilities to children. The belief that the child is teachable and has "reason," as well as the idea that a child has a fixed personality and common sense, tends to coincide with the 5–7 shift. Children begin to be assigned child-care tasks and other household and domestic responsibilities during this period. If 5–7 is the age of onset of this shift, the 8- to 10-year-old period is frequently seen as the time when the child has attained full competence. Children appear by this point to be capable of performing more complex tasks, which may require a more holistic understanding of context, and have the ability to integrate and coordinate different sets of information. There may be a maturational basis, then, for the assignment of responsibility to children during this period.

However, the pancultural attainment of these cognitive and social skills does not of course lead to domestic task responsibility and child care in the absence of cultural requirements and familial roles encouraging them. In societies using shared management, there does appear to be a correlation between the ages when such responsibilities are initiated (5–7), the ages when independent performance becomes more generally expected (8–10), and the maturational potentials of the child during these same developmental periods.

Antecedents of Sibling Care

LeVine and White (this volume, Chapter 10) emphasize four ecocultural features that are associated with the transformation from shared caretaking to conjugal-parental care: the transformation of agrarian societies to urban-industrial ones; the demographic transition from high to low birth and death rates; the rise of mass schooling; and public interest in children and childhood as a unique and special stage in life. These authors also emphasize that there are a variety of pathways from one pattern to the other, and many cultural differences in how they are applied. Shared caretaking and conjugal-parental caretaking each has specific kinds of ecocultural contexts, and activity settings, in which socialization for parenting occurs. These activity settings are shaped by a mix of ecological constraints and opportunities, as well as cultural goals for children and parents. They have shown a broad transformation around the world in the past 200 years from shared management with a large sibling and family group to parental management of small families, but also show considerable cultural variability. The hypothesis is that parental roles and training for parenting vary due to differences in ecocultural conditions, including cultural goals; these conditions effect the shaping of activity settings within which training for parenting occurs.

A useful way to view the context in which sibling care and shared management occur is to consider their association with more general ecocultural conditions that have been shown to affect the organization of child care and human development around the world (Bronfenbrenner, 1979; Super & Harkness, 1980; R. LeVine, 1977; Whiting & Whiting, 1978). One such list has come from the collaborative work of Whiting and Edwards (in preparation). Sibling care is favored over other strategies because in some ways it is an effective adaptation to family and community needs for safety and security, provides some protection from mortality risks, fits with other familial tasks and subsistence requirements, and supports the development of other social skills and cultural ideals valued in a community.

There are three general conditions of family environment that are likely to influence how shared child management occurs, the extent to which it occurs, and hence the ways in which children are trained in parenting skills: (1) the availability of various family and domestic group members to perform parenting activities and take responsibility for them; (2) cultural and parental goals regarding the valued developmental outcomes for children, including differences between boys and girls; and (3) the kind of continuity maintained among the sibling/cousin group across the life span.

1. *Availability of personnel.* Large families, and/or societies with joint, stem, or extended domestic group residence patterns which pool large groups of children together, encourage shared care of children. A daily routine which takes both parents away from the home for work or other activities, or a heavy work load for adult women in particular, encourages sibling care. Shared care is encouraged further if large coresident families are present. High fertility may also encourage sibling care if women are pregnant and/or breast-feeding an infant or toddler for most of their own active parenting years. These mothers will often devote more attention and care to the younger, more vulnerable children in their large families. Higher maternal involvement in infant care and a heavy work load force the care of older children out into the courtyard and the sibling group, and make child labor important for survival. Cultural rules restricting women to the home, as in some areas of the Middle East or South Asia, increase the availability of nonparent adult women and tend to encourage large family compounds. In these contexts, sibling care occurs along with care by mothers and other women.

2. *Cultural ideas regarding sex-role training and child development goals.* A family cultural style of responsibility, compliance, and obedience and deference to elders encourages an emphasis on the indirect control functions of parenting rather than on the direct, continuing intense emotional involvement of a parent with each child. Beliefs in the importance of training girls for domestic and child-care skills also are associated with early sex-role specialization.

3. *A sibling group that shares important survival and reproductive obligations throughout the life span.* Sibling caretaking systems anticipate later functions shared by the sib group. These include the management and distribution of family inheritance and marriage payments; mutual needs for protection and defense; and arrangement of marriages, initiation rites, and other life-passage ceremonies. Joint care of children within such sib groups seems to go along with functional interdependence of siblings across the life

span. Sibling care as a form of parent training anticipates the fact that as adults these children will assume joint responsibility for their families' cultural and economic continuity.

There do not appear to be data available to support the view that sibling care optimizes inclusive genetic fitness. McKenna (1979 and Chapter 6, this volume) reviews the data on functional and sociobiological correlates of alloparenting. He finds wide diversity in its forms among primates and cautions against a strict inclusive fitness hypothesis as to its functions or origins. Such parenting practices appear to evolve as part of a system of social institutions, and the use of nonparental caretakers can exist for many reasons other than the genetic fitness of parents, offspring, or siblings. The variety of ecocultural features that seem associated with sibling care in human cultures supports this view.

Emlen (1982a, b) has presented a model of cooperative breeding in birds which includes both inclusive fitness and ecological variables. He points out that cooperative breeding is relatively rare, and occurs only when the cost to a bird of leaving the nest is very high compared to the cost of delaying departure. In contrast, shared care of children in human societies is widespread, and is not associated with severe costs in alternative modes of care. Emlen's model refers to *adults* delaying departure from their natal home, who then assist other birds in rearing offspring, whereas sibling caretaking refers to *juveniles* assisting in the care of their parents' (or their aunts', uncles', or cousins') children.

The ecocultural features associated with sibling care and shared management of children are those which make child care more efficient, make families more adaptive in their subsistence efforts, and promote wider parental and cultural goals regarding appropriate socialization for children.

These three broad ecocultural conditions encouraging both shared child management and early training of children in child-care activities can also be broken down into more specific variables. Each of these alone does not produce shared management; but a confluence of several of them appears to make it more likely for children to learn how to care for younger children early in life.

• *Subsistence work cycle characteristics,* including wage work, work load, returns to labor-intensive investment, tending crops or animals, distance of work settings from the home, and the role of migration or transhumance in subsistence. Sibling care and shared management should be associated with wage work away from the home, subsistence tasks done away from the home, heavier work loads, labor-intensive economies, and the periodic migration of some family members, such as in the case of seasonal or recurrent migration (e.g., Ross and Weisner, 1977). This kind of subsistence pattern requires flexibility in child-care responsibilities, and usually means that there will be continuous changes in domestic group personnel available to help in child care as children grow up. Shared functioning and early training in parenting skills should be more common under such conditions.

• *Health status and demographic characteristics* of the community, including mortality, availability of health care, birth control, fertility, family size, and residence patterns. Sibling care should be associated with large, coresident families, customs encouraging fosterage, adoption, and exchange of children between households, higher fertility, and low use of birth control. These conditions increase the range of available personnel in the household to help with child care and to learn the various roles and tasks needed to manage the family group.

• *Community safety,* such as dangers from automobiles, wild animals, community violence, warfare and raiding, and so on. Sibling care should be associated with greater environmental dangers, particularly those outside the household. Sibling care is more likely to occur where older boys and young men become involved in security and protection of the home and community. They will probably move away from the home in adolescence and young adulthood, leaving older girls and others in the domestic group responsible for child care and domestic management. These conditions may increase the need for regular monitoring and care of young children by others, and increase the likelihood that fathers and younger males are not around the home and available to assist in these tasks.

• *Division of labor* by age and sex, and the differential prestige of work activities. Shared and sibling care should be associated with sex role-specific and age-ranked tasks. Many sibling care systems are associated with clear authority hierarchies and patterns of rank and deference. Sibling care tasks typically entail (White, Burton, and Brudner, 1977) expectations that children, especially girls, will participate in the domestic task system and remain near the home.

• *Role of women* in the community and social supports for women; degree of autonomy and independence of women; institutional supports, such as female work groups and mutual aid societies; polygyny and cowives in the home; importance of church and women's ceremonial groups. The presence of such social supports for women is often associated with shared management of children and sibling caretaking. Greater female interdependence in work and cultural activities ouside the home appears related to increased interdependence and sharing of child-care and parenting functions within the domestic group as well. Maternal control of the organization of child care and the domestic domain is also associated with shared care.

• *Role of the father:* Greater male involvement in family protection and subsistence support functions outside the home, and less paternal involvement in the domestic domain, seem to be associated with more use of sibling care. The active presence of men in supportive roles in the domestic domain, especially those involving direct care of children, would generally be associated with less need for sibling care.

• *Parental sources of information* about child care, including formal education, and modernity. Modernity and education seem to reduce exclusive reliance on sibling care, and increase variability in the available parental alternatives. There is great diversity in the choices and short-term strategies employed by such parents (Leiderman and Leiderman, 1977).

• *Community and familial heterogeneity,* particularly large differences in wealth, the presence of castes, or oppression and dominance of some groups over others. Sibling care seems influenced by such heterogeneity and differences in rank or wealth to the extent that servants or other dependent groups perform domestic work, including child care, and thus replace siblings.

Correlates and Consequences of Sibling Care

Sibling care has been directly or indirectly linked to a variety of cognitive, personality, and social relational outcomes in children (Weisner and Gallimore, 1977). "Polymatric" care of infants and young children, for instance, has been associated with a more diffused attachment to the mother and a stronger, enduring attachment to other significant caretakers (Leiderman and Leiderman, 1974a, 1974b; Levy, 1968). Maternal influence on subsequent behavioral outcomes is not necessarily displaced by nonmaternal caretakers, however. For instance, Munroe and Munroe (1980) studied the Logoli, a high sibling care culture in western Kenya, and found that infants with more maternal involvement during infancy showed evidence of more labile affective expression five years later. Indeed, learning to monitor the mother's wishes and gaining her favor through one's position in the sibling group is an important skill in sibling-care systems.

Sibling care is associated with earlier sex role training for girls in the areas of domestic management, responsibility and compliance, and prosocial and nurturant behavior. Some of these behaviors may generalize to some non-child-care situations (Whiting and Whiting, 1975; B. Whiting, 1983; Draper, 1975). Young children are likely to participate in play groups that include more older girls than boys and younger children of both sexes (Ember, 1981; Whiting and Edwards, 1973). Wenger (1983) provides an excellent example of the system of childhood socialization in a middle-level horticultural society, the Giriama of Kenya. The Giriama encourage responsible domestic work and nurturance toward young children, and emphasize these roles more for girls than for boys. In Wenger's study, girls (controlling for age and available targets for interaction) are more likely to be assigned child-care and domestic tasks, are less often found alone and in pure play and social situations, and are more often directed toward these activities and situations by adult women.

Sibling caretaking is also associated with customs such as fosterage, adoption, and child lending. One reason for the movement of children between households is the provision of assistance in child care to kin. E. Goody (1982) and J. Goody (1969) have documented fosterage for West African societies, and Carroll (1970) and Gallimore and Howard (1968) for Oceania. Weisner (1982) describes the practice among the Abaluyia of western Kenya of sending a young girl to help her older sister with the sister's children, or to care for elderly parents. The numbers involved in such child exchanges are high; Gallimore et al. (1974) reported adoption rates of 23% in their Hawaiian-American samples, and Goody reports that of 106 sibling groups studied in three communities in Ghana, only 20, 25, and 23%, respectively, did *not* have a member fostered out for the purpose of learning occupations, as an aid to kin, or for other reasons (E. Goody, 1982, p. 157).

Training for interdependence and affiliation, not autonomous independence and achievement, among the peer group is associated with sibling care and shared management child-care systems (Gallimore, Boggs, and Jordan, 1974; Weisner, 1982). Children learn to work within "pivot roles" (Levy, 1973); i.e., roles where the child must at one moment defer to an elder child or mother and not long after become the primary caretaker of the home, assuming responsibility and utilizing decision-making skills. Some authors have argued that these roles produce sophisticated social skills, empathy, and role flexibility (Tharp et al., in press), while others have suggested that they lead to an early "hardening" of some aspects of personality and values (Mead, 1968; Ritchie and Ritchie, 1979). Ochs and Schieffelin (in press) present material from Samoa which suggests a resolution to this issue. They point out that sibling care giving often occurs in societies already very concerned with deference and hierarchy. Thus, a Samoan child's behavior is fluid across the day, depending on whether older, more senior family members or caretakers are present. A cross-sectional view during a period of the day when the mother, an older sister, and the father are within view or hearing might show a child caretaker displaying a somewhat rigid, limited behavioral pattern, with little vocalization or active, direct responsibility, due to the nature of the child's low status rank in that setting at that point in time. A later point in the day might find the child to be relatively senior in rank and in charge, directing other children and displaying quite different behaviors. Their interpretation is that the sibling caretaking hierarchy and its associated training for parenting teaches *positional awareness* and sensitivity, both in the family system generally and with respect to caretaking in particular. The result seems to be flexibility in child-care styles—but within clear and early-acquired situationally and socially defined limits. In societies where deference, hierarchy, and authority are focal cultural and familial concerns, this may prove to be a general pattern (cf. LeVine, 1973).

Children growing up in cultures practicing sibling caretaking have shown a more field dependent cognitive style (Cohen, 1969; Witkin et al., 1974; Park and Gallimore, 1975). This cultural difference in response pattern may be due in part to generalized cultural expectations of conformity and compliance pressures in societies which also practice sibling caretaking. There are no studies separating children within a culture who have had different levels of sibling care exposure and testing them on similar cognitive measures. Munroe and Munroe (1983; in press) however, clearly show birth-order effects for memory, pattern completion, and block design tests, favoring early-born children. They speculate that caretaker roles among older children, and corresponding differences in maternal involvement in child care, may contribute to these differences. Blake (this volume, Chapter 13), Zajonc and Markus (1975), and others have also noted a general decrement in mean IQ and school achievement measures correlated with increased family size and birth order. Sibling caretaking roles are associated with larger family sizes both culturally and in the incidence of sib care among families within a community. However, it is not known if there is an independent effect of participation in sibling caretaking (whether as caretaker or as charge) on IQ scores or school achievement. Some indirect evidence suggests that there is no such relationship independent of family size (Leiderman and Leiderman, 1974a; Weisner, in preparation), but research is needed on this issue.

In any event, IQ and school-related cognitive skills are unlikely to be strongly related to sibling care experience. School skills involved manipulation of symbols disassociated from everyday, enterprise-engaged activity; they require context-independent manipulation of language, with adults as teachers. In contrast, functional or adaptive measures of competence, which attempt to assess situated intelligence and social sensitivity, are the kinds of talents that might have stronger associations with sibling caretaking within societies. Nerlove et al. (1974, 1975), cited earlier, identified two such dimensions self-managed sequencing skills and voluntary social activity that were associated with both community judgments of smartness in children and cognitive test measures. Children with such skills may be selecting themselves for sibling care, or may be differentially selected by mothers for this role. In turn, participation in sibling care appears to encourage the development of these skills in all children in a culture.

Beginning with Minturn and Lambert (1964), efforts to replicate findings from cross-cultural data within cultures has been difficult (see Munroe and Munroe, 1980; Shweder, 1979a, 1979b; Lewis and Ban, 1977). In general, it is safer to make cultural-level statements about differences between sibling care and nonsibling care cultures, subcultures, or communities, than to predict intracultural or individual difference outcomes for particular children. One reason for this is that every child in a family constellation has his or her own unique interpersonal "environment." Family size, birth order, or birth spacing effects are far stronger in *group* comparisons across families than they are in accounting for individual differences within a family or school or classroom (Scarr and Grajek, 1982). In addition, cultural expectations regarding socialization for parenting are transmitted through mechanisms other than direct, individual experience. A child's direct exposure to sibling care in its own family may be low or absent; but if this same child participates in a culture characterized by such a pattern, the child's training for parenting is affected. Weisner, Gallimore, and Tharp (1982), for example, found that sibling care among urban Hawaiian-Americans was pervasive and culturally recognized as a pattern of caretaking, yet also highly variable in the family's and individual child's experience. The quality of this cultural experience is described in the next section.

The Quality of Social Relationships

Tharp et al. (1984) illustrate many of the qualities of social network relations in shared care families. The Hawaiian-American or Abaluyia mother may be alternately warm or gruff and busy, but there is an understood, intense *belonging* and shared sense of responsibility between parents and children. Families encourage interdependence (not autonomous independence); responsibility to others (not expectations of services from adults); shared work and functions (rather than particular, specialized tasks); shared resources (not private space and possessions); cooperation and affiliation (not competition and individual achievement); and deference to parents (not egalitarian discussions and family "democracy").

"Children are accustomed to flexible rearrangements of work schedules and responsibilities worked out within the sibling group. Adult supervision is usually mediated by older siblings. Thus children have considerable independence, felt autonomy and competence" (Tharp et al., 1984, p. 12). There is not the same Western middle class tightrope walk between emotional and economic dependency of children on adults on the one hand, and early pressure for autonomy and independent competence outside the home on the other.

Hawaiian children are expected not to make trouble for parents— but they are expected to stand up for themselves, to be "tough" (Ibid.). Children become very sensitive to dominance relationships, along with caretaking responsibilities. Hence, life in the sibling group is not a cooperative, supportive, romantic idyll for children. Some sense of this is gained from interviews with 70 Kenyan mothers regarding what events within their sibling/courtyard group need their intervention. Most mothers mentioned more than one event. In order of frequency of mention they include: child being beaten up by others, or threatened and harassed; lack of food, and children arguing over food; child needing help with schoolwork; child being sick; child needing money or other resources and being unable to get them from other children. These examples show the two major situations in which mothers actively become involved: intervention in physical and verbal teasing or harassment when requested; and provision of resources or information children can't or won't provide for each other.

Teaching of younger children and learning from parents and older children occurs less through verbal instruction and control and more through mixed modes of coparticipation in the task or activity being learned; through modeling and demonstrations, or through nonverbal example (Ochs, 1982; Jordan, 1981a, 1981b).

> . . . emphasis is on learning from models, shared-functioning, and on direct assistance by intervention in performance when error occurs. Learning occurs in a mode of "enterprise-engagements" in which the learner is actually engaged in performing, in some degree, the skill or task that he is learning . . . . Emphasis is not on "I'll tell you how to do it," but on "watch," "listen," "participate," "try" (Tharp et al., 1984, pp. 14–15).

The feeling of being enmeshed in the sibling or domestic compound group and doing important work competently is "one of the main ways to initiate, confirm, and signal friendship and good feeling among a group of people" (Ibid., p. 37).

The emotional or subjective experience of training for child care in particular, and future parenthood more generally takes shape along with these feelings. These are affective tones and feelings that are probably carried into adulthood through the sharing of parenting and caretaking between adults and other children in one's community. A well-established, shared caretaking community is an emotionally satisfying experience. Parenting is thus accompanied by a personal and cultural confirmation of cohort and kin membership, as well as by the more familiar feelings of intense love and protectiveness parents have for their children.

MOTHERS' AND CHILDREN'S INTERACTION: A KENYAN RURAL-URBAN EXAMPLE

Direct naturalistic observations of the social behavior of children in shared function, sibling-care cultures show high proportions of prosocial as well as task and chore behaviors. Data from the Abaluyia of western Kenya illustrate this pattern. The Abaluyia sample consists of 24 matched pairs of families. Half the families lived in their rural clan homeland, and their matched pairs lived in an urban housing estate in Nairobi. Each urban male household head was matched with his rural counterpart by age, formal education level, and local lineage membership. The sample used for field observations of children's social behaviors consisted of all children living in the rural homesteads or urban rooms with these 48 matched pairs of men.

The matched rural-urban sample design allows for a systematic comparison between the evolved cultural patterns of behavior which characterize these Abaluyia families, on the one hand, and the localized ecocultural conditions which permit or encourage sibling caretaking, on the other. In the urban setting very few older children were available for child care, since most remained in the rural area to attend school and to do domestic and farm work. As a result, urban mothers were involved in more direct interaction with their children, and also had fewer tasks and chores to perform in the city. The rural-urban comparisons suggest which features of shared function families persist, even in these changed urban circumstances, and which are modified by ecocultural features of city life.

Abaluyia children spend their time in rather large sibling groups which may also include other children and some adults. The rural group size mode is 5 to 7, the urban (salient others excluding strangers) peaks at 2 to 3, with another mode at 6 to 7. There is more variety in the personnel actually available and salient for children in the *rural* setting, even though the potential numbers and variety are, of course, greater in town. Rural homesteads, however, include more different kinds of kin, usually have older children present, and, of course, have a wide range of friends and neighbors available to help and to visit.

The data analyses are based on 168 home observations 30 minutes long of 63 different children aged 2 to 8. The social behaviors are summarized by the proportion of each type (nurturance, aggression, chores, and so on) for two age categories (2 to 4 or 5 to 8), sex of child, location (rural or urban), and dyad types (child–child, or child–mother) (see Figures 9.1 and 9.6)[1]

A 30-minute continuous running written record was taken in the field of children's social behavior. The children targeted for observation were between the ages of 2 and 8, and everyone with whom these children interacted, regardless of age, was included in the observations. Data were subsequently coded using a modified version of the behavior code developed for the Six Cultures Project (Whiting and Whiting, 1975). Field observers were trained local students familiar to the families. Protocols were independently coded, with the rule that no category with reliability coefficients under .70 were retained. Most categories had agreements well over this minimum level. Reliability and validity were also assessed by obtaining a set of field protocols written simultaneously by two observers visiting the same homestead. These protocols were subsequently divided into interacts and scored by independent coders. Results indicated that the specific sequence of behaviors recorded were not necessarily identical (as to either

---

[1]The age of the target of interaction is not specified. Whiting and Edwards (in preparation) have examined these same dyad types in greater detail, broken down by both subject and target age, and have found age-of-target effects. However, for the general purpose of contrasting Abaluyia urban and rural profiles across broad behavior descriptions like nurturance or sociability, the aggregate data are most useful.

order or behavior type), but the overall proportions of the various behavior categories, summed across the 30-minute observation period, were not significantly different across pairs of observers. This result suggests that these observational procedures reliably capture the *patterning* of interactional styles within the family, but do not necessarily capture the details of each moment-to-moment interaction sequence. Such a level of precision could only be attained in the field by major changes in the mechanics of recording—by using fully precoded recording formats, for example, and/or videotaping of field data for later coding.

Figure 9.1 shows the overall levels of nurturance observed between children and between mothers with their children. Nurturance includes providing direct care; providing resources, such as food; and providing emotional support and comfort to others. Girls display nearly as much nurturant behavior as do mothers. The magnitude of these proportions is particularly large for girls, ranging from 9% of all girls' social behaviors (for girls showing nurturance to boys in the country), up to 17% (for girls showing nurturance to boys in town). Mothers showed nurturance scores ranging from 12.5 to 17.5%. Boys receive more nurturance from mothers and their sisters and female cousins in the city than in the country, and boys are less likely than their sisters to offer nurturance to others in either locale. Boys in the city are in or near their urban room more, with less opportunity to roam, and are less likely to be in caretaking roles.

Providing emotional support and comfort, in contrast to providing resources such as food or direct care, shows a pattern similar to that for overall nurturance (Figure 9.2). However, mothers are somewhat more likely than child caretakers to provide such emotional support, especially with younger children. (There were relatively few young boys in the observations, and this may have skewed the exceptional data for nurturance shown by rural girls to boys.)

Mothers are substantially more likely than children to give instructions and orders in the performance of child-care tasks, as Figure 9.3 shows. Mothers gave such direction some 8–12% of the time, compared to from 0 to 3% for children. Girls continue to offer directions regarding child care more than to boys.

Mothers are more actively directive regarding all chores and tasks, not only those related to child care (Figure 9.4): mothers' directives concerning all tasks range from 12 to 20% of their interactions, compared to none to 1.5% for children. These African parents command, manage, and verbally direct; siblings and children collaborate with one another in doing tasks and chores, including child care.

When these children are not involved in tasks and chores, they are usually engaged in friendly sociability: shows of friendliness and affection, physical contact and sitting together, seeking one or another out for shared social activities, and play (Figure 9.5). The child–child proportions for

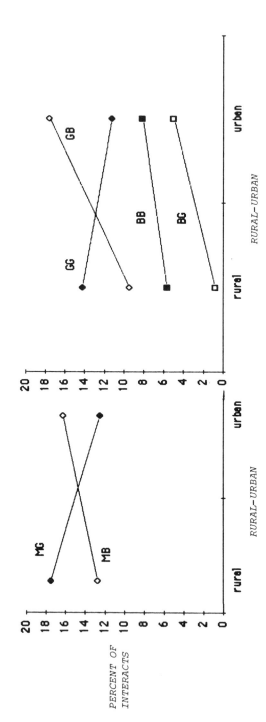

FIGURE 9.1. Nurturant interactions (direct care and emotional support) by dyad and rural-urban residence. GG, girls to girls; GB, girls to boys; BB, boys to boys; BG, boys to girls; MG, mothers to girls; MB, mothers to boys. *Left*, mothers to children; *right*, child to child.

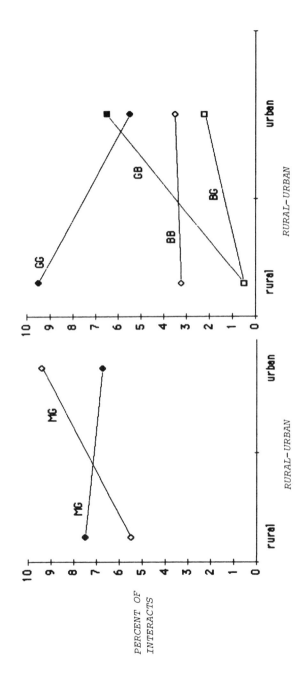

FIGURE 9.2.   Emotional support and comfort, by dyad and rural–urban residence. GG, girls to girls; GB, girls to boys; BB, boys to boys; BG, boys to girls; MG, mothers to girls; MB, mothers to boys. *Left,* mothers to children; *right,* child to child.

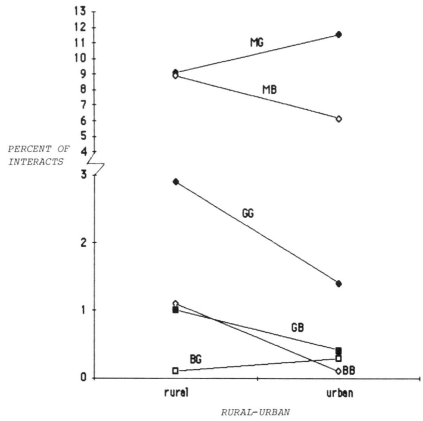

FIGURE 9.3.   Requests and instructions regarding child caretaking, by dyad and
rural-urban residence. GG, girls to girls; GB, girls to boys; BB, boys to
boys; BG, boys to girls; MG, mothers to girls; MB, mothers to boys.
Top, mothers to children; *bottom,* child to child.

sociability range in magnitude from 21 to 46%, with girls somewhat more
likely to be involved in such interactions; mothers' sociability scores range
from 6 to 10.5%.

But children also try to dominate and disrupt each others' activities
(Figure 9.6). They engage in physical assaults and insults, seek to annoy
each other, and try to get other children to submit to their demands. This is
so more often with boys than with girls, although boys are less rambunctious
in the city with other boys. This result appears due to the ecological features
of urban versus rural households. In the city mothers are present more of the
time, and older boys are seldom in the city for long periods. Older siblings
are often not present to watch over their activities. In general, dominance
and disruptiveness increases among city children due to these features.

City life does not substantially reduce the amount of child–child nurtur-

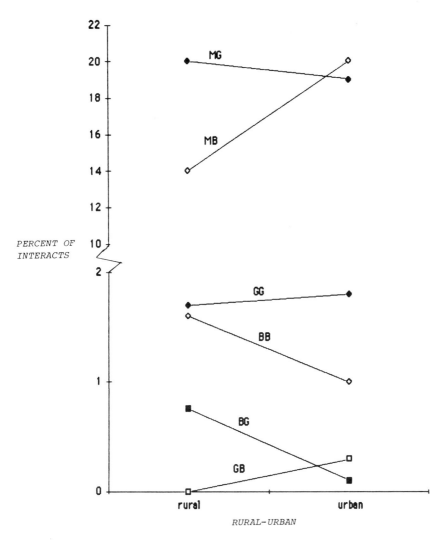

FIGURE 9.4. Requests and instructions regarding domestic tasks and chores, by
dyad and rural-urban residence. GG, girls to girls; GB, girls to boys;
BB, boys to boys; BG, boys to girls; MG, mothers to girls; MB,
mothers to boys. *Top*, mothers to children; *bottom*, child to child.

ance or the number of tasks and chores children are expected to do.
However, the absence of older children in urban households does appear to
increase the extent to which mothers directly intervene and respond to
children's requests, and the degree to which they give instructions and
directions to their children. Disruptiveness among the smaller, younger,
more crowded sibling group also increases in town.

Although city life in Nairobi hardly exemplifies the ecological conditions

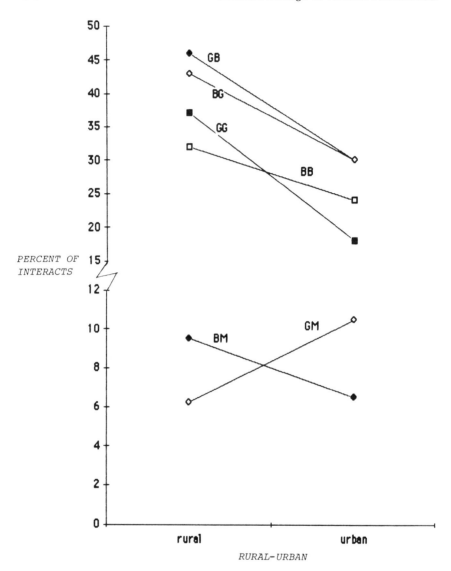

FIGURE 9.5.   Sociable interaction (affection, physical contact, seeks proximity,
sitting together), by dyad and rural-urban residence. GG, girls to girls;
GB, girls to boys; BB, boys to boys; BG, boys to girls; GM, girls to
mothers; BM, boys to mothers. *Top*, child to child; *bottom*, child to
mother.

that promote sibling and other nonparental care of children, the families in
this sample in fact participate part-time in rural cultural life, so the influence
of rural customs persists in modified form in the city. The city-dwelling
families in this sample intend to return to their rural homes, and there is, in

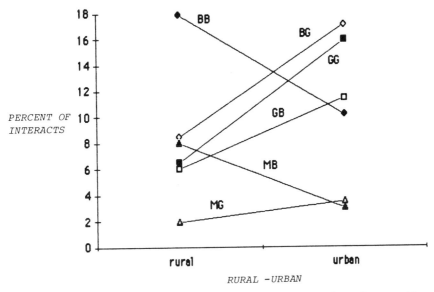

FIGURE 9.6.   Dominance (physical assaults, insulting, annoying others, seeking submission) by dyad and rural-urban residence. GG, girls to girls; GB, girls to boys; BB, boys to boys; BG, boys to girls; MG, mothers to girls; MB, mothers to boys.

fact, frequent commuting back and forth by most family members, including children. The features of child caretaking that persist are those related to: (1) the expected performance of chores and tasks by children; (2) the preference for girls doing child-care and domestic tasks; and (3) the continued nurturance and prosocial behavior shown between children. Those features that change include: (1) increased disruptiveness among family members and (2) increased direct intervention and involvement of mothers in domestic activities and child management.

MOTHERS' VIEWS OF SHARED MANAGEMENT AND SIBLING CARETAKING

This chapter began with a glimpse of one African girl's view of her experience with child care in Kenya. She vacillated between her pleasure and confidence in her experience, and the annoyance and insecurity she felt in the role. In her report and in other discussions with her, however, there was little doubt that she considered this experience a central part of normal development. Whatever other personal experiences she had as a child, not to have been given any responsibility and training in child-care roles within her extended family group would have implied a lack of acceptance. The same pattern of feelings about this kind of training for parenting—ambivalence along with a sense of cultural acceptance—emerges from the data available on mothers' views of sibling care and other forms of nonparental care. The mother's views also reflect a distinction between *control* and authority over the domestic domain (which is still clearly seen as under maternal direction), and *responsibility* for work as part of that daily routine (which is seen as widely shared with others).

In interviews 73 urban Hawaiian mothers were asked a series of questions about assignment of domestic and child-care tasks to children (Weisner *et al.*, unpub. ms.). Two independent dimensions emerged from a factor analysis of these items: a *responsibility expectation* dimension and a *task assignment* factor. The first dimension taps the concern for control and compliance; the second focuses on domestic management aspects of a shared caretaking milieu. Mothers emphasized the importance of generalized expectations of responsibility for other children independently from their reports of how they specifically assigned jobs to children (e.g., bathing younger sibs, taking them on shopping trips, cooking, and so on). Regardless of any particular child's experience (due to the particular family vagaries of birth order, sex, or family size), he or she learns to deal with other children within the shared management and responsibility patterns characterizing sibling care arrangements.

Seventy Abaluyia mothers in Kenya were also asked about their views of child training and preparation for parenting (Weisner, n.d.). These semistructured interviews probed for the individual feelings and opinions of these mothers, in addition to obtaining their more culturally stereotyped responses. In order of mention and importance to this group of mothers, parental goals included:

- Knowing the proper Abaluyia customs—particularly concerns for respect and deference
- Eating properly (good diet, sufficient food)
- Health and safety of children
- Doing work properly
- Understanding how to talk to strangers and to be hospitable, including cooperating and playing well with other children
- Doing well in school and securing employment
- Respect for parents and compliance to adult requests
- Religious training (for Christian mothers)
- Learning English and Kiswahili

We also asked the African mothers about the costs and benefits they saw in the practice of sibling caretaking; how sib care related to other kinds of tasks and chores for children, and how sib care was changing with the growth of schooling for girls and boys. There were maternal worries about how well children are being prepared for a changing and uncertain economy. Mothers' responses to the interviews items on these topics can be summarized as follows:

- Competence, obedience, and the attention children should pay to the hierarchy within the family and domestic group were emphasized as important skills learned by children in the sib group;
- Boys and girls can and should assume child-care duties if needed, but girls are preferred for reasons of convenience and role training;
- Mothers usually mixed domestic tasks and child care in their answers, and typically had to be prompted to separate the two kinds of tasks;
- Verbal and maternal "stimulation" being provided for each child is seldom mentioned; on the other hand, school-learned literacy training is frequently mentioned as a valued trade-off for less sibling care help for mothers in the home.

Mothers did not view child care, and training for it, as a particularly special, high-level skill, outside of its general merits for inculcating family responsibility. Of the mothers, 68% believed that going to school was preferable to a child staying home for sibling care purposes, since school widened a child's opportunities. But the remaining 32% emphasized traditional role training benefits in preparing for marriage and rearing healthy children. In either event, however, sibling care experience continues outside school time; the two are not viewed as mutually exclusive childhood experiences.

Of the African mothers in this sample, 74% reported that as children they had been sent out to others' homes to do child care while they were growing up, and/or had had substantial sib care responsibilities in their own homes. These mothers tended to be oldest or earlier-born children in their own families (but not statistically significantly more so). In addition, 54% of the mothers reported that they had had relatives or hired maids in their own homes doing domestic and child care-related duties during their own childhoods. These characteristics of the mothers' own families of origin and their own sibship parity might have been influential in their decisions as parents concerning sibling care and in their attitudes toward the practice. However, statistical relationships were not found between parents' own childhood experiences and their responses to interview items regarding sibling care and parenting in their own families of procreation. Parents with different childhood experiences in their family of orientation were neither more nor less likely to practice sibling care now that they were parents themselves, and were neither more nor less likely to promote its value. Mothers' formal educations and their own current family size appear to be better predictors of differences in attitudes and practice. Three educational levels were compared: no schooling ($N = 26$), 1–4 years of primary school ($N = 19$), and 5–10 years of school ($N = 22$); data for 3 women was lacking. Age and educational experience remain partially confounded, however, since younger mothers have more formal education. There is a tendency for better educated, younger mothers to report that sibling care limits their children if it is a major ongoing role; that it can teach children to be passive, and that this is not good in today's Kenyan society. More educated mothers also emphasized the menial nature of domestic work, including child care. Better educated women more often distinguished between goals concerning their children's future as parents, on the one hand, and as adult workers, on the other. The contrasting view among uneducated mothers is that these goals are one and the same, and that sibling care trains for respect, for being a proper Luyia child, and for learning to share and cooperate as adult parents later in life. These latter themes were clear in the analysis of interview data, but none reached statistical significance.

Mothers who believed that sibling care is declining at present in turn more often emphasized the obvious effect of schooling in removing children from the home for part of the day. These mothers more often had migrated to Nairobi for periods of time, and had had their own family group divided between city and country. Even these mothers, however, emphasized that control and management remained, as always, in their (the mothers') own hands. This fact had not changed, in their view. They felt that *younger* preschool-age children were now far more involved in sibling care and less lazy than they would have been allowed to be in the past, since they were now taking on more tasks and child-care roles. Leiderman and Leiderman (1977) also found such a child-care pattern in their more acculturated Kikuyu samples.

Of mothers in our sample, 38% reported sending their own children to relatives' homes to help with domestic tasks and child care. Parents believe that this practice is declining due to schooling, available cash for hiring help, and parents' increasing reluctance to send their children to do such "menial" work. Some mothers emphasized that this practice has been used for sending away somewhat troublesome children, children who were harder to manage, in hopes that a new family setting and work tasks might benefit such a child. This practice may be declining, but is still culturally accepted.

Parkin (1979, pp. 329–333) and Wenger (1983, pp. 185–188) have suggested that the terminology used to describe work in many Bantu languages encodes many of the cultural ideas about sibling caretaking and shared functioning reflected in these Abaluyia women's interviews. Among the Giriama, for example, girls before marriage " . . . are likely to live at a close relative's home as a *mu-kazi* [worker]. In this role she helps look after young children in the homestead. . . . This role, they say, is so named because it is an unmarried girl's 'work', and also prepares her for the 'work' she will have when she married . . . The use of the suffix -*kazi* [work], or a similar form, to denote a woman or female roles is in fact widespread in Bantu languages" (Parkin, 1979, p. 329). The *Mkazi* is in this sense a woman who participates in the sociocultural work of the village and kin group, combining subsistence, reproduction, and parenting roles. *Kazi* in its original cultural meanings retains a sense of female gender, familial continuity, sustenance. Sibling caretakers as *mukazi* had a subordinate but enmeshed role in this system. A sibling caretaker is learning parenting as cultural work—the "work" of fertility, of the soil, of cultural continuity.

But contemporary ideas about work are beginning to alter conceptions of the child caretaker role and the roles of girls and women in the subsistence economy. In the current world economy *Kazi* means paid work, a job, as opposed to subsistence work. This change separates *-kazi* as a part of domestic subsistence responsibilities from *-kazi* for wages (Parkin, 1979). This distinction is similar to that expressed by the Abaluyia mothers about the changing importance of schooling and urban migration vis-a-vis sibling caretaking skills and training for parenting. If one enters an Abaluyia household today and asks where an absent male migrant wage worker is, the (Kiswahili) response would probably be, "ameenda kazini" (he or she has gone to work, or to the place of work). One then looks about the homestead, with cooking, clothes washing, food preparation, and child tending going on all around, and asks what others in the homestead are doing. A typical reply might be, "sisi tuko nyumbani, tu" (we are just here at home). As males have migrated in search of wage employment beyond their own local communities, the traditional blending of work done for one's home compound and participation in kin and parenting roles has begun to be transformed. The status attached to work for the homestead has declined, and thus the status of the *mukazi* and the status of girls and women within this system relative to wage employment is lower. Traditionally, training for parenting occurred within a system in which women were major contributors to the subsistence economy; parenting skills were embedded in this larger context. One of the effects of the penetration of the world economy on middle-level societies in much of the world appears to be the increased separation and alienation of parenting from other forms of work children are trained for throughout childhood and adolescence.

CONCLUSION

The Polynesian and African examples used in this chapter illustrate a style of sibling care that includes recognized caretaker roles and responsibilities and sharing of nurturance and discipline. Yet it is also clearly a family system where mothers and fathers retain overall control. Both conditions (maternal control and culturally recognized role training) vary among sibling care societies. For instance, older girls in some black American households act as "boss girl," managing virtually all aspects of household and child care (e.g., Stack, 1974, 1975) without much maternal control. Indeed, many of these girls may soon have children of their own who will be incorporated in these same households. And sibling-care roles are not always well-defined or named. Children watch out for each other without the clear role assignment and hierarchical domestic structure that characterizes the kinds of societies focused on here. Cohorts of children play with one another, and in the course of the day children offer nurturance and advice to one another without having had the role training within the domestic group that characterizes many middle-level African and Polynesian societies. A good deal of nonformal training in child caretaking skills occurs in the context of such groups, whether or not there is a more organized cultural plan and value attached to nonparental child care.

Sibling care occurs along with continued maternal involvement in child care and domestic management. Ethnographic data, mother interviews, and systematic observations all are consistent on this point. Maternal and child roles are not mutually exclusive ones; the term shared management, or shared parenting, further emphasizes this point. The involvement of mothers in direct caretaking is greater during infancy and the early toddler periods, but continues with the help of others throughout childhood.

The contrast between the North American middle-class model and the shared management model is between two different kinds of training for parenting—not between the absence of such training in America and its presence elsewhere. Many students of sibling relationships in Western cultures (e.g., Dunn, 1983; Bryant, 1982) show clearly that Western children are learning about relationships and caregiving, just as are the African or Hawaiian children in the preceding examples. The relevant contrasts are in the ecocultural pressures in each respective society, and in the cultural goals and desires regarding social replacement that are reflected in how children learn parenting.

Training for parenting is changing as societies around the world face intense cultural, ecological, and demographic changes which affect their adaptive choices and their family functions. In many parts of the world catastrophes of war, exploitation, and ecological degradation make any attempt to find a culturally viable pattern of parental training secondary to a struggle for sheer survival and safety. It does not seem as though either of the two opposing patterns of child care and parent training sketched herein is likely to continue in its pure form. The data available on the effects of ecocultural changes on child socialization and parenting in the contemporary non-Western world do not suggest a linear evolution toward the Western middle-class, ideal-typical pattern. Rather, a tremendous variety of adaptive family forms is emerging around the world, in Western and non-Western societies alike. These transformations are influenced by survival pressures, as well as by proactive family efforts to implement their cultural goals and ideals for their children in new circumstances (Weisner, 1982). This is what should be expected; after all, the ecocultural conditions promoting sibling care itself are diverse and can vary widely, and did not characterize human families until the recent evolutionary past. At the same time, the variables reviewed here that seem linked to patterns of parental training (ecocultural conditions; cultural values and relationship styles; the performance of parental functions essential for development) continue to be powerful in shaping the further evolution of parenting.

SUMMARY

In many societies around the world training for parenthood is an apprenticeship experience, learned along with the performance of domestic and subsistence tasks within shared-function family systems. In such shared caretaking families, child-care skills are acquired first, followed only gradually by autonomy from parents and siblings, and then by full managerial control of a household. Parenting skills are learned within the sibling group which continues to remain functionally interdependent throughout the life span, helping with and feuding over inheritance, marriage arrangements, or needs for community defense and protection. Child-care and parenting roles are widely diffused within a group of kin. In contrast, in our own society establishment of a new household typically comes first, followed by acquisition of a mate and marriage and only then by parenthood and child care.

Training for parenting in shared management systems is a joint process involving mothers and the sibling group. There may be a series of stages in how such societies develop parenting skills: (1) training in direct child care (feeding, carrying, etc.); (2) provision of emotional and affective support and comfort; (3) teaching, supervision, and monitoring of others doing these tasks, along with the mother; and (4) assumption of the primary responsibility for providing shelter, food, and protection for the child and the family.

Data from the Abaluyia of Kenya and Hawaiian-Americans are used to illustrate the process of acquiring parenting skills in a shared function, sibling caretaking system. Girls in the Kenya studies do over twice as much direct child care as boys and show proportions of nurturant and emotionally supportive interactions similar to those of mothers. Mothers are far more likely to show managerial, directive, and commanding behaviors, however, then sibling caretakers. Task and chore performance by children is also high compared to Western samples. Interviews with Kenyan and Hawaiian-American mothers show that their views on child caretaking and training for parenthood combine two independent dimensions: (1) the importance of children learning generalized responsibility within the family, including compliance; and (2) specific needs for domestic management and task performance. There is also a statistically nonsignificant tendency for more educated Kenyan mothers to report that heavy sibling care responsibilities teach children to be too passive and compliant.

ACKNOWLEDGMENTS

The preparation of this paper has been supported by the Department of Psychiatry and Biobehavioral Sciences, UCLA. Data from Kenya were collected with the assistance of the Child Development Research Unit, University of Nairobi and Harvard University, John and Beatrice Whiting, Directors, through a grant from the Carnegie Corporation. Additional support came from the Academic Senate Faculty Research Fund, UCLA. Data on Hawaiian-American families were collected with support from the Kamehameha Early Education Project, Roland Tharp and Ronald Gallimore, Co-Principal Investigators, supported by the Bernice P. Bishop Estate, Honolulu, Hawaii. Professor Jill Korbin made helpful comments on an earlier draft.

REFERENCES

Barry, H., III, and Paxson, L. M. Infancy and early childhood: Cross-cultural codes 2. *Ethnology*, 1971, *10*, 466–508.

Bronfenbrenner, U. *The Ecology of Human Development*. Cambridge, MA: Harvard University Press, 1979.

Brown, J. Cross-cultural perspectives on middle-aged women. *Current Anthropology*, 1982, *23*(2), 143–156.

Bryant, B. K. Sibling relationships in middle childhood. In M. Lamb and B. Sutton-Smith (Eds.), *Sibling Relationships: Their Nature and Significance Across the Lifespan*. Hillsdale, NJ: Erlbaum, 1982, pp. 87–121.

Carroll, V. (Ed.). *Adoption in Eastern Oceania*. Honolulu, HI: University of Hawaii Press, 1970.

Cohen, R. Conceptual styles, culture conflict, and non-verbal tests of intelligence. *American Anthropologist*, 1969, *7*, 828–55.

Draper, P. !Kung women: Contrasts in sexual egalitarianism in foraging and sedentary contexts. In Rayna R. Reiter (Ed.), *Toward an Anthropology of Women*. London: Monthly Review Press, 1975, pp. 77–112.

Draper, P. Social and economic constraints on child life among the !Kung. In Richard B. Lee and Irven De Vore (Eds.), *Kalahari Hunter-Gatherers: Studies of the !Kung San and Their Neighbors*. Cambridge, MA: Harvard University Press, 1976, pp. 200–217.

Dunn, J. Sibling relationships in early childhood. *Child Development*, 1983, *54*(4), 787–811.

Ember, C. A cross-cultural perspective on sex differences. In R. H. Munroe, R. L. Munroe, and B. Whiting (Eds.), *Handbook of Cross-Cultural Human Development*. NY: Garland STPM Press, 1981, pp. 531–581.

Emlen, S. T. The evolution of helping. I. An ecological constraints model. *The American Naturalist*, 1982, *119*(1), 29–39. (a)

Emlen, S. T. The evolution of helping. II. The role of behavioral conflict. *The American Naturalist*, 1982, *119*(1), 40–53. (b)

Gallimore, R., Boggs, J. W., and Jordan, C. *Culture, Behavior and Education: A Study of Hawaiian-Americans*. Beverly Hills, CA: Sage Publications, 1974.

Gallimore, R., and Howard, A. Hawaiian life style. In R. Gallimore and A. Howard (Eds.), *Studies in a Hawaiian Community: Na Makamaka O Nanakuli*. Honolulu, HI: PAR no. 1, B. P. Bishop Museum, 1968, pp. 10–16.

Goody, E. N. *Parenthood and Social Reproduction: Fostering and Occupational Roles in West Africa*. Cambridge: Cambridge University Press, 1982.

Goody, J. Adoption in cross-cultural perspective. *Comparative Studies in Society and History*, 1969, *11*, 55–78.

Jordan, C. *Educationally effective ethnology: A study of the contributions of cultural knowledge to effective education for minority children*. Dissertation, UCLA, 1981. Microfilm from University Microfilms Library Services, Ann Arbor, MI. (a)

Jordan, C. The selection of culturally compatible teaching practices. *Educational Perspectives*, 1981, *20*(1), 16–19. (b)

Konner, M. J. Maternal care, infant behavior and development among the !Kung. In R. B. Lee and I. DeVore (Eds.), *Kalahari Hunter-Gatherers: Studies of the !Kung San and Their Neighbors*. Cambridge, MA: Harvard University Press, 1976, pp. 218–245.

Korbin, J. *Child Abuse and Neglect. Cross-Cultural Perspectives*. Berkeley, CA: University of California Press, 1981.

Langness, L. L., and Frank, G. *Lives. An Anthropological Approach to Biography*. Novato, CA: Chandler and Sharp Publishers, Inc., 1981.

Leiderman, P. H., and Leiderman, G. F. Affective and cognitive consequences of polymatric infant care in the East African highlands. *Minnesota Symposium of Child Psychology*, 1974, *8*, 81–110. (a)

Leiderman, P. H., and Leiderman, G. F. Familial influences on infant development in an East African agricultural community. In E. J. Anthony and C. Koupernek (Eds.), *The Child in His Family. Children at Psychiatric Risk*, Vol. 3. NY: Wiley, 1974. (b)

Leiderman, P. H., and Leiderman, G. F. Economic change and infant care in an East African agricultural community. In P. Herbert Leiderman, S. R. Tulkin, and Anne Rosenfeld (Eds.), *Culture and Infancy*. NY: Academic Press, 1977, pp. 405–438.

LeVine, R. A. Patterns of personality in Africa. *Ethos*, 1973, *1*(2), 123–152.

LeVine, R. A. Child rearing as cultural adaptation. In P. Herbert Leiderman, Steven R. Tulkin, and Anne Rosenfeld (Eds.), *Culture and Infancy*. NY: Academic Press, 1977, pp. 15–28.

LeVine, S. *Mothers and Wives: Gusii Women of East Africa*. Chicago, IL: University of Chicago Press, 1979.

Levy, R. I. Child management structure and its implications in a Tahitian family. In E. Vogel and N. Bell (Eds.), *A Modern Introduction to the Family*. NY: The Free Press, 1968.

Levy, R. I. *Tahitians. Mind and Experience in the Society Islands*. Chicago, IL: University of Chicago Press, 1973.

Lewis, M., and Ban, P. Variance and invariance in mother–infant interaction: A cross-cultural study. In P. Herbert Leiderman, Steven R. Tulkin, and Anne Rosenfeld (Eds.), *Culture and Infancy*. NY: Academic Press, 1977, pp. 329–356.

McKenna, J. J. Aspects of infant socialization, attachment, and maternal caregiving patterns among primates: A cross-disciplinary review. *Yearbook of Physical Anthropology*, 1979, *22*, 250–286.

Mead, M. *Growing Up in New Guinea. A Comparative Study of Primitive Education.* NY: Dell, 1968.

Minturn, L., and Lambert, W. *Mothers of Six Cultures.* NY: Wiley, 1964.

Munroe, R. H., and Munroe, R. L. Infant experience and childhood affect among the Logoli: A longitudinal study. *Ethos,* 1980, *8,* 295–315.

Munroe, R. L., and Munroe, R. H. Birth order and intellectual development in East Africa. *Journal of Cross-Cultural Psychology,* 1983, *14,* 3–16.

Munroe, R. L., and Munroe, R. H. Birth order and its psychological correlates in East Africa. In R. Bolton (Ed.), *The Content of Culture: Constance and Variance.* New Haven CT: HRAF Press, in press.

Nerlove, S. B., Roberts, J. M., Klein, R. E., Yarbrough, C., and Habicht, J. P. Natural indicators of cognitive development: An observational study of rural Guatemalan children. *Ethos,* 1974, *2*(3), 265–295.

Nerlove, S. B., Roberts, J. M., and Klein, R. E. Dimensions of listura ("smartness"): Community judgements of rural Guatemalan children. In P. Draper (Chair.), *Experimental Correlates of Cognitive Abilities.* Symposium presented at the biennial meeting of The Society for Research in Child Development, Denver, April 1975.

Ochs, E. Talking to children in Western Samoa. *Language in Society,* 1982, *11,* 77–104.

Ochs, E., and Schieffelin, B. Language acquisition and socialization: Three developmental stories and their implications. In R. Shweder and R. LeVine (Eds.) *Culture Theory. Essays on Mind, Self, and Emotion.* NY: Academic press, 1984, pp. 276–320.

Park, H. T., and Gallimore, R. Cognitive style in urban and rural Korea. *Journal of Cross-Cultural Psychology,* 1975, 6, 227–237.

Parkin, D. The categorization of work: Cases from coastal Kenya. In S. Wallman (Ed.), *Social Anthropology of Work.* London: Academic Press, 1979.

Ritchie, J., and Ritchie, J. *Growing Up in Polynesia.* Sydney, Australia: George Allen and Unwin, 1979.

Rogoff, B., Sellers, J. J., Pirrotta, S., Fox, N., and White, S. H. Age of assignment of roles and responsibilities to children: A cross-cultural survey. *Human Development,* 1975, *18,* 353–369.

Rogoff, B., Newcombe, N., Fox, N., and Ellis, S. Transitions in children's roles and capabilities. *International Journal of Psychology,* 1980, *15,* 181–200.

Ross, M. H., and Weisner, T. S. The rural-urban migrant network in Kenya: Some general implications. *American Ethnologist,* 1977, *4*(2), 359–375.

Scarr, S., and Grajek, S. Similarities and differences among siblings. In M. E. Lamb and B. Sutton-Smith (Eds.), *Sibling Relationships: Their Nature and Significance Across the Lifespan.* Hillsdale, NJ: Erlbaum, 1982, pp. 357–382.

Shweder, R. A. Rethinking culture and personality theory Part I: A critical examination of two classical postulates. *Ethos,* 1979, *7*(3), 255–278. (a)

Shweder, R. A. Rethinking culture and personality theory Part II: A critical examination of two more classical postulates. *Ethos,* 1979, *7*(4), 279–311. (b)

Stack, C. *All Our Kin: Strategies for Survival in a Black Community.* NY: Harper and Row, 1974.

Stack, C. Who raises black children? Transactions of child givers and child receivers.

In T. R. Williams (Ed.), *Socialization and Communication in Primary Groups*. The Hague: Mouton, 1975, pp. 183–205.

Super, C. M., and Harkness, S. (Eds.). *Anthropological Perspectives on Child Development. New Directions for Child Development* No. 8. San Francisco, CA: Jossey Bass, 1980.

Tharp, R. G., Jordan, C., Speidel, G. E., Hu-pei Au, K., Klein, T., Calkins, R. P., Sloat, K. C. M., and Gallimore, R. Product and process in applied developmental research: Education and the children of a minority. In M. E. Lamb, A. L. Brown, and B. Rogoff (Eds.), *Advances in Developmental Psychology*, Vol. III. Hillsdale, NJ: Erlbaum, 1984, pp. 91–141.

Weisner, T. S. Urban-rural differences in sociable and disruptive behavior of Kenya children. *Ethnology*, 1979, *18*(2), 153–172.

Weisner, T. S. As we choose: Family life styles, social class, and compliance. In J. G. Kennedy and R. B. Edgerton (Eds.), *Culture and Ecology: Eclectic Perspectives*. Washington, D.C.: American Anthropological Association, 1982, pp. 120–141.

Weisner, T. S. Sibling interdependence and child caretaking: A cross-cultural view. In Michael E. Lamb and Brian Sutton-Smith (Eds.), *Sibling Relationships: Their Nature and Significance Across the Lifespan*. Hillsdale, NJ: Erlbaum, 1982, pp. 305–327.

Weisner, T. S. Sibling caretaking experience and school achievement among the Abaluyia of western Kenya. In preparation.

Weisner, T. S., and Gallimore, R. My brother's keeper: Child and sibling caretaking. *Current Anthropology*, 1977, *18*(2), 169–191.

Weisner, T. S., Gallimore, R., and Tharp, R. G. Concordance between ethnographer and folk perspectives: Observed performance and self-ascription of sibling caretaking roles. *Human Organization*, 1982, *41*(3), 237–244.

Weisner, T. S., Gallimore, R., Jordan, C. Unpacking cultural effects on classroom learning: Hawaiian peer assistance and child-generated activity. Unpublished manuscript.

Wenger, M. *Gender role socialization in an East African community: Social interaction between 2- to 3-year-olds and older children in social ecological perspective*. Doctoral dissertation, Graduate School of Education, Harvard University, 1983.

White, D. R., Burton, M. L., and Brudner, L. A. Entailment theory and method: A cross-cultural analysis of the sexual division of labor. *Behavior Science Research*, 1977, *12*, 1–24.

Whiting, B. B. (ed.). *Six Cultures: Studies of Child Rearing*. NY: Wiley, 1963.

Whiting, B. The Genesis of Prosocial Behavior. In D. Bridgeman (Ed.), *The Nature of Prosocial Development: Interdisciplinary Theories*. NY: Academic Press, 1983, pp. 221–242.

Whiting, B. *Transcultural code for social interaction*. Unpublished manuscript.

Whiting, B., and Edwards C. P. A cross-cultural analysis of sex differences in the behavior of children aged three through eleven. *Journal of Social Psychology*, 1973, *91*, 171–88.

Whiting, B., and Edwards, C. P. *The Company They Keep: The Genesis of Gender Role Behavior*. In preparation.

Whiting, B. B., and Whiting, J. W. M. *Children of Six Cultures: A Psycho-cultural Analysis.* Cambridge, MA: Harvard University Press, 1975.

Whiting, J. and Whiting, B. A strategy for psychocultural research. In G. P. Spindler (Ed.), *The Making of Psychological Anthropology.* Los Angeles, CA: University of California Press, 1978, pp. 41–62.

Witkin, H. A., Price-Williams, D., Bertini, M., Christiansen, B., Oltman, P. K., Ramirez, M., and Van Meel, J. Social conformity and psychological differentiation. *International Journal of Psychology,* 1974, 9, 11–29.

Zajonc, R. B., and Markus, G. B. Birth order and intellectual development. *Psychological Review,* 1975, 82, 74–88.

10 PARENTHOOD IN SOCIAL TRANSFORMATION

Robert A. LeVine
Merry White

INTRODUCTION

During the past 200 years the conditions of child development in much of the world have changed more drastically
than they had in millennia—perhaps since the spread of
agrarian conditions after 7000 B.C. The history of this recent
change can be traced numerically, with school enrollments
rising and infant mortality rates falling as countries industrialized, populations moved to the city, and families reduced
their fertility. It can be told as a moral tale, with the
elimination of child labor and illiteracy, when parents and
public policymakers alike recognized the rights and expanded the opportunities of children. It can be, and often is,
looked upon as a struggle for the welfare of children that is
not yet won, particularly since many of the conditions
abolished in the industrial countries (e.g., high infant mortality, illiteracy,
and child labor) still exist in the Third World.

However one regards this shift, it represents a fundamental change not
only in the means by which children are raised but in the reasons for which
they are brought into the world and the goals they pursue during their lives.
It is a change that is only beginning to be understood in terms of its history,
its causes, and its contemporary directions. This chapter provides an
overview of its major elements, particularly in the West, and considers its
implications for the comparative analysis of parenthood and child development. The social changes reviewed here have undermined traditional
agrarian conceptions of the life span, particularly the centrality of fertility
and filial loyalty in the social identities of men and women. This shift has
occurred in the industrial countries of the West, Eastern Europe, and Japan.
It has been occurring, and continues, in certain countries of the Third World,
although not uniformly within those countries. That the shift deserves to be
called "revolutionary" can hardly be disputed; the question is whether it
should be thought of as one revolution or many. Are all the socioeconomic,
demographic, educational, and ideological changes involved but different
aspects of one comprehensive process of social transformation (e.g., "modernization"), or separable processes that happen to be linked in particular

historical cases? Are the sequences and outcomes of recent change—particularly in Japan and the Third World—replicating those of the past, particularly of 19th century Europe and the United States?

This question, even in specific regard to family life, has long concerned sociologists, but many chose to answer it by assuming there was a unitary process driving history in a single direction. More empirical knowledge, however, has made theories of global modernization, like the classical Marxist stages of history, seem examples of what Hirschman (1971) has called "paradigms as a hindrance to understanding": Sociologists prevented taking diversity seriously enough, until documentation of diversity overwhelmed the very theories that had denied their importance. Fortunately, social scientists have brought a wealth of new evidence to bear on questions of historical change in family life and the conditions of child development in social and cultural settings throughout the world. This points to a history of the family adapting to specific local conditions rather than moving in one preordained direction.

The abandonment of unilinear evolution as a conceptual framework for analyzing social change in family life does not mean the denial of recurrent trends that can be documented and are clearly significant. On the contrary, those broad trends must be the starting point for our inquiry. This chapter begins with a brief consideration of the radically diverse perspectives from which children are viewed in the contemporary world, both in the private contexts of family life and in the public contexts of national and international policy. Then questions follow: How did it come to be this way? How did human societies develop such differing perspectives on children? This amounts to asking how—given a world with primary agrarian perspectives only two centuries ago—did some societies move so far from these perspectives?

THE MEANINGS OF CHILDREN: DIFFERENCES AND SIMILARITIES IN THE CONTEMPORARY WORLD

In contrast with agrarian values common to much of the world two centuries ago, the cultures of contemporary industrialized countries, particularly their middle-class subcultures, tend to value parent-child relationships that provide unilateral support—economic, emotional, and social—to children, with parents not expected to receive anything tangible in return. The period of such support in Western societies has been lengthening, from childhood through adolescence into adulthood, and the proportion of family resourses devoted to children has been increasing.

The current state of the evidence has been summarized by Hoffman and Manis (1979):

> [The] economic value of children is particularly salient among rural parents and in countries where the economy is primarily rural. In addition, children are often

seen as important for security in old age. Children are valued for this function, particularly in an age where there is no official, trusted, and acceptable provision for the care of the aged and disabled.

In a highly industrialized country like the United States, however, with a government-sponsored social security system, children are less likely to have economic utility. Even their utility in rural areas might be lessened because of rural mechanization and the greater availability of hired help. And, since the cost of raising children is higher in the more urban and industrially advanced countries, children are not likely to be seen as an economic asset (p. 590).

When a national sample of Americans was asked about the advantages of having children, only 3.1% of the white mothers with more than 12 years of schooling gave answers involving economic utility (Hoffman and Manis, 1979, p. 585). The rest of that subsample mentioned a variety of social, emotional, and moral benefits. The responses of East Asian mothers to this question help to place the American figure in a global context (Table 10.1).

In the industrial countries, Japan and Taiwan, the proportion of urban middle-class respondents mentioning the economic utility of children is virtually identical to that of the more educated white mothers in the United States, despite differences in culture. In the Philippines, a largely agrarian country, the proportion of the urban middle class perceiving economic benefits in children is ten times higher. Within each of the three Asian countries, with national policies of old-age assistance held constant, the rural proportion is at least twice as high as that of the urban middle class. While such figures from one limited question are only suggestive, they show the magnitude of the differences in attitudes and their powerful association with agrarian life both within and between contemporary countries.

The fact that the majority of middle-class parents in industrial countries expect no tangible return from children can be seen as paradoxical, not only from the perspective of utilitarian economics, which assumes that substantial investment must be motivated by the expectation of material return, but also from the viewpoint of agrarian cultures, in which reciprocity between the generations is a basic principle of social life. It does not seem

TABLE 10.1. Advantages of Having Children: Percentage Mentioning Economic Utility[a]

	Urban middle class	Rural
Japan	2	11
Taiwan	3	36
Philippines	30	60

[a]Source: Arnold, 1975, Table 4.4.

paradoxical to most contemporary Westerners, who take it for granted that the parent-child relationship is exempted from ideas of material return and long-term reciprocation.

Indeed, the Western notion that the welfare of children should represent the highest priority for society as well as parents and that children should be unstintingly supported without calculation of reward—a revolutionary idea in world history—has established itself as an unchallengeable principle of international morality. The most fervent support for the idea, however, continues to come from northwestern Europe and the United States, where the public defense of children is an established cultural tradition, religious and secular, generating symbols used to arouse intense emotions, mobilize voluntary activity, and subsidize programs of action.

What is most remarkable about this basically Western ideology that has been accepted in international forums as a universal moral code is that it entails a passionate concern with the welfare of *other people's children*. In other words, it presumes that the current well-being and future development of children are the concern and responsibility not only of their parents but of a community—local, national, and international—that is not based on kinship. Westerners are proud, for example, of the long and ultimately successful campaign against child labor waged by reformers in their own countries, but their ideology requires that such benefits be extended to all children everywhere. In some Western countries such as Sweden, the Netherlands, and Canada, there is more concern with and activity on behalf of poor children in Third World societies than there is among the privileged segments of the latter societies. This gap in cultural values belies the apparent consensus embodied in United Nations declarations and points to the radical disagreement about practices such as child labor that would emerge if Western reformers tried harder to implement their ideas as global programs of action. How did the West acquire its contemporary cultural ideals concerning parent–child relationships and other people's children? That is the question to be explored in this chapter, in terms of four topics: (1) the shift from agrarian to urban-industrial institutions, (2) the demographic transition, (3) mass schooling, and (4) the rise of a public interest in children.

THE SHIFT FROM AGRARIAN TO URBAN-INDUSTRIAL INSTITUTIONS

The industrialization of Europe and North America made its primary impact on the family through the rise of wage labor and bureaucratic employment as alternatives to agricultural and craft production, the consequent separation of the workplace from the home and of occupational from kin-based roles and relationships, the migration from rural villages to concentrated settlements where jobs were available, and the penetration of labor market values into parental decisions regarding the future of children. Each of these channels needs to be analyzed in terms of how it operated to alter the assumptions on which agrarian parents had based their conceptions of childhood.

The rise of wage labor and bureaucratic employment meant first that an increasing number of children would make their future living through jobs that were unfamiliar to their parents and which the latter could not teach them. This was in itself a break with the agraian tradition, in which the work roles of one generation largely replicated that of its forebears: If a parent had not himself mastered the skills his child would live by, he had kin, neighbors, or friends who had. Under the new conditions, however, increasing numbers of parents would have to acknowledge that they lacked not only the specific competencies required by their children for future work, but also the social connections with others who had the skills.

This decline in the parental capacity to provide training for subsistence was accompanied by a loss of supervisory control, as children and adults worked in factories, shops, and offices under other supervisors. The dual role of the agrarian parents as nurturers and supervisors of their immature and adult children working at home—a role they could transfer to foster parents through apprenticeship in domestically organized craft workshops— was not possible when employers and foremen had no social ties with the parents of their laborers. This set the stage for the abuses of child labor that ultimately led to its abolition.

Equally significant, however, was the liberation of adult workers from parental supervision in domestic production, even as they were exploited by industrial employers. Industrialism in the West cast off the kinship model of relationships that had prevailed in craft production in favor of a rationalistic and contractual model of work relationships now thought of as bureaucratic. Industrial paternalism was not unknown, but the polarization of work versus family roles and relationships rose with increasing mass production, labor migration, and the creation of a heterogeneous work force that lacked preexisting social ties or common origins. The workplace required of employees not only skills but conformity to a new code of social behavior not foreshadowed in the domestic group; it resocialized workers and gave them new identities distinct from those of birth and marriage. But since work for a particular firm was often not permanent, identification with it as an object of loyalty and idealization was the exception rather than the rule. Industrial employment was contractual, and the social identities of workers came to incorporate this sense of contractual distance from the firm. Sprung loose from the permanence of agrarian kin and community affiliations and from the parental control involved in domestic production, the more mobile industrial workers found new identities in religious sects, national-ism, voluntary associations—and in the ideals of organizations like trade unions and professional associations that were organized by occupation but offered membership more permanent than employment with any firm was likely to be. Whether one views this trend as facilitating personal autonomy or promoting anomie and social disintegration, it meant the greater salience of models of behavior that were not based on domestic relationships. It also meant a decline in parental control as an expectable concomitant of work roles.

Large-scale industrialization draws people from the countryside into concentrated settlements, either large cities with many functions or specialized industrial communities such as mining and mill towns, and this relocation is likely to have a great impact on the family. This does not mean the breakup of family and kin networks, for social historians and anthropologists have shown how resourceful rural migrants were and are in preserving these ties after moving to the city. But urbanization eroded many of the premises on which agrarian family values rested. The availability of residential housing, wild game, and assistance from neighbors, for example, had been taken for granted in many rural areas, but the migrant to the city found such resources to be commodities that had to be purchased, and at a steep price. Many more consumer goods were available in urban centers, and material aspirations quickly rose, but migrants had to develop a new awareness of what things cost in relation to their limited incomes. Thus, urbanization encouraged families to examine the choices in their lives in explicitly economic terms.

The family's recognition of having moved from country to city in order to better its economic position through employment was another important, if indirect, influence on the parent–child relationship. In the rural areas it had been possible to see one's residence, occupation, and social position as simply inherited together from the past and therefore fixed, but the knowledge of having moved to where jobs were inevitably gave subjective priority to occupation and earnings as the source of the family's position, and it encouraged the younger generation to think of improving their lives through maximizing their incomes.

In the cities and increasingly even outside them, the influence of the labor market on parental thinking and family decision-making grew. Childhood was seen as a time for offspring to acquire whatever skills would enhance their future employability in a competitive labor market where workers outnumbered jobs. The uncertainties inherent in this situation brought new anxieties to parents. In the agrarian past, the future position and livelihood of a son was preordained through inheritance of land and an inherited role in domestic production, that of a daughter through marriage. Parents helped their children marry and start a household, but (except where primogeniture was the rule) did not have to find occupations for their sons. The rise of industrial employment eroded the predictability inherent in this agrarian situation, forced parents to concern themselves more broadly with what would become of their children once they grew up, and offered hope for success in the future labor market only through adequate preparation in childhood. The domestic group, once the setting for the entire life cycle in its productive as well as relational dimensions, became a temporary nest for the nurturance of fledglings who would leave to wrest a living from an uncertain and competitive outside world. Parent–child relations, once conceived as a lifelong structure of reciprocity, were increasingly thought of as a support and nurturance system provided by adults to their immature offspring, leaving the future relationship ambiguous.

By moving to cities, European families in the 19th century were moving closer to expanding urban school systems and enhancing the likelihood that their children would become enrolled. As the population of each country became more concentrated through urbanization, the difficulties of distributing formal education were reduced and literacy grew. Urban populations were in fact generally more exposed than rural ones to the laws and programs of increasingly active and bureaucratized national governments, and schooling provided children contact with the symbols and doctrines of the national state.

Urbanization became a mass phenomenon in the 19th century as European villagers migrated to cities and towns in Europe, North and South America, Australia, and New Zealand, and they have continued to do so throughout the present century. In 1800 only 7.3% of the population of all these regions (including in South America only Argentina, Chile, and Uruguay) lived in settlements of at least 5000 people; by 1900 it was 26.1% and in 1980 it was 70.2%. Western Europe urbanized earliest and most heavily. Great Britain had by 1850 become the first major country with more than half its population residing in cities; by 1900 the figure was 77%, and by 1980 it was 91%. The major industrial cities of England and Germany grew to ten times their size and those of France grew by five times in the course of the 19th century alone. These figures show how large was the proportion of families affected by industrial employment. Urban migrants did not necessarily lose their kin ties nor the significance of kinship in their lives, but their livelihoods and those of their children depended on the labor market. This was an irreversible change, and it reached into the countryside, commercializing work relationships in agriculture and inducing even rural parents to regard wage labor as a major alternative way of life for their children.

Thus, industrialization and urbanization changed the economic basis of family life (i.e., the role of the family as a productive unit) and replaced the local age-sex hierarchy of rural communities with new social identities and sources of motivation centered on the urban occupational structure. This trend has long been known in general terms, but it is only in recent decades that social historians have investigated whether and how particular Western countries fit into the general picture. Did they all start at the same place? Did they change in the same ways in terms of sequence and intensity? Did they arrive at the same outcomes in terms of resultant patterns of family life and child development? While the evidence is far from complete, the answer to all these questions is NO.

It has been shown, for example, that contractualism in property relations within and outside the family, as well as the separation of adolescent and preadolescent children from their parents, has a much longer history in England than on the Continent, and MacFarlane (1977) argues that these patterns antedate even England's preindustrial economic development, representing a cultural tradition that sets England apart from the rest of Europe. While his cultural argument is subject to controversy, there is no dispute concerning English primacy in industrial development and urbanization and in the utilitarian ideology of market relationships that social scientists have seen as an integral part of the urban-industrial transformation. In other words, England, along with its American colonies and the Calvinist communities of the Netherlands, Geneva, and Scotland, may in the 17th century have had many of the social and psychological characteristics that the rest of Europe did not acquire until the urban-industrial transformation of the mid-19th century.

Similarly, the preindustrial family structures of the Western countries were far from identical, and some of them can plausibly be seen as preparing rural families for urban life under industrial conditions. Wherever the rules of inheritance did not permit the division of family land, for example, the "stem family" in rural populations assured only the heirs of a future on the parental land and created for the other sons something closer to the uncertainty of the industrial labor market. This situation in Sweden and Ireland was a factor in early (i.e., pre-19th century) migration of rural labor to urban markets at home and abroad. The United States, with its lack of a feudal tradition and expanding rural as well as urban settlements, provided more opportunities for migration into newly established communities that were less dominated by inherited kinship and status relationships than those of Europe. Thus, the Western countries, far from being homogeneous in culture and family structure before major industrial and urban development, were significantly varied in ways that bore directly on how they would enter and experience that historical transition.

It is equally clear that the processes of industrial and urban development were not the same throughout the West. France, for example, never became urbanized to the extent that England did. A much larger proportion of Frenchmen remained in rural villages, participating in agriculture. In Italy and the United States, urban growth and industrialization were heavily concentrated in the northern regions, leaving the south rural and "underdeveloped" down to the present, but this was not the case in smaller and more densely populated countries like the Netherlands. Hence, the suddenness of the shift from agrarian to urban-industrial conditions, the proportions of the population that were uprooted from rural areas and absorbed in the urban labor force, the continuity of urban centers with a preindustrial culture, and many other factors were variable among (and within) the Western countries and are highly relevant to family life and the raising of children.

Do such historical variations make a difference in terms of late 20th century outcomes? Not if outcomes are measured only by economic indicators such as gross national product per capita and demographic indicators such as birth and death rates for all the countries of the contemporary world. In these comparisons, the Western countries stand out (with Japan) at the high end economically and the low end demographically—particularly in contrast with the Third World. There are major differences among the Western countries, however, in the results of industrial and urban development, especially in regard to the quality of life.

The contrast between the United States and virtually all of Europe in residential mobility, for example, is enormous and of great significance in how occupational identities and local ties affect childhood and adult experience. Divorce, female participation in the work force, and the extent of government welfare entitlements are other widely varying quantitative factors that affect both the individual life course and family life among the Western countries. On the qualitative side, the salience of social class divisions, trade union affiliations, and religious participation represent other variables that create differing contexts for life experience in the several countries of the West.

It is clear, then, on the basis of available evidence that industrial and urban development has not simply homogenized Western countries as social environments for the development of children. These countries did not enter the transition from agrarian life at the same places, did not undergo quite the same historical experiences, and did not arrive at identical destinations in terms of the conditions of family life and childhood. Their similarities in the urban-industrial transitions are well established, particularly in comparison with other parts of the world, but neither the process nor the outcome of the transition should be considered uniform.

THE DEMOGRAPHIC TRANSITION

Between the late 18th and mid-20th centuries Western birth and death rates declined drastically, eliminating the agrarian expectations of natural fertility and a relatively short life as normal features of the human condition. The impact on family life was as great as that of the more or less concomitant decline in domestic production and child labor. So many conditions affecting the family were changing during that time, however, that the connections between socioeconomic and demographic change are matters of theoretical controversy rather than straightforward fact.

"Demographic transition theory" (Caldwell, 1982, pp. 117–133) includes all historical formulations that assume the inevitability and irreversibility of declining birth and death rates and the coupling of those declines to each other and to other socioeconomic trends, regardless of those factors to which the change is attributed. From this chapter's perspective, demographic transition theory is interesting not only because it attempts to make sense of secular trends affecting parents, but because it explicitly suggests parallels between 19th century Europe and the contemporary Third World. Recent research in historical demography makes possible comparisons between what happened in the West and Japan and what is now happening in the rest of the world.

The basic facts have been succinctly summarized by van de Walle and Knodel (1980, p. 5):

> In the first half of the 19th century, there were two general levels of birth rates in Europe. West of an imaginary line running from the Adriatic to the Baltic Sea, birth rates were under 40 per 1,000 persons per year—the result of late marriage and wide spread celibacy—and death rates were in the 20's. East of the line, universal and early marriage made for birth rates above 40 per 1,000—not unlike those in much of Asia and Africa today—while death rates were in the 30's. Now, at the end of the transition, most birth rates are under 15 per 1,000 in Western Europe and only a little higher in Eastern Europe. And death rates on both sides of the line are down to about 10 per 1,000.

The magnitude of these shifts, particularly if they are considered irreversible, deserves to be emphasized: Contemporary Europeans bear only one third as many children and have a death rate only half as high as Europeans in the early 19th century. The decline in infant mortality was even more precipitous, from early 19th century rates of about 200 infant deaths in every 1000 births to about 10 at present; contemporary Europeans thus lose only 1/20th as many infants as their forebears in 1800. Similar changes occurred at roughly the same time in North America and Australia.

The timing, sequence, and socioeconomic concomitants of these shifts are important to an understanding of how they might have affected, and been affected by, parental attitudes. Crude death rates, though not infant mortality, dropped moderately and gradually throughout the 19th century, then more steeply after 1900. The onset of mortality decline, probably in the late 18th century, was well in advance of improvements in medicine and has been attributed by McKeown (1976) to the greater availability of potatoes and maize, which improved the diet of ordinary people and made them more resistant to infection. Fertility, having increased in the late 18th century, began to decline around 1880 (much earlier in France, Switzerland, and the United States), had dropped substantially by 1920, and continued its decline in the mid-20th century. Infant mortality declined little in the 19th century, except in Sweden, but dropped precipitously between 1900 and

1920 (due to improved water and sanitation and the pasteurization of milk), continuing its decline thereafter.

When European parents started to limit the number of their children, they had not yet experienced the enhanced probability of infant survival that came with the 20th century. Thus, the *onset* of fertility decline cannot be attributed to the greater parental confidence in child survival that follows reduced infant mortality. Whatever their reasons for limiting births (which are still a matter of speculation), they accomplished it through abstinence and withdrawal—methods theoretically available to all humans—rather than through advances in contraceptive technology. Parents in the 19th century were healthier on the average and living longer than their forebears, and they had large families that were less likely to be disrupted by the death of a parent during the reproductive years. The drop in infant mortality that followed the onset of fertility decline probably strengthened the trend but could not have instigated it.

Deliberate birth limitation on the scale that occurred in Europe and North America in the late 19th and early 20th centuries was unprecedented in human history, and seems to have marked a turning point in concepts and conditions of child development. The small-family ideal that emerged represented a departure from agrarian values toward a view of parent–child relations attuned to an urban-industrial economy, one in which each child signified increased costs and reduced contributions.

The relations of fertility decline to the urban-industrial transition and the spread of schooling are discussed below. At this point it should be noted that each of the major demographic trends of the 19th and 20th centuries seems to have been instigated by changes in socioeconomic conditions and subsequently amplified by use of new medical technologies rather than the other way around. Thus, the decline in crude death rates around 1800 may have resulted from an improved diet due to the more abundant and nutritious food supply of early capitalistic economies, though the trend was certainly strengthened later on by better medical care. Fertility decline began because married couples decided to limit births and used existing techniques, though their efforts were later facilitated by the availability of contraceptive technology. Infant mortality may have begun to decline after fertility was limited due to better parental care for each of fewer children, though the trend was powerfully strengthened by public sanitation (water and sewerage), the pasteurization of milk, immunization, and more effective drugs. In other words, demographic transition should not be seen as the simple result of changes in biotechnology but rather as the outcome of parental responses to changing socioeconomic conditions.

The West, Eastern Europe, and Japan arrived at roughly the same demographic destination by the last quarter of the 20th century, with only a few exceptions. Their birth and death rates are low and vary within a narrow range. They did not begin the demographic transition at the same place, however, and did not move along identical pathways to their present positions. In other words, it would be a mistake to conclude that their current similarities in comparison with Third World societies are the outcomes of the same historical process or represent a shared historical background. This is particularly important to bear in mind when attempting to generalize from their past patterns of change in order to forecast what is possible and probable for the Third World.

As historical demography is pursued in greater depth, more country-specific patterns—including features of the pretransitional social order—are identified as having been crucial to the process of demographic transition. Wrigley (1983), for example, argues that household formation in England from the 17th century was sensitive to the cost of living. Couples postponed marriage—and therefore childbearing—when prices were high, thus reducing the birth rate. The customary practices by which families regulated the establishment of reproductive unions in response to economic conditions constitute a type of influence on fertility prior to the industrial revolution that might have facilitated the English fertility transition at a later date.

In France and the United States the secular decline in birth rates began before 1800—perhaps a century before the rest of Europe—and probably for different reasons. In both countries, however, the decline was initiated before industrialization and urbanization. This is particularly noteworthy because neither France nor the United States became as urban in the proportions of their populations living in cities as England and some of the other industrial countries. In other words, the forefront of fertility decline in the 19th century occurred in settings characterized by agrarian, or at least predominantly rural, conditions, contradicting the view that fertility decline is inexorably linked to urbanization.

A recent comparison of fertility decline in Japan and Sweden also emphasizes the influence of country-specific pretransitional characteristics—in this case the patriarchal stem family, which is shared by those two countries but not by others in their respective regions (Mosk, 1983). Here again the evidence points to the conclusion that the demographic transition encompasses varied trajectories to the same destinations.

MASS SCHOOLING

There were schools in Europe from ancient times, but until the 19th century a relatively small proportion of children attended them. In the 50 years between 1840 and 1890 primary school attendance was enormously broadened and became compulsory in Western Europe, North America, and Australia. This marks one of the most radical shifts in the parent–child relationship in human history. Mass schooling must be seen as both a reflection of powerful antecedent trends in social, political, and economic conditions and a determinant of subsequent changes in reproduction and family life. The extension of schooling in the individual life span and its expansion across the globe have proved to be irresistible and apparently irreversible tendencies, fundamentally altering the way children are regarded.

How did mass schooling affect the parent–child relationship? First, it kept children out of full-time productive work and minimized their economic contributions to the family. It furthermore established in a public and unavoidable way that childhood was dedicated to preparation for adult roles outside the family. It gave children a certain kind of power vis-à-vis their parents, either because the latter saw their better educated children as bearers of potentially higher social status or because the children themselves, having gained access to a new world of valuable skills and information, asserted themselves more within the family. Assertive, school-going children cost more than compliant children who work under parental supervision in domestic production; they required a larger share of family resources for their clothes, for space in which to study, and for the satisfaction of the consumer tastes they acquired outside the home. Their demands, implicit and actual, were strongly supported by the wider society, particularly after compulsory school legislation, which had the effect of informing parents that the state had officially determined how their offspring should spend their time during childhood.

The parental response to this revolutionary change was initially to minimize its impact, then to devise strategies to maximize the advantages it offered. At first children enrolled in school were frequently kept home when their work was needed, as attested by daily attendance figures. In 1869-1870, for example, although 57% of the United States population aged 5 to 17 was enrolled in school, only 35% attended daily. Even those children who did attend daily were probably required to perform chores at home and to "make themselves useful" to their parents. Caldwell (1982, pp. 117–131) has argued that so long as this was the case, parents could realistically consider numerous offspring advantageous even if they were not directly involved in domestic production. Eventually, however, the advantages of children in performing household chores must have been outweighed by their rising costs to the family, particularly if parents could not count on benefiting from their children's future wages, thus creating an economic incentive for birth control. According to Caldwell's theory, however, this shifting cost-contribution ratio was subjectively experienced in terms of parental ideology rather than economic calculation.

A new model of parenthood arose, with the goal of optimizing life chances for each of a few children through extended education and a measure of adult attention that had formerly been reserved for heirs to the throne. "Quality" replaced "quantity" as the focus of child-rearing efforts, first in the middle classes but with a rapid spread into other classes.

The new model was effective as a strategy for optimizing the competitive position of offspring in a labor market that increasingly favored more education and personal autonomy, but what did it do for parents? Not very much in material terms, for economic "returns" to parents were usually unfavorable. The code of filial reciprocity that had prevailed in agrarian communities was no longer binding on adult children, at least to a dependable degree. But something happened which cannot be accounted for in strictly economic terms; parents came to identify with the children in whom they had invested so much of themselves as well as their resources, and they were able to derive subjective satisfaction from the economic and reproductive careers of their children even in the absence of material support. The history of ideological sources of this subjective satisfaction is considered in the following section.

The history of schooling in the West varied from one country to another. Before 1800 schooling (often limited to literacy acquisition) was widespread in England, Scotland, the United States, the Netherlands, and Prussia. In these countries, between 40 and 60% of the entire male population attended school, if only for a few years, and became literate. In the rest of Europe smaller proportions ever attended school or became literate. Thus, the 19th century opened with major differences in educational development among the countries of Europe.

Schooling was extended through diverse forms of organization. Prussia pioneered the development of a governmentally planned and hierarchically organized school system, and France also built a centrally controlled national network of schools. England, on the other hand, had a wide and unregulated variety of religious and private schools, many of them of poor quality, until late in the 19th century, and never imposed the bureaucratic controls found in France. In the United States schools were built and managed under state and local control (and financing), with a degree of decentralization unknown in Europe. These institutional variations affected long-range outcomes, for variability in school quality by social class in England and by locality (which is correlated with social class) in the United States have remained strong into present times. Hence, the relations of schools to the central government and to the national system of social status have varied widely across Western countries.

THE RISE OF PUBLIC INTEREST IN CHILDREN

There can be no doubt that European attitudes toward children changed radically during the 19th century, but the changes had so many expressions and concomitants that they are not simple to describe or explain. Furthermore, ideas spread more quickly from one country to another than economic, demographic, and institutional patterns, and became harder to isolate for analysis. Most of the revolutionary ideas of the 19th century had been formulated in earlier centuries, and questions remain as to when their impact was fully felt. Stone (1977) and Plumb (1980) trace some of these ideas to the second half of the 17th century in England. On the Continent, the ideas formulated by Rousseau in *Emile* early in the 18th century were basic to the changing concepts of child development and education a century and more later. Pestalozzi, the 18th century Swiss educator, spread these concepts to Prussia before 1800.

This complex intellectual and social history is still being investigated by professional historians and remains an area of controversy. From a comparative perspective, however, its outlines are clear. Western conceptions of childhood after 1500 reflected a growing and changing debate over freedom, individualism, and authority. At first this debate was conducted in religious terms and was associated with the rise of Protestant Christianity. Calvinism conceptualized the child as born with a will of its own, but viewed this as symptomatic of original sin, to be subdued by parental authority in the interests of moral virtue and divinely sanctioned moral order. Later, philosophers such as Locke and Rousseau proposed the natural goodness of the child and an acceptance of the child's playful impulses as beneficial for education and individual development. Such ideas grew in influence during the 18th century, particularly in the arts (e.g., the poetry of William Blake) and in philosophical discourse on education (e.g., Pestalozzi). During the same period liberal political theory—emphasizing individual freedom rather than obedience to authority—not only developed but was dramatically promulgated through the American and French revolutions. In the 19th century literary and artistic romanticism established an emotional climate on which the struggle for children's rights as a form of political liberation could draw. It was during the 19th century, then, that the sentimental idealization of childhood combined with the liberal notion that children had enforceable rights, was expressed in such cultural phenomena as the novels of Dickens and the legislative struggle against child labor.

Much of the complexity of this history derives from the fact that the debate over freedom versus constraint in childhood has not led to a final resolution but continues even today, in issues specific to contemporary contexts. Furthermore, the Western countries represent a variety of experiences with this debate in terms of the particular sequences of intellectual discourse, public policy, and effects on family life. What distinguishes the Western ideology as a whole from that of many non-Western cultures is not so much the preference for freedom, even for children, as the definition of freedom as liberation from authority—a polarity that pits options (freedom to choose) against ligatures (social constraints) in the struggle for a better life. This struggle, this morality play on behalf of children, provided the basic terms in which the modern European conceptions of the child emerged during the 19th century.

The new ideas were hostile to agrarian models of obedience and reciprocity. Focusing on childhood as a distinct and valuable phase of life, they emphasized autonomy and the child's development as a separate and equal human being, supported and protected, by loving parents as he developed his capacities to make free and intelligent choices. In philosophy, literature, and the arts, these ideas were advanced and elaborated. In psychology and child study they were justified on scientific grounds. In politics they inspired legislation to defend children against exploitation in factories and to restrict parental control. And in the family they inspired an emotional commitment that knew no precedent except in the rearing of royal princes.

The relationship of these ideas to the socioeconomic trends reviewed above and to the larger cultural ideologies from which they were derived deserves more intensive research. It is clear that these ideas were important in forming the emotional attitudes of parents and policymakers alike and thus had an important impact. It also seems true, however, that the emotional component, and particularly the sense of a struggle for children against those who do them harm, was stronger in some countries than in others. In some European countries, then, the cause of children gained a political constituency of reformers crusading against the status quo, while in others reforms were enacted, perhaps somewhat later and more peacefully as simply necessary steps required of every civilized society.

All these trends focused more public and private attention on childhood and the development of children than had previously been the case in European societies and in agrarian societies generally. Children were as never before depicted as valuable, lovable, innocent but intelligent individuals, to be cherished, protected, defended, and developed. Public and private poles of this general tendency might seem to have been in conflict, for the public laws prohibiting child labor and compelling school attendance embodied the assumption that the citizenry bore a collective responsibility for other people's children in addition to their own offspring, while romantic sentimentalism promoted an intensification of the parent–offspring bond in the most private and exclusive terms. Both poles, however, were based on the notion that every individual child was uniquely valuable to his own parents *and* to the wider society—an idea compatible with Western traditions but newly applied to children in the context of a secular national state.

The ideological complementarity of these two poles can be seen in the presumption that parents who cherished their own children would be able to support the public cause of all children through a process of identification, i.e., by imagining how they would feel if their own children were the victims of neglect or exploitation. Similarly, the argument that the development of children represented a national resource for public investment was expected to evoke in parents a complementary "investment" in the educational and occupational aspirations of their own offspring. In the larger cultural ideology that emerged, then, the potential conflict between public and private interests in children was not only conceptually reconciled but embedded in the idea of their convergence to the benefit of children.

CONCLUSIONS

All the trends reviewed above favor the bearing of *fewer* children receiving *more* attention (and other resources) over a *longer* period of their lives than was typical in agrarian societies. Changing economic, demographic, and structural conditions led Western parents in the late 19th century to perceive the allocation of greater resources to each child as enhancing the future advantage of the child in an increasingly competitive environment. Changing ideological conditions motivated their willingness to commit resources to each child without expecting a material return and to define their commitment in emotional and moral terms from which economic considerations were expunged. Similar trends have been observed in Japan and in some Third World countries as they have moved from agrarian to urban-industrial conditions.

This brief overview has also indicated differences among Western countries in the conditions of family life and child development before 1800, in the processes and sequences of change during the 19th and 20th centuries, and in the outcomes as of the present time. European countries were not homogeneous to begin with and are not homogeneous today, however much they contrast with other countries in the world. Moreover, their advances in formal education and the regulation of birth and death were not achieved by taking the same steps in the same order, but through various pathways reflecting the diversity of their socioeconomic and cultural conditions. This historical record suggests that family change will continue to reflect the diversity of settings in which it occurs. Those who formulate policy will have to pay close attention to the unique resources and limits of each setting rather than assume a universal series of prerequisites for replicating progress.

In attempting to explain how the West was transformed from its agrarian condition, it is not only diversity in local settings that must be taken into account but temporal diversity in the circumstances under which each major change occurred in a given country. Each secular trend showed at least two surges, often 80 or 100 years apart. Fertility began its major decline in the 19th century but fell sharply after World War I. Infant mortality dropped after 1900 but continued to decline thereafter until it reached present levels. The spread of primary schooling was a 19th century phenomenon, but secondary schooling as a mass process did not occur until the 20th century. New concepts of the child and education arose between the mid-17th and early 19th centuries but did not have their major institutional impact until much later. In each case the socioeconomic and ideological conditions affecting the consciousness of parents were different by the time the later surge occurred, and different social forces were mobilized to advance the trend. This makes it possible for largely economic factors to have determined the first surge and largely ideological factors the second, or vice versa. It means that secular trends cannot be treated as single historical events and that the telescoping of historical process in "late developing countries" cannot be treated as replicating lengthy European antecedents.

The general shift from "quantity" to "quality" as objectives of parental behavior is somewhat analogous to the contrast between r-selection and K-selection among animal species: r-selected species, adapted to dispersion in relatively unexploited habitats, bear numerous offspring at one time, provide minimal postpartum care, and have high rates of offspring mortality; K-selected species, adapted to more densely occupied and competitive environments, bear few offspring, provide lengthy and attentive parental care, and have low rates of offspring mortality (Wilson, 1975). There is a similarity between animal ecology and human history in the inverse relationship or "trade-off" between number of offspring and amount of parental energy expended per individual offspring as generating distinctive (and equally successful) strategies for adapting to different levels of competition.

The analogy is a limited one, however, and not only because it leaves out the distinctive channels through which adaptation is accomplished in each case: genetic and embryological mechanisms in animal ecology and the impact of social processes on parental consciousness for human history. In the human situation, the quantity-quality trade-off as an abstraction fails to capture the fact that parents in agrarian and industrial societies (unlike animals of different species) do not share a single set of reproductive goals: The economic utility of children as young labor and future old-age support, so important in agrarian settings, is minimized in industrial populations. In other words, offspring are not experienced as fulfilling the same goals for all humans. Furthermore, the parental commitment differs not only in its distribution over time and number of offspring but in other ways that need to be specified: e.g., the confident expectation by agrarian parents of filial reciprocation, the emotional intensity of unilateral commitment by parents in industrial societies. In both cases, their concepts of child care are related to broader cultural ideologies not specific to the parent–child relationship, e.g., the ideologies of patrilineal kinship and humanitarian liberalism. Finally, the analogy between animal adaptation and human history, however useful it is as a starting point, implies a greater uniformity of adaptive responses to environmental competitiveness than is shown by the available historical and ethnographic evidence. A theoretical model that encompasses the broad historical shift from quantity to quality in human parenthood, and cultural diversity in the ends and means of parenthood within each historical phase, is needed.

The following formulation can be proposed. For every society there is probably an optimal strategy of parental investment, i.e., a most efficient way of maximizing culture-specific parental goals through regulation of fertility and amount of parental energy expended per child. The optimal strategy is a function of: (1) the expectable lifetime costs and contributions of each child to parents (a concept similar to Caldwell's net flow of wealth between generations, but extended to include as costs and contributions anything that counts as such in a particular culture), and (2) the means available to enhance the lifetime cost-contribution ratio of a child from the average parent's point of view. The expectable cost-contribution ratio and the means available for its enhancement are in turn conditioned by prevalent socioeconomic and demographic parameters such as labor market dependence, child labor laws, compulsory schooling, urbanization, birth and infant mortality rates—plus an array of options and constraints specific to certain societies, e.g., rural landholding and inheritance patterns, white-collar employment.

The optimal strategy of parental investment for a society may not be formulated as such by its members, but it is recognized by them in their concepts of parental success and failure. The African polygynous husband with six wives and fifty children approximates an ideal in a certain kind of agrarian society, while the barren woman or man without descendants constitutes a recognizable case of failure there. Conversely, the couple raising two highly educated children is an ideal image for a Western urban society in which failure is represented by a woman with ten neglected children. Thus, the optimum strategy, though a hypothetical construct, is represented in parental consciousness through prevalent cultural models.

Insofar as there are optimal strategies of parental investment adapted to broad categories of societies, such as agrarian and industrial societies, they should be thought of as constaining variation in the cultural models of parenthood within each category but not determining the symbolic content that motivates parents to commit themselves to implementing the strategy. Each society provides the symbolic content from its own traditions and prepares its members from their early years to become emotionally respon- sive to the symbols involved. This results in diverse implementations of a given strategy in different societies of a particular category. A cultural model of parenthood, then, reflects both a general strategy of parental investment and culture-specific prototypes for the symbolic action of parents.

At their extremes, agrarian societies contrast with industrial societies in their optimal strategy of parental investment along a quantity-quality dimension. Agrarian societies can be defined to include those in which the majority live by domestic food production involving child labor and are characterized by high birth and death rates and little schooling. Industrial societies can be defined as not only meaning a majority living by wage labor in cities but with low birth and death rates and children going to school instead of work. With such a polarized comparison it is possible to claim that for all agrarian societies the optimal strategy is to maximize the number of offspring because they contribute more than they cost and are in any event unlikely to survive in numbers exceeding demand. Similarly, one can claim that for industrial societies the optimal strategy is to minimize the number of offspring because they cost more than they contribute and have excellent—hence economically excessive—survival chances, and to provide each one with intensive and extended preparation for competition in the labor market. The evidence indicates, however, that variations in cultural models of parenthood within each of these two polar types, while not incompatible with these claims, are not trivial. Among agrarian societies parental attitudes and practices varied between preindustrial England and continental Europe (Macfarlane, 1977) and between what might be called the patriarchal cultures of Africa, the Middle East, India, and China, and the less patriarchal cultures of Southeast Asia and the Pacific.

Among industrial societies there are significant variations that can be illustrated by contemporary Japan and the United States. Despite their common commitment to minimizing the number of births and maximizing schooling, Japanese and American married couples differ in the means they typically adopt to enhance the life chances of their children. Japanese mothers become intensively involved in their young children's learning of school subjects, so they can help them with homework and preparation for exams as part of their broader definition of their identity as primary caretakers of their children. They are less likely than American mothers to work outside the home during their children's school years. American families, however, are more likely to devote themselves to their children's futures through residential mobility, i.e., moving to communities reputed to have less crime and better schools, even when the costs involved mean mothers must work for the family to afford them. There is a difference in family priorities, in concepts of what children need and who should provide it. Although middle-class Japanese and Americans could be said to share an optimal strategy of parental investment, the social conditions in which they live (e.g., availability of housing, frequency of crime, variability in the standards of schools) and their cultural models of learning (see White and LeVine, 1985) differ sufficiently to lead to different styles of parental commitment. Each style incorporates a central feature derived from the respective traditions of the two countries: for Japan, the intense devotion of women to domestic tasks of economic value; for the United States, the residential mobility of the family in search of a better life. Thus, styles of parental commitment are not simply predictable from optimal strategies of parental investment, at least as broadly defined for agrarian and industrial societies. There is no reason to believe that the continuing global transformation of family life will eliminate diversity in models of parenthood or their realization in differing styles of parental commitment.

CHANGES IN THE LIFE COURSE

The changes in parenthood and the family on which this chapter has focused are related to a different structure of the life course in agrarian and urban-industrial societies. Here a distinction must be made between what parents want *for* their children and what they want *from* them. Parents in all societies want similar things for their children: health, economic security, and the optimization of local cultural values. Differing customary patterns of parental behavior can be seen as cultural responses to the jeopardy in which particular environments put the attainment of these goals (LeVine, 1974). Thus, peoples with high infant and child mortality will have parental practices designed to protect health and survival; those with competitive or unstable economies will have customs focused heavily on the early development of economic skills, and so forth. Parents do not differ fundamentally in the hopes that they have for their children, but in their perceptions—conditioned by folk knowledge—of the chances that the hopes will be fulfilled. Perceiving different hazards, they devise local solutions that become traditional prescriptions for parental behavior. Since traditions often change slowly or partially, the parental practices of two peoples like the Japanese and Americans are likely to vary even after the major environmental parameters that helped shape them are no longer sources of difference.

When it comes to what parents want *from* their children, however, there are the fundamental differences between agrarian and urban-industrial societies with which this chapter began. Agrarian parents want, and consider themselves entitled to, economic returns in the short run (child labor) and the long term (old-age security). These goals, and the expectation that they will be fulfilled, are predicated on a different conception of the life course than that prevailing in urban-industrial societies. Where the family depends on child labor for economic subsistence, parents are strongly motivated to continue bearing children as long as possible, i.e., until the woman reaches menopause and even longer in polygynous societies where men may take younger wives to prolong their own reproductive careers. Thus, being the parent of a young child is seen as a property of adulthood in general, not only young adulthood or any other limited period within the adult life course. In contrast with the expectation of urban-industrial parents for low fertility and confinement of childbearing to young adulthood, the agrarian expectation is that the raising of children is a normal accompaniment of family life in all its phases.

The restricted period of parenthood within the life course of adults in urban-industrial societies is a major change from the agrarian past, and one that both reflects and reinforces the diminished salience of the parent–child relationship and other kin ties as defining attributes of social identity in those societies. This is clearly seen with respect to the issue of old-age security. In the agrarian context, the parental expectation of being helped by children in old age was not based on a hope of filial generosity. On the contrary, it was predicated on a social organization that connected children and parents in active relationships throughout the life span. Where there was domestic production, significant family property, and residential stability, at least some of the children were likely to be neighbors and co-workers of their parents until the latter died. Where there were also corporate descent groups, the parent–child relationship was publicly embedded in a system of intergenerational continuity and reciprocity that included a code of mutual assistance and conferred a social identity on each person.

In other words, the self-definition of a person in an agrarian society was likely to be based on kinship ties in which parentage was salient—not only when children were young but in their adulthood as well. Where parents did look to their children for assistance in old age—and this was not universal, particularly among the preindustrial societies of the West—it was as part of a local organization of relationships that defined each person's participation in society. The urban-industrial transformation was a growth of new forms of social participation not defined by kin and locality and not necessarily involving parentage, thus reducing the salience of those relationships in the social identities and self-evaluation of adults. Concepts of the parent–child relationships as a lifelong bond between adults gave way to a concept of parenthood as the raising of offspring to an autonomous maturity in which their future relationship was optional. Where parents had seen their old age as the time when the benefits of parenthood—in social respect from the community as well as kin—were most expectable, it came to be seen as the time when, for many, the nest was empty and parenthood was largely finished. The prolongation of the life span and the institutional provision of old-age pensions have also contributed to urban-industrial conceptions of the adult life course in which parenthood is an intermediate phase of adulthood, with an increasingly salient postparental phase.

ACKNOWLEDGMENT

This chapter is based on a paper published as Chapter 3 of *Human Conditions: The Cultural Basis for Educational Development* by Robert A. LeVine and Merry White, London: Routledge and Kegan Paul, 1986. The research was supported by the Bernard van Leer Foundation.

REFERENCES

Arnold F., Bulatao, R., Burikpakdi, C., Chung, B., Fawcett, J., Iritani, T., Lee, S., and Wu, T. *The Value of Children. Vol. I: Introduction and Comparative Analysis.* Honolulu, HI: East-West Population Institute, 1975.

Caldwell, J. *Theory of Fertility Decline.* NY: Academic Press, 1982.

Caldwell, J. Direct economic costs and benefits of children. In R. Bulatao and R. Lee (Eds.), *Determinants of Fertility in Developing Countries.* NY: Academic Press, 1983.

Hirschman, A. O. *A Bias for Hope.* Princeton, NJ: Princeton University Press, 1971.

Hoffman, L., and Manis, J. The value of children in the United States: a new approach to the study of fertility. *Journal of Marriage and the Family,* 1979, *41,* 583–96.

LeVine, R. A. Parental goals: A cross-cultural view. *Teachers College Record,* 1974, *76,* 226–239.

MacFarlane, A. *The Origins of English Individualism.* Cambridge, MA: Cambridge University Press, 1977.

McKeown, T. *The Modern Rise of Population.* NY: Academic Press, 1976.

Mosk, C. *Patriarchy and Fertility: Japan and Sweden, 1880–1960.* NY: Academic Press, 1983.

Plumb, J. The new world of children in eighteenth century England. In V. Fox and M. Quitt (Eds.), *Loving, Parenting and Dying.* NY: Psychohistory Press, 1980.

Stone, L. *The Family, Sex and Marriage in England, 1500–1800.* NY: Harper & Row, 1977.

van de Walle, E., and Knodel, J. Europe's fertility transition: new evidence and lessons for today's developing world. *Population Bulletin,* 1980, *34*(6).

White, M., and LeVine, R. What is an Ii ko? In H. Stevenson and K. Hakuta (Eds.), *Child Development in Japan and the United States.* Philadelphia, PA: Witt. Freeman, 1985.

Wilson, E. *Sociobiology: The New Synthesis.* Cambridge, MA: Harvard University Press, 1975.

Wrigley, E. The growth of population in eighteenth century England: a conundrum resolved. *Past and Present,* 1983, *98,* 121–150.

11 HISTORICAL PERSPECTIVES ON THE DEVELOPMENT OF THE FAMILY AND PARENT–CHILD INTERACTIONS

Maris A. Vinovskis

OVERVIEW

The perception and treatment of children and parent–child relationships have experienced major changes during the past 300 or 400 years. While most Western families have always been small and nuclear, the sharp boundary between the modern American family and the rest of society is a recent development. Although parents have historically been responsible for their children, they were not always closely attached to them as infants. Nor have young children been perceived and treated the same throughout history. Whether or not children were once seen as miniature adults, it is clear that they were regarded as capable of considerable intellectual training at a very early age. Furthermore, while historians differ amongst themselves on the existence or meaning of adolescence in earlier times, most of them agree that the life course of youth has changed considerably during the past several hundred years.

Parent–child relationships have also changed over time. Parental involvement in early child care has grown considerably since the Middle Ages, but the role of the father in the catechizing and educating of young children has diminished. At the same time, parental control over children has been greatly diminished in areas such as sexual behavior or choice of a career or spouse.

The relationship between parents and children is influenced by many factors and can vary over time. Alterations in the composition and size of the household as well as its interactions with the outside can affect the experiences of children growing up within it. Similarly, changes in the roles of parents or servants, for example, may affect the socialization of the young by that household. And any changes in the perceptions of the nature of children or their appropriate role in society is likely to influence their dealings with parents and other adults.

During the past 20 years historians have reexamined the nature of the family as it once was as well as the changes in the perception and treatment of children (Degler, 1980b; Vinovskis, 1977, 1983a). Most of these efforts, however, have been focused on some particular aspect of the family of the child, with less attention paid to their interaction. This chapter will attempt to bring together some of these diverse studies and suggest how parenting and child development may have been different in the past than it is today. Although this analysis will draw upon historical examples from all of Western Europe since the 16th century, its primary focus will be on 17th, 18th, and 19th century England and America. Furthermore, while there are many different possible definitions of family, throughout this chapter, family will refer to members of the same kin living under one roof (Stone, 1977).

NATURE OF THE FAMILY AND HOUSEHOLD IN THE PAST

The social context of parenting and child development is very much affected by the nature of the residence in which the child is reared. The traditional assumption (Wirth, 1938; Parsons, 1943) is that most children in the past grew up in extended households. After marriage, they continued to live with their parents and supported them in their old age. As a result, young children frequently grew up in large households where their grandparents as well as their parents played an important role in their upbringing.

Accordingly, the extended Western preindustrial household was transformed into an isolated nuclear one as the result of the disruptive impact of urbanization and industrialization (often incorrectly combined under the term "modernization") in the 19th and 20th centuries. While this new nuclear household was supposedly better suited to the needs of the modern economy in terms of providing a more mobile and less kin-oriented labor force, the tasks of child rearing and care of the elderly were seen to have suffered in the process.

Recent historical research has cast considerable doubt on the idea that the Western family evolved from extended to nuclear due to the onset of urbanization and industrialization. As Laslett (1972) and his associates have argued, most households in preindustrial Western Europe were already nuclear and therefore could not have been transformed by any recent economic changes. While some variations did exist in household size, these were surprisingly small and mainly due to the presence or absence of servants of boarders and lodgers rather than relatives. Furthermore, instead of the nostalgic view of children growing up in large families, Laslett (1972) contends that most households were actually quite small (mean household size was about 4.75).

Critics (Berkner, 1972, 1973) of the use of a mean household size point out that studying the average size of families at any given moment is misleading and incorrect because individual families increase and decrease in size and complexity over time. While only a small proportion are extended at any particular instance, a much larger proportion of them may have been extended at some point. Berkner (1972) in particular notes the prevalence of the stem family in Austria, where one of the male children continues to live with the parents after he marries and then inherits the farm after the father dies.

Although the critics of the use of mean household size are correct in questioning its conceptual and analytical utility, it is not likely that many families in preindustrial England or America had married children routinely living with them (Degler, 1980a; Vinovskis, 1977, 1983a). While single servants or boarders and lodgers frequently resided in the same household (Demos, 1970; Modell and Hareven, 1973), it was expected that married couples would establish their own separate, independent households. In some parts of Western Europe, however, such as southern France (Flandrin, 1979) or the Baltic provinces (Plakens, 1975), multigenerational households were more common. Furthermore, while mean household size was usually quite small in Western Europe (Laslett, 1972), it was considerably larger in colonial New England (Greven, 1972) because of the higher fertility and lower mortality of that region.

Even if most Western European families had always been small and nuclear, it does not mean that the social context in which children were brought up in a household remained the same. As Aries (1962) has pointed out, the medieval family was very different from its modern counterpart in that the boundary between the household and the larger society was not as rigidly drawn and the role of parents, servants, or neighbors in the socialization of children was not as differentiated and clear-cut. Stone's (1977) analysis of the late medieval and early 16th century English family confirms and expands upon many of Aries's findings. While Stone acknowledges that his categorization and periodization of the changes in English families is limited by the sources and the overlapping of these ideal family types to some degree in practice, his framework provides a useful point of departure for this analysis.

The English in the late medieval period maintained only weak boundaries between their families and the rest of society, and family members were oriented more toward kin relationships among the upper classes and toward neighbors among their poorer counterparts (Stone, 1977). Marriage among property-owning classes in 16th-century England was a collective decision involving not only the family but also other kin. Individual considerations of happiness and romantic love were subservient to the need to protect the long-term interests of the lineage. Relationships within the nuclear family were not much closer than those with neighbors, relatives, or other friends.

According to Stone (1977), this open lineage family gave way to a restricted patriarchal nuclear family that predominated from 1580 to 1640, during which time loyalties to lineage, kin, and local community declined as allegiances to the state and church and kin within the household increased. As a result, the boundary between the nuclear family and the other members of society increased, while the authority of the father as head of the household within that family was enhanced. Both the state and the church provided new theoretical and practical support for patriarchy within the family, which was coupled with a new interest in children. Fathers now had added incentive to ensure that their offspring internalized the values of submissiveness to them even if it meant breaking their will at an early age. This drive toward parental dominance was particularly characteristic of the Puritans, who tended to be especially anxious about their children's upbringing. Concern about children continued as they developed, and upper-class parents sought to control their choices of both a career and a spouse.

Finally, Stone (1977) sees the growth of the closed domesticated nuclear family after the mid-17th century among the upper bourgeoise and squirarchy caused by the rise of affective individualism. The family was now increasingly organized around the principle of personal autonomy and bound together by strong affective ties. The separation between the members of the nuclear family and their servants or boarders and lodgers widened, along with the distance between the household and the rest of society. Physical privacy became more important, and the idea of the individual's right to pursue his own happiness became more acceptable.

While the causes of the changes or the exact timing among the different social classes of the move from the open lineage family to the closed domesticated nuclear family are not always clear or agreed upon (Trumbach, 1978), the occurrence of that shift is generally accepted. Children growing up in 15th-century England, for example, encountered a very different social environment in their homes and neighborhoods from those in the 18th and 19th centuries. Thus, the close-knit affective nuclear family that is most prevalent today is really only the latest stage in the longer evolution of households and family life in Western Europe in the past 500 years.

Throughout most of the preindustrial period the household also functioned as the central productive unit of society. Children received training in their own homes regarding their future occupations or were employed in someone else's household (Mitterauer and Sieder, 1982). But as the economic functions of the household were transferred in the late 18th- and 19th centuries to the shop or the factory, the home environment in which the children were raised changed. Rather than being closely integrated into neighborhood activities and serving as an economic focal point, the household increasingly became a haven or escape from the outside world (Cott, 1977; Lasch, 1977). Furthermore, as members of the nuclear family increasingly distanced themselves from others, they came to expect and cherish more from each other emotionally (Mitterauer and Sieder, 1982). As a result, whereas children growing up in the 15th century were expected and encouraged to interact closely with many other adults besides their own parents, those in the 18th and 19th centuries came to rely more upon each other and their own parents for their emotional needs.

While major changes in the nature of the family occurred in Western

Europe, such changes were less dramatic in America due to the fact that when the New World was settled the closed domesticated nuclear family was already prevalent in England (Stone, 1977). The families that migrated to the New World, especially the Puritans, brought with them the ideal of a close and loving family (Demos, 1970; Morgan, 1966, first pub. 1944). While the economic functions of the American household were altered in the 19th century, the overall change was less than the shift from an open lineage family to the closed domesticated nuclear family in Western Europe. Thus, although the relationship between parents and their children, for example, has not remained constant in America during the past 300 years, the extent of that change is probably less than in Western Europe.

CHANGING PERCEPTIONS AND TREATMENT OF CHILDREN

Having surveyed some of the changes in the nature of the household and the way they might affect the environment in which children were raised, the way those children were perceived and treated will now be considered. Since it is impossible, of course, to survey child development in its entirety, the focus will be confined to only three aspects: (1) parental love of children, (2) intellectual capabilities of young children, and (3) youth.

Parental Love of Children

It is commonly assumed that one of the basic characteristics of human beings is the close and immediate attachment between the newborn child and the parents—especially the mother. Consequently, child abandonment or abuse today is puzzling to many Americans, since these practices seem to contradict what is perceived to be a deeply ingrained feeling toward one's own children.

Maternal indifference to infants, however, may have been common during the Middle Ages (Aries, 1962; Stone, 1977). Parents did not pay much attention to newborn infants and did not display much grief if they died. According to Aries, the lack of affection toward and attention to infants continued until the 16th and 17th centuries, and Shorter (1975) argues that it persisted into the 18th and 19th centuries among the ordinary people of Western Europe. A few studies (Pollock, 1983), however, question the extent of maternal indifference and inattention in the past and thereby tend to minimize any of the more recent changes perceived by other historians.

As evidence of parental indifference to infants, scholars point to the casualness with which deaths of young children were accepted and sometimes seemingly encouraged or at least tolerated. Although overt infanticide was frowned upon and increasingly prosecuted in the 16th century, it still may have been quite common in parts of Western

Europe (Langer, 1975). There also seems to be agreement that the practice of leaving infants at foundling hospitals or with rural wet nurses during the 17th, 18th, and 19th centuries resulted in very high mortality rates (Badinter, 1981). The prevalence of wet-nursing is indicated by the fact that in the first two decades of the 19th century approximately half of the infants born in Paris were nursed commercially, even though this often resulted in more than one quarter of those infants dying (Sussman, 1977). In addition, the natural children of the wet nurses also suffered and were more apt to die because they did not receive sufficient nourishment (Lehning, 1982). Whether the decision to abandon an infant to a charitable institution or to a wet nurse was mainly the result of the mother's economic desperation, the difficulty of raising an out-of-wedlock child, or a lack of attachment for the young infant is not clear. But the fact that many well-to-do, married women casually chose to give their infants to wet nurses, despite the apparent higher risks of mortality, suggests that not everyone using this form of child care was driven to it by dire circumstances (Shorter, 1975).

While the practice of overt infanticide and child abandonment may have been relatively widespread in parts of Western Europe (such as France), it does not seem to have been as prevalent in either England or America (Hoffer and Hull, 1981; Stone, 1977). Indeed, authorities in both those countries prosecuted cases of infanticide in the 16th and 17th centuries more vigorously than most other forms of murder and emphasized the importance of maternal care of the young child. Furthermore, the use of wet nurses (employed by upper-class English women) became unfashionable by the end of the 18th century (Trumbach, 1978).

Although there is considerable disagreement on the extent and timing of parental indifference to infants in Western Europe, almost everyone is agreed on its presence as well as its subsequent demise. Though few individuals (Pollock, 1983) have begun to challenge this interpretation—at least in its more extreme forms—most observers still concur that by the 17th and 18th centuries (or perhaps even later among French peasants and workers) parents expressed more interest in and affection for their children (Demos, 1970; Morgan, 1966; Stone, 1977, Trumbach, 1978). Indeed, the deep affection and attachment to one's own children became one of the major characteristics of the closed domesticated nuclear family. By the 19th century many observers began to even criticize parents for being too child-centered (Wishy, 1968).

While the gradual change in the reactions of parents to their newborn undoubtedly improved the situation of children generally, parents still could, if they chose, abuse their own children as long as such abuse did not result in death. Gradually, however, the state began to intervene to protect the child from harm inflicted at the workplace or at home. Yet it was not until the late 19th century that reformers in England were able to persuade lawmakers to pass legislation to protect children from abusive parents, since the parent–child relationship was regarded as sacred and beyond state intervention (Behlmer, 1982). Ironically, efforts to prevent cruelty against animals preceded those to accomplish the same ends for children by nearly half a century (Turner, 1980).

Intellectual Capabilities of Young Children

Child developmentalists sometimes portray the nature and capabilities of the young as invariant across cultures and over time, without taking into consideration how much of the behavior of those children can be explained by parental and societal expectations. Yet historically the perceptions and treatment of the child have been quite varied.

Some of the earliest studies (Earle, 1899) of children in colonial America yielded the observation that a distinct phase of childhood did not exist. Children were expected to think and behave as adults from a very early age. As Fleming (1933, p. 60) noted, "Children were regarded simply as miniature adults. . . . " This perception of children received strong reinforcement from Aries (1962), who argued that medieval society in general did not distinguish between children and adults and that the idea of childhood as a separate and distinct stage did not emerge until the 16th and 17th centuries.

Some recent scholars (Demos, 1970, 1974; Zuckerman, 1970) of the colonial American family have continued the idea that children were perceived and treated as miniature adults. But others (Axtell, 1974; Stannard, 1975, 1977; Kaestle and Vinovskis, 1978, 1980) have questioned this interpretation by pointing out that the New England Puritans were aware that children had different abilities and temperaments from adults and that child rearing should be molded to those individual differences (Moran and Vinovskis, 1983).

Young children in colonial America, however, were perceived as being more capable intellectually at an early age than their counterparts today. The Puritans believed that children should be taught to read the Bible as soon as possible because it was essential for everyone's salvation. The importance of early reading was reinforced for them by their expectation that children were likely to die at any moment and therefore had to be spiritually prepared for this eventuality (Slater, 1977; Stannard, 1975, 1977; Vinovskis, 1972, 1976, 1981b). Indeed, the notion that children could and should learn to read as soon as they could talk was so commonly accepted by educators (Locke, 1964) that they did not feel the need to elaborate upon it in their writings (Kaestle and Vinovskis, 1978, 1980).

The idea of early childhood learning received a powerful boost in the first third of the 19th century, when the infant school movement swept the United States (May and Vinovskis, 1977; Kaestle and Vinovskis, 1978, 1980). The focus on special classes for very young children was imported from England, where infant schools had been created to help disadvantaged poor children. While most infant schools in America were initially intended to help poor children, they were quickly adopted by middle-class parents once it became evident that they were useful in helping children to develop. By the 1830's and 1840's in Massachusetts, for example, nearly 40–50% of 3-year-old children were attending schools and learning to read. Although some infant-school teachers were reluctant to focus on intellectual activities such as reading, pressures from parents forced most of them to provide such instruction.

During the first two centuries of settlement in the New World, the idea that 3- and 4-year-old children were intellectually capable of learning to read had gone virtually unchallenged in theory as well as practice and was reinforced by the infant-school movement of the late 1820's. Yet in the 1830's this viewpoint became strongly and successfully contested. Amariah Brigham, a prominent physician, published a popular book (1833) in which he argued that the early intellectual training of children seriously and permanently physically weakened their growing young minds and often led to insanity in later life. His dire warnings were accepted and repeated by educators as well as writers of child-rearing manuals. As a result, crucial financial support for the infant schools from the middle-class reformers dropped precipitously, and many such institutions were forced to close. Although parents were much slower than physicians and educators in abandoning early childhood education, by the 1850's and 1860's virtually no very young children (3 or 4 year olds) could be found in Massachusetts schools. Interestingly, when the kindergarten movement was popularized in the United States in the 1860's and 1870's by Mary Peabody, a former Massachusetts infant-school teacher, it was restricted to children at least 5 or 6 years old and deliberately avoided intellectual activities such as reading.

This example of the changing attitudes on when a child could and should learn to read illustrates how alterations in the perception of children can greatly affect the type of socialization provided for them in early life. It also demonstrates how sudden and dramatic shifts in the perceptions of the child can alter the basic pattern of child care that had been accepted unquestioningly for several centuries. One might even speculate that as society becomes increasingly willing to incorporate the latest scientific and medical findings in the care of the young, and as social institutions such as the schools become more willing and able to determine how and when parents educate their children, the likelihood of frequent swings in child-rearing practices may increase.

Youth

Although the historical study of youth is now attracting more research (Gillis, 1974; Kett, 1977), there is still little agreement among scholars on the changes that occur in this phase of the life course. The recognition of adolescence as a particular stage of development in the past, for example, has not been conclusively demonstrated. Some historians (Demos and Demos, 1969) see its emergence only in the late 19th or early 20th century, as a result of the introduction of more career choices and the sharper discontinuities in young people's lives due to urban-industrial development. Others (Hiner, 1975) have challenged that interpretation by arguing for the presence of adolescence in the early 18th century. Some individuals (Kett, 1977) have moved away from the issue of adolescence as a particular stage and focused instead on the changes in the lives of youth as they move from a state of dependence to one of independence, signaled by the establishment of their own household.

Rather than trying to analyze the individual emotional turmoil and tension that is often associated with adolescence today, many historians are studying other aspects of teenage development, such as patterns of school attendance and labor force participation. Here the debate, usually among economic and educational historians, revolves not around the life course experiences of the individual, but on those differences in the experiences among various ethnic groups or classes (Vinovskis, 1983). Scholars like Thernstrom (1964) argue that early school leaving in 19th century America was mainly the result of ethnic rather than class differences, as Irish parents were more willing to have their children leave school in order to help the family earn enough money to purchase their own home. Other historians (Katz and Davey, 1978; Bowles and Gintis, 1976) reject this ethnic interpretation and contend that the real cause of variations in school attendance was class differences. Finally, some analysts (Kaestle and Vinovskis, 1980) offer a more pluralistic interpretation that recognizes the importance of both the ethnicity and class of the parents as well as the type of community in which the children are raised.

While historians may be moving toward more agreement on the patterns of school attendance and labor force participation among youth, they are simultaneously beginning to disagree on the importance of that education. Whereas Thernstrom (1964) and most other social historians simply assumed that education was an important factor in the social functioning and mobility of 19th-century teenagers, Graff (1979) questions the benefits and necessity of literacy and education altogether. Thus, historians who have been content to analyze the patterns and causes of teenage school attendance are now being forced to reexamine its actual meaning and impact on the lives of those children.

Although American historians have tried to analyze the patterns of school attendance and labor force participation of teenagers in the past as well as the existence of adolescence as a stage of the life course, surprising little has been done to explore the changes in teenage sexuality, pregnancy, or childbearing (Vinovskis, 1982). This is somewhat surprising, since the issue of the so-called "epidemic" of adolescent pregnancy has become so visible and symbolically important to policymakers in Washington today (Vinovskis, 1981a).

In early America, adolescent sexuality, pregnancy, and childbearing were not perceived to be particular problems (Vinovskis, 1982). Althought the age of menarche in colonial New England biologically was low enough for teenage parenting to occur, few became pregnant because of the stringent 17th-century prohibitions against premarital sexual relations and the fact that few women married in their early teens. Even if teenage girls were sexually active and did become pregnant, their age was less of a factor in how society reacted than their general behavior. In other words, early Americans were more concerned about premarital sexual relations in general than the age of the women involved. Only in the late 19th and early 20th centuries is there differentiation between teenage and adult sexual behavior, with a more negative connotation attached to the former.

Throughout most of the 17th, 18th, and 19th centuries there was little onus attached to teenage marriages as long as the couple was self-supporting. Since opportunities for careers for single or married women outside the home were limited, the handicaps currently associated with early childbearing did not seem as severe. Furthermore, the relatively small number of teenage marriages during these years compared to the situation today also minimized the attention that was paid to teenage childbearing in the past.

Indeed, only in the post-World War II period has the issue of teenage pregnancy and childbearing become such a major public concern. Ironically, the greatest attention to it has come during the late 1970's and early 1980's, even though the rates of teenage pregnancy and childbearing peaked in the United States in the late 1950's (Vinovskis, 1981a).

PARENT–CHILD RELATIONS

Thus far this chapter has dealt with changes in the nature of the household as well as in the perception and treatment of children over time. Two issues in the relationship between parents and children: (1) parental responsibility for early child care and (2) parental control of children should also be considered.

Parental Responsibility for Early Child Care

In modern American society it is assumed that the parents have the primary responsibility for child care until the children are enrolled in schools where they will receive most of their educational instruction. When the behavior of parents seriously threatens the well-being of the young child, the state can intervene to protect it, but this does not occur frequently. Furthermore, the physical care and early socialization of the child is almost always the responsibility of the mother—even if both parents are employed.

Historically, the primary responsibility for the upbringing of young children belonged almost exclusively to the parents, especially the father. Although in some periods and societies, such as 17th- and 18th-century New England (Moran and Vinovskis, 1983), the state or church intervened in order to assure that the children were properly catechized and instructed, it was not until the late 19th and early 20th centuries that the state was willing to remove the young child from the direct supervision of negligent or abusive parents (Behlmer, 1982). It should also be noted, however, that although the state valued the family in the past, it was not irrevocably committed to it when that family was incapable of supporting its own members. Thus, in early America destitute families were sometimes disbanded and the children placed in other households in order to reduce the welfare costs to the rest of the community (Rosenkrantz and Vinovskis, 1977).

If the responsibility for early child care usually resided with the parents, they did not always provide that care themselves. In the medieval household, for example, servants as well as neighbors complemented the care given the young child by the parents or their older siblings (Aries, 1962; Stone, 1977). In addition, as was discussed previously, many women in the past willingly or out of economic necessity relinquished the nurturing of their infants to a wet nurse (Shorter, 1975; Sussman, 1977).

By the 17th and 18th centuries, particularly in England and America, parents increasingly cared for their own young children and began to limit assistance from nonfamily members (Morgan, 1966; Stone, 1977). This trend was caused in large part by the growing affection and self-centeredness among the immediate family members in the closed domesticated nuclear family. Furthermore, parental involvement in the upbringing of their own children was especially evident among the Puritans, who insisted on the importance of the family in providing for the spiritual as well as the physical needs of the young child (Moran and Vinovskis, 1982, 1983).

As the family began to play a more active role in the care of its young children, there was often a division of labor between the parents. The mother provided for the physical needs of the child while the father, as head of the household, attended to its spiritual and educational development. Indeed, the Puritans saw the father as the primary catechizer of children and household servants (Moran and Vinovskis, 1983).

The importance in these areas of the Puritan father was reversed in the 18th and 19th centuries, as men stopped joining churches and therefore were deemed less suitable for overseeing the religious upbringing of their children (Moran, 1979, 1980). New England Puritans came to rely more upon the mothers who, although they were less literate than the husbands, continued to join the churches. By the end of the 18th and early 19th centuries, the mother's role in early childhood care and socialization was clearly established (Kuhn, 1947; Moran and Vinovskis, 1983). The only major change thereafter was the growing role of the schools in the provision of formal education for the young child, as parents usually willingly relinquished that task to reluctant schoolteachers who had tried to limit the entry of young children into their classrooms (Kaestle and Vinovskis, 1980).

Thus, although parents have usually been assigned the primary responsibility for the care and socialization of the young child in Western society, they have not always provided those services themselves. During the past 300 or 400 years, however, parents have increasingly nurtured and socialized, at least to some degree and frequently with the assistance of specialized institutions such as schools or churches, their own children. While the direct involvement of parents in early child care and education has grown, that of other nonrelated members of the household or of the neighbors has diminished; the family today is more private and self-centered than its medieval counterpart. Finally, although the father played a more important role in the catechizing and educating of young children in certain time periods and cultures, the primary provider of care and affection for the young child was usually the mother or her female substitute. The mother's role in the upbringing of the young child increased during the 18th and 19th centuries as fathers became too busy or uninterested in sharing more fully in the raising of their young offspring. While child-rearing manuals continued to acknowledge the importance of the father for the care of the young, they also recognized that the mother had become the major figure in the performance of that task (Demos, 1982).

Parental Control of Children

Throughout most of Western development, parents exercised considerable control over children as long as they remained in the home. Children were expected to be obedient to their parents and to contribute to the well-being of the family. During much of this time, parents arranged the marriages of their children and greatly influenced their choice of careers.

In the medieval period, the interests of the lineage and kin were more important than those of the individual (Aries, 1962; Stone, 1977). Children were not only expected to acquiesce to the requests of parents, but also to the interests of the larger kinship network. Marriages were arranged in order to further the goals of the family and its kindred.

The emergence of the restricted patriarchal nuclear family weakened the claims of the lineage and kin on the allegiances of the children as the nuclear family grew closer together. The emphasis on the authority of the father as the head of the household, however, reinforced parental control over the children.

It was not until the arrival of the closed domesticated nuclear family that the rights of children as individuals were clearly recognized and acknowledged. Increasingly, children were allowed not only to veto an unsatisfactory marriage partner, but even to choose someone they loved (Stone, 1977; Trumbauch, 1978). While dating this erosion of parental power in the selection of a child's mate may vary from one society to another, it probably occurred in America between the late 18th and early 19th centuries (Smith, 1973).

Parents tried to determine not only whom children should marry, but also when. According to Greven (1970), the second generation in 17th-century Andover, Massachusetts were prevented from early marriages by the unwillingness of their fathers to relinquish legal control over the land they had set aside for their sons. While this argument is plausible, Greven has been unable to establish it statistically (Vinovskis, 1971). Indeed, while there is little doubt that parents often tried to influence the timing as well as the partner of their child's marriage, very few of the existing historical studies are able to ascertain the relative importance of the role of the parents—especially since many of the children may have willingly acquiesced in this process anyway. Yet the idea that a child has rights independent of and superior to those of the parents is a relatively recent development in Western society.

In Western Europe children were also often expected to turn over almost all their earnings directly to the parents—sometimes even after they had left home (Shorter, 1975). Under these circumstances, the economic value of children to the family was considerably enhanced, since the additional labor or revenue from a grown child could be substantial. Although children frequently contributed some of their outside earnings to their parents in the United States, it does not seem to have been as common as in Western Europe—especially among the native-born population (Dublin, 1979). This difference in parental control over the earnings of children probably reflects both the greater individuality and freedom of the child in the 19th-century American family and the fact that these families were not as economically destitute as their European counterparts. Certainly among some immigrant groups in the United States there seems to have been a stronger tradition of children, particularly girls, turning over their pay envelopes to the parents (Hareven, 1982).

Over time parental control of children has been significantly diminished. Whereas in the medieval and early modern periods parents had almost unlimited control over the behavior of their children in their own households, such is no longer the case. Although parents may still influence the choice of a child's mate or career, they cannot determine them. In addition, the idea of a child giving most of his/her outside wages to the parents seems anachronistic and inappropriate today. Indeed, the development of children's rights has proceeded so far and rapidly that society is in the midst of a backlash as efforts are being made to reassert parental rights in areas such as the reproductive behavior of minor children.

CONCLUSION

This brief historical survey of the nature of the family and household, the perception and treatment of children, and parent–child relationships suggests that major changes have occurred in these areas during the past 300 to 400 years. While most Western families have always been small and nuclear, the sharp boundary between the modern American family and the rest of society is a recent development.

Although parents have been responsible for their children, they were not always closely attached to them as infants. Nor were young children perceived and treated the same throughout history. Whether or not children were once seen as miniature adults, it is clear that they were regarded as capable of considerable intellectual training at a very early age. Furthermore, while historians differ amongst themselves on the existence or meaning of adolescence in the past, most of them agree that the life course of youth has drastically changed during the past several hundred years.

Finally, parent–child relationships have changed over time as well. Parental involvement in early child care has grown greatly since the Middle Ages, but the role of the father in the catechizing and educating of young children has diminished. At the same time, parental control over the behavior of children has been greatly diminished in areas such as sexual behavior or choice of a career or spouse.

Although there have been major changes in the way society treats children, it would be very difficult to agree on the costs and benefits of those trends from the viewpoint of the child, the parents, or society. While many applaud the increasing individualism and freedom for children within the family, others lament the loss of family responsibility and individual discipline. While an historical analysis of parents and children cannot resolve such issues, it can provide us with a better appreciation of the flexibility and resilience of the family as an institution for raising the young.

SUMMARY

Major changes have occurred during the past 300 to 400 years in the perceptions and treatment of children. Although parents have been responsible for their children, they were not always closely attached to them as infants. Whether or not children were once seen as miniature adults, it appears that they were regarded as capable of considerable intellectual training at a very early age. The existence and definition of adolescence has also changed considerably over time.

Parent–child relationships have changed as well. Parental involvement in early child care has grown considerably since the Middle Ages, but the role of the father in catechizing and educating young children has diminished. At the same time, parental control over the behavior of children has been greatly diminished in areas such as sexual behavior or choice of a career or spouse.

ACKNOWLEDGMENTS

Research was supported by the Program in American Institutions at the University of Michigan.

REFERENCES

Aries, P. *Centuries of Childhood: A Social History of Family Life*. R. Baldick (trans.). NY: Vintage Books, 1962.

Axtell, J. *The School Upon a Hill: Education and Society in Colonial New England*. New Haven, CT: Yale University Press, 1974.

Badinter, E. *Mother Love: Myth & Reality*. NY: MacMillan, 1981.

Behlmer, G. K. *Child Abuse and Moral Reform in England, 1870–1908*. Stanford, CA: Stanford University Press, 1982.

Berkner, L. K. Recent research on the history of the family in Western Europe. *Journal of Marriage and the Family*, 1973, *35*, 395–405.

Berkner, L. K. The stem family and the developmental cycle of the peasant household: An eighteenth-century Austrian example. *American Historical Review*, 1972, *77*, 398–418.

Bowles, S., and Gintis, H. *Schooling in Capitalist America: Educational Reform and the Contradictions of Economic Life*. NY: Basic Books, 1976.

Brigham, A. *Remarks on the Influence of Mental Cultivation and Mental Excitement upon Health*, 2d ed. Boston, MA: Marsh, Capen and Lyon, 1833.

Cott, N. F. *The Bonds of Womanhood: "Woman's Sphere" in New England, 1780–1835*. New Haven, CT: Yale University Press, 1977.

Degler, C. *At Odds: Women and the Family in America from the Revolution to the Present*. NY: Oxford University Press, 1980. (a)

Degler, C. Women and the family. In M. Kammen (Ed.), *The Past Before Us: Contemporary Historical Writings in the United States*. Ithaca, NY: Cornell University Press, 1980, pp. 308–326. (b)

Demos, J. *A Little Commonwealth: Family Life in Plymouth Colony*. NY: Oxford University Press, 1970.

Demos, J. The American family in past time. *American Scholar*, 1974, *43*, 422–446.

Demos, J. The changing faces of fatherhood: A new exploration in American family history. In S. H. Cath, A. R. Gurwitt, and J. M. Ross (Eds.), *Father and Child: Developmental and Clinical Perspectives*. Boston, MA: Little, Brown, 1982, pp. 425–450.

Demos, J., and Demos, V. Adolescence in historical perspective. *Journal of Marriage and the Family*, 1969, *31*, 632–638.

Dublin, T. *Women at Work: The Transformation of Work and Community in Lowell, Massachusetts, 1826–1860*. NY: Columbia University Press, 1979.

Earle, A. M. *Child Life in Colonial Days*. NY: MacMillan, 1899.

Flandrin, J. L. *Families in Former Times: Kinship, Household and Sexuality in Early Modern France*. R. Southern (trans.). Cambridge: Cambridge University Press, 1979.

Fleming, S. *Children and Puritanism: The Place of Children in the Life and Thought of the New England Churches, 1620–1847*. New Haven, CT: Yale University Press, 1933.

Gillis, J. R. *Youth and History*. NY: Academic Press, 1974.

Graff, H. J. *The Literacy Myth: Literacy and Social Structure in the Nineteenth-Century City*. NY: Academic Press, 1979.

Greven, P. J. The average size of families and households in the province of Massachusetts in 1764 and in the United States in 1790: An overview. In P. Laslett (Ed.), *Household and Family in Past Time*. Cambridge: Cambridge University Press, 1972, pp. 545–560.

Greven, P. J. *Four Generations: Population, Land, and Family in Colonial Andover, Massachusetts*. Ithaca, NY: Cornell University Press, 1970.

Hareven, T. K. *Family Time & Industrial Time: The Relationship Between the Family and Work in a New England Industrial Community*. Cambridge: Cambridge University Press, 1982.

Hiner, N. R. Adolescence in eighteenth-century America. *History of Childhood Quarterly*, 1975, *3*, 253-280.

Hoffer, P. C., and Hull, N. E. H. *Murdering Mothers: Infanticide in England and New England, 1558–1803*. NY: New York University Press, 1981.

Kaestle, C. F., and Vinovskis, M. A. From apron strings to ABCs: Parents, children, and schooling in nineteenth-century Massachusetts. In J. Demos and S. S. Boocock (Eds.), *Turning Points: Historical and Sociological Essays on the Family*. Chicago: University of Chicago Press, 1978, pp. S39–S80.

Kaestle, C. F., and Vinovskis, M. A. *Education and Social Change in Nineteenth-Century Massachusetts*. Cambridge: Cambridge University Press, 1980.

Katz, M. B., and Davey, I. E. School attendance and early industrialization in a Canadian city: A multivariate analysis. *History of Education Quarterly*, 1978, *18*, 271–294.

Kett, J. F. *Rites of Passage: Adolescence in America, 1790 to the Present*. NY: Basic Books, 1977.

Kuhn, A. L. *The Mother's Role in Childhood Education*. New Haven, CT: Yale University Press, 1947.

Langer, W. Infanticide: A historical survey. In L. deMause (Ed.), *The New Psychohistory*. NY: The Psychohistory Press, 1975, pp. 55–68.

Lasch, C. *Haven in a Heartless World: The Family Beseiged*. NY: Basic Books, 1977.

Laslett, P. (Ed.). *Household and Family in Past Time*. Cambridge: Cambridge University Press, 1972.

Lehning, J. R. Family life and wetnursing in a French village. *Journal of Interdisciplinary History*, 1982, *12*, 645–656.

Locke, J. *Some Thoughts Concerning Education*. Abridged and edited by F. W. Garforth. Woodbury, NY: Barron, 1964.

May, D., and Vinovskis, M. A. A ray of millenial light: Early education and social reform in the infant school movement in Massachusetts, 1826–1840. In T. K. Hareve. (Ed.), *Family and Kin in American Urban Communities, 1800–1940*. NY: Watts, 1976, pp. 62–99.

Mitterauer, M., and Sieder, M. *The European Family: From Patriarchy to Partnership.* K. Oosterveen and M. Horzinger (trans.). Chicago, IL: University of Chicago Press, 1982.

Modell, J., and Hareven, T. K. Urbanization and the malleable household: An examination of boarding and lodging in American families. *Journal of Marriage and the Family*, 1973, *35*, 467–479.

Moran, G. F. Sisters in Christ: Women and the church in seventeenth-century New England. In J. W. James (Ed.), *Women in American Religion*. Philadelphia, PA: University of Pennsylvania Press, 1980, pp. 47–64.

Moran, G. F. Religious renewal, Puritan tribalism, and the family in seventeenth-century Milford, Connecticut. *William and Mary Quarterly*, 3rd Series, 1979, *36*, 236–254.

Moran, G. F., and Vinovskis, M. A. The Puritan family and religion: A critical reappraisal. *William and Mary Quarterly*, 3rd Series, 1982, *39*, 29–63.

Moran, G. F., and Vinovskis, M. A. *The great care of Godly parents: Early childhood in Puritan New England*. Paper presented at Biennial Meeting of the Society for Research in Child Development, Detroit, April, 1983.

Moran, E. S. *The Puritan Family: Religion and Domestic Relations in Seventeenth-Century New England*. NY: Harper and Row, 1966.

Parsons, T. The kinship system of the contemporary United States. *American Anthropologist*, 1943, *45*, 22–38.

Plakens, A. Seigneurial authority and peasant family life: The Baltic area in the eighteenth century. *Journal of Interdisciplinary History*, 1975, *4*, 629–654.

Pollock, L. *Forgotten Children: Parent–Child Relations from 1500 to 1900*. Cambridge: Cambridge University Press, 1983.

Rosenkrantz, B. G., and Vinovskis, M. A. Caring for the insane in anti-bellum Massachusetts: Family, community, and state participation. In A. J. Lichtman and J. R. Challinor (Eds.), *Kin and Communities: Families in America*. Washington, D.C.: Smithsonian Institution Press, 1977, pp. 187–218.

Shorter, E. *The Making of the Modern Family*. NY: Basic Books, 1975.

Slater, P. G. *Children in the New England Mind: In Death and in Life*. Hamden, CT: Archon Books, 1977.

Smith, D. S. Parental power and marriage patterns: An analysis of historical trends in Hingham, Massachusetts. *Journal of Marriage and the Family*, 1973, *35*, 406–418.

Stannard, D. E. Death and the Puritan child. In D. E. Stannard (Ed.), *Death in America*. Philadelphia, PA: University of Pennsylvania Press, 1975, pp. 9–29.

Stannard, D. E. *The Puritan Way of Death: A Study in Religion, Culture, and Social Change*. New Haven, CT: Yale University Press, 1977.

Stone, L. *The Family, Sex and Marriage in England, 1500–1800*. NY: Oxford University Press, 1977.

Sussman, G. D. Parisian infants and Norman wet nurses in the early nineteenth century: A statistical study. *Journal of Interdisciplinary History*, 1977, *7*, 637–654.

Thernstrom, S. *Poverty and Progress: Social Mobility in a Nineteenth-Century City.* Cambridge, MA: Harvard University Press, 1964.

Trumbach, R. *The Rise of the Egalitarian Family: Aristocratic Kinship and Domestic Relations in Eighteenth-Century England.* NY: Academic Press, 1978.

Turner, J. *Reckoning with the Beast: Animals, Pain, and Humanity in the Victorian Mind.* Baltimore, MD: Johns Hopkins Press, 1980.

Vinovskis, M. A. American historical demography: A review essay. *Historical Methods Newsletter,* 1971, *4,* 141–148.

Vinovskis, M. A. Mortality rates and trends in Massachusetts before 1860. *Journal of Economic History,* 1972, *32,* 184–213.

Vinovskis, M. A. Angels, heads and weeping willows: Death in early America. *Proceedings of the American Antiquarian Society,* 1976, *86,* 273–302.

Vinovskis, M. A. From household size to the life course: Some observations on recent trends in family history. *American Behavioral Scientist,* 1977, *21,* 263–287.

Vinovskis, M. A. An epidemic of adolescent pregnancy? Some historical considerations. *Journal of Family History,* 1981, *6,* 205–230. (a)

Vinovskis, M. A. *Fertility in Massachusetts from the Revolution to the Civil War.* NY: Academic Press, 1981. (b)

Vinovskis, M. A. *Adolescent sexuality, pregnancy, and childbearing in early America: Some preliminary speculations.* Paper presented at the SSRC Conference on School-Age Pregnancies and Parenthood, Belmont Conference Center, Maryland, May, 1982.

Vinovskis, M. A. American families in the past. In J. B. Gardner and G. R. Adams (Eds.), *Ordinary People and Everyday Life: Perspectives on the New Social History.* Nashville, TN: American Association for State and Local History, 1983, pp. 115–137. (a)

Vinovskis, M. A. Quantification and the analysis of antebellum education. *Journal of Interdisciplinary History,* 1983, *13,* 761–786. (b)

Wirth, L. Urbanism as a way of life. *American Journal of Sociology,* 1938, *44,* 1–24.

Wishy, B. *The Child and the Republic.* Philadelphia, PA: University of Pennsylvania Press, 1968.

Zuckerman, M. *Peaceable Kingdoms: New England Towns in the Eighteenth Century.* NY: Alfred A. Knopf, 1970.

IV | THE LIFE SPAN AND PARENTAL INVESTMENT IN MODERN SOCIETY

12 DEMOGRAPHIC TRENDS IN HUMAN FERTILITY, AND PARENTING ACROSS THE LIFE SPAN

Dennis P. Hogan

INTRODUCTION

Since 1960 the nature of marriage, childbearing, and parenting among Americans has changed greatly. The age at first marriage of American men and women has risen and the probability of that marriage ending in separation and divorce has increased tremendously. These trends, however, do not indicate that Americans are abandoning marital relationships. The rate of remarriage among persons whose first marriage has terminated also has increased, ensuring that a substantial proportion of the adult lifetimes of American men and women continue to be spent within marriage (Cherlin, 1981). Also, the survivorship probabilities of husbands and wives have improved, reducing the chance that a marriage will end through death.

Decreases in the size of families desired by wives and their husbands, coupled with improved contraceptive efficacy in preventing unwanted births, have caused dramatic reductions in marital fertility rates (Westoff & Ryder, 1977). These reductions are associated with fewer births per woman, and fewer children who require parenting. Although the age at which women experience their first birth has increased in recent years, fewer births have meant an earlier average age for women at the completion of childbearing (Rindfuss & Bumpass, 1976). A decreased number of years between the first and last birth is also common.

Taken together, these nuptial and childbearing behaviors of Americans herald a demographic revolution that has remarkable implications for the parenting activities of men and women over their life spans. They are of major significance regarding the types of parenting received by children over their lifetimes. Moreover, there are major racial differences in nuptial, reproductive, and residential behaviors, resulting in a substantial divergence in the parenting activities of blacks and whites.

This chapter documents the most important shifts in the nuptial and childbearing behaviors of American couples. It describes the consequences of these new behaviors for the prevalence and incidence of parenting activities over the lifespan of Americans during the 1980's. The implications of these adult behaviors for the types of parenting received by American children from birth until age 18 are also discussed. This analysis highlights the increased variability in the reproductive and parenting behaviors of American men and women, and the emergence of distinct patterns between blacks and whites, especially those blacks in lower socioeconomic levels.

DATA

The data for this analysis were obtained from three sources: (1) the High School and Beyond study, a 1980 national survey of high school sophomores and seniors and their parents; (2) the Young Chicagoans Survey, a sample survey of black teenagers living in Chicago in 1979; and (3) published tabulations of data collected by the U.S. Bureau of the Census. The data sources for the Census Bureau tabulations vary but include the decennial censuses of the United States, the vital registration system, and the monthly Current Population Survey (CPS). The CPS is best known as the source of the monthly labor force data (on labor force participation, employment, and unemployment) for the American civilian noninstitutional population. In addition, the CPS includes supplementary questions each March to obtain data about the household and family characteristics of the population. Periodically, the June CPS includes supplemental questions on the birth expectations and fertility experiences of women of reproductive age. These supplementary CPS data (reported in the *Current Population Reports* of the Census Bureau) are the major source of descriptive data for this analysis. Tabulations from the High School and Beyond study and the young Chicagoans Survey provide insights into the causes and consequences of the trends and differentials in marriage, fertility, and parenting behaviors of young persons that are documented by the Census Bureau data.

The Current Population Survey samples in 1980 and 1981 were initially selected from the 1970 census files, with coverage of all 50 states and the District of Columbia. The sample is continually updated to reflect new construction and changing patterns of residence. The 1981 CPS sample is located in 629 areas comprising 1133 counties, independent cities, and minor civil divisions. Of the approximately 69,000 occupied households eligible, 66,000 were successfully interviewed. Overall undercoverage of the population (resulting from missed households and missed persons within sample households), compared to the level of the decennial census, is about 5% (U.S. Bureau of the Census, 1982a). Unlike the decennial census, the CPS gathers data through personal interviews with a representative of each sample household. The CPS interviewers are carefully trained about the details of the complex CPS questionnaires, in addition to receiving general training about techniques of personal interviewing. As a result of its careful design and execution, the Current Population Survey provides excellent data on the marriage, childbearing, and parenting activities of the American population.

The High School and Beyond study, sponsored by the National Center for Education Statistics, is a longitudinal survey of American high school sophomores and seniors who were first interviewed in the spring of 1980. The study respondents are a nationally representative sample of 58,728 sophomores and seniors in 1016 high schools. The response rate for the survey was 84%. A representative sample of 7201 students from 312 high schools was selected for inclusion in a supplementary parent survey. The data from one parent of each student was collected in the fall of 1980 through a combination of mailed-out questionnaires, telephone interviews, and personal interviews. A total of 6564 parents responded to the survey, for a completion rate of 91.2%. In combination with student response rates, the overall completion rate for sophomores and seniors and their parents was 76.6% (Hogan, 1985). Unless otherwise indicated, tabulations from the High School and Beyond Survey appearing in this chapter are based on the full student sample.

The High School and Beyond Survey collected a variety of information from the student respondents concerning their demographic characteristics, social origins, school experiences, and aspirations for the future. Most importantly for this analysis, the students were asked: "At what age do you expect to . . . (a) get married? and (b) have your first child?" They were given precoded responses permitting them to specify the expected year or age at each event, that they had already experienced the transition, or that they did not expect to do the transition. Sophomores were asked whether they would consider having a child before marriage. The parents' questionnaire obtained basic demographic data on the parents and their families and asked: "At what age do you expect (name) to . . . (a) get married? and (b) have his/her first child?" Precoded response categories identical to those of the student respondents were used. In this analysis, the data are used to measure parental influences on children's plans about the timing of marriage and parenthood. The data also provide insights into racial differences in attitudes about premarital parenthood.

The 1979 Young Chicagoans Survey was conducted by the Research Division of the Chicago Urban League. It collected extensive information about the demographic, social, economic, and fertility characteristics of teenage respondents through personal interviews by trained female interviewers. The 1078 black female respondents to this survey were selected by means of two randomly drawn two-stage area probability samples of households in the city of Chicago. All females aged 13 to 19 who were resident in sample households were selected for interview. The first sample of 388 respondents was designed to be representative of the population of black teenage girls resident in Chicago in 1979. The second independent sample of 690 respondents was designed to represent the population of black teenage girls living in the poor, primarily black areas of Chicago's West Side (Near West Side, East Garfield Park, and Lawndale). According to the Urban League, the survey nonresponse rate was less than 10% (Hogan & Kitagawa, 1985). This analysis uses data from the Young Chicagoans Survey to identify those blacks with the highest rates of premarital adolescent pregnancy and to characterize the living arrangements of their children.

METHODS

Trends and Period Comparisons

It would be ideal to be able to characterize the parenting activities of persons at each age over the life span. If there were a society in which the major features of nuptiality, fertility, and child rearing had remained constant for an extended period of time (50 years or longer) and could reasonably be expected to remain unchanging during the lifetimes of persons currently living, persons born in different years would share common parenting experiences at each age. Representative population data for any year would be adequate to describe the typical parenting responsibilities of persons at each age. This description would characterize the earlier parenting experiences of those persons now in their later adult years, and would accurately project the future parenting experiences of persons now in their early adult years.

However, there have been major changes over time in the demographic factors that determine the parenting experiences of Americans. Many of the most important changes (e.g., the age at first marriage, the timing of first birth, and the number of children born during the reproductive lifetime) have occurred on an intercohort basis (Ryder, 1969; Hogan, 1981; Evans, 1983a,b). That is, a group of persons born during the same year (a birth cohort) share a common demographic history which differs in significant ways from that of earlier and later birth cohorts. These demographic differences result from the unique social histories that characterize each birth cohort, and the effects of such histories on their demographic behaviors.

For example, some birth cohorts faced particularly unfavorable economic conditions in their early adult years. Cohort members responded to these circumstances by postponing marriage and delaying fertility. Other birth cohorts faced relatively good economic conditions; they married and began childbearing at earlier ages (Ryder, 1969; Easterlin, 1980; Hogan, 1981). These early decisions have persisting consequences for parenting activities over the life span, since they determine the number of children that must be raised and the parental ages when these responsibilities will be greatest. Thus, the age-specific patterns of parenting differ between birth cohorts.

Demographers distinguish between "real" cohort and "synthetic" cohort descriptions. Real cohort descriptions examine the age-specific experiences of individuals who are born at the same point in time as they progress through their lifetimes. Such comparisons describe the actual experiences of a group of persons. Studies that use real cohort methods are able to describe only the part of the cohort's history that has already occurred. It is possible to characterize the complete life-span experiences of persons only after the cohort members have lived their entire lives.

Synthetic cohort methods describe the age-specific characteristics of members of a society at a given point in time. These characteristics indicate what the age patterns of a phenomenon would be for a hypothetical group of individuals (i.e., a synthetic cohort) born into a society and experiencing during their lifetimes the age-specific rates characteristic of the particular year in question. A major advantage of the synthetic cohort method is that it permits the analyst to examine the most recent data available. Researchers interested in describing current social changes consequently tend to rely on period data and synthetic cohort methods.

Real cohort and synthetic cohort methods provide identical information about a phenomenon over the life span only in the case of a static society such as the one described above. A great deal of attention has gone into the ways in which the age-specific experiences of cohorts are translated into the age-graded behaviors of individuals during each period. Analysts also have attempted to develop methods for projecting the future behaviors of real cohorts in order to facilitate intercohort comparisons, but these techniques have met with decidedly mixed success (Hogan, 1984). Consequently, there is no satisfactory way to relate the period data available on the parenting behaviors of individuals at different ages to the actual parenting experiences of real birth cohorts over their life span.

This chapter describes *trends* in the marriage, childbearing, and parenting behaviors of Americans using the period data available from the Census Bureau tabulations. Other investigators have derived data regarding marriage and childbearing activities of real birth cohorts, and this work is cited at relevant points in this chapter. However, similar data have not been derived for the parenting behaviors of birth cohorts.

The *current* marriage, childbearing, and parenting activities of American men and women who are at different points in their life span are also characterized. This analysis is based on the most recent period data (1980 in the case of fertility and 1981 for marriage and parenting) released by the Census Bureau. These data will show the prevalence and incidence of parenting activity for persons by age (in 1980 or 1981), providing some idea of the characteristic age-graded patterns of these behaviors over the life span. However, recent intercohort changes in the timing and number of children born to women mean that these data should not be interpreted as a synthetic cohort description of parenting over the life span of real cohorts.

The current marriage and parenting decisions of young men and women will determine the shape of parenting behaviors over the life span of adults during the remainder of this century. Many of the most significant changes in marriage and fertility involve persons in these birth cohorts, and it is among them that racial differences are most pronounced. To help clarify the antecedents of these trends, this chapter directs attention to factors determining the early behaviors of members of these cohorts and their expectations for the future.

Gender and Race Comparisons

Women marry earlier and become parents at younger ages than men. These differences produce gender variations in the age-patterning of parenting activities over the life span. Of course, the biology of human reproduction means that the life changes entailed by childbearing (at least during and immediately after the pregnancy) are greater among females. Social conventions in the allocation of child-care responsibilities create important gender differences in the nature and intensity of child-care activities. This analysis thus describes the parenting behaviors of males and females separately. '

The marriage, separation, and divorce behaviors of blacks and whites have diverged in recent years (Cherlin, 1981). There are persistent racial differences in the timing of the first birth, and increased racial differences in the marital status of the mother at the time of the first birth (Kitagawa, 1981; Zelnik, Kanter & Ford, 1981). There has, on the other hand, been an intercohort convergence in the number of children ever born to black and white women (Evans, 1983b). As a result, quite different patterns of parenting are found among blacks and whites. Therefore, this chapter describes the parenting behavior of blacks and whites, by gender, whenever the available data permit.[1]

RESULTS

For most Americans the initiation of parenting activities occurs when a husband and wife experience the birth of a child. The timing of that event depends upon the age at marriage of the couple, their decisions about the desirability and timing of a birth, the fecundity of the couple, and their contraceptive efficacy. The nature of subsequent parenting responsibilities for the husband and wife will depend upon the continuation of their

[1]It also would have been possible to present data on the parenting behaviors of the Spanish origin population of the United States. This has not been done herein because the CPS sample of this population segment is too small to provide reliable data on marriage, childbearing, and parenting behavior by sex and detailed age group.

marriage and child custody arrangements should their marriage end. The level of parenting activities also depends upon the fertility of the couple after the birth of their first child. Of course, there are many variations from typical patterns. Some persons become parents before marriage—a premarital pregnancy itself may prompt marriage. Some married couples never have children. Men and women sometimes become parents after their first marriage ends, either extramaritally or with a new spouse. Nonetheless, the parenting behaviors of American couples cannot be understood adequately without consideration of their marital experiences

Marriage

Trends in Marriage. Most Americans marry at some point during their lifetimes (U.S. Bureau of the Census, 1975, Series A.160–171; U.S. Bureau of the Census. 1983, Table 49). At the beginning of the 20th century more than 83% of the males age 35–44 had been married. The percentage increased to more than 90% by 1960 and has remained at this high level through 1980. Nearly 90% of the women age 35–44 had been married in 1900, and this proportion continued to increase over the course of the 20th century. Thus, most women marry while they are of reproductive age.

Although the lifetime prevalence of marriage has remained high throughout the 20th century, the age patterns of marriage have shown tremendous intertemporal variability. Before 1940 only about one quarter of the women age 18–19 and half the women 20–24 had married. During the post-World War II period early marriage became much more common, with about one third of the women age 18–19 and nearly two thirds of the women age 20–24 being ever married. Between 1960 and 1980 the age pattern of marriage returned to the levels observed in the first half of the century. While the proportion that had married at each age is somewhat lower, the marriage behaviors of males show a similar temporal pattern.

There are significant racial differentials in the percentage of persons ever married by age (U.S. Bureau of the Census, 1982b, Table 1). Among white women age 20–24 in 1981, nearly half had been married, compared to fewer than three tenths of the black women. These racial differences narrow somewhat over the reproductive years, but the prevalence of first marriage among blacks and whites is not equal except among women who have passed their reproductive years. Similar patterns characterize the males.

The later age at marriage observed among blacks in 1981 represents the continuation of a long-term pattern (Cherlin, 1981; Hogan, 1978). In the past, racial differences have resulted from a pattern of delayed marriage rather than nonmarriage among blacks. For example, 75% of black women in the birth cohort of 1930 did not marry until 25.5 years of age, compared to 23.5 years of age among whites, even though 93% of the blacks and 96% of the whites in that birth cohort married before age 45 (Thornton & Rodgers,

1983, Tables 2-1, 2–3, 2–5, and 2–7). It is not yet certain whether the delays in marriage currently being observed among young blacks will result in substantial nonmarriage in the more recent birth cohorts. However, synthetic cohort nuptiality tables derived from the 1980 CPS indicate that 92% of all white women but only 77% of black women will marry should current rates continue (Espenshade, 1982).

Marital Dissolution. Perhaps the most remarkable change in the nuptial behavior of American men and women is the dramatic increase in the proportion of marriages that end in separation and divorce. Synthetic cohort calculations indicate that only 14% of first marriages among white women ended in separation in 1950–1954, compared to 42% in 1975–1979 (Cherlin & McCarthy, 1983, Chapter 6, Table 1). First marriages often are of brief duration—an estimated 21% of the white women married in 1975–1979 separated from their husbands within 5 years (Cherlin & McCarthy, 1983, Chapter 6, Table 2).

Marriages among blacks are somewhat more likely to end in separation and less likely to end in divorce than marriages among whites. Among women first married in 1959, 57% of the blacks and 26% of the whites separated by 1979, but of these only 71% of black marriages had been ended by a formal divorce, compared to 92% of the white marriages. Synthetic cohort estimates suggest that 42% of the white marriages and 64% of the black marriages that occurred in 1979 will end within 20 years (Thornton & Rodgers, 1983, Table 3–2). Because of higher mortality rates among blacks, there is a greater chance during the early adult years that a black marriage will end through the death of the spouse (most often the husband).

Remarriage. Blacks have a substantially lower rate of remarriage following the termination of their first marriage, and this difference has widened over time. The annual number of remarriages per 1000 divorced or widowed persons age 14–54 increased among white women, from 83 in 1960–1965 to 112 in 1975–1980, while declining from 74 to 46 among blacks (Espenshade, 1983, Table 6). Synthetic cohort calculations for 1980 indicate that the lifetime probability of remarriage following divorce is 0.75 among white women compared to only 0.60 among blacks (Espenshade, 1982).

Current Marital Status. Considered in combination, the racial differences in rates of marriage, separation and divorce, and remarriage mean that the average black spends fewer of the adult years married and living with a spouse than the average white, and this difference has widened over time (Cherlin, 1981). In 1960–1965 white women spent a total of 38.8 years of their lifetime married, compared to 27.5 years among blacks. By 1975–1980 the comparable figures were 33.3 years among whites and 16.3 among blacks (Espenshade, 1983, Tables 9 and 10).

Racial differences in the likelihood of being currently married with a spouse present are observed even among 18- to19-year-old persons, and the likelihood widens substantially with increased age. Whereas more than three quarters of all white women age 30–54 were living with their husband in 1981, fewer than half the black women of these ages were living with a husband. Indeed, by 1981 there is no age at which a majority of black women are living with a husband. Among whites, in contrast, a majority of women are living with a husband from ages 25 to 64. Only after age 65 does increased widowhood reduce the proportion of white women who are currently married to less than 50% (U.S. Bureau of the Census, 1982b, Table 1).

Because of their later ages at marriage, a majority of men are not living with a wife until age 25–29 among whites and 30–34 among blacks. Men are less likely than women to have a marriage end through the death of the spouse, and men have higher rates of remarriage than women (Cherlin, 1981). As a result, a somewhat greater proportion of men than women of each race are likely to be living with a spouse after age 34 (U.S. Bureau of the Census, 1982b, Table 1).

Interpretations. The causes of the changing marriage, divorce, and remarriage behaviors of American whites and blacks are not fully understood. Cherlin (1981) has noted that the older ages at marriage observed in recent years represent a return to the more "normal" patterns of the past, whereas the early marriages of the 1950's were unusual. Research by Easterlin (1980), Evans (1983a), and Hogan (1981) has demonstrated that young people marry at earlier ages when the economic situation is relatively good (low unemployment rates, high wages for young workers, and good unemployment benefits in case of job loss), government transfer programs are advantageous for young married couples (G.I. Bill benefits for married students, FHA and VA housing loans), and the demographic situation of the cohort is favorable (i.e., the birth cohort is small relative to preceding and succeeding cohorts).

Among individuals some activities of the early life course (such as school enrollment or active duty in the armed forces) are associated with marriage delays, in part because they place the person in a relatively unattractive marriage market position and because they represent activities that are to some extent incompatible with the roles of spouse and parent (Hogan, 1978). Recent delays in marriage by American women are strongly associated with increases in college and graduate/professional school enrollments among females, and with their higher rates of labor force participation.

Furthermore, the introduction of better methods of contraception during the early 1960's and the legalization of abortion has enabled sexually active unmarried women to avoid accidental pregnancies that often "necessitated" marriages in previous birth cohorts. The sexual revolution of the past two decades has coincided with these changes in contraceptive efficacy, allowing men and women to engage in sexual relations outside of marriage without undue fear of an ill-timed pregnancy. Furthermore, some couples now live together prior to marriage, enabling them to enjoy many aspects of married life without legal commitments. These changes have, in essence, reduced the opportunity costs previously associated with delays in marriage and with a separated or divorced status.

The delays in first marriage among blacks may be especially pronounced because of a relatively unfavorable marriage market facing black women (Goldman & Westoff, 1982). In the United States black men face considerably higher mortality risks during their teens and twenties, in part as a result of the greater risk of a violent death (Farley, 1980). In addition, blacks are more frequently absent from residential communities because of their higher rates of military service and institutionalization during the early adult years.[2] Finally, the unemployment rate of black men is substantially higher than that of white men, reducing their attractiveness as marriage partners.[3] Thus, black women face unavoidable delays in marriage should they desire a spouse who is black and gainfully employed.

The initial increases in the probability of separation and divorce observed during this century were counterbalanced by increases in the joint survival probabilites of couples. For example, of males surviving to age 50, 65% of the persons who were born in 1870 and 69% of those born in 1930 were married and living with their first wives, even though the percentage of marriages ending through separation and divorce increased from 7.5% for the cohort of 1870 to 23% for the cohort of 1930 (Uhlenberg, 1978, Table 2.6). However, recent increases in separation and divorce have not been counterbalanced by further declines in mortality; divorces are occurring earlier and more often involve couples with young children than in the past.

Although the demography of the rising divorce rate is well documented, there are no convincing explanations of its causes. Certainly the better economic opportunities available to women have enabled many wives to terminate marriages that might otherwise have remained intact (Hannan, Tuma, & Groeneveld, 1977). However, the economic costs of divorce, and especially of child care, are still disproportionately borne by the wife (Cherlin, 1981; Cherlin & McCarthy, 1983). Finally, as discussed below, the

---

[2]Although data could not be located on military service rates by age, sex, and race, the higher rate of military service among blacks is indicated by the racial composition of the military—19.0% of the personnel of the armed forces in 1979 were black, compared to 10.5% of the total American population aged 18 years and over (calculated with data from U.S. Bureau of the Census, 1983, Tables 33 & 615). Among men aged 20–29 in 1970, 2.2% of the blacks and 0.6% of the whites were inmates of institutions other than prisons. An additional 2.1% of black men but only 0.4% of the white men were prison inmates (calculated from U.S. Bureau of the Census, 1973a, Table 53, 1973b, Tables 2 & 3).

[3]In 1980 the unemployment rate of black men ages 20–34 was 15.9%, compared to 7.7% among the whites (U.S. Department of Labor, 1981, Table 3).

TABLE 12.1. Distribution of Women by Number of Children Ever Born, by Age and Race: 1980[a]

Race and age	Number of births (% distribution)						
	Total	0	1	2	3	4	5 or more
Whites							
40–44	100.0	10.1	9.5	26.1	24.1	15.7	14.7
35–39	100.0	12.2	10.4	34.4	23.5	12.3	7.2
30–34	100.0	20.2	19.2	35.6	16.3	5.6	3.1
25–29	100.0	38.7	25.4	25.0	8.4	1.8	0.7
20–24	100.0	66.9	20.1	10.4	2.1	0.5	0.0
18–19	100.0	87.5	10.7	1.6	0.2	0.1	0.1
Blacks							
40–44	100.0	10.6	11.0	12.9	11.6	14.9	39.1
35–39	100.0	10.1	13.1	20.9	20.4	14.9	20.6
30–34	100.0	15.2	21.0	25.9	20.6	9.3	8.1
25–29	100.0	23.4	28.3	27.4	12.1	5.0	3.8
20–24	100.0	43.8	31.4	16.0	5.8	2.2	0.8
18–19	100.0	70.8	22.6	4.9	1.7	0.0	0.0

[a]Source:U.S. Bureau of the Census. *Current Population Reports,* Series P-20, No. 375, Table 12.

changing nature of child-care responsibilities (due to fewer children born and a younger age for parents at the birth of the last child) may have reduced the costs of divorce for both spouses.

Parenting

Childbearing. The number of children borne differs substantially by age and race (Table 12.1). In 1980 nearly 30% of the black women age 18–19 had at least one child, compared to 12% of the white women. Among women 20–24, well over half the blacks had at least one child compared with only one third of the whites. These differences reflect the earlier timing of first births among black women rather than a substantial racial difference in the proportion of women who remain childless—about 90% of the women age 35–44 had at least one birth among both races.

The larger number of children born to women in the birth cohorts age 35–44 in 1980 are the result of their higher lifetime levels of fertility. The differences in number of children born to women who are different ages in the 18–34 range are the result of the older women's longer period of exposure to fertility. Among white women age 18–34 in 1980, the expected number of births during the lifetime averages 2.0–2.2, with little evidence of intercohort variation. Among black women age 18–24, the expected number of births is roughly similar to that of whites (about two births per

TABLE 12.2. Cumulative Percent of Women Bearing a First Child Within Selected Intervals After First Marriage, by Period of Marriage and Race[a]

	Interval			
Race and period of first marriage	Before first marriage	After first marriage (months)		
		7	12	24
Whites				
1930–1939	3.2	8.8	25.3	47.9
1940–1949	3.2	8.2	27.4	53.4
1950–1959	4.3	13.1	36.4	63.7
1960–1969	5.1	18.9	39.0	60.1
1970–1974	6.1	18.6	29.6	45.4
Blacks				
1930–1939	17.9	30.4	43.7	57.4
1940–1949	25.2	38.5	50.4	60.5
1950–1959	28.8	44.1	56.0	71.3
1960–1969	34.6	52.2	64.5	76.9
1970–1974	37.5	52.5	62.0	72.5

[a]Source: U.S. Bureau of the Census. Statistical Abstract of the United States: 1980, Table 98.

woman), while black women age 25–34 expect about 2.5 births. In 1980 more than 85% of the births expected by women of both races occur by age 30–34 (U.S. Bureau of the Census, 1981, Table 12.2).

By age 30–34 only about 20% of the white women and 15% of the black women remain childless (Table 12.1). Based on the level and tempo of fertility experienced by these women to date, Evans (1983b) estimates that about 15% of the whites and 10% of the nonwhites in these birth cohorts will remain childless. Thus, most American women during the 1980's are assuming parenting roles, and most elect to do so by age 35.

The most common number of children borne to women age 30–34 in 1980 was two (36% of the whites and 26% of the blacks), but a substantial proportion of women of both races have three children (16% of whites and 21% of blacks). Very few white women age 30–34 (9%) have had more than three children, compared to 17% of the blacks. Evans (1983b) projects the mean completed family size of *mothers* in these cohorts as 2.6 among whites and 2.8 among nonwhites.

Thus, current fertility data suggest that most American women continue to become mothers, and that the number of children these women have will be moderate compared to earlier birth cohorts. There is little evidence that substantial proportions of American women plan to forego motherhood. Black women become mothers at earlier ages than whites, and give birth to somewhat more children, resulting in greater parenting responsibilities compared to whites.

The parenting responsibilities of women 40 and older in 1980 are much greater than those of younger women due to the legacy of higher fertility rates during the later 1950's and early 1960's. Fully 90% of these women became mothers and almost 80% had at least two births. More than one third (35%) of the white women and half (54%) the black women had four or more children during their reproductive years. While only 5% of these white women had seven or more births, fully one fifth (21%) of the black women age 40–44 in 1980 had given birth to seven or more children (U.S. Census Bureau, 1981, Table 12). Thus, American women who were born before 1940 and were entering middle age in the 1980's have experienced substantially greater parenting responsibilities than will be experienced by women born during the post-World War II era.

Marriage and Parenthood. Although blacks marry at later ages than whites, black women experience motherhood at an earlier age. Taken together, these behaviors are associated with a greater tendency among blacks for motherhood to occur prior to marriage. Among women who married for the first time in 1970–1974 (the most recent marriage cohort for which data are available), 38% of the blacks but only 6% of the whites had a birth prior to marriage (Table 12.2). This racial differential has not changed greatly in recent years, with roughly similar proportions observed in the marriage cohort of 1960–1969. Between the marriage cohorts of 1930–1939 and 1970–1974, the percentage of women who were mothers at the time of marriage doubled among both whites and blacks. However, the absolute increase was low among whites (increasing from 3 to 6%) but much more dramatic among blacks (from 18 to 38%). Thus, while the percentage of white women becoming mothers prior to marriage has always been low, a substantial proportion of black women have experienced premarital motherhood for the past 50 years. The high proportion of black women now becoming mothers before marriage represents an intensification of this historical pattern.

The proportion of premaritally conceived first births born during the first 7 months of marriage provides an indication of the extent to which persons attempt to link the achievement of parenthood to a marital relationship. Nearly two thirds of premaritally conceived first births occurred within marriage among white women first married in 1970–1974, a proportion that is similar to that observed for the marriage cohort of 1930–1939. Among blacks, 41% of the premaritally conceived births occurred within marriage for the cohort of 1930–1939, compared to 29% for the cohort of 1970–1974. Among whites, therefore, a premarital pregnancy that is carried to term commonly is associated with marriage, whereas among black women this linkage has become quite weak.

The racial difference in rate of childbearing outside marriage is especially remarkable among young persons. In 1978 the out-of-wedlock birth rates per 1000 unmarried women was 13.8 among whites 15–19 and 18.5 among those 20–24. Among blacks the rates were 90.3 for women 15–19 and 114.2 for those 20–24 (Dryfoos & Bourque-Scholl, 1981, Table 30). Statistics from Chicago are typical of the changes experienced in the black populations of major metropolitan areas (Hogan & Kitagawa, 1985). The percentage of births to Chicago teenagers that were to unmarried females increased from 42% in 1956 to 76% in 1978, when 43% of the births to white teenagers and 91% of the births to black teenagers were to unmarried females. Furthermore, because of decreases in the fertility rates of married adult women, the proportion of births that are to unmarried teenagers has increased substantially among blacks (Kitagawa, 1981). Of all births occurring in Chicago in 1978, only 6% among whites but 28% among blacks were to unmarried teenagers.

Many of the women who married for the first time during the Great Depression delayed parenthood until they had been married for some years. As shown in Table 12.2, 52% of the newly married white women and 43% of the black brides delayed parenthood beyond the first 2 years of marriage in the marriage cohort of 1930–1939. In contrast, during the peak of the baby boom years few women waited until they had been married 2 years before having their first child. In the marriage cohort of 1960–1964 only one third of all white women and one fifth of all black women delayed parenthood until the third year of marriage. Since 1970 it has again become common for newly married white women to postpone parenthood beyond the first 2 years of marriage (the experience of 55% of the cohort of 1970–1974), but few blacks (27%) follow this pattern.

Social Factors in Premarital Parenthood. Thus, the cohorts of young persons now reaching adulthood are making decisions about the timing and sequencing of marriage and parenthood that depart from previous post-World War II patterns. While white actions to delay marriage and postpone childbearing within marriage are not historically unique, the extent to which young black women are becoming parents prior to marriage is unprecedented. These racial differences in patterns of marriage and parenthood have major implications for the parenting activities of adults and for the family environments of children, as discussed below. It is, therefore, useful to describe the social factors underlying the decisions made by adolescents about the timing and sequencing of marriage and parenthood.

During their teens young persons develop aspirations for their adult lives and begin to form tentative plans to achieve those ambitions. This includes the formation of educational and career plans as well as anticipations about marriage and parenthood. These plans develop in the context of the adolescents' social environment, and evolve under the influences of parents, peers, and teachers (Hogan, 1985; Sewell & Hauser, 1980; Sewell & Shah, 1968).

Data from the 1980 High School and Beyond survey indicate that more than 85% of the males and females of both races expect to marry and become parents during their lifetimes. The anticipated timing of marriage and childbirth is responsive to the influences of parents and the educational and career plans of the parents (Hogan, 1985). Sons and daughters of parents with nontraditional sex role attitudes expect to delay marriage and parenthood in order to achieve a degree of career success before assuming the responsibilities of parenthood. Children of college-educated parents expect to marry and have their first child at older ages than children of less-educated parents, in part because their parents have encouraged them to have high educational aspirations. The expectations of parents about the ages at which their children will marry and have children are strongly associated with the adolescents' own plans. Among teenagers, females with high educational aspirations expect to marry and become parents at later ages than other females. Young women who plan to have a career in the paid labor force expect to delay family formation, and this pattern does not differ according to the occupation desired. Despite anticipated delays in family formation, neither young women nor men expect to remain single or childless as a result of nontraditional sex role attitudes or educational or career aspirations.

Black teenagers expect to become parents at the same ages as whites, but they have later expected ages at marriage. Multivariate analyses of the High School and Beyond data indicate that, net of controls for differing social class and income of family of origin, black adolescents have expected age-specific rates of marriage that are 36% lower than those of whites, but expected age-specific rates of parenthood that are only 2% lower (tabulations not shown). As a result, the anticipated timing of parenthood in relation to marriage differs significantly by race and gender, with 21% of the black males and 17% of the black females expecting to become parents prior to marriage, compared to fewer than 2% of the whites (Tables 12.3). It appears that single parenthood is considered a viable option by a substantial number of young blacks but by very few whites. The responsibilities associated with parenthood, in particular single parenthood, hamper educational and occupational achievements of both males and females (Card and Wise, 1978; Hofferth and Moore, 1979; Trussell, 1976). This fact seems to influence the family formation plans of young blacks, as the proportion expecting to have a child prior to marriage declines substantially with increased educational aspirations (Table 12.3).

These findings suggest that the high rate of premarital parenthood among blacks during the 1980's may result, at least in part, from the attitudes, expectations, and behaviors of an identifiable segment of the black population (Hogan & Kitagawa, 1985; Stack, 1975; Suttles, 1968; Wilson, 1978, 1982). Poverty, coupled with uncertain prospects for economic success, are hypothesized to lower the educational and career aspirations of young blacks, reducing the opportunity costs of single parenthood. Growing up in

TABLE 12.3. Percentage of American High School Students Expecting to Become
          Parents Prior to First Marriage, by Gender, Race, and Educational
          Aspirations: 1980

	Gender and race[a]			
	White		Black	
Educational aspirations	Females	Males	Females	Males
High school diploma or less	1.8	2.2	34.0	31.7
Some college or vocational school	1.8	1.5	21.7	30.5
College degree or higher	0.6	1.1	10.0	12.2
Total	1.0	1.4	16.5	21.0

[a]Persons of Hispanic ancestry are not included in these figures.

a large family that is female-headed or exposure to other female-headed families is hypothesized to increase the acceptability of single parenthood. Finally, the ability of parents to influence the plans of their children and control their daily behavior is expected to be less in single-parent, large families, especially those where peer contacts in poor ghetto neighborhoods are strong.

Analyses of the High School and Beyond data were conducted to determine the effects of theoretically important variables on the probability that: (1) a black sophomore is willing to consider having a child while unmarried; and (2) a black sophomore or senior expects to become a parent prior to marriage. The results of this analysis are displayed in Table 12.4. For both males and females, more of the teenagers from a lower-class social background are willing to consider unmarried parenthood, and a greater proportion expect to become unmarried parents. Blacks growing up in a home lacking the presence of *both* parents, especially those in a home headed by the mother alone, are more likely to anticipate premarital parenthood. Finally, the social environments of black adolescents affect the probability that a student will anticipate premarital parenthood, with students attending schools with poor reputations more likely to expect single parenthood. Further multivariate analyses of the High School and Beyond data indicated that black students from unfavorable ("high-risk") home environments (father not present, low socioeconomic status, lax parental supervision of behavior), in peer groups not conducive to college attendance, with poor academic ability and achievements, and with low educational aspirations, are especially likely to anticipate unmarried parenthood. A model estimating the joint effects of these variables shows that only 34% of sophomores who are "low risk" on these social background and personal characteristics are willing to consider having a child while unmarried, compared to 71% of the "high-risk" sophomores. Only 4% of

TABLE 12.4. Anticipations of Unmarried Parenthood Among Black High School Students, by Gender and Social Background: 1980

Gender and social background	Anticipations	
	Percentage willing to consider unmarried parenthood	Percentage expecting to be an unmarried parent
Females		
Social class	*	**
High	44.3	11.2
Medium	49.8	19.3
Low	55.5	22.2
Parents present	**	**
Father and mother	43.4	14.4
Mother and other	52.9	17.5
Mother alone	57.0	23.4
Other arrangements	50.7	21.3
School reputation in community	*	**
Average or above	45.5	14.2
Below average	53.1	22.7
Males		
Social class	*	**
High	55.7	15.4
Medium	57.8	21.7
Low	67.3	27.4
Parents present	*	*
Father and mother	52.8	18.9
Mother and other	61.5	24.4
Mother alone	64.3	26.8
Other arrangements	67.6	20.5
School reputation in community		
Average or above	56.2	18.5
Below average	61.5	24.7

$*p < .05; **p < .001$

the low-risk students expect to become parents prior to marriage, compared to 48% of the high-risk students.[4]

Hogan and Kitagawa (1985) analyzed the influences of family background, social environments, and personal characteristics on the probability of premarital pregnancy using the Young Chicagoans Survey data. Tabulations from this study indicate that black teenagers in Chicago who are from families lacking at least one parent, families in the lower social class, and

[4]Tabulations of the results of these mulitivariate models are available from the author upon request.

TABLE 12.5. Fertility Experiences of Black Females Ages 13 to 19 in Chicago, by Social Background: 1979

	Fertility experiences		
Social background	Sexually active (%)	Pregnant by 1979 (%)	Pregnant by age 19 (%)
Social class	*	**	**
Upper	29.0	10.2	23.1
Middle	35.5	17.7	39.6
Lower	37.8	21.8	57.1
Parents' marital status		**	
Married	31.6	13.9	30.3
Not married	36.1	18.6	45.7
Neighborhood quality	**	**	**
High	30.7	14.2	25.4
Medium	32.5	15.4	42.0
Low	42.2	22.6	52.0

*$.05 \leq p < .10$
**$p < .05$

very low-quality (poor, highly segregated) neighborhoods have significantly higher raters of pregnancy (Table 12.5). These higher rates accumulate over the early life course so that by age 19 there are very substantial differentials in the probability of premarital pregnancy. The final product of the Hogan and Kitagawa study was the estimation of a mulitivariate, continuous-time, semi-Markov model of the rate of premarital pregnacy. This model demonstrates that 57% of black teenagers who are from high-risk social environments (lower class, resident in a ghetto neighborhood, from a nonintact family, with five or more siblings, a sister who became a teenage mother, and lax parental control of dating) will become pregnant by their eighteenth birthdays, compared to only 9% of those from low-risk environments (upper class, resident in a good neighborhood, intact family, four or fewer siblings, no sister who became a teenage mother, and strict parental control of dating). Differences in age at initiation of sexual intercourse account for a substantial proportion of these differences, but teenagers from high-risk social environments also are less likely to be effective contraceptors (Hogan, Astone & Kitagawa, 1985). Thus, data on the attitudes, expectations, and behaviors of teenagers support the hypothesis that the decreased linkage between marriage and parenthood observed among black Americans is concentrated in that segment of the black population that has been excluded from benefits in the broader system of social stratification.

Parenting and Child Care. These marriage and fertility behaviors together determine the family building practices of American men and women. Data on the percentage of women having one or more children and on the completed family sizes indicate the extent to which these women will be mothers. Although the Census Bureau does not collect data on paternity, the male patterns of parenthood undoubtedly resemble those of females, except that the age at which men first become parents is somewhat higher.

Child-care activities typically begin with the entry of a newborn infant into the home. As children age and leave the parental household the daily activities involved in raising a child end, although parenting activities continue. Parents sometimes avoid these daily child-care activities. Some fathers never acknowledge paternity and avoid all parenting responsibilities. Other parents (especially unmarried teenage mothers) avoid child-care responsibilities by placing their children in the household of another (often the grandmother of the child). When a marriage ends through separation or divorce, child care and parenting become distinct, with one parent (usually the mother) assuming daily caretaking responsibilities and the other parent (typically the father) continuing to act as a parent without involvement in daily child care. Other persons live in households with children who are not their own (for example, grandchildren), increasing their child-care activities.

Thus, the parenting and child-care activities of Americans differ in important ways. The marriage and fertility behaviors of Americans determine the extent to which they will be parents of children, and the distribution of these activities over the life span. Other information is needed to characterize the daily child-care activities of Americans of different ages during the 1980's. This topic follows.

Child-Care Responsibilities

Measures. The Bureau of the Census does not collect data on actual child-care responsibilities. However, it does publish data distinguishing different types of households, the relationships of persons within households, and the age distributions of household members. These data can be used to characterize the coresidential arrangements of adults and children, indicating the extent to which adults engage in child care (the presence of one or more children in the household) and the number of children being raised.

This discussion will begin with a description of the presence of sons or daughters in married couple families, according to the age of the family householder. Under Census Bureau procedures adopted children and stepchildren are combined with biological children as "own children." The householder refers to the person (or one of the persons) in whose name the housing unit is owned or rented (maintained). If the house is owned or rented jointly by a married couple, the person who is considered the householder is designated by the Current Population Survey respondent from the household, and may be either the husband or the wife. The householder refers to the husband in 96% of these married-couple families (U.S. Bureau of the Census, 1982b, Table 2).

Since a husband and wife constitute a family whether or not children are present, there are no definitional problems in describing the percentage of such married couple families with children in the household. Under Census Bureau procedures, a household that does not include both a husband and wife is not a family unless a relative of the householder is present. Since this relative is in most cases a son or daughter, it is not appropriate to present data on the percentage of such families with own children present.

In order to characterize the typical child-care activities of adults without restricting attention to married couples, data on the presence of persons under age 18 in households (most of whom are the own children of the householder) by type of household are used (married couple or female householder without husband present). These data are presented by age of householder. Since most householders in married couple households are male, and there are gender differences in age at parenthood, considerable caution should be exercised in comparing the age-specific data for households with married couples and female householders.[5]

Own Children. Most married couples have children present in their household from shortly after the time they marry until the householder (hereafter, "husband") is in late middle age (Figure 12.1). More than three quarters of all married couples have one or more children living with them from the time the husband is age 30 until he is 54. Children begin leaving the home thereafter, but even among households with husbands age 55–64, about one third of white couples and half of black couples have at least one of their own children living with them.

These age patterns are similar for whites and blacks, although child-care activities begin somewhat earlier among black couples (because of the earlier age at parenthood of black women and the more frequent occurrence of premarital parenthood). Among older couples (householder 65 and over), blacks are somewhat more likely than whites to have a child living with them. This results both from the historically higher fertility levels of this group and from the somewhat later age at which black children leave the parental home (U.S. Bureau of the Census, 1982b, Table 2).

Of course, the child-care activities of many of these families involve a son or daughter who is well beyond the early years of childhood, when the responsibilities are the greatest. The percentage of married couples with one

[5]In 1981, 52% of the married couple households and 29% of all female-headed households included children, compared to only 9% of the male-headed households (U.S. Bureau of the Census, 1982a: Table 22). Because male-headed households with children present are rare, the Census Bureau does not publish data on them by age of householder.

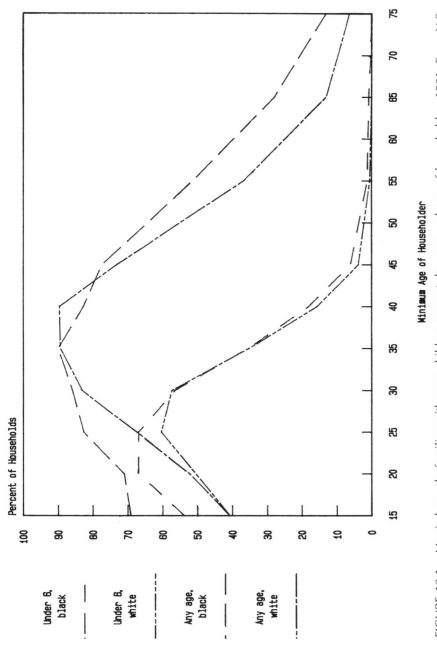

Percent of Households

Minimum Age of Householder

Under 6, black

Under 6, white

Any age, black

Any age, white

FIGURE 12.1. Married couple families with own children present, by race and age of householder: 1981. From U.S. Bureau of the Census, 1982a, Table 3.

or more children of preschool age (under 6 years) is shown in Figure 12.1. About half the white couples and two thirds of the black couples are raising a young child when the husband is age 20–24. Among whites, responsibilities for young children peak when the husband is age 25–34, with young children present in more than 57% of all married couple families. The presence of young children declines rapidly with age, characterizing fewer than one third of couples with a husband age 35–39 and one fifth of couples with a husband age 40–44. Thus, responsibility for the care of young children is concentrated in the early life span of Americans, although responsibilities for children residing with the family continue well into middle age.

Cohabitation and Child Care. Since 1960 increased numbers of men and women have decided to live together as sexual partners without marrying. By 1981, 5.3% of the females and 5.5% of the males age 18–64 who were not living with a spouse were sharing a household with one other adult of the opposite sex. Such coresidential arrangements peak at 11.0% of the females and 11.6% of the males among persons age 25–34 (U.S. Bureau of the Census, 1982a, Tables 1 & 7). Of course, these figures do not by any means represent the proportion of persons with a long-term sexual partner, many of whom maintain separate households. Additional individuals live together as sexually active roommates in households shared with other adults.

Many of the persons involved in coresidential arrangements with a partner of the opposite sex will already have become a parent, either in a former marriage or extramaritally. Thus, many may have child-care responsibilities either for their own children or for the children of their partner. Of all persons age 18–64 living with a sexual partner, 29% of the females and 30% of the males share a household with one or more children (persons under age 18) present. Child-care responsibilities of sexual partners peak at age 25–34 for both sexes, with 41% of the females and 34% of the males living in a household with one or more persons under age 18 (U.S. Bureau of the Census, 1982a, Tables 1 & 7). Although child-care responsibilities among unmarried coresidential partners do not approach the high levels experienced by married couples, such child-care arrangements represent the emergence of a new form of parenting among Americans in the 1980's.

Children in Households. Among whites, married couple households are much more likely than female-headed households to include members under age 18 (Figure 12.2). More than half of all married couple white households with a householder age 54 or under include a child. This figure is more than 80% among householders who are 30–44. A similar age patterning is observed among female householders, but the percentage of such households is about 20 points less at each age up to 54. More than 60% of households headed by women age 30–44 include one or more children.

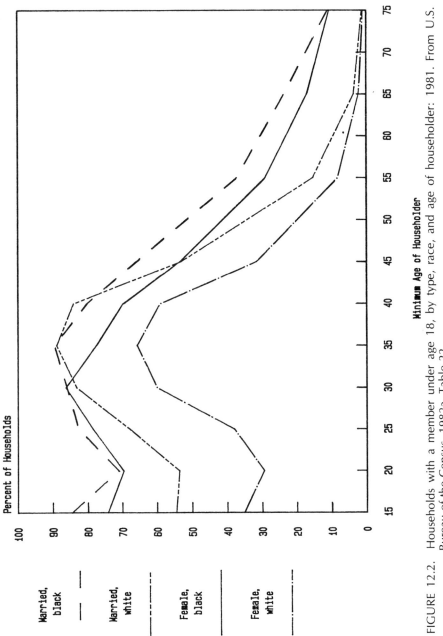

Percent of Households

Minimum Age of Householder

Married, black ———
Married, white – – –
Female, black —————
Female, white —··—··—

FIGURE 12.2. Households with a member under age 18, by type, race, and age of householder: 1981. From U.S. Bureau of the Census, 1982a, Table 22.

Black married-couple households are more likely than white households to include children among the young (householders under age 30) and among the old (45 and older), but there are no racial differences in the presence of children in families where the husband is age 30–44. The child-care responsibilities of black women who head their own households are very great. Among householders under age 35, the likelihood that a child will be present in a black household is equally high whether that household consists of a married couple or is headed by an unmarried female. Black women heading their own households are much more likely than white women to have children living with them. Until age 30 fewer than 40% of the white households headed by females include children, compared to more than 70% of the black households. This pronounced racial differential is apparent at every point in the life span.

Because of the moderate fertility rates of American women, the average number of children living in American households is relatively low, even when attention is restricted to those households with one or more children (Figure 12.3). Indeed, the average number of children in households with children present is never greater than 2.3 among whites and 2.5 among blacks. Thus, the intensity of child-care responsibilities among Americans in the 1980's is moderate, even though parenthood remains a nearly universal choice.

The mean number of children present in households that include at least one child is higher among blacks than among whites at every age (Figure 12.3). Once again, the relatively intense parenting activities of black women heading their own households are apparent, with these women having more children on average to care for than black married couples at every age from 20–39, and more children on average than white married couple households (for householders age 20–74).

The Experiences of Children

Thus far this chapter has focused on the family building and child-rearing experiences of adults over their life span. Because of differential fertility (in childlessness, mean family size, and mean age at childbirth), the experiences of a population of adults who are potential parents need not be exactly parallel to the parental experiences of children. Therefore, trends and differentials in the living arrangements of American children will now be considered.

In 1960, 69% of all black children and 92% of white children were living with both parents (Table 12.6). These proportions had declined substantially by 1970, and the pace of the decline accelerated thereafter. By 1980, only 42% of black children were living with both parents, compared to 83% of white children. Most of the corresponding increases occurred in the

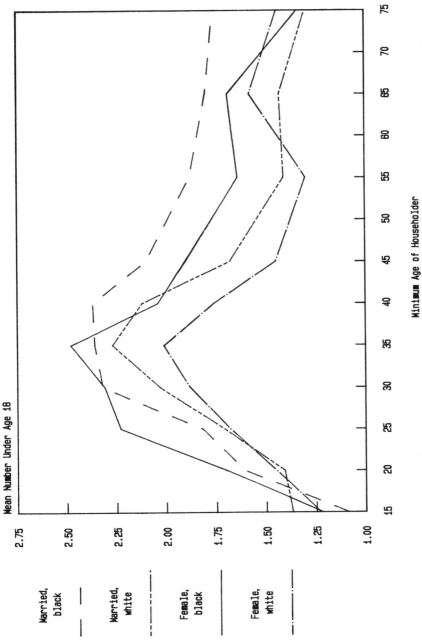

FIGURE 12.3. Mean number of persons under age 18 in households with at least one member under age 18, by type and age of householder: 1981. From U.S. Bureau of the Census, 1982a, Table 22.

339

TABLE 12.6. Presence of Parents, for Persons Under 18 Years Old by Race[a,b]

| | Percentage distribution | | | | | |
| | Black | | | White | | |
Presence of parents	1960	1970	1980	1960	1970	1980
All children living in families	100.0	100.0	100.0	100.0	100.0	100.0
Living with both parents	69.2	58.1	42.2	91.9	89.2	82.7
Living with mother only	20.6	29.4	43.8	6.2	7.8	13.5
Married, spouse absent	—	16.2	16.1	—	2.8	3.8
Widowed	—	4.2	4.0	—	1.7	1.7
Divorced	—	4.6	10.9	—	3.1	7.0
Never married	—	4.4	12.8	—	0.2	1.0
Living with father only	2.1	2.2	2.0	1.0	0.9	1.6
Neither parent	8.2	10.4	12.1	0.8	2.2	2.2

[a]Data for 1960 are for blacks and other races. This slightly inflates the proportion of children living with both parents and deflates the share living with the mother only relative to what the distribution would have been if only blacks had been considered. Figures for 1970 and 1980 exclude persons under 18 years old who are heads and wives of heads of families and subfamilies.
[b]Source: U.S. Bureau of the Census. *Social Indicators III*, Table 1/14 (for 1960). *Statistical Abstract of the United States: 1981*, Table 73 (for 1970 and 1980).

percentage of children who were living with their mothers only. By 1980, the most common living arrangement for black children was a mother-headed family—44% of blacks under age 18 were living with their mothers only. In contrast, only 14% of white children lived with the mother only.

The proportion of children living with widowed mothers was 4% among blacks and 2% among whites in both 1970 and 1980. By 1980, 11% of the black children and 7% of the white children lived with divorced mothers, a substantial increase since 1970. The proportion of children whose parents were separated (children living with married, spouse-absent mother) was 16% among blacks and 4% among whites in 1980, figures that were largely unchanged from 1970. The most remarkable change over the decade involved the increased proportion of black children living with never-married mothers (from 4% in 1970 to 13% in 1980). In contrast, only 1% of white children in 1980 lived with never-married mothers. These changes are a direct consequence of the loosened connections between marriage and parenthood among blacks that were discussed above.

In recent years there has been considerable public attention to fathers raising their children alone. Among whites there has indeed been a pronounced increase (60%) in the proportion of children raised by the father, but this increase has been from such a small base (1.0% in 1960) that very few children (1.6%) were included in this category in 1980 (Table 12.6). Indeed, fewer than 10% of white children and 4% of the black children who were not living with both parents were living with the father. While it is possible that the upward trend in fathers with child-care responsibilities may continue, it is apparent that men ordinarily have children living in the household with them only when they are married or living with a female partner.

The living arrangements of children do not differ significantly between males and females (U.S. Bureau of the Census, 1982b, Table 4). Among whites, the percentage of children living with both parents is 87% at ages under 3, but declines with increasing age to 79% at 15–17 years. Percentages of white children living with the mother alone show compensating increases over the course of childhood. The percentage of black children living with both parents in 1981 is relatively unchanging with age, being 41% for children under 3 and 44% among children age 15–17. Among black children under age 3, 37% live with the mother only. This increases to about 45% for children age 6–17.

As discussed above, the Current Population Survey regards stepchildren and adopted children as the "own children" of adults. Conversely, many of the children who are counted as living with both parents in fact are living with a mother and stepfather, or in some other family arrangement. Given the substantially higher rates of remarriage among whites, the CPS tabulations thus may provide a misleading picture of racial differences in the types of living arrangements of children, with this distortion increasing with age of the child (since biological parents will have had more time to divorce and remarry).

A recent study by Furstenberg, Nord, Peterson, & Zill (1983) reported data on types of parental living arrangements of children born in 1965–1969 over their early life course. Among children born 1965–1967 and observed at age one, 8% of the whites and 32% of the blacks were from families in which the biological parents were no longer (or had never) married. By age 13, 25% of the whites and 51% of the blacks had experienced a disrupted family. Furthermore, the likelihood of experiencing a disrupted family by age 13 was even higher for children born in 1968–1969, reaching 32% among the whites and 70% among the blacks. Thus, blacks are about twice as likely to experience the disruption of their parental family as are whites.

Once disruption occurs, white women are much more likely to remarry, as discussed above. Remarriage occurs within 5 years of the disruption of the parental family among 56% of the whites, but only among 13% of the blacks. Thus, when the parental family of a white child is disrupted it is likely that a new parental family consisting of mother and stepfather will be constituted, whereas among blacks the disruption of the parental relationship commonly results in a permanent shift to a matrifocal family. For many blacks the disruption of the parental family represents the permanent loss of the father—48% of the black children with a nonresidential father have had no contact with him for the last 5 years, compared to 29% of the whites (Furstenberg et al., 1983).

TABLE 12.7. Living Arrangements of Children of Black Teenage Mothers in Chicago, by Social Background of the Mother: 1979

	Percentage distribution				
Social background	Three generation	Two-parent nuclear	Single mother	Other	Total
Social class*					
Average or above	46.3	14.8	22.2	16.7	100.0
Below average	67.4	5.6	14.6	12.4	100.0
Parent's marital status*					
Married	56.3	6.3	31.3	6.3	100.0
Not married	60.4	9.9	13.5	16.2	100.0
Neighborhood quality**					
Average or above	49.4	12.6	19.5	18.4	100.0
Below average	78.4	2.0	15.7	3.9	100.0
Total	59.4	9.1	17.5	14.0	100.0

*$.05 \le p < .10$
**$p < .05$

Very few white children (2%) lived with neither parent in 1980, compared to 12% of black children (Table 12.6). Black children are most likely to live with neither parent during the first 3 years of life (20% in 1981). This pattern declines to 15% among children age 3–5, and to below 10% thereafter (U.S. Bureau of the Census, 1982b, Table 4). Presumably, most of these children are living with grandparents (grandmothers), but the CPS data to determine this are not published. Tabulations from the Young Chicagoans Survey indicate that 14% of the children of black adolescents lived apart from the mother, and nearly all of these lived with the grandmother.

Carol Stack (1974, 1975), based on an ethnographic study of a black community, has persuasively argued that black matrifocal families survive through the utilization of social network support systems that provide emotional and material support in times of need. These support arrangements are especially characteristic of persons in the lower socioeconomic class who are resident in poor, segregated neighborhoods. Such support networks should be apparent in the residential arrangements of teenage mothers and their children.

Tabulations from the Young Chicagoans Survey on the living arrangements of children of black adolescents in Chicago provide support for Stack's observations (Table 12.7). Overall, 59% of these children live in a three-generation family (with mother and grandmother), and this percentage is significantly higher among those families of below average social status (67%) and resident in poor, segregated neighborhoods (78%). In contrast, adolescent mothers are most likely to be living alone with their child(ren) if they are from higher social status families where both the father and mother were present. Thus, those black teenagers from social backgrounds associated with high rates of premarital parenthood are able to rely on their parental families for social support during the difficult early years of parenthood.

Consequences of Family Structure. When the Moynihan report drew attention to the large racial differential in the percentage of children growing up in female-headed families, more than two thirds of the black children were living with both parents (Moynihan, 1965). By 1980 this figure had declined to 42%, yet there has been no renewal of the discussion about the effects of black family structure on the welfare of children. This absence of further research is due, at least in part, to the controversy sparked by Moynihan's report (Wilson, 1982).

There is clear evidence that maternal-headed households are substantially more likely to be poor (Farley, 1977; Wilson, 1982). Even after controls are introduced for income level, children raised in one-parent households have slower rates of cognitive development, a higher incidence of personality disorders (Rutter, 1980; Kellam, Ensminger, & Turner, 1977), and a greater likelihood of becoming unmarried mothers while adolescents (Hogan & Kitagawa, 1985). Growing up in a maternal-headed household also is associated with depressed socioeconomic achievements during the later life span, in cases where the mother did not work at a paid job (Blau & Duncan, 1967).

As pointed out by critics of the Moynihan report, many of the negative sequelae of mother-headed households can be ameliorated by an extended family network (Rainwater & Yancey, 1967). Specifically, it has been shown that the presence of a grandmother in black families has beneficial consequences for both the mother and the child (Kellam, Ensminger, & Turner, 1977). Although such arrangements are common for teenage mothers and their first child, extended family coresidence remains relatively rare. In 1981 only 6.5% of the black children living with their mother (with the father absent) lived in a household headed by a grandparent (U.S. Bureau of the Census, 1982b, Table 4). While extended kin assistance networks need not involve coresidence (Stack, 1975), these observations about the family structures of black children in the 1980's indicate the need for more attention to this subject (Wilson, 1982; Taub & Wilson, 1982).

Researchers have recently devoted a great deal of attention to documenting the increased rates of marital instability and remarriage of American couples. However, the consequences of these changes in adult nuptial behaviors for children have received little attention. The issue can no longer remain simply the consequences of growing up in an intact or a broken home. Researchers must now direct attention to the consequences of different family structures for: (1) the social and economic environments of children; (2) children's social, intellectual, and emotional development; and (3) the educational aspirations, attainments, career achievements, and family formation patterns of adolescents as they become adults. Such research will not be easy since these new patterns of parenting show considerable interindividual variability in the causes of the disruption of the biological parental family, its timing in the child's life course, the subsequent living arrangements, and form of contact with residential and nonresidential parents, stepparents, siblings, stepsiblings, and half-siblings.

CONCLUSIONS

Declining fertility rates have reduced the number of children that persons will have during their lives and diminished the parenting responsibilities of Americans in the 1980's. Despite these changes there is no evidence that Americans are, in large numbers, deciding to forego parenting activities. Most men and women marry, and most first marriages result in children. Data on the birth expectations of adolescents and women of reproductive age indicate that parenting remains a preferred life activity among Americans, and these expectations will provide a basis for the reproductive decisions of men and women during the 1980's.

Other changes have increased parenting responsibilities. Improved survivorship of children and adults means that the children born to a person usually will be alive at the time of the parent's death. Thus, the parenting responsibilities that begin with the birth of a child can be expected to continue throughout the remaining lifetime, although the nature of those responsibilities will change as the children reach adulthood. Of course, these increases in longevity also mean that many persons now reach middle age with responsibilities for their own children and grandchildren, as well as for aging parents.

Increases in rates of separation and divorce are associated with a decreasing proportion of men and women who are currently married and living with a spouse. The responsibility for children born to these disrupted marriages disproportionately falls on the mothers. In this sense, the child-rearing responsibilities of many women are greater than in the past, despite reductions in average completed family size.

The prevalence of marriage and parenthood does not differ by race— among blacks as well as whites, most persons marry and become parents during their lifetimes. Both blacks and whites have decreased their completed family sizes, although only the most recent cohorts show a convergence in the number of children born. Despite these similarities, the family building patterns of blacks and whites have diverged in important ways. Blacks are much less likely than whites to be married and living with a spouse at any point in the life span; indeed, there is no age at which a majority of black women live with husbands. Marriage and parenthood no longer are strongly linked in the black population, with a large percentage of black women bearing their first child prior to marriage.

As a result of these racial differences in marriage and fertility, blacks have greater parenting and child-care responsibilities than whites. Among husband–wife couples, black families are more likely to have one or more children present at the young and later middle ages. The number of children present in such families is on average higher. The most remarkable racial difference in the parenting activities of Americans during the 1980's involves the fact that black women are much more likely than white women to be heads of their own household. These households are very likely to include one or more young children. During the early adult years black female-headed households are more likely than black husband–wife households to have at least one child present. Households headed by black women are more likely to include children than white married-couple or female-headed households at virtually every age. Finally, the average number of children in black families is larger than in white ones, this differential being especially pronounced for black female-headed families.

These patterns of parenting and child rearing have important implications for the types, of families in which American children are growing up in the 1980's. Nearly all white children are born to husband and wife families. As these children age, an increased proportion are raised in mother-headed families due to the dissolution of their parents' marriage. Nonetheless, high rates of remarriage guarantee that a large proportion of white children live in two-parent families from birth until age 18. The family experiences of black children are much different. By 1976 only half the black births were to married women (Kitagawa, 1981, Table 1/10). By 1981 more black children lived in mother-headed families than lived in mother and father families. Very few of these mother-headed families included grandparents or other related adults. Finally, a substantial number of black children were not living with either parent in 1981, and this situation was most common in infancy.

Thus, the remarkable changes in nuptial and fertility behaviors of American men and women have had major effects on their parenting and child-rearing activities. It is clear that Americans have not abandoned family living arrangements, nor have they abandoned parenthood. However, the family living arrangements and parenting activities experienced by Americans over their lifetimes display dramatic changes. Among blacks these are nothing short of revolutionary. Further alterations in the parenting activities of Americans during the 1980's are anticipated. The research agenda of social scientists during this decade must include projects to document and explain these changes, and investigate their consequences for the lives of black and white men and women and for their children.

SUMMARY

This chapter documents important changes in the nuptial and childbearing behaviors of American men and women. It describes the consequences of these changes for the prevalence and incidence of parenting activities over the life span of Americans during the 1980's. The implications of these adult behaviors for the types of parenting received by American children from birth until age 18 are discussed. This analysis highlights the increased variability in the reproductive and parenting behaviors of American men and women, and the emergence of distinct patterns between blacks and whites, especially those blacks belonging to the lower socioeconomic class.

ACKNOWLEDGMENTS

The initial draft of this paper was written while the author was a Fellow at the Center for Advanced Study in the Behavioral Sciences, supported in part by a grant from the John D. and Catherine T. MacArthur Foundation. Research support for parts of this analysis were provided by grants from the Spencer Foundation and National Institute of Child Health and Human Development (Grant No. 1-R01-HD-14980-01).

References

Blau, P., and Duncan. O.D. *The American Occupational Structure.* NY: Wiley, 1967.

Card, J.J., and Wise, L.L. Teenage mothers and teenage fathers: The impact of early childbearing on the parents, personal and professional lives. *Family Planning Perspectives*, 1978, *10*, 199–205.

Cherlin, A.J. *Marriage, Divorce, Remarriage.* Cambridge, MA: Harvard University Press, 1981.

Cherlin, A.J., and McCarthy, J. *Demographic analysis of family and household structure.* Final Report to the National Institute of Child Health and Human Development, Contract NO1-HD-12802, 1983.

Dryfoos, J.G., and Bourque-Scholl, N. *Factbook on Teenage Pregnancy.* NY: Guttmacher Institute, 1981.

Easterlin, R. *Birth and Fortune: The Impact of Numbers on Personal Welfare.* NY: Basic Books, 1980.

Espenshade, T.J. *Longitudinal analysis of family and household structure.* Progress report to NICHD on Contract N01-HD-02849, November 30, 1982.

Espenshade, T.J. *Black-white differences in marriage, separation, divorce, and remarriage.* Presented at the annual meeting of the Population Association of America, Pittsburgh, 1983.

Evans, M.D. *Modernization, economic conditions and family formation: Evidence from recent white and nonwhite cohorts.* Unpublished Ph.D. dissertation at the University of Chicago, Department of Sociology, 1983. (a)

Evans, M.D. *The emergence of a modern fertility pattern: a comparison of white an nonwhite cohorts.* Presented at the annual meeting of the Population Association of America, Pittsburgh, 1983. (b)

Farley, R. Trends in racial inequalities: Have the gains of the 1960s disappeared in the 1970s? *American Sociological Review,* 1977, *42,* 189–208.

Farley, R. Homicide trends in the United States. *Demography,* 1980, *17,* 177–178.

Furstenberg, Jr., F.F., Nord, C.W., Peterson, J.L., and Zill, N. The life course of children of divorce. *American Sociological Review,* 1983, *48,* 656–668.

Goldman, N., and Westoff, C.F. *Demography of the U.S. marriage market.* Presented at the annual meeting of the Population Association of America, San Diego, 1982.

Hannan, M.T., Tuma, N.B., and Groeneveld, L.P. Income and marital events: Evidence from an income-maintenance experiment. *American Journal of Sociology,* 1977, *82,* 1186–1211.

Hofferth, S.L., and Moore, K.A. Early childbearing and later economic well-being. *American Sociological Review,* 1979, *44,* 784–815.

Hogan, D.P. The effects of demographic factors, family background, and early job achievement on age at marriage. *Demography,* 1978, *15,* 161–175.

Hogan, D.P. *Transitions and Social Change: The Early Lives of American Men.* NY: Academic Press, 1981.

Hogan, D.P. Cohort comparisons in the timing of life transitions. *Developmental Review,* 1984, *4,* 289–310.

Hogan, D.P. Parental influences on the timing of early life transitions. In Zena Smith Blau (Ed.), *Current Perspectives on Aging and the Life Cycle,* Vol. 1. Greenwich, CT: JAI Press, 1985, pp. 1–59.

Hogan, D.P., and Kitagawa, E.M. The impact of social status, family structures, and neighborhood on fertility of black adolescents. *American Journal of Sociology,* 1985, *90,* 825–855.

Hogan, D.P., Astone, N.M., and Kitagawa, E.M. Social and environmental factors influencing contraceptive use among black adolescents. *Family Planning Perspectives,* 1985, *17,* 165–169.

Kellam, S.G., Ensminger, M.E., and Turner, R.J. Family structure and the mental health of children. *Archives of General Psychiatry,* 1977, *34,* 1012–1022.

Kitagawa, E.M. New life-styles: marriage patterns, living arrangements, and fertility outside of marriage. *Annals of the American Academy of Political and Social Sciences,* 1981, *453,* 1–27.

Moynihan, D.P. *The Negro Family: The Case for National Action.* Washington, D.C.: U.S. Department of Labor, Office of Policy Planning and Research, 1965.

Rainwater, L., and Yancey, W.L. *The Moynihan Report and the Politics of Controversy.* Cambridge: MIT Press, 1967.

Rindfuss, R.R., and Bumpass, L.L. How old is too old? Age and the sociology of fertility. *Family Planning Perspectives,* 1976, *8,* 226–230.

Rutter, M. *Changing Youth in a Changing Society: Patterns of Adolescent Development and Disorder.* Cambridge, MA: Harvard University Press, 1980.

Ryder, N.B. The emergence of a modern fertility pattern: United States, 1917–1966. In S.J. Behrman et al. (Ed.), Fertility and Family Planning: A World View. Ann Arbor, MI: University of Michigan Press, 1969, pp. 99–126.

Sewell, W.H., and Hauser, R.M. The Wisconsin longitudinal study of social and psychological factors in aspirations and achievements. Research in Sociology of Education and Socialization, 1980, 1, 59–99.

Sewell, W.H., and Shah, V.P. Social class, parental encouragement, and educational aspirations. American Journal of Sociology, 1968, 73, 559–572.

Stack, C. Sex roles and survival strategies in an urban black community. In M.Z. Rosaldo & L. Lamphere (eds.), Woman, Culture, and Society. Stanford, CA: Stanford University Press, 1974, pp. 113–128.

Stack, C. All Our Kin: Strategies for Survival in a Black Community. NY: Harper and Row, 1975.

Suttles, G.D. The Social Order of the Slum. Chicago, IL: University of Chicago Press, 1968.

Taub, R., and Wilson, W.J. Toward a new understanding of motivation and economic mobility of the poor: An ethnographic approach. Research proposal submitted to the U.S. Department of Health and Social Services, Assistant Secretary for Planning and Evaluation, 1982.

Thornton, A., and Rodgers, W.L. Changing patterns of marriage and divorce in the United States. Final Report to the National Institute of Child Health and Human Development, Contract N01-HD-02850, 1983.

Trussell, T.J. Economic consequences of teenage childbearing. Family Planning Perspectives, 1976, 10, 184–190.

Uhlenberg, P. Changing configurations of the life course. In T.K. Hareven (ed.), Transitions: The Family and the Life Course in Historical Perspective. NY: Academic Press, 1978, pp. 65–97.

U.S. Bureau of the Census. Census of the Population: 1970, Vol. I. Characteristics of the Population, Part I, United States Summary-Section I. Washington, D.C.: Government Printing Office, 1973. (a)

U.S. Bureau of the Census. Census of the Population: 1970, Subject Reports, Final Report PC (2)-4E, Persons in Institutions and Other Group Quarters. Washington, D.C.: Government Printing Office, 1973. (b)

U.S. Bureau of the Census. Historical Statistics of the United States, Bicentennial Edition, Part 2. Washington, D.C.: Government Printing Office, 1975.

U.S. Bureau of the Census. Current Population Reports, Series P-20, No. 375. Washington, D.C.: Government Printing Office, 1981.

U.S. Bureau of the Census. Current Population Reports, Series P-20, No. 371. Washington, D.C.: Government Printing Office, 1982. (a)

U.S. Bureau of the Census. Current Population Reports. Series P-20. No. 372. Washington, D.C.: Government Printing Office, 1982. (b)

U.S. Bureau of the Census. Statistical Abstract of the United States: 1981. Washington, D.C.: Government Printing Office, 1983.

U.S. Department of Labor, Employment and Unemployment: A Report on 1980. Bureau of Labor Statistics, Special Labor Force Report 244. Washington, D.C.: Government Printing Office, 1981.

Westoff, C.F., and Ryder, N.B. *The Contraceptive Revolution*. Princeton, NJ: Princeton University Press, 1977.

Wilson, W.J. *The Declining Significance of Race: Blacks and Changing American Institutions*. Chicago, IL: University of Chicago Press, 1978.

Wilson, W.J. *Urban poverty, social dislocations, and public policy*. Presented at the University of Chicago Conference on The Future of Our City, Chicago, 1982.

Zelnik, M., Kantner, J., and Ford, K. *Sex and Pregnancy in Adolescence*. Beverly Hills, CA: Sage, 1981.

13 DIFFERENTIAL PARENTAL INVESTMENT: ITS EFFECTS ON CHILD QUALITY AND STATUS ATTAINMENT

Judith Blake

A principal finding of research on social stratification in the United States is that men's educational attainment is the single most important known determinant of their occupational status (Blau and Duncan, 1967; Featherman and Hauser, 1978; Sewell and Hauser, 1980). The saliency of educational attainment in the achievement process has focused major research effort on the determinants of schooling differences. From this effort it is clear that parental socioeconomic status explains only a share of the variance in offsprings' schooling (Blau and Duncan, 1967; Featherman and Hauser, 1978; Sewell and Hauser, 1980), and even then, questions have been raised about how differential class background operates, through family structure, to create educational differentials. For example, the pioneering work of William Sewell and his colleagues has demonstrated the importance of parental encouragement to achieve educationally as intervening between stratificational variables (like parents' socioeconomic status) and educational attainment of offspring (Sewell, Haller, and Portes, 1969; Sewell, Haller, and Ohlendorf, 1970; Sewell and Hauser, 1972, 1975).

Sewell's work on family structure as a mediating link between the class hierarchy and individuals' schooling stimulated the author's interest in sibsize as a determinant of educational levels. Her research has shown that the number of siblings a person has is an important familial variable affecting educational attainment, since adults who have few siblings achieve substantially higher educational levels than those who come from large families (Blake, 1981; Duncan, 1965, 1967; Featherman and Hauser, 1978). This inverse relation between sibsize and educational achievement includes the smallest sibsize of all—the only child (Blake, 1981). Moreover, the relation is not simply a function of differential socioeconomic endowment among the parents of small and large families. Even when major background characteristics of the parents are controlled, the relationship persists (Figure 13.1). In fact, since only children are more likely than children from other small families to suffer certain persistent parental disadvantages (among them broken homes and lower family income), control for parental background factors will often accentuate the overall inverse relationship between achievement and sibsize. The means in Figure 13.1 have been adjusted, using multiple classification analysis, for one or both parents' educational attainment, father's occupation or family income, whether the family was broken while the respondent was growing up, whether it was from a Southern background (or farm background), and respondent's age.

Why is there an inverse relationship between educational attainment and sibsize? Although it is not possible definitively to adduce causality with any data now available, it is possible, through the use of modern, large-scale data sets and multivariate analysis, to shed some light on the causal mechanisms involved. For example, children from small families achieve higher scores on tests of intelligence and are more encouraged by their parents to aspire toward higher education. Elsewhere, documentation has been provided of the differential encouragement, holding parental socio-economic status constant, that children from small and large families receive, and the importance of its influence on college plans (Blake, 1981). This initial result has been borne out by a number of additional studies not reported on here. It has been suggested that differential encouragement is related to the dilution of parental interaction and attention that occurs with increasing sibsize.

Here, emphasis will be put on a consideration of intelligence and sibsize, with a view to establishing the nature of the relationship using more adequate controls than heretofore has been possible and understanding some of the causal mechanisms involved. Finally, given the fact that the parents of large families are, of course, overrepresented genetically in the next generation (see Table 13.1), the question will be addressed as to whether their children are proportionately represented among the more endowed intellectually, despite any inverse relationship between sibsize and IQ that may be found.

Past Research on Sibsize and Intelligence

In 1956 Anne Anastasi summarized the research to date on sibsize and intelligence (Anastasi, 1956). The results of 110 studies showed that customarily the relationship was inverse. In deviant cases confounding factors and selection biases were clearly operating.

More recent studies, some on exceptionally large data sets, have confirmed the inverse relationship of sibsize and various measures of ability or achievement (Belmont and Marolla, 1973; Breland, 1974; Claudy, Farrell, and Dayton, 1979). However, in two instances where the inverse relationship exists generally, the only child constitutes something of an exception because it performs less well than do children of other small- or medium-sized families. These instances are the Dutch data analyzed by Belmont and

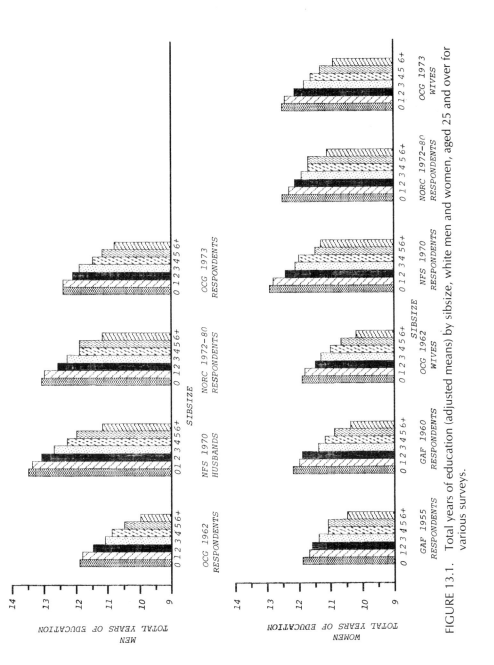

FIGURE 13.1.   Total years of education (adjusted means) by sibsize, white men and women, aged 25 and over for various surveys.

353

TABLE 13.1. Percentage Distribution of Whites by Sibsize in Various United States Surveys from National Samples of Adults and Children[a]

| | Sibsize | | | | | | | | |
Survey	0	1	2	3	4	5	6+	Total	N
Adults									
Growth of American Families Study, 1955									
Female respondents	8	15	16	14	12	9	26	100	(2,713)
Growth of American Families Study, 1960									
Female respondents	10	19	18	18	15	11	9	100	(2,961)
Occupational changes in a generation, 1962									
Male respondents	6	13	15	14	11	10	31	100	(18,485)
Wives	7	14	16	14	12	9	28	100	(15,569)
National Fertility Study, 1970									
Female respondents	7	19	20	16	11	8	19	100	(5,359)
Husbands	7	20	20	15	11	8	19	100	(4,976)
Occupational changes in a generation, 1973									
Male respondents	7	16	18	15	11	9	24	100	(26,963)
Wives	7	17	18	15	11	9	23	100	(21,416)
National Opinion Research Center, General Social Survey, 1972–1980									
Males and females	6	15	17	14	11	9	28	100	(10,644)
Children									
Health Examination Survey, Cycle II, 1963–1965									
Males and Females	4	21	26	21	11	6	11	100	(4,511)
Health Examination Survey, Cycle III, 1966–1970									
Males and females	7	22	26	16	10	6	13	100	(3,310)
Youth in Transition, 1966									
Male respondents	6	22	25	20	12	6	8	100	(1,911)

[a]Note. These tabulations come from a forthcoming monograph on sibsize and educational attainment, by the author, involving the secondary analysis of numerous large-scale data sets.

Marolla, and a cohort taking the National Merit Scholarship Qualifying Examination (in 1965) analyzed by Breland. The Belmont and Marolla and Breland results by sibsize are presented in Figure 13.2.

In considering these results for only children, it must be noted that the studies did not control for selective factors peculiarly affecting such youngsters. Regarding the Belmont and Marolla findings on young Dutch-

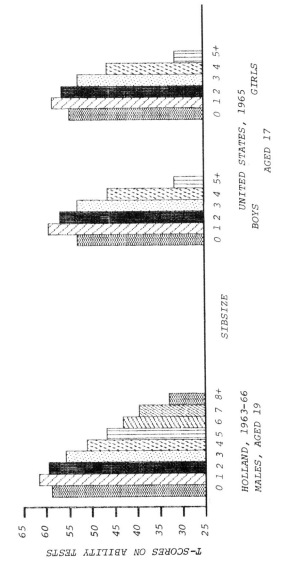

FIGURE 13.2. T-Scores on ability tests by sibsize for 19-year-old dutch males, and 11th-grade students taking the U.S. National Merit Scholarship Qualifying Examination Test.

men born during the period 1944–1947, probably the most acute selection, as has been discussed in detail elsewhere, concerns the effects of the famine in Holland on all lastborn and apparently lastborn children, including only children (Blake, 1981). In brief, since the famine drastically affected fertility, fetal mortality, and infant deaths, being an only child or other lastborn child was a status that would occur selectively in those families worst hit by the famine (those families in which the woman could not become pregnant or stay pregnant to term, or in which a next-born child would die). Moreover, since the adult death rate was adversely affected as well, many only and lastborn children who were born during the 1944–1947 period were partially or completely orphaned by the famine, and, hence, remained "lastborn." Again, on average this excess adult mortality would occur more often in those families worst affected by the famine. Since severe starvation in childhood is known to adversely affect intellectual functioning, it is hardly surprising that only and other lastborn children in the Dutch data evidence an unexpectedly sharp drop in performance on the Raven Progressive Matrices test.

Although the selective effects of the famine were probably crucial in the Dutch data, overriding other effects, the fact is that all of the data sets analyzed for this chapter (and for a forthcoming monograph on sibsize and achievement) indicate that, relative to children from other small families, only children suffer from some particular familial handicaps. As may be seen from Table 13.2, only children invariably come from broken families in higher proportions than do children from other sibsizes. The disruption of their parents' marriages is doubtless the reason, in many cases, that these children are singletons. Moreover, since most of the children reside with their mothers after the family is disrupted, the family's income level is adversely affected compared to children from other small families that remain intact (Table 13.2). In addition, because unusually high proportions of only children are born to older parents (Table 13.2), the parents of singletons tend to be somewhat less educated than the parents of children in other small families (the two- and three-child families with which the only child is usually compared). Finally, the incidence of infant and child health problems (particularly low birth weight and its possible sequelae) is greater among only children.

Turning to Breland's findings on the approximately 800,000 participants in the National Merit Scholarship Qualifying Examinations in 1965 (Figure 13.2), it is important to be aware that, for this group, there were no controls for background characteristics, including race. This point is often misinterpreted in discussions of the Breland article since he also mentions, but does not present, sibsize data for a small sample of finalists in 1962, where some parental background data were apparently available. Thus, the somewhat less distinguished performance of the only child in the 1965 data is easily accounted for by the overrepresentation among only children of broken

TABLE 13.2. Background Characteristics of White Respondents by Sibsize from Selected Surveys

Survey	Sibsize							n
	0	1	2	3	4	5	6+	
Percentage in broken family while respondent a child[a]								
GAF 1955	39	22	24	18	19	21	15	(2,713)
GAF 1960	29	15	15	12	13	12	15	(2,961)
OCG 1962	23	14	14	14	13	16	14	(18,485)
NFS 1970	30	15	18	19	21	21	19	(5,359)
OCG 1973	22	13	13	13	14	15	15	(26,963)
NORC 1972–1980	31	18	20	20	22	23	25	(10,644)
HES Cycle II 1963–1965	26	11	8	9	7	6	18	(4,511)
HES Cycle III 1966–1970	25	14	12	10	14	17	16	(3,310)
YIT 1966	27	15	14	16	21	22	29	(1,911)
Family income under $5,000 (%)								
HES Cycle II	30	22	19	26	32	41	55	(4,511)
HES Cycle III	23	12	11	10	20	31	38	(3,310)
Mother's education less than high school complete (%)								
HES Cycle II	34	30	29	36	41	55	59	(4,511)
HES Cycle III	30	30	29	33	41	53	55	(3,310)
Mother's education college 4 plus (%)								
HES Cycle II	18	22	21	17	16	10	11	(4,511)
HES Cycle III	18	24	21	18	15	10	13	(3,310)
Father's education less than high school complete (%)								
HES Cycle II	44	34	30	36	46	51	65	(4,511)
HES Cycle III	39	37	33	37	46	45	57	(3,310)
Father's education college 4 plus (%)								
HES Cycle II	18	32	33	24	25	23	9	(4,511)
HES Cycle III	22	28	34	28	20	23	12	(3,310)
Mothers over thirty at birth of child (%)								
HES Cycle II	45	25	25	21	22	23	38	(4,511)
HES Cycle III	53	23	17	12	10	9	15	(3,310)
Fathers over thirty at birth of child (%)								
HES Cycle II	55	42	40	39	38	44	50	(4,510)
HES Cycle III	63	43	35	29	23	15	34	(3,310)

[a]For OCG 1962 and 1973 and NFS 1970, the figures are for respondents only.

families, families with less educated parents and lower incomes, and a disproportionate number of blacks. Moreover, since only children are being compared with those of other sibsizes, it must be remembered that singletons are disproportionately likely to finish high school and be encouraged to go to college. Hence, they are less selected for academic performance by the age of the NMSQEs takers than are children from larger sibsizes, among whom many have been weeded out by age 17.

Given the importance, when studying IQ and sibsize, of controlling for
such background factors as parental educational attainment, income, family
intactness, and race, in addition to avoiding selective factors such as
"surviving" the educational process and intending to go to college, this
analysis has been based on data that allow such possible confounders to be
taken into account. It may be mentioned, parenthetically, that controlling for
parents' educational attainment introduces at least a partial control for
parents' own IQ. In other words, insofar as some might argue that the inverse
association of IQ and sibsize is simply a result of the inverse association of
parental IQ and number of children ever born (Spaeth, 1976; Scarr and
Weinberg, 1978), the control for parents' education helps to offset the
confounding effect that could result if less intelligent parents had larger
families.

METHOD

The Data Bases

The research reported on here is based on two cycles of the Health
Examination Survey conducted by the National Center for Health Statistics.
Between 1960 and 1970 three cycles of the Health Examination Survey
were completed. Each focused on a different age grouping—Cycle I on ages
18 through 79, Cycle II on ages 6 through 11, and Cycle III on ages 12
through 17. Cycle I was begun in 1960 and completed in 1962; Cycle II was
begun in 1963 and completed in 1965; Cycle III was begun in 1966 and
completed in 1970. Only Cycles II and III will be considered here. They
were based on probability samples of noninstitutionalized children and
youths. Cycle II included 7119 children out of the 7417 originally sampled,
and Cycle III included 6768 young people out of the 7514 originally
sampled. To avoid severe problems of statistical interaction, only the data on
white, non-Hispanics have been used, thereby reducing the number in
Cycle II to 4511 and that in Cycle III to 3310. A portion of this reduction is
also due to the difficulty of ascertaining sibsize for some of the young people
in the surveys.

Data on sibsize were derived from information on the number of children
in the household. Although a question was asked of parents concerning
whether any children lived elsewhere, no information was obtained on the
number of such children. Among those young people who had six or more
siblings in the household (an open-ended category), the lack of data on the
number of siblings living elsewhere did not present a problem. But it was
necessary to exclude from the analysis all other cases where there were
siblings who lived elsewhere, since it was not possible to ascertain the total

number of siblings. There is no reason to believe that such cases represent instances of particularly wide spacing.[1]

The general format of both Cycle II and Cycle III was a physical examination by physicians and dentists in a mobile unit, and psychological and ability testing by trained psychologists. Additional information on health and behavior, as well as parental background information, was derived from a parent questionnaire, a youth questionnaire (in the case of 12 to 17 year olds), a questionnaire sent to the school, and data from the young person's birth certificate that were combined with the examination and test results when the findings from all parts of the survey were processed. The files from both cycles were obtained from the National Center for Health Statistics and the analysis reported on here was conducted by the author. More detailed descriptions of the surveys may be found in reports by the National Center for Health Statistics (National Center for Health Statistics, 1964, 1969).

A major advantage of the Health Examination Surveys is that they are not keyed to school populations and, hence, are not selecting only those children who have remained in school. Since the data on adults show a direct relationship between sibsize and the probability of dropout (prior to high school graduation), it is important to avoid this selection by sibsize as much as possible. Nonetheless, because the population sampled consists of noninstitutionalized children, there is some (unknown) selection against children whose problems are extreme enough to require institutionalization, or who are in institutions for other reasons, such as orphanhood or parental desertion. However, these data sets afford unique opportunities for controls,

---

[1]There is a popular tendency, in thinking about the influence of sibsize, to fixate on unusual and extreme conditions, such as exceptionally wide (or close) spacing between offspring, when accounting for sibsize differences. Actually, wide spacing has been uncommon in the United States at least since mid-century, because of both the decline in infant and child mortality (which created "spaces" in the past) and the decline in breast-feeding, as well as the fact that since World War II American women appear to have preferred relatively close spacing and an early end to childbearing (Bumpass, Rindfuss, and Janosik, 1978; Whelpton, Campbell, and Patterson, 1966). Recent trends in family formation and reproduction (1970's and 1980's) do not bear on the data sets used here. A question might be raised, however, about whether children from widely spaced families were deleted when the cases of those who had siblings living elsewhere were dropped. As far as large families are concerned, all cases in the open-ended category of six and over were kept in. Thus, the fact that children from these family sizes are shown to have lower IQ's is not due to selective deletion of widely spaced youngsters. Among the children from sibsizes three, four, and five, the findings on the relation of IQ and sibsize do not differ if the cases that have been deleted are included, indicating that particularly wide-spaced youngsters were not selectively removed among these large sibsizes. Indeed, it would be expected, without selectivity on spacing, that some siblings of the 12 to 17 year olds (and even 6 to 11 year olds) in large families would have already left home. The fact that widely spaced children from small families have been deleted would be expected to understate the inverse relationship of sibsize and IQ.

and avoid many of the more flagrant problems of selection by sibsize that occur when special groups are sampled.

The author's overall research on sibsize and achievement has utilized survey data on both adults and children. The analysis of the surveys of adults has concentrated on educational attainment according to sibsize. The surveys of young people have been used to understand the marked inverse relationship between total educational accomplishment and attainment at each stage of the educational process (so-called continuation ratios) and sibsize.

The Wechsler Intelligence Scale for Children (WISC)

Both Cycle II and Cycle III of the Health Examination Survey employed a short form of the Wechsler Intelligence Scale for Children (WISC). The WISC was first published in 1949 as an extension, to children, of the already well-known Wechsler test for adults. The Wechsler tests had their inception in their author's broad view that "intelligence" implies a global ability to act purposively, think rationally, and deal with the personal environment effectively (Glasser and Zimmerman, 1967; Kaufman, 1979; Matarazzo, 1972; Wechsler, 1958). The test, consisting of 12 subtests, endeavored to take account of more than purely logical (what, today, might be called "left hemisphere") functioning, and to recognize that cognitive functions are an integral part of personality in general. For these reasons, unlike the Stanford-Binet, the subtests are not ranked hierarchically, but are accorded equal weight.

Six of the subtests measure verbal abilities and six measure what Wechsler called performance. The latter is roughly equivalent to what psychologists now call perceptual organization (spatial organization, and so on). An important additional difference from the Stanford-Binet is that the Wechsler has abandoned the Binet notion of mental age and evaluates test performance on the basis of distributions of representative samples of persons of comparable chronological age. The WISC scores presented here are standardized for age and sex and have a mean of 100 and a standard deviation of 15. The subtest scores have a mean of 50 and a standard deviation of 10.

In spite of Wechsler's vision concerning a more inclusive and holistic approach to intelligence testing, the Wechsler tests are, in content, lineal descendents of the Binet. As a consequence, the Wechslers are criticized today (as is the Stanford-Binet) for not including more material that reflects intuitive, right-hemisphere functioning. This criticism is voiced especially regarding their use for testing blacks. An additional problem with the Wechsler for clinical purposes is that it is insensitive at the extremes of intellect—exceptionally gifted and exceptionally handicapped children are somewhat underestimated relative to the Stanford-Binet. Nonetheless, the WISC correlates highly with the Stanford-Binet (correlations in the .80s) in most studies.

Does the WISC measure "ability" or "achievement"? Sidestepping what has become a raging controversy, Wechsler maintained that it measures accrued achievement, plus personality factors such as drive and persistence. Its purpose is to predict future learning, and it is very good at that, especially for white, non-Hispanic young people. However, subtests of the WISC are designed to tap into different kinds of achievement, and to depend on different sorts of past influence in the subject's life. They are also differentially predictive of future academic attainment. In particular, the Vocabulary subtest of the Verbal battery appears to be deeply influenced by the home environment and cultural influences within it, outside reading, and school learning. A number of the Performance (perceptual organization) subtests, such as Block Design, are regarded as less dependent on past levels of personal and cultural enrichment, and more influenced by personality characteristics such as field dependence and independence, as well as ability to work under time pressure. For white, non-Hispanic (so-called Anglo) young people, the Vocabulary subtest is the single best predictor of future academic achievement (Kaufman, 1979).

Although for clinical purposes it is desirable to use the full complement of subtests (in addition, of course, to numerous other diagnostic tools), it is not uncommon to use "short forms" of the WISC to describe the intellectual level of groups (Kaufman, 1979; National Center for Health Statistics, 1973). A short form, made up of various combinations of two or more subtests, is used to estimate the Full Score. A large number of studies of special populations (gifted, mentally retarded, and so on) have found high correlations between the Vocabulary and Block Design combination and the Full Scale. A special study of schoolchildren by Mercer and Smith in Riverside, California (performed under contract to the National Center for Health Statistics) found that, for Anglo children, the Vocabulary and Block Design subsets were the optimal combination to estimate the Full Score. For this group of children, the Vocabulary/Block Design combination had a .867 correlation with the Full Scale (National Center for Health Statistics, March, 1972). It is worth noting as well that a number of investigators have confirmed Wechsler's own data indicating that Vocabulary and Block Design are the most reliable subtests of the WISC scale. It has also been reported that these subtests are the most highly loaded on the so-called "general" factor of intelligence in factor analyses of the WISC. In light of this evidence, and of the time constraints of the Cycle II and Cycle III examinations, the Vocabulary and Block Design dyad was used for both Cycle II and III of the Health Examination Surveys. The total WISC scores presented are the unweighted sum of the dyad of subtests.

Clearly, the two cycles of the Health Examination Survey for young people provide an extraordinary range of information in addition to sibsize. These data, for example, make it possible to analyze dependent variables according to sibsize controlling for a number of important "background" variables of the parents, as well as for many additional predictors such as infant health (including birth weight), current health, and mother's and father's age at birth. The Wechsler data to be discussed here were analyzed using the following predictors: sibsize, mother's education, father's education, family income, mother's labor force activity, intactness of family, region, and community size.

Parenthetically, no data on birth order will be presented here, although detailed analyses have been done on this variable. The fact is that for all the data sets available to the author, no statistically significant birth order effects on IQ are evident once controls have been instituted for sibsize and familial background factors. Moreover, an extensive review of other studies in which birth order effects appear to have occurred indicates that such effects are a result of systemative confounding factors.

Method of Analysis

The data have been analyzed using a form of dummy variable multivariate regression—Multiple Classification Analysis (MCA). This technique makes no assumptions about linearity, and allows categorical as well as numerical predictors. Among the statistics available, the output provides values for bivariate relationships between predictors and the dependent variable (unadjusted means), and values that have been adjusted for the other predictors in the equation (adjusted means). The "eta" is a measure of the zero-order correlation, and the "beta" is essentially the equivalent of the standardized regression coefficient in ordinary regression. The "betas" of MCA thus allow a comparison between the rank order of predictors within a given regression equation. As is the case with all standardized regression coefficients, "betas" cannot be compared among equations. The R^2 in MCA, percentage variance explained, has the same meaning as in ordinary regression. The values for R^2 presented in this chapter have been adjusted for degrees of freedom.

RESULTS

Figure 13.3 summarizes the WISC findings by sibsize for Cycles II and III. As can be seen, the results are materially affected by controls for parental background characteristics, with only children, and particularly children from large families, being brought up sharply in their scores when the adjusted coefficients are considered. Despite the fact that the scores for

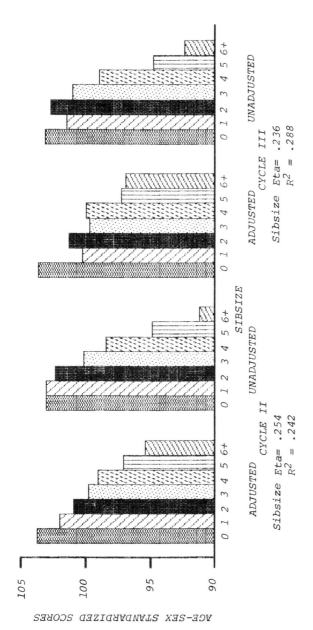

FIGURE 13.3. Age-sex standardized scores on the WISC, adjusted and unadjusted for parental characteristics. Data for white boys and girls, Health Examination Survey, Cycles II and III. As described in the text, the WISC score is a composite of two subsets, Vocabulary and Block Design. Scores have been adjusted through Multiple Classification Analysis, for mother's and father's education, family income, family intactness, mother's usual activity, region, and community size.

363

TABLE 13.3. Beta Coefficients for Predictors Used in Multiple Classification Analysis of the WISC and the Vocabulary and Block Design Components of WISC[a]

	Beta coefficients	
Predictor	Cycle II	Cycle III
WISC total		
Mother's education	.241	.221
Father's education	.145	.221
Sibsize	.142	.129
Family income	.129	.134
Region	.076	.099
Mother's activity	.067	.086
Community size	.050	.048
Family intact	.014	.019
R^2	.242	.288
Vocabulary		
Mother's education	.240	.239
Sibsize	.200	.154
Father's education	.157	.234
Family income	.137	.119
Region	.087	.134
Community size	.063	.055
Mother's activity	.055	.081
Family intact	.015	.014
R^2	.286	.327
Block design		
Mother's education	.172	.146
Father's education	.098	.157
Family income	.090	.111
Region	.088	.065
Sibsize	.060	.072
Mother's activity	.053	.070
Community size	.031	.031
Family intact	.029	.034
R^2	.100	.130

[a]White boys and girls, Health Examination Survey, Cycles II and III.

children from large families are greatly improved by adjustments, the relationship between sibsize and intelligence is inverse, and the only child clearly excels. It is noteworthy that the effects of sibsize are more marked and linear among the younger children (those in Cycle II) than among the older ones (those in Cycle III).

Among younger children (Cycle II), the relative importance of sibsize (as shown by the beta coefficients in Table 13.3) is approximately equal to the importance of father's education. Both father's education and sibsize are only exceeded in importance by mother's education. Among older children, mother's and father's education are most (and equally) important, and sibsize is clearly less important.

As was pointed out earlier, the two components of the short version of the WISC considered in Cycles II and III, Vocabulary and Block Design, represent very different aspects of measured IQ. When the WISC scores are disaggregated into their components (Figures 13.4 and 13.5) , it is evident that the major influence of all background factors, including sibsize, is on Vocabulary. For Block Design the amount of variance explained by such factors is one third that explained when the same predictors are applied to Vocabulary. Moreover, the relative importance of sibsize (see beta rankings in Table 13.3) is slight for Block Design, but a major influence for Vocabulary.

Finally, the question may be posed as to whether, in spite of the inverse relationship of sibsize and intelligence, parents of large families do not reap an advantage because their genes are disproportionately represented among the highly intelligent in the next generation. This would result from the fact that children brought up in large families are so much more prevalent in a population than children brought up in small ones (Table 13.1). Indeed, as is summarized in Table 13.4, three quarters or more of the respondents in all our samples have two or more siblings (come from families of three or more children), and typically half or more of the respondents come from families of four or more children. This picture is, of course, very different from the one that relates to the number of children ever born to women, since 20th century fertility among women in the United States has been quite low. The high proportion of the population from large families suggests that, with regard to any given characteristic such as superior intelligence, one might expect a correspondingly high representation. What do the data from Cycles II and II show?

Figures 13.6 and 13.7 present the results of a multiple classification analysis in which the WISC scores (Figure 13.6) and the Vocabulary scores (Figure 13.7) are plotted against sibsize as the dependent variable, controlling for all the parental background variables heretofore used in this chapter. For the WISC, the groupings rank from 1 (low) to 7 (high), and for the Vocabulary, from 1 (low) to 5 (high). From these figures it is evident that the lowest scorers on these scales come from sibsizes substantially above the sibsize mean, and the highest scorers come from sibsizes below the sibsize mean.

In effect, the reproductive success (in the biological sense) of the parents who have invested in large sibsizes has not gained them anything like proportionate representation among the ranks of the highly intelligent in the next generation. In fact, the children of large families are disproportionately represented among the less able intellectually.

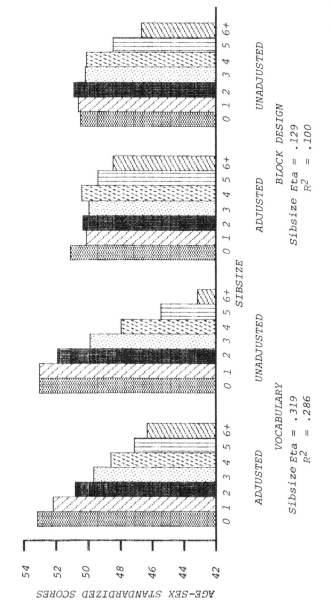

FIGURE 13.4. Age-sex standardized scores on Vocabulary and Block Design components of the WISC, adjusted and unadjusted for parental characteristics. Data for white boys and girls, from Health Examination Survey, Cycle II. Scores have been adjusted through Multiple Classification Analysis, for mother's and father's education, family income, family intactness, mother's usual activity, region, and community size.

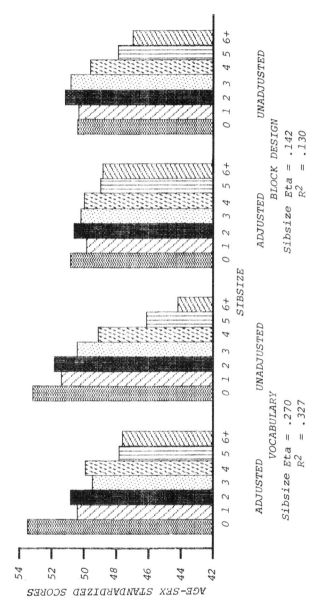

FIGURE 13.5. Age-sex standardized scores on Vocabulary and Block Design components of the WISC, adjusted and unadjusted for parental characteristics. Data for white boys and girls from Health Examination Survey, Cycle III. Scores have been adjusted through Multiple Classification Analysis, for mother's and father's education, family income, family intactness, mother's usual activity, region, and community size.

367

TABLE 13.4. Size of Family of Orientation of Respondents in Various Surveys, Summarized from Sibsize Distributions in Table 13.1

	Size of family or orientation (%)	
Survey	Three or more children	Four or more children
Adults		
GAF 1955		
Female respondents	77	61
GAF 1960		
Female respondents	71	53
OCG 1962		
Male respondents	81	66
Wives	79	63
NFS 1970		
Female respondents	74	54
Husbands	73	53
OCG 1973		
Male respondents	77	59
Wives	76	58
NORC 1972–1980		
Males and females	79	62
Children		
HES Cycle II, 1963–1965		
Males and females	75	49
HES Cycle III, 1966–1970		
Males and females	71	45
YIT 1966		
Males and females	71	46

DISCUSSION

Two surveys, Cycles II and III of the Health Examination Survey, provided data for the analysis of scores by sibsize on a short form of the WISC, controlling for major parental background variables of the young people involved. Both surveys were independent of schools for their sampling frames and, hence, do not involve selection of individuals who have been able to remain in school. A principal result of introducing controls is to offset negative influences on the intelligence of the only child, and to demonstrate that such children conform to the marked inverse relationship between sibsize and intelligence. This relationship is especially sharp among the youngest children, those in Cycle II, who were aged 6–11. The diminution of the effects of sibsize on intelligence as children get older may be due to the fact that, with age, nonfamilial influences partially dilute such effects. For example, the marginal effect of schooling may be greater for children from larger families, bringing them closer to those who have greater advantages at home. However, only children at later ages maintain their

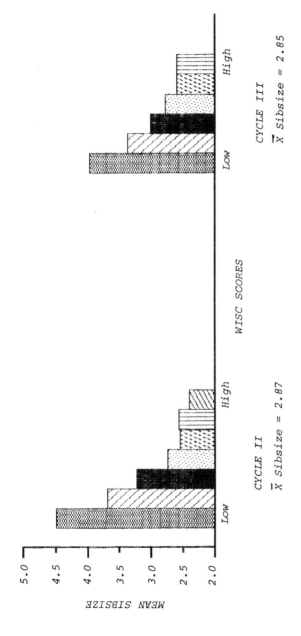

FIGURE 13.6. Adjusted mean sibsize by level of score on the WISC. Data for white boys and girls from Health Examination Survey, Cycles II and III. Sibsize means have been adjusted for differences in mother's education, father's education, family income, mother's activity, region, community size, and family intactness. Due to the small number of Cycle III respondents (20) scoring in the highest category, the two highest WISC score catagories (6 and 7) have been combined for representation in this figure.

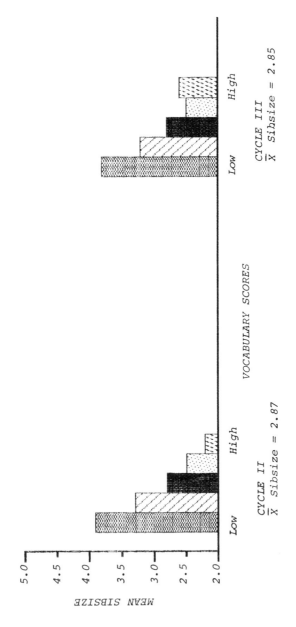

FIGURE 13.7. Adjusted mean sibsize by level of score on the vocabulary component of the WISC. Data for white boys and girls from Health Examination Survey, Cycles II and III. Sibsize means have been adjusted for differences in mother's education, father's education, family income, region, mother's activity, community size, and family intactness.

stellar position, arguing that, for them, some familial advantage continues as an important factor in their lives. Another reason for the relative improvement in scores of older children who come from large families is that, by ages 12–17, some of the most intellectually disadvantaged may have died (such as those with Down's syndrome) or been institutionalized.

Why is there an inverse relationship between intelligence and sibsize even after controls for differentials in home advantages? As Anastasi has suggested, two other explanations are of major importance (Anastasi, 1956). One is that large families are more prevalent among parents who are themselves genetically less able, and, on average, this genetic incapacity is transmitted to their children. A second is that large families, regardless of socioeconomic status, have invested fewer resources per child. In particular, such families can muster less parental concentration, attention, and interaction per child. Such diminished parental input is not compensated by the effect of siblings on each other.

As for differential genetic endowment by sibsize, controls for the educational attainment of both parents take some account of this factor, insofar as it may, indeed, operate. Moreover, the lack of a sibsize effect on measures of nonverbal ability suggests that a genetic explanation may be unfounded. Turning to whether there is evidence that a dilution of parental inputs causes a reduction in measured intelligence, it is fortunate to have some guidelines. As Anastasi noted almost 30 years ago, certain aspects of measured intelligence vary consistently with adult contact and interaction— primarily verbal development. It is also true that verbal ability is the single best predictor (at least among Anglo children in the United States) of academic achievement (Matarazzo, 1972). Some existing findings (unfortunately lacking controls for parental socioeconomic status) suggest strongly that it is the verbal aspects of measured intelligence that are primarily responsible for the association of intelligence scores and sibsize (Nisbet, 1953; Breland, 1974). In a set of unusual research papers, Marjoribanks, and Marjoribanks and Walberg, have made additional contributions to this issue (Marjoribanks, 1972; Marjoribanks and Walberg, 1975; Walberg and Marjoribanks, 1973; Walberg, 1976). Controlling for the parents' socioeconomic status, these researchers have measured directly what they call "family environment" variables of schoolchildren (pressure for achievement, activeness, intellectuality, and independence, as well as mother and father dominance). Also included were two variables relating to whether English was spoken and the use of a second language, since the research was done in Canada. The family environment variables were negatively related to sibsize, and positively related to ability—particularly verbal ability. The Marjoribanks-Walberg research indicates that sibsize is related to ability through the family environment variables, and that the relation is specific for verbal ability.

Using the Health Examination Surveys, it is possible to disaggregate the

WISC scores into their two components—Vocabulary and Block Design (Figures 13.3 and 13.4). From this analysis, it is evident that the major influence of sibsize is on Vocabulary. It would thus appear that the strong association of sibsize with educational attainment can be explained, in part, by the association of sibsize with the verbal aspects of measured intelligence. Moreover, since verbal ability is known to depend on adult–child interaction, particularly parent–child interaction, it seems highly probable that the elevated scores of children from small families are partially a result of the greater parental inputs per child that are possible in such families. It is also suggestive that the sibsize influence is more marked among younger than among older children. In sum, children from small families are not only encouraged more, they are also apparently afforded the requisite amounts of parent–child interaction that tend to result in high scores on verbal ability, which, in turn, is a strong independent predictor of educational achievement.

Consequently, although parents of small families have not maximized reproductive "fitness," they are very good at rearing children who can compete well educationally and who, therefore, have access to the most interesting and lucrative occupations. Parents of few children have sacrified genetic maximization in succeeding generations in order to produce high-quality children from an educational point of view.

Can it be claimed that actually the parents of large families also have a high representation among the most intelligent, simply because, among the larger number of siblings, some will be represented among the best? Such an outcome would not be precluded by the inverse relationship between sibsize and intelligence. It certainly would help to explain why, among able people, there are many from large families. Coming from a large family is the norm rather than the exception, as has been seen. Even so, the results reported on here, using sibsize as a dependent variable and IQ as a predictor, have shown that there is an excess of young people from large families among the least intelligent, and a deficit of respondents from large families among the most intelligent. In effect, there is an inverse relationship of sibsize by intelligence, as well as an inverse relationship of intelligence by sibsize.

CONCLUSION

The results presented here show that, on average, the verbal ability of children is strongly affected by whether parents must divide their time and attention among many or few offspring. Small families, those of one or two children, appear to be highly advantaged child-rearing units from the point of view of cognitive ability because parents are not precluded from major investments per child. Since it is already known, from data on adults, that sibsize bears a strong negative relation to educational attainment, these findings concerning cognitive ability are part of a larger picture rather than an isolated piece of information. Youngsters from small families are smarter, and their cognitive ability is of a type that is very important for educational achievement. These factors make the findings on education more credible and more understandable. In addition, the analysis herein has suggested that human parents, as distinct from those in other species, are well advised to invest their efforts in a few cognitively enriched children because a large family, on average, is a high-risk venture when it comes to child quality.

SUMMARY

In prior research a marked negative effect of number of siblings on educational attainment has been found among adults, even after controls for parental socioeconomic characteristics. This is interpreted as a result of the dilution of parental resources—both economic and personal—in large families. The effect of sibsize on educational attainment has led to an interest in specifying further how number of siblings operates to curtail education. In this chapter, special attention is given to the influence of sibsize on intellectual ability using two large-scale data sets for youngsters ages 6–11 and 12–17. Particular attention is devoted to verbal ability, since that is strongly influenced by parental interaction and serves as a major predictor of educational success. After controlling for parental socioeconomic background and family intactness, a strong negative association is found between sibsize and verbal ability, with the only child scoring well above children from other sibsizes. By contrast, the relationship between sibsize and nonverbal ability is weak. Conflicting results concerning the relative ability of only children in some other research are explained in terms of lack of controls for parental background and selection bias. It thus appears that the negative association of sibsize and educational attainment can be understood, in part, by the inverse relationship of sibsize with the verbal aspects of measured intelligence. Moreover, since verbal ability is known to depend on adult–child interaction, particularly parent–child interaction, it seems highly probable that the elevated scores of children from small families are partially a result of the greater parental inputs per child that are possible in such families.

Clearly, parents of small families have not maximized reproductive "fitness" in the genetic sense because their representation in succeeding generations is relatively small. Parents of many children, by contrast, epitomize reproductive "fitness," but, on average, sacrifice child quality in the cognitive and educational sense. Can it be argued, however, that the large-family reproductive strategy is actually successful in terms of child quality, because even a small proportion of a large number may add up to a major representation in the next generation of persons from large families among the cognitively endowed? One way of testing this idea is to regress ability on sibsize. When this is done, relatively few from large families are found to be among the most able, and a major overrepresentation is found among the least able. Hence, from the point of view of their offspring's ability to function amid the complexity of human societies, parents would seem best advised to limit the size of their families and invest in "quality."

ACKNOWLEDGMENT

The support of the Russell Sage Foundation and the Fred H. Bixby Foundation is gratefully acknowledged. Inas El-Attar and Wendy Chang assisted with data processing and computing, and Hannah Balter and Jennifer Frost Bhattacharya provided general research assistance. The Data Archives Library of the UCLA Institute for Social Science Research made the Health Examination Survey data files available.

REFERENCES

Anastasi, A. Intelligence and family size. *Psychological Bulletin*, 1956, *53*, 187–209.
Belmont, L., and Marolla, F. A. Birth order, family size, and intelligence. *Science*, 1973, *182*, 1096–1101.
Blake, J. Family size and the quality of children. *Demography*, 1981, *18*, 421–442.
Blau, P. M., and Duncan, O. D. *The American Occupational Structure*. NY: Wiley, 1967.
Breland, H. M. Birth order, family configuration, and verbal achievement. *Child Development*, 1974, *45*, 1011–1019.
Bumpass, L. L., Rindfuss, R. R., and Janosik, R. B. Age and marital status at first birth and the pace of subsequent fertility. *Demography*, 1978, *15*, 75–86.
Claudy, J. G., Farrell, W. S., Jr., and Dayton, C. W. *The Consequences of Being an Only Child: An Analysis of Project Talent Data*. Palo Alto, CA: American Institutes for Research, 1979.
Duncan, B. *Family Factors and School Dropout: 1920–1960*. Ann Arbor, MI: University of Michigan, mimeo, 1965.
Duncan, B. Education and social background. *American Journal of Sociology*, 1967, *72*, 363–372.
Featherman, D. L., and Hauser, R. M. *Opportunity and Change*. NY: Academic Press, 1978.
Glasser, A. J., and Zimmerman, I. L. *Clinical Interpretation of the Wechsler Intelligence Scale for Children (WISC)*. NY: Grune and Stratton, 1967.
Kaufman, A. S. *Intelligence Testing with the WISC-R*. NY: Wiley, 1979.
Marjoribanks, K. Ethnic and environmental influences on mental abilities. *American Journal of Sociology*, 1972, *78*, 323–337.
Marjoribanks, K., and Walberg, H. J. Family environment: Sibling constellation and social class correlates. *Journal of Biosocial Sciences*, 1975, *7*, 15–25.

Matarazzo, J. D. *Wechsler's Measurement and Appraisal of Adult Intelligence*. Baltimore, MD: Williams and Wilkins, 1972.

National Center for Health Statistics. *Plan, Operation, and Response Results of a Program of Children's Examinations*. Vital and Health Statistics. PHS Pub. No. 1000-Series 11-No. 1. Washington, D.C.: U.S. Government Printing Office, 1964.

National Center for Health Statistics. *Plan and Operation of a Health Examination Survey of U.S. Youths, 12–17 Years of Age*. Vital and Health Statistics. PHS Pub. No. 1000-Series 1-No. 8. Washington, D.C.: U.S. Government Printing Office, 1969.

National Center for Health Statistics. *Subtest Estimates of the WISC Full Scale IQs for Children*. Vital and Health Statistics. Series 2, No. 47. DHEW Pub. No. (HSM) 72-1047. Washington, D.C.: U.S. Government Printing Office, 1972.

National Center for Health Statistics. *Intellectual Development of Youth as Measured by a Short Form of the Wechsler Intelligence Scale*. Vital and Health Statistics. Series 11, No. 128. DHEW Pub. No. (HRS) 74-1610. Washington, D.C.: U.S. Government Printing Office, 1973.

Nisbet, J. D. *Family Environment: A Direct Effect of Family Size on Intelligence*. London: Cassel, 1953.

Scarr, S., and Weinberg, R. R. The influence of "family background" on intellectual attainment. *American Sociological Review*, 1978, *43*, 674–692.

Sewell, W. H., and Hauser, R. M. Causes and consequences of higher education: Models of the status attainment process. *American Journal of Agricultural Economics*, 1972, *54*, 851–861.

Sewell, W. H., and Hauser, R. M. *Education, Occupation and Earnings: Achievement in the Early Career*. NY: Academic Press, 1975.

Sewell, W. H., and Hauser, R. M. The Wisconsin longitudinal study of social and psychological factors in aspirations and achievements In A.C. Kerckhoff (Ed.), *Research in Sociology of Education and Socialization*. Greenwich, CT: JAI Press, 1980, pp. 59–99.

Sewell, W. H., Haller, A. O., and Ohlendorf, G. W. The educational and early occupational status attainment process: replication and revision. *American Sociological Review*, 1970, *35*, 1014–1027.

Sewell, W. H., Haller, A. O., and Portes, A. The educational and early occupational attainment process. *American Sociological Review*, 1969, *34*, 82–92.

Spaeth, J. L. Cognitive complexity: A dimension underlying the socioeconomic achievement process. In W. H. Sewell, R. M. Hauser, and D. L. Featherman (Eds.), *Schooling and Achievement in American Society*. NY: Academic Press, 1976.

Walberg, H. J. Family environment and cognitive development. *Review of Educational Research*, 1976, *46*, 527–551.

Walberg, H. J., and Marjoribanks, K. Differential mental abilities and home environment: A canonical analysis. *Developmental Psychology*, 1973, *9*, 363–368.

Wechsler, D. *The Measurement and Appraisal of Adult Intelligence*. Baltimore, MD: Williams and Wilkins, 1958.

Whelpton, P. K., Campbell, A. A., and Patterson, J. E. *Fertility and Family Planning in the United States*. Princeton, NJ: Princeton University Press, 1966.

14 CHILDREN IN THEIR CONTEXTS: A GOODNESS-OF-FIT MODEL

Richard M. Lerner
Jacqueline V. Lerner

Ideas implicit in one discipline are often unrecognized in another. Thus, it is useful to begin this chapter with an observation that is obvious to sociologists but which, until relatively recently, was not of great concern to developmental psychologists. All humans are invariantly born into a social network, typically a family. The family, too, is embedded in a social system, just as children are in a family with parents and vice versa. The adult's development as a parent, then, as well as the development of his or her spousal relationship, may well be affected by characteristics of the child. Moreover, the social relations that exist within a family are influenced by the broader social context.

For instance, the mores regarding parental behavior (e.g., regarding the appropriateness of maternal employment),the resources available to support the parent role (e.g., availability of quality day care), and the laws and mores pertinent to marital interaction (e.g., regarding divorce), exist in a given historical era and may be expected to affect the parent/spouse, the child, and the parent–child relationship; such influences may thereby affect individual and joint developmental patterns.

With individual development having such potential bidirectional links to a changing social context, two points may be made. First, an exclusively psychological analysis of individual development must be avoided and, instead, models that emphasize the multilevel bases of human functioning *and* the connections among levels must be sought. Second, if the course of human development is responsive to changes at multiple levels of analysis, then the processes of development are more plastic than often previously believed (Brim & Kagan, 1980; R. Lerner, 1984).

An increasing number of developmental psychologists have come to recognize that what happens on any one level of analysis systematically influences what happens on all others (Baltes, Reese, & Lipsitt, 1980; R. Lerner & Busch-Rossnagel, 1981; Nesselroade & von Eye, 1985). As a result, there is a growing theoretical and empirical literature that supports the two points made above (Baltes *et al.*, 1980; Belsky, 1981, 1984; Belsky,

Lerner, & Spanier, 1984; Bronfenbrenner, 1979; J. Lerner, 1983; R. Lerner, 1981, 1982, 1984; R. Lerner & Busch-Rossnagel, 1981; R. Lerner & Spanier, 1978, 1980; Parke & Tinsley, 1982). To a great extent, this literature has been associated with a life span view of human development. Since the life-span perspective provides the developmental framework with which this discussion of children in their contexts is approached, it will be useful to present some of its key ideas. Reciprocal relations between individuals and their social context are emphasized by this perspective. Therefore, after the life-span perspective is presented, a model of individual-social context relations which tries to depict the implications of such relations for child development will be explored.

THE LIFE SPAN VIEW OF HUMAN DEVELOPMENT

The "life span view of human development" (Baltes, 1979; Baltes et al., 1980) has become crystallized as a set of interrelated ideas about the nature of human development and change. In combination, these ideas present a set of implications for theory building, for methodology, and for scientific collaboration across disciplinary boundaries. There are perhaps two key propositions or assumptions of the life-span perspective. These have been labeled *embeddedness* (R. Lerner, Skinner, & Sorell, 1980) and *dynamic interaction* (R. Lerner, 1978, 1979, 1984). From these propositions an interrelated set of implications is derived, and these propositions and implications constitute the key concepts in current life span thinking.

Embeddedness and Dynamic Interactionism

The idea of embeddedness is that the key phenomena of human life exist at multiple levels of being (e.g., the inner-biological, individual-psychological, dyadic, social network, community, societal, cultural, outer physical-ecological, and historical); at any one point in time variables from any and all of these levels may contribute to human functioning. However, it is important to have a perspective about human development that is sensitive to the influences of these multiple levels because the levels do not function in parallel; they are not independent domains. Rather, the variables at one level influence and are influenced by the variables at the other levels. There is a *dynamic interaction* among levels of analysis: As such, each level may be a product and a producer of the functioning and changes at all other levels.

The import of the two key assumptions of the life-span perspective are that, first, individual developmental phenomena occur in the context of the developmental and nondevelopmental phenomena of other levels of analysis. Second, developments and/or changes on one level influence and are influenced by developments and/or changes at these other levels. There are at least three major implications of the ideas of embeddedness and dynamic interactionism.

1. *The Potential for Plasticity.* The idea that changes at one level are reciprocally dependent on changes at other levels suggests that there is always some possibility for altering the status of a variable or process at any or all levels of analysis. However, it must be emphasized that this potential for plasticty is not construed by life-span developmentalists to mean that there are no limits or constraints on change. For instance, by virtue of its structural organization, a system delimits the range of changes it may undergo (Brent, 1984), and such a structural constraint holds for any level of analysis. In addition, the possibility that developmental and nondevelopmental phenomena at one point in life may influence functioning at later points is explicitly recognized by life-span developmentalists in the concept of developmental embeddedness (R. D. Parke, personal communication, December, 1982).

2. *The Potential for Intervention.* This implication derives from the plasticity of developmental processes. Given potential plasticity, it follows that means may be designed to prevent, ameliorate, or enhance undesired or nonvalued developments or behavior.

3. *The Person as a Producer of His/Her Own Development.* A final implication is one that will lead to a presentation of the model of individual-context relations. It has been noted that any level of analysis is an influence on other levels. For individual psychological development, this means that the person may affect the context that affects him or her. By influencing the context, the person provides feedback to himself or herself; in other words, the individual is a producer of his/her own development (R. Lerner, 1982; R. Lerner & Busch-Rossnagel, 1981).

The individual may act as a producer of his/her own development in three ways. First, the person may accomplish this as a consequence of constituting a distinct stimulus to others (e.g., through characteristics of physical and/or behavioral individuality); second, as a consequence of his/her capabilities as a processor of the world (e.g., in regard to cognitive structure and mode of emotional reactivity); and last, as a consequence of his/her behavioral agency (Bakan, 1966; Block, 1973). Indeed, the individual's developing competency to behaviorally shape and/or select his/her contexts is the instance of the most flexible means by which the person may act as a producer of his/her own development.

Conclusions

It is only during its relatively recent history that developmental psychology has focused on embeddedness of children in their families *and* on the bidirectional relations between individual development and contextual change. Moreover, central within this focus is the idea that children possess characteristics of individuality which, in the context of bidirectional relations, may allow them to be agents in their own development. Apparently, however, this key idea remains incompletely assimilated by developmental psychologists. About 15 years ago Bell (1968) published his influential paper on a reinterpretation of the direction of effects in socialization research. However, later Hartup (1978) still found it useful to remind colleagues that socialization is best viewed as a reciprocal process rather than one involving a unidirectional social molding of children by parents. Even more recently, Scarr (1982; Scarr & McCartney, 1983) argued that a child's organismic characteristics, represented by his or her genotype, may be the "driving force" of cognitive, personality, and even social developments.

It is important to emphasize, however, that Scarr (1982; Scarr & McCartney, 1983), as well as other scholars who have argued for the role of the child as an agent in his or her own development (e.g., Thomas & Chess, 1977), does *not* view the characteristics of children that promote their own development as acting in a predetermined or fixed manner. Instead, the *probabilistic* character of such "child effects," and of development in general, is emphasized. This stress occurs because the reciprocal nature of all child effects is taken seriously. The context enveloping a child is composed of, for example, a specific physical ecology and the other individually different and developing people with whom the child interacts (e.g., parents and siblings). This context is as unique and changing as is the child individually distinct. No one can say completely in advance what particular features of the context will exist at a specific time in a given child's life. As a consequence, it is possible to speak only probabilistically of the effects a given child may have on his or her context; of the feedback the child is likely to receive from the context; and of the nature of the child's development that will therefore ensue.

Thus, child effects are not as simple as they may seem at first. Indeed, the probabilism of development represents a formidable challenge for theory and research. To understand how children may influence their own development, more is needed than just a conceptualization of the nature of the individual characteristics or processes involved in such effects. In addition, there is a need to conceptualize and operationalize the features of the context, or of the ecology, wherein significant interactions occur for the child. As Bronfenbrenner (1979) has so eloquently said, however, psychologists are neither readily prone nor typically adequately trained to do this. There is yet one other conceptual task as well. It is to devise some means, some model, by which child effects and contextual features may be integrated. Then, a last and by no means unidimensional task, is to translate all this conceptualization into methodologically sound research.

There is no laboratory within which all the above tasks have been accomplished. However, progress has been made in developing a conceptual model with which such child effects may be empirically studied. Data in support of the model derive from work in several laboratories. Accordingly, this research will be reviewed after the general details of the model are presented; the model has been labeled the "goodness-of-fit model of person-context relations."

THE GOODNESS-OF-FIT MODEL

Both individuals and the world they inhabit are composed of multiple "levels of being" or, more simply, multiple dimensions. These dimensions are thought to be interdependent and developing and/or changing over time. Several essays have tried to describe such person-context complexity, and one such description is presented in Figure 14.1.

It should be emphasized that this figure is only *descriptive* of the relations that theorists (e.g., Belsky, 1984; Bronfenbrenner, 1979; Schneirla, 1957; Tobach & Schneirla, 1968) and researchers (e.g., Baltes, Baltes, & Reinert, 1970; Nesselroade & Baltes, 1974; Thomas & Chess, 1977) have noted are involved in person-context relations. Thus, Figure 14.1 presents a descriptive and not a theoretical model. Indeed, the bidirectional arrows in the figure correspond to relations identified in various portions of the child, adolescent, or adult development empirical literatures.

To illustrate the use of the model, the reader's attention is directed to a construct that relates to the authors' own research and to major portions of this chapter: temperament. The child development literature contains studies examining the relationship, within-the-child, of temperament and other characteristics of individuality, such as personality (Buss & Plomin, 1975) or cognitive status variables (such as "social referencing"; Campos, 1980–81; Feinman & Lewis, 1983). In turn, other studies examine how the child's temperamental individuality influences the parent–(typically the mother–)child relationship (Crockenberg, 1981) and/or the mother's emotional adjustment (Brazelton, Koslowski, & Main, 1974). Such studies provide data constituting "child effects" on their significant others—others which, to developmental psychologists (Belsky et al., 1984), are a component of the child's context, here an interpersonal one. These studies comprise one portion of the bidirectional effects (here of child→parent) discussed in the child development literature (e.g., Bell, 1974; Belsky, 1984; Belsky et al., 1984; R. Lerner & Spanier, 1978; Lewis & Rosenblum, 1974; Scarr & McCartney, 1983).

These child→parent studies stand in contrast to those that examine how parental characteristics—such as temperament (Thomas, Chess, & Birch, 1970), or demands on the child regarding the child's temperament (Thomas, Chess, Sillen, & Mendez, 1974), or cognitive status (e.g., stage of cognitive

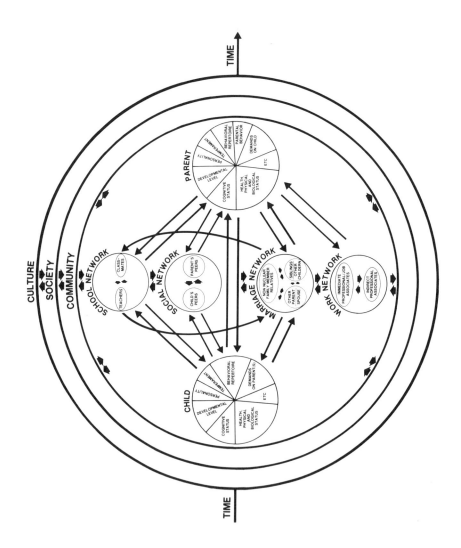

FIGURE 14.1. A dynamic interactional model of child and parent development (from R. Lerner, 1984, p. 144).

development; Sameroff, 1975)—influence the child; such studies are parent →child ones, and provide the other direction of effect to complement child → parent studies. Other studies in the temperament literature examine the influence of the parent's social network on the child's temperament, on the mother's characteristics, or on the parent–child relationship (e.g., Crockenberg, 1981); in turn, some studies examine how children with different temperaments "produce" different responses in their social (e.g., school) network (Palermo, 1982). Still other studies examine how child-temperament ⇄ parent-demand relations vary in relation to their embeddedness in different social classes or communities (Thomas *et al.*, 1974) or in different culture settings (Super & Harkness, 1981).

In summary, several of the interrelations illustrated in the model in Figure 14.1 are found in the extant temperament literature. While relatively few of the studies in this literature assess both directions of relation between one component (or level) of the model and another (cf. Bell, 1974; Lewis & Lee-Painter, 1974), the bidirectionality of relations discussed in this litera-ture (e.g., Bell, 1974; Belsky *et al.*, 1984; Lewis & Rosenblum, 1974; R. Lerner & Spanier, 1978) emerges when studies are integrated within a model like the one presented in Figure 14.1. Finally, by helping integrate extant studies, the model also points to child temperament-social context relations that are uninvestigated but that may be of potential importance.

This use of the model for furthering research points out other features of the model that should be stressed. It probably would not be useful or even possible to do research testing the model as a whole. Instead, this or similar representations (e.g., Belsky, 1984) of person-context relations can guide the selection of individual and ecological variables in one's research, and provide parameters about the generalizability of one's findings. That is, this representation should serve as a reminder that we need to consider whether the results of a given study may be generalized beyond the particular individual and ecological variable studied herein and applied to other community, societal, cultural, and historical contexts.

To illustrate how the model of Figure 14.1 may be used as a guide for the selection of variables from the individual and contextual levels depicted (i.e., the interpersonal and physical features of the settings within which one lives), the authors of this chapter may show how our own research is based on selected components of the model. In Figure 14.2 the "restricted" or "reduced" model used in our research on child temperament ⇄ context relations is shown.

First, the studies conducted by our collaborators and us have focused on how the demands regarding temperament held by a child's parents, teachers, or peers are associated with different levels of adaptation, or adjustment, among children with various repertoires of temperamental individuality (e.g., J. Lerner, 1983; J. Lerner, R. Lerner, & Zabski, 1985; Palermo, 1982; Thomas *et al.*, 1974; Windle *et al.*, 1986).

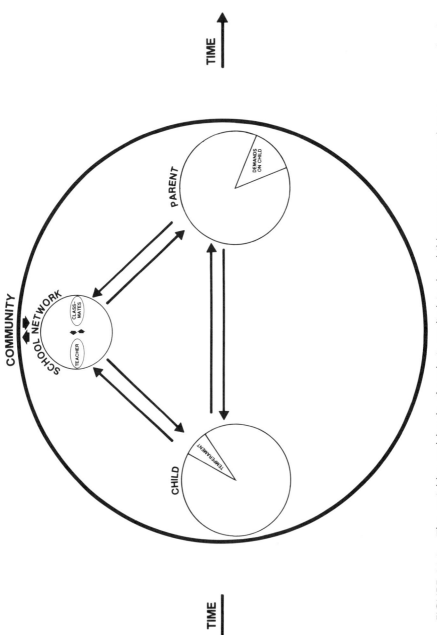

FIGURE 14.2. The variables and levels of analysis studied in the child temperament-social context research of J. Lerner and R. Lerner (1983).

Second, the parent-demands→child-temperament relations and the school-network demands→child-temperament relations examined in these studies have been contrasted with child-temperament→parent-demand relations, or child-temperament→parent-demand versus school-network demands relations; the contrasts have occurred in studies appraising how a child's temperament at one time of measurement may lead at another time of measurement either to changes in parents' demands (Thomas et al., 1974) and/or to differing imports for child adjustment when the child moves from the home to the school context (Korn, 1978; Thomas et al., 1974).

It is important to emphasize a last use of the descriptive model shown in Figure 14.1. When the relations depicted in the figure are used, as in Figure 14.2, for the selection of a reduced or a restructured model to guide research, such use should be theory-guided. That is, as implied above, Figure 14.1 and other such figures show that there needs to be three components of theory-guided research studying person-context relations, and these components are all represented by the selections involved in our temperament research, as illustrated in Figure 14.2. That is, there needs first to be some conceptualization of the nature of the attributes of the person one is interested in studying (i.e., of temperament in our case). Second, there needs to be some conceptualizations of the feature of the person's context one wishes to explore (i.e., of the demands of the parental or of the school contexts, in our case) and a rationale for why this portion of the context is pertinent to the personological attribute being assessed (i.e., in our case, we need a rationale about why contextual demands are relevant to the study of child temperament). Third, and most important, there needs to be some conceptualization of the *relationship* between the individual attribute and the contextual feature.

This third point allows the goodness-of-fit model to be introduced. The person and the context described in Figures 14.1 and 14.2 will be individually distinct as a consequence of the unique combination of genotypic and phenotypic features of the person and of the specific attributes of his or her context. The presence of such individuality is central to understanding the goodness-of-fit model. As a consequence of charac- teristics of physical individuality [for example, in regard to body type or facial attractiveness (Sorell & Nowak, 1981)] and/or of psychological individuality [for instance, in regard to conceptual tempo or temperament (Kagan, 1966; Thomas & Chess, 1977)], children promote differential reactions in their socializing others; these reactions may feed back to children, increase the individuality of their developmental milieu, and provide a basis for their further development. T. C. Schneirla (1957) termed these relations "circular functions." It is through the establishment of such functions in ontogeny that people may be conceived of as producers of their own development (R. Lerner & Busch-Rossnagel, 1981). However, this circular functions idea needs to be extended. In and of itself the notion is mute regarding the specific characteristics of the feedback (for example, its positive or negative valence) a child will receive as a consequence of its individuality. What may provide a basis of the feedback?

Just as a child brings his or her singular characteristics to a particular social setting, there are demands placed on the child by virtue of the physical and/or by the social components (i.e., by the significant others) in the setting [the "context" in our tems (J. Lerner & R. Lerner, 1983)]. It is these demands that provide the functional significance for a given temperament attribute, which, congruent with the demands of a significant other (e.g., a parent), should produce a positive adjustment (adaptation). If that same attribute is incongruent with such demands, a negative adjustment would be expected. To illustrate, consider the case of the child in his or her family context and of the psychosocial and physical climate promoted by the parents. Parents can vary in their cognitive and behavioral attributes (e.g., in regard to their child-rearing attitudes and parenting styles; Baumrind, 1971); parents can vary, too, in the physical features of the home they provide. These parent-based psychosocial and physical characteristics constitute presses for, or demands on, the child for adaptation. Simply, parent characteristics are "translated" or "transduced" into demands on the child.

These demands may take the form of, first, attitude, values, or expectations held by parents (or, in other contexts, by teachers or by peers) regarding the child's physical or behavioral characteristics. Second, demands exist as a consequence of the behavioral attributes of parents (or, again, of teachers or of peers); these people are significant others with whom the child must coordinate, or fit, his or her behavioral attributes for adaptive interactions to exist. Third, the physical characteristics of a setting (such as the noise level of the home, or the presence or absence of access ramps for the motorically handicapped), constitute contextual demands. Such physical presses require the child to possess certain behavioral attributes for the most efficient interaction within the setting to occur.

The child's individuality in differentially meeting these demands provides a basis for the feedback he or she gets from the socializing environment. For example, considering the demand "domain" of attitudes, values, or expectations, teachers and parents may have relatively individual and distinct expectations about behaviors desired of their students and children, respectively. Teachers may want students who show little distractibility, since they would not want attention diverted from a lesson by the activity of children in the classroom. Parents, however, might desire their children to be moderately distractible—for example, when they require their children to move from television watching to the dinner table or to bed. Children whose behavioral individuality was either generally distractible or generally not distractible would thus differentially meet the demands of these two contexts. Problems of adjustment to school demands or to home might thus develop as a consequence of a child's lack of match, or "goodness of fit," in either or both settings.

Similarly, considering the second type of contextual demands that exist—those that arise as a consequence of the behavioral characteristics of others in the setting—problems of fit might occur when a child who is highly irregular in such biological functions as eating, sleep-wake cycles, and toileting behaviors interacts in a family setting composed of highly regular and behaviorally scheduled parents and siblings. In turn, considering the third type of contextual demands that exist—those that arise as a consequence of the physical characteristics of a setting—a child who has a low threshold for response and who is also highly distractible might find it problematic to perform efficiently in a setting with high noise levels: for instance, in a crowded home, or in a schoolroom situated near the street in a busy urban area; such a child might not perform well on tasks such as studying or taking an examination that necessitate concentration and/or attention.

Thomas and Chess (1977, 1980, 1981) and we [J. Lerner, 1983; J. Lerner & R. Lerner, 1983) have argued that adaptive psychological and social functioning do not derive directly from either the nature of the person's characteristics of individuality per se or the nature of the demands of the contexts within which the person functions. Rather, if a person's characteristics of individuality fit or exceed the demands of a particular setting, adaptive outcomes (i.e., those associated with good personal adjustment and positive social interaction) in that setting will accrue. Those people whose characteristics match most of the settings within which they exist should receive supportive or positive feedback and should show evidence of the most adaptive (i.e., adjusted, positive) behavioral functioning. In turn, of course, mismatched people whose characteristics are incongruent with (that is, fell short of) the demands of one or most settings should show personally maladjusted and/or negative social functioning.

The goodness-of-fit concept describes the status of the relationship between a child and his or her setting as it exists at one point in time. However, in the concern with "circular functions" between children and their contexts, it is clear that fit established at one time will have implications for the future history of feedback and developmental outcomes. As such, to appraise the developmental import of goodness of fit, in effect, a longitudinal series of "snapshots" of the person-context relation must be taken. Changes in what is seen in the "snapshot" can be understood as a consequence of whether the feedback, derived as a consequence of the fit at one point in time, leads to changes in the person, the setting, or both.

This sequence of bidirectional relations can best be appraised by observations over time. Repeated measures of both child and context characteristics are required in order to describe the child's effects on the context, the context's feedback to the child, the child's further development, and so forth. Moreover, because children exist in more than one context, and because behavior in one context affects behavior in others, goodness of fit should be appraised in several contexts.

To date there have been no tests of the goodness-of-fit model that fulfill *all* these requirements. Previous research bearing on the use of this model provides only incomplete support because it has suffered from several limitations. For instance, most research has focused on cross-sectional patterns of covariation, not on repeated observations. When longitudinal assessments have been made, problems of either retesting effects and/or attrition have occurred. Second, such research has failed to include assessments of both child characteristics and contextual demands, thus leaving the "goodness of fit" between a child and his or her context to be inferred indirectly. Third, processes linking child and context typically have not been assessed. Fourth, much research has assessed children in only one context. Thus, as was illustrated by the above discussion on the features and uses of the descriptive model presented in Figure 14.1, rather than finding bidirectional relations appraised in one single investigation, bidirectional relations between child temperament and context have to be constituted largely on the basis of unidirectional relations (child→context ones *or* context→child ones) assessed in several independent studies.

Some of these limitations apply to the authors' own research; most important is that, to date, none of the research has provided *longitudinal* assessments of: characteristics of the person; demands pertinent to these characteristics placed by parents on him or her; and the precise reactions evoked in significant others when a child fits or does not fit with demands. Nevertheless, it is believed that the weight of the evidence, derived from both the studies in other laboratories as well as in our own, lends support to the goodness-of-fit model. Summarized below, then, are the major findings of this research.

TESTS OF THE GOODNESS-OF-FIT MODEL

Because temperament has been identified (Thomas & Chess, 1977) as a key dimension of behavioral individuality in infancy and throughout childhood, tests of the goodness-of-fit model within developmental psychology have typically focused on this construct. By temperament we mean only behavioral style—that is, how a child does whatever it does (Thomas & Chess, 1977). For example, because all children engage in eating, sleeping, and toileting behaviors, the absence or presence of such contents of the behavior repertoire would not differentiate among them. But whether these behaviors occur with regularity (i.e., rhythmically), or with a lot of or a little intensity might serve to differentiate among children.

Much of the research literature supporting the use of the goodness-of-fit model is derived either directly from the Thomas and Chess New York Longitudinal Study (NYLS) or associated with independent research that has adopted their conceptualization of temperament. The contribution of the NYLS data set is considered first.

The NYLS

Within the NYLS data set, information relevant to the goodness-of-fit model exists as a consequence of the multiple samples present in the project. First, the NYLS core sample is composed of 133 white, middle-class children of professional parents. In addition, a sample of 98 New York City Puerto Rican children of working-class parents has been followed for about 14 years. Each sample subject was studied from at least the first month of life onward. Although the distribution of temperamental attributes in the two samples was not different, the import of the attributes for psychosocial adjustment was quite disparate. Two examples may suffice to illustrate this distinction.

First to be considered is the impact of low regularity or rhythmicity of behavior, particularly in regard to sleep–wake cycles. The Puerto Rican parents studied by Thomas and Chess (1977; Thomas, Chess, Sillen & Mendez, 1974) were very permissive. No demands in regard to rhythmicity of sleep were placed on the infant or child. Indeed, the parents allowed the child to go to sleep any time the child desired, and permitted the child to awaken any time as well. The parents molded their schedule around the children. Because parents were so accommodating, there were no problems of fit associated with an arrhythmic infant or child. Indeed, neither within the infancy period nor throughout the first 5 years of life did arrhythmicity predict adjustment problems. In this sample arrhythmicity remained contin-uous and independent of adaptive implications for the child (Korn, 1978; Thomas et al., 1974).

In white, middle-class families, however, strong demands for rhythmic sleep patterns were maintained. Thus, an arrhythmic child did not fit with parental demands, and consistent with the goodness-of-fit model, ar-rhythmicity was a major predictor of problem behaviors both within the infancy years and across time through the first 5 years of life (Korn, 1978; Thomas et al., 1974).

It should be emphasized that there are at least two ways of viewing this finding. First, consistent with the idea that children influence their parents, it may be noted that sleep arrhythmicity in their children resulted in problems in the parents [e.g., reports of stress, anxiety, anger (Chess & Thomas, 1984; Thomas et al., 1974)]. Such an effect of child temperament on the parent's own level of adaptation has been reported in other data sets wherein, for instance, infants who had high thresholds for responsiveness to social stimulation and thus were not soothed easily by their mothers evoked intense distress reactions in their mothers and a virtual cessation of maternal care-giving behaviors (Brazelton et al., 1974). Therefore, it is possible that the presence of such child effects in the NYLS sample could have altered previous parenting styles in a way that constituted feedback to the child that was associated with the development of problem behaviors in him/her.

In turn, a second interpretation of this finding arises from the fact that problem behaviors in the children were identified initially on the basis of parental report. It may be that irrespective of any problem behavior evoked in the parent by the child and/or of any altered parent–child interactions that thereby ensued, one effect of the child on the parent was to increase the probability of the parent labeling the child's temperamental style as problematic and reporting it to the NYLS staff psychiatrist. Unfortunately, the current state of analysis of the NYLS data does not allow us to discriminate between these obviously nonmutually exclusive possibilities.

However, the data in the NYLS do allow us to indicate that the parents in the middle-class sample took steps to change their arrhythmic children's sleep patterns; and as most of these arrhythmic children were also adaptable, low rhythmicity tended to be discontinuous for most children. That the parents behaved to modify their child's arrhythmicity is also an instance of a child effect on its psychosocial context. That is, the child "produced" in his/her parents alterations in parental care-giving behaviors regarding sleep. That these "child effects" on the parental context fed back to the child and influenced his/her further development is consistent with the finding above that sleep arrhythmicity was discontinuous among these children.

Thus, in the middle-class sample early infant arrhythmicity tended to be a problem during this time of life but proved to be neither continuous nor predictive of later problems of adjustment. In turn, in the Puerto Rican sample, infant arrhythmicity was not a problem during this time of life but was continuous and—because in this context it was not involved in poor fit—was not associated with adjustment problems in the child in the first 5 years of life. (Of course, this is not to say that the parents in the Puerto Rican families were not affected by their children's sleep arrhythmicity; as was the case with the parents in the middle-class families, it may be that the Puerto Rican parents had problems of fatigue and/or suffered marital or work-related problems due to irregular sleep patterns produced in them as a consequence of their child's sleep arrhythmicity; however, the current nature of data analysis in the NYLS does not allow an investigation of this possible "child effect" on the Puerto Rican parents.)

However, the data do underscore the importance of considering fit with the demands of the psychosocial context of development by indicating that arrhythmicity did begin to predict adjustment problems for the Puerto Rican children when they entered the school stystem. Their lack of a regular sleep pattern interfered with their obtaining sufficient sleep to perform well in school and, in addition, often caused them to be late to school (Korn, 1978; Thomas *et al.*, 1974). Thus, before age 5 only one Puerto Rican child presented a clinical problem diagnosed as a sleep disorder. However, almost 50% of the Puerto Rican children who developed clinically identifiable problems between ages 5 and 9 were diagnosed as having sleep problems.

Another example may be given illustrating how the differential demands existing between the two family contexts provide different presses for adaptation. This example pertains to differences in the demands of the physical contexts of the families.

As noted by Thomas *et al.* (1974), as well as by Korn (1978), overall there was a very low incidence of behavior problems in the Puerto Rican sample children in their first 5 years of life, especially when compared to the corresponding incidence among the core sample children. However, if a problem was presented at this time among the Puerto Rican sample it was most likely to be a problem of motor activity. In fact, across the first 9 years of their lives, of those Puerto Rican children who developed clinical problems, 53% were diagnosed as exhibiting problematic motor activity. Parents complained of excessive and uncontrollable motor activity in such cases. However, in the core sample's clinical group only one child (a child with brain damage) was characterized in this way. It may be noted here that the Puerto Rican parents' reports of "excessive and uncontrollable" activity in their children does constitute, in this group, an example of a child effect on the parents. That is, a major value of the Puerto Rican parents in the NYLS was child "obedience" to authority (Korn, 1978). The type of motor activity shown by the highly active children of these parents evoked considerable distress in them, given their perception that their children's behavior was inconsistent with what would be expected of obedient children (Korn, 1978).

Of course, if the middle-class parents had seen their children's behavior as excessive and uncontrollable, it may be that—irrespective of any major salience placed on the value of child obedience—problems would have been evoked in the middle-class parents, and feedback to the child, derived from such evocation, would have ensued. Thus, an issue remains as to why the same (high) activity level should evoke one set of appraisals among the Puerto Rican parents but another set among the middle-class parents (i.e., in the latter group no interpretation of "excessive and uncontrollable" behavior was evoked). Similarly, it may be asked why high activity level is highly associated with problem behavior in the Puerto Rican children and not in the middle-class children. The key information needed to address these issues may be related to the physical features of the respective groups' homes.

In the Puerto Rican sample the families usually had several children and lived in small apartments. Even average motor activity tended to impinge on others in the setting. Moreover, and as an illustration of the embeddedness of the child-temperament–home-context relation in the broader community context (see Figures 14.1 and 14.2 above), it may be noted that even in the case of the children with high activity levels, the Puerto Rican parents were reluctant to let their children out of the apartment because of the actual dangers of playing on the streets of East Harlem. In the core sample, however, the parents had the financial resources to provide large apartments or houses for their families. There were typically suitable play areas for the children both inside and outside the home. As a consequence, the presence of high activity levels in the homes of the core sample did not cause the problems for interaction that they did in the Puerto Rican group. Thus, as Thomas et al. (1968, 1974) emphasize, the mismatch between temperamental attribute and physical environmental demand accounted for the group difference in the import of high activity level for the development of behavioral problems in the children.

In sum, data from the NYLS are not fully consonant with the methodology required for a direct and complete test of the goodness-of-fit model. For example, measures of temperament were not directly related to measures of the context. However, in spite of such limitations, the NYLS data set provides results compatible with the goodness-of-fit model. Data independent of the NYLS also lend some support.

The Research of Super and Harkness

Support both for the generalizability of the temperamental attributes studied by Thomas and Chess (1977, 1980, 1981) and for the goodness-of-fit model is provided in a cross-cultural study by Super and Harkness (1981), who studied infants in a rural farming community in Kenya named Kokwet and infants in suburban families living in the metropolitan Boston area.

They report that the dimensions studied in the NYLS "are not, by and large" (p. 79) artifacts of the American setting. In both samples the dimensions of mood, adaptability, intensity of reaction, and rhythmicity, or regularity, of biological functions (eating, sleeping, elimination) were identified in interview as well as naturalistic observational data. However, because of cultural differences between the two settings, the imports of these temperamental attributes were quite different; and as Super and Harkness report, children with the same temperament attribute scores had different fits and different developmental outcomes as a consequence of the different contextual demands.

In many homes in their Boston sample, physical space was altered in anticipation of the arrival of the baby (e.g., a room was decorated for the infant). Typically the mother made arrangements to change her schedule once the baby arrived. However, in none of these families was there more than one person generally at home during most of the day (i.e., typically either the mother or a baby-sitter was present). This one-to-one ratio of care-giver to infant presents a limitation on the moment-to-moment flexibility of the care giver; he or she cannot engage in noncare-giving activities when the infant makes unanticipated demands.

The people of Kokwet (Kipsigis) create a much different niche for an infant. In the first months of life the baby is in the exclusive care of the mother and is rarely separated from physical contact with her. Such constant and close physical contact is not at all characteristic of the mother–infant relationship in the Boston sample. Moreover, in Kokwet the mother is rarely alone with the infant. During the day an average of five additional people are in the house.

Some of the impact of these cultural differences may be seen by considering the dimensions of rhythmicity and adaptability. In the Boston sample the infant's activities are often highly temporally scheduled in order to meet the needs of both the mother and infant. In Kokwet, however, the baby spends much of his or her waking day being held or sitting on the lap of the mother while she is pursuing her duties. As noted, if the mother needs a break or has to do a task where the infant cannot be carried, the infant is attended to by another nearby care giver. Within this situation the infant is free to sleep at will and nurse at the mother's breast virtually at will (at most the mother is only a short walk away).

Thus, an infant who does not show rhythmicity of sleeping and eating would not have a problem of fitting the cultural demands imposed by the Kokwet setting and would not be likely to evoke negative reactions in the mother as a consequence of this feature of its temperament; that is, even mothers who were themselves not particularly adaptable could adjust easily to the infant's behavior of the moment through using the "support network" (the other care givers present in the context, in this case) at hand as a consequence of the cultural system. However, an infant in the Boston setting who had the same low level of rhythmicity would not fit well with the demands imposed on him or her. Moreover, if this infant was low in adaptability the problems related to fit—for example, the schedule the mother tried to impose—would be enhanced, and the potential problems for adequate development would be increased. Such problems would likely be enhanced if such an infant were coupled with a mother low in adaptability, given her lack of immediate social support. In turn, an infant in Kokwet who had a low adaptability score would not have a poor fit because there is no schedule imposed on him or her to which adaptation is required, and, as noted, his/her mother's level of adaptability is not the issue it may be within the Boston setting.

Super and Harkness (1981) point out that there are several developmental consequences of these cultural differences in the meaning of temperament.

For example, although it starts out similarly, by 4 months of age the sleep-wake cycle of Boston and Kokwet infants is quite different, with the average Boston infant sleeping for 8 hours a night and the average Kokwet infant continuing to wake briefly and nurse. In addition, maternal impressions of the infant are different in each setting. The Kokwet mothers are not concerned with characteristics like negative mood, low rhythmicity, and low adaptability, and do not view them as indicative of long-term problems. However, the Boston mothers in the Super and Harkness sample have precisely the opposite evaluation of these temperamental attitudes (e.g., they view these temperament characteristics as undesirable and as presenting immediate and potentially long-term problems). Thus as in the NYLS data set, the same temperamental characteristic has a different impact on others as a consequence of its embeddedness in a different cultural context.

There is evidence for the use of the goodness-of-fit model in contexts other than the home and in regard to relationships other than that of parent–child. A key context of childhood and adolescence is the school, and focal relationships in such a setting are those between children and teachers and between children and peers. There is some direct, albeit cross-sectional, evidence that children who show differential matches with the demands of their school context have different individual and interpersonal functioning. This support is derived from a series of studies in the Lerners' laboratory.

Research in Our Laboratory

Although most current temperament research invovles an emphasis on infants or young children, our research has included a focus on the late childhood-to-late adolescent age range. As noted, the concern with temperamental individuality derives from a theoretical interest in person-context relations, and this period of life contains a much wider and richer array of contexts within which people function than is the case in infancy. This is especially true considering that from childhood through late adolescence new contexts, such as the workplace, become salient; moreover, the person plays an increasingly more active role in selecting his or her settings and associates.

Procedures in Testing the Model. Our research, to date, has followed a general methodological strategy. First, in order to measure temperament, one of two instruments has been used: the Dimensions of Temperament Survey, or the DOTS; and the Revised Dimensions of Temperament Survey, or the DOTS-R. The DOTS measures five temperament attributes (attention span-persistence versus distractibility; adaptability-approach versus withdrawal; activity level; rhythmicity; and reactivity). The DOTS-R measures seven temperament attributes: activity level (general); activity level (sleep); rhythmicity; attention span-distractibility; approach-withdrawal; mood; and flexibility-rigidity.

In accordance with the goodness-of-fit model, the second measurement task is to assess a feature of the child's context relevant to his or her temperament. As explained earlier, there are at least three contextual presses, or demands, that may be relevant to a child's temperament. These are: expectational demands about temperament held by significant others, demands imposed by the temperaments of significant others, and the demands on behavior style imposed by the physical ecology. To date, the focus has been mostly on the expectational type of demands, although the results of one study wherein the authors assessed the demands imposed by the temperament of a significant other will be discussed.

In using the DOTS to assess the expectational demands about temperament held by a child's significant others, items have been recast to relate to the preferences held by either parents, teachers, or peers. For example, a DOTS item pertinent to persistence is: "I stay with an activity for a long time." To assess a parent's expectational demands for this item, it is recast to read, "I want my child to stay with an activity for a long time."

With the DOTS-R a somewhat different, more explicitly theory-guided approach to measuring expectational demands has been taken.Thomas and Chess (1977), as part of their NYLS, conducted extensive interviews with parents. If a child had particular scores on a specific set of five of the nine temperament attributes they assessed in the NYLS, it was difficult for the parent to have positive interactions with the child. The five attributes comprising the "difficult-to-interact-with" child are low rhythmicity, slow adaptability, high intensity, negative mood, and withdrawal. In addition, a short attention span and high level of distractibility also present difficulty in interaction, but primarily in the school for teachers (J. Lerner, R. Lerner, & Zabski, 1985).

The point here is that the levels of scores, or the "signs" of the difficult child, present problems only because they constitute a basis of poor interaction between the child and a significant other in his or her context. And the attribute provides a basis for poor interaction because it is not something the significant other wants or expects from the child. In other words, temperamental difficulty resides not in the child per se, not in a particular level of a particular attribute being possessed. Rather, difficulty derives from the failure of an attribute to facilitate positive interaction between a child and the significant others comprising his/her context. It is the context, then, that defines what is difficult.

Super and Harkness (1982) have made this point quite clear. They stress that people in different contexts may have distinct ideas about how difficult a given temperamental attribute may be. They term the belief system of people of a particular context an *ethnotheory*, and believe that in different contexts there exist different ethnotheories of temperamental difficulty.

Following the lead of Super and Harkness, we have used the DOTS-R items to formulate a means to assess the ethnotheory of temperamental difficulty held by the parents, the teachers, and the peers of the children being studied. For instance, the DOTS-R item, "My child gets sleepy at different times every night," is rated by a parent in respect to how difficult it would be for the parent to interact with his or her child *if* the child always showed the behavior described in the item. It should be reiterated, however, that unlike the NYLS and the Super and Harkness (1981) research, the data being presented does not include information about the reactions evoked in significant others when a child fits or does not fit with the others' demands.

While such direct measurement will need to be included in future tests of the model, to date the nature of such "child effects" on the basis of the ethnotheory score has been inferred, and these inferences have been used to predict outcomes in the child (that is, to predict the presumed result of feedback to the child). These procedures constitute the third and last piece of the general methodology—putting temperament scores and demands together. In effect, the goodness-of-fit model is used to formulate the inference that the specific demands of the significant others comprising a child's context (e.g., teachers in school, parents at home) allow one to predict or explain any relation between temperament and psychosocial functioning. Thus, the general hypothesis guiding the integration of child temperament scores and demand scores from significant others is that a given temperament score will be positively related to adaptive psychosocial functioning when, on the basis of the demand score, it promotes adaptive child-context interactions; in turn, temperament will be negatively related to adaptive psychosocial functioning when it is incongruent with the demands of the context.

In sum, using this three-pronged approach to research, we have begun to test the goodness-of-fit model of person-context relations. As this research has progressed, increasing evidence in support of the model has been obtained. Some of this support will be presented below.

Results of the Tests of the Model. In an initial study, using an early version of the DOTS, J. Lerner (1983) measured eighth graders' temperaments and the demands for behavioral style in the classroom maintained by each subject's classroom teacher and peer group. Those subjects whose temperaments best matched each set of demands had more favorable teacher ratings, better grades, and more positive peer relations and fewer negative peer relations than did subjects whose temperaments were less well matched with either teacher and/or peer demands. Moreover, fit in one context predicted fit in the other context. As such, temperamental fit with the teacher-predicted not only the teacher-related criterion measures, but also the criterion measures derived from the peer context. Similarly, fit with peer demands predicted both peer-related and teacher-related criterion measures.

Further support for the use of the model is derived from the already noted study by J. Lerner et al. (1985), which provides evidence that temperament-context fit also covaries with actual academic abilities. The J. Lerner (1983) study demonstrated that good temperament-expectational demands fit related to favorable peer and teacher ratings and to teacher assigned grades, but no relation between actual academic abilities and fit was assessed. Such a relation was found by J. Lerner et al. (1985). That is, for several temperament dimensions measured on the DOTS, fourth grade students whose self-rated temperament best fit teacher demands not only had better teacher ratings of ability and adjustment but also scored better on two standardized achievement tests—the Stanford Achievement Test for Reading and the Comprehensive Test of Basic Skills—than did children whose fit was poorer.

In another study, Palermo (1982) used the DOTS to assess fifth graders' ratings of their own temperaments, the fifth graders' mothers' ratings of their children's temperaments, and the demands for behavioral style held by the teachers and mothers of the fifth graders. Outcome measures included teacher ratings of classroom ability and adjustment, classroom peers' sociometric appraisals of each subject's positive and negative peer relations, and mother's reports of problem behaviors shown at home. Again, better fit children had more favorable scores on teacher-, peer-, and mother-derived outcome measures than did less well fit children. Most interestingly, the best predictors were fit scores computed between mother-rated temperament and teacher demands. In other words, Palermo's (1982) data illustrate that temperament is not a within-the-person phenomenon; scores for goodness of fit between temperament rated by one source (the mother) and demands derived from another independent source (the teacher) not only were the best predictors of adaptation within the mother- and teacher-rated contexts but also within a third, independent (peer) context.

After the completion of the J. Lerner (1983), the J. Lerner et al. (1985), and the Palermo (1982) studies the work on the measurement of temperament and expectational demands turned from the use of the DOTS to the use of the DOTS-R and to assessment of ethnotheory. In one project reported to date (R. Lerner et al., 1986; Windle et al., 1986), temperament and its fit with contextual demands was studied among early and late adolescents. Among the former group the relations between temperament and dimensions of perceived competence, as measured by Harter's (1982) Perceived Competence Scale, could be accounted for by the goodness-of-fit model. Harter's scale measures four components of perceived competence—cognitive, social, physical, and general self-worth. Use of this scale was predicated on the view that children who have positive interactions with significant others should come to perceive themselves as competent actors, at least in regard to those features of self-evaluation likely to be influenced by feedback from others. The cognitive, social, and self-worth components are particularly relevant in this regard. No predictions were made regarding the physical component; this factor was included for exploratory purposes.

It was expected that temperament scores that diverged *most* from the teachers' ethnotheory scores would be associated with high—that is, positive—scores on these three components of perceived competence. The teachers reported that high general activity level, high sleep activity level, low rhythmicity, low (i.e., negative) mood, low attention span, low flexibility, and low approach (or conversely high withdrawal) would present difficulties for interaction. Thus, positive correlations were expected between cognitive, social, and general perceived competence, on the one hand, and rhythmicity, flexibility, mood, attention span, and approach, on the other. In turn, negative correlations between these competence domains and the two activity attributes were expected. For 14 of the 21 relationships for which predictions were made (that is, for 67%) significant correlations were found, and all of these were in the expected direction. Moreover, the multiple correlations between temperament and each of the three relevant competence domains are significant.

These results were essentially cross-validated within the late-adolescent sample. Here the ethnotheories of both parents (mostly mothers) and peers (i.e., other college students) were studied. It was found that, for both groups, high general and sleep activity level and low rhythmicity, flexibility, approach, and attention span, and low (i.e., negative) mood constitute temperamental levels that are rated to make for difficulty in interaction. As such, it was predicted that high scores on the temperament attributes of rhythmicity, mood, flexibility, attention span, and approach would vary positively with favorable scores on the cognitive, social, and general components of the Perceived Competence Scale and, in addition, would vary negatively with high scores on the Center for Epidemiologic Studies-Depression Scale, the CES-D scale. In turn, low scores on general and sleep activity level were expected to vary negatively with high scores on the three competence components and positively with CES-D scores. It should be noted that the CES-D was used by Windle et al. because of the findings that failure to meet the demands of one's context (i.e., failure to be interactively competent) may be associated with feelings of depression (Seligman, 1975). For 17 of the 28 relationships for which predictions were made (that is, for 61%), significant correlations were found. All were in the expected direction. Finally, it was again found that the multiple correlations between temperament and each of the three relevant competence domains were significant.

Thus, as was found with early adolescents, the assessment of late adolescents indicates that knowledge of the fit between a young person's temperament and the expectational demands of his or her context aids substantially in understanding the relationship between temperament and adaptive psychosocial functioning.

Finally, in regard to a last study completed to date in our laboratory, Windle and R. Lerner (1984) studied 153 young adult dating dyads; i.e., college students engaged in exclusive dating relationships. Each dyad

member's temperament and demands/expectations for partner's temperament were measured. Within-dyad temperament-temperament and
demand-demand correlations for each of five temperament attributes, or
corresponding demands, were calculated. These correlations were compared to those that existed within 98 randomly formed dyads, i.e., dyads
formed by randomly pairing 98 nondating college males with 98 nondating
college females. Within the dating dyads, three of five temperament-
temperament correlations (for adaptability, rhythmicity, and reactivity) and
five of five demand-demand correlations were significant. In the "random
dyads" only one of five temperament-temperament correlations were
significant. Moreover, the magnitude of six of the eight significant correlations in the dating dyads was significantly greater than the corresponding
correlation in the "random dyads." Thus, in this study, temperament-
temperament fit and demand-demand fit seem to mark the relation between
a person and a significant other in his/her social context. Such congruence
appears to be absent among late adolescents not engaged in exclusive
dating or intimate relationships—a type of social relationship believed to be
central to adequate psychosocial functioning during the late adolescent
portion of life. This observation leads to some final conclusions.

CONCLUSIONS

As emphasized above, none of the studies done to date in any laboratory
fulfill all the methodological requirements. Research should be extended to
include a direct assessment of the behavioral exchanges that occur when fit
is or is not achieved; in this way a richer understanding may be gained of the
processes that lead to positive or negative psychosocial outcomes. Specifically, more longitudinal information is needed about: the precise reactions
evoked in parents (or other care givers) as a consequence of a child's fitting
or not fitting parental demands; the feedback given to the child as a
consequence of such child effects on their care givers; and the further child
developments influenced by such feedback.

Nevertheless, despite these lacunae, the results of the studies summarized
allow the inference that at a given point in development neither children's
nor adolescents' attributes per se, nor the demands of their settings per se,
are the key predictors of their adaptive functioning. Instead, the *relationship*
between the child and his or her context seems most important in home,
peer, and school settings. This relationship is invariably complex and, as has
been illustrated, requires that the study of child effects involves three
components: first, an attribute of child individuality must be measured;
second, a feature of the context theoretically relevant to that domain of child
individuality must be appraised; and third, a model must be formulated that
specifies the nature and implications of the relationship between child and

context. We believe the findings reviewed here suggest that the goodness-of-fit model is a useful one to employ in such a study of child effects, and that it is deserving of further testing and refinement.

SUMMARY

Using ideas associated with a life-span view of human development, we present a goodness-of-fit model of the relationships between the developing characteristics of children and presses or demands for adaptation present in their contexts. Within this model characteristics of physical or behavioral individuality promote differential reactions in socializing others; these reactions feed back to children and provide a basis for their further development. The nature of the feedback (e.g., its positive or negative valence) is determined by whether the child's characteristics match or mismatch the attitudes, values, or expectations of significant others; the behaviors of significant others; or physical features of the setting. Good fits (or matches) are predicted to be associated with adaptive development; poor fits are expected to be associated with maladaptive development. The use of this model for understanding the nature and import of a child's relations to his/her context is evaluated by review of research pertinent to the study of characteristics of temperamental or behavioral style individuality. Although several methodological limitations of this research are noted, results are sufficiently positive to encourage further tests of the model.

ACKNOWLEGMENTS

The authors were supported in part by grants from the John D. and Catherine T. MacArthur Foundation and from the William T. Grant Foundation. Jay Belsky is thanked for his contributions to a previous draft of this manuscript.

REFERENCES

Bakan, D. The Duality of Human Existence. Chicago, IL; Rand McNally, 1966.
Baltes, P. B. Life-span developmental psychology: Some converging observations on history and theory. In P. B. Baltes and O. G. Brim, Jr. (Eds.), Life-Span Development and Behavior, Vol. 2. NY: Academic Press, 1979.
Baltes, P. B., Reese, H. W., and Lipsitt, L. P. Life-span developmental psychology. Annual Review of Psychology, 1980, 31, 65–110.
Baltes, P. B., Baltes, M. M., and Reinert, G. The relationship between time of measurement and age in cognitive development of children: An application of cross-sectional sequences. Human Development, 1970, 13, 285–268.

Baumrind, D. Current patterns of parental authority. *Developmental Psychology Monographs*, 1971, *4* (1, Pt. 2).

Bell, R. Q. A reinterpretation of the direction of effects in studies of socialization. *Psychological Review*, 1968, *75*, 81–95.

Bell, R. Q. Contributions of human infants to caregiving and social interaction. In M. Lewis and L. A. Rosenblum (Eds.), *The Effect of the Infant on Its Caregiver*. NY: Wiley, 1974.

Belsky, J. Early human experience: A family perspective. *Developmental Psychology*, 1981, *17*, 3–23.

Belsky, J. The determinants of parenting: A process model. *Child Development*, 1984, *55*, 83–96.

Belsky, J., Lerner, R., and Spanier, G. *The Child in the Family*. Reading, MA: Addison-Wellesey, 1984.

Block, J. H. Conceptions of sex roles: Some cross-cultural and longitudinal perspectives. *American Psychologist*, 1973, *82*, 512–526.

Brazelton, T. B., Koslowski, B., and Main, M. The origins of reciprocity in mother-infant interaction. In M. Lewis and L. A. Rosenblum (Eds.), *The Effect of the Infant on Its Caregiver*. NY: Wiley, 1974.

Brent, S. B. *Psychological and Social Structure: Their Organization, Activity, and Development*. Hillsdale, NJ: Erlbaum, 1984.

Brim, O. G., Jr., and Kagan, J. Constancy and change: A view of the issues. In O. G. Brim, Jr., and J. Kagan (Eds.), *Constancy and Change in Human Development*. Cambridge, MA: Harvard University Press, 1980.

Bronfenbrenner, U. Toward an experimental ecology of human development. *American Psychologist*, 1977, *32*, 513–531.

Bronfenbrenner, U. *The Ecology of Human Development*. Cambridge, MA: Harvard University Press, 1979.

Buss, A., and Plomin, R. *A Temperamental Theory of Personality Development*. New York: Wiley-Interscience, 1975.

Campos, J. J. Human emotions: Their new importance and their role in social referencing. *Annual Report Research and Clinical Center for Child Development*. Sapporo, Japan: Faculty of Education, Hokkaido University, 1980–1981.

Chess, S., and Thomas, A. *The Origins and Evolution of Behavior Disorders: From Infancy to Early Adult Life*. NY: Brunner/Mazel, 1984.

Crockenberg, S. B. Infant irritability, mother responsiveness, and social support influences on the security of infant-mother attachment. *Child Development*, 1981, *52*, 857–865.

Feinman, S., and Lewis, M. Social referencing at ten months: A second-order effect on infants' responses to strangers. *Child Development*, 1983, *54*, 878–887.

Harter, S. The perceived competence scale for children. *Child Development*, 1982, *53*, 87–97.

Hartup, W. W. Perspectives on child and family interaction: Past, present, and future. In R. M. Lerner and G. B. Spanier (Eds.), *Child Influences on Marital and Family Interaction: A Life-Span Perspective*. NY: Academic Press, 1978.

Kagan, J. Reflection-impulsivity: The generality and dynamics of conceptual tempo. *Journal of Abnormal Psychology*, 1966, *71*, 17–24.

Korn, S. *Temperament, vulnerability, and behavior*. Paper presented at the Louisville Temperament Conference, Louisville, KY, September, 1978.

Lerner, J. V. The role of temperament in psychosocial adaptation in early adolescents: A test of "goodness of fit" model. *Journal of Genetic Psychology*, 1983, *143*, 149–157.

Lerner, J. V., and Lerner, R. M. Temperament and adaptation across life: Theoretical and empirical issues. In P. B. Baltes and O. G. Brim, Jr. (Eds.), *Life-Span Development and Behavior*, Vol. 5. NY: Academic Press, 1983, pp. 197–231.

Lerner, J. V., Lerner, R. M., and Zabski, S. Temperament and elementary school children's actual and rated academic performance: A test of a "goodness of fit" model. *Journal of Child Psychology and Psychiatry*, 1985, *26*, 125–136.

Lerner, R. M. Nature, nurture, and dynamic interactionism. *Human Development* 1978, *21*, 1–20.

Lerner, R. M. A dynamic interactional concept of individual and social relationship development. In R. L. Burgess and T. L. Huston (Eds.), *Social Exchange in Developing Relationships*. NY: Academic Press, 1979.

Lerner, R. M. Adolescent development: Scientific study in the 1980s. *Youth and Society*, 1981, *12*, 251–275.

Lerner, R. M. Children and adolescents as producers of their own development. *Developmental Review*, 1982, *2*, 342–370.

Lerner, R. M. *On the Nature of Human Plasticity*. NY: Cambridge University Press, 1984.

Lerner, R. M., and Busch-Rossnagel, N. Individuals as producers of their development: Conceptual and empirical bases. In R. M. Lerner and N. A. Busch-Rossnagel (Eds.), *Individuals as Producers of Their Development: A Life-Span Perspective*. NY: Academic Press, 1981.

Lerner, R. M., and Spanier, G. B. A dynamic interactional view of child and family development. In R. M. Lerner & G. B. Spanier (Eds.), *Child Influences on Marital and Family Interaction: A Life-Span Perspective*. NY: Academic Press, 1978.

Lerner, R. M., and Spanier, G. B. *Adolescent Development: A Life-Span Perspective*. NY: McGraw-Hill, 1980.

Lerner, R. M., Skinner, E. A., and Sorell, G. T. Methodological implications of contextual/dialectical theories of development. *Human Development*, 1980, *23*, 225–235.

Lerner, R. M., Lerner, J. V., Windle, M., Hooker, K., Lenerz, K., and East, P. L. Children and adolescents in their contexts: Tests of a goodness of fit model. In R. Plomin and J. Dunn (Eds.), *The Study of Temperament: Changes, Continuities, and Challenges*. Hillsdale, NJ: Erlbaum, 1986.

Lewis, M. and Lee-Painter, S. An interactional approach to the mother-infant dyad. In M. Lewis and L. A. Rosenblum (Eds.), *The Effect of the Infant on Its Caregiver*. NY: Wiley, 1974.

Lewis, M., and Rosenblum, L. A. (Eds.). *The Effect of the Infant on Its Caregiver*. NY: Wiley, 1974.

Nesselroade, J. R., and Baltes, P. B. Adolescent personality development and historical change: 1970–1972. *Monographs of the Society for Research in Child Development*, *39* (1, Serial No. 154), 1974.

Nesselroade, J. R., and von Eye (Eds.). *Individual Development and Social Change: Explanatory Analysis*. NY: Academic Press, 1985.

Palermo, M. *Child temperament and contextual demands: A test of the goodness of fit model*. Unpublished dissertation, The Pennsylvania State University, 1982.

Parke, R. D., and Tinsley, B. The early environment of the at-risk infant: Expanding the social context. In D. Bricker (Ed.), *Intervention with At-Risk and Handicapped Infants: From Research to Application*. Baltimore, MD: University Park Press, 1982.

Radloff, L. S. The CES-D scale: A self-report depression scale for research in the general population. *Applied Psychological Measurement*, 1977, *1*, 385–401.

Sameroff, A. L. Transactional models in early social relations. *Human Development* 1975, *18*, 65–79.

Scarr, S. Development is internally guided, not determined. *Contemporary Psychology*, 1982, *27*, 852–853.

Scarr, S., and McCartney, K. How people make their own environments: A theory of genotype→environment effects. *Child Development*, 1983, *54*, 424–435.

Schneirla, T. C. The concept of development in comparative psychology. In D. B. Harris (Ed.), *The Concept of Development*. Minneapolis, MN: University of Minnesota Press, 1957.

Seligman, M. E. P. *Helplessness: On Depression, Development and Death*. San Francisco, CA: Freeman, 1975.

Sorell, G. T., and Nowak, C. A. The role of physical attractiveness as a contributor to individual development. In R. M. Lerner and N. A. Busch-Rossnagel (Eds.), *Individuals as Producers of Their Own Development: A Life-Span Perspective*. NY: Academic Press, 1981.

Super, C. M., and Harkness, S. Figure, ground and gestalt: The cultural context of the active individual. In R. M. Lerner & N. A. Busch-Rossnagel (Eds.), *Individuals as Producers of Their Development: A Life-Span Perspective*. New York: Academic Press, 1981.

Super, C., and Harkness, S. *Constitutional amendments*. Presentation at the 1982 Occasional Temperament Conference, Salem, MA., October 28–29, 1982.

Thomas, A., and Chess, S. *Temperament and Development*. NY: Brunner/Mazel, 1977.

Thomas, A., and Chess, S. *The Dynamics of Psychological Development*. NY: Brunner/Mazel, 1980.

Thomas, A., and Chess, S. The role of temperament in the contributions of individuals to their development. In R. M. Lerner and N. A. Busch-Rossnagel (Eds.), *Individuals as Producers of Their Own Development: A Life-Span Perspective*. NY: Academic Press, 1981.

Thomas, A., Chess, S., and Birch, H. G. *Temperament and Behavior Disorders in Children*. NY: New York University Press, 1968.

Thomas, A., Chess, S., and Birch, H. G. The origin of personality. *Scientific American*, 1970, *223*, 102–109.

Thomas, A., Chess, S., Sillen, J., and Mendez, O. Cross-cultural study of behavior in children with special vulnerabilities to stress. In D. F. Ricks, A. Thomas, and M. Roff (Eds.), *Life History Research in Psychopathology*. Minneapolis MN: University of Minnesota Press, 1974.

Tobach, E., and Schneirla, T. C. The biopsychology of social behavior of animals. In

R.E. Cooke and S. Levin (Eds.), *Biologic Basis of Pediatric Practice*. NY: McGraw-Hill, 1968.

Windle, M., and Lerner, R. M. The role of temperament in dating relationships among young adults. *Merrill-Palmer Quarterly*, 1984, 30, 163–175.

Windle, M., Hooker, K., Lenerz, K., East, P. L., Lerner, J. V., and Lerner, R. M. Temperament, perceived competence, and depression in early- and late-adolescents. *Developmental Psychology*, 1986, 22, 384–392.

15 PARENT–CHILD RELATIONS IN LATER LIFE: TRENDS AND GAPS IN PAST RESEARCH

Gunhild O. Hagestad

INTRODUCTION

Parents and children in modern society spend decades of life together, with a growing number of them experiencing half a century or more of shared lives. During the majority of those years, the children will be adults and parents themselves. This unprecedented duration of parent–child ties and the growing prevalence of multigenerational families present researchers with new challenges and opportunities. Yet most work on parent–child relations considers only a small fragment of their shared lives—the first decade. Moreover, work that *has* considered adults and their parents has tended to suffer from conceptual and methodological shortcomings.

The focus of this chapter is parents and children in the last few decades of their relationship. It will review past work dealing with the period following the midpoint of the children's lives, i.e., roughly the age of 40. During this life phase the children are also likely to be parents of young adult offspring. Most modern families have one or more generations who occupy the roles of both parent and child. Such bridge generations offer immense challenges to research on parent–child relationships over time, but past work has not given them the attention they deserve.

After a brief overview of recent demographic changes that have reshaped family ties, main trends in research on parents and adult offspring will be examined. This chapter argues that much of the current knowledge on the later phase of parent–child ties has come about because social scientists have responded to pressing social and political issues, rather than having as their primary goal the building of systematic knowledge on the nature and significance of this long-term family bond. Some key gaps in existing work are identified, and some suggestions are made for ways to view parent–child ties within the contexts of the entire life span and evolving vertical family bonds. Such an approach would need to identify constructs and themes that hold significance in all phases of parent–child ties.

THE CHANGING DEMOGRAPHY OF PARENT–CHILD
RELATIONSHIPS

Two aspects of recent demographic change are of particular interest here: the unprecedented duration of parent–child ties and the rise of multigenerational families (Hagestad, 1986a). Among individuals born around the turn of the century, a substantial number lost their parents before reaching adulthood. Uhlenberg (1980) estimates that in the 1900 birth cohort, one of every four experienced the death of at least one parent before reaching the age of 15. The corresponding figure for children born in the 1970's is one of 200. The same author suggests that among middle-aged couples in 1900, 10% had two or more parents living. The corresponding figure for 1976 was 47%.

Parents and children not only share more life years than ever before, they also increasingly find themselves part of an intergenerational context that includes multiple parent–child links. Four-generation families are now common (Shanas, 1980; Townsend, 1968); five or six generations in the same family are not unheard of. While it has long been recognized that parent–child pairs represent vertical links that make families continuous systems across historical time, this era is unique in the extent to which several such links can be observed at one point in time. For example, in a four-generation family there are three "tiers" of parent–child relationships and two generations of members who simultaneously occupy the roles of parent and child.

These trends reflect two sets of demographic changes: increased general life expectancy and altered rhythms of family formation. American women now live close to eight decades, but have fewer children and finish their childbearing earlier in life than women did previously. Consequently, an acceleration of generational turnover has been witnessed.

Research on parents and children has in no way kept up with demographic change. Indeed, most of it has defined "child" in the chronological sense, not as a family role that is occupied as long as there is a surviving parent (Hagestad, 1984). Our thinking—and our language— make it difficult to visualize a 70-year-old child who is retired, frail, and widowed.

Since the child development movement early in this century, it has been recognized that the study of parent–child relationships is critical to under-standing the developing child. With the more recent awareness that development and change are lifelong processes, the impact of parent–child ties on *human development* should now be examined. In seeking such wider understanding, new bridges need to be built across disciplines and traditions of research.

ALPHA AND OMEGA VIEWS OF PARENT–CHILD RELATIONS

Past research on parents and children has taken two distinct directions (Hagestad, 1982, 1984). One body of work has focused on young children and their parents. Here "child" is defined chronologically and the parent is for the most part assumed to be in the early decades of adulthood. A recent review of 1970's research on parent–child relationships (Walters & Walters, 1980) concludes that even in current work the emphasis is on young children and their parents. Authors claiming to take a life-span perspective typically just extend considerations of child development into adolescence—still covering less than one fourth of the span of the individual's life that is likely to include the *role* of child. Thus, the analytic focus is on the very beginning of a long relationship career, on the *Alpha* phase of parent–child ties.

A second body of work has concentrated on the last years of the parent–child relationship, between aged parents and middle-aged offspring. This *Omega* phase typically is not discussed under the heading of parent–child relations, but is found under such key words as "intergenerational relations," "older families," "families in later life," and "kin relations" (Lee, 1980; Streib & Beck, 1980; Troll et al., 1979). The *Journal of Marriage and the Family* has had two "decade review issues" summarizing scholarly work on the family in the 1960's and 1970's. In both issues the early and late phases of parent–child ties were addressed in separate articles. Yet only the first article had the words parent and child in the title.

These two distinct traditions of work have, for the most part, been carried out by researchers who were trained in different disciplines and who publish in quite separate journals. The Alpha phase has predominantly been the domain of psychologists with an interest in child or developmental psychology; the Omega phase has mostly been addressed by gerontologists and family sociologists. The latter tradition of research has tended to focus on questions that reflect pressing social issues and the needs of planners and policymakers, rather than on a systematic program of basic research aimed at building knowledge of parents and children across the life span.

FOUR DECADES OF RESEARCH ON ADULTS
AND THEIR PARENTS

Data on parent–child relations in adulthood have often been created because of a wider set of social or political concerns. This research has evolved through three distinct phases, responding to key social issues that emerged in four decades. First, there was the "isolated nuclear family debate" of the 1950's and 1960's. Then came "the great generation gap scare" triggered by the 1960's, and finally, the growing recognition that this is, indeed, an aging society during the 1970's and 1980's (Hagestad, 1986a). Responding to the fact that the most rapidly growing segment of the population is found among those over the age of 80, more and more research has focused on "parent caring" (Lieberman, 1978), its organization and costs.

In 1943, Talcott Parsons published an article on American kinship that may have provided more fuel for research in family sociology than any other single piece of writing. Parsons was echoing a sociological preoccupation with "urbanism as a way of life," especially that urbanization tends to break down primary group ties (e.g., Wirth, 1938). He argued that in urban-industrial society, kinship is functionally less important than in other settings or earlier times; that the nuclear family is typically geographically and economically isolated from kin; and that these developments are inescapable consequences of societal change. A popular statement of similar arguments appeared later in Vance Packard's *Nation of Strangers*. A derivative of the view that kin ties are weak in contemporary American society was the argument that old people are isolated and uncared for. This has proven to be a resilient myth that Shanas (1979) has called a *Hydra*—a multiheaded monster that is impossible to kill. Since the 1950's thousands of pages have been devoted to dispelling such myths. As a response to Parsons's propositions, an impressive series of articles and books maintained that kin ties in contemporary United States are strong. The key element in such kin networks is the parent–child relationship, which is characterized by high frequency of contact, extensive exchange of goods and services, and even geographic proximity (e.g., Adams, 1968, 1970; Hill *et al.*, 1970; Shanas & Streib, 1965; Shanas *et al.*, 1968; Sussman & Burchinal, 1962; Troll, 1971). Family historians also entered the debate, reasoning that this nation and most of the countries from which its immigrants hailed never had an extended family structure as the predominant family form (e.g., Demos, 1979; Held, 1984; Laslett, 1965, 1977). Research that constituted a contribution to the debate stirred by Parsons was for the most part descriptive. Much of it concentrated on *family structure*, such as household structure and residential propinquity. It also provided considerable descriptive material on *kin contact* and *exchange of goods and services* across generations.

Events of the late 1960's rallied researchers to focus on new concepts and variables. Now the attention was focused on *consensus, similarity,* and *intergenerational transmission*—or the absence of them. This decade stirred a great deal of concern over possible chasms between young and old in society. There was widespread fear that values and attitudes of the young were so different from those of their elders that continuity was threatened, in society at large as well as in families. Consequently, between 1965 and

1975 an impressive body of research explored the existence of generation gaps. In family research the typical study in this tradition gave attitude measures to young adults and their parents, or to middle-aged individuals and their parents. Data analyses looked for either similarities or differences between generations on such measures. (For overviews, see Bengtson et al., 1976; Troll & Bengtson, 1979.) By the mid-1970's new concerns had emerged.

The proportion of the population in advanced old age increased dramatically in the 1970's and 1980's, and a growing number of scholars turned their attention to the costs and strains of intergenerational support. In particular, a great deal of attention has been focused on the costs of parent caring. There is growing awareness that families often have multiple members in advanced old age—individuals who are in need of constant attention and care. If there is a theme in the last decade of research on parent–child relations in later life, it is likely to be the strains experienced by middle-aged children of aged parents. A fairly typical recent title says, "They Can't Do It All: Aging Daughters With Aged Mothers" (Brody & Lang, 1982).

Based on these four decades of research, there are some dimensions of parent–child relationships about which considerable knowledge exists, while others have been left largely unexplored. Several excellent overviews have been written on this body of research (e.g., Bengtson & Schraeder, 1982; Streib & Beck, 1980; Troll & Bengtson, 1979; Troll et al., 1979). They have identified the following six key issues in the study of adults and their parents: (1) family structure, (2) patterns of contact, (3) consensus and similarity, (4) norms and expectations, (5) patterns of support, and (6) the affective quality of ties. Across all six issues, contrasts between men and women have formed a recurrent theme.

Each of these issues will be discussed in a bit more detail. The goal is not to provide a comprehensive review of research, but to identify main themes and that which has been left unasked or unanswered.

Family Structure

Bengtson and Schraeder (1982) list three main structural characteristics of families that have been considered in the study of parent–child relations among adults: household composition, family demographic composition, and geographic proximity. The census is our main source of information about household structure. From census material we know that most elderly live alone or with a spouse. Only a small segment live with a child (Mindel, 1979; Soldo, 1980; Soldo & Lauriat, 1976). When such coresidence occurs, it is most likely to involve older women and their daughters.

The fact that the census uses the individual and the household—but not the family—as units of analysis has limited resulting knowledge of the demographic composition of families. For example, estimates of how many adults have parents living are found either in general mortality estimates or in data from large-scale surveys. In a Social Security Administration study from the 1970's (Murray, 1973) it was found that among individuals aged 58–59, nearly one fourth had at least one living parent. Among persons aged 62–63, 12% had surviving parents. These figures appear to have risen during the past decade. A more recent national survey (National Retired Teachers Association, AARP, 1981) found that 40% of individuals aged 55–59 had at least one living parent. Among those aged 60–64, the figure was 20%. There seems to be no data set on the middle-aged that combines information on number of living parents with number of young adult children. Shanas (1980) estimates that 90% of older people who have living children also have grandchildren, and 46% have great-grandchildren. However, there is no reliable information on how common four- and five-generation families are, and how many of them have members of all generations living in the same community.

As discussed by Rossi (Chapter 3, current volume), one thing known about contemporary American families is that because of the nearly 8-year difference in life expectancy between men and women, combined with age differentials at marriage, most older women are widows, while most older men are married. It is also known that the oldest surviving member of a family lineage is likely to be a woman, and that mothers and daughters frequently share some experiences and roles of old age, such as being grandmothers, retirees, and widows.

There is hope that it will soon be recognized that in an aging, divorcing, and remarrying society, "family" cannot be equated with "household," and census material needs to be organized accordingly. Demographic data on *family units*, not individuals or households (Hagestad, 1981), is needed, along with information on family structures across several generations, their population pyramids and dependency ratios. Such data are important for predictions regarding needed support, housing, and services. They would also give researchers a baseline, enabling them to judge the representativeness of intergenerational samples or to decide about how to draw stratified samples to pursue questions regarding specific subgroups of families or individuals. Some work currently in progress uses Norwegian census data to explore the age structure of families for successive cohorts of Norwegian children during this century (Hagestad, 1986b). Norwegian census material allows researchers to link records of parents and children, as well as to trace individuals across time (i.e., several censuses). Dutch researchers are also currently exploring the possibility of developing parameter estimates for family lineage composition across several generations (Knipscheer, personal communication).

Survey research has provided descriptive data on the geographic proximity of parents and children. Much of this research was triggered by the isolated nuclear family debate. Troll et al. (1979) report finding 25 major surveys on residential patterns, all amply demonstrating that most adults have some close relatives who live nearby. This has particularly been reported for elderly parents. Shanas and co-workers (Shanas et al., 1968; Shanas, 1979) have repeatedly found that over 80% of the elderly live less than an hour away from at least one child. Unknown, however, are the conditions under which there is great distance and little contact between adults and their parents (Lee, 1980).

In part, the gaps in knowledge of family proximity and contact are due to problems of asymmetry. As Brody (1981) notes: "The usual view of the family tree is downward from the perspective of the old" (p. 473). Troll et al. (1979) comment that "it is hard to decide whether Adams' finding that one third of his young adults live near their parents compares with the figures of Shanas et al. (1968) who only asked about one child per parent" (p. 85).

Patterns of Contact

The isolated nuclear family debate made it important to demonstrate that, even though they do not have common residence, adults and their parents nevertheless keep in touch. Troll et al. (1979) found almost as many surveys on frequency of family contact as on residential propinquity. Family members keep in touch through visits, phone calls, and letters.

In her campaign to dispel the myth that the elderly are alienated from their families, Shanas (Shanas et al., 1968; Shanas, 1979) has repeatedly reported data indicating that nearly 80% of the elderly see a child weekly or more. However, there is an asymmetry problem here as well. Shanas coments on this issue in one of her papers: "Adult children see their parents often. Where there are several children, only one child may be a steady visitor, but one is enough" (Shanas, 1975, p. 176). That might be, but the danger, as can be seen in a number of recent publications, is to disregard the asymmetry problem and infer that because the majority of elderly parents have frequent contact with a middle-aged child, the majority of middle-aged children have regular contact with elderly parents. It is possible that new insight into parent–child dynamics could be gained if family members who do not keep in touch, or "family black sheep" who have not been heard from in years, were studied. In other words, research needs to develop profiles for contact and affective ties between elderly parents and each of their children in order to resolve the asymmetry problem.

Some recent work in Europe as well as the United States has attempted to address intrafamily differences among children. Knipscheer (1980) used ratios to describe the proportion of all children in a family who engage in certain types of activities with elderly parents. He found considerable intrafamily variability. Similar findings are reported in a survey of Swedish families (Teeland, 1978). In a recent U.S. survey, Aldous and co-workers (Aldous, Klaus, & Klein, 1985) asked parents to identify the adult child to whom they gave the most comfort, and the child from whom they received the most comfort. The study found that intrafamily complexity and diversity in parent–child relations increased with family size. The data also indicated that "the loved one" and "the loving" children tended to be daughters who lived geographically close.

It has repeatedly been argued that women are the linchpin of family contact. They are the kinkeepers, the family correspondents who orchestrate family get-togethers, keep track of birthdays and anniversaries, and make the phone calls (Berardo, 1967; Hagemann-White, 1984; Hill et al., 1970; Lehr, 1984; Rosenthal, 1981). In a study of couples with school-aged children, Nye and coworkers (Nye, 1976) concluded that "of all the roles in this study, the kinship role as we have presently analyzed it is most normatively weighted toward one sex—the female" (pp. 154–155).

Consensus, Similarity and Socialization

The Chapter 16 by Bengtson (in this volume) addresses intergenerational consensus, which he has defined as "the extent of agreement or similarity in general values or orientations, in specific sociopolitical attitudes, or in beliefs" (Bengtson et al., 1976). Concerns about degree of consensus between parents and children peaked as a result of the 1960's and the discussion of generation gaps. In this literature there was a great deal of emphasis on "intergenerational transmission" from parents to children. Ironically, many such publications occurred during an era when a view of socialization as a unidirectional process between a "socializer" and a "socializee" was being replaced with conceptualizations that treated it as a mutual, reciprocal process (e.g., Bell, 1968; Lewis & Rosenblum, 1974)— typically in studies of young children and their mothers. It is possible that the intense concern about gaps and intergenerational continuity made researchers in the Omega tradition slow to study mutual socialization between parents and adult children. In the Alpha tradition, reconceptualizations of socialization came as a result of new views of children, most importantly discarding what Hartup (1978) called "the social mold view" of life's first decade. However, the concept of reciprocal socialization also says something about parents, and recognizes that adults change too.

It is paradoxical that the growing emphasis on individual development as a lifelong process, which has characterized the field of psychology in the last decades, did not lead to a major push for research on how adults and their parents mutually shape each other's life patterns and behaviors. A number of authors have discussed how patterns of socialization may change as parents and offspring mature and age (e.g., Bengtson & Black, 1973; Brim,

1968; Mortimer & Simmons, 1978; Riley *et al.*, 1972). For example, Brim argues that as parents age and become more dependent, "reversed social-ization" takes place, wherein the children become the main socializers. Thus, he sees changing patterns of influence between parents and offspring as a result of individual maturation and aging. Other writers consider this to be the product of historical change. The best known example of such a view is Mead's *Culture and Commitment* (1970), in which she calls the older generations "immigrants in time," individuals who must turn to the young for necessary knowledge and skills. Most of these discussions, however, are not embedded in empirical studies.

Recent reviews (Lerner & Spanier, 1979; Mortimer & Simmons, 1978) demonstrate that there is very limited empirical material on how adults and their parents mutually shape each other's lifestyles, outlooks, and values. At the present time considerably more is known about patterns of mutual influence between infants and their mothers (e.g., Lewis & Rosenblum, 1974) than about how parents and offspring influence one another during adulthood.

There are other peculiar contrasts between discussions of parent–child socialization in literature on adults and writings on young children and their parents. Research on generation gaps tended to focus on the products or outcomes of socialization (similarities and differences in values and attitudes). The attitudes measured, furthermore, typically focused on views of society at large, a world outside the family. Research on young children and parents focused on *process*, and the main emphasis was on ways of relating within the family. When there was discussion of influence from child to parent, it typically centered on parenting, i.e., the shaping of the parent's behavior toward the child. The interest centered on how the needs of young children are met in interactions with parents. It was argued that not only do parents impose a set of expectations on offspring, but the latter also, from the very early phases of life, find ways to shape parents' behaviors. Thus, socialization was not seen primarily as a process of *transmitting* expectations, but of *creating* them through ongoing interaction. Continuity, in this perspective, does not become a question of similarity, but of the maintenance of an interactional system that is comprised of changing individuals with changing needs and resources. This view assumes a great deal of variability across and within parent–child pairs, depending on phases of development and individual difference factors such as temperament.

In multigenerational families, members of different generations represent quite different historical circumstances and life experiences. In their inter-actions across generational lines, they have to find a modicum of "common ground." In a heterogenous, changing society such common ground is not readily provided by the surrounding community, but has to be developed through interactional negotiation. The main unit of such negotiation is the

414 Modern Society: Life Span, Parental Investment

parent–child dyad. The creation of family continuity no doubt involves influence from old to young—"what is passed on" along generational lines. However, intergenerational continuity can no longer be described as a matter of a simple, unidirectional process of transmission from old to young or "the extent to which people in different generations replicate each other" (Troll & Bengtson, 1979).

Some of my own research has explored patterns of communication and influence among three generations of adults in 148 Chicago-area families. This work has repeatedly demonstrated the great variability in those issues that engage attention, time, and energy in families. When families seek to find common ground for relating across generations, the critical question may not be *how* to think on certain issues, but *what* to think about at all. Families vary a great deal in what they consider worthy of attention—what they think should be taken seriously. They expend a great deal of effort on finding a set of concerns that engages all of them but that is not likely to bring out differences great enough to be disruptive. In some families the focus may be money and its management; in others it may be sports and the outdoors; in others political issues form the core of "the common base." Because of the considerable interfamily variability in such themes, standard-ized attitude measures may not be helpful in capturing the key areas of concern to families. The measures may demonstrate intergenerational differences that do not matter and totally miss life concerns critical to some family units. Families also have mechanisms for suppressing dissimilarities that *could* make a difference. For example, they create "demilitarized zones": silent agreements regarding what *not* to discuss (Hagestad, 1981).

The Chicago data also pointed to variations between men and women in what they emphasize in their search for common ground across generations. Contrasts between the sexes fell along the lines of Parsons and Bales' (1955) distinction between "instrumental" and "emotional-expressive" leadership. Grandfathers and fathers chose as their focus of attention involvements in nonfamily spheres such as work, education, and finances. Particularly for grandfathers in the study (most of them born around the turn of the century), cohort changes in the rest of society appeared to present potential threats to a common base in relations with the younger generations. Women, on the other hand, concentrated attention on relationships *within* the family. The mothers and grandmothers in the study appeared to think of themselves as "ministers of the interior," specialists on internal family dynamics.

Similar contrasts between men and women also emerged in relation to conflict and strain. When other family members discussed fathers and grandfathers, views on social issues were by far the most commonly mentioned "sore spots." Race relations, social policy, and sex roles were commonly identified as touchy subjects around grandfathers and fathers. In discussions of mothers and grandmothers, reported troublespots were topics related to interpersonal issues, particularly in the family realm. These findings are remarkably similar to a recent study of German families (Lehr, 1982), which found that intergenerational disagreements among men focused on nonfamily spheres, while conflicts among women typically occurred over how to relate within the family.

Some recent work on young adults and their parents further illustrates the mother's role as specialist on interpersonal relations. Filsinger and Lamke (1983) examined interpersonal competence in parents and young adult children and concluded that "the mother appeared to have the greatest effect on the interpersonal life of the child" (p. 79). Other work has reported that adolescents and young adults are more likely to perceive their outlooks and attitudes as similar to those of their mothers than those of their fathers (e.g., Acock & Bengtson, 1978). This trend holds for both sons and daughters, but is most pronounced for daughters.

In the Chicago families, women seemed more ready to accept influence "up" generational lines from their children than men. It was particularly in relations to the outside world, areas such as views on social issues, involvement in work and education, and changing styles in dress and grooming that Chicago grandmothers and mothers recognized "reversed socialization" from the young (Hagestad & Snow, 1977). However, they were not ready to heed similar efforts when the young focused on how to run a family, even though the interviews with the younger generations indicated that such influence had been attempted.

Norms and Expectations

Recently several authors have argued that family life has become less regulated by societal norms and community control. Families have become more self-contained social groups, setting their own norms in their own private spheres (Aries, 1978; Gadlin, 1977; Hess & Waring, 1979; Riley, 1983). Burgess and Locke (1953) discussed an historical change from "institution" to "companionship," a steady moving away from the 19th century situation in which relationships between husbands and wives, parents and children "were based on socially sanctioned mutual obligations that transcended personal affection and sentiment" (Hareven, 1977, p. 64).

There are also discussions of how rapid demographic changes have caught us off guard and created "cultural lags." There are now new forms of family relationships for which there are few culturally shared expectations (Hess & Waring, 1979; Laslett, 1977). An example would be parents and children who are both old and in need of help. Hess and Waring argue that contemporary intergenerational relationships among adults are anomic: "Clear normative prescriptions are lacking at the same time the range of choices of what to do is expanding" (p. 242). In her discussion of contemporary intergenerational relations, Kreps (1977) asks: "Will there be sufficient mutuality of interest to hold them together?"

In examining factors that serve to bind adults and their parents, authors have explored norms and expectations, functional interdependence through exchange, and affective ties. First, a brief look at how researchers have tried to assess the expectations held by parents and children about how to relate.

In research on normative expectations in the Alpha phase of parent–child relations, nearly all the emphasis has been on how parents ought to behave, while in studies on the Omega phase, most of the attention has been focused on how children should behave. Knipscheer (1984) suggests that normative expectations regarding parental behavior toward adult offspring are, for the most part, proscriptions—rules for what not to do. Examples would be not to interfere in the lives of children and not to become overly dependent on them. In contrast, normative expectations regarding children's behavior constitute prescriptions, or statements of what they should do—as exemplified by one of the ten commandments.

Several authors have suggested that a sense of moral obligation on the part of children may be the main factor in maintaining steady contact between adults and their parents (Adams, 1968; Knipscheer, 1980; Teeland, 1978). A moral imperative may be followed regardless of personal affection, which may explain why no consistent relationship has been demonstrated between rates of contact and feelings of emotional closeness with parents (Lee, 1980; Troll et al., 1979; Walker & Thompson, 1983). Bott (1972) says of adults in her study of London families: "They felt that amicable relations should be kept up with parents even though they did not always like them" (p. 129).

It has been suggested that many parents would like to have more contact with children than they report expecting, because of norms and values protecting the independence of children and proscriptions against interfering in their lives (e.g., Hawkinson, 1965; Kerckhoff, 1965; Knipscheer, 1980; Teeland, 1978). Hawkinson found that while the majority of his elderly respondents *wished* for more visits from their children, less than 10% *expected* more. Margaret Clark (1969), who has written extensively on the cultural contexts of aging, says of elderly parents:

> They are the very people who, in their earlier roles as parents, as the guardians and advocates of the cultural norms and constraints, have insisted that their children learn and practice self-reliance. They have believed, and have taught the present generation of adults to believe, that dependency—except in young children—is weak, psychopathic, immoral, or un-American. . . . Yet these same advocates are now those who—if they live long enough—will really need other people (p. 71).

In the last decade, a good deal of research has explored expectations regarding *help* to parents in need of care. Seelbach (1977, 1978) found that women expected somewhat more help from offspring than did men. Studies have often compared the expectations of parents and children. It is a commonly reported finding that children are more ready than parents to state that the younger generation should provide help to needy elderly parents (e.g., Brody et al., 1984; Knipscheer, 1984; Wake & Sporakowski, 1972). Brody and co-workers (Brody, 1979; Brody et al., 1983, 1984), in a recent study of three generations of adult women, found that it is important to distinguish between types of help. All three generations agreed that children are the best sources of emotional aid (providing confidante relationships and advice, for example), but "It is clear that this emphasis on children to satisfy emotional needs is not coupled with wanting children to provide financial or instrumental help." They continue: " . . . family ties and responsibility . . . are seen as quite different from money and concrete services. . . . " (Brody et al., 1984, p. 745).

As other authors have reported (e.g., Hill et al., 1970; Knipscheer, 1984), Brody found that the main type of help expected by elderly parents is emotional support and companionship. The oldest group of women were the most receptive to formal, nonfamily services, while the youngest women were the most in favor of family-provided service. The middle generation held intermediate views. The authors attribute these contrasts to "youthful idealism" on behalf of the young adult women. The middle-aged and older women, on the other hand, were often responding on the basis of actual caretaking experiences. These researchers also point to the importance of going beyond values and attitudes to an examination of concrete family experiences. They found that women who thought that adult children should help with the expenses of widowed mothers were themselves not providing much help to an elderly mother. Those who shared residence with their mothers and gave a great deal of help were the least likely to be in favor of children as sources of financial help. Women living with their mothers ranked children low as potential providers of time-intensive services.

Brody is among a growing number of scholars who express apprehension that current social expectations regarding family help to the elderly are unrealistic, given recent demographic and social change (see also Fischer & Hoffman, 1983). She asks: "At what point does the expectation of filial responsibility become social irresponsibility?" (Brody, 1979, p. 286). In several papers she voices concern that too much of the burden of care falls on the middle ages, particularly women. Sussman (1983) has focused on formally stated norms, such as family responsibility laws. He suggests that family supports may be given more weight in the near future because of recent trends to remove various types of support from the public domain. There is a growing literature on the legal aspects of intergenerational support and its costs (Schorr, 1980). Recent court cases have tended to state middle-aged individuals' obligation to support two generations when they are in need: young adult children and aging parents. By far, the most rapidly growing social science literature on adults and their parents addresses various aspects of support and help, particularly from child to elderly parent.

However, very little research has actually considered both sets of parent–child relations in which the middle-aged are typically involved.

Patterns of Support

Following the isolated nuclear family debate, there was a good deal of descriptive research demonstrating a wide array of support across generational lines. It has been found that family members still share goods and services (Adams, 1968; Hill et al., 1970; Shanas et al., 1968; Troll & Bengtson, 1979) and serve one another as reliable sources of continuing human contact, emotional support, and confidante relationships (Babchuk, 1978; Shanas, 1979; Townsend, 1957). This research has also pointed to the uniqueness of the parent–child bond as a unit of intergenerational exchange (Lopata, 1978).

In spite of all the research, there is still considerable "pluralistic ignorance" about families and support (Shanas, 1979). In Brody's research (Brody et al., 1983) all generations agreed that children should help take care of their elderly parents. Yet 80% in all three groups also agreed that "these days adult children do not take care of elderly parents as they did in the past." Research on widowhood has repeatedly pointed to children, particularly daughters, as the mainstay of widows' support system (Bankoff, 1983; Lopata, 1979; Treas, 1977).

During the last decade a great deal of attention has focused on the provision of care for the very old, prompted by a virtual population explosion among individuals over the age of 80. It has been well documented that most elderly adults prefer independent living. However, many of them face a time in old age when they require steady care (Frankfather et al., 1981). It is estimated that 80% of such care is provided by family members, usually wives and daughters (Brody & Lang, 1982; Troll et al., 1979; U.S. GAO, 1977).

In addition to direct care, women also carry a "worry burden." In a recent Canadian study, two thirds of women over 50 who had a living parent said they worried about the parent's health (Marshall, Rosenthal, & Synge, 1983). Several authors suggest that the need for parent caring (Lieberman, 1978) is changing the lives of many women in their middle years. Tobin and Kulys (1980) call the view of the empty nest years as a time of carefree personal growth a myth. Increasingly, concerns are expressed that parent caring may lead to a sense of overload and stress, which may threaten middle-aged women's physical as well as mental health—and, in turn, create a bleak outlook for their own old age (Archbold, 1982; Brody, 1981; Lehr, 1984; Robinson, 1983; Robinson & Thurner, 1979). New needs among the younger generation have also emerged. It is becoming clear that the state of the economy, as well as high divorce rates among young adults, are putting new strains on middle-aged parents. A growing number of their mature offspring are now turning to them for shelter as well as emotional and financial support.

There is insufficient knowledge on the extent to which needs of children and parents are factors in middle-aged women's decisions regarding paid employment. However, there is little doubt that women's work may now help even out imbalances between family income and family needs the way men's moonlighting (Oppenheimer, 1974)—or the employment of adolescent and young adult offspring still living at home—did in the past (Modell et al., 1976: Oppenheimer, 1981). It has been common, especially in the popular press, to suggest that when women are in the labor force, they will spend less time and effort on kin tending. There is little empirical evidence to support this claim. Indeed, a recent study by Stoller (1983) found that employment significantly reduced care giving to aging parents among sons, but this was not a statistically significant trend for daughters. It is also not clear that increased labor force participation among women led to altered *expectations* regarding kin responsibilities. Brody et al. (1984) found that the majority of older women in their study felt that working daughters should adjust their work schedules to help out an elderly parent. These researchers also found that for some types of assistance, such as personal care, the respondents deemed help from sons unacceptable.

There seems to be good reason to worry about what Friedan (1981) has called "the superwoman squeeze"—the overload experienced by middle generation women who provide support for both children and parents, in addition to facing the demands of workday life and household maintenance. Brody (1981), Hagemann-White (1984), and Lehr (1984) suggest that legislation and supportive services must be developed to allow women an optimal level of family involvement, one which permits independent interests and lives.

Several authors have discussed the way men and women in the middle generation end up being intergenerational "patrons" (Hill et al., 1970) who give to both young and old, and the fact that the oldest and the youngest generations receive more help than they give (Adams, 1968; Hill et al., 1970; Irving, 1972; Kennedy & Stokes, 1982; National Council on Aging, 1975). Cheal (1983), in a recent discussion of monetary transfers across generations, calls this "the curvilinear model" of intergenerational support. His proposed alternative model is one of "continuous redistribution," in which resources are transferred from old to young in successive generations. This means that the oldest of the three generations receives the least, the youngest is given the most.

There is little doubt that the past work on exchange of support between adults and their parents has failed to grasp the complexities of such exchanges. Discussions of how giving and receiving are balanced need to consider dimensions of time, multiple dimensions of support, and the full set of parent–child linkages within a family lineage. Balancing may occur over much longer spans of time than has been considered in research (Hill *et al.*, 1970; Rosenmayr, 1978), and there may be complex patterns of balancing across domains of support as well as across relationships involving more than one generation. For example, a middle-aged woman confronted with the task of caring for her terminally ill mother may receive attention, affection, and advice from young adult children. This support from the young may reduce the potential strain and sense of imbalance in the relationship to the older generation.

Research on support between parents and children has not covered the range of support identified in the rapidly growing literature on support networks. In his well-known volume on the subject, House (1981) identifies four main types of help: instrumental aid, emotional concern, information (about the environment), and appraisal (data related to self-evaluations and self-esteem). In research on parents and children, too much of past discussion has centered on the first type, and far too little has been done on the last two dimensions. Recent work has pointed out that children often form informational bridges between the elderly and bureaucratic structures (Shanas & Sussman, 1977, 1981). This was illustrated in interviews with the two older generations in the Chicago families. The latter study also found middle-aged children and children-in-law to be key sources of financial advice for older women, especially widows. As was briefly discussed above, it has been suggested that under conditions of rapid social change, parents turn to their children for information needed to "keep up with the times." A current example in many American middle-class families would be children introducing parents to the world of computers.

No work has systematically explored the extent to which parents and children in the adult years seek each other out as sources of information and the life domains in which such support is most frequently given. In general, informational support is vastly understudied in work on intergenerational exchanges. For example, little or no research has considered the importance of parents in the construction of personal biographies, and the fact that parents are unique informants about our personal pasts as well as family pasts.

The last dimension of support identified by House—appraisal—has received considerable attention in the work on early parent–child ties. The importance of parental feedback for the development of identity and self-esteem has been repeatedly emphasized. However, there is an amazing paucity of information—even speculation—on how adults and their parents affect each other's sense of competence and self-worth. Less cautious observers of social life, such as columnists and comedians, make us laugh at how most of us never grow beyond the need for parental approval. (An example would be the Smothers brothers' recurrent theme of "Mom always liked you better.")

Some authors have offered provocative discussions of how parental support and encouragement may have intergenerational ripple effects. For example, positive appraisal and other types of support from parents may aid the offspring's transition into parenthood (e.g. Belsky & Tolan 1981; Wandersman, Wandersman, & Kahn, 1980). Tinsley and Parke (1984) present cross-cultural work that has demonstrated ways in which grand-mothers may serve as "stabilizers" of mothers, resulting in greater maternal warmth and competence (Minturn & Lambert, 1964; Rohrer, 1975). In an American sample, Abernathy (1973) found that frequency of contact between women and their own mothers was the best predictor of the women's sense of competence in the role of parent. There is little doubt that intergenerational "second-order effects" of support is an exciting research frontier. However, before it can be fully explored, new conceptual and methodological tools for assessing the emotional quality of ties between adults and their parents are needed.

Affective Quality of Ties

Although many authors have proclaimed the importance of sentiment and emotional ties between parents and adult offspring, very little research has tried to assess these aspects of the relationship (Bengtson & Schraeder, 1982; Walker & Thompson, 1983). Indeed, in their longitudinal study of father–child relationships in later life, Mitteness and Nydegger decided not to even speak of "closeness": "We asked fathers what 'closeness' meant, only to discover such a lack of consensus that we felt justified in not using closeness as a construct describing relationships" (Mitteness & Nydegger, 1982, p. 2). They add that for these fathers, all over the age of 45, words like "love," "caring," and "affection" were uncomfortable terms that were extremely difficult for them to discuss. The work by Nydegger and associates is unique in several respects. It is one of the few studies that has attempted to measure negative affect as well as positive feelings between parent and child.

Most commonly, a sense of closeness has been assessed through single item indicators (Bengtson & Schraeder, 1982; Cicirelli, 1981, 1983). Even with such crude measurements, there are two highly consistent findings: Parents will describe the relationship more positively than the child, and reported closeness shows distinct sex differences. It has commonly been found that younger generations more readily report family strain and conflict than do members of the older generations (e.g., Bengtson & Kuypers, 1971; Hagestad, 1984; Troll & Bengtson, 1979). Furthermore, parents are less likely than children to report changes in the relationship and will more often describe the relationship as "good" and close (Bengtson & Black, 1973; Bengtson & Kuypers, 1971; Hagestad, 1984; Knipscheer & Bevers, 1981;

Wilen, 1979). This trend has been observed between both elderly adults and their children and young adults and their parents.

Measures of parent–child closeness frequently do not distinguish between mothers and fathers, daughters and sons, but when they do, affective dimensions of relationships seem to vary by gender. In their study of individuals in four stages of life, Lowenthal and co-workers (Lowenthal *et al.*, 1975) found that in all four groups, both men and women said that they felt close to their mothers twice as often as they reported feeling close to their fathers. Similar trends were found in a study of nearly 800 undergraduates (Hagestad & Fagan, 1974). Furthermore, daughters appear to feel more closeness to parents than do sons (Cicirelli, 1983), and parents also appear more likely to name daughters as their favorite children (Aldous *et al.*, 1983).

The area of emotional ties better than any other aspect of parent–child relations demonstrates the limitations of past conceptualizations in considering parents and children over dimensions of time. There are highly limited data available, both on how needs and patterns of support or closeness vary across phases of parent–child ties. Although several authors have argued for the importance of seeing attachment between parents and children as a lifelong phenomenon (e.g., Kalish & Knudtson, 1976; Troll & Smith, 1976), no empirical work has seriously confronted the conceptual and measurement issues implied by such a view. Very little is known about how the needs for closeness and its definitions change over the life span. There is also extremely limited knowledge about how the developmental needs and resources of parents and children interact in what Hill and Mattessich (1979) call "developmental reciprocities." Work on the early part of the parent–child relationship has delineated stages according to the age of children. Research on the Omega phase of parent–child ties has concentrated on the age of parents (Alpert & Richardson, 1980). Very little work has considered the complex interactions between two sets of lives.

The combinations of developmental issues confronted by parents and children will, of course, depend on the timing of parenthood. The long-term consequences of parenthood timing and age differences between parents and children have, for the most part, been unexplored. Some work by Rossi (1980) should inspire further research in this regard. She studied relations between middle-aged women and their children and found that the mothers who had their children late had more problematic relations with them in mid-life than women who bore their children earlier. With regard to instrumental support, Oppenheimer's (1981) pioneering work suggests that the timing of parenthood in two generations shapes the needs and resources as well as "life cycle squeezes" of parent–child pairs. Building on the work by Erikson (e.g., Erikson, 1982), Kivnick (1983) has discussed how intergenerational ties provide opportunities for individuals to "preview" and "review" life phases different from their own by observing close family members confronting their developmental tasks. Such a perspective, which encourages a consideration of the combinations of life issues represented in a given family, would seem to imply that timing of parenthood may influence the likelihood of psychodynamic "life cycle squeezes"—times when emotional resources of the family are spread too thin.

Finally, the dimension of historical time and possible cohort contrasts have, for the most part, been neglected in work on affective ties between parents and children. No discussions have been offered on the possibility that cultural change has led to altered expectations regarding intimacy and closeness between generations. It is quite possible, for example, that children who spent their adolescent years in the 1960's have quite different definitions of what it means to be close to someone than many of their parents, who may have been young in the 1930's. This, of course, would present complex issues of measurement in the comparison of parent–child perceptions of closeness.

KEY SHORTCOMINGS IN RESEARCH ON THE OMEGA PHASE

This chapter has argued that most work on parent–child relations in later life has been triggered by debates on the role of the family in modern society rather than by an interest in building systematic knowledge about the nature and significance of parent–child relationships. Three sets of social concerns have produced the bulk of studies on adults and their parents: (1) the isolated nuclear family debate, (2) the generation gap scare, and (3) the growing concern over family care for the very old. Questions raised in such discussions have given rise to six main research themes: family structure, patterns of contact, consensus, norms and expectations, patterns of support, and affective ties. Three decades of work on adults and their parents reveals not only distinct substantive gaps, but also methodological and conceptual limitations in contemporary studies of these parent–child ties.

Specifically, this genre of research suffers from two serious limitations:

1. It has tended to focus on one parent–child dyad at a time, disregarding the fact that adults in contemporary society spend several decades being both parents and children. Nearly all work on adults and their parents has disregarded this dual linkage, either by gathering data on only one dyad or by using data analysis strategies that lose the intrafamily connections.

2. It has, for the most part, utilized concepts and constructs that would have little or no applicability in studies of young children and their parents. Consequently, no foundation has been laid for understanding dynamics of parent–child bonds across the duration of their relationship, and few links can be made between Alpha and Omega research.

Any understanding of many of the issues discussed above will remain limited as long as research strategies only allow the examination of one set of parent–child relations. Parent caring and its strains cannot be understood if the support and strain experienced by the middle generation of care giving children in their *other* parent–child relationship is disregarded—that with their grown children. Insights into the relationships between young adults and their parents might be incomplete without information regarding the extent to which the parents' ties to their own parents represent emotional security and support or a drain on material or emotional resources. Furthermore, in an examination of stability and change in parent–child relations over time and over more than one nuclear family, members of middle generations become crucial informants. They can be examined in the roles of both parent and child—one important strategy in attempting to understand continuity in such relationships over time.

In looking at more than one set of parent–child dyads, great care should go into the data analysis phase of the research. It is very easy to lose the intrafamily connections. For example, in many studies that included members of three generations, support, contact, and consensus were compared in the relations between parents (G2) and grandparents (G1) and between parents (G2) and grandchildren (G3). The typical strategy has been to compare means in the two types of dyads, which, of course, means that the family has been lost as a unit of analysis. Much effort is needed in developing new data analysis schemes for the creation of family data incorporating three or more generations.

How much stability might be found in parenting behaviors across the parent's adult years? Do individuals exhibit "parenting styles" that remain characteristic of them through the ages of 25, 45, 65, and 85? Do parent–child pairs display consistency in interactional patterns across the different phases of their relationship? Are there normal, predictable changes in parent–child relations across the spans of their individual lives and the career of their relationship? What triggers such changes? On what dimensions would it make sense to start looking for continuity and change? Do parenting styles and interaction patterns "run in families?" The answers to all these questions is that we do not know. However, if they are tackled, even more basic issues must be confronted. First and foremost, the study of the beginning and the end of parent–child relations cannot be continued in two separate research enterprises.

CONCLUSION: THE NEED FOR NEW BRIDGES

In reading this chapter many researchers whose work has focused on young children and their parents may find few familiar themes or constructs. Proximity and rates of contact are not interesting issues between small children and their parents. In the first years of life, norms, expectations, and consensus are not critical issues, either. Support is assumed to be fairly one-sided as long as the children are young. Only in regard to the sixth issue—emotional quality of ties—is there some common ground.

Clearly, to build bridges between the Alpha and the Omega traditions requires a reexamination of our constructs. Concepts that are sufficiently general to allow for instances in all phases of the parent–child relationship must be developed. There are a number of such constructs in classical work from the Alpha tradition. Attachment was already mentioned. The concepts of control and support (Sears et al., 1957) have figured heavily in research on parenting styles. It is surprising that power and dominance have been ignored in the study of adults and their parents. Interviews in the Chicago study often provided glimpses of intrafamilial power struggles. These families also illustrated that parent–child dyads between adults show a great deal of variability on dimensions such as degree of mutuality and the ratio of positive, supportive interactions and controlling, negative interactions. Such constructs have been applied in observational research on troubled families (e.g., Burgess, 1979; Patterson & Reid, 1970), but there appears to be no work on parent–child relations in later life that has sought to measure them.

In attempting to fill the data gap left by the Alpha and Omega traditions, new uses must be made of existing research material. For example, it may be possible to follow up studies of parenting carried out in the 1950's and 1960's. There are, of course, some unique data sets that include observations on three generations of parents and children over a long span of time. The most outstanding example is likely to be the Berkeley Studies, which span half a century. Several investigators are currently working on parent–child relations in these data (e.g., Clausen et al., 1981; Elder et al., 1986).

The last part of this century will have parents and children who share six and seven decades of life. This new demographic picture presents a wide range of human potentials and challenges. It also offers researchers new opportunities to seek knowledge on the relationship that forms a core for human development from beginning to end. To maximize these opportunities, researchers from both the Alpha and the Omega view of this relationship need to join forces, coordinate their questions, and inform one another.

SUMMARY

Recent demographic change has made parent–child relationships longer-lasting than ever before in human history. A growing number of aging individuals now have parents living. Research on parents and children does not cover the many decades of shared lives between them. Two distinct and separate bodies of work exist on this subject. One focuses on young children and their parents; the other on the elderly and their children. Between the two there is an empirical and theoretical gap. Research on adults and their parents has been motivated by social and political concerns regarding the impact of industrialization and urbanization on family ties, the possibility of generation gaps, and family care for a rapidly growing population of frail elderly. Because of these concerns and the many policy-related issues facing families in an aging society, research on the later phases of parent–child relations has not had a life-span orientation. Furthermore, it has used few of the concepts that are central in work on early parent–child ties, and little work has recognized the intergenerational context of parent–child dyads. Research has failed to take into account the fact that the children of aging parents are themselves parents. It is high time that concepts and research designs are developed that can be utilized in research across all phases of parent–child relations and across several generations in a family lineage.

REFERENCES

Abernathy, V. Social network and response to the maternal role. *International Journal of Sociology and the Family*, 1973, *3*, 86–92.

Acock, A. C., and Bengtson, V. L. On the relative influence of mothers and fathers: A covariance analysis of political and religious socialization. *Journal of Marriage and the Family*, 1978, *40*(3), 519–530.

Adams, B. N. *Kinship in an Urban Setting*. Chicago, IL: Markham Publishing Company, 1968.

Adams, B. N. Isolation, function, and beyond. American kinship in the 1960's. *Journal of Marriage and the Family*, 1970, *32*, 575–597.

Aldous, J. *Family Careers: Developmental Change in Families*. NY: John Wiley, 1978.

Aldous, J., Klaus, E., and Klein, D. M. The understanding heart: Aging parents and their favorite children. *Child Development*, 1985, 56, 303–316.

Alpert, J. L., and Richardson, M. S. Parenting. In L. W. Poon (Ed.), *Aging in the 1980's*. Washington, D.C.: APA, 1980, pp. 441–454.

Anspach, D., and Rosenberg, S. Working class matricentricity. *Journal of Marriage and the Family*, 1972, *34*, 437–442.

Archbold, P. G. All-consuming activity: The family as caregiver. *Generations*, 1982, Winter, pp. 12–13.

Aries, P. The family and the city. In A. Rossi, J. Kagan, and T. K. Hareven (Eds.), *The Family*. NY: Morton & Co., 1978, pp. 227–235.

Arling, G. The elderly widow and her family, neighbors, and friends. *Journal of Marriage and the Family*, 1976, *38*, 757–767.

Babchuk, N. Aging and primary relations. *Aging and Human Development*, 1978, 9, 137–151.

Bankoff, E. A. Social support and adaptation to widowhood. *Journal of Marriage and the Family*, 1983, *45*(4), 827–841.

Bell, R. Z. A reinterpretation of the direction of effects in studies of socialization. *Psychological Review*, 1968, *75*, 81–95.

Belsky, J., and Tolan, W. J. Infants as producers of their own development: An ecological analysis. In R. M. Lerner and N. A. Busch-Rossnagel (Eds.), *Individuals* as *Producers of Their Own Development: A Life-Span Perspective*. NY: Academic Press, 1981.

Bengtson, V., and Black, O. Intergenerational relations: Continuities in socialization. In P. Baltes and K. W. Schaie (Eds.), *Life Span Developmental Psychology*. NY: Academic Press, 1973.

Bengtson, V., and Cutler, N. Generations and intergenerational relations: Perspectives on age groups and social change. In E. Shanas and R. Binstock (Eds.), *Handbook on Aging and the Social Sciences*. NY: Van Nostrand Reinhold, 1976.

Bengtson, V., and Kuypers, J. A. Generational difference and the "developmental stake." *Aging and Human Development*, 1971, *2*, 249–260.

Bengtson, V., and Schraeder, S. S. Parent–child relations. In D. J. Mangen and W. A. Peterson (Eds.), *Research Instruments in Social Gerontology: Vol. 2. Social Roles and Social Participation*. Minneapolis, MN: University of Minnesota Press, 1982, pp. 115–187.

Bengtson, V., Olander, E. B., and Haddad, A. A. The "generation gap" and aging family members: Toward a conceptual model. In J. F. Gubrium (Ed.) *Time, Roles, and Self in Old Age*. NY: Human Sciences Press, 1976.

Berardo, F. M. Kinship interaction and communications among space-age migrants. *Journal of Marriage and the Family*, 1967, *29*, 541–554.

Blenkner, M. The normal dependencies of aging. In R. A. Kalish (Ed.), *The Dependencies of Old People*. University of Michigan/Wayne State University, Institute of Gerontology, Ann Arbor, Michigan, 1969.

Bott, E. *The Family and Social Network*: Roles, norms and external relationships, 2nd ed. NY: Free Press, 1972.

Brim, O. G. Adult Socialization. In J. A. Clausen (Ed.), *Socialization and Society*. Boston, MA: Little, Brown, Inc., 1968.

Brody, E. M. The etiquette of filial behavior. *Aging and Human Development*. 1970, *1*(1), 87–94.

Brody, E. M. Aged parents and aging children. In P. K. Ragan (Ed.), *Aging parents*. Los Angeles, CA: University of Southern California Press, 1979, pp. 267–288.

Brody, E. M. Women in the middle and family help to older people. *The Gerontologist*, 1981, *21*, 471–480.

Brody, E. M. and Lang, A. They can't do it all: Aging daughters with aged mothers. *Generations*, 1982, Winter, 18–20.

Brody, E. M., Johnsen, P. T., Fulcomer, M. C., and Lang, A. M. Women's changing roles and help to elderly parents: Attitudes of three generations of women. *Journal of Gerontology*, 1983, *38*(5), 597–607.

Brody, E. M., Johnsen, P. T., and Fulcomer, M. C. What should adult children do for elderly parents? Opinions and preferences of three generations of women. *Journal of Gerontology*, 1984, *39*, 736–746.

Burgess, E. W., and Locke, H. J. *The Family: From Institution to Companionship*. NY: American Book Co., 1953.

Burgess, R. L. Child abuse: A social interactional analysis. *Advances in Clinical and Child Psychology*. 1979, *2*, 141–172.

Cheal, D. J. Intergenerational family transfers. *Journal of Marriage and the Family*, 1983, *45*(4), 805–813.

Cicirelli, V. G. *Helping Elderly Parents: Role of Adult Children*. Boston, MA: Auburn House, 1981.

Cicirelli, V. G. Adult children and their elderly parents. In T. H. Brubaker (Ed.), *Family Relationships in Later Life*. CA: Sage Publications, 1983, pp. 31–47.

Clark, M. Cultural values and dependencies in later life. In R. Kalish (Ed.), *The Dependencies of Old People*. MI: Institute of Gerontology, The University of Michigan, 1969.

Clausen, J. A., Mussen, P. H., and Kuypers, J. Involvement, warmth, and parent–child resemblances in three generations. In D. H. Eichorn, J. A. Clausen, N. Haan, M. P. Honzik, and P. H. Mussen (Eds.), *Present and Past in Middle Life*. NY: Academic Press, 1981.

Demos, J. Images of the American family: Then and now. In V. Tufte and B. Meyerhoff (Eds.), *Changing Images of the Family*. New Haven, CT: Yale University Press, 1979.

Dowd, J. J. Aging as exchange: A preface to theory. *Journal of Gerontology*, 1973, 30, 584–594.

Elder, G. H., Caspi, A., Downey, G. Problem behavior and family relationships: A multigenerational analysis. In A. Sorensen, F. Weinert, and L. Sherrod (Eds.), *Human Development: Multidisciplinary Perspectives*. Hillsdale, NJ: Erlbaum, 1986.

Erikson, E. H. *The Life Cycle Completed*. NY: W. W. Norton & Company, 1982.

Filsinger, E. E., and Lamke, L. K. The lineage transmission of interpersonal competence. *Journal of Marriage and the Family*, 1983, 45(1), 75–81.

Fischer, D. H. *Growing Old in America*. NY: Oxford University Press, 1977.

Fischer, L. R. Transitions in the mother–daughter relationship. *Journal of Marriage and the Family*. 1981, 43, 613–622.

Fischer, L. R. Mothers and mothers-in-law. *Journal of Marriage and the Family*, 1983, 45(1), 187–193.

Fischer, L. R., and Hoffman, C. Who cares for the elderly: The dilemma of family support. In M. Lewis and J. Miller (Eds.), *Social Problems and Public Policy*. Guilford, CT: JAI Press, 1983.

Frankfather, D. L., Smith, M. J., and Caro, F. G. *Family Care of the Elderly*. Lexington, MA: Lexington Books, 1981.

Friedan, B. *The Second Stage*. NY: Summit Books, 1981.

Gadlin, H. Private lives and public order: A critical view of the history of intimate relations in the U.S. In G. Levinger and H. Rausch (Eds.), *Close Relationships: Perspectives on the Meaning of Intimacy*. Amherst, MA: University of Massachusetts Press, 1977.

Hagemann-White, C. The societal context of women's role in family relationships and responsibilities. In V. Garms-Homolova, E. M. Hoerning, and D. Schaeffer (Eds.), *Intergenerational Relationships*. Lewiston, NY: C. J. Hogrefe, Inc., 1984, pp. 133–143.

Hagestad, G. O. Problems and promises in the social psychology of intergenerational relations. In Fogel et al. (Eds.), *Aging: Stability and Change in the Family*. NY: Academic Press, 1981.

Hagestad, G. O. Parent and child: Generations in the family. In T. M. Field, A. Huston, H. C. Quay, L. Troll, and G. E. Finley (Eds.), *Review of Human Development*. NY: John Wiley, 1982.

Hagestad, G. O. The continuous bond: A dynamic, multigenerational perspective on parent–child relations. In M. Perlmutter (Ed.), *Minnesota Symposium on Child Psychology*, Vol. 17. Hillsdale, NJ: Erlbaum, 1984.

Hagestad, G. O. The aging society as a context for family life. *Daedalus*, 1986, *115*(1), 119–139. (a)

Hagestad, G. O. *The age structure of families in an aging society: Four decades of Norwegian data.* Paper prepared for the Annual meetings of the American Sociological Association, New York City, New York, September. 1986. (b)

Hagestad, G. O., and Fagan, M. *Patterns of fathering in the middle years.* Paper presented at the annual meetings of the National Council on Family Relations, St. Louis, MI, October, 1974.

Hagestad, G. O., and Snow, R. *Young adult offspring as interpersonal resources in middle age.* Paper presented to the annual meeting of the Gerontological Society, San Francisco, 1977.

Hareven, T. K. Family time and historical time. *Daedalus*, 1977, *106*, 57–70.

Hartup, W. W. Perspectives on child and family interaction: Past, present, and future. In R. M. Lerner and G. B. Spanier (Eds.), *Child Influences on Marital and Family Interactions: A Life-Span Perspective.* NY: Academic Press, 1978.

Hawkinson, W. Wish, expectancy, and practice in the interaction of generations. In A. Rose and W. Peterson (Eds.), *Older People and Their Social World.* Philadelphia, PA: F. A. Davis Co., 1965.

Held, T. Generational co-residence and the transfer of authority: Some illustrations from Austrian household listings. In V. Garms-Homolova, E. M. Hoerning, and D. Schaeffer (Eds.), *Intergenerational Relationships.* Lewiston, NY: C. J. Hogrefe, Inc., 1984, pp. 41–53.

Hess, B. B., and Waring, J. M. Parent and child in later life: Rethinking the relationship. In R. M. Lerner and G. B. Spanier (Eds.), *Child Influences on Marital and Family Interaction.* NY: Academic Press, 1978.

Hill, R., Foote, N., Aldous, J., Carlson, R., and MacDonald, R. *Family Development in Three Generations.* Cambridge, MA: Schenkman, 1970.

Hill, R., and Mattessich, P. Family theory and life-span development. In P. Baltes and O. Brim, Jr. (Eds.), *Life-Span Development and Behavior*, Vol. 2. NY: Academic Press, 1979.

House, J. S. *Work Stress and Social Support.* Reading, MA: Addison-Wesley, 1981.

Irving, H. *The Family Myth.* Toronto: Copp Clark, 1972.

Johnson, E. S. Good relationships between older mothers and their daughters: A causal model. *The Gerontologist*, 1978, *18*(3), 301–306.

Kalish, R. A., and Knudtson, F. W. Attachment vs. disengagement: A life-span conceptualization. *Human Development*, 1976, *19*(2), 171–181.

Kennedy, L., and Stokes, D. Extended family support and the high cost of housing. *Journal of Marriage and the Family*, 1982, 44(May), 311–318.

Kerckhoff, A. C. Nuclear and extended family relationships: A normative and behavioral analysis. In E. Shanas and G. F. Streib (Eds.), *Social Structure and the Family: Generational Relations.* Englewood Cliffs, NJ: Prentice-Hall, 1965.

Kivnick, H. *Intergenerational relations: Personal meaning in the life cycle.* Paper presented at the annual meetings of the Gerontological Society of America, San Francisco, CA, 1983.

Knipscheer, C. *Oude mensen en hun sociale omgeving.* Gravenhage: Vuga-Baekerij's, 1980.

Knipscheer, C. The quality of the relationship between elderly people and their adult children. In V. Garms-Homolova, E. M. Hoerning, and D. Schaeffer (Eds.),

Intergenerational Relationships. Lewiston, NY: C. J. Hogrefe, Inc., 1984, pp. 90–101.

Knipscheer, C., and Bevers, A. *Older Parents and Their Middle-Aged Children: Symmetry or Asymmetry in Their Relationships.* Paper presented in the symposium "Generations: Conflict and Cooperating" for the XIIth International Congress of Gerontology, Hamburg, July, 1981.

Kreps, J. Intergenerational transfers and the bureaucracy. In E. Shanas and M. B. Sussman (Eds.), *Family, Bureaucracy, and the Elderly.* Durham, NC: Duke University Press, 1977.

Lang, A. M., and Brody, E. M. Characteristics of middle-aged daughters and help to their elderly mothers. *Journal of Marriage and the Family,* 1983, *45*(1), 193–203.

Laslett, P. *The World We Have Lost.* NY: Scribner's 1965.

Laslett, P. Characteristics of the Western family considered over time. *Journal of Family History.* 1977, *2(Summer),* 89–115.

Lee, G. R. Children and the elderly: Interaction and morale. *Research on Aging,* 1979, *1,* 335–360.

Lee, G. R. Kinship in the seventies: A decade review of research and theory. *Journal of Marriage and the Family,* 1980, *42*(4), 923–934.

Lee, G. R., and Ellithorpe, E. Intergenerational exchange and subjective well-being among the elderly. *Journal of Marriage and the Family,* 1982, *44,* 217–224.

Lehr, U. The role of women in the family generation context. In V. Garms-Homolova, E. M. Hoerning, and D. Schaeffer (Eds.), *Intergenerational Relationships.* Lewiston, NY: C. J. Hogrefe, Inc., 1984, pp. 125–133.

Lerner, R. M., and Spanier, G. B. (Eds.), *Child Influences on Marital and Family Interaction: A Life-Span Perspective.* NY: Academic Press, 1979, pp. 1–22.

Lewis, M., and Rosenblum, L. A. *The Effect of the Infant on Its Caregiver.* NY: Wiley, 1974.

Lieberman, G. L. Children of the elderly as natural helpers. *American Journal of Community Psychology,* 1978, *6,* 489–498.

Lopata, H. Z. Contributions of extended families to the support systems of metropolitan area widows: Limitations of the modified kin network. *Journal of Marriage and the Family,* 1978,*40,* 355–364.

Lopata, H. Z. *Women as Widows.* NY: Elsevier, 1979.

Lowenthal, M. F., Thurner, M., Chiriboga, D., and Associates. *Four Stages of Life.* San Francisco, CA: Jossey-Bass, Inc., 1975.

Marshall, V. W., Rosenthal, C. J., and Synge, J. Concerns about parental health. In E. Markson (Ed.), *Older Women.* Boston, MA: Lexington, 1983.

Mead, M. *Culture and Commitment: A Study of the Generation Gap.* NY: Langman, 1970.

Mindel, C. H. Multigenerational family households: Recent trends and implications for the future. *The Gerontologist,* 1979, *19*(5), 456–463.

Minturn, L. A., and Lambert, W. W. *Mothers of Six Cultures: Antecedents of Childbearing.* NY: Wiley, 1964.

Mitteness, L. S., and Nydegger, C. N. *Dimensions of parent–child relations in adulthood.* Paper presented at 35th annual meetings of The Gerontological Society of America, November 22, 1982.

Modell, J., Furstenberg, F. F., Jr., and Hershberg, T. Social change and transitions to adulthood in historical perspective. *Journal of Family History*, 1976, *1*, 7–32.

Mortimer, J., and Simmons, R. "Adult socialization." *Annual Review of Sociology*, 1978, *4*, 421–454.

Murray, J. Family structure in the preretirement years. *Social Security Bulletin*, 1973, *36*(10), 25–45.

Mutran, E., and Reitzes, D. C. Intergenerational support activities and well-being among the elderly: A convergence of exchange and symbolic interaction perspectives. *American Sociological Review*, 1984, *49*, 117–130.

National Council on the Aging. *The Myth and Reality of Aging in America*. Washington, D.C.: National Council on the Aging, 1975.

National Retired Teachers Association. American Association of Retired Persons. *National Survey of Older Americans*, No. 6, Washington, DC, Aughor: 1981.

Nydegger, C. N., and Mitteness, L. S. Old fathers and aging children: Marriage is a major source of strain. *Generations*, 1982 (Winter), 16–17.

Nye, F. I. (Ed). *Role Structure and Analysis of the Family*. Beverly Hills, CA: Sage, 1976.

Oppenheimer, V. K. The life cycle squeeze: The interaction of men's occupational and family life cycles. *Demography*, 1974, *11*, 227–245.

Oppenheimer, V. K. The changing nature of the life-cycle squeezes: Implications for the socioeconomic position of the elderly. In R. W. Fogel, E. Hatfield, S. B. Kiesler, and E. Shanas (Eds.), *Aging: Stability and Change in the Family*. NY: Academic Press, 1981.

Packard, V. *Nation of Strangers*. NY: McKay Co., 1972.

Parsons, T. The kinship system of the contemporary United States. *American Anthropologist*, 1943, *45*, 22–38.

Parsons, T., and Bales, R. F. *Family: Socialization and Interaction Process*. NY: The Free Press, 1955.

Patterson, G. R., and Reid, J. B. Reciprocity and coercion: Two facets of social systems. In C. Neuringer and J. D. Michael (Eds.), *Behavior Modification in Clinical Psychology*. NY: Appleton-Century-Crofts, 1970.

Ragan, P. K. (Ed.). *Aging Parents*. Los Angeles: University of Southern California Press, 1979.

Riley, M. W. The family in an aging society: A matrix of latent relationships. *Journal of Family Issues*, 1983, *4*, 439–454.

Riley, M. W., Johnson, M. E., and Foner, A. (Eds.), *Aging and Society: A Sociology of Age Stratification*, Vol. 3. NY: Russell Sage Foundation, 1972.

Robinson, B. Validation of a caregiving strain index. *Journal of Gerontology*, 1983, *38*, 344–348.

Robinson, B., and Thurner, M. Taking care of aged parents: A family cycle transition. *Gerontologist*, 1979, *19*, 586–593.

Rohrer, R. *They Love Me, They Love Me Not: A World-Wide Study of the Effect of Parental Acceptance and Rejection*. New Haven, CT: HRAF Press, 1975.

Rosenmayr, L. *A view of multigenerational relations in the family*. Paper presented at the 9th World Congress of Sociology, Uppsala, Sweden, 1978.

Rosenthal, C. J. *Kinkeeping: A task in the familial division of labor*. Paper presented at the combined annual meetings of the Gerontological Society of America and the Canadian Association on Gerontology, Toronto, November, 1981.

Rosow, I. Intergenerational relationships: Problems and proposals. In E. Shanas and G. F. Streib (Eds.), *Social Structure and the Family: Intergenerational Relations.* Englewood Cliffs, NJ: Prentice-Hall, 1965.

Rossi, A. S. Aging and parenthood in the middle years. In P. B. Baltes and O. G. Brim, Jr. (Eds.), *Life-Span Development and Behavior.* NY: Academic Press, 1980.

Schmidt, M. G. Failing parents, aging children. *Journal of Gerontological Social Work,* 1980, *2,* 259–268.

Schorr, A. L. *"Thy Father and Thy Mother . . . :" A Second Look at Filial Responsibility and Family Policy.* SSA Publication No. 13–11953. Washington, DC: U.S. Department of Health, Education, and Welfare, 1980.

Sears, R. R., Maccoby, E. E., and Levin, H. *Patterns of Child Rearing.* Evanston, IL: Row, Peterson, 1957.

Seelbach, W. C. Gender differences in expectations for filial responsibility. *The Gerontologist,* 1977, *17,* 421–425.

Seelbach, W. C. Correlates of aged parents' filial responsibility expectations and realizations. *Family Coordinator,* 1978, *27,* 341–350.

Shanas, E. Family relationships. In L. Brown and E. Ellis (Eds.), *Quality of Life, Vol, III: The Later Years.* Acton, MA: Publishing Science Group, 1975.

Shanas, E. Social myth as hypothesis: The case of the family relations of old people. *Gerontologist,* 1979, *19,* 3–9.

Shanas, E. Older people and their families: The new pioneers. *Journal of Marriage and the Family,* 1980, *42*(9), 9–15.

Shanas, E., and Streib, G. (Eds.), *Social Structures and the Family: Generational Relations.* NY: Prentice-Hall, 1965.

Shanas, E., and Sussman, M. B. (Eds.), *Family, Bureaucracy, and the Elderly,* Durham, NC: Duke University Press, 1977.

Shanas, E., and Sussman, M. B. The family in later life: Social structure and social policy. In R. W. Fogel, E. Hatfield, S. B. Kiesler, and E. Shanas (Eds.). *Aging: Stability and Change in the Family.* NY: Academic Press, Inc., 1981, pp. 211–233.

Shanas, E., Townsend, P., Wedderburn, D., Friis, H., Milhoj, P., and Stenhouwer, J. *Old People in Three Industrial Societies.* London/NY: Atherton and Routledge Kegan Paul, 1968.

Soldo, B. J. America's elderly in the 1980s. *Population Bulletin,* 1980, *35*(4), 1–47.

Soldo, B. J., and Lauriat, P. Living arrangements among the elderly in the United States: A log-linear approach. *Journal of Comparative Family Studies,* 1976, *7*(Summer), 351–366.

Stoller, E. P. Parental caregiving by adult children. *Journal of Marriage and the Family,* 1983, *45*(4), 851–858.

Streib, G. F., and Beck, R. W. Older families: A decade review. *Journal of Marriage and the Family,* 1980, *42,* 937–956.

Sussman, M. B. 1981 Burgess address: Law and legal systems: The family connection. *Journal of Marriage and the Family,* 1983, *45*(1), 9–23.

Sussman, M. B., and Burchinal, L. Kin family network: Unheralded structure in current conceptualizations of family functioning. *Marriage and Family Living,* 1962, *24,* 231–240.

Teeland, L. *Keeping in Touch*. Gothenburg, Sweden: University of Gothenburg Monograph, 1978.

Tinsley, B. R., and Parke, R. D. Grandparents as support and socialization agents. In M. Lewis (Ed.), *Beyond the Dyad*. NY: Plenum, 1984.

Tobin, S., and Kulys, R. The family and service. In C. Eisdorfer (Ed.), *Annual Review of Gerontology and Geriatrics*, Vol. 1, NY: Springer, 1980, pp. 370–399.

Townsend, P. *The Family Life of Old People*. London: Routledge and Kegan Paul, 1957.

Townsend, P. Emergence of the four-generation family in industrial society. In B. L. Neugarten (Ed.), *Middle Age and Aging*. Chicago, IL: University of Chicago Press, 1968, pp. 255–257.

Treas, J. Family support systems for the aged. *The Gerontologist*, 1977, *17*, 486–491.

Treas, J. Intergenerational families and social change. In P. K. Ragan (Ed.), *Aging Parents*. Los Angeles, CA: University of Southern California Press, 1979, pp. 58–66.

Troll, L. E. The family of later life: A decade review. *Journal of Marriage and the Family*, 1971, *33*, 263–290.

Troll, L. E., and Bengtson, V. L. Generations in the family. In W. R. Burr, R. Hill, F. I. Nye, and I. L. Reiss (Eds.), *Contemporary Theories About the Family*, Vol. 1. NY: The Free Press, 1979, pp. 127–161.

Troll, L. E., and Smith J. Attachment through the life span: Some questions about dyadic bonds among adults. *Human Development*, 1976, *19*(2), 156–170.

Troll, L. E., Miller, S. J., and Atchley, R. C. *Families in Later Life*. Belmont, CA: Wadsworth, 1979.

Turner, J. G. Patterns of intergenerational exchange: A developmental approach. *International Journal of Aging and Human Development*, 1975, *6*(2), 111–115.

Uhlenberg, P. Death and the family. *Journal of Family History*, 1980, *5*, 313–320.

U.S. General Accounting Office. *Report to the Congress: The well-being of older people in Cleveland, Ohio*. Washington, D.C.: Document No. HRD–77–70, 1977.

Wake, S. B., and Sporakowski, M. An intergenerational comparison of attitudes towards supporting aged parents. *Journal of Marriage and the Family*, 1972, *34*, 42–48.

Walker, A. J., and Thompson, L. Intimacy and intergenerational aid and contact among mothers and daughters. *Journal of Marriage and the Family*, 1983, *45*(4), 841–849.

Walters, J., and Walters, L. H. Parent–child relationships: A review, 1970–1979. *Journal of Marriage and the Family*, 1980, *42*, 807–822.

Wandersman, L. P., Wandersman, A., and Kahn, S. Social support in the transition to parenthood. *Journal of Community Psychology*, 1980, *8*, 332–342.

Wilen, J. B. *Changing relationships among grandparents, parents, and their young adult children*. Paper presented at the annual meeting of the Gerontological Society, Washington, D.C., 1979.

Wirth, L. Urbanism as a way of life. *American Journal of Sociology*, 1938, *44*, 1–24.

Wood, V., and Robertson, J. F. Friendship and kinship interaction: Differential effects on the morale of the elderly. *Journal of Marriage and the Family*, 1978, *40*, 367–375.

16 PARENTING, GRANDPARENTING, AND INTERGENERATIONAL CONTINUITY*

Vern L. Bengtson

Parenting, at least within the human group, has always been a hazardous enterprise. Parents invest prodigious amounts of time, energy, and material resources in the uncertain hope of producing offspring who will be happy, healthy, and wise—and who will, hopefully, validate at least some of their parents' principles. But their offspring are continually changing, as is the social environment within which they are growing up. One of the things parents strive for is continuity: indicators in the behavior of their children that they have achieved transmission of what is best or better than in their own lives. One of the things children strive for is distinctiveness: a better way of life, a more successful social order.

Thus, parenting represents a classic human paradox involving social manifestations of generational distinctiveness or continuity. On the one hand, there is the process of generational turnover and replacement. This implies change—both biological and social. Children are not mere replicas of their parents; they represent subtly new genetic combinations in interaction with a unique developmental environment (Rossi, 1980). They also represent social innovation, as new participants in existing social systems (Wood and Ng, 1980). The product of unique sociohistoric influences, children are the carriers of new perspectives and commitments that represent the potential for change in the existing social order (Elder, 1978).

On the other hand, there is substantial biosocial continuity across generations, seen in genetic and social similarities between parents and children. Despite change and the impulse of distinctiveness, the inertia of tradition persists through decades and across generations and cohorts, even in the rapidly changing world of science (see Cohen, 1985; Kuhn, 1962). Historical comparisons suggest more stability through time in groups and societies than we commonly acknowledge (Allen, 1952). Social continuity is attempted most directly in the efforts of the older generation to transmit and preserve. Upholding a social order they have created, perhaps

*With the assistance of Donna Polisar.

struggling to preserve positions of power, the *ancien régime* attempts to enhance continuity in the face of generational succession and innovation.

Other chapters in this volume have examined biosocial aspects of the process of parenting: across species, across cultures, and across the life span. In this chapter the focus is on the consequences of that process, seen in the context of tensions between social continuity and of innovation between generations. First, an instance of the macrosocial dilemmas of parenting will be examined, what future historians might look to as a modern example of the classic struggle of continuity and distinctiveness between social generations—the protest movements of the 1960's, with their indicators of generational rebellion and age-group cleavage. Second, some conceptual distinctions that help in understanding the generational causes of these movements will be explored: cohort, lineage, and period effects, whose operations are important in charting social change. Third, there will be a focus on issues of distinctiveness and influence in generational processes, reviewing some evidence in values and opinions of contrasts or similarities among youth, parents, and grandparents.

GENERATIONS AND THE DECADE OF PROTEST

The paradox of generational continuity or change appears as a recurrent theme in human writings, from Greek tragedy up to today's daily newspaper. The succession of one generation by another involves tension between stability and innovation, reflected in the lives of individuals and social groups as they move through time.

The puzzle of continuity across generations, or its lack, involves two quite different problems reflecting two contrasting levels of analysis. The first concerns macrosocial manifestations of stability or change through time, and the effects of generational turnover or cohort succession on broad patterns of social organization and culture.

At the societal level, social systems go through what Ryder (1965) described as "demographic metabolism" for the entry of new cohort members and departure of the old. As Matilda Riley (1976, 1985) has pointed out, variable cohort flow leads to alteration in the age stratification of societies. Fertility, mortality levels, trends, and relationships among demographic groups and social positions are relevant variables here (Riley, 1985). Given the birth rate, the dependency ratio, economic conditions, and political trends, the question becomes: are existing social structures and available roles appropriate to the population of birth cohorts growing up and moving into adulthood? If they are not, there is clear indication of possible upcoming social change; the structures of existing society will be altered by the sheer size of a population moving into adult positions. Cherlin (1981) has discussed the potential "generation crunch" as social changes result from current demographic trends. The rapidity of change creates periods of transition in which role strain (i.e., conflicts between cohort-related roles of female, daughter, wife, mother, career person) may be experienced because individuals have not yet been socialized to the consequences of a particular structural change; they have not had enough "rehearsal" time in the negotiation of life-course change. There is, of course, danger in a simplistic one-to-one juxtaposition of population processes and subsequent social change; but that cohort size influences macrosocial developments has become an incontrovertible argument (see Cherlin, 1981; Elder, 1984; Easterlin, 1980; Riley, 1976, 1984; Ryder, 1965).

The second level of analysis, the microstructural, focuses on the face-to-face negotiation of generational turnover and its social manifestations. The most obvious context is the family, a "unit of interacting personalities" (Burgess, 1926) comprised of individuals at different levels in the unfolding succession of generations. Here the paradox of continuity versus change is most immediate, as family members negotiate norms, roles, and values consistent with their life-cycle positions. As Hagestad (1984) has pointed out, the negotiation of similarity versus individuation is complex, delicate, and unending—as well as frequently unnoticed. Outside the family (in microsocial encounters characterizing the workplace, the school, and voluntary organizations) interaction between "social generations" may be less affect-laden, but it still involves the negotiation of continuity or innovation between actors who have different "developmental stakes" in the maintenance of existing structures and patterns because of their differences in generational position (Bengtson and Kuypers, 1971).

The recent history of social movements in America provides a useful example of both macro- and microlevel phenomena involved in problems of parenting. More generally, they illustrate complex issues of generational succession and social change. Between 1960 and 1970 Americans became concerned about the prospect of political and social cleavages between age groups, which appeared to be pulling society apart, and the "generation gap" suddenly became a cliché. Parenting, in the Benjamin Spock era, became viewed as a macrosocial problem (Leventman, 1982).

Five distinct but related social movements which had cohort- and generational-related overtones characterized this "decade of protest."

First was the emergence in 1959–1961 of the civil rights movement, in which predominantly youthful whites and blacks marched together to protest the discrepancy between values of equality and actions of organized discrimination. The "freedom riders" and their peaceful protests culminated in bloody confrontations that troubled an entire nation, suddenly aware that some of their youth were serious about social change. One legacy was the emergence of the New Left, with its innovative articulation of Marxist themes applied to old social inequities (Breines, 1982).

The second movement started out more lightheartedly: the free speech movement, begun in Berkeley in May, 1964, was portrayed by the press as an attempt to shock the establishment by shouting obscenities over loud-speakers within the hallowed halls of academe (Nassi, 1981). But the issues were much more serious—college students questioning the legitimacy of their elders' complete control over educational governance, including the right to absolutely free speech. The student movement was born and quickly spread across the nation, revolutionizing academic decision-making and instructional mores.

Students appeared in classrooms with nonnegotiable demands regarding curricula; they "sat in" administrative offices to change *in loco parentis* rules. Academic administrators, benign authority figures representing un-wanted parental control, were being challenged as never before (Miller and Gilmore, 1975). Expressions of student unrest in the 1960's were often interpreted as social manifestations of generational conflict (see Bettleheim, 1965). From another perspective, however, the movement represented cohort expressions of age-related strivings for personal autonomy and social justice (Flacks, 1967; Feuer, 1969).

At the same time, American military involvement in Southeast Asia was escalating in what Barbara Tuchman (1984) describes as a classic case of "the march of folly." The antiwar movement, beginning in 1965–1966 and manned by predominantly youthful protesters in deadly earnest, drove one President from office and shook the views of America's elders concerning American foreign policy. The Kent State killing of four students by National Guardsmen presented the spectre of law-and-order at any cost in the face of peaceful protest. By 1969 virtually every 4-year college in the nation had experienced some form of organized protest on the part of youth questioning the moral and legal basis for an undeclared war directed by their elders (Wood and Ng, 1980). Most families probably experienced the disquieting effects of intergenerational confrontation about the war. It was a sobering spectacle of "America betraying herself" (Tuchman, 1984) in the eyes of many youths. The legacies of the antiwar movement are still with us (Surrey, 1982), and many of today's voters had their ideologies shaped by the rhetoric of that struggle (Wheeler, 1984).

The fourth major social movement of this decade, the women's move-ment, began quietly in the 1960's and is today the most obviously active of any of the five. Deckard (1983) discusses the political, sociological, and psychological issues of the women's movement and concludes that gener-ational distinctiveness was not one of its major foci. In order to create fundamental change, Deckard asserts that more than a decade of protest has been required. The women's movement has shown its strength and flexibil-ity with the passage of time. Adaptation of tradition and consciousness raising has touched all groups (Freeman, 1975).

The women's movement is, in this context, perhaps the least indicative of generational cleavages, since its most visible spokeswomen have not been college-age youth. But it is also perhaps the least co-opted by other interest groups and subsequent political or economic developments. In a recent examination of women students in business school, Cancian (1980) reviews the social and structural processes that contribute to the explanation and understanding of developments in the acceptance and endorsement of women in a male-dominated area of expertise. Continuing indicators of economic inequities between males and females suggest that the impetus to change is very much present as younger generations of women come of age.

The fifth social movement of the 1960's involved styles and philosophy of life more than policy-oriented issues. This has been termed the counter-culture movement (Leventman, 1982; Yinger, 1982). Groups of youth began espousing values and behaviors that ran counter to the ethos of productivity, cleanliness, and capitalism that appeared to characterize their parents' generation. Long hair, secondhand clothes, communal living, recreational use of drugs, casual sex—all reflected an emerging life style in clear contrast to middle-aged, middle-class conventions of the 1960's. Their shock value was significant. Charles Reich (1970) called it "the greening of America."

Margaret Mead (1970) gave the movement a more scholarly, and even more radical, interpretation. She suggested that these youth were "immi-grants in time" moving into a new cultural configuration and reversing prior mechanisms of socialization. Whereas in hundreds of previous generations of human society children had learned from their parents, Mead suggested that social and technological innovation had accelerated so rapidly that in the next generation children would have to teach their parents how to survive, what is good or valuable, and what is bad or maladaptive. The "counterculture" was for Mead a radical departure, and the older genera-tion had better learn from it—and adapt. In one of the most memorable quotes of this period, Edgar Friedenberg (1969) gave the following judgment: "Young people today aren't rebelling against their parents: they're *aban-doning* them" (p. 219). Middle-class parenting, in this perspective, was simply irrelevant to the cultural epoch that lay ahead.

COHORT, LINEAGE, HISTORICAL PERIOD

How can one account for such contrasts between cohorts of youth and elders (and generations of parents and children) as seemed to surface in this decade of protest? What are the causes of social differences and similarities between cohorts and generations? Three concepts may be useful in explain-ing the change and continuity in intergenerational comparisons evident between 1960 and 1970: cohort, lineage, and period effects. Although all three effects are interrelated, each provides a slightly different perspective for viewing the succession of generations and subsequent social change (Bengtson, Cutler, Mangen, & Marshall, 1985). And each reflects the fact that parenting and its outcomes must be considered on three levels of change and development: individual, family, and historical (Aldous, 1978; Elder, 1984; Hareven, 1977; Hagestad, 1984).

The *cohort effect*, or what may be less elegantly termed the potential "cohort gap" between individuals of different ages, refers to real or apparent differences between groups born at different points in historical time. In 1987, those who were born in 1965 compared with those born in 1925 can be expected to evidence somewhat different personal or sociopolitical concerns as well as life experiences. A first reason concerns processes of biosocial development, phrased as maturation and aging: born in different points in time, the members of these cohorts are at different points in the human life cycle—at different stages psychologically, physiologically, and sociologically. Second, because each cohort grew up in different points in historical time, they will also have experienced common sociopolitical events differently, as those events were encountered at different stages of life-span development. The war in Vietnam was undoubtedly experienced quite differently by most 20 year olds compared to their 50-year-old parents, and these differences were reflected in public opinion data showing contrasts between cohorts (Cutler, 1976). There are good reasons for the existence of contrasts between individuals born at different points in time, either on the basis of maturation or cohort experience. There are, in short, good reasons for manifestations of a cohort-level generation gap.

Karl Mannheim (1952) was the first modern sociologist to explicitly relate social change to age cohort effects. Because in the process of generational succession there is a "continuous emergence of new participants in the cultural process," (p. 293) "each new generation comes to live within a specific, individually acquired, framework of usable past experience, so that every new experience has its form and its place largely marked out for it in advance" (p. 296). He further pointed out that "members of any one generation can only participate in a temporally limited section of the historical process" (p. 296). It is because each new age cohort comes afresh upon the social scene and can see it with a new perspective that new variations of old themes occur. It is from this fresh contact with existing social structures and values that a new "Weltanschauung," a new spirit of the age, evolves.

Mannheim also proposed the independent effect of what he termed the "generational unit"—members of a birth cohort who become "forerunners" in the pursuit of new alternatives to existing styles or causes. Not all people born at the same time share the same socialization or perceive historical events in the same way. "Only where contemporaries are in a position to participate as an integrated group in certain common experiences can we rightly speak of community of location of a generation" (p. 298). Mannheim's notion of generation as a social unit is, however insightful, somewhat imprecise. While "the sociological phenomenon of generations is ultimately based on the biological rhythm of birth and death," his suggestion that we try "to understand the generation as a particular type of social location" (p. 290–291) does not provide researchers with a clear conceptual definition upon which they might build. As a result of Mannheim's imprecision, Kertzer (1983) criticizes use of the term "generation" in discussions of cohort contrasts. The problem, Kertzer asserts, lies in the conceptual ambiguity of generation. Each author's interpretation is an attempt to clarify, yet contradictory meanings prohibit the ability to compare studies using generation, or they tend to produce conflicting results and conclusions. Certainly no single characterization of youth in the 1960's would be completely descriptive of all members of that cohort (Laufer and Bengtson, 1974). Rather, a range of styles can be discerned, including revivalists, communalists, and freaks. Although all of these youth were members of the same birth cohort, they are clearly not of the same generational unit. As Braungart (1984) has noted, other social structural variables such as social class, race, and geographic location can be expected to influence intracohort differentiations.

The *lineage effect*, or lineage gap, refers to real or perceived differences between generations within families. The family is a structure of social organization in which there are a series of statuses defined by ranked descent. Fathers and mothers, sons and daughters, grandchildren and grandparents, all form successive links in the flow of biological and social generations. This conceptual tool was used by the very first recorded historians to put in order events of history: writers of the Old Testament set off historical periods by lineage; time of a particular event was frequently indexed by reference to the life span of a particular ancestor in the lineage chain.

Even though lineage descent is an easily measureable phenomenon for social scientists, it becomes complex in two ways. The first is suggested by Hagestad's (1981) aphorism that "generations do not file into families by cohort." The second reflects the transfer from the microsocial level of a particular family to the macrosocial level of large aggregates such as the population of a nation. The term generation is very inexact in terms of social boundaries. Reference can be made to the generation of American college students today and one can assume, although the term has been used imprecisely, that at least the reference is to a group of individuals most of whom share a birthdate of 18 to 22 years earlier. But if reference is made to the parental generation of the same students, the referent is a group whose ages may vary considerably. The timing of the births of children varies to a much greater extent than the timing of entry into college. This occurs for two reasons: the timing of first births may not be normatively patterned, and the spacing and number of children within a family interacts with parental age.

Such differences in timing of generations within lineages may have important consequences. Linda Burton (see Burton and Bengtson, 1985) examined psychosocial consequences of the grandparental role in two groups of grandmothers—those who assumed the grandparental role "early" in chronological years (age 27–34) versus those who assumed the role "on time" (age 40 and above). In some of the families, Burton was able to interview the great-grandmothers and even one great great grandmother. There was one six-generation family in the sample in which the 91-year-old great great grandmother was living alone, while the young mother and infant were living with the 29-year-old grandmother. In this lineage, four of the six generations of women gave birth to their first child when they were between 11 and 14 years of age. This case illustrates two points: first, timing of first pregnancy may be transmitted from generation to generation. Second, families are differentiated by age and by generational membership, but that differentiation does not necessarily coincide with the normative pattern of events found within a particular cohort (Elder, 1984).

Are there inevitable differences between cohorts (or "generations") by virtue of differential status as parent or child? Much of 20th century psychology has assumed so, following the suggestions of Freud. The notion is that an inevitable and perhaps useful rebellion occurs as young children wish, first of all, to become their parents, and second, to take over many of the prerequisites and power of parents (Bettleheim, 1965). The theme of such generational conflict within families frequently appears throughout western literature. The aged King Lear at the end of Shakespeare's tragedy— an embittered king seeing his wishes disrespected, and crying, "Oh, the infamy that is to be a parent!" His words indeed reflect a lineage gap.

But there is another and opposite dimension to the lineage effect—the processes of intergenerational socialization in which generations attempt to influence each other. Most often this is seen in transmission effects from parents to children; but, as will be noted later, transmission and influence are best seen as bidirectional (Hagestad, 1984; Glass, Bengtson, & Dunham, 1986). At any rate, the intended product of socialization is some degree of similarity in values and opinions, and the process involved is intergenerational interaction geared to enhancing similarity between parents and children.

As Tamara Hareven (1977) has noted, the historical trends in family demography have created striking contrasts in intergenerational contact and interactions today compared with the last century. Declining fertility has effected differences simply in the number of individuals per generation within a given family. Moreover, much more contact takes place today between generations geographically distant from each other than at any other time in American history because of advances in telecommunications and travel technology.

Whether the quality of intergenerational contact has changed as much as the quantity over the last century is not as certain. However, evidence from 19th century American diaries and novels suggests that disaffection between generations was often resolved by the younger generation moving west to the frontier and having little further contact with the older generation (Vinovskis, 1978).

The third explanation, the *period effect*, involves comparisons of perceptions, events, or attitudes at a given point in time to those of another time. An Arab proverb claims that "men resemble their times more than they do their fathers." It is to period effects that this proverb refers.

When examining relationships between generations or between age groups within society, it is instructive to compare them to other periods of history. Over a decade later, pronouncements like Friedenberg's (1969) and Mead's (1970) quoted above concerning new generational configurations in our culture appear almost quaint. On contemporary college campuses there are few reminders that the 1960's clash between generations was so pervasive and portentous (Breines, 1982; Braungart & Braungart, 1986). Age groups do not seem to oppose each other much; rather, as in the 1950's, all age groups today appear vaguely concerned about high prices, taxes, jobs, and America's foreign policy. The 1958 of Eisenhower, not the 1984 of Orwell, seems the more appropriate analog to today's America. Perhaps the apparent swing of the pendulum is exactly the point: That both change and continuity are exhibited by social groups comprised of different generations at contrasting points of historical time.

Throughout the philosophical and moral literature of Western civilization are encountered the laments of older generations concerning the young. Plato's observations about the young being undisciplined, unmotivated, and taking drugs is often repeated today as solace for those in the middle generation who may find that their own children's lack of industry fails to meet their ideals. It is possible that the so-called generation gap is really not more serious even in today's fast-changing society than it was a hundred years ago. It is possible that there is an inevitable "period gap," which only seems to reflect generational cleavages (the youth being the most outspoken advocates of new interpretations and events).

In short, it is necessary to distinguish among three conceptual causes of the differences that appear between generations. Each effect—cohort, lineage, and period—may create natural and inevitable differences in the attitudes, values, and behaviors of the individuals involved in the negotiation of intergenerational interaction. But each also can be seen as effecting some degree of continuity. Maturational changes can be expected to bring children closer to their parents' orientations as they mature in adulthood; lineage effects involve mutual influence between generations and therefore greater similarity; period effects involve all contemporaneous generations experiencing similar sociohistorical events and adapting to them in parallel, if not in series. In sum, age groups reflected in generations and cohorts must be seen as social units moving through time, exhibiting both change and continuity.

What do these perspectives suggest about the causes of social movements in the 1960's and their roots in generational cleavage? Was this a classic case of "generational rebellion," at the macrosocial or microsocial level of analysis; and if not, what were its more likely antecedents?

Certainly cohort effect explanations are the most plausible. At the macrosocial level the antecedents of these social movements can surely be traced to one factor involving the succession of generations: population processes that resulted in a "baby boom" coming of age. The sheer numbers of youthful recruits into the social order could have been expected to change existing configurations of both roles and ideologies. That few commentators had noted this or predicted the massive social resulting changes is perhaps surprising—especially in the wake of classroom-building and school expansion that occurred in the 1950's as these "baby boomers" went off to elementary school. But Americans are notoriously optimistic, and perhaps optimism breeds conservatism in terms of the belief that things will pretty much stay the same and get better. Certainly most people expect that their children will have a better life than they had—a hope that, in today's economic climate, is perhaps unrealistic. That the protesters of the 1960's are today mostly middle-class producers and consumers worrying about mortgages and financing their children's college education does not deny that their sociopolitical ideology was affected by their cohort experiences (see Fendrich, 1974; Wheeler, 1984).

At the microsocial level the predictors of the five social movements are less clear. Certainly there was evidence of contrasts in values and sociopolitical attitudes between social movement participants and their parents. However, having and/or espousing different values is not necessarily a rejection of one's parents, or is it an invalidation of the transmission of values via one's parents. Deutscher (1973) has suggested that Americans are socialized to believe from early childhood that change is both inevitable and good. If Americans do have a national ethos that applauds and internalizes progress (i.e., change), as Deutscher asserts, familial continuity may merely be expressed in different forms. With the passage of time, sociohistorical events tailor these changing forms. Yet, in speaking of changing configurations in the life course, Uhlenberg (1978) cautions that it is important not to ignore the remarkable stability *and* adaptability of the American family. Temporal dimensions create shifts in demographic and social aspects of the family life course (Bengtson and Treas, 1980). These subsequent shifts give rise to questions and future challenges in parenting, grandparenting, and intergenerational continuity.

It does not appear to be the case that the young radicals of the 1960's were "rebelling" against their parents (Flacks, 1967). On the contrary, the left-wing college students were, as a group, more in political agreement with their parents—liberals themselves—than were the less active, more conservative students Flacks and his associates interviewed (Whalen and Flacks, 1981; Wood and Ng, 1980). A similar conclusion was drawn by Keniston

(1968) in his analysis of the psychosocial development of "young radicals." These studies suggest that the youthful protestors in the forefront of 1960s social movements were implicitly carrying out an agenda of intergenerational continuity, not change, and applying parental pronouncements of involvement, consistency, and principled living far more extensively than their parents had foreseen.

Moreover, their actions undoubtedly influenced their parents—and their grandparents. Nowhere is this more clear than in the rapid adoption by middle-class, middle-aged Americans by 1970 of the paraphernalia of counterculture style: blue jeans and beards and bell-bottomed pants, not to mention increased use of psychotropic drugs and a greater openness in exploring "The Joys of Sex" (Comfort, 1968). In the political realism, the influence of youth on their elders is less clear, since the issues of age cleavage quickly became co-opted by other sociopolitical issues—Watergate, the energy crisis, inflation—in a classic example of period effects muting the cohort or lineage contrasts evident a few years earlier.

DISTINCTIVENESS AND INFLUENCE

Two assumptions can be seen in analyses concerning parent–child interaction prior to the "decade of protest." The first deals with the inevitability of substantial differences, if not conflict, between parents and children (Bettleheim, 1965; Davis, 1940; Mannheim, 1952). As new cohorts of youth become independent adults, they attempt to maximize their distinctiveness from the parental generation. The second assumption concerns the direction of influence in socialization. Most studies examining similarity between youth and parents adopted a unidirectional model of transmission, in which influence is seen as passing down the generations from parent to child, from elder to youth. This assumption is based on the earlier one that individuals' potential for change and development is highest at the beginning of life and is minimized after adolescence.

However, recent evaluations of intergenerational interaction (see Acock, 1984; Hagestad, 1981; Glass, Bengtson & Dunham, 1986) are based on an alternative assumption, that the interactions involved in socialization affect all participants, whatever their time of life. This leads to two corollaries. The first is that distinctiveness between parents and youth is modified by processes enhancing solidarity between generations; the second, that socialization is bilateral, not unidirectional. If youth adopt new behaviors and values, for example, it is plausible that these will influence and perhaps modify the prior orientations of their parents. From this perspective, each interacting generation will change, develop, or be socialized anew in the ongoing process of negotiating generational emergence. This logic is consistent with the emerging life-course perspective within the sociology of aging (Dannefer, 1984; Featherman, 1981: Featherman & Lerner, 1986).

Socialization and Transmission

Socialization can best be seen as a process of ongoing negotiation between generations representing the assumption of new age-related roles, a process that can be viewed both within and outside the family. Relations between parents and children at each stage of the life course reflect influence processes that are both reciprocal and continuously changing. The patterns of such influence within families are altered, directly or indirectly, by societal processes that themselves can be viewed in generational themes, and that derive from period and cohort themes, on the one hand, and family themes, on the other.

For example, in the process of transition into adulthood, a new cohort of youth, or at least what can be called, following Mannheim (1953), a band of "forerunners" in that cohort may strike a unique theme or keynote that sets the group apart from its parents and elders, as happened in the 1960's. But as the research by Flacks (1967) and his associates suggests, such a keynote often derives from the salient leitmotivs of the forerunner's families; power and persistence of the archetypal message within the culture depends upon its congruence with the emerging thrusts of ongoing historical processes.

Transmission has the connotation of sequentially passing on information in a linear fashion from one unit of a system to another (such as generations within a family). But it is important to note that transmission also implies exchange—that the actions of each unit in the sequence are influenced by the actions of the others (Dowd, 1981). In short, there is feedback among elements of the system. Under such conditions sequence or causal ordering may be difficult to ascertain.

This is the case in regard to questions concerning intergenerational transmission or contrast in the 1960's. Indications of similarities or differences between parents and children compared at one point in time can be used to examine three issues involved in generational analysis (Bengtson, Furlong, & Laufer, 1974). The first involves descriptions concerning the degree of similarity or difference between generations. To what extent do parents, children, and grandchildren appear to be distinctive from or to replicate each other in behaviors, attitudes, and orientations? A second issue concerns the causes of generational contrast or similarity. Can differences between generations within a given family be attributed to contrasts in developmental or ontogenetic status, or are they better traced to cohort effects—to being born and coming of age at different points of history, evidencing the differential influence of sociohistorical trends (Elder, 1978)? The third issue concerns sequence. Is it at all possible to infer "transmission" from evidence of "similarity"? If so, who influences whom—do parents not learn from their children, as well as the reverse (Glass, Bengtson & Dunham, 1986)?

Distinctiveness

Two theoretical extremes are evident in examinations of similarity or contrast among generations. One emphasizes the inevitability of differences because of different locations in developmental and historical time. Each cohort must deal anew with issues of identity, intimacy, values, and appropriate behaviors as it moves into adulthood and comes into what Mannheim (1952) termed "fresh contact" with established configurations of culture. This contrast between youthful idealism and establishment folkways is especially true in periods of rapid social change (Davis, 1940; Reich, 1970). Mead (1970) argued that in the "prefigurative" culture that was emerging since Sputnik, the old must learn from the young, since the pace of contemporary technosocial change is accelerating so rapidly.

The opposite position minimizes generational contrasts. Apparent differences between generations are temporary; children differ from their parents primarily because of ontogenetic developmental status (Adelson, 1970). Adolescents are different from older adults, but when youth in turn become middle-aged or old, they will then presumably resemble their parents and grandparents. The stereotypic portrayal of the "Yuppies" cohort emerging to espouse conservative values after their youthful protest indiscretions were outgrown is an example.

An accurate picture of generational distinctiveness probably lies between these two extremes. But relevant to both extremes may be the "generational stake" each cohort has in maximizing or minimizing its perception of continuity (Bengtson & Kuypers, 1971). On the one hand, parents may wish to minimize their offspring's distinctiveness. The perspective of middle-aged parents on the next generation is in part a product of their own life-span status (as postulated in Erickson's (1950) Stage 7 concerning "generativity" needs). The effort and commitment parents have invested in raising their children, their present diminished influence on them, as well as the recognition of their own mortality, make it important that the next generation "carry on." On the other hand, their children, establishing what Erikson (1950) calls "identity" distinctiveness, are looking forward to an independently constructed life ahead. Needing to express their uniqueness, they may minimize apparent continuities with their parents—grandparents. Each generation, thus, has a different "stake" in the intergenerational continuity or distinctiveness. (See discussions of this point in Lerner, 1975: and Lerner & Knapp, 1975.)

One study attempted to explore the distinctiveness of value orientations across three generations shortly after the "decade of protest," examining contrasts and similarities among grandparents, parents, and young adult grandchildren. Over 2000 respondents were asked to rank in order of importance 16 items reflecting various goals or orientations (Bengtson and Lovejoy, 1973). Some contrasts were evident between generations. "Achievement," for example, was ranked highest by the middle-aged parents, significantly lower by youth, and still lower by grandparents. "Personal freedom" was ranked very high by youth, but two scale points lower by the grandparents—a pattern seen also in "skill" and "exciting life."

While value differences between generations are reflected in these data, there are also similarities; what is most interesting is that many of the differences run counter to usual expectations. On the item, "a world at peace," the youth who appeared to be in the forefront of peace demonstrations in the 1960's. But of the three groups it was the grandparents who ranked this value highest. Similar patterns appeared on "service to mankind" and "equality of mankind"—valued highest by the grandparents, next by the grandchildren, and last by the parents. These scores on humanistic values suggested that some stereotypes about generational differences in orientations were inaccurate. Not only are there similarities in value rankings, but the differences that do exist run counter to stereotypic expectations. There is, in short, little in these data to support the proposition of generational distinctiveness in values.

Another issue addressed in this study is the question of family lineage (socialization) versus cohort membership (age) factors in defining value orientations. To what extent are patterns of family socialization apparent from the values data—in light of the generation or age group contrasts just reviewed? In a two-way analysis of variance, value orientations were examined in terms of cohort versus lineage effects (Bengtson, 1975). It was found that through three generations value similarities could be traced suggesting some degree of lineage continuity in orientations. However, there was more agreement on values *within* the grandparent, parent, and child cohorts than there was *between* generations within the family, pointing to the operation of cohort effects within these family lineages. These results suggest that direct parent–child socialization attempts will produce values in the child that are similar to, but not necessarily replications of, those of the parent.

The most explicit evidence of bidirectional influence is found in Hagestad's (1977, 1982, 1984) analyses of child interaction and socialization (see Chapter 15 of this volume). In her 1972 dissertation research examining role changes in the "empty nest" transition, 119 mothers of college-age children were asked whether they felt their children had tried to influence them during the past 2 or 3 years and whether such efforts had been successful. Three-fourths of the sample recalled such attempts, and about two-thirds of these reported them to have had an effect. A number suggested that without such influence they would have found the events of the late 1960's to be much more foreign and threatening. One woman volunteered, "You think that boys with long hair are a strange and dangerous species until your own son becomes one of them and you discover that he is still the same kid—honest, concerned about the world around him, not wanting to hurt anybody" (Hagestad, 1977, p. 19). Thus, perceptions of distinctiveness are not incompatible with perceptions of bidirectional influence.

Influence

The issue of perception—of attribution to the other—is important in exploring apparent generational dissimilarities as well as influence. Several studies (Gallagher, 1976; Lerner, 1975; Thompson & Walker, 1982) demonstrate the difference between actual attitudes or values expressed by youth and parent respondents and the attitudes and values each perceives the other to have. Each generation warps the attitudes of the other, though in opposite directions. Late-adolescent children exaggerate the difference between their own attitudes and those of their parents while their parents minimize this difference. The actual differences fall between these two extremes. The discrepancy between actual and perceived orientations may indeed enter into the negotiation of differences involved in cross-generational influence during primary socialization (Bengtson & Black, 1973) and into adulthood.

The contrast between actual versus perceived differences takes on importance in examination of the outcome of parental influence attempts. In the socialization of attitudes, which is the better predictor of youths' orientations: What parents actually think (their stated attitudes), or what their children think they think (perceived attitudes which their children attribute to them)?

One line of theory—that of behaviorists—suggests that the *actual* opinions or goals of parents constitute the most predictive model of influence. Another theoretical perspective—represented by cognitive psychologists and symbolic interactionists—would suggest, instead, that the orientations *attributed* to the parent by the child are more influential.

In one examination of this issue (Acock and Bengtson, 1980), the stated attitudes of mothers, fathers, and youths from 466 family triads were examined on nine political and religious questions (affect attitudes). The young adult children were also asked to predict their mothers' and fathers' responses (attributed attitudes). The research question involved the path of influence in the "social construction of reality" evidenced between generations. By exploring the actual versus perceived attitudes of similarity between parents and youth, an attempt was made to resolve contradictions between claims of similarity and claims of differences between generations. The attitude items touched upon work, government, law and order, business, college demonstrators, civil rights, welfare, marijuana, and religion.

Results indicated several findings. The most consistent evidence was that the generation gap was far more apparent in the minds of the children than actually appeared in divergence with parents' actual reports of their sociopolitical attitudes. There was a persistent misperception on the part of the children based perhaps on the assumption of an age-related polarization between children and their parents; the result was a discrepancy between perceived (attributed) attitudes and actual opinions of parents. Although male children were somewhat more liberal or less traditional than female children (on 6 out of the 9 items), the differences were not statistically significant; both daughters and sons shared this misperception.

Sherif et al. (1965) noted that an individual's opinion in one situation often becomes an "anchor" in the placement of other opinions. Perhaps parents become anchored according to children's experiences, and the children begin to see disagreement as polarization and agreement as assimilation. Misattribution may be caused by the meaning of generational contrasts in the form of ontogenetic development—the "generational stake" (Bengtson and Kuypers, 1971) that reflects different levels of investment in particular relationships; the lack of communication between generations; deliberate misrepresentation as reflected in the (parental) adage, "Do what I say, not what I do"—since parents often expect rebellion and overcompensate by exaggerating their conventionality (tradition becomes parents' anchor).

In this study, the attributed parental attitudes (what children perceived in their parents) were much more predictive of the children's own attitudes, than were the actual opinions currently stated by the parents. Children also perceived strong parental consensus, between mothers and fathers, while actual similarity between their attitudes was slight. The cohort group-level findings were characterized by the term "polarized misattribution."

The major implication of this study is that children are strongly influenced by parental attitudes, but only as these attitudes are perceived (attributed)— not as they actually are. If children have perceived and thereby construct a generation gap, it is important to recognize the construction and to pursue its source. The distinction between actual and perceived attitudes is crucial in attempting to explain contradictory research findings regarding parent–child contrasts or similarities in socialization outcomes. It is also essential for socialization theorists to pay closer attention to attribution processes when charting intergenerational processes of influences, for example, in the transmission of value orientations.

CONCLUSIONS

The classic problem of generations—reflecting distinctiveness and change versus continuity and tradition—continues to be a rich agenda for scholarly interest in macrosocial and microsocial investigations of parenting. Social scientists looking at the processual flow of generational turnover and replacement are beginning to emphasize the biosocial and sociohistorical influences in both distinctiveness and continuities across cohorts and generations. This chapter has focused on the dynamics of parenting and the consequences of biosocial, sociohistorical, and demographic shifts within the context of familial and macrosocial tensions. These tensions are dialectical in that they reflect both social continuity and social innovation. Despite the American ethos of change, researchers note substantial continuity across generations. Each emerging cohort may be convinced that it produces a unique content and form; each cohort may also believe that past generations cannot understand what is being experienced. This perspective of distinctiveness and uniqueness may be, paradoxically, one of the traditions that is maintained over time within the context of successive generations.

The research reviewed in this chapter leads to six conclusions:

1. The impact of demographic trends is played out in social movements; often the demographic metabolism can be linked to themes of social change, as can be seen in the civil rights movement, the free speech movement, the antiwar movement, the women's movement, and the counterculture movement which characterized the "decade of protest" at a macrosocial level.

2. Individual struggles for independence and autonomy require renegotiation as generations succeed each other and as cohorts flow through differential developmental stages. Here, however, microlevel changes are not as clear as macrolevel successions.

3. Differences between parents and youth do not necessarily indicate rejection of parents' values or norms, and similarities are not tantamount to a consensus with parents' values. New commitments frequently reflect parents' orientations, though they may be expressed in a distinctive way; nevertheless, continuity often resides within innovation.

4. Both social and social-structural (environmental) factors contribute to the subsequent interaction between generations. Distinctiveness between parents and youth is often modified by processes that enhance the solidarity between generations.

5. Cohort, lineage, and period effects account for many of the apparent inconsistencies between and among generations; each succeeding generation has its own "definition of the situation." Cohort effects indicate factors related to real or apparent differences between individuals born at different

points in historical time. Lineage effects represent the bidirectional nature of intergenerational socialization. Period effects reflect the impact of sociohistorical events as they produce change and continuity in different social groups (i.e., social generations) at different points in time.

6. Apparent generational contrasts may be caused by children's polarized misperceptions of parents' attitudes—or, to a lesser degree, by parents' misattribution of childrens' attitudes. Children's own attitudes seem to be more accurately predicted by their attributed evaluations of their parents' opinions. In any event, the reciprocal influence of parents and children is an important consideration in socialization theory.

ACKNOWLEDGMENT

Preparation of this paper was supported by grants #MH-38244 of the National Institute on Mental Health and #AG-04092 and #5T32AG00037 of the National Institute of Aging.

REFERENCES

Acock, A.C., and Bengtson, V.L. On the relative influence of mothers and fathers: A covariance analysis of political and religious socialization. *Journal of Marriage and the Family,* 1978, *40* (3), 519–530.

Acock, A.C., and Bengtson, V.L. Socialization and attribution processes: Actual versus perceived similarity among parents and youths. *Journal of Marriage and the Family,* 1980, *42* (3), 501–515.

Acock, A.C. Parents and their children: the study of intergenerational difference. *Sociology and Social Research,* 1984, *69,* 2–22.

Adelson, J. What generation gap? *New York Times Magazine,* 1970 (Jan. 18:10 ff).

Aldous, J. *Family Careers: Developmental Change in Families.* NY: John Wiley, 1978.

Allen, F. *The Big Change: America Transforms Itself, 1900–1950.* NY: Harper and Row, 1952.

Bengtson, V.L. The 'generation gap': A review and typology of social-psychological perspectives. *Youth and Society,* 1970, *2* (1), 7–32.

Bengtson, V.L., and Black, K.D. Intergenerational relations and continuity in socialization. In P. Baltes and K.W. Schaie (Eds.), *Life-Span Developmental Psychology and Socialization.* NY: Academic Press, 1973, pp. 207–234.

Bengtson, V.L., and Kuypers, J.A. Generational differences and the 'developmental stake'. *Aging and Human Development,* 1971 *2* (1), 249–260.

Bengtson, V.L. and Laufer, R.S. (Eds.). Youth, generations, and social change. Special 2-Volume number of *Journal of Social Issues,* 1974, *39* (2,3).

Bengtson, V.L., and Lovejoy, M.C. Values, personality, and social structure: An intergenerational analysis. *American Behavioral Scientist,* 1973, *10* (6), 880–912.

Bengtson, V.L., and Treas, J. The changing family context of mental health and aging.

In J.E. Birren and R.B. Sloane (Eds.), *Handbook of Mental Health and Aging*. Englewood Cliffs, NJ: Prentice-Hall, 1980.

Bengtson, V.L., Furlong, M.J., and Laufer, R.S. Time, aging, and the continuity of the sociological structures: Themes and issues in generational analysis. *Journal of Social Issues*, 1974, *30* (2), 1–30.

Bengtson, V.L., Cutler, N.E., Mangen, D.J., and Marshall, V.W. Generations, cohorts, and relations between age gruops. In R. Binstock and E. Shanas (Eds.), *Handbook of Aging and Social Sciences*, NY: Van Nostrand Reinhold, 1985.

Berger, P., and Luckman, W. *The Social Construction of Reality*. NY: Anchor, 1965.

Bettelheim, B. The problem of generations. In E. Erikson (Ed.), *The Challenge of Youth*. NY: Anchor, 1965, pp. 76–109.

Braungart, R.G. Historical generation and youth movements: A theoretical perspective. *Research in Social Movements, Conflict and Change,* Vol. 6, Greenwich, CT: JAI Press, 1984, pp. 95–142.

Braungart, R.G., and Braungart, M.M. Life course and generational politics. *Annual Review of Sociology*, 1986, *12*.

Breines, W. *Community and Organization in the New Life: 1962–1968*. NY: Praeger, 1982.

Burgess, E.W. The family as a unit of interacting personalities. *Family*, 1926, *7*, 3–9.

Burton, L.C., and Bengtson, V.L. Black grandmothers: Issues of timing and continuity in roles. In V. Bengtson and J. Robertson (Eds.), *Grandparenthood*. Beverly Hills, CA: Sage Publications, 1985, pp. 304–338.

Cancian, F.M. Rapid.social change: Women students in business schools. *Sociology and Social Research*, 1980, 66 (2), 169–183.

Cherlin, A. Remarriage as an incomplete institution. *American Journal of Sociology*, 1978, *84*, 634–650.

Cherlin, A. A sense of history: Recent research on aging and the family. In B. Hess and K. Bond (Eds.), *Leading Edges*. Washington, DC: National Institute of Health, 1981, (November) pp. 21–50.

Cohen, J.B. *Revolution in Science*. Cambridge, MA: Harvard University Press.

Comfort, *The Joys of Sex*. NY: Random House, 1968.

Cutler, N.E. Generational analysis and political socialization. In S.A. Renshon (Ed.) *Handbook of Political Socialization: Theory and Research*. NY: Free Press, 1976.

Dannefer, D. Adult development and social theory: a paradigmatic reappraisal. *American Sociological Review*, 1984, *49*, 100–116.

Davis, K. The sociology of parent-youth conflict. *American Sociological Review*. 1940, *5* (4), 523–534.

Deckard, B.S. *The Women's Movement*, 3rd Ed. NY:Harper & Row Publishers, 1983.

Dowd, J.J. *Stratification Among The Aged*. Monterey, CA: Brooks-Cole, 1980.

Easterlin, R.A. *Birth and Fortune*. NY: Basic Books, 1980.

Elder, G.H. Jr. Approaches to social change and the family. In J. Demos and S.S. Boocock (Eds.), *Turning Points*. Chicago, IL: University of Chicago Press, 1978, pp. 1–38.

Elder, G.H. Jr. Family and kinship in sociological perspective. In R. Parke (Ed.), *The Family*. Chicago, IL: University of Chicago Press, 1984.

Erickson, E.H. *Childhood and Society*. NY: Norton, 1950.

Esler, A. Youth in revolt: The French generation of 1830. In R.J. Bezucha (Ed.), *Modern European History*. Lexington, MA: D.C. Heath, 1972.

Featherman, D. Social stratification and mobility: two decades of cumulative social science. *American Behavioral Scientist*, 1982, *24* (3): 364–85.

Featherman, D., and Lerner, R.M. Ontogenesis and sociogenesis: Problematics for theory and research about develoment and socialization across the lifespan. *American Sociological Review*, 1986.

Fendrich, J.M. Activists ten years later: A test of generational unit continuity. *Journal of Social Issues*, 1974, *31*, 95–118.

Feuer, L. *The Conflict of Generations*. NY: Basic Books, 1969.

Flacks, R. The liberated generation: An exploration of the roots of student protest. *Journal of Social Issues*, 1967, *239*, (July), 52–72.

Freeman, J. *The Politics of Women's Liberation*. NY: David McKay Co., 1975.

Friedenberg, E. Current patterns of generational conflict. *Journal of Social Issues*, 1969, *25* (2), 21–38.

Fries, J.F. Aging, natural death, and the compression of morbidity. *New England Journal of Medicine*, 1980, *303* (3), 130–135.

Gallagher, B.J. Ascribed and self-reported attitude differences between generations. *Pacific Sociological Review*, 1976, *19*, 317–332.

Glass, J., Bengtson, V.L., and Dunham, C. Attitude similarity in three generation families: socialization, status inheritance, or reciprocal influence. *American Sociological Review*, 1986 (October).

Hagestad, G.O. Role change in adulthood: The transition to the empty nest. Unpublished manuscript, Committee on Human Development, University of Chicago, 1977.

Hagestad, G.O. Problems and promises in the social psychology of intergenerational relations. In R.W. Fogel, E. Hatfield, S.B. Kiesler, and E. Shanas (Eds.), *Aging*. NY: Academic Press, 1981.

Hagestad, G.O. Life-phases analysis. In D.J. Mangen and W. Peterson (Eds.), *Research Instruments in Gerontology*, Vol. 1. Minneapolis, MN: University of Minnesota Press, 1982.

Hagestad, G.O. The continuous bond: A dynamic multigenerational perspective on parent–child relations between adults. In M. Perlmutter (Ed.), *Minnesota Symposia on Child Psychology*, Vol. 17. Hillsdale, NJ: Earlbaum, 1984, Chap. 5.

Hareven, T.K. Family time and historical time. *Daedalus*, 1977, *106*, 57–70.

Hernes, G. Structural change in social processes. *American Journal of Sociology*, 1976, *82* (November), 513–547.

Jennings, M.K., and Niemi, R.C. *Generations and Politics*. Princeton, NJ: Princeton University Press, 1981.

Keniston, K. *Young Radicals: Notes on Committed Youth*. NY: Harcourt, Brace, Jovanovich, 1968.

Kertzer, D.I. Generations as a sociological problem. In R.H. Turner and J.F. Short, Jr. (Eds.), *Annual Review of Sociology*, Vol. 9. Palo Alto, CA: Annual Reviews, Inc., 1983, pp. 125–149.

Kuhn, T. *The Structure of Scientific Revolutions*. Chicago, London: The University of Chicago Press, 1962.

Lerner, R.M. Showdown at the generation gap: Attitudes of adolescents and their parents toward contemporary issues. In H.D. Thornberg (Ed.), *Contemporary Adolescence: Readings*. Belmont, CA: Wadsworth, 1975.

Lerner, R.M., and Knapp, J.R. Actual and perceived intergenerational attitudes of late adolescents and their parents. *Journal of Youth and Adolescence*, 1975, *4*, 17–36.

Leventman, S. (Ed.). *Counterculture and Social Transformation: Essays in Negativistic Themes in Sociological Theory*. Springfield, IL: Charles C. Thomas, 1982.

Mannheim, K. The problem of generations. In D. Kecskemeti (Ed.), *Essays on the Sociology of Knowledge*. London: Routledge & Kegan Paul Ltd, 1952, pp. 276–322.

Mead, M. *Culture and Commitment: A Study of the Generation Gap*. NY: Longmans, 1970.

Miller, J., and Gilmore, K. *Revolt at Berkeley*. NY: American, 1975.

Nassi, A.J. Survivors of the sixties: Comparative psychosocial and political development of former Berkeley student activities. *American Psychologist,* 1981, *36* (7), 753–761.

Nassi, A.J., and Abramowitz, S.I. Transition or transformation? Personal and political development of former Berkeley free speech movement activists. *Journal of Youth and Adolescence*, 1976, *8*, 21–35.

Reich, C. *The Greening of America*. NY: Dell, 1970.

Riley, M.W. Aging and social systems, In R.H. Binstock and E. Shanas (Eds.), *Handbook of Aging and Social Sciences*. NY: Van Nostrand Reinhold Co., 1976.

Riley, M.W. Age strata and aging. In R. Binstock and E. Shanas (Eds.), *Handbook of Aging and the Social Sciences*. NY: Van Nostrand Reinhold Co., 1985.

Rossi, A.S. Aging and parenthood in the middle years. In P. Baltes and O.G. Brim (Eds.), *Life-Span Development and Behavior,* Vol. 2. NY:Academic Press, 1980.

Ryder, N.B. The cohort as a concept in the study of social change. *American Sociological Review*, 1965, *30* (6), 834–861.

Schaie, K.W. A general model for the study of developmental problems. *Psychological Bulletin*, 1965, *64*, 72–107.

Sherif, M., Sherif, C., and Nebergall, R.E. *Attitude Change: The Social Judgment-Involvement Approach*. Philadelphia, PA: W.B. Saunders, 1985.

Sprey, J., and Matthews, S. Contemporary grandparenthood: A systematic transition. *Annals of American Academy of Political and Social Science,* 1982, *464* (November), 91–103.

Surrey, D.S. *Choice of Conscience: Vietnam Era Military and Draft Resisters in Canada*. NY: Praeger, 1982.

Thompson, L., and Walker, A.J. Mothers and daughters: Aid patterns and attachment. Unpublished paper presented at the annual Gerontological Society of America meeting, Boston, November, 1982.

Treas, J., and Bengtson, V.L. The demography of mid- and late-life transitions. *Annals of American Academy of Political and Social Science*, 1981, *464*, November, 11–21.

Treas, J., and Bengtson, V.L. Family in later years, In M. Sussman and S. Steinmetz (Eds.), *Handbook on Marriage and the Family*. NY: Plenum, 1984.

Troll, L., and Bengtson, V.L. Youth and their parents: Feedback and intergenerational influence in socialization. In R.M. Lerner and G.B. Spanier (Eds.) *Child Influences in Marital and Family Interaction: A Life-Span Perspective*. NY: Academic Press, 1978, pp. 215–240.

Troll, L., and Bengtson, V.L. Generations in the family. In W. Burr, R. Hill, I. Reiss, and I. Nye (Eds.), *Theories about the Family*, Vol. 1. NY: The Free Press, 1979, pp. 127–161.

Tuchman, B. *The March of Folly*. NY: Harper and Row, 1984.

Uhlenberg, P. Changing configurations of the life-course. In T. Hareven (Ed.), *Transitions*. NY: Academic Press, 1978, pp. 66–98.

Vinovskis, M.A. Recent trends in American historical demography: Some methodological and conceptual considerations. *Annual Review of Sociology*, 1978, *4*, 603–627.

Whalen, J., and Flacks, R. The Isla Vista "bank burners" ten years later: Notes on the fate of student activists. *Sociological Focus*, 1982, *13* (3), 215–236.

Wheeler, J. *The Vietnam Generation*. NY: Random House, 1984.

Wood, J.L., and Ng, W.C. Socialization and student activism: Examination of a relationship. In L. Kriesberg (Ed.), *Research in Social Movements, Conflicts, and Change*. Greenwich, CT: JAI Press, 1980, pp. 21–43.

Yinger, J.M. *Countercultures*. NY: Free Press, 1982.

INDEX

A

G

Gender differences
  in age of marriage and
    childbearing, 320
  biological components of, 64–72
  in brain, 66–70
  in competence, 119–122
  evolutionary perspective on,
    62–63
  in fetal development, 66
  in future, 71–72
  in intergenerational closeness,
    421–422
  in intergenerational common
    ground, 414–415
  in intergenerational contact, 412
  in involvement with children,
    125–134
  of offspring, and fertility of
    parent, 224
  in parental investment, 191–192,
    200
  in parental styles, 122–125
  in parenting, 54–61, 63, 69,
    113–115
  in reproductive strategies, 116
  in sensitivity, 119–122
  in sensory modalities, 68, 69, 70
  in sibling caretaking, 242, 244,
    246
  in social and cognitive skills,
    68–69, 70
  in social behavior, 66–70
Generational stake, 447, 450
Generational unit, 440
Generation crunch, 436–437
Generation gap
  as cohort gap, 440–441, 443,
    444
  in decade of protest, 437
  as lineage gap, 441–443
  perception of, 450
  as period gap, 443

and socialization, 412, 413
Genetic relatedness, 15, 211,
  215–217
Genital shaving, 48
Geographic proximity, in
  intergenerational relations,
  410–411
Gerbils, initiation of reproduction
  in, 92
Giriama, sibling caretaking by,
  247–248
Goodness-of-fit model, 381–388
  for adaptability and rhythmicity,
    392–394
  for interaction with adolescents,
    395–399
  for motor activity, 391–392
  for sleep-wake cycles, 389–391
  tests of, 388–399
Grandmother
  in female-headed household,
    343
  and sense of competence of
    mother, 421
Green monkeys, lactation in, 95

H

Hawaiian-Americans, sibling
  caretaking among, 241–242,
  248, 250, 260
Health Examination Survey,
  358–360
Hemispheres, of brain, 70
Heterogeneity, and sibling
  caretaking, 247
High School and Beyond Study,
  316, 317
Historical change
  in family, 187–188, 226–227,
    295, 296–299
  in family size, 187–188,
    191–194, 296
  in household, 296–299